# Cooking for Today

# Cooking for

# Today

**Edited by Hyla O'Connor**

CHARTWELL
BOOKS INC.

This edition first published 1976 by
Chartwell Books Inc.
A Division of Book Sales Inc.
110 Enterprise Avenue
Secaucus, New Jersey 07094

ISBN 0 7064 0468 8

# Contents

# Introduction

Today's cook is a busy cook; speed and planning are the essence of her work. That's what this book is all about. Cooking for Today sets out to help you enjoy entertaining and everyday cooking.

In the first section 'Basic Recipes and Techniques', all the essential cookery methods are given, as well as a comprehensive collection of recipes from soups to desserts, sauces and cakes. There are also illustrated step-by-step recipes for 13 classic dishes.

'For the Hostess' includes all the information and specially planned time-saving recipes which the busy hostess needs. There are chapters on wines, aperitifs and brandies; suggestions for setting the table; recipes to be cooked in advance, with advice on freezing and meals to cook in a hurry with suggestions for using a pressure cooker, mixer and blender.

'Entertaining' gives a series of menus for specific occasions from dinner parties and informal buffets to children's parties, Christmas and other family occasions, easy weekends and barbecues. As well as complete recipes there are timetables and lots of handy hints.

In 'Information', a selection of helpful advice is given on subjects including planning a party, basic equipment and herbs and spices.

*Smoked haddock and cheese flan (page 200)*

# Basic Recipes
and Techniques

# SOUPS

Soups may be thin and clear, thick and creamy, hot, cold, or so full of meat and vegetables that they make a nourishing meal in themselves. Whatever kind of soup you are planning to make, the basis will always be a tasty stock. Nowadays there are many readymade stock preparations available, the most popular being bouillon cubes, which make an acceptable stock and save an enormous amount of time and trouble. Beware of the strength of the seasoning if using a bouillon cube and don't add more until you have tasted the finished soup; remember, too, that cubes do not give 'body' to a soup in the same way as bone stock. There is nothing to beat a rich home-made stock – a pressure cooker cuts time and if you own a freezer it is easy to keep stock by freezing it in 2½ cup or 1¼ cup quantities.

White stock – which can be made from veal or mutton bones, or poultry carcasses – is used for the pale, delicately flavored soups. It can also be used for one of the darker soups with the addition of a few drops of gravy browning. However, a brown stock – made from bones and beef first browned in the oven – is really more satisfactory for a dark soup. It is essential for consommé to use a really tasty brown stock. Turn to the end of the section for stocks.

## SOUPE A LA PAYSANNE
*6 servings*

2 carrots, peeled
½ turnip, peeled
1 stalk celery
2 leeks
2 tablespoons butter
Salt and pepper
5 cups brown stock
Bouquet garni (2–3 stalks parsley, 1 bay leaf, 1 sprig thyme)
Croûtons

Cut the carrot and turnip into cubes; thinly slice the celery and leeks. Cook the vegetables in about 2 cups of boiling water for 3 minutes. Drain and rinse in cold running water. Drain well. Melt the butter in a 2½-quart saucepan. Add the vegetables and cook, stirring occasionally, for about 5 minutes. Add the stock. Bring to a boil and carefully skim top of soup. Add the bouquet garni. Cover and simmer for 20–30

*French onion soup, a classic dish, can almost make a meal in itself*

*Use up surplus garden lettuce in a tasty lettuce and onion soup*

minutes. Remove the bouquet garni and skim thoroughly, using absorbent paper towels. Season to taste.
Pour into a preheated bowl and serve with croûtons on the side.

## SUSAN'S GERMAN SOUP
*4 servings (a meal in itself)*

5 cups household stock
½ pound potatoes, diced
2 leeks, sliced
2 small turnips, diced
3 carrots, sliced
1 red or green pepper, sliced
2 stalks celery, sliced
½ pound unsliced bacon, rind removed
½ pound Mettwurst sausage

Combine the stock and potatoes in a large saucepan. Cook until the potatoes are tender. Put the potatoes and stock through a sieve or purée in a blender. Return to the saucepan. Add the leeks, turnips, carrots, pepper, celery and bacon. Cover and simmer gently for 1½–2 hours. Remove the skin from the Mettwurst and cut into slices at a 45° angle. Add to the soup and simmer for 15 minutes. Adjust seasoning if necessary. Remove the bacon and cut into bite-sized

pieces. Return to the saucepan and serve the soup piping hot.

## FRENCH ONION SOUP
*4 servings*

¼ cup butter or margarine
Sugar
1 pound onions, thinly sliced
3¾ cups brown stock
Salt and pepper
½ cup grated Gruyère or Emmenthal cheese
4 thin slices French bread, toasted
White wine, optional

Melt the butter in a large saucepan. Add a pinch of sugar and the onions. Cook slowly until the onions are well browned and soft. Stir in the stock. Bring to a boil. Lower heat, cover and simmer for 30 minutes. Season to taste.
Pour the mixture into 4 flameproof soup bowls. Sprinkle the cheese on the slices of French bread and float one on each bowl of soup. Place under a hot broiler and cook until the cheese melts and bubbles. Serve at once, with more grated cheese if desired.
*Note:* A dash of dry white wine may be added to the soup just before turning into the bowls.

## MINESTRONE
*4–6 servings*

1 small leek, shredded
1 onion, finely chopped
1 clove garlic, crushed
2 tablespoons butter or margarine
5 cups white stock
1 carrot, cut into thin strips
1 turnip, cut into thin strips
1 stalk celery, thinly sliced
¼ small head cabbage, finely shredded
3 green beans, thinly sliced
¼ cup green peas
4 tomatoes, peeled and diced
2 slices bacon, chopped and fried
¼ cup elbow macaroni
Salt and pepper
Grated Parmesan cheese

Sauté the leek, onion and garlic in melted butter until soft but not browned. Add the stock and bring to a boil. Add the carrot, turnip and celery. Simmer for 20–30 minutes. Add the cabbage, beans and peas and simmer for 20 minutes. Stir in the tomatoes, bacon and macaroni. Season to taste. Simmer gently for about 10–15 minutes until the macaroni is tender. Serve piping hot with plenty of Parmesan cheese.

## MAMA'S LEEK SOUP
*3–4 servings*

2–3 leeks
¼ cup butter or margarine
1 package (1 ounce) white sauce mix
2½ cups milk
¼ cup grated Cheddar cheese
Salt and pepper
Croûtons

Wash the leeks and cut in thin slices. Melt the butter in a saucepan. Add the leeks, cover and cook slowly for about 10 minutes or until tender. Remove from heat. Sprinkle the sauce mix over the leeks and stir well. Gradually add the milk, stirring until smooth. Cook, stirring constantly, until the mixture thickens and comes to a boil. Put the mixture through a sieve or purée in a blender. Return to the saucepan, add the cheese and season to taste. Heat, but *do not boil*. Add more milk if desired for a thinner soup. Serve piping hot with croûtons.

## LETTUCE AND ONION SOUP
*6 servings*

¼ cup butter or margarine
1 large onion, finely chopped
1 large head lettuce, shredded
5 cups chicken stock
Salt and pepper
⅓ cup heavy cream

Melt the butter in a saucepan. Add the onion and cook until soft but not browned. Add the lettuce and cook for just a few minutes, stirring constantly. Add the stock and salt and pepper to taste. Bring to a boil. Lower heat, cover and simmer for 5–7 minutes. Purée the mixture in a blender. Return to saucepan and bring to a boil. Remove from heat and stir in the cream, mixing well. Serve immediately.

## SPLIT PEA SOUP
*8 servings*

2 cups dried split peas, yellow or green
1 onion, sliced
2 stalks celery, sliced
1 carrot, sliced
1 ham bone
¼ bay leaf
2 quarts water
3 cups milk
2 tablespoons butter or margarine
1 teaspoon salt
⅛ teaspoon pepper
Chopped parsley

Wash the peas. Soak in cold water for several hours or overnight (if quick-cooking peas are used, do not soak). Put the peas, onion, celery, carrot, ham bone, bay leaf and water into a large soup pot. Bring the mixture to a boil. Lower heat, cover and simmer for about 2 hours or until the peas are tender. Remove from heat and cool slightly. Remove ham bone. Put the mixture through a sieve or food mill, then return to soup pot. Add the milk, butter, salt and pepper. Heat thoroughly but *do not boil.* Serve sprinkled with chopped parsley.

## COCK-A-LEEKIE
*4 servings*

1 stewing chicken, 2½ – 3 pounds
5 cups stock or water
4 leeks, sliced
Salt and pepper
6 prunes, optional

Put the chicken in a large saucepan with the stock or water, leeks and seasoning. Bring to a boil. Lower heat, cover and simmer for

*An oxtail makes a rich, meaty soup for a cold day*

*Consommé princesse, the clearest of soups garnished with asparagus*

about 3 hours or until the chicken is tender. Remove the chicken, and cut into fairly large pieces. Serve the soup with the chicken pieces or serve separately, with the chicken as a main course.
*Note:* If prunes are used, soak them overnight in cold water. Halve and remove pits. Add to the soup about 30 minutes before the end of cooking time.

## CREAM OF CELERY SOUP
*4 servings*

2 tablespoons butter or margarine
1 whole bunch celery, chopped
¼ cup flour
2½ cups chicken stock
1 blade mace
1 teaspoon lemon juice
Salt
Freshly ground pepper
2 carrots, finely diced
1¼ cups milk

Melt the butter in a large saucepan. Add the celery and cook gently for about 5 minutes. Add the flour and cook, stirring constantly, for a few minutes. Remove from heat and stir in the stock, mace, lemon juice, salt and pepper. Return to heat and bring

to a boil, stirring. Lower heat, cover and simmer for 20 minutes. Remove mace and discard.
Purée the soup in a blender. Return to the saucepan. Add the carrots and simmer for about 15 minutes until tender. Remove from heat and stir in the milk. Taste for seasoning. Serve piping hot.

## POTATO AND ONION SOUP
*4 servings*

¼ cup butter or margarine
2 large onions, thinly sliced
1 pound potatoes, diced
2½ cups chicken stock
1¼ cups milk
Salt and pepper
2 tomatoes, peeled and seeded
¼ cup grated Cheddar cheese
1 tablespoon chopped parsley

Melt the butter in a saucepan. Add the onions and fry gently for about 10 minutes. Add the potatoes, cover and simmer over very low heat for 10 minutes. Add the stock. Bring to a boil, lower heat and simmer until the potatoes are soft. Purée the mixture in a blender. Return to saucepan and stir in the milk. Season to taste. Slice the tomato

in strips and add to the soup with the cheese and parsley. Heat the mixture, but *do not boil.* Serve piping hot.

## OXTAIL SOUP
*6 – 8 servings*

1 oxtail, cut in pieces
2 tablespoons butter or margarine
2 onions, chopped
1 carrot, sliced
2 stalks celery, sliced
7½–10 cups brown stock
2 slices bacon, chopped
Bouquet garni
Salt and pepper
3¾ tablespoons flour
Port wine, optional
Lemon juice

Wash and dry the oxtail and trim off any excess fat. Fry the oxtail in the hot butter with the vegetables for 5 minutes, or until evenly browned. Cover with the stock and bring to a boil. Add the bacon, bouquet garni and seasoning. Lower heat, cover and simmer for 3–4 hours, or until meat is tender, skimming occasionally. Strain soup, reserving stock and oxtail and discarding the vegetables. Remove the meat from the bones and cut up in small cubes. Return the meat and stock to soup pot. Combine the flour with a little water or port wine to make a smooth paste. Stir a little hot liquid into the flour mixture, then return it to the stock. Bring to a boil, stirring until the mixture boils. Cook for about 5 minutes. Add a squeeze of lemon juice and more salt and pepper if necessary.

## CONSOMMÉ PRINCESSE
*4 servings*

5 cups home-made brown stock (bouillon cubes will not do for this soup)
¼ pound lean beef
⅝ cup cold water
1 carrot, cut up
1 small onion, cut up
Bouquet garni
1 egg white
1 small can asparagus tips
Salt
2½ teaspoons sherry, optional

Remove any fat from stock. Cut the meat, with the grain, into very small shreds. Cover with the water and stand for 15 minutes. Combine the meat, water, vegetables, stock and bouquet garni in a large soup pot. Add the egg white. Heat the stock gently, stirring constantly with a whisk until

*Gazpacho, modern-style*

a froth starts to form. Stop whisking and bring the mixture to a boil. Reduce heat immediately and simmer *gently* for 2 hours. (If the liquid boils too rapidly, the froth will break and cloud the consommé.)

Line a collander with 4 layers of damp cheesecloth. Place over a large bowl. Pour the soup through, keeping the froth back at first with a spoon, then let it slide out onto the cheesecloth. Pour the soup through the cloth and through the filter of egg white a second time. The consommé should now be clear and sparkling.

Meanwhile, heat the asparagus in a small saucepan. Drain thoroughly. Reheat the consommé, adding salt if necessary and a

small amount of sherry. Serve piping hot with a few asparagus tips in each serving dish.

### SHRIMP CHOWDER
*4 servings*

1 large onion, sliced
1 tablespoon butter or margarine
⅝ cup boiling water
3 medium potatoes, diced
Salt and pepper
1 pound shrimp, cleaned and cooked
2½ cups milk
¼ – ½ cup grated Cheddar cheese
Chopped parsley

Cook the onion in the hot butter until soft but not browned. Add the boiling water, potatoes and seasoning. Cover and simmer

*Shrimp chowder – a party soup*

gently for 15–20 minutes or until the potatoes are just cooked. Add the shrimp and milk and heat thoroughly. Stir in the cheese. Serve piping hot topped with chopped parsley.

### GAZPACHO MODERN–STYLE
*4 servings*

1 pound very ripe tomatoes, peeled and sliced
1 small onion, finely chopped
1 small green pepper, seeded and chopped
1 clove garlic, crushed
1¼ tablespoons wine vinegar
1¼ tablespoons olive oil
1½–2 tablespoons lemon juice
Salt and pepper
1 small can tomato juice, optional
¼ cucumber, peeled and diced
1 thick slice bread, toasted and diced

Purée the tomatoes, onion, green pepper, garlic, vinegar and olive oil in an electric blender. Turn into a large bowl. Stir in the lemon juice and season to taste. Chill thoroughly. If desired, dilute with chilled tomato juice just before serving. Serve with a topping of diced cucumber and toast cubes.

## STOCKS

### BROWN STOCK
*makes about 6 cups*

1 pound small marrow bones
2 pounds shin of beef
7½ cups water
2 sprigs parsley
Pinch of thyme
Pinch of marjoram
1 small bay leaf, crumbled
1 carrot, sliced
1 medium onion, chopped
1 stalk celery, sliced
5 peppercorns
½ tablespoon salt

Put the marrow bones in a large soup pot. Cut the beef in pieces and add to the bones with the water and remaining ingredients. Bring to a boil. Skim foam from top of stock. Lower heat, cover and simmer for 4–5 hours. Strain the mixture into a large bowl. Chill in refrigerator overnight. Skim off any fat from cold stock. Keep in refrigerator no longer than 2 or 3 days.
*Note:* Brown stock can be put in small containers and frozen for later use.

### WHITE STOCK
*makes about 8½ cups*

2½ pounds knuckle of veal or meaty veal bones
¼ cup white wine
Lemon juice
12½ cups cold water
1 large onion, sliced
3 carrots, sliced
Bouquet garni
1 teaspoon salt
4 peppercorns

Wipe the knuckle with a damp cloth. Put into a large soup pot. Cover with cold water and bring to a boil. Skim off any foam and scum from top of liquid. Drain and rinse the knuckle. Return to soup pot. Pour in the wine and reduce to about 2 tablespoons. Add a squeeze of lemon juice and the water. Bring to a boil and skim top of liquid. Add the vegetables, bouquet garni, salt and peppercorns. Bring to a boil. Lower heat, cover partially and simmer for 4 hours. Strain the mixture into a large bowl. Chill in refrigerator overnight. Skim off any fat from cold stock. Keep in refrigerator no longer than 2 or 3 days.
*Note:* White stock can be put in small containers and frozen for later use.

### HOUSEHOLD STOCK
*makes about 10 cups*

2 pounds left-over beef bones, chicken or turkey bones
1 pound sliced vegetables, including onion, carrot, leek, celery, mushrooms or desired vegetables
3 tablespoons fat
Bouquet garni
Salt
Peppercorns

Chop up the bones and carcass. Spread the bones in a flat baking pan. Bake in a fairly hot oven (400°F.) just long enough to brown bones lightly. Cook the vegetables in hot fat in a large soup pot for about 10 minutes. Add the browned bones to the cooked vegetables. Add remaining ingredients and enough water to cover. Bring to a boil and skim off foam or scum on top of liquid. Reduce heat, cover and simmer for 3–4 hours. Strain into a large bowl. Chill in refrigerator overnight. Skim off any fat from cold stock. Keep in refrigerator no longer than 2 or 3 days.

*Minestrone, an Italian soup*

# PATES & TERRINES

A pâté is essentially a blend of different meats – principally liver and pork – which has been ground finely, well seasoned and cooked slowly. Because of the high proportion of liver used they tend to be very rich and only small portions should be allowed per serving – particularly as pâté is generally served as an appetizer accompanied by toast.

The most famous (and the most expensive) of these mixtures is, of course, pâté de foie gras, made from the livers of specially fattened geese, but you can follow our recipes and make your own pâté maison quite simply and inexpensively. Apart from the delicate fish ones, most pâtés will keep quite happily for a week in the refrigerator – in fact, this can even improve the flavor.

Anything that can be prepared and cooked ahead of time is a boon for a busy hostess, so this makes pâté an ideal choice for a formal dinner party.

Terrines are generally more robust than pâtés and of a coarser texture. They are not really suitable – except in minute quantities – as appetizers, because of their richness. However, terrines make a wonderful main course for a lunch or supper, served accompanied by salad. They are also particularly suitable to serve at an informal party when you have been out of doors for most of the day. Serve hot soup first and follow it with a selection of 2–3 rich terrines, accompanied by lashings of crusty French bread and even the heartiest appetite will be satisfied. The essential difference in the cooking of terrines and pâtés is that terrines are cooked in the dish from which they will be served – properly a terrine, but a suitably shaped casserole or loaf pan will do just as well. They are wrapped in fatty bacon and after cooking should be pressed with a heavy weight to compress the layers of meat really tightly together. Pâtés are usually at least partially cooked before molding and are served either turned out and sliced, or in individual dishes.

## COUNTRY PATE
*12 servings*

¼ cup butter or margarine
2 large onions, chopped
½ pound lean bacon, chopped
½ pound fresh side pork with fat or fat back cut in strips
¾ pound pork liver, diced
¾ pound round steak, finely diced
½ pound lean veal, diced
3 cloves garlic, crushed
⅝ cup dry red wine
5 tablespoons brandy
2 bay leaves
Salt and pepper
Dash Worcestershire sauce
Bacon fat
1 egg, beaten

Melt the butter in a large saucepan. Add the onions and bacon and fry until golden brown. Add the remaining ingredients, except the egg. Bring to a boil. Lower heat, cover and simmer for 30 minutes. Strain off liquid and reserve. Put the meat and vegetable mixture through the food chopper twice using the finest blade. Mix thoroughly with the reserved strained liquid and beaten egg. Taste and season if needed. Butter an 8 in. by 5 in. by 3 in. baking pan and line with aluminum foil. Pat the mixture into the pan. Place in a larger pan half-filled with boiling water. Cook in a moderate oven (350°F.) for 1½ hours. Remove from oven and cool. Chill in refrigerator for at least 12 hours. Turn out of pan and cut in thin slices to serve.

## HOME-MADE PATE DE FOIE
*6 servings*

1 pound chicken livers
½ cup pork fat
1 small clove garlic, crushed
Pinch of mixed herbs
Salt
Freshly ground black pepper
1 thin slice cooked tongue
1 small truffle, optional
Aspic jelly
Truffle or black olives for garnish

Cut the chicken livers in small pieces and combine with the pork fat, garlic and mixed herbs. Season lightly with salt and pepper. Heat a thick, heavy skillet. When piping hot, add the liver mixture. Cook, stirring constantly, until the chicken livers change color. Add 1–2 tablespoons water, lower heat and simmer for about 5 minutes. Purée the mixture in a blender. Cut the tongue into tiny diamond shaped pieces and chop the truffle. Combine with chicken livers. Taste for seasoning. Line the bottoms of tiny soufflé dishes or custard cups with a thin layer of plain aspic. Decorate with thin slices of truffle or black olive. Chill until firm. Fill each dish with the chicken mixture, spreading it smoothly on the top. Chill until firm. Unmold to serve.

## THRIFTY PATE
*6 servings*

1¼ pounds fresh lean side pork with fat or lean fat back
½ pound pork or beef liver
¼ pound lean bacon
1 large onion, chopped
1 small clove garlic
1 teaspoon salt
Freshly ground black pepper
2 tablespoons butter or margarine, melted

Dice the pork in small pieces. Rinse and dry the liver. Cut in chunks. Put the pork, liver, bacon, onion and garlic through food chopper three times. Mix in salt and pepper.

Turn into a 1½-quart terrine or small casserole. Cover with a piece of aluminum foil. Place in a roasting pan half-filled with hot water. Bake in a cool oven (300°F.) for 1½ hours.

Remove from oven and remove foil. Place a double thickness piece of aluminum foil over top of pâté. Place weights on top and refrigerate until thoroughly chilled. Remove weights and pour melted butter over top of pâté. Chill until ready to serve.

## HUNTER'S PATE
*16 servings*

1 pound boneless rabbit or hare meat
1 pound fresh side pork with fat or fat back
½ pound pork liver
1 pound pork sausage
½ pound garlic sausage
1 cup chopped onions
3¾ tablespoons sherry
2½ tablespoons chopped parsley
2½ teaspoons dried sage
Salt and pepper
1 pound bacon

Cut the rabbit meat into small pieces. Put the pork, liver, sausage, garlic sausage and onion through the food chopper. Mix in the rabbit, sherry, parsley, sage, salt and pepper.
Line a 9 in. by 5 in. by 3 in. terrine or baking pan with slices of

*Chicken liver pâté is a rich starter for a dinner party*

bacon, leaving overhanging ends to lap over top of pâté. Spoon in the mixture and smooth top. Fold bacon edges over top of pâté. Cover with aluminum foil and place in a larger baking pan half-filled with boiling water. Cook in a warm oven (325°F.) for about 3 hours. Remove from oven and cool in pan. When cold, remove from pan, wrap in aluminum foil and refrigerate. Cut in thick slices for serving.

## POTTED BEEF
*6 servings*

1 pound round steak, cut into ½-in. cubes
⅝ cup beef stock
1 clove
1 blade mace
Salt and pepper
¼ cup butter or margarine, melted
Fresh bay leaves for garnish

Combine the steak, stock, clove, mace, salt and pepper in a small casserole. Cover and cook in a moderate oven (350°F.) for 2½–3 hours or until beef is very tender. Remove the clove and mace. Strain off the stock and reserve. Purée the meat in a blender until very smooth. Turn into a bowl. Stir in 2 tablespoons of the melted butter and enough of the reserved stock to moisten the beef. Press into 6 small soufflé dishes or custard cups. Cover with remaining melted butter and chill until firm. Serve garnished

with a fresh bay leaf if desired.

## CHICKEN LIVER PATE
*10 servings*

1½ pound chicken livers
6 tablespoons butter or margarine
1 medium onion, finely chopped
1 large clove garlic, crushed
1 tablespoon heavy cream
2½ tablespoons tomato paste
3¾ tablespoons sherry or brandy

Rinse and dry the chicken livers. Fry in hot butter until they change color. Reduce heat, add the onion and garlic. Cover and cook for 5 minutes. Remove from heat and cool. Stir in the cream, tomato paste and sherry. Purée in a blender until smooth. Turn mixture into individual dishes. Cover tops with melted butter, if desired. Chill well before serving.

## SMOKED TROUT PATE
*6 servings*

½ pound smoked trout
¼ cup butter or margarine
1½ cups fresh white breadcrumbs
Finely grated rind and juice of 1 lemon
Salt
Freshly ground black pepper
Pinch of nutmeg
⅝ cup light cream

Skin and bone the trout and chop the fish very fine. Melt the butter in a small skillet. Toss lightly with breadcrumbs, lemon rind

and juice. Season well with salt, pepper and nutmeg. Blend in the chopped fish and cream. Spoon the mixture into 6 ramekins or small soufflé dishes. Chill thoroughly before serving.

## FRESH SALMON PATE
*8 servings*

¼ cup butter or margarine
½ cup all-purpose flour
2 cups milk
1 bay leaf
Salt and pepper
¼ teaspoon nutmeg
½ pound haddock or cod fillet, skinned
1 pound fresh salmon, skinned and boned
Grated rind and juice of 1 lemon
1 tablespoon chopped parsely
2 eggs, beaten
Melted butter
Parsley sprigs
Lemon slices

Melt the butter in a small saucepan. Stir in the flour and cook for 2–3 minutes. Remove from heat and stir in the milk. Cook, stirring constantly, until the mixture thickens and comes to a boil. Add the bay leaf, salt, pepper and nutmeg. Boil gently for 2–3 minutes. Remove bay leaf and discard.
Finely chop the haddock and three-quarters of the salmon. Add to the sauce together with the lemon rind, juice, chopped parsley and beaten eggs. Blend well. Divide the mixture into buttered ramekins. Brush the tops with melted butter and decorate with slices of the remaining salmon. Place them in a large baking pan half-filled with hot water. Cook in a cool oven (300°F.) for about 40 minutes. Remove from hot water and cool. Chill well before serving. Serve garnished with parsley sprigs and lemon slices.

## KIPPER PATE
*4 servings*

¼ pound kipper fillets
2½ tablespoons dry white wine
Freshly ground black pepper
½ cup butter or margarine, softened

Skin the fillets, cut in pieces and place in a bowl. Cover with wine and stand for 12 hours, turning occasionally. Purée in a blender until smooth or work with a pestle in a mortar. Turn into a bowl and season with pepper. Add the butter and beat until the mixture is smooth. Divide between 4 small soufflé dishes or custard cups. Chill. Serve with hot toast.

## TUNA PATE
*6–8 servings*

**2 cans (7 ounces each) tuna, drained**
**2 packages (3 ounces each) cream cheese, at room temperature**
**2 teaspoons horseradish**
**½ teaspoon Worcestershire sauce**
**½ cup onion, finely chopped**
**1 clove garlic, crushed**
**½ teaspoon celery salt**
**3 tablespoons mayonnaise**
**¼ teaspoon pepper**

Flake the tuna fish into a bowl. Add the cream cheese and mix thoroughly. Add the remaining ingredients and blend well. Pack into a crock or bowl. Refrigerate thoroughly before serving.

## TERRINE OF DUCK, LIVER AND PORK
*10–12 servings*

**1 pound duck meat (approximated yield from a 3½ pound roasting duck)**
**¼ cup Marsala**
**1½ pounds fatty fresh side pork with fat or fat back**
**1 pound calf's liver**
**1 medium onion**
**2 cloves garlic**
**1 medium orange**
**1 teaspoon salt**
**Freshly ground black pepper**
**½ teaspoon dried thyme**
**Sliced fatty bacon**
**4 bay leaves**

Cut the duck meat into long strips. Place in a bowl. Cover with Marsala and refrigerate for 6 hours. Keep small pieces and scraps of duck separate. Dice the pork and liver. Put through food chopper together with the duck scraps, onion and garlic. Place the ground mixture in a bowl and blend in the juice from half the orange, salt, pepper, thyme and Marsala drained from the duck strips. Line a 6-cup terrine or casserole with bacon slices, leaving the ends long enough to envelop the terrine mixture completely. Spoon one-third of the ground meat mixture into the terrine on top of bacon slices. Lay half the strips of duck meat along the length of the terrine. Repeat the layers, finishing with the meat mixture. Wrap the bacon ends over the top of the meat layers. Slice the remaining half orange and lay on top of bacon slices. Top with bay leaves. Cover and place in a baking pan half filled with hot water. Cook in a warm oven (325°F) for about 2½ hours.

When cooked, remove the lid and place a piece of aluminum foil over top of pâté, leaving the orange slices and bay leaves in place. Press the pâté down firmly with a small plate. Place a 2-pound weight, such as a can of fruit, on top of the plate and allow the terrine to cool.

## LIVER TERRINE
*4–6 servings*

**1 pound pork liver**
**¼ pound fatty bacon**
**3–4 anchovy fillets**
**4 eggs, beaten**
**1 clove garlic, crushed**
**1¼ cups thick white sauce**
**Salt and pepper**
**12 slices fatty bacon**

Grind the liver, fat bacon and anchovy fillets. Purée in a blender until smooth. Turn into a mixing bowl. Stir in the beaten eggs, garlic, white sauce and seasoning to taste. Line a shallow casserole or baking dish with bacon slices. Spoon the liver mixture into casserole. Cover with ends of bacon slices. Place the casserole in a baking pan half filled with hot water. Cook in a warm oven (325°F.) for 2 hours. Remove from hot water and place a piece of aluminum foil over top of terrine. Press down firmly with a small plate. Place a 2-pound weight, such as a can of fruit, on top of plate and allow terrine to cool. Chill before serving.

## TERRINE OF VEAL AND CHICKEN
*6–8 servings*

**¾ pound boneless chicken meat**
**1 pound lean veal**
**¼ pound chicken livers**
**5 tablespoons dry white wine**
**1 clove garlic, crushed**
**Pinch of mixed spices**
**1 cup fresh white breadcrumbs**
**Salt**
**Freshly ground black pepper**
**Sliced fatty bacon**
**2 bay leaves**
**Sprig of thyme**

Put the chicken, veal and chicken livers through the food chopper, using the medium cutter. Stir in the white wine, garlic, spices and breadcrumbs. Season well with salt and pepper.
Line a 5–6-cup terrine or oval casserole with overlapping slices of bacon, making sure they are long enough to envelop the top of the casserole. Spoon in the meat mixture and lap the bacon slices back over the meat. Lay a bay leaf

*Many terrines are encased in slices of fatty bacon*

or two and a sprig of thyme on top. Cover. Place in a baking pan half filled with hot water. Cook in a warm oven (325°F.) for about 2½ hours. Remove from hot water and let cool. When cool, pour off any juices into a small bowl. Chill the terrine and juices. When the juices are on the point of setting, spoon carefully over top of terrine. Serve in dish.

## TERRINE OF DUCK
*6 servings*

**1¾ pounds duck breasts**
**2½ teaspoons salt**
**1 pound fresh side pork with fat or fat back**
**1 pound lean veal**
**¼ pound pork, fat back**
**⅝ cup dry white wine**
**1 clove garlic, crushed**
**Freshly ground black pepper**
**1½ envelope (½ tablespoon) unflavored gelatin**
**1 cup chicken bouillon**
**1 small orange, thinly sliced**

Place the duck portions in a roasting pan. Sprinkle with salt. Roast in a warm oven (325°F.) for 40 minutes. Cut the pork and veal into small cubes. Cut 4–6 very thin strips from the pork fat and

reserve for topping. Put the pork, veal and remaining pork fat through food chopper. Add the wine, garlic, salt and pepper and mix thoroughly.
Remove duck from oven and let cool. Remove the skin and cut the meat into small cubes.
Put half of the pork and veal mixture in a 1½–2-quart terrine or casserole. Cover top of mixture with duck meat. Spoon the remaining mixture over top of duck and smooth out. Arrange the reserved strips of pork fat in a lattice design on top of mixture. Cover top of terrine with aluminum foil. Place the terrine in a roasting pan half-filled with hot water. Cook in a warm oven (325°F.) for 1½–2 hours. Remove terrine, remove foil and stand for 15 minutes. Cover top with a double thickness of aluminum foil. Place weights on top and chill thoroughly.
Soften the gelatin in chicken bouillon. Place in a pan of hot water and stir until dissolved. Remove from heat and chill until the consistency of egg whites. Place orange slices on top of pâté. Pour gelatin carefully over top. Chill thoroughly before serving.

*Kipper pâté is the simplest to make*

# GARNISHES

Suitable decorations add good looks as well as flavor to food and drink – but they must be very fresh, and preferably quite simple and comparatively small. The garnish for any particular dish should be decided on beforehand. Colors should be chosen to tone with both the food and the serving dish – two, or at most three, colors are sufficient. Sometimes ingredients which are an integral part of the recipe can also add decorative value.

## VEGETABLE AND SALAD GARNISHES

**Turned mushrooms** have a nicely tailored look. You need to use large button mushrooms and 'turn' them with a small, sharp-pointed knife, by making a series of cuts from the top of the cap to the base at intervals. Then repeat in the opposite direction to remove each narrow 'fillet'. Sauté the mushrooms in butter.

**Baby turnips** can be 'turned' prettily in the same way.

**Carrot curls** look crisp on open sandwiches, and in salads (or served as cocktail nibblers). Scrape raw carrots and slice them lengthwise and paper thin, using a vegetable peeler. Roll up, fasten with a toothpick and put them in iced water until they curl. Serve on or off the picks.

Another simple way to cut carrots raw is with a fondant cutter or tiny pastry cutter – simply scrape and slice the carrots then flute the edges by stamping out with a cutter.

**Pickle fans** always stay fresh, and suit hot or cold dishes. Make lengthwise cuts almost to the end of each gherkin, from the 'flower' end. Spread carefully to form an open fan.

**Radish roses** to garnish open sandwiches or cold meat platters are always popular. Cut off a narrow slice from the root end of each radish, then cut thin 'petals' from stem to root.

Put into iced water until the cuts open to form petals.

To make radish water lilies, make 4–8 small deep cuts, crossing in the center of the radish at the root end. Leave in iced water to open out.

**Celery curls** are made by cutting the celery into strips about ½ in. wide and 2 in. long and then slitting one or both ends in narrow strips almost to the center. Leave the pieces in iced water for an hour until the fringed ends curl.

**Scallions** split down the stem and left in cold water will open out in the same way.

## ORANGE OR LEMON GARNISHES

**Citrus twists** look cool on an iced drink or on top of a chiffon dessert. Using a sharp-edged vegetable peeler, start to remove a strip of peel from the narrow end of a lemon, orange or grapefruit. Work in a continuous spiral, removing only the colored part of the peel. Let the peel twist naturally as a garnish.

**Orange and lemon slices,** deftly twisted, suit fish and chicken dishes and may be used wherever these flavors are present in a recipe. Slit the slice through the rind to the centre, then twist in opposite directions. A double twist with 2 slices gives more emphasis.

## SAVORY GARNISHES

**Croûtons** are small, fancy-shaped pieces of bread which are fried or toasted. Cut the slices of white bread ¼–½ in. thick, remove the crusts and then either cut the bread into ¼–½ in. cubes and fry them, or leave the slices whole and broil them before cutting up. Use as a garnish for soups.

Croûtons cut into larger triangles and crescents are used as a garnish for ground meat or au gratin dishes.

**Cheese triangles** are good with soups and savories. Butter 6 slices of crustless bread and arrange close together on a cookie tray. Sprinkle ¼ cup finely grated cheese over. Bake in a moderate oven (350°F.) for about 40 minutes. Overlap around the edge of a savory dish or float on puréed soups.

**Fleurons** Roll out some puff, flaky or rough puff pastry to ¼ in. thickness, then stamp it into shapes with small fancy cutters, or cut with a sharp knife into squares, triangles or diamonds. To make crescents, which are a traditional shape, use a small round cutter; place it about ½ in. on to the edge of the pastry for the first cut, then move the cutter a further ½ in. inwards and cut again, making a crescent. Continue the length of the pastry, moving the cutter ½ in. each time. Place the fleurons on a cookie tray, brush the tops with beaten egg and bake in a very hot oven (450°F.) until well risen, golden brown and crisp, 7–10 minutes.

**Buttered crumbs** Melt 2 tablespoons butter and add 2 cups fine white breadcrumbs. Let them absorb the fat, forking the mixture several times. Spread out on cookie trays and dry in the oven on its lowest setting. When ready, they are cream-colored and dry. Stored in a screw-top jar or plastic bag in a cool place, these will keep fresh for 2 months. Use dry for coating rissoles; toss with butter or grated cheese for topping other dishes.

**Crunchy topper** Fry 1 cup fresh white breadcrumbs in 3 tablespoons butter until golden brown. Sift together 2 cups self-rising flour, 1 teaspoon salt, pepper and ½ teaspoon dried onion powder. Stir in 3¾ tablespoons salad oil and enough milk to give a soft dough. Drop tablespoons of the dough into buttered crumbs and roll into balls in the crumbs. Arrange on top of a casserole about 50 minutes before serving. Bake, uncovered, in a fairly hot oven (375°F.).

# SAVORY SOUFFLES AND MOUSSES

*A traditional soufflé dish is round and straight sided; it is smooth inside and fluted outside. Plain white china is the most common color, but brown earthenware, colored china and ovenproof glass are also available. In some classic soufflé recipes it is recommended that a paper band be tied round the outside of the dish to come about 3 in. above the rim. After cooking, the paper is peeled away and the soufflé still stands well above the edge of the dish. This is not strictly necessary, though, as a good soufflé will rise well without it and looks just as attractive. Simply butter the dish and dust with breadcrumbs or Parmesan cheese. The paper is necessary to give a 'risen' appearance to a cold soufflé.*

A hot soufflé is made on a base of a thick white sauce, or panada, flavored with meat, fish, cheese or vegetables. Egg yolks are beaten in to make it rich and the egg whites are beaten separately until really stiff and then folded in gently with a rubber spatula. The amount the soufflé rises depends on the air whipped into the egg whites: the air expands in the oven heat and raises a hot soufflé, and gives bulk to a cold one. Don't beat or stir in the egg whites rapidly.

To cook a soufflé place in the oven at 350–375°F. for 30–45 minutes, until well risen and brown on top. Be careful not to open the door of the oven too early in the cooking or your soufflé will collapse! To test when a hot soufflé is ready, open the oven door after 30 minutes and give the dish a slight movement without taking it out. If the crust moves considerably in the center, leave it a little longer. Serve a hot soufflé straight from the oven – it will spoil if kept for more than a few moments. This unfortunately makes a soufflé an unsuitable choice for a dinner party, when you cannot rely on the guests being precisely on time – but give the family a treat from time to time.

Cold soufflés and mousses are less temperamental and make ideal party dishes. They are set with gelatin and a mousse may be served in the dish or turned out of a mold on to a flat serving platter – a ring mold is often used. To turn out a molded mousse, dip the mold quickly into hot water and invert it on to a wet plate; the mousse will then slip easily out of the mold and slide into place on the plate if it is not quite central.

## CHEESE SOUFFLE
*4 servings*

**4 large eggs**
**3 tablespoons butter or**
    **margarine**
**¼ cup flour**
**1¼ cups milk**
**1½ cups grated Cheddar cheese**
**Salt and pepper**

Lightly butter a 1½-quart soufflé dish. Preheat oven to 350°F. Separate the eggs. Melt the butter in a saucepan. Stir in the flour and cook for 2–3 minutes. Remove from heat and stir in milk. Cook over moderate heat, stirring constantly, until mixture is smooth and thick. Add the egg yolks, one at a time, beating well. Stir in the cheese and season to taste. Beat the egg whites until stiff. Fold into the yolk mixture, quickly and evenly, with a rubber

*Red house soufflé*

spatula. Turn the mixture into the soufflé dish. Bake in center of oven for about 45 minutes or until well risen and browned. Serve immediately.

## RED HOUSE SOUFFLE
*6 servings*

¾ cup butter or margarine, divided
½ pound onions, thinly sliced
1 package (10 ounces) frozen corn
½ pound tomatoes, peeled and thickly sliced
2½ tablespoons chopped parsley
1 cup flour
2½ cups milk
Salt
Freshly ground black pepper
1½ cups grated sharp Cheddar cheese
6 eggs, separated

Butter a 2-quart soufflé dish. Preheat oven to 350°F. Heat ¼ cup butter in a skillet, add the onion and cook until soft but not browned. Add the corn and continue cooking for 5 minutes. Remove from heat and fold in the tomatoes and parsley. Melt the remaining butter in a saucepan. Stir in the flour and cook for 2–3 minutes. Remove from heat and stir in the milk. Cook over moderate heat, stirring constantly, until the mixture boils and is smooth and thick. Add the tomato mixture to half of the cream sauce and blend well. Season to taste. Turn the mixture into the soufflé dish. Add the cheese to the remaining sauce and stir until well blended. Add the egg yolks and beat well. Season to taste. Beat the egg whites until stiff. Fold into the sauce with a rubber spatula.
Spoon the mixture over top of vegetables. Place in center of oven and bake for about 1 hour or until well risen and golden brown. Serve immediately.

## BACON AND ONION SOUFFLE
*4 servings*

6 tablespoons butter or margarine, divided
6 slices lean bacon, chopped
½ pound onions, chopped
1¼ tablespoons chopped parsley
Salt and pepper
6 tablespoons flour
1¼ cups milk
3 egg yolks
4 egg whites

Butter a 1½-quart soufflé dish. Preheat oven to 375°F. Melt 2

*Cold ham soufflé will satisfy the heartiest appetite*

tablespoons of the butter in a small skillet. Add the bacon and fry for 2–3 minutes. Add the onions and continue cooking until tender. Remove from heat. Add the parsley and season to taste. Melt remaining butter in a saucepan, stir in the flour and cook for 2–3 minutes. Remove from heat and stir in milk. Cook over moderate heat, stirring constantly, until the mixture comes to a boil and is smooth and thick. Mix half the sauce with half the bacon and onion mixture. Spoon into the soufflé dish.
Beat the egg yolks, one at a time, into the remaining white sauce. Beat the egg whites until stiff. Fold into the white sauce with a rubber spatula. Fold in the remaining bacon mixture. Spoon into the soufflé dish. Bake in top part of oven for 45 minutes or until well risen and golden brown. Serve immediately.

## MARROW (ZUCCHINI) SOUFFLE
*4 servings*

1 pound vegetable marrow or large zucchini, peeled
¼ cup butter or margarine
¼ cup flour
1¼ cups milk
Salt and pepper
2½ teaspoons dried summer savory
3 eggs, separated
1 cup grated Cheddar cheese

Butter a 1½-quart soufflé dish. Preheat oven to 375°F. Cut the marrow in half lengthwise and remove seeds. Cut into thick slices. Cook in boiling, salted water until tender, but still firm. Drain thoroughly. Chop in large chunks.
Melt the butter in a saucepan. Stir

in the flour and cook for 2–3 minutes. Remove from heat and stir in the milk. Cook over moderate heat, stirring constantly, until the mixture comes to a boil and is thick. Season with salt and pepper. Combine half the sauce with the marrow and savory. Spoon into the soufflé dish.
Beat the egg yolks into the remaining sauce. Stir in the cheese. Add more seasoning if necessary. Beat the egg whites until stiff. Fold into sauce mixture with a rubber spatula. Spoon over the marrow mixture in the soufflé dish. Bake for about 30 minutes or until well risen and lightly browned. Serve at once.

## SPINACH SOUFFLE
*4 servings*

7 tablespoons butter, divided
1 large onion, sliced
1 pound fresh spinach, partially cooked and chopped
Salt
Freshly ground black pepper
¼ teaspoon grated nutmeg
¼ cup flour
1¼ cups milk
3 large eggs, separated
6 tablespoons grated Parmesan cheese

Butter a 1-quart soufflé dish. Preheat oven to 375°F. Melt 3 tablespoons of the butter in a saucepan. Add the onion and cook until tender. Add the spinach and cook about 2 minutes longer. Season lightly with salt, pepper and nutmeg.
Melt the remaining butter in a saucepan. Stir in the flour and cook for 2–3 minutes. Remove from heat and stir in the milk. Cook over moderate heat, stirring constantly, until mixture comes to a boil. Season and add half the

sauce to the spinach and onion. Turn into the soufflé dish and place on a cookie tray. Beat the egg yolks and most of the cheese into the remaining sauce, reserving a little cheese to sprinkle over the soufflé. Beat the egg whites stiffly. Fold carefully into the sauce with a rubber spatula. Spoon over the mixture in the soufflé dish. Sprinkle remaining cheese over top. Place in center of oven and bake for about 40 minutes or until well risen and lightly browned. Serve at once.

## COLD HAM SOUFFLE
*4 servings*

2 tablespoons butter or margarine
¼ cup flour
1¼ cups milk
4 large eggs, separated
5 teaspoons unflavored gelatin
5 tablespoons water
½ pound cooked ham, finely ground
½ teaspoon chopped tarragon
⅝ cup light cream
Salt and pepper
Watercress and ham slices for garnish

Cut a piece of aluminum foil long enough to go around the top of a 3-cup soufflé dish. Fold the foil into a long strip about 4 in. wide and lightly butter one side. Fasten around the top of the dish with tape or string so that it will stand about 3 in. above the rim of the dish.
Melt the butter in a saucepan. Stir in the flour and cook for 2–3 minutes. Remove from heat and stir in the milk. Cook over moderate heat, stirring constantly, until the mixture comes to a boil and thickens. Remove from heat and beat in the egg yolks, one at a time.
Soften the gelatin in the water, then dissolve over a pan of hot water. When it has dissolved, add it to the white sauce. Chill in refrigerator, stirring occasionally, just until mixture begins to set.
Stir in the ground ham, tarragon and cream. Season to taste.
Beat the egg whites until stiff. Fold into the ham mixture, carefully but thoroughly. Turn into prepared soufflé dish. Refrigerate until firm.
To remove collar, wet a small spatula and run it carefully around between foil and soufflé. Gently peel away foil. Serve garnished with watercress and rolled slices of ham.

*Smoked haddock is the basis for this appetizing savory mousse*

## SMOKED HADDOCK MOUSSE
*6 servings*

**1 small carrot, cut up**
**1 small onion, cut up**
**1¼ cups milk**
**1 bay leaf**
**3 parsley sprigs**
**6 peppercorns**
**3 tablespoons butter or margarine**
**¼ cup flour**
**1¼ cups unflavored liquid gelatin, made from unflavored gelatin**
**½ pound smoked haddock**
**3 hard-cooked eggs**
**1¼ tablespoons chopped parsley**
**⅝ cup heavy cream, whipped**
**Juice and grated rind of 1 small lemon**
**Salt**
**Freshly ground black pepper**
**Parsley sprigs**

Combine the carrot, onion, milk, bay leaf, parsley and peppercorns in a saucepan. Bring to a boil. Remove from heat and let stand for 10 minutes.

Melt the butter in a small saucepan. Stir in the flour and cook for 1–2 minutes. Remove from heat. Strain the vegetables from the milk and stir the warm milk into the butter mixture. Cook over moderate heat, stirring constantly, until mixture comes to a boil. Remove from heat and stir in all but 3 tablespoons of the liquid gelatin. Cool.

Meanwhile, poach the fish in water to cover for 10 minutes. Drain, discard the bones and skin and flake the fish. Chop 2 of the hard-cooked eggs. Combine with the flaked fish and parsley.

Fold the whipped cream into the cooled white sauce. Fold in the lemon rind and juice and the fish mixture. Season to taste. Turn the mixture into a 1½-quart soufflé dish. Chill. Slice the remaining egg and arrange over the surface of the mousse with sprigs of parsley. Remelt remaining gelatin and dilute with 3 tablespoons water. Spoon over garnish on top of mousse. Chill.

## SALMON AND ASPARAGUS MOUSSE
*(Do not attempt this recipe unless you have an electric blender)*
*8 servings*

**4 envelopes (4 tablespoons) unflavored gelatin**
**2 cups chicken bouillon**
**2 tablespoons butter**
**¼ cup flour**
**1¼ cups milk**
**¼ teaspoon dry mustard**
**Pinch of cayenne**
**Salt and pepper**
**1¼ tablespoons cider vinegar**
**3 eggs, separated**
**2 cans (7½ ounces each) salmon, drained**
**⅝ cup heavy cream, lightly whipped**
**1 package (10 ounces) asparagus spears, cooked and cooled**

Combine 2 envelopes unflavored gelatin with chicken bouillon in a small bowl. Set bowl in a pan of hot water and dissolve. Cool and chill just until it begins to set. Pour a little gelatin into an 8-in. spring-form pan with a plain base or into a 2-quart fluted mold. Coat the sides of the fluted mold with gelatin. Chill. Pour more gelatin into the mold until it is ¼ in. deep. Chill. Reserve at least 6 tablespoons liquid gelatin. Melt the butter in a small saucepan. Stir in the flour and cook for 2–3 minutes. Remove from heat and stir in the milk. Cook over moderate heat, stirring constantly, until the mixture comes to a boil and is thickened. Season with mustard, cayenne, salt and pepper. Beat in the vinegar and egg yolks. Cook over low heat for a few more minutes. Add the drained, flaked salmon, stir well and check seasoning.

Put the 6 tablespoons liquid gelatin in a bowl. Add 2 remaining envelopes unflavored gelatin and let soften. Place over hot water until dissolved, then add to the salmon mixture. Put about half the mixture into the container of an electric blender and blend until smooth. Turn out into a bowl and repeat with remaining mixture. Let stand until just about ready to set. Fold in the whipped cream. Beat the egg whites until stiff and fold into the salmon mixture. Spoon into the prepared pan or fluted mold. Chill until the mixture is set.

To unmold, hold a warm cloth around the sides of the pan, release the clip and remove ring. Warm the base and slide the mousse on to a serving platter. Or, dip the mold in hot water and invert on to a damp serving platter. Garnish with asparagus spears. Serve immediately.

## SHRIMP MOUSSE
*4 servings*

**3 envelopes (3 tablespoons) unflavored gelatin**
**1 cup cold chicken bouillon**
**½ pound whole, cooked shrimp**
**2½ cups milk**
**1 small onion, cut up**
**1 small carrot, cut up**
**2 cloves**
**1 bay leaf**
**3–4 peppercorns**
**3 tablespoons butter or margarine**
**6 tablespoons flour**
**2 eggs, separated**
**Salt and pepper**
**⅝ cup dry white wine**

Soften 1 tablespoon gelatin in the chicken bouillon in a bowl, then set bowl in a pan of hot water and dissolve. Pour a thin layer of gelatin in bottom of a 1½-quart mold. Add a few shrimp for decoration and chill. Put the milk, onion, carrot, cloves, bay leaf and peppercorns in a saucepan. Bring to a boil. Turn off heat, cover and let stand for 15 minutes. Strain and discard the vegetables.

Melt the butter in a saucepan. Stir in the flour and cook for 2–3 minutes. Remove from heat and stir in milk. Cook over moderate heat, stirring constantly, until mixture comes to a boil and thickens. Remove from heat and cool slightly. Beat in egg yolks. Season to taste. Soften remaining 2 tablespoons gelatin in white wine in a bowl. Set bowl in a pan of hot water to dissolve. Stir dissolved gelatin into white sauce. Chop the remaining shrimp and fold into the sauce. Chill just until mixture begins to set. Beat the egg whites until stiff. Fold into the shrimp mixture. Spoon into the prepared mold. Chill until set. To serve, dip mold into hot water and invert on to a damp serving platter. Garnish as desired.

## SHRIMP RICE MOUSSE
*4 servings*

**½ cup long grain rice**
**2 tablespoons (2 envelopes) unflavored gelatin**
**1¼ cups cold water**
**½ pound cooked shrimp, roughly chopped**
**⅝ cup mayonnaise**
**½ cup cooked peas**
**2 stalks celery, chopped**
**Salt**
**Freshly ground black pepper**
**⅝ cup heavy cream, whipped**
**Sliced cucumber**

Cook the rice according to package directions. Drain. Soften the gelatin in cold water in a small bowl. Set bowl over a pan of hot water and dissolve. Remove from heat and cool, stirring occasionally. Reserve a few of the shrimp for garnish and fold the rest into the mayonnaise. Stir in the peas, celery and dissolved gelatin. Season to taste. Fold in the whipped cream and rice. Cool.

When nearly set, turn the mousse into a 1-quart mold that has been rinsed with cold water. Chill thoroughly. When set, dip the mold quickly into hot water and invert on to a wet plate or serving platter. Garnish with reserved shrimp and sliced cucumber. Serve immediately.

# CHEESE AND CHEESE DISHES

When cheese is made, the best and richest part of the milk, the curd, is separated from the whey, the watery part, pressed and allowed to mature. The quality of the milk and the animal from which it came (whether cow, goat or ewe, or even camel or buffalo), give rise to a wide range of different types of cheese. Local conditions of climate and vegetation, different methods of making it and varying storage conditions during ripening affect the cheese so that almost no cheeses taste the same.

Cheese is an important source of protein, fat and minerals in the diet and is one of the tastiest savory foods, whether eaten in its natural state or cooked and combined with other foods. Remember never to cook cheese for longer than it takes to heat through and melt — over-heating makes it tough and indigestible.

## CONTINENTAL CHEESES

**Bel Paese** Italian; rich, creamy cheese; mild flavor; made usually from October to June.

**Brie** French; soft farm cheese made from whole milk and mold-inoculated; creamy-white, with a brownish, slightly moldy crust; mild, rich flavor; made in flat rounds 1–1½ in. thick and about 14 in. across, but also available, boxed, in wedges; does not keep well. Not good for cooking.

**Camembert** French; made from creamy cows' milk inoculated with a white mold; creamy-white, with a light crust similar to Brie; delicious at its best, when starting to soften, but if allowed to over-ripen it becomes too soft and generates unpleasant gases. Made in rounds 4–5 in. across and sold boxed; also sold in individually wrapped portions.

**Danish Blue** White, crumbly cheese with blue veining produced by mold; sharp, salty taste.

**Demi-sel** French; soft cream cheese; sold in small, square, foil-wrapped packs.

**Dolcelatte** Italian; a milder, creamier form of Gorgonzola.

**Edam** Dutch; firm, smooth cheese; ball shaped, bright red outside, deep yellow inside; mild flavor. Good for cooking; low in calories. Also made in other countries but only the Dutch has the true flavor.

**Emmenthal** Swiss (also French, Italian and Austrian); similar to

*Reading clockwise from bottom left: Camembert, Sage Derby, Leicester, Lancashire, Emmenthal, Danish Blue, Edam, Boursin and Brie*

19

Gruyère but slightly softer in texture, with larger 'eyes'. Excellent for fondues, quiches, etc.

**Fontainebleau** French; soft, fresh cream cheese.

**Fromage à la crème** Soft cheese made from sour milk; served softened with a little milk and with sugar and cream.

**Gorgonzola** Italian; semi-hard, blue veined cheese; sharp flavor.

**Gouda** Dutch; similar to Edam in texture but creamier and with a better flavor, and a yellow skin. Usually made as large rounds but also exported as small cheeses.

**Gruyère** Swiss (also French and Italian); hard cheese honeycombed with 'eyes' or holes caused by rapid fermentation of the curd; pale yellow; distinctive, fairly sweet taste; good uncooked but also cooked in many classic European dishes.

**Havarti** Danish; smooth, light yellow cheese with numerous holes, large and small. Full flavored, with a piquant aftertaste. Foil wrapped.

**Limburger** Belgian (also German and French); semi-hard whole milk cheese; full flavored and strong smelling.

**Mycella** Danish; has the golden yellow color of rich cream, with green veining.

**Mysöst (Gietöst)** Norwegian; whey cheese, made principally from goats' milk; hard and dark brown; sweetish flavor.

**Parmesan** Italian; the hardest of all cheeses; pale straw color and full of tiny holes, like pin-pricks; used finely grated in cooked dishes or sprinkled on top of hot dishes such as pasta, rice and soups.

**Petit Suisse (Petit Gervais)** French; unsalted cream cheese; very mild; sold in small, cylindrical, foil-wrapped packs.

**Pommel** French; unsalted double cream cheese; not unlike Petit Suisse.

**Pont l'Evêque** French; semi-hard cheese, salted repeatedly while maturing; yellow; made in small squares. Somewhat similar to Camembert and should be eaten soft and not too ripe.

**Port-Salut** French; semi-hard, round cheese; creamy yellow; mild flavor; should be eaten while still slightly soft.

**Roquefort** French; ewes' milk cheese layered with a culture of molded breadcrumbs (the same mold as that inoculated into Stilton); made only during the lambing season and only in the Roquefort district; white, curd-

*Reading clockwise from top left: Cheddar, Jarlsberg, Stilton, Bleu de Bresse, Port-Salut, Windsor Red and Raybier*

like cheese, mottled with blue veins; sharp, peppery taste.

**Samsoe** Danish; firm in texture with regular holes, and a mild, sweet nut-like flavor. Cuts well into thin slices or cubes.

## BRITISH CHEESES

### HARD CHEESES

**Blue Vinney (Blue Dorset)** Hard cheese made from skimmed cows' milk; white with a blue vein; rather strong flavor.

**Caerphilly** A soft, crumbly, whole milk cheese, eaten when about 10 days old; white; creamy, mild flavor; best uncooked.

**Cheddar** Hard, yellow, whole milk cheese; slightly salty and varying in flavor from mild to quite strong; good cooked or uncooked. The cheddaring process is easily mechanized and carried out under factory conditions and the cheese is therefore produced in many parts of the world, other than the United States, notably New Zealand, Australia and Canada. 'Farmhouse' Cheddar is still usually considered the best.

**Derby** Hard, close-textured, white cheese; mild when young but developing a full flavor as it matures; sage leaves sometimes added to give a green cheese known as **Sage Derby**.

**Double Gloucester** Hard, orange-yellow cheese; close, crumbly texture; rich flavor similar to mature Cheddar.

**Dunlop** Scottish cheese similar to Cheddar, but more moist and with a closer texture.

**Lancashire** A fairly hard cheese but crumbly when cut; mild, tangy flavor when new, developing as the cheese matures; excellent for cooking.

**Leicester** Hard cheese; orange-red color; mild, slightly sweet flavor.

**Stilton** Semi-hard, double cream cheese (i.e. made from rich milk to which extra cream is added); white with evenly distributed blue veining caused by a mold inoculated into the cheese; the rind should be a dull, drab color, well crinkled, regular and free from cracks; best after 6–9 months. Made only during May to September. A milder, white Stilton is also available. Not suitable for cooking.

**Wensleydale** Double cream cheese originally matured until blue; now usually sold white and unripe, when it is mild and flaky.

### SOFT CHEESE

**Cream cheese** Made from cream only; may be heavy cream cheese (from cream with a 45–50 per cent fat content) or light cream cheese (made from cream with a 25–30 per cent fat content); made in small quantities as it keeps for only 6–7 days; soft and rich. Available plain or flavored with herbs, fruit, nuts, etc.

**Curd cheese** Made by the same method as cream cheese, but from milk; soft, but slightly firmer than cream cheese and not so rich.

**Cottage cheese** Made from the same method again, but using skimmed milk; very soft, loose-textured, rather flavorless cheese. Mixes well with salads and used for making cheesecake. Available plain or flavored with herbs or fruit.

### STORING CHEESE

The drier, harder cheeses will keep well when stored correctly, but softer cheeses deteriorate quickly, so should be bought only as required. To store cheese, wrap it loosely in plastic, aluminum foil or waxed paper – trap some air in the package

otherwise the cheese will sweat and mold will grow quickly – then place it in a cool larder or refrigerator. If you keep it in the refrigerator, make sure that it is brought to room temperature for serving. Wrap different types of cheeses separately, so that one does not take on the flavor of another. Pre-packaged cheese keeps well in the refrigerator, but once opened it should be re-wrapped and stored as for fresh cheese. Soft cheeses, including Brie, Camembert and cream cheese, freeze well.

Cottage cheese and cream cheeses have a comparatively short life and must be kept covered in the refrigerator.

### PRESENTING THE CHEESE BOARD

A cheese board or platter is one of the best ways of finishing a meal; many people prefer the sharp flavor to a sweet, and others will return to cheese after the sweet, to finish off the last of a dry wine or to enjoy a glass of port.

A good cheese board does not have to offer the number of cheeses that might be available in a restaurant, but there should be a good variety. A balance of hard and soft cheeses, mild and full flavored ones is the most important consideration and the colors and shapes of the pieces make it more interesting visually. A fairly modest but well-balanced board would offer, say, Cheddar, Stilton or Roquefort, Brie and Gouda. Many people will be delighted if you offer something new or unusual for them to try.

The board itself may be any attractive platter large enough to hold your chosen selection without looking crowded. For a small selection, an old-fashioned china dish with its own cover is ideal – these are usually a pretty shape and they are prefectly designed for keeping the cheese in good condition, covered but airy. For more pieces, a well-scrubbed bread board or a meat dish serves the purpose, and may also be large enough to accommodate a garnish such as celery, or a small bunch of grapes. For a big party use a tray or the top of a cart; the first has handles, the latter wheels and either will overcome the problem of lifting a very heavy board carrying a large selection of cheeses. Provide 2 or 3 knives so that the person taking Cheddar does not get unwelcome traces of Stilton with it.

*Spaghetti con formaggio is covered in melted cheese*

To go with the cheese, offer a selection of plain and sweet cookies, and a few salty crackers, or a basket of chunky breads or rolls. Several small dishes of fresh, unsalted butter, in small chunks or individual pats, saves endless passing of a single dish. Nothing looks more attractive or goes better with cheese than a big bowl of fresh fruit. Polished apples and pears, freshly washed peaches and nuts are probably the most popular at this stage of the meal. Again, make sure there are enough dessert knives to go round – it is difficult to skin a peach with an ordinary table knife.

For a change, try serving a selection of crisp salad vegetables with the cheese. Quartered lettuce hearts, chunks of celery, endive leaves, tomato wedges, small whole radishes and carrot sticks all go down well, with the addition of a little salt.

## SPAGHETTI CON FORMAGGIO
*2 servings*

⅓ **pound spaghetti**
½ **pound lean bacon, chopped**
1 **onion, coarsely grated**
2 **tablespoons butter**
½ **pound button mushrooms, sliced**
**Salt**
**Freshly ground black pepper**
1¼ **tablespoons salad oil**
⅓ **pound sharp Cheddar cheese, grated**
**Chopped parsley**

Cook the spaghetti in boiling salted water for 10 minutes. Put the chopped bacon in a skillet and fry gently for 3 minutes, stirring occasionally with a wooden spoon. Add the onion and cook for 1 minute. Add the butter and sliced mushrooms, season lightly and cook for 4 minutes, stirring occasionally. Drain the spaghetti and return it to the pan with the salad oil. Using 2 forks, coat the spaghetti in oil until it glistens. Turn the spaghetti into a flameproof dish and spoon the bacon and mushroom mixture on top. Sprinkle with the grated cheese and broil under a heated broiler for 30 seconds or just until the cheese is melted. Sprinkle with chopped parsley.

## ASPARAGUS AU GRATIN
*6 servings*

1 **pound asparagus, fresh or frozen**
¼ **cup butter or margarine**
5 **tablespoons flour**
2½ **cups milk**
3⅓ **tablespoons port**
¼ **cup grated Parmesan cheese**
¾ **cup grated Cheddar cheese**
**Salt and pepper**

Trim fresh asparagus to even lengths. Plunge fresh or frozen asparagus into boiling salted water, bring to a boil and boil for 5 minutes. Drain well.
Butter a shallow au gratin dish and arrange the asparagus in the bottom. Melt the butter in a saucepan. Stir in the flour and cook for 1-2 minutes. Remove from the heat and stir in the milk. Cook over medium heat, stirring constantly, until the mixture comes to a boil and thickens. Stir in the port, Parmesan cheese and half of the Cheddar cheese. Adjust seasoning.
Pour the sauce on top of the asparagus. Sprinkle the remaining Cheddar over the top. Bake in a fairly hot oven (400°F.) for about 20 minutes.

## CAULIFLOWER AU GRATIN
*4 servings*

2 **pounds potatoes**
2 **eggs**
2½ **tablespoons milk**
**Salt and pepper**
2 **pounds cauliflower**
1 **can (10½ ounces) condensed cream of celery soup**
¼ **pound Cheddar cheese**
½ **cup buttered breadcrumbs**

Peel the potatoes and cook in boiling salted water until tender. Drain and put through a sieve back into the pan. Beat 1 egg and add 2 tablespoons of it to the pan. Beat well. Season. Put the potatoes in a pastry bag with a large star nozzle, pipe the potato around the edge of a shallow au gratin dish, and brush with the remainder of the beaten egg.

Brown in a fairly hot oven (400°F.) for about 20 minutes. Meanwhile, break the cauliflower into flowerets. Cook in boiling salted water until tender but not mushy. Drain well and arrange in the center of the potatoes.
In a saucepan, beat together the soup, the second egg, milk and cheese. Heat until piping hot, stirring. Adjust seasoning. Pour over the cauliflower. Top with the buttered crumbs. Return to the oven and heat until piping hot.

## MUSHROOMS WITH GRUYERE
*4-6 servings*

1½ **pounds button mushrooms**
¼ **cup butter**
⅝ **cup water**
2½ **tablespoons lemon juice**
1 **clove garlic**
**Salt and pepper**
2½ **pounds potatoes, cooked**
2 **tablespoons warm milk**
2 **tablespoons butter**
**Pinch of nutmeg**
1 **egg yolk**
½ **cup grated Gruyère cheese**

Wipe the mushrooms with a damp cloth. In a large saucepan, melt the butter in the water, add the lemon juice, garlic, salt and pepper. Add the mushrooms and cook without covering over a fairly high heat until the moisture has evaporated, about 25 minutes. Watch carefully at the end of cooking time so as to not burn the mushrooms. Remove garlic clove.
Sieve the potatoes and cream with the milk, butter, seasonings and egg yolk. Beat well. Pipe the potato in a border around a flameproof dish. Place under a hot broiler just long enough to brown top lightly. Spoon the mushrooms into the center of the potato border and sprinkle with the grated cheese. Return to the broiler just long enough to melt the cheese. Serve at once.

## CORN AND CHEESE OMELET
*2 servings*

4 **eggs**
2½ **tablespoons water**
**Salt**
**Freshly ground black pepper**
2 **tablespoons butter**
1 **can (8 ounces) creamed corn**
¼ **cup grated Cheddar cheese**

Beat 2 eggs lightly with 1 tablespoon water. Season to taste.

*A quick and appetizing supper – asparagus au gratin*

Heat 1 tablespoon butter in a heavy-bottomed skillet, tilting the pan to grease the whole surface. Pour in the egg mixture. Stir gently with the back of a fork, from the sides towards the center, until no liquid egg remains. Stop stirring and cook a little longer to lightly brown the omelet underneath. Meanwhile, heat the corn in a separate pan.

When the egg mixture has almost set, spread half the corn down the center and towards one side. Sprinkle with 2 tablespoons cheese. Tilt the pan and let the omelet fold over. Repeat for the second omelet. Serve at once.

## VEAL CORDON BLEU
*4 servings*

**4 veal escalopes, 6-7 ounces each**
**4 slices lean cooked ham**
**4 slices Gruyère cheese**
**¼ cup butter**
**3⅓ tablespoons salad oil**
**1¼ cups rich brown stock, page 10**
**⅝ cup Madeira**
**Freshly ground black pepper**

Put the escalopes between two pieces of waxed paper. Pound with the side of a cleaver or other heavy object to about ¼ in. thick. Remove paper. Top each with a slice of ham cut to fit. Cover half with a slice of cheese and fold escalopes in half. Secure with toothpicks.

Melt the butter and oil in a large skillet. Fry the escalopes quickly on each side. Reduce heat and cook for about 6 minutes on each side until tender and golden brown. Add the stock and Madeira and simmer on top of the stove for 5 minutes.

Remove the meat to a heated serving platter and keep hot. Season the juices with black pepper and boil rapidly to reduce. Take the toothpicks from the meat, cover with the juices and serve.

## CHEESE FRITTERS
*2 servings*

**¼ cup butter**
**6 tablespoons flour**
**1¼ cups milk**
**Salt**
**Freshly ground black pepper**
**½ teaspoon dry mustard**
**⅓ pound Edam cheese, rinded and diced**
**1 can (8 ounces) button mushrooms, drained**
**1 egg, beaten with a little salt**
**½ cup dried breadcrumbs**
**Oil for deep frying**

Melt the butter in a small pan. Stir in the flour and cook for 1 minute. Remove from heat and stir in the milk. Cook over medium heat, stirring constantly, until the mixture comes to a boil and thickens. Season well with salt, pepper and mustard. Remove from heat.

Add the diced cheese and the mushrooms and blend well. When the mixture is cool, shape into fritters with a spoon. Coat with the beaten egg and roll in the breadcrumbs. Pat the crumbs on very firmly and carefully shake off any excess. Let stand a while for crumbs to set.

Heat the oil to 350°F. Fry the fritters for 5 minutes, turning to brown all sides. Drain thoroughly on paper towels.

Serve at once with green salad and potato chips.

*Orange cheesecake is a delicious dessert for a special occasion*

## ORANGE CHEESECAKE
*6-8 servings*

**3 oranges**
**Juice of 1 lemon**
**2 envelopes unflavored gelatin**
**2 eggs, separated**
**1¼ cups milk**
**6 tablespoons sugar**
**2½ cups cottage cheese**
**⅝ cup heavy cream, whipped**

*For crumb base:*

**1 cup graham cracker crumbs**
**¼ cup sugar**
**¼ cup butter, melted**
**3 oranges, peeled and sectioned**

Finely grate the rind of 2 oranges, squeeze the juice from 3 and add the lemon juice. Put 4 tablespoons of the mixed juices in a small bowl and sprinkle the gela-

tin over the top.

Beat together the egg yolks, milk and 4 tablespoons sugar. Turn into a saucepan and cook over low heat, stirring, for a few minutes until hot. Add the softened gelatin mixture and stir continuously until dissolved.

Let cool until just starting to set, then add the grated orange rind and ½ cup more of the mixed juices. Sieve the cheese and beat it into the orange mixture with an electric beater, or put the cheese and the orange mixture in a blender and blend until smooth. Beat the egg whites until stiff, beat in 2 tablespoons sugar and beat until stiff. Fold quickly into the cheese mixture. Fold in the cream.

Turn mixture into a 9-in. spring-form pan. Combine the cracker crumbs, sugar and melted butter and toss lightly. Spread over the

cheese mixture and press lightly with a spatula. Chill thoroughly. To serve, turn out of the pan on to a cake plate. Garnish with overlapping sections of orange and a whirl of whipped cream.

## CHEESE WHEEZIES
*2 servings*

**½ pound sausage meat**
**Six 1-in. cubes Cheddar cheese**
**Dried breadcrumbs**
**Oil for deep frying**
**1 can (16 ounces) kernel corn**
**4 tomatoes, halved**
**Black pepper**
**Watercress**

Divide the sausage meat into 6 equal-size pieces and wrap it around the cheese cubes. Roll into balls and dip in breadcrumbs

until well coated and then reshape.

Heat the oil to 350°F. and fry the sausage balls for about 5 minutes, until golden brown. Turn the wheezies once or twice so that they cook evenly. Meanwhile, heat the corn in a saucepan over low heat. Sprinkle the tomatoes with pepper and broil under a hot broiler until piping hot.

Arrange the wheezies on the corn on individual plates and garnish with the broiled tomatoes and watercress.

## CHEESE SCONES AND GHERKIN BUTTER
*Makes 9*

**2 cups self-rising flour**
**1 teaspoon baking powder**
**Pinch of salt**
**3 tablespoons butter or margarine**
**½ cup grated strong Cheddar cheese**
**1 teaspoon dry mustard**
**⅝ cup milk**

*For gherkin butter:*

**½ cup butter or margarine**
**Dash of Tabasco sauce**
**2 small gherkins, chopped**
**1½ tablespoons chopped capers**
**Salt and pepper**

Sift together the flour, baking powder and salt. Cut in the fat with a pastry blender or two knives until the mixture resembles fine breadcrumbs. Stir in the cheese and mustard. Add enough milk to make a fairly soft, light dough. Roll out on a lightly floured board to about ¾ in. thick. Cut into rounds with a 2½-in. round cutter. Place the rounds on an ungreased, preheated cookie tray and sprinkle the tops with flour.

Bake near the top of a hot oven (425°F.) for about 10 minutes. Cool on a wire rack.

To make the gherkin butter, cream the butter, stir in Tabasco sauce, gherkins and capers, season to taste.

## BLUE CHEESE DRESSING
*3½ tablespoons French dressing*
*1 tablespoon blue cheese*
*1 scallion, snipped*

Beat the French dressing to emulsify it thoroughly. Break up the blue cheese as finely as possible and mix into dressing with scallion. Serve spooned over lettuce wedges.

# CHOOSING YOUR MEAT

*All meat needs to be hung in a suitable temperature and for the correct length of time before it is sold, otherwise it is tough and tasteless. Any reputable butcher will see that this is done.*

*A shoulder of lamb has more fat but also more flavor than the leg*

## BEEF

**What to look for**

1. The lean should be bright red, the fat a creamy yellow.
2. There should be small flecks of fat through the lean; this fat (called marbling) helps to keep the lean moist and tender when the meat is cooking.
3. There should be no line of gristle between lean and fat – this usually suggests the meat has come from an old animal and it may be tough.

**Chuck and blade**
Fairly lean with no bone, suitable for stewing and casseroles. Allow 6–8 ounces per serving.

**Rib**
A large roast, sold on the bone or boned and rolled. Usually roasted. With bone, allow 8–12 ounces per serving; without bone, allow 6–8 ounces per serving. (Wing rib is sirloin without the fillet.)

**Sirloin**
A large roast including the undercut which is particularly tender. Usually sold on the bone, but also boned and rolled. Almost always roasted. With bone, allow 8–12 ounces per serving; without bone, allow 6–8 ounces per serving.

**Rump**
Cut into steaks for broiling and frying; no bone.

**Aitchbone**
A big roast with a large bone, often boned or partially boned for convenience when carving. Usually roasted, but also boiled and braised. Sometimes salted and boiled. Allow 12 ounces per serving.

**Topside**
A lean roast with no bone; good flavor. Usually slow roasted, but also braised and pot roasted. Allow 6–8 ounces per serving.

**Silverside**
A boneless roast needing long, slow cooking such as braising. Allow 8–12 ounces per serving.

**Flank** (*the belly – may be thick or thin*)
A boneless cut, rather coarse. Needs slow, moist cooking such as stewing, braising or pot roasting. Allow 6–8 ounces per serving.

**Brisket**
A fatty roast but with a good flavor; sold on and off the bone. Slow roast, braise or stew; often salted for boiling. With bone, allow 8–12 ounces per serving; without bone, allow 6–8 ounces per serving.

## LAMB, MUTTON

**What to look for**

1. The younger the animal the paler the meat; in a young lamb it is light pink, while in a mature animal it is light red.
2. A slight blue tinge to the bones suggests that the animal is young.
3. The fat is firm and white, or creamy colored.

**Scrag and middle neck**
A high proportion of bone and fat but a good flavor. Suitable for stews and casseroles. Allow 8–12 ounces per serving, on the bone.

**Best end of neck**
A series of tiny cutlets that may be divided up and fried or broiled, or left whole and roasted. Two roasts, back to back, form a crown of lamb. Allow 12 ounces per serving.

**Loin**
A prime cut sold on the bone or boned, stuffed and rolled for roasting, or divided into chops for broiling or frying. When roasting with the bone, allow 12 ounces per serving; without bone, allow 4–6 ounces per serving.

**Chump**
Cut into chops for broiling, frying and casseroles. Allow 1–2 chops per serving.

**Leg**
A good cut for roasting. With bone, allow 12 ounces per serving. Cut the meat off the bone for kebabs etc.

**Breast**
A rather fatty cut, usually boned, stuffed and rolled. Roasted, braised, stewed. With bone, allow 8–12 ounces per serving.

**Shoulder**
A large roast with more fat, but often with more flavor, than the leg. Usually roasted. Allow 12 ounces per serving on the bone.

## VEAL

**What to look for**

1. The meat should be light in color, fine textured, pale pink, soft and moist; avoid flabby, wet meat.
2. If the meat looks bluish or mottled it generally means it comes from an older animal or is rather stale.
3. The fat – of which there is very little – should be firm and pinkish or creamy white.

**Best end of neck**
Sold on the bone, or boned, stuffed and rolled. Suitable for roasting, braising and stewing; if divided into cutlets, suitable for sautéing or frying. With bone, allow about 1 pound per serving.

**Loin**
A prime cut for roasting, either on the bone or boned, stuffed and rolled. Also used for sautés and braised or divided into chops for broiling or frying. With bone, allow 8 ounces per serving.

**Fillet**
Sold in the piece for roasting (usually boned and stuffed before cooking), or cut into thin slices or escalopes for frying. Without bone, allow 4–6 ounces per serving.

**Shoulder**
An awkward shape but suitable for roasting if boned, stuffed and rolled. Portions of shoulder meat are often sold for pies and stews. With bone, allow 1 pound per serving.

## PORK

**What to look for**

1. The lean should be pale pink, moist and slightly marbled with fat.
2. There should be a good outer layer of firm, white fat, with a thin, elastic skin; if the roast is to be roasted, get the butcher to score the skin.
3. The bones should be small and pinkish (which denotes a young animal).

**Spare rib**
A fairly lean cut, good for roasting, but can be cut up for braising and stewing. Also divided into chops for broiling and frying. With bone, allow 8–12 ounces per serving.

**Loin**
A prime cut which often includes the kidney. Best roasted, it can be cooked on the bone or boned and stuffed; also divided into chops for broiling. With bone, allow 8–12 ounces per serving; without bone, allow 4 ounces per serving.

**Leg**
A prime cut, but rather large, so it is often cut into 2. Roasted on the bone or boned and stuffed. Sometimes pickled for boiling. With bone, allow 8–12 ounces per serving; without bone, allow 4 ounces per serving.

**Belly**
A fatty cut, usually sold salted for boiling. May be roasted or braised, cut into strips for frying or ground for pâtés. Allow 4–6 ounces per serving.

**Hand and spring**
The foreleg, a little on the fatty side. Suitable for roasting, boiling and stewing. Hand is good salted and boiled. Allow 12 ounces per serving.

# CARVING A ROAST

*When a roast is well carved, the meat looks nice on the plate and goes further. Carving is an art most people can master, given a good knife. If you tell the butcher how you want to serve the meat, he will prepare the roast the easiest way for carving.*

In order to carve successfully, the one essential tool is a long-bladed, sharp knife. To maintain the sharpness, use a steel or a patent sharpener every time you carve. (To use a steel, draw each side of the blade in turn smoothly down and across with rapid strokes, holding the blade at an angle of 45° to the steel.) Careless sharpening can inflict permanent damage on the knife or your finger!

Also essential is a sharp 2-pronged fork to hold the meat, with a guard to protect your hand should the knife slip. The final accessory is a meat dish with sharp prongs to hold the meat in place – this is by no means necessary, but it is extremely helpful.

Meat is usually best cut against the grain, except when it is very tender (undercut, for instance, is cut with the grain). The grain of the meat runs lengthwise along the carcass, hence roasts are carved from the outside to the center of the animal.

Before you start to carve, examine the structure of the roast, and notice the exact distribution of bone, lean meat and fat. Carve standing up and use long, even strokes, keeping the blade at the same angle throughout, to give neat, uniform slices. As you carve, move the knife to and fro, cutting cleanly without bearing down on the meat, which presses out the juices. Serve the carved slices on to really hot plates.

Beef and veal (except fillet) are carved very thinly, but pork and lamb are cut in slices about ¼ in. thick. If the roast has a bone, take the knife right up to it, so that eventually the bone is left clean.

## BEEF

### Sirloin of beef on the bone
Stand the roast on its back with the fillet uppermost. First carve out the flank, then remove the fillet from the bone and carve both these into thin slices. Then turn the roast so that the upper-cut is on top, making a long slice against the back bone. Further slices will then separate easily.

### Rib
Stand the roast on edge on the bone. Slice downwards along the full length of the roast, cutting each slice down to the bone (if necessary, cutting behind the ribs to free the meat) and slanting a little away from the cut edge, so that the bone is left clean. Support the slices with the fork to prevent them breaking.

### Boneless joints
Carve against the grain, usually horizontally. In the case of a long piece of roast fillet, carve downwards.

## VEAL

### Stuffed breast
Cut downwards in fairly thick slices, right through the roast. Remove the string from each part of the joint as it is carved.

### Chump end leg
The bone is sometimes removed and replaced by stuffing. Cut across the grain (i.e. horizontally) into medium-thick slices, right across the roast.

If the bone has been left in, cut the meat in long slices following the shape of the bone. When the bone is reached and cleared, turn the roast over and continue carving vertically on the other side.

### Loin
One of the few roasts carved with the grain of the meat. Carve long slices down the length of the back, turning the knife to follow the bone and release the slices. Then turn the roast round to complete the cut. Take smaller slices from the chump end and turn the roast over and remove smaller slices.

## LAMB

### Leg
Begin by cutting a wedge-shaped slice from the center of the meatier side of the roast. Carve slices from each side of the cut, gradually turning the knife to get larger slices and ending parallel to the bone. Turn the roast over, remove the fat, and carve in long flat slices along the leg.

### Shoulder
Cut a long thick slice down to the bone from the center of the meatier side of the roast. Carve small slices from each side of the hump on the blade bone down to the shank until the whole surface is clean.

Turn the roast over, remove the fat and carve in horizontal slices.

### Best end of neck
Remove the chine bone then cut down between the ribs, dividing the roast into cutlets.

### Saddle
First carve the meat from the top of the roast in long slices, cutting downwards, to and parallel with the backbone. Do this at each side of the bone, taking about 4 slices from either side of the saddle.

### Stuffed breast
Cut downwards in fairly thick slices, right through the roast.

## PORK

### Loin of pork
Sever the chine bone from the chop bones and put to one side. Divide into chops by cutting between the bones.

### Boned and rolled
Remove the string from each part of the roast as it is carved. Cut through the crackling where it was scored half-way along the roast. Lift off the crackling and cut into pieces. Carve the meat into slices.

### Leg
Use the point of the knife to cut through the crackling; it is usually easier to remove it and then divide it into portions. Carve as for leg of lamb, but medium-thick.

### Spring
Remove the rib bones underneath, then turn the crackling back on top. Remove some of the crackling before carving. Distribute fat and lean evenly by cutting alternate slices from either end until the bone is reached. Turn the roast over and carve the meat from the other side of the bone.

## HAM

Roasts for boiling are usually boned and rolled. Carve as for boned and rolled beef, but in slightly thicker slices.

Cold cooked ham is best carved on a ham stand as this supports the awkwardly shaped roast. A specially long thin knife is used. Carve in the thinnest possible slices, as for leg of lamb.

# ROASTING

There is no method of cooking that can give a tastier result than roasting, with so little trouble. Plainly roasted meat, served with fresh vegetables and rich gravy is considered one of the best possible meals.

Meat to be roasted must be prime quality, tender and juicy. Roasting is a quick method of cooking, and will not break down tough, sinewy fibres; roasts that are likely to be at all tough should be pot roasted, braised or casseroled. Guidance as to which cuts are suitable is given in the section 'Choosing your meat', but be guided by your butcher as well – only roast those pieces which he recommends and you will not have cause for complaint.

## TRADITIONAL ROASTING

It is traditional to roast in the oven at a high temperature – 425°F. This sears the roast quickly on the outside, giving a good meaty flavor, and is the ideal way when you know the meat is of prime quality – well hung and tender. Many people prefer to roast at 375°F. This is the best way if in doubt about quality and for small roasts, as it keeps the roast more moist than the higher temperature, there is less shrinkage and the meat is likely to be more tender, though the flavor may not be quite as good. Before starting to cook, arrange the shelves in the oven so that there is room for the roast and so that the meat will be in the center. Preheat the oven; if the meat is placed in a cold oven and heated too slowly, the juices will run too freely, leaving the roast dry and tasteless.

Put the roast in the roasting pan so that the cut surfaces are exposed and the fattest part is on top; this automatically bastes the roast. If the natural fat is meagre, top the meat with some dripping or shortening. During cooking, spoon the hot fat and juices over the meat from time to time, to keep it moist and juicy. Never pierce the meat with a fork or knife as this will allow the juices to escape, leaving the roast dry. For those who like less fatty meat, it is a good idea to place the roast on a rack in the roasting pan, so that it is kept free of the dripping. This is particularly convenient if roast potatoes or Yorkshire pudding are being cooked, as they can be placed under the rack and will absorb all the juices and the flavor of the meat.

## COVERED ROASTING

Roasting in a covered pan, in aluminum foil or in a transparent roasting bag helps to keep the oven clean. It also keeps the meat moist; because this method is also partly steaming, it breaks down the fibres more thoroughly than conventional roasting, making the meat more tender and rendering the fat almost to nothing. To crisp the outside of the roast, remove the lid or open the foil 30 minutes before the end of the cooking time; transparent roasting bags allow the roast to brown without this. This is a good method for a roast that you suspect may be slightly tough, or if your family doesn't like any fat at all on meat. It does, however, tend to destroy some of the true open-roasted flavor. Potatoes cooked with a covered roast will not brown.

## FROTHING

If you like a particularly brown, crisp outside to the meat, sprinkle with flour and salt 15 minutes before the end of the cooking time and leave uncovered.

*Score the skin of pork to allow the crackling to cook crisply through*

*Use an evenly shaped roast for successful spit roasting*

## CRACKLING

The outside skin of pork is left on to form 'crackling'. Make sure this is scored deeply and evenly at ¼-in. intervals all over the roast, or it will be extremely difficult to carve. To make the crackling extra crisp and golden brown, rub salad oil and salt into the skin before cooking.

## MEAT THERMOMETERS

A meat thermometer is an infallible guide to when the roast is cooked. Insert it into the thickest part of the roast (but not against the bone) before you start cooking. The thermometer then registers the temperature at the innermost part of the roast and when it shows the correct internal temperature (see chart), the meat is correctly cooked. This is particularly useful with beef, ensuring that you can have it rare, medium or well done, just as you wish. (It is of course necessary to work out the approximate cooking time, so that you know what time to start cooking.)

## SPIT ROASTING (OR ROTISSERIE COOKING)

Spit roasting is a development of the original method of cooking meat in front of an open fire. (The closed-oven method now commonly used should more properly be called baking.) The flavor of spit roasted meat is as different from oven roasted as the latter is from that of meat roasted in a covered pan. Gas and electric cookers are available fitted with a spit, or you can buy a separate, electrically operated model. On a cooker, the spit is best if fitted to the broiler unit – spit roasting in

the oven shows very little difference from ordinary oven roasting. But either way the meat browns more evenly than oven roasted meat and needs even less attention, since it is completely self basting.

Any roast, with bone or boneless, that is suitable for quick roasting may be roasted on a spit. It must, however, be shaped as evenly as possible, so that it will revolve steadily (e.g. a shoulder of lamb on the bone is not really satisfactory). If it is not a compact shape, remove the bone, stuff the roast if you wish, roll it and tie with string. Frozen meat must be completely thawed before cooking starts.

First turn on the heat and allow the broiler or oven to become very hot. Push the shaft through the meat, push the holding forks into place on either side and secure them, to hold the meat firmly in place. Place the loaded shaft in position and start the motor. Allow the shaft to revolve several times before you leave it, to make sure that there is no obstruction and it is turning evenly. Cook the meat on full heat for 5 minutes or according to the manufacturer's instructions, to sear the surface, then reduce the heat and cook for the appropriate time. Individual manufacturers recommend different cooking times, so follow the instructions given with your model. If you wish, the roast may be basted from time to time with the juices and fat from the drip tray, though this is not strictly necessary. To vary the flavor, try adding fruit juice or cider to the juices, or more conventionally a sliced onion or a clove garlic.

## COOKING TIMES AND OVEN TEMPERATURES

| **Beef** on the bone | | 425°F. | 15 min. per pound plus 15 min. (rare) |
| | | 425°F. | 20 min. per pound plus 20 min. (medium) |
| | | 375°F. | 25 min. per pound (medium-well done) |
| | boned and rolled | 425°F. | 20 min. per pound plus 20 min. (rare) |
| | | 425°F. | 25 min. per pound plus 25 min. (medium) |
| | | 375°F. | 30 min. per pound (medium-well done) |
| **Lamb** on the bone | | 425°F. | 20 min. per pound plus 20 min. |
| | | 350°F. | 27 min. per pound plus 27 min. |
| | boned and rolled | 425°F. | 25 min. per pound plus 25 min. |
| | | 250°F. | 35 min. per pound plus 35 min. |
| **Veal** on the bone | | 425°F. | 25 min. per pound plus 25 min. |
| | boned and rolled | 425°F. | 30 min. per pound plus 30 min. |
| **Pork** on the bone | | 425°F. | 25 min. per pound plus 25 min. |
| | boned and rolled | 375°F. | 30–35 min. per pound plus 35 min. |

## USING A MEAT THERMOMETER

| Meat | | Temperature of meat | Results |
| --- | --- | --- | --- |
| **Beef** | Rare | 140°F. | Very rare when hot, but ideal when cold. |
| | Medium | 160°F. | Brown meat, but with blood running from it; pale pinkish tinge when cold. |
| | Well done | 170°F. | Well cooked. Tends to be dry when cold. |
| | Very well done | 180°F. | Fibres breaking up; fat rendered down. |
| **Lamb** | | 180°F. | Moist, brown meat. |
| **Veal** | | 180°F. | Moist, pale meat. |
| **Pork** | | 190°F. | Moist, pale meat. |

# ACCOMPANIMENTS FOR ROASTS

## YORKSHIRE PUDDING
*for beef*

**1 cup all-purpose flour**
**Pinch of salt**
**1 egg**
**1¼ cups milk**
**2 tablespoons lard or pan drippings**

Sift together the flour and salt. Make a well in the center and break in the egg. Sift in half the liquid and beat the mixture with a beater until it is smooth. Add the remaining liquid gradually and beat until well mixed.
Put the lard or dripping in an 8-in. square baking pan and heat it in the oven. Pour in the batter and bake in a hot oven (425°F.) for about 30 minutes or until well risen. Cut into squares and serve at once.

## HORSERADISH CREAM
*for beef*

**2½ tablespoons grated horseradish**
**2½ teaspoons lemon juice**
**2½ teaspoons sugar**
**Pinch of dry mustard**
**⅝ cup heavy cream**

Combine the horseradish, lemon juice, sugar and mustard. Whip the cream just until it is soft, then fold in the horseradish mixture.

## HORSERADISH SAUCE
*for beef*

**⅝ cup white sauce**
**1-2 tablespoons grated horseradish**
**1¼ tablespoons vinegar**

Mix the ingredients thoroughly and serve warm.

## MINT SAUCE
*for lamb*

**Small bunch of mint, washed**
**2½ teaspoons sugar**
**1¼ tablespoons boiling water**
**1-2 tablespoons vinegar**

Strip the mint leaves from the stalks and put with the sugar on a board. Chop finely. Put in a gravy boat, add the boiling water and stir until the sugar is dissolved. Stir in the vinegar to taste.
Let the sauce stand for 1 hour before serving.

*Most people like roast beef slightly rare*

## MINT JELLY
*for lamb*

**6 pound cooking apples**
**5⅝ cups water**
**Bunch of fresh mint**
**Sugar**
**5⅝ cups vinegar**
**6-8 tablespoons chopped mint**
**Green coloring (optional)**

Wash and roughly chop the apples; do not pare or core. Put in a large pan with the water and mint and simmer until really soft and pulpy. Add the vinegar and boil for 5 minutes. Strain through a jelly cloth. Measure the extract and return it to the pan with 1 pound sugar to 2½ cups of extract. Stir until the sugar has dissolved. Boil rapidly until a 'jell' is obtained on testing a few drops on a cold saucer.
Stir in the chopped mint and a few drops of coloring, if required. Skim and turn into warm, dry jars. Seal tightly.

## RED-CURRANT JELLY
*for lamb*

**3 pound red-currants**
**2½ cups water**
**Sugar**

Wash the fruit but do not remove the stalks. Put into a pan with the water and simmer gently until the currants are very soft and pulpy. Strain through a jelly cloth. Measure the extract and return it to the pan with 1 pound sugar to 2½ cups of extract. Stir until the sugar has dissolved and then boil rapidly until a 'jell' is obtained on testing a few drops on a cold saucer.
Skim, turn into warm, dry jars

and seal.
Cranberry jelly is made in the same way.

## APPLE SAUCE
*for pork*

**1 pound cooking apples, pared and cored**
**2 tablespoons butter**
**Sugar, optional**

Slice the apples into a pan, add 2-3 tablespoons water and simmer, covered, until soft – about 10 minutes. Beat to a pulp with a wooden spoon, then sieve or purée in an electric blender if wished. Stir in the butter and add a little sugar if the apples are very tart.

## GOOSEBERRY SAUCE
*for pork*

**½ pound gooseberries, washed and stalks removed**
**2 tablespoons butter**
**Sugar, optional**

Stew the fruit in as little water as possible, until soft and pulped. Beat well then sieve the fruit or purée in a blender. Add the butter and a little sugar if the fruit is very sour.

## CUMBERLAND SAUCE
*for ham and mutton*

**1 orange**
**1 lemon**
**5 tablespoons red-currant jelly**
**5 tablespoons port**
**2½ teaspoons cornstarch**
**2½ teaspoons water**

Pare the rind thinly from the orange and lemon, cut into strips. Cover with water and simmer for

5 minutes. Squeeze the juice from both fruits. Put the red-currant jelly, orange juice and lemon juice in a pan and stir until the jelly dissolves; simmer for 5 minutes and add the port. Blend the cornstarch and water to a smooth paste and stir in the red-currant mixture. Return the sauce to the pan and re-heat, stirring until it thickens and is clear. Drain the strips of rind and add to the sauce.

## SAGE AND ONION STUFFING
*for pork*

**2 large onions, chopped**
**2 tablespoons butter**
**2 cups fresh breadcrumbs**
**2 teaspoons dried sage**
**Salt and pepper**

Put the onions in a pan of cold water, bring to the boil and cook until tender – about 10 minutes. Drain well, add the other ingredients and mix well.

## PRUNE AND APPLE STUFFING
*for pork*

**4 ounces prunes, soaked and pitted**
**8 ounces cooking apples, pared and cored**
**Just under 1 cup cooked long grain rice**
**2 ounces shredded suet**
**2 ounces almonds, blanched and shredded**
**Salt and pepper**
**Juice and grated rind of ½ a lemon**
**1 egg, beaten**

Cut the prunes into quarters and roughly chop the apples. Mix the fruit, rice, suet and nuts. Season to taste, add the lemon rind and juice and bind with beaten egg.

## CELERY STUFFING
*for pork and lamb*

**4 stalks celery, thinly sliced**
**2½ tablespoons salad oil**
**1 onion, finely chopped**
**Juice and grated rind of 1 orange**
**Salt and pepper**
**2 cups fresh white breadcrumbs**

Place the celery in a pan, cover with boiling water and simmer for 15–20 minutes, until tender. Heat the oil and sauté the onion until golden.
Drain the celery and put it in a bowl; mix with the onion, orange juice and rind. Season well and add the crumbs. Mix carefully.

27

# BROILING

*Broiling is a primitive method of cooking in which the food is cooked by direct heat from an open flame. One of the best ways of broiling is over charcoal, but this is obviously an outdoor party method now – we normally settle for the more conventional gas and electric broilers.*

*The principle remains the same though. The broiler should be heated before it is needed, to allow it to get really hot. The meat or fish is brushed with oil or melted butter if it is very lean and placed under the heated grid, on a grill pan. Cooking is then started with the broiler on full heat, and if the food starts to burn, the broiler heat is lowered.*

## BROILING MEAT

Since broiling is a quick method of cooking, it is suitable only for the best cuts of meat; fresh, underhung meat and the poorer cuts will remain tough. Many meats benefit from marinating first; for the marinade, mix 2 parts salad oil with 1 part vinegar or lemon juice, add a little chopped onion and some salt and pepper. Keep turning the meat in this marinade for about 2 hours. The remaining marinade may then be used in a sauce to serve with the meat. If you are not marinating, simply sprinkle the meat with salt and pepper (for beef use pepper only), and brush with a little oil or melted butter.

Steak, chops, kidneys, tender liver, sausages, bacon and fish are the foods usually broiled; the only vegetables suitable for this method of cooking are tomatoes and mushrooms.

**Steak** Marinate the meat for 2 hours, or brush with melted butter or oil. Cook under high heat for 1 minute on each side, then drop to a lower heat and cook for the required time, turning the meat from time to time.

Broiling times in minutes:

| Thickness | Rare | Medium | Well done |
|---|---|---|---|
| ¾ in. | 5 | 9–10 | 14–15 |
| 1 in. | 6–7 | 10–12 | 15 |
| 1½ in. | 10 | 12–14 | 18–20 |

**Chops, lamb and pork** Remove any skin and central bone, and trim neatly. If the chops are unshapely, tie with string or fasten with a skewer; alternatively, remove all the bone, roll neatly and tie or skewer into place.

Broiling times: 10–15 minutes (lamb), 15–20 minutes (pork).

**Liver** Wash, wipe and cut into slices ¼–½ in. thick. Broiling time: 5–10 minutes.

**Kidneys** Wash, skin and cut in half. Remove the core and, if liked, thread on to a skewer to make handling easy. Broiling time: 10 minutes.

**Bacon and ham** Lean slices, cut thick, require brushing with oil or melted butter. For thinly cut slices, cook for 2–3 minutes, until the fat is transparent on one side, then turn and cook the other side. Thick slices may take 10–15 minutes.

**Sausages** Prick the sausages and broil slowly, under a medium heat, turning frequently until well browned all over. Broiling time: 15–20 minutes.

## MIXED GRILL
*4 servings*

**4 rib lamb chops**
**2 lamb's kidneys**
**4 tomatoes**
**4 mushrooms**
**Melted butter or oil**
**Salt and pepper**
**½ pound pork sausages**
**4 slices bacon**
**Watercress and lemon slices to**
   **garnish**

Trim the chops of fat. Halve and remove hard core from kidneys. Halve the tomatoes and trim the ends of the mushrooms stalks. Brush the chops, kidneys, tomatoes and mushrooms with fat or oil and season. Heat the broiler. Place the tomatoes, cut side up, and the mushrooms, stalk side up, in the broiler pan, where they will be basted by the juices from the other food and will cook without further attention.

Place the rack in place on the pan and put the chops, sausages and kidneys on the rack. Broil 3–4 in. from source of heat for 14–16 minutes, turning the food on the rack frequently to ensure even cooking. The kidneys will probably be cooked first, so remove these and keep them warm. Replace them with the bacon slices and cook for a further 3–5 minutes.

Serve the mixed grill on a large heated platter. Garnish with watercress and lemon. Traditional accompaniments are potato chips or skinny French fries.

*Note:* Small pieces of fillet of beef or tender sirloin steak may be substituted for the lamb chops. A small portion of calf's or lamb's liver is sometimes included.

## NOISETTES OF LAMB

These are prepared from a whole rib roast of lamb. Ask the butcher to chine the meat, but not to cut through the rib bones.

Remove the chine bones, skin the meat and remove all the rib bones. Season the inside of the meat with salt, freshly ground pepper and herbs and roll it up tightly, starting from the thick end, rolling towards the flap and wrapping it around. Tie securely at 1½ in. intervals. Using a sharp knife, cut up in portions, with the string coming in the center of each one.

Brown quickly on both sides under a hot broiler. Place the broiler pan further from the source of heat and broil for 10–15 minutes, turning once, or as desired.

Top with pats of savory butter.

## BROILING FISH

Most fish can be broiled, though the drier types are better cooked in other ways. The fish should be seasoned, sprinkled with lemon juice and brushed liberally with melted butter (except for oily fish such as herrings).

Fillets and large fish should be placed directly in the broiler pan rather than on the rack of the pan.

**Cutlets and fillets.** Broil first on one side for 3–10 minutes, depending on thickness, then turn with a flat pancake turner. Brush with fat and broil the second side. Serve very hot with a garnish of broiled tomato halves or parsley sprigs and a sauce.

**Whole fish** Wash and scale the fish. Score it with a sharp knife in 3–4 places on each side (this allows the heat to penetrate the thick flesh more quickly), season and brush with melted butter, if required. Line the broiler pan with foil to catch the juices, place the fish in the pan and broil rather slowly, so that the flesh cooks thoroughly without the outside burning.

Turn the fish once or twice, handling it carefully to prevent breaking. To test whether the fish is done, insert the back of a knife next to the bone to see if the meat comes away easily. Serve with maître d'hôtel butter or melted butter, lemon wedges and chopped parsley.

## BROILED FISH FILLETS WITH PUFFY SAUCE
*4–6 servings*

**4–6 fish fillets**
**½ cup mayonnaise**
**Pinch of cayenne**
**1 tablespoon chopped parsley**
**2 tablespoons chopped pickle**
**1 egg white, beaten stiff**

Pre-heat broiling compartment and pan for 10 minutes. Wipe the fillets with a damp cloth. Place the fillets skin side down in pre-heated broiling pan 2 in. from source of heat. Broil about 5 minutes. Combine the remaining ingredients. Spread evenly over top of fish. Broil for 3 minutes or until sauce is puffed and golden brown.

## DEVILED FISH STEAKS
*4 servings*

**4 fish steaks**
**2 tablespoons prepared mustard**
**1 tablespoon salad oil**
**2 tablespoons horseradish**
**1 teaspoon salt**

Place the fish steaks on a broil-and-serve platter or in the broiling pan. Combine the remaining ingredients and spread half of the mixture on the steaks. Pre-heat broiling compartment. Broil 2 in. from source of heat for 4 minutes. Turn steaks over. Cover with the remaining mixture. Broil for 7–8 minutes or until fish flakes easily with a fork.

## ACCOMPANIMENTS FOR BROILED MEAT OR FISH

### SAVORY BUTTERS
*Serve the savory butters chilled and cut into pats, 1 pat on each portion of meat or fish.*

**Anchovy butter** Beat 1 part anchovies (pounded to a paste) with 2 parts butter or margarine. A little spice or flavoring may be added, but take care with salt – anchovies are very salty themselves.

**Maître d'hôtel butter** Beat ½ cup butter, mix in 2½ tablespoons finely chopped parsley and a squeeze of lemon juice with salt and a pinch of cayenne.

**Chutney butter** Beat ¼ cup butter or margarine with ¼ cup chutney and ¼ teaspoon lemon juice until well blended.

**Black butter (for meat)** Melt ¼ cup butter in a pan and heat until dark brown in color but not burned. Add 1¼ tablespoons wine vinegar, a little salt and freshly ground black pepper and 1 teaspoon chopped parsley. Pour over the meat while it is still hot.

**Black butter (for fish)** Heat ¼ cup butter until it is lightly browned. Add 1¼ tablespoons vinegar, 2 teaspoons capers, cook for 2–3 minutes and pour over the hot fish. Sprinkle with chopped parsley and serve at once.

**Garlic butter** Crush a large clove garlic. Beat it well into the butter and season lightly with salt and pepper.

**Horseradish butter** Soften ½ cup butter and add 2½ tablespoons

*Noisettes of lamb topped with maître d'hôtel butter*

*Whole fish should be scored 2 or 3 times before broiling*

creamed horseradish. Beat them well together.

**Green butter** Wash a small bunch of watercress and dry thoroughly. Chop finely. Beat ½ cup of the watercress into ½ cup softened butter until well blended.

## MATCHSTICK POTATOES

Pare the potatoes and cut them into matchstick size slivers. Let them soak in cold water for at least 30 minutes. Drain and dry thoroughly on paper towels. Fry in deep hot fat for 3 minutes; drain on paper towels. Before serving, reheat the fat and fry for a further 3 minutes.

## SAUTÉ POTATOES

Pare the potatoes as thinly as pos-sible. Cook in boiling salted water until just tender. Drain thoroughly and cut the hot potatoes into ¼ in. thick slices. Fry slowly in a little hot butter, turning them once so that they are crisp and golden on both sides. Drain well on paper towels and serve sprinkled with a little chopped parsley or chives.

## GAME CHIPS

Pare the potatoes and slice into very thin rounds using a vege-table peeler. Soak in cold water for 30 minutes. Dry thoroughly on paper towels.
Fry in deep hot fat for 3 minutes. Remove from the fat and drain on paper towels. Before serving, reheat the fat and fry the potatoes for a further 3 minutes.

*Broiled ham slice is delicious with a fruit garnish*

## MAÎTRE D'HÔTEL POTATOES

**1 pound potatoes**
**1¼ tablespoons olive oil**
**Salt**
**Freshly ground black pepper**
**Chopped parsley**
**1¼ tablespoons vinegar**

Boil the potatoes in their skins and pare them while still warm. Cut into ¼ in. thick slices. Heat the oil in a skillet, add the remain-ing ingredients and toss the sliced potatoes in the mixture until well heated. Serve at once.

## CRISP FRIED ONION RINGS

**4 large onions, cut into ¼ in.**
  **thick slices**
**Milk**
**Flour**
**Salt and pepper**
**Fat for deep frying**

Separate the onion slices into rings. Dip in the milk and then in flour seasoned with salt and pep-per. Heat the fat so that when one ring is dropped in, it rises to the surface surrounded by bubbles. Gradually add the rest of the rings to the hot fat and fry for 2–3 minutes or until golden brown. Drain on paper towels, season and serve while piping hot.

## CARROTS COWAN

**1 bunch carrots**
**Salt**
**1 tablespoon butter**
**2½ tablespoons brown sugar**
**Juice of 1 orange**

Trim and scrape the carrots. Slice thinly if old, leave whole if young and tender. Simmer in salted boiling water for about 15 minutes or until cooked. Drain thoroughly. Add butter, sugar and orange juice. Heat gently to melt the butter and dissolve the sugar. Simmer for 5 minutes before serving.

## GLAZED CARROTS

**¼ cup butter**
**1 bunch young carrots, cleaned**
  **and left whole**
**3 lumps sugar**
**¼ teaspoon salt**
**Stock**
**Chopped parsley**

Melt the butter in a pan. Add the carrots, sugar, salt and enough stock to come half-way up the car-rots. Cook gently without a lid, shaking the pan occasionally, until the carrots are soft. Remove

from the pan and keep them hot. Boil the liquid left in the pan rapidly until it is reduced to a rich glaze. Replace the carrots a few at a time, turning them until all sides are well coated with glaze. Serve sprinkled with parsley.

## SAUTE CUCUMBER

Pare the cucumber and cut in half lengthwise. Cut into dice and cook very gently in butter in a covered pan for 10-15 minutes. Serve with a cream sauce or melted butter.

## CREAMED SPINACH

Allow ½ pound uncooked spinach for each serving. Wash spinach well in several waters to remove all grit and strip off any coarse stalks. Chop roughly. Pack into a saucepan or large kettle with only the water that clings to the leaves after washing. Heat gently, turning the spinach occasionally, then bring to a boil and cook gently until soft, 10–15 minutes. Drain thoroughly. Push through a nylon sieve or purée the spinach in a blender. Add 1–2 tab-lespoons cream, some salt and pepper. Reheat before serving.

## SAVORY LEMON SAUCE

**Rind and juice of 1 lemon**
**1¼ cups of white sauce, using**
  **half milk and half fish or**
  **chicken stock**
**1–2 teaspoons sugar**
**Salt and pepper**
**1–2 tablespoons light cream**

Simmer the lemon rind in the milk and stock for 5 minutes. Strain and use the liquid to make a white sauce. When it has thick-ened, stir in the lemon juice and sugar. Season to taste.
If the sauce is too sharp, stir in a little light cream before serving with broiled fish or chicken.

## BLACK BUTTER SAUCE

**¼ cup unsalted butter**
**2 tablespoons tarragon vinegar**
**Salt and pepper**
**2½ teaspoons chopped parsley**

Cut the butter into small pieces and put in a small heavy sauce-pan. Heat butter until it is golden brown color, then remove from the heat and cool. Meanwhile, put the vinegar in another small heavy saucepan and boil rapidly to reduce to about half the origi-nal quantity. Stir in the butter and reheat. Season and add parsley. Serve with broiled fish.

# FRYING

*Frying is a quick method of cooking, giving a tasty, succulent result. Natural fat makes an important contribution to the flavor of many foods, and frying in fat can add extra flavor where this is lacking in the original.*
*Fry tender cuts of meat – steaks, chops, lambs' or calves' liver and kidney, gammon and bacon slices. Do not fry the poorer cuts of meat as these need long, slow cooking to break down the tough fibers and if fried will remain hard and tough. Most fish can be fried, and it is a particularly good method of cooking for those with little natural flavor or color.*
*Fried eggs and egg dishes such as pancakes and omelets are traditional favorites and a large selection of vegetables can be fried. Certain sweet foods – doughnuts, fruit fritters – are also fried.*

Frying may be done in shallow fat, or by completely submerging the food in deep fat; either way there are certain basic rules for success.

1. Never add the food to the pan until the fat reaches the correct frying temperature (see chart and individual recipes). If the fat is not hot enough it will soak into the food, instead of sealing the outside crisply, and the result will be soggy and unpleasant.

2. Do not add too much food to the pan at once, as this lowers the temperature of the fat. Add a small piece at a time. Maintain the temperature by carefully controlling the heat.

3. Never overload the pan, or foods will start to stew rather than fry.

4. After frying, drain foods thoroughly on absorbent paper towels.

## Shallow fat frying

For shallow frying, use a small quantity of fat in a shallow skillet. This method is suitable for steaks, chops, liver, young chicken, sausages, fish steaks, white fish such as sole, and pancakes – all these need only sufficient fat to prevent them sticking to the pan. Made-up dishes such as fish cakes and rissoles can also be shallow fried, but need enough fat to half-cover them. In this case, most of the foods require a coating of batter or egg and breadcrumbs. Salad oils, shortening, dripping and butter are all

*Dip in beaten egg, then press the breadcrumbs on well*

### Deep fat frying guide

| Food | Size | Temperature | Time |
| --- | --- | --- | --- |
| **French Fried potatoes** Fry for 5 minutes at 360°F., remove from pan and raise temperature to 380°F. Fry for a further 3 minutes | ¼ in. thick | 360°F. 380°F. | 5 minutes 3 minutes |
| **Potato croquettes** (egg and breadcrumb coating) | 3½ in. long | 375°F. | 3–4 minutes |
| **Scotch eggs** (egg and breadcrumb coating) | 3½ in. by 3½ in. | 325°F. | 10 minutes |
| **Chicken Kiev** (egg and breadcrumb coating) | 4 in. by 2½ om' © ©325°F. (approx.) | | 15 minutes |
| **Fritters (using fritter batter)** pineapple rings apple rings banana | ¼ in. thick ¼ in. thick 1 banana cut in half lengthwise | 350°F. 350°F. 375°F. | 5 minutes 4 minutes 2–3 minutes |
| **Rechauffé** dishes | | 360–380°F. | as recipe |
| **Fish fillets** (egg and breadcrumb or batter coating) | approx. ½ in. thick | 350–360°F. | 5–10 minutes |
| **Doughnuts** | | 350–360°F. | 5–10 minutes |

suitable for shallow frying. When frying with butter, put a little oil in the pan first to keep the butter from browning; when the oil is hot add an equal quantity of butter, then add more butter as the food starts to color.

## Deep fat frying

The food is cooked in sufficient fat to cover it completely. This method is used for batter-coated fish, whitebait, French fried potatoes, doughnuts and made-up dishes such as croquettes and fritters. A deep pan and a wire basket are needed, with enough fat to come about three-quarters of the way up the pan; clarified beef fat (for less delicate foods), shortening and oil are all suitable. The fat must be pure and free from moisture to prevent spitting or boiling over. After frying, cool the fat and strain it into a bowl or wide-necked jar and cover; store it in a cool place for future use.

## COATING BATTER – 1

**1 cup flour**
**Pinch of salt**
**1 egg**
**⅝ cup milk or milk and water, approximately**

Mix together the flour, salt, egg, and sufficient liquid to give a stiff batter which will coat the back of a spoon; beat well until smooth. Dip the food into the batter, holding the pieces on a skewer or fork, and drain slightly before putting into the hot fat.

## COATING BATTER – 2

**1 cup flour**
**Pinch of salt**
**1¼ tablespoons oil**
**1 egg, separated**
**2½–4 tablespoons water or milk and water**

Mix together the flour, salt, oil and egg yolk with sufficient water to give a stiff batter which will coat the back of a spoon; beat until smooth. Just before using, beat the egg white stiffly and fold it into the batter. Dip the food pieces into seasoned flour before coating them with the batter.
This method gives a lighter, crisper batter than the first recipe.

## EGG-AND-CRUMBING

Have a beaten egg on a plate and some fresh white or dry breadcrumbs on a paper towel or in a shallow dish. Dip the food in the egg and lift it out, letting it drain for a second or two. Transfer it to the crumbs and tip the paper backwards and forwards until the food is well covered. Press in the crumbs with a spatula, then shake the food to remove any surplus. Alternatively, have the crumbs in a plastic bag and shake the food pieces inside the bag until they are covered.

Do not use this method if the food is likely to break up.

## MUSTARD STEAKS
*4 servings*

**4 filet of beef steaks**
**Salt and pepper**
**1¼ tablespoons salad oil**
**¼ cup butter**
**⅝ cup heavy cream**
**2 teaspoons French mustard**

Sprinkle the steaks with salt and pepper. Heat the oil and butter in a heavy skillet. Fry the steaks for 3–5 minutes on each side. Remove from pan and keep hot. Pour the cream into the skillet and cook, without boiling, until thick. Stir in the mustard and pour the mixture over the steaks just before serving.

## PEPPER STEAK
*4 servings*

**1 ounce white peppercorns**
**1½ pound boneless sirloin steak, cut 1 in. thick**
**1¼ tablespoons salad oil**
**2 tablespoons butter**
**2½ tablespoons brandy**
**⅝ cup dry white wine**
**2½ tablespoons heavy cream**
**Salt and pepper**

Crush the peppercorns roughly and coat both sides of the steak with them. Press into steak with the hands. Heat the oil and butter in a very heavy skillet. Fry the steak, turning once, for 6–10 minutes or as desired. Place on a heated serving platter and keep hot. Pour off the fat, leaving the peppercorns in the pan. Pour in the brandy and wine, add the cream and warm through. Taste and season. Pour over the steak and serve at once.
*Note:* For a less pungent flavor, try canned green peppercorns.

## HAMBURGERS
*4 servings*

**1 pound lean ground beef**
**½ onion, grated**
**Salt and pepper**
**Fat**

Combine meat, onion and generous amounts of salt and pepper.

*Hamburgers – a favorite lunch-time snack*

Shape into 4 round flat cakes. To cook, shallow fry in a little fat, allowing 4–6 minutes on each side. Hamburgers can be served rare or well done, according to personal preference.
### Variations
Traditionally, hamburgers contain no other ingredients, but they can be varied by adding any of the following when mixing the meat and seasoning:
½–1 cup grated cheese
1 tablespoon chopped sweet pickle
1–2 tablespoons prepared mustard
1 teaspoon mixed herbs
1 tablespoon chopped parsley
A few sliced mushrooms
2 tomatoes, peeled and chopped
Alternatively, when the hamburgers are cooked, top them with a fried or poached egg or with a sprinkling of grated cheese.
Serve in a plain, soft bun with onion rings, slices of tomato and American relish on top, or accompanied by a salad.

## CHICKEN MARYLAND
*4 servings*

**3 pound roasting chicken, cut into 8 portions**
**2½ tablespoons seasoned flour**
**Beaten egg**
**2 cups fresh white breadcrumbs**
**1¼ tablespoons salad oil**
**6 tablespoons butter**
**2 tablespoons flour**
**1¼ cups chicken stock**
**⅝ cup dairy sour cream**
**Salt and pepper**
*For corn fritters:*
**½ cup all-purpose flour**
**Salt and pepper**
**1 egg, beaten**
**⅝ cup milk**
**1 can (8 ounces) whole kernel corn, drained**
**Fat for frying**
*For fried bananas:*
**1 banana per serving**

Discard the skin from the chicken pieces. Dip each piece of chicken in the seasoned flour, then coat with egg and breadcrumbs, patting the crumbs firmly on to the chicken. Heat the oil in a large skillet and add the butter. When the butter is melted, add the chicken. Reduce the heat and cook slowly, allowing 35–45 minutes, until evenly browned on all sides and well cooked. Drain on paper towels and keep warm. Fry bananas (see below).
Pour off all but 2 tablespoons of the fat. Stir in the flour and cook for 2 minutes. Remove from heat and stir in the stock and sour cream. Cook over moderate heat, stirring constantly, until thickened. *Do not boil.* Check seasoning. Serve the chicken surrounded by corn fritters and fried bananas, with the gravy in a sauceboat.

### Corn fritters
Sift the flour and seasoning into a bowl, make a well in the center and add the beaten egg and ¼ cup milk. Beat until smooth. Add enough milk to give a thick coating consistency and then stir in the corn. Fry the batter in spoonfuls in shallow fat for about 5 minutes, turning once.

### Fried bananas
Peel the bananas and cut into 3-4 pieces. Fry in the hot chicken fat. Keep warm.

## LIVER, BACON AND MUSHROOMS
*4 servings*

**1 pound calves' liver**
**Seasoned flour**
**4 slices lean bacon, chopped**
**1-2 onions, chopped**
**Fat or oil**
**¼ pound mushrooms, sliced**

Wash and trim the liver and cut

into thin strips. Toss in seasoned flour to coat. Fry the bacon until the fat begins to run, add the onion and cook for 5 minutes or until soft, then add the mushrooms and liver. Add a little more fat if necessary and continue frying over a gentle heat, stirring from time to time, until the meat is just cooked, about 5–10 minutes.

## FRIED SWEETBREADS
*4 servings*

**1 pound lambs' or calves' sweetbreads**
**Juice of ½ lemon**
**Salt and pepper**
**1 egg, beaten**
**1 cup fresh white breadcrumbs**
**8 slices bacon**

Soak the sweetbreads in cold water for 3–4 hours. Drain. Put in a pan and cover them with cold water and lemon juice. Bring the water slowly to the boil and simmer for 5 minutes. Drain. Cover sweetbreads with cold water until they are firm and cold. Strip off any stringy unwanted tissue.
Press the sweetbreads well between sheets of paper toweling. Slice, season and dip into the beaten egg. Cover with breadcrumbs, patting on to both sides of slices. Cut the bacon into pieces and fry lightly until just crisp; drain and keep hot. Fry the sweetbreads in the bacon fat until golden brown. Serve sweetbreads with bacon on top. Serve with tartar or tomato sauce.

## FRIED SHRIMP

**½ pound shelled large shrimp**
**Seasoned flour**
**1 cup all-purpose flour**
**Pinch of salt**
**1¼ tablespoons oil**
**1 egg yolk**
**2–3 tablespoons water or milk and water**
**Fat for deep frying**

If fresh shrimp are used, remove the dark vein. If frozen, thaw and drain well. Dip in seasoned flour. Mix together the flour, salt, oil and egg yolk with sufficient liquid to give a stiff batter which will coat the back of a spoon. Beat until smooth. Dip the shrimp in the batter. Heat the fat until a cube of bread dropped into it takes 20–30 seconds to brown. Fry the shrimp a few at a time, until they are golden brown. Drain and serve with tartar or tomato sauce (see pages 57 and 58).

## PAN FRIED FISH
*6 servings*

**6 small fish, cleaned and dressed**
**1 teaspoon salt**
**⅛ teaspoon pepper**
**1 egg**
**1 tablespoon milk**
**1 cup breadcrumbs, cracker crumbs or cornmeal**
**Fat for frying**

Wash the fish and be sure that they are well cleaned inside. Pat dry with paper towels. Sprinkle both sides with salt and pepper. Beat the egg lightly and beat in the milk. Dip the fish in the egg and roll in the crumbs. Pat the crumbs into the fish on all sides. Melt about ⅛ in. fat in a very heavy skillet.

Heat the fat, but do not allow it to smoke. Fry the fish until well browned and crispy on both sides, about 10 minutes, depending on thickness of the fish. Drain on paper towels. Serve immediately with lemon or tartar sauce.

## FLUFFY CODFISH BALLS
*6 servings*

**2 cups salt codfish, flaked**
**4 cups diced raw potatoes**
**2 eggs, lightly beaten**
**2 tablespoons butter or margarine, melted**
**⅛ teaspoon celery salt**
**⅛ teaspoon pepper**
**Fat for frying**

Wash the codfish in cold water and drain well. Cook in a saucepan with the potatoes until the potatoes are tender. Drain well. Mash. Add the eggs, butter and seasonings. Beat the mixture until light and fluffy. Heat fat at least 1 in. deep in a skillet to 370°F. on a deep fat thermometer. Drop the mixture from a tablespoon into the hot fat and fry until golden brown on all sides. Drain on paper towels and serve at once.

## FISH FILLETS A LA WILLIAM
*4 servings*

**¼ cup blanched slivered almonds**
**6 tablespoons butter or margarine, divided**
**4 medium tomatoes, peeled and chopped**
**½ clove garlic, crushed**
**½ teaspoon dried tarragon**
**Salt and pepper**
**4 fillets of sole or flounder**
**Seasoned flour**

Heat the slivered almonds in 1 tablespoon of the butter, stirring

*Some of the nicest fritters have a sweet filling*

occasionally, until lightly browned. Set aside. Combine the tomatoes, garlic, 1 tablespoon butter, tarragon and seasonings in a saucepan. Bring to a boil and simmer for 5 minutes. Dust the fillets lightly in seasoned flour. Heat the remaining 4 tablespoons of butter in a skillet. Quickly brown the fillets in the butter on both sides. Arrange the tomato mixture in a heated serving platter. Place the fish fillets on top and cover with the toasted almonds.

## CHIPPED POTATOES (FRENCH FRIES)

**allow about ½ pound potatoes per serving**

Pare the potatoes and cut into ¼–½ in. slices, then into strips ¼–½ in. wide. (For speed, several slices can be put on top of one another and cut together, or use a special chipper.) Place in cold water and let stand for at least 30 minutes to remove excess starch. Drain well and dry with a cloth. Heat oil in a deep fat fryer until when one chip is dropped in it rises to the surface immediately, surrounded by bubbles. Put enough potatoes into the basket to about quarter fill it and lower carefully into the hot fat. Cook for 6–7 minutes, remove and drain on paper towels. Repeat this process until all the potatoes have been cooked.

Just before serving, reheat the fat, test the temperature, and fry the potatoes rapidly or until crisp and brown. Drain well on paper towels and serve at once, sprinkled with salt.

## DOUGHNUTS
*makes 10–12*

**1 teaspoon sugar**
**¼ cup milk, approximately**
**1 package active dry yeast**
**2 cups all-purpose flour**
**½ teaspoon salt**
**¼ cup butter or margarine**
**1 egg, beaten**
**Preserves**
**Deep fat for frying**
**Sugar and cinnamon mixture**

Dissolve the sugar in the milk in a saucepan. Warm the milk slightly and add the yeast. Let stand in a warm place until frothy –about 15 minutes. Mix together the flour and salt. Cut in the butter or margarine with a pastry blender. Add the yeast and egg and mix to a soft dough, adding a little more milk if necessary. Beat well until smooth. Cover and let rise until doubled in bulk. Knead lightly on a floured board and divide into 10–12 pieces. Shape each one into a circle, put 1 teaspoon preserves in the center and draw up the edges to form a ball, pressing firmly to seal edges together. Place on a greased pan. Let stand for 15 minutes.

Heat the fat until it will brown a cube of bread in 40 seconds. Fry the doughnuts, fairly quickly, until golden brown, about 5–10 minutes, according to size. Drain on paper towels and toss in sugar mixed with a little cinnamon. Serve warm.

Alternatively, shape the doughnuts into rings, removing a small circle from the center of each ring. In this case, do not add the preserves but let rise and then fry. Roll in sugar and cinnamon

before serving.

## FRUIT FRITTERS WITH LIQUEUR
*4 servings*

**8 canned pineapple slices, drained**
**2½ tablespoons Kirsch**
**1 cup all-purpose flour**
**Pinch of salt**
**1 egg**
**⅝ cup milk**
**Fat for deep frying**
**Sugar and cinnamon mixture**

Soak the pineapple rings in the Kirsch. Sift together the flour and salt. Make a well in the center and break in the egg. Add half the milk gradually and beat the mixture until smooth. Add the remaining milk and beat until well mixed. Heat the fat until it is hot enough to brown a cube of bread in 1 minute. Dip the pineapple slices in the batter and fry in the fat until golden on both sides. Drain on paper towels and toss lightly in cinnamon-sugar mixture. Serve hot.

## CONTROLLED PAN FRYING

There are now available electric skillets and deep-fat fryers with built-in thermostatic controls. Any food that can be fried in the normal way can be fried in a temperature-controlled skillet and they are particularly useful for foods needing a high degree of accuracy in the fat temperature to achieve the correct result. Once the desired temperature is reached, the thermostat maintains it automatically with only small variations.

The deep-fat fryers are most useful if you cook in any quantity, as you can generally cook larger amounts more quickly than by the ordinary deep frying method. These fryers prevent the fat spitting in your face or spattering over the hob. Although they take a rather larger quantity of fat than the normal deep fryers, it can, of course, be used repeatedly.

Shallow-fat frying in a controlled-temperature skillet is often more satisfactory than in an ordinary skillet, as the heat is evenly spread, giving a more level temperature overall. Dry-frying (i.e. with little or no fat) can be very successful in this type of skillet, in particular those with a 'non-stick' or easy-clean finish. Controlled-temperature skillets can also be used for braising, pot roasting and stewing.

# STEWS AND CASSEROLES

A casserole can be anything from an inexpensive, tasty meal for the family to the richest of dinner party dishes. Long, slow cooking breaks down tough fibres and draws out the full flavor.

In the main, casserole dishes use the cheaper, tougher cuts that require long cooking to make them tender, but these cuts often have the most taste. Add vegetables and a rich, home-made stock and the result is a meal to be proud of. For a party dish, add cream or sour cream to the cooking liquid to make a really delicious sauce. For many casserole recipes, the ingredients are fried first. This can either be done in a skillet, transferring the food to a casserole afterwards, or it can be done in a flameproof casserole, using the same pan for top-of-the-stove and oven cooking.

If you are using one pan only, be careful to discard the excess fat before adding liquid.

## VEAL AND OLIVE CASSEROLE
*5-6 servings*

**2 pound veal stew meat, cubed**
**¼ cup flour**
**2 tablespoons butter or margarine**
**2½ tablespoons salad oil**
**1 clove garlic, finely chopped**
**½ can (6 ounces) tomato paste**
**1 beef bouillon cube**
**2½ cups boiling water**
**1 bay leaf**
**Pinch of thyme**
**Pinch of marjoram**
**12 pitted black olives**
**¼ pound mushrooms, sliced**
**Salt and pepper**
**½–¾ cup long grain rice**
**12 small stuffed olives**

*For glazed onions:*
**12 small onions**
**Butter**
**2½ tablespoons brown sugar**
**2½ tablespoons vinegar**
**2½ tablespoons port**

Coat the veal cubes with flour and brown on all sides by frying in the heated mixed butter and oil. Transfer meat to a casserole. Add the garlic, tomato paste, bouillon cube, boiling water and the herbs. Cook in a moderate oven (350°F.) for 1½ hours. After the first hour add the black olives and sliced mushrooms. Toss lightly and adjust seasoning.

To glaze the onions, cook them gently in butter in a pan with the lid on, shaking occasionally. Meanwhile, put the sugar, vinegar and port in a pan and cook until a thick syrup is formed. When the onions are cooked, put them into the syrup and boil it for a few minutes, until the onions are well coated.

Cook the rice in plenty of boiling salted water for 12–15 minutes or until tender.

Serve the casserole with the cooked rice and garnish with the stuffed olives and glazed onions.

## VEAL AND RICE PAPRIKA
*4 servings*

**2 tablespoons butter or margarine**
**1 pound lean veal, cut into small pieces**
**3 onions, finely sliced**
**1 teaspoon paprika**
**1 tablespoon tomato paste**
**1⅞ cups stock**
**¾ cup long grain rice**
**⅝ cup dairy sour cream**
**Salt and pepper**
**Chopped parsley**

Melt the butter in a skillet. When hot, add the veal and fry briskly. Transfer the meat to a casserole and fry the onions until tender. Stir in the paprika, tomato paste and stock. Pour over the veal, cover and cook in a warm oven (325°F.) for 1 hour or until veal is tender. Add the rice, cover and cook for 30 minutes or until the rice is cooked.

Gently heat the sour cream in a

small saucepan. Turn into casserole and lightly fork cream through the rice. Season to taste and sprinkle with parsley.

## OLD-FASHIONED BEEF STEW
*6 servings*

**2 pound boneless beef chuck, cubed**
**3 tablespoons flour**
**3 tablespoons butter or pan drippings**
**Salt**
**¼ teaspoon pepper**
**6 cups water**
**12 small white onions**
**2 cups yellow turnip, diced**
**6 carrots, cut into chunks**
**4 medium potatoes, cut up**

Dredge the meat with the flour. Heat the butter or drippings in a Dutch oven. Add the beef and brown well on all sides. Add 2 teaspoons salt, pepper and water. Bring to a boil. Lower heat and simmer, covered, for 1½ hours or until meat is almost tender. Add remaining ingredients and simmer for 45 minutes or until vegetables are tender. Add more salt if needed. Serve piping hot.

## PORK RIBS WITH SPICED SAUCE
*4 servings*

**2 pound country spare ribs, cut into serving pieces**
**1¼ tablespoons salad oil**
**2 tablespoons butter**
**½ pound onions, finely chopped**
**1 tablespoon flour**
**½ teaspoon ground ginger**
**1¼ cups chicken stock**
**2½ tablespoons white wine vinegar**
**1 can (8 ounces) cranberry sauce**
**¼ teaspoon dried rosemary**
**Salt**
**Freshly ground black pepper**
**Chopped parsley**

Trim the spare ribs of excess fat. Heat the oil in a large skillet. Add the butter and on the point of browning add the meat. Fry briskly and brown on both sides. Remove meat and place in a casserole. Add the onions to the pan and fry until tender. Stir in the flour and ginger and cook for 1 minute. Stir in the stock, vinegar, cranberry sauce, rosemary and seasoning. Bring to a boil, stirring. Pour sauce over meat in casserole. Cover the casserole and cook in a warm oven (325°F.) for 1½ hours.
Remove the meat from the cas-

serole. Skim off as much fat as possible. Lift off any remaining fat by laying paper towels on top of the liquid. Carefully remove the fat with the towels. Reduce the juice by ⅓ by boiling hard in a pan, or in the casserole if it is flameproof. Return the meat to the casserole and reheat. Sprinkle with parsley and serve.

## SCANDINAVIAN PORK
*4 servings*

**4 pork chops**
**2 fresh herrings or other small oily fish**
**4 medium potatoes**
**4 onions**
**Butter**
**¼ cup flour**
**2½ cups milk**
**2 eggs**
**Salt and pepper**
**Parsley**

Trim the chops of excess fat and rind. Cut the heads and tails off the herrings and fillet them. Slice the potatoes and onions thinly. Butter a large ovenproof dish, put in a layer of potato, a layer of onion, then 2 chops and 2 herring halves, and a further layer of potato and onion. Add the remaining 2 chops and herring halves, then fill in round the sides and cover the top with the rest of the onion and potato. Put a few small lumps of butter on top and cook, uncovered, in a moderate oven (350°F.) for 1 hour.
Combine the flour with a little of the milk to make a smooth paste. Beat in the eggs and gradually add the rest of the milk. Season to taste. Pour this mixture over the casserole. Return casserole to the oven and bake for 30 minutes or until the custard on top is set. Garnish with parsley to serve.

## CHICKEN AND WALNUTS
*6 servings*

**3½–4 pound roasting chicken, cut into serving pieces**
**2½ tablespoons sherry**
**2 teaspoons sugar**
**3¾ tablespoons salad oil**
**½ pound button mushrooms, sliced**
**1 can (6 ounces) water chestnuts, drained and diced, optional**
**2½ cups chicken stock**
**2½ tablespoons cornstarch**
**1 cup walnut halves**
**2 tablespoons butter**

Remove the skin from chicken pieces. Place in a dish and pour the sherry and sugar over chicken. Let stand for 1–2 hours.

*Veal and rice paprika, finished with dairy sour cream*

Heat the oil in a skillet. Drain the chicken pieces and brown in the oil. Place the mushrooms and water chestnuts in a large casserole and arrange the chicken pieces on top. Pour over the chicken juices and stock. Cover the casserole and cook in a moderate oven (350°F.) for 2 hours.
Drain off the liquid, keeping the chicken hot. Combine cornstarch and a little water to make a paste. Stir into the liquid and cook until clear and thickened. Brown the walnuts in melted butter for 4–5 minutes. Drain on paper towels. Arrange the chicken, mushrooms and water chestnuts on a serving platter and pour some of the thickened chicken gravy over the top. Garnish with the browned walnuts. Serve the remaining gravy separately.

## POULET A L'ORANGE
*4 servings*

**1 roasting chicken, cut into serving pieces**
**2½ tablespoons salad oil**
**1 package (1¼ ounces) white sauce mix**
**1¼ cups milk**
**2 medium oranges**
**White grapes**

Fry the chicken pieces in the hot oil until well browned. Remove from pan and place in a casserole. Make up the sauce mix according to directions on the package, using the milk. Thinly pare the rind, free of all white, from 1½ oranges and cut in thin strips. Add the strips to the sauce, together with the juice of 1 orange. Pour the sauce over the chicken. Cover the casserole and

*Chicken, cooked with orange and garnished with grapes*

35

*Marinated beef with olives for a French-style casserole*

bake in a fairly hot oven (375°F.) about 45 minutes or until the chicken is tender. Cut the remaining orange in slices and use it for garnish along with the grapes.

## MARINATED STEAK POT
*6 servings*

**2 pound boneless chuck steak**
**2½ tablespoons garlic vinegar**
**¼ cup butter or pan drippings**
**6 tablespoons flour**
**¼ pound tiny onions**
**¼ pound button mushrooms**
**¼ pound bacon, diced**
**2½ cups beef stock**
**1 bay leaf**
**1 tablespoon tomato paste**
**Bouquet garni**
**Chopped parsley**

Cut the meat into 1 in. squares.

Put into a deep bowl and toss with garlic vinegar. Cover the bowl with plastic wrap and let stand overnight.

Melt the butter or drippings in a skillet. Drain the meat, reserving the juices. Dredge the meat with flour. Fry the meat cubes until brown on all sides. Remove the meat from the pan and place in a casserole with a tight lid. Add the onions, mushrooms and bacon to drippings in skillet and fry for 5 minutes. Pour the mixture from the skillet over the top of the meat in the casserole.

Pour the stock into the skillet and stir to loosen the sediment in the bottom of the pan. Add the bay leaf, tomato paste and bouquet garni. Bring to a boil. Pour the mixture over the meat. Cover the casserole tightly and cook in a

warm oven (325°F.) for 1½ hours or until meat is tender. Discard the bay leaf and bouquet garni. Serve sprinkled generously with chopped parsley.

## FRENCH BEEF AND OLIVE CASSEROLE
*4 servings*

*For marinade:*
**3¾ tablespoons salad oil**
**1 carrot, sliced**
**1 onion, sliced**
**2–3 stalks celery, cut into 1 in. pieces**
**⅝ cup red wine**
**⅝ cup wine vinegar**
**Bunch of fresh herbs**
**1 clove garlic, crushed**
**Few peppercorns**
**Salt and pepper**

**1½ pound round steak, trimmed**
**⅔ pound bacon**
**⅝ cup red wine**
**½ cup black olives**
**½ cup green olives**
**3–4 tomatoes, peeled and sliced**

Make up the marinade as follows. Heat the oil and add the vegetables. Fry until brown. Add the remaining ingredients and bring to a boil. Simmer for 15 minutes. Allow to cool. Cut the meat into thick chunks and cover with the marinade.

Fry the bacon to extract the fat. Remove bacon from pan and crumble. Drain the beef from marinade and fry in the hot bacon fat. Pour the beef and fat into a casserole. Add the crumbled bacon, marinade, wine and olives. Cover tightly and cook in a warm oven (325°F.) for 1½–2 hours.

Shortly before serving, remove any excess fat and add the sliced tomatoes. Serve with buttered noodles and grated cheese.

## CASSEROLE OF RABBIT
*4 servings*

**1 rabbit, cut into serving pieces**
**½ cup seasoned flour**
**¼ cup butter or pan drippings**
**1 onion, sliced**
**1 beef bouillon cube**
**2½ cups stock or water**
**2 carrots, diced**
**1 stalk celery, chopped**
**Bouquet garni**
**1 tablespoon catsup**
**Pinch of ground nutmeg**
**Salt and pepper**
**Fried croûtons**

Soak the rabbit pieces in cold salted water to remove the blood. Dry the pieces well and toss in

seasoned flour. Heat the butter or drippings in a skillet. Add the rabbit pieces, a few at a time, and fry until lightly browned. Remove rabbit and place in a casserole. Add onion to pan and fry gently for a few minutes. Stir in the remaining flour and fry until lightly browned. Add the bouillon cube with stock or water and stir until dissolved and the mixture is boiling.

Pour over the rabbit in casserole. Add the carrots, celery, bouquet garni, catsup and nutmeg. Cover and cook in a moderate oven (350°F.) for about 2 hours or until rabbit is tender.

Remove the herbs, adjust seasoning and serve the casserole garnished with fried croûtons.

## POULET EN COCOTTE
*4 servings*

*For stuffing:*
**¼ pound sausage meat**
**2 tablespoons fresh white breadcrumbs**
**1 chicken liver, chopped**
**2 tablespoons chopped parsley**
**Salt**
**Freshly ground black pepper**

**3–3½ pound roasting chicken**
**5 tablespoons butter or margarine**
**½ pound bacon, cut up**
**1 pound potatoes**
**⅓ pound shallots**
**1 bunch small carrots**
**Chopped parsley**

Combine the stuffing ingredients in a bowl until well blended. Adjust seasoning. Stuff the chicken at the neck end. Plump up and secure with a skewer. Truss the bird as for roasting and season well.

Melt the butter or margarine in a large skillet. Add the chicken and fry, turning until browned all over. Place the chicken and butter in a large casserole and add the bacon. Cover and cook in a moderate oven (350°F.) for 15 minutes.

Meanwhile, cut the potatoes into 1 in. cubes. Remove the casserole from the oven and baste the chicken with drippings. Surround the chicken with the potatoes, shallots and carrots, turning them over in the fat. Season. Cover and return to oven and cook for 1½ hours. Garnish with chopped parsley.

Have a heated serving platter ready for carving the chicken but serve the vegetables and juices straight from the casserole.

*Rabbit is delicious in a casserole*

## NAVARIN OF LAMB
*4 servings*

2 pound lamb stew meat
¼ cup shortening or pan
   drippings
2½ tablespoons flour
2½ teaspoons salt
½ teaspoon pepper
3¾ tablespoons tomato paste
2½ cups hot water
Bouquet garni (including cut
   clove garlic)
4 onions, sliced
4 carrots, sliced
4 small turnips, sliced
8 small potatoes

Cut the meat into serving-size pieces. Melt 2 tablespoons shortening or drippings in a skillet. Brown the meat, a few pieces at a time. Dredge with seasoned flour and brown again. Gradually stir in the tomato paste and hot water. Add the bouquet garni. Bring to a boil, reduce heat, cover and simmer for 1 hour.

Melt 2 tablespoons shortening or drippings in a pan and fry the onions, carrots and turnips until lightly browned. Stir vegetables into the meat mixture and simmer for 30 minutes. Discard the bouquet garni. Add the potatoes and simmer for 30 minutes until tender. Skim off fat and adjust seasoning before serving.

## LAMB JULIENNE
*6 servings*

3⅓ tablespoons flour
1¼ teaspoons curry powder
2½ teaspoons salt
Freshly ground black pepper
2 pound lamb stew meat, cubed
Oil for frying
3¾ cups water or chicken stock
8 small onions
8 carrots

*For crispy dumplings*
3 tablespoons butter
1 cup fresh white breadcrumbs
2 cups self-rising flour
1¼ teaspoons salt
½ teaspoon onion powder
3¾ tablespoons corn oil
Milk

Sift together the flour, curry powder, salt and pepper. Toss the lamb cubes in this mixture. Fry the meat in the hot oil until well browned. Stir in any excess flour. Gradually stir in the water or stock and bring to a boil, stirring. Pour meat into a casserole. Add the onions. Cover and cook in a warm oven (325°F.) for 1 hour. Cut the carrots into long thick

*A fish casserole makes a pleasant change from meat and poultry*

matchsticks and add to the meat. For crispy dumplings, melt the butter in a pan. Stir in the crumbs and cook gently, stirring frequently, until golden.

Sift together the flour, salt and onion powder. Stir in the oil and enough milk to make a soft but manageable dough. Shape into balls. Coat with crumbs and arrange in the casserole on top of the meat and vegetables. Cover and cook for 1 hour.

## SUMMER LAMB CASSEROLE
*4 servings*

2 pound lamb stew meat
2 teaspoons salt
½ teaspoon pepper
2½ cups water
1 bunch carrots, sliced
1 pound small new potatoes,
   scraped
½ pound fresh peas
1 tablespoon tomato paste
Chopped fresh mint

Put the meat in a shallow flameproof casserole. Add the salt, pepper and water and bring to a boil. Add the carrots. Cover the casserole and cook in a warm oven (325°F.) for about 1 hour. Add the potatoes and peas to the casserole and cook for about 30 minutes or until meat and vegetables are tender. Adjust seasoning and stir in the tomato paste. Cook an additional 10 minutes. Serve sprinkled with fresh mint.

## FISH AND BACON CASSEROLE
*6 servings*

¼ pound bacon, chopped
3 onions, chopped
1 tablespoon butter or margarine
1½ pound fillet of white fish
Salt
Cayenne
1 teaspoon Worcestershire sauce
1 can (8 ounces) tomato sauce
⅝ cup water

Fry the bacon and onions in melted butter until onion is tender. Put alternate layers of bacon and onion and fish into a casserole, sprinkling each layer with salt and a very little cayenne.

Mix the Worcestershire and tomato sauces with the water. Pour over the fish. Cover casserole and cook in a moderate oven (350°F.) for 45 minutes.

## CIDERED HADDOCK CASSEROLE
*4-6 servings*

1–1½ pound haddock or cod
   fillet, skinned
½ pound tomatoes, peeled and
   sliced
6 button mushrooms, sliced
1 tablespoon chopped parsley
Salt
Freshly ground black pepper
⅝ cup cider
2 tablespoons fresh white
   breadcrumbs
2½ tablespoons grated Cheddar
   cheese

Wipe the fish. Cut into cubes and place in an ovenproof baking dish. Cover with the sliced tomatoes and mushrooms, parsley and seasonings. Pour the cider over the top.

Cover with foil and cook in a moderate oven (350°F.) for 20–30 minutes. Sprinkle with breadcrumbs and cheese. Turn oven temperature up to 425°F. and bake casserole just long enough to brown the crumbs.

## SWEETBREAD HOTPOT
*4 servings*

1 pound sweetbreads
1 onion, chopped
½ pound fresh peas
¼ pound mushrooms, sliced
2 tablespoons butter or
   margarine
½ cup all-purpose flour
2½ cups white stock
Salt
Freshly ground black pepper
1 teaspoon mixed dried herbs
Toast for garnish

Soak the sweetbreads in salted water for about 1 hour. Drain. Cover with fresh water, bring slowly to a boil. Drain.

In a flameproof casserole, fry the onion, peas and mushrooms very slowly for 5 minutes in hot butter. Add the flour and stir until cooked. Stir in the stock slowly. Cook, stirring constantly, until mixture comes to a boil. Season and add herbs.

Chop the sweetbreads and add to the casserole. Cook in a warm oven (325°F.) for about 2 hours until sweetbreads are tender. Serve garnished with triangles of toast.

---

**Handy hint**

When reheating casseroles and stews, bring quickly to boiling point, then simmer for 15 minutes or for as long as necessary to heat through thoroughly. Keeping meat warm, but not boiling, for long periods may encourage the growth of fresh bacteria.

Lamb julienne

# BRAISING

Braising is a combination of baking and steaming. It is suitable for both the less expensive roasting cuts and stewing meats – particularly such cuts as leg of mutton, rib, brisket or silverside of beef, best end of neck of lamb or knuckle of veal, pork spare ribs and, of course, poultry and game (especially the tougher, boiling birds). It gives a delicate flavor to the food and a tender, moist consistency. A split calf's foot added to the pan will make it even more succulent.

Start with a fairly generous cut, as it will shrink a little in the cooking. Many vegetables can also be successfully braised.

Meat is cooked by laying it on a bed of vegetables (called a mirepoix) half covered with liquid, and either cooked in the oven at 300–325°F., or simmered on top of the stove. The liquid may be stock, wine or cider. The meat may be braised either as a whole piece, or boned and stuffed, or sliced. Prepare the vegetables you plan to use in the mirepoix – e.g. an onion, a carrot, a small turnip, 2 stalks of celery – by peeling and trimming in the usual way and cutting into pieces. Use enough to make a 2 in. layer in the bottom of the pan.

Put about 2 tablespoons pan drippings and a few bacon rinds into a flameproof casserole. Fry the meat in the hot fat until well browned all over. Take out the meat, add the vegetables, seasoning and a bouquet garni to the pan and place the meat on top. Add sufficient stock or water to half-cover the mirepoix. Bring to the boil, cover and simmer gently, basting every 15–20 minutes for half the cooking times until the meat is tender. (For a roast under 3 pound allow 2 hours.) Slice the meat and serve with vegetables, in the cooking juices.

Alternatively, coat the meat in seasoned flour and fry in melted pan drippings. Remove the meat from the pan, fry the vegetables and continue as in the first method. Cover, and cook in the oven at 325°F. until the meat is tender. To serve, the vegetables are usually piled round the meat and the liquid (made into a sauce) is poured over them.

To braise vegetables, fry lightly first, then season, add a little liquid and cook slowly in the oven.

*Chicken absorbs the flavors of herbs and vegetables braised with it*

## BRAISED CELERY
*4 servings*

**4 small bunches celery, trimmed and scrubbed**
**¼ cup butter**
**Stock**
**Salt and pepper**

Tie each head of celery securely to hold the shape. Fry lightly in 3 tablespoons butter for 5 minutes or until golden brown. Put in an ovenproof dish. Add enough stock to come half-way up the celery, sprinkle with salt and pepper and add the remaining butter. Cover and cook in a moderate oven (350°F.) for 1–1½ hours. Remove the string and serve with the cooking liquid poured over the top.

## BRAISED ENDIVE
*4 servings*

**1½ pound endive**
**2 tablespoons butter**
**¼ teaspoon grated nutmeg**
**Juice of ½ a lemon**
**⅝ cup chicken stock**
**2 teaspoons cornstarch**
**1¼ tablespoons cold water**
**Salt and black pepper**
**Chopped parsley**

Plunge the trimmed endive into boiling water for 1 minute. Drain and rinse with cold water. Drain again. Butter a large casserole. Lay the endive in the bottom in a single layer. Dot with butter. Stir the nutmeg and lemon juice into the stock and pour over the endive. Cover with a lid and cook in a warm oven (325°F.) for about 1½ hours. Blend the cornstarch with the water. Drain the juices from the casserole into a small saucepan. Add the cornstarch and bring to a boil, stirring constantly. Boil for 1 minute. Adjust the seasoning and pour the sauce over the endive. Sprinkle with parsley and serve.

## SWEET-SOUR RED CABBAGE
*4 servings*

**2 pound red cabbage, shredded**
**2 medium onions, sliced**
**2 cooking apples, pared and chopped**
**2½ teaspoons sugar**
**Salt and pepper**
**Bouquet garni**
**2½ tablespoons water**
**2½ tablespoons red wine vinegar**
**2 tablespoons butter or margarine**

In a casserole, layer the cabbage, onions, apples, sugar and seasoning. Put the bouquet garni in the center. Pour the water and vinegar over the layers. Cover tightly and cook in a cool oven (300°F.) for about 2½ hours. Just before serving, add the butter and mix well.

## CHICKEN IN A POT
*6 servings*

**¼ pound sausage meat**
**2½ tablespoons fresh white breadcrumbs**
**1 chicken liver, chopped**
**2½ tablespoons chopped parsley**
**3½ pound roasting chicken**
**3⅓ tablespoons salad oil**
**Salt**
**Freshly ground black pepper**
**4 stalks celery, thickly sliced**
**2 leeks, thoroughly washed and sliced**
**½ pound small turnips, cut up**
**1 bunch carrots, sliced**
**Juice of ½ a lemon**
**Bouquet garni**
**Chicken stock made from giblets**
**Chopped parsley**

In a bowl, combine the sausage meat, breadcrumbs, liver and parsley. Stuff the chicken with this mixture and truss with skewers or string. Heat the oil in a large pan. Season the skin of the bird and fry in the oil until golden brown on all sides.

Place the browned chicken in a large casserole. Put the celery, leeks, turnips and carrots in the remaining oil in the pan. Cover and cook gently for 5 minutes, stirring occasionally. Drain off the fat and pack the vegetables around the chicken in the casserole. Add the lemon juice, bouquet garni and enough stock to give a depth of about 1 in. in the bottom of the casserole.

Cover tightly. Place on a cookie tray and cook in a moderate oven (350°F.) for about 1½ hours until both the chicken and vegetables are tender.

Arrange the chicken and vegetables on a large serving platter. Keep warm in the oven. Skim off any surplus fat from the juices with a spoon. Bring to a boil and reduce liquid slightly. Adjust the seasoning and sprinkle with parsley. Pour the juice over the chicken and serve at once.

## BRAISED PORK AND RED CABBAGE
*6 servings*

1½ pound lean pork
1 tablespoon butter or margarine
1½ tablespoons salad oil
1 pound cooking apples, pared and cored
1 pound red cabbage, finely shredded
2½ tablespoons flour
3¾ tablespoons wine vinegar
2½ cups stock
Salt
Freshly ground black pepper

Cut the pork into thin strips ½ in. wide. Cut each strip in half. Melt the butter and oil in a skillet until bubbling. Season the pork and fry until well browned on all sides. Reduce heat and simmer for 10–15 minutes. Cut the apples into thick slices.

Place a good third of the red cabbage in a deep casserole, add some apple slices and half the meat. Continue the layers, finishing with the apple slices. Blend the flour with the vinegar. Gradually add the stock and stir until well blended. Taste and adjust seasoning. Bring to a boil and cook, stirring constantly, for 2–3 minutes. Pour into casserole, cover and cook in a moderate oven (350°F.) for 2 hours or until pork is tender.

## BRAISED BEEF WITH SOUR CREAM AND MUSHROOMS
*6 servings*

3½ pound thick flank steak
1 can (16 ounces) plum tomatoes
2 beef bouillon cubes
½ pound onions, cut up
½ pound carrots, cut up
1 pound button mushrooms, stalks removed
¼ cup butter or margarine
1 cup dairy sour cream
Chopped parsley

Cut the meat into thin strips. Put the tomatoes in a large flameproof casserole and crumb in the bouillon cubes. Arrange the meat in the center with the onions, carrots and mushroom stalks around the sides. Cover tightly, preferably with foil and a lid. Cook in a warm oven (325°F.) for about 2 hours.

Remove the lid and gently turn the meat in the juice. Cover, reduce heat to 300°F. and cook for 1 hour or until tender.

Slice the mushroom caps. Melt the butter and fry the mushrooms just until tender. Discard the vegetables from the casserole, leaving the strips of beef. Add the mushrooms and the cream. Reheat carefully, but do not boil. Adjust the seasoning and serve sprinkled with chopped parsley.

## BRAISED DUCKLING WITH TURNIPS
*4 servings*

3½ pound roasting duckling, cut into quarters
Salt
Freshly ground black pepper
2 large onions, chopped
1 pound small turnips, cut up
2 stalks celery, chopped
1 teaspoon dried thyme
2½ cups brown stock
1 tablespoon cornstarch
1¼ tablespoons chopped parsley

Place the duckling pieces in a roasting pan and season well. Cook, uncovered, in a fairly hot oven (400°F.) for 20 minutes or until well browned. Remove from pan and drain well on paper towels.

Place the onions, turnips and celery in the bottom of a flameproof casserole. Sprinkle thyme on the vegetables and lay the duckling pieces on top. Pour over the stock. Cover and cook in a fairly hot oven (375°F.) for about 1 hour.

Combine the cornstarch with a little water to make a smooth paste. Stir into the casserole juice. Bring to a boil and cook for 1–2 minutes. Arrange the duckling and vegetables on a hot serving platter, pour the juices over and garnish with parsley.

## BRAISED PIGEONS WITH GOLDEN SPAGHETTI
*4 servings*

2-3 slices bacon, diced
1 carrot, diced
Small piece turnip, diced
2 stalks celery, chopped
1 onion, chopped
4 pigeons, halved
3¾ cups stock
Bouquet garni
Salt and pepper
1¼ tablespoons cornstarch
⅓ pound spaghetti
½ cup butter
Chopped parsley

Put the bacon and vegetables into a flameproof casserole. Lay the halved pigeons on top. Add enough stock almost to cover. Add the bouquet garni and seasoning. Cover casserole tightly and cook on top of the stove for 1 hour, over moderate heat, until the pigeons are almost tender.

*Preparing braised endive*

Place the casserole in a moderate oven (350°F.) and cook, uncovered, for 45 minutes or until the stock is reduced and the pigeons are browned. Thicken the stock with cornstarch, if necessary. Meanwhile, cook the spaghetti in boiling salted water until tender. Drain. Add the butter and toss well until the spaghetti is well coated and glistening. Serve the pigeons on a hot serving platter, surrounded by spaghetti and garnished with chopped parsley.

## BRAISED HAM
*12 servings*

½ a smoked ham, about 7 pound
1 onion, cut up
1 carrot, cut up
1 turnip, cut up
Bouquet garni
5 cups stock
3 tomatoes, peeled and sliced
A few mushrooms, sliced, optional
1¼ cups rich brown sauce
⅝ cup sherry, optional

Soak the ham overnight in cold water. Drain.

Place it in a large kettle and add just sufficient water to cover. Add the onion, carrot, turnip and bouquet garni. Bring to a boil and simmer for 1¾ hours. Remove the ham and peel off the rind.

Put the ham in a deep casserole. Add the stock, tomatoes and mushrooms. Cover tightly and cook in a moderate oven (350°F.) for about 2 hours.

Remove ham and place on a warm serving platter. Strain the stock into a saucepan. Bring to a boil and boil rapidly to reduce the volume by half. Brush mixture over top of ham. Add the brown sauce and sherry to the remaining mixture, boil up and serve as gravy with the ham.

## BRAISED SWEETBREADS
*4 servings*

1 pound frozen lambs' sweetbreads, thawed
1 large carrot, diced
1 onion, diced
2 stalks celery, diced
1¼ tablespoons salad oil
Salt and pepper
1¼ cups white stock
3 slices bacon
2½ teaspoons cornstarch
Parsley

Soak the sweetbreads in cold water for 4 hours, changing the water several times. Put into fresh cold water in a saucepan. Bring to a boil. Lift out the sweetbreads and rinse under cold running water. Remove the black veins and skin. Wrap lightly in a cloth or a piece of muslin. Place on a board, stand a weighted plate on top and let cool.

Fry the vegetables in half of the heated oil until tender. Place them in the bottom of a casserole just large enough for the sweetbreads. Add the seasoning and enough stock just to cover the vegetables. Slice the sweetbreads, arrange on the vegetables and top with bacon slices.

Cover the casserole and cook in a fairly hot oven (375°F.) for ½–¾ hour, basting occasionally with the juices. Increase the oven temperature to 425°F. and remove lids. Cook for 10 minutes. Strain the liquid into a saucepan. Mix the cornstarch with a little

*Vermouth is the ideal flavor with this delicious sole*

cold water. Add to liquid and cook until clear and thickened. Pour over the sweetbreads. Garnish with parsley.

## BRAISED VEAL CUTLETS
*4 servings*

5 tablespoons butter
4 veal cutlets, trimmed
¼ pound cooked ham, chopped
1¼ tablespoons chopped onion
1¼ tablespoons chopped parsley
Salt and pepper
⅝ cup dry red wine

Melt 4 tablespoons butter in a skillet. Add the cutlets and fry until golden brown on both sides. Remove cutlets and set aside. Fry the ham and onion just until onion is tender. Stir in the parsley and season well. Cover the cutlets with this mixture, place carefully in a flat casserole and add the wine and sufficient water to come half-way up the meat. Cover and cook in a moderate oven (350°F.) for 45 minutes. Remove the cutlets and keep warm. Bring the liquid to a boil and reduce it slightly. Stir the remaining butter into the sauce and pour over the cutlets.

## ORANGE-BRAISED PORK CHOPS
*4 servings*

6 tablespoons butter or margarine
½ pound onions, sliced
4 pork chops
Salt and pepper
1 teaspoon dry mustard
2 teaspoons sugar
1 tablespoon flour
3 large oranges
⅝ cup dry white wine

Heat 2 tablespoons of the butter in a skillet. Add the onions and cook gently until light golden brown, then remove from the skillet. Trim any excess fat from the chops. In a small bowl, mix together the salt and pepper, mustard, sugar and remaining butter. Spread on one side of each chop. Fry the chops until golden on both sides. Remove from the skillet, stir in the flour and blend well.

Coarsely grate the rind from 2 oranges and add to the pan with the onions. Squeeze the juice from 2 oranges and make up to ⅝ cup of liquid with water. Stir into the skillet and cook, stirring, until mixture comes to a boil. Stir in the wine.

Peel the remaining orange and cut it into sections. Arrange the chops in a flameproof pan. Add the orange sections. Pour on the onion and wine sauce. Cover and simmer on top of the stove for 40 minutes or until chops are tender.

## BOEUF EN DAUBE
*6 servings*

2½ pound top or bottom round beef roast
2 tablespoons butter or margarine
2½ tablespoons salad oil
½ pound onions, finely sliced
1 bunch carrots, finely sliced
½ pound salt pork, rinded and cubed
1¼ cups dry white wine
⅝ cup beef stock
1 teaspoon dried basil
½ teaspoon dried rosemary
1 bay leaf
½ teaspoon powdered mixed spice
Salt and pepper
6 pitted black olives

Tie the beef firmly with string. Melt the butter and the oil in a Dutch oven. Add the beef and brown well on all sides. Remove the beef and set aside. Fry the vegetables and salt pork in the Dutch oven until golden brown. Return beef to Dutch oven. Pour over the wine and stock and stir in the herbs and seasonings. Bring to a boil. Cover and cook in a warm oven (325°F.) for 2½–3 hours or until fork tender. About 30 minutes before the end of the cooking time, add the olives. When cooked, remove the string from the meat and slice. Skim the fat from the juices and serve from the casserole.

## BRAISED SOLE
*4 servings*

2½ pound sole fillets
Salt and pepper
5 tablespoons butter
Fresh white breadcrumbs
2 shallots, chopped
1½ teaspoons finely chopped parsley
7½ tablespoons dry vermouth

Season the fish with salt and pepper. Melt 2 tablespoons of the butter. Dip fillets in the butter then coat well with breadcrumbs. Combine the shallots and parsley and spread over the bottom of a greased baking dish. Lay the fillets on top. Melt the remaining butter and pour over the fish. Spoon the vermouth carefully around the fish; do not pour it over the top.

Cook, uncovered, in a very hot oven (450°F.) for 10–15 minutes or until the fish is cooked. Transfer to a hot serving platter and keep warm. Pour the liquid into a small saucepan and boil rapidly until reduced by half. Pour over the fish and serve immediately.

## HERRINGS BRAISED IN WINE
*6 servings*

1 cup dry red wine
2 thick slices onion
1 carrot, sliced
1 celery stalk, sliced
1 bay leaf
6 peppercorns
Salt and pepper
6 herrings or other small oily fish
Sauté button mushrooms

Place the wine, sliced vegetables, bay leaf, peppercorns and seasoning in a small saucepan. Cover and simmer for 30 minutes. Arrange the herrings in a single layer in an ovenproof baking dish. Strain the wine mixture over the fish, adding a little water if necessary, almost to cover the fish. Cover and cook in a warm oven (325°F.) for 1 hour. Garnish with sauté button mushrooms before serving.

### Handy hint

When browning meat in fat, choose a large, deep pan to prevent splashing the cooker and yourself with fat.

*Boeuf en daube is a classic braised dish*

# VARIETY MEATS

*Ragoût of liver*

## LIVER

**Ox liver** has a strong flavor and is often rather tough and coarse-textured. Best used for casseroles.
**Calf's liver** is very tender and has a delicate flavor. It can be lightly broiled or fried, but over-cooking makes it hard and dry.
**Lamb's liver** has a slightly stronger flavor than calf's. It is suitable for broiling or frying.
**Pig's liver** has a pronounced distinctive flavor and a softer texture. It is best casseroled and makes an excellent pâté.
Allow ¼ lb. liver per serving.

## SAVORY LIVER
*4 servings*

1 pound lambs' liver
1 cup fresh white breadcrumbs
1 tablespoon chopped parsley
1 teaspoon mixed dried herbs
2 tablespoons suet, chopped
Salt and pepper
Grated rind of ½ a lemon
Milk
4 slices bacon
⅝ cup stock or water

Wash and slice the liver and arrange in a shallow casserole. Combine the breadcrumbs, parsley, herbs, suet, seasoning and lemon juice. Stir in enough milk to make the mixture stick together. Spread the stuffing on the liver and place the bacon slices on top. Pour in the stock or water.
Cook, covered, in a moderate oven (350°F.) for 30–45 minutes or until liver is tender. Remove the lid for the last 15 minutes to crisp the bacon.

## RAGOUT OF LIVER
*4 servings*

1 pound lambs' liver
5 tablespoons seasoned flour
1 onion, sliced
4 slices bacon, chopped
2 tablespoons fat or oil
1⅞ cup stock
2 tablespoons white raisins
1 apple, pared and grated
1 teaspoon tomato paste
Hot cooked rice

Wash and trim the liver and cut into small pieces. Coat with seasoned flour. Fry the liver, onion and bacon in the hot fat or oil until golden brown. Add the stock to the skillet and bring to a boil, stirring constantly. Add the raisins, apple and tomato paste and simmer for 20 minutes.
Serve with hot cooked rice.

## LIVER MARSALA
*4 servings*

1 pound calves' or lambs' liver
Lemon juice
Seasoned flour
¼ cup butter
4 tablespoons Marsala
⅝ cup stock
Broiled tomato halves
Parsley

Slice the liver, sprinkle with lemon juice and coat with seasoned flour. Melt the butter in a skillet. Fry the liver quickly on both sides until lightly browned. Stir in the Marsala and stock and simmer until the meat is just cooked and the sauce syrupy.
Arrange the liver on a serving platter and garnish with broiled tomato halves and parsley.

## KIDNEY
**Ox kidney** has a fairly strong flavor. It needs slow, gentle cooking to make it tender. It is usually cooked with steak in casseroles and pies, or curries. Allow ¼ pound kidney to 1 pound steak.
**Calf's kidney** is more tender and delicate in flavor than ox kidney, but is used in the same ways. One kidney will serve 1–2 people and is usually sold chopped.

**Lamb's kidneys** are usually the best, being small, well-flavored and tender enough to broil or fry, either whole or in halves. The skin and white 'core' should be removed for cooking. Allow 2 per serving.
**Pig's and sheep's kidneys** are similar to lamb's but are slightly larger and not quite so tender. Pig's kidney has a strong flavor. They can be halved and broiled or fried, or used in stews, curries, or casseroles. Allow 1–2 per serving, depending on size.

## KIDNEYS IN RED WINE
*4 servings*

¼ cup butter or margarine
1 onion, chopped
4–6 sheeps' kidneys
3¾ tablespoons flour
⅝ cup red wine
⅝ cup stock
Bouquet garni
1 tablespoon tomato paste
Salt and pepper
6 mushrooms, sliced

Melt the butter and fry the onion until golden brown. Wash, skin and core the kidneys and cut into small pieces. Add to the skillet with the onions and cook for 5 minutes, stirring occasionally.

Stir in the flour and cook for 1 minute. Add the wine and stock and bring slowly to a boil, stirring. Add the bouquet garni, tomato paste and seasoning. Simmer for 5 minutes. Add the mushrooms and simmer for 5 minutes. Remove the bouquet garni, check seasoning and serve.

## KIDNEY ROYALE
*4 servings*

8 lambs' kidneys
3 tablespoons butter or
  margarine
1 medium onion, chopped
2 pimientos
Salt
Freshly ground black pepper
2½ tablespoons Irish whiskey
5 tablespoons dairy sour cream
Hot cooked rice
Chopped parsley

Halve the kidneys. Remove and discard the skin and cores, then cut into pieces. Melt the butter in a skillet and fry the onion gently, about 5 minutes, till transparent but not colored. Add the kidneys and fry for about 10 minutes. Stir in the pimientos. Season and simmer for 5 minutes. Warm the whiskey gently, pour over the kidneys and ignite with a kitchen match. When the flames have died out remove the pan from the heat. Stir in the sour cream and reheat without boiling.
Arrange the hot cooked rice around the edge of a serving platter and pile the kidneys in the center. Garnish generously with chopped parsley.

## SWEETBREADS

**Ox sweetbreads** need slow, gentle cooking in a casserole.
**Calf's sweetbreads** are more tender than ox, but are also best stewed or casseroled.
**Lamb's sweetbreads** are tender, with a fine delicate flavor. They can be fried, or casseroled. Allow ¼ lb. sweetbreads per serving.

## FRIED SWEETBREADS
*4 servings*

1 pound lambs' or calves'
  sweetbreads
Juice of ½ a lemon
Beaten egg
Dry breadcrumbs
Oil for deep frying

Soak the sweetbreads for 3–4 hours in cold water. Drain. Place in a saucepan and cover with cold water and lemon juice. Bring slowly to a boil and simmer for 5 minutes. Drain. Cover with cold

water and let stand until sweetbreads are firm and cold. Strip off any stringy unwanted tissue. Press the sweetbreads well between paper towels to absorb all the moisture. Slice and dip in the beaten egg and breadcrumbs. Fry in the hot oil until golden. Serve at once with tartar or tomato sauce.

## CREAMED SWEETBREADS
*4 servings*

1 pound sweetbreads
Juice of ½ a lemon
½ an onion, chopped
1 carrot, chopped
Few parsley stalks
½ bay leaf
Salt and pepper
3 tablespoons butter or
  margarine
6 tablespoons flour
1¼ cups milk
Squeeze of lemon juice
Chopped parsley

Soak the sweetbreads for 3-4 hours in cold water. Drain. Put in a pan, cover with cold water and lemon juice. Bring slowly to a boil and simmer for 5 minutes. Drain and leave in cold water until they are firm and cold. Strip off any stringy unwanted tissues. Slice sweetbreads.
Put the sweetbreads, vegetables, herbs and seasoning in a pan with water to cover and simmer gently until tender, ¾–1 hour. Drain and keep hot, retaining 1¼ cups of the cooking liquid. Melt the butter in a saucepan. Stir in the flour and cook for 1 minute. Remove the pan from the heat and gradually stir in the milk and the sweetbread liquid. Cook over moderate heat, stirring constantly, until mixture thickens and comes to a boil. Season well and stir in lemon juice. Return sweetbreads to pan and heat gently. Serve sprinkled with chopped parsley.

## HEART
**Ox heart** is the largest and tends to be rather tough unless cooked long and slowly. It can be parboiled whole and then roasted, or cut up and braised or stewed, but in any case it needs strong seasonings and flavorings. An ox heart weighs about 3–4 pound and serves 4–6 people. It can be bought sliced.
**Calf's heart** is small and more tender, but still needs slow cooking. It may be roasted, braised or stewed. 1 calf's heart will serve 2 people.
**Lamb's heart** is more tender than

*Try lambs' kidneys flamed in Irish whiskey – kidney royale*

ox or calf's and has a fine flavor. It is usually stuffed and either roasted or braised. Allow 1 per serving.

## RICH CASSEROLED HEART
*4 servings*

1 ox heart, 2½–3 pound
¼ cup fat or oil
2 onions, sliced
¼ cup flour
1¼ cups stock
3–4 carrots, grated
½ small turnip, grated
1 orange
6 walnut halves, chopped

Slice the heart, removing the tubes. Wash well in cold running water. Fry in hot fat until lightly brown. Remove from pan and place in a casserole. Fry the onions in the hot fat and add to the casserole. Stir the flour into the fat and cook, stirring, until just browned. Add the stock, bring to a boil and simmer, stirring, for 2–3 minutes or until slightly thickened. Pour over the heart and onions in the casserole. Cover and cook in a cool oven (300°F.) for 2½– 3 hours. Add the grated carrots and turnip and cook for 1 more hour.
Pare the rind from the orange. Cut into shreds. Cover with water in a saucepan and boil for 10–15

minutes. Drain. Add the orange rind and walnuts for the last 15 minutes.

## STUFFED HEART CASSEROLE
*4 servings*

4 small lambs' hearts
2½ tablespoons seasoned flour
2 tablespoons fat or oil
2½ cups stock
1 onion, sliced
4 stalks celery, sliced
3 carrots, sliced
1 tablespoon cider, optional

*For stuffing:*
2 cups fresh breadcrumbs
1 medium onion, finely chopped
3¾ tablespoons melted butter
2½ teaspoons mixed dried herbs
Salt and pepper

Wash the hearts, slit open and remove any tubes. Wash again. Mix the ingredients for stuffing and fill the hearts with the mixture. Tie them into their original shape with string. Coat with seasoned flour. Brown quickly in hot fat or oil.
Place the hearts in a casserole. Add the stock. Cover and cook in a moderate oven (350°F.) for 2½ hours, turning frequently. Add the onion, celery, carrots and cider for the last 45 minutes.

*Sweetbreads are delicious coated with egg and breadcrumbs and fried*

# POULTRY AND GAME

*Poultry is the term used for all birds reared specially for the table. It includes chicken, duck, goose and turkey. Game refers to wild birds and animals that are hunted for food, but which are protected by law at certain seasons.*

*The most common game birds are grouse, partridge, pheasant, wild duck, black game and ptarmigan; the only protected animals are deer. Hare, pigeon and rabbit are usually grouped with game although they are not protected. Pigeon and rabbit are sometimes reared specially for the table; both are prepared in much the same ways as game and it is therefore convenient to include them.*

## CHICKEN

A very young chicken (6–8 weeks old, weighing 1–2 pound) is usually broiled, fried or baked. A broiler (12 weeks old, weighing 2½–3½ pound) is cooked in the same way. (Frozen chickens are usually broilers.) There is, of course, no reason why these birds should not be casseroled or braised. A roaster (4–5 pound) and a capon (up to 10 pound) both look and taste very appetizing when stuffed and roasted. Boiling fowl (18 months old, weighing 4–7 pound) are boiled or casseroled; the meat is too tough to roast.

## TURKEYS, DUCKS, GEESE

Whole turkeys are most commonly roasted, stuffed with 1 or 2 kinds of stuffing. Cut pieces may be made into a variety of casserole dishes.

Ducks may be roasted, casseroled or braised. They are rich and are therefore usually served with a sharp-flavored sauce or accompaniment such as apple sauce or orange salad. Ducklings are more commonly eaten than fully grown ducks. Buy a duck or duckling weighing at least 3 pound, otherwise the proportion of bone is too high.

Geese (average weight 9–10 pound) are usually roasted, though they can be casseroled. Again they are rich in fat and need something to offset this.

*Game birds tend to dry out when roasting, so bard with bacon slices*

## GAME BIRDS

Generally speaking, the more simply game is cooked, the better. For young birds there is no better way than roasting. For older birds that are likely to be tough, braising or casseroling are better. Since game birds lack fat, it is usual to bard the breast before roasting with slices of fat bacon and to baste frequently with fat during cooking. Sometimes a lump of butter or a piece of juicy steak is put inside the bird before it is cooked, to keep it moist.

## HARE AND RABBIT

Hares may be roasted (if young), fricasseed or braised. They are usually hung for 7–10 days before cooking. Rabbits may be cooked almost any way suitable for other kinds of meat, but only young, tender ones should be roasted or fried; they also make a good pie filling and adapt well to jellied molds.

## VENISON

This is the meat of the red deer. The haunch is the prime cut and this and the other better-quality cuts roast and fry well. Venison, which should be well hung, does tend to be rather dry; so bard or

lard it and marinate before cooking. The back and breast may be casseroled or braised.

## PREPARATION

Most poultry and game are now sold ready for cooking, that is hung, cleaned or drawn where appropriate, and plucked or skinned. However, since many of the birds are stuffed before cooking, you need to be able to truss them at home (trussing keeps the bird a good shape, so that it looks attractive and is easy to carve).

*Note:* Poultry are cooked without the feet, but game feet are left on for cooking.

## TRUSSING

There are two ways of trussing, using either a trussing needle and fine string or a skewer and string. First stuff the bird if required, then fold the neck skin under the body and fold the wing tips back towards the backbone so that they hold the neck skin in position. Make a slit in the skin above the vent and put the tail (the 'parson's nose') through.

If you are using a trussing needle, thread it with fine string and insert it close to the second joint of the right wing; push it right

through the body, passing it out to catch the corresponding joint on the other side. Then insert the needle in the first joint of the left wing, pass it through the meat at the back of the body, catching the wing tips and the neck skin, and bring it out through the first joint of the wing on the right side. Tie the ends of the string in a bow. To secure the legs, re-thread the needle, insert it through the gristle beside the parson's nose and tie the legs and tail firmly together. If you are using a skewer, insert it right through the body just below the thigh bone and turn the bird over on its breast. Catching in the wing tips, pass the string under the ends of the skewer and cross it over the back. Turn the bird over and tie the ends of the string round the tail, at the same time securing the drumsticks.

## FROZEN BIRDS

Both poultry and game are frequently sold frozen. *The bird must be thoroughly thawed before cooking starts.* A single piece of chicken will take 2–3 hours to thaw; a whole chicken or game bird 12–24 hours, depending on size. A large turkey may take up to three days.

## ROAST CHICKEN

Wipe the inside of the bird with a clean, damp cloth and stuff the neck end. Don't stuff too tightly as the stuffing mixture tends to swell and might split the skin. To add flavor if left unstuffed, put a lump of butter with some herbs, an onion or a wedge of lemon in the body. Truss. Brush the chicken with oil or melted butter and sprinkle with salt and pepper. Place a few slices of bacon over the breast if you wish.

Cook at 375°F., allowing 20 minutes per pound plus 20 minutes. Baste occasionally and put a piece of aluminum foil over the breast if it seems to be browning too quickly.

Alternatively, wrap the bird in foil before cooking, with the join along the top, or use a transparent roasting bag, following the instructions. Allow the same cooking time but open the foil for the final 15–20 minutes to allow the bird to brown.

Serve with roast potatoes and green vegetables or a tossed green salad; also bread sauce and thin gravy made from the giblets.

To roast a very small bird, spread with softened butter and put a lump of butter inside. Wrap in buttered paper and cook for only about 30–45 minutes, according to size. Remove the paper for the last 15 minutes to brown the breast.

## ROAST TURKEY

Stuff and truss and spread with softened butter or dripping. Cover the breast with slices of fat bacon.

Cook either at 325°F., basting regularly, or at 450°F., wrapping the bird in foil first and unwrapping it for the last 30 minutes. In either case turn it once, for even browning.

Cooking times – at 325°F.
6–8 pound 3–3½ hours
8–10 pound 3½–3¾ hours
10–12 pound 3¾–4 hours
12–14 pound 4–4¼ hours
14–16 pound 4¼–4½ hours
16–18 pound 4½–4¾ hours

Cooking times – at 450°F.
6–8 pound 2¼–2½ hours
8–10 pound 2½–2¾ hours
10–12 pound 2¾ hours
12–14 pound 3 hours
14–16 pound 3–3¼ hours
16–18 pound 3¼–3½ hours

If preferred, use a large roasting bag and follow directions.
Serve with roast potatoes and Brussels sprouts; thin gravy, bread sauce and cranberry sauce.

## ROAST DUCK

*allow 12–14 ounces per serving*

Stuff at the tail and truss as for chicken, except that the wings are not drawn across the back. Prick the skin all over with a fine skewer and sprinkle the breast with salt and pepper.
Cook at 375°F. for 20 minutes per pound.
Serve with apple sauce, new potatoes, peas and thin brown gravy, or orange salad, or with bigarade sauce.

## ROAST GOOSE

*8 servings*

Stuff and truss. Sprinkle with salt and place in a roasting pan on a wire rack, as goose tends to be fatty. Cover the breast with waxed paper or foil. A sour apple put in the roasting pan will add extra flavor to the gravy.
Cook at 400°F. for 15 minutes per pound plus 15 minutes, without basting. Alternatively, cook at 350°F. for 25–30 minutes per pound. Remove the paper for last

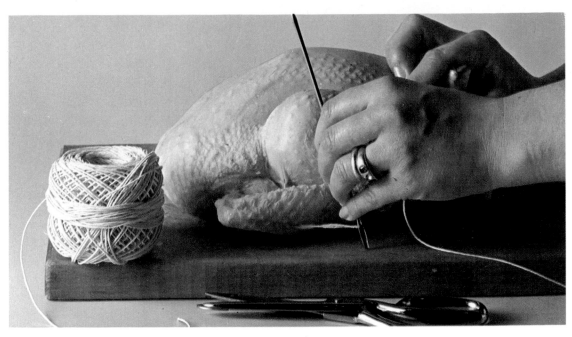

*Trussing a chicken for roasting, using fine string and a special trussing needle*

30 minutes to brown skin. Serve with gravy and apple or gooseberry sauce.

## ROAST GROUSE

*2–3 servings*

Truss, season inside and out and lay some fat bacon over the breast. Put a lump of butter inside and place the bird on a slice of toast. Cook at 400°F. for 30 minutes, basting frequently. After 20 minutes, remove the bacon, dredge the breast with flour, baste well and cook for a further 10 minutes. Serve the grouse on the toast on which it was roasted, with thin gravy, fried crumbs and French fried potatoes.

## ROAST PARTRIDGE

*1–2 servings*

Season the inside with salt and pepper, replace the liver and add a lump of butter. Truss. Cover the breast with slices of bacon fat. Cook at 450°F. for 10 minutes, then reduce the temperature to 400°F. and cook for a further 10–20 minutes, according to size. Partridge should be well cooked. Serve with fried crumbs, clear gravy, watercress, orange sauce and quarters of lemon.

## ROAST PHEASANT

*4–5 servings*

Wipe the bird inside and out and put a lump of butter, flavored with herbs and lemon juice, inside. Truss and cover the breast with slices of fat bacon. Cook at 450°F. for 10 minutes, then reduce the temperature to 400°F. and continue cooking for 30–40 minutes,

according to size. Baste frequently with butter; 15 minutes before the end, remove the bacon, dredge with flour and baste well. Serve as for partridge.

## ROAST WILD DUCK

*Mallard serves 4–5*
*Pintail serves 2*
*Widgeon serves 2*
*Teal serves 1*

Truss like a domestic duck and spread with softened butter. Cook at 425°F., basting frequently. Allow 20 minutes for teal, 30 minutes for mallard and widgeon – they should on no account be overcooked. Half-way through the cooking time, pour a little port or orange juice over the bird. Serve with thin gravy and orange salad or bigarade sauce.

## ROAST VENISON

*For marinade:*
**2 carrots, chopped**
**2 small onions, chopped**
**1 stalk celery, chopped**
**6 peppercorns**
**Parsley stalks**
**1 bay leaf**
**3 blades of mace**
**Red wine**

The best part for roasting is the saddle, but for a small piece use the loin or a fillet cut from the saddle. Place the vegetables and flavorings for the marinade in a large container, put in the venison and add sufficient wine to half cover it. Leave to marinate for 12 hours, turning the meat 2–3 times.
It was traditional to cover the meat with a paste made by mixing flour and water to a stiff dough

(allow about 3 pound flour to a saddle) and rolling it out to ½ in. thickness. Nowadays, however, the meat is usually brushed generously with oil and wrapped loosely in foil. Roast in the center of the oven at 325°F., allowing 25 minutes per pound; 20 minutes before the end of cooking time, remove foil or paste, dredge meat with flour and return to oven to brown. Serve hot with thick gravy and red-currant or cranberry jelly.

## GAME CHIPS

Pare the potatoes and slice very thinly into rounds. Soak in cold water, dry and fry in deep fat for about 3 minutes (fill frying basket only ¼ full). Remove the chips from the fat and drain well.
Just before serving, reheat the fat and fry the chips rapidly for a further 3 minutes, until crisp and brown. Drain well on paper towels and serve.

## FRIED CRUMBS

**1–2 cups fresh white breadcrumbs**
**2 tablespoons butter**

Fry the crumbs in the butter until golden brown.

## BREAD SAUCE

**1 medium onion**
**2 cloves**
**2 cups milk**
**Salt**
**A few peppercorns**
**1½ tablespoons butter**
**1½ cups fresh white breadcrumbs**

*The richness of duck can be offset by the sharp orange tang of bigarade sauce*

Stick the onion with the cloves and place in a saucepan with the milk, salt and peppercorns. Bring almost to boiling point and leave in a warm place for about 20 minutes.

Remove the peppercorns and add the butter and the breadcrumbs. Mix well and allow to cook very slowly for about 15 minutes, then remove the onion. Serve hot.

## BIGARADE SAUCE

3 oranges (use bitter ones, e.g. Seville, when available)
1 lemon
1 tablespoon sugar
1¼ tablespoons vinegar
2½ tablespoons brandy
1 tablespoon cornstarch

Grate the rind from 1 orange and squeeze the juice from all of the oranges and the lemon. Melt the sugar in a pan with the vinegar and heat until it is a dark brown caramel. Add the brandy, orange and lemon juice to the caramel and simmer gently for 5 minutes. Drain the excess fat from the pan in which the duck was roasted and add the grated rind and the orange sauce to the sediment. Stir in the cornstarch blended with a little water, return the pan to the heat, bring to a boil and cook for 2–3 minutes, stirring.
Adjust seasoning.

## ORANGE SALAD

2 oranges, pared
Chopped tarragon or mint
French dressing, page 54
Endive or crisp lettuce leaves

Divide the oranges into sections, removing all the skin, pith and seeds. Alternatively, cut across in thin slices, using a saw-edged knife.

Put the orange in a shallow dish, sprinkle with tarragon or mint and pour the dressing over; let stand for a short time.

Spoon the orange on to a bed of endive or lettuce to serve.

## APRICOT STUFFING

*for chicken; make double this quantity to stuff the neck end of a turkey*

¼ pound dried apricots
1½ cups fresh white breadcrumbs
¼ teaspoon mixed spice
¼ teaspoon salt
¼ teaspoon pepper
1¼ tablespoons lemon juice
2 tablespoons butter, melted
1 egg, beaten

Soak the apricots in cold water overnight. Drain off the liquid. Chop the fruit. Stir in the remaining ingredients and blend lightly.

## APPLE AND CELERY STUFFING

*for duck; use double the quantity for goose*

3 slices bacon, chopped
2 tablespoons butter or margarine
2 onions, chopped
2 stalks celery, chopped
4 medium cooking apples, pared and cored
1½ cups fresh white breadcrumbs
2½ tablespoons chopped parsley
Sugar to taste
Salt and pepper

Fry the bacon in the butter for 2–3 minutes until golden brown. Remove from pan with a slotted spoon. Fry the onions and celery for 5 minutes and remove from the pan with a slotted spoon. Slice the apples into the pan and fry for 2–3 minutes, until soft. Combine all ingredients in a mixing bowl and blend well.

## VEAL STUFFING

*for turkey*

½ pound lean veal, trimmed and diced
⅓ pound lean bacon, diced
2 onions, finely chopped
¼ cup butter or margarine
3 cups fresh white breadcrumbs
2 large mushrooms, chopped
2½ teaspoons finely chopped parsley
Salt
Freshly ground black pepper
Pinch of cayenne
Pinch of ground mace
2 eggs, beaten
Milk, optional

Mix the veal and bacon and put twice through a food chopper. Place in a bowl and beat well. Fry the onions lightly in a little of the butter until soft, but not colored, about 2–3 minutes. Add to the meat.

Add the breadcrumbs, mushrooms, remaining butter, seasonings and spices. Add the eggs and blend well. If the mixture is too stiff, add a little milk.

## TURKEY A LA KING
*4 servings*

½ pound button mushrooms
1 small green pepper, seeded
¼ cup butter
6 tablespoons flour
1 jar (6½ ounces) pimiento, drained and diced
⅝ cup turkey stock
⅝ cup milk
Tabasco sauce
4 cups diced, cooked turkey
Salt and pepper
1–2 tablespoons sherry

Wipe the mushrooms and remove the stems but do not peel. Cut in thick slices. Cut the pepper in thin slices. Melt the butter in a saucepan and sauté the mushrooms and pepper for 10 minutes. Stir in the flour and cook for 1 minute. Remove from heat and stir in the pimiento, stock and milk. Cook over moderate heat, stirring constantly, until mixture comes to a boil. Reduce heat, add a few drops of Tabasco and the turkey. Season to taste and simmer on very low heat for 15 minutes, or until piping hot. Add the sherry, reheat and serve with hot cooked rice.

## CHICKEN CHASSEUR
*4 servings*

1 roasting chicken, cut in quarters
Seasoned flour
1¼ tablespoons salad oil
2 tablespoons butter or margarine
1 onion, chopped
4–5 mushrooms, sliced
2 tomatoes, peeled and seeded
1¼ cups espagnole sauce (page 58) or rich gravy
5 tablespoons dry white wine
Salt and pepper
Chopped parsley

Coat the chicken pieces in seasoned flour. Heat the oil and butter in a heavy skillet. Add the chicken and fry until golden brown on all sides. Remove the chicken and place in a casserole or baking dish in a single layer. Add the onion and mushrooms to the fat in the skillet and fry gently for 5 minutes. Drain off the fat. Dice the tomatoes and add to the onion and mushrooms. Add the espagnole sauce or gravy, the wine and seasoning. Blend well. Pour over the chicken. Cover and cook in a moderate oven (350°F.) for about 1¼ hours or until chicken is tender. Sprinkle with chopped parsley before serving.

*Grilled grouse à l'américaine makes a quick 'company' dish*

## GROUSE A L'AMERICAINE
*4 servings*

2 young grouse
¼ cup butter
Salt and pepper
2 cups fresh breadcrumbs
Cayenne
4 slices bacon
4 tomatoes, halved
¼ pound button mushrooms
Watercress

Slit the grouse down the back and flatten. Brush with melted butter and season with salt and pepper. Preheat broiling compartment and pan. Place the grouse in the pan and broil about 3 in. from the source of heat for 5 minutes. Turn breast side up, sprinkle with breadcrumbs and dust lightly with cayenne. Broil for about 20 minutes, turning frequently.
Roll up the bacon and broil, with the tomatoes and mushrooms, until cooked. Serve around the grouse on the serving platter and garnish with watercress.

## SALMI OF PARTRIDGE OR PHEASANT
*4 servings*

2 partridges or 1 pheasant, lightly roasted
1 shallot, chopped
1 orange, pared and sectioned
⅝ cup stock
1¼ cups espagnole sauce, page 58
⅝ cup red wine
White grapes, skinned and seeded
Red-currant jelly

Remove the skin from the birds; cut off the breast and the legs and set aside. Break up the remaining carcasses into small pieces and put in a pan with the shallot, orange rind and stock. Simmer for 30 minutes. Strain the stock from the pan and combine with the espagnole sauce and wine in a saucepan. Add the breast and legs of the partridge and simmer for about 10 minutes or until the meat is heated through. Arrange the meat on a serving platter. Boil

the sauce until it is reduced to a syrupy consistency. Pour it over the game and garnish with a few grapes, orange sections and red-currant jelly.

## POULET AU GRAND MARNIER
*4–6 servings*
*For stuffing:*
6 tablespoons butter
¼ pound onions, finely chopped
3 stalks celery, finely chopped
1 teaspoon dried marjoram or oregano
½ pound cooked ham, finely chopped
½ teaspoon grated orange rind
3 cups fresh white breadcrumbs
1¼ tablespoons Grand Marnier
Salt
Freshly ground black pepper

3½–4 pound roasting chicken
1 tablespoon butter
Salt and pepper
Juice of 2 oranges
2½ tablespoons Grand Marnier
½ pound cherries, pitted
¼ cup sugar
1 tablespoon flour
1¼ cups water
Parsley sprigs

Melt 2 tablespoons of the butter in a large saucepan. Add the onion and celery. Cover with a lid and simmer for 10 minutes. Add remaining butter and allow to melt. Stir in the herbs, ham, orange rind, breadcrumbs and Grand Marnier. Mix well together and season to taste. Use this to stuff the chicken, then truss in the usual way.
Smear 1 tablespoon butter over the chicken. Sprinkle with salt and pepper. Put the chicken and its washed giblets in a roasting pan. Pour the juice of 1 orange over the chicken. Roast in a fairly hot oven (375°F.) for about 1½–2 hours; 15 minutes before the end of cooking time spoon the Grand Marnier over the breast. Meanwhile, squeeze the juice from the remaining orange and put in a small pan with the cherries and the sugar. Cook over gentle heat. Remove the chicken from roasting pan. Discard the trussing string and keep the chicken warm on a serving platter.
On top of the stove, reduce the pan juices to about 2 tablespoons by boiling rapidly. Stir in the flour and cook for 1 minute. Add the water and cook, stirring constantly, until the mixture comes to a boil. Bubble for 1–2 minutes. Season well.

Drain the cherries and arrange them around the chicken. Add the cherry juice to the thickened pan juices. Pass the mixture through a sieve. Garnish the chicken with parsley and serve the sauce separately.

## HUNTER'S CASSEROLE
*4 servings*

3½ pound rabbit, skinned and cut into small pieces
Salt
Freshly ground black pepper
2½ tablespoons salad oil
1 tablespoon butter
⅝ cup dry white wine
1 clove garlic, crushed
4 tablespoons chopped parsley

Season the rabbit pieces. Heat the oil and butter in a heavy pan. Fry the rabbit briskly on all sides until golden brown. Remove the rabbit and place in a casserole. Drain the excess fat from the pan juices. Add the wine, garlic and 2 tablespoons chopped parsley. Adjust the seasoning and heat for a few minutes. Pour the sauce over the rabbit. Cook in a fairly hot oven (375°F.) for about 45 minutes or until rabbit is tender. Remove the meat from the bones. Return to the sauce and cook for 15 minutes. Sprinkle with remaining chopped parsley.

## PIGEONS IN CREAM
*6 servings*

6 pigeons
½ cup butter
⅝ cup stock
2½ tablespoons red-currant jelly
1¼ cups heavy cream
Salt and pepper
1¼ tablespoons brandy
Chopped parsley

Wash the pigeons and trim away the claws and undercarriage bones. Fry in the butter until well browned. Place in a casserole, breast side down, with the butter and juices. Add the stock. Cover tightly. Cook in a warm oven (325°F.) for about 2 hours or until very tender. Remove the birds from the casserole and keep warm. Pour the juices into a small saucepan. Boil rapidly to reduce by half. Stir in the red-currant jelly and cream, season to taste. Bring to a boil. Reduce heat to simmer. Warm the brandy, ignite with a kitchen match and pour flaming over the sauce. Pour the sauce over the birds and sprinkle with chopped parsley.

*Poulet au Grand Marnier, generously garnished with cherries*

# VEGETABLES

Vegetables add interest and flavor to the day's meals and many of them are also a good source of vitamins and minerals. For example, a helping of potatoes and a green vegetable will supply most (if not all) of the daily Vitamin C requirements.

## Storing and preparation

Buy vegetables in prime condition and store in a cool, airy place – a vegetable rack in a well ventilated cupboard is ideal, or the vegetable compartment of a refrigerator. Green vegetables should be used as soon as possible after gathering, while their Vitamin C value is at its highest. All vegetables should be prepared with care and as near to the time of cooking as possible, to retain flavor and Vitamin C content.

## Serving

Serve vegetables as soon as they are cooked – they tend to deteriorate when they are kept hot and some develop unpleasant, strong smells. Serve them slightly under- rather than over-cooked and drain them well if they have been boiled. Serve all vegetables really hot, especially if fried. Don't cover them with a lid or they will become soggy. A sprinkling of salt and pepper improves most vegetables – especially fried ones, where no salt is used in the cooking process. Add a lump of butter to boiled or steamed vegetables when serving.

## GLOBE ARTICHOKES

Cut off the stem close to the base of the leaves and take off the outer layer of leaves and any others which are dry or discolored. Soak the artichokes in cold water for about 30 minutes to ensure they are clean; drain well (upside down).

Cook them in boiling salted water until the leaves will pull out easily – about 20–40 minutes, depending on size – and drain upside down. Serve them with melted butter or hollandaise sauce (page 58). Globe artichokes may also be served cold, with a vinaigrette dressing.

Allow 1 artichoke per serving as a starter.

## JERUSALEM ARTICHOKES

Scrub the artichokes; using a stainless steel knife or peeler, peel them quickly and immediately plunge them into cold water, to prevent discoloration. A squeeze of lemon juice or a few drops of vinegar added to the water helps to keep them a good color.

Cook in boiling salted water to which a little lemon juice or vinegar has been added for about 30 minutes, until just soft. Drain, garnish with finely chopped parsley and serve with melted butter or a white, cheese, or hollandaise sauce (page 58).

1 pound makes 2–3 servings.

## ASPARAGUS

Cut off the woody end of the stalks and scrape the white part lightly, removing any coarse spines. Tie in bundles with all the heads together and place upright in a deep saucepan or special asparagus pan of boiling salted water. Boil for 10 minutes, then lay them flat and continue cooking until just soft – a further 5–6 minutes (this does not apply when cooking in a special pan). Alternatively, lay the bundles in the bottom of a saucepan with the heads all pointing in the same direction and have one side of the pan slightly off the heat, so that the heads are in the cooler part; allow about 15 minutes.

Drain well and untie the bundles before serving with melted butter or hollandaise sauce (page 58). Don't overcook asparagus – it is better to have to discard more of the stem part than to have the tips mushy.

Allow 8–12 stems per serving.

## BEETS

Cut off the tops 1 in. or so above the beet, then wash, taking care not to damage the skins or they will 'bleed' while boiling. Boil in salted water until tender, from 1–2 hours depending on the age of the beet. When they are cooked, pare off the skin and cut the beets into cubes or slices. Serve hot coated with a white sauce or butter. Serve cold in a little vinegar.

Allow ¼ pound per serving.

## BUTTERY SHREDDED BEETS

*4–6 servings*

**6 medium beets**
**½ teaspoon salt**
**⅛ teaspoon garlic salt**
**⅛ teaspoon pepper**
**2 tablespoons butter or margarine**

Peel beets and grate on a medium grater. Place in a skillet. Sprinkle with salt, garlic salt and pepper and dot with butter. Simmer, covered, for 20–30 minutes or

until tender. Serve with vinegar or lemon wedges.

## GLAZED BEETS
*4 servings*

**12 small beets, cooked**
**2 tablespoons butter**
**1 teaspoon sugar**
**Salt and pepper**
**Grated rind of 1 lemon**
**1 teaspoon chopped chives**
**2 teaspoons chopped parsley**
**Juice of ½ lemon**
**1 tablespoon capers**

Remove the skin, stalks and root ends from the beets. Melt the butter in a saucepan and add the beets, sugar, salt, pepper and lemon rind. Toss the beets in the pan over medium heat until they are well coated. Add the remaining ingredients and heat thoroughly. Serve piping hot.

## BROCCOLI
Select broccoli with tender, firm stalks and tightly closed heads, with no yellow color. Cut off large leaves and a slice from the lower stalk. With a vegetable peeler remove the tough skin from the stem. Wash well. If stalks are large, make lengthwise slits in the bottom almost up to the flowerets. Lay them flat in a skillet and cook in 1 in. boiling salted water, covered, for 10–15 minutes. Serve with butter or hollandaise sauce (page 58).
1 pound makes 2–3 servings.

## BRUSSELS SPROUTS
Buy green, fresh-looking sprouts. Avoid yellow spots or worm holes. Wash the sprouts, removing any discolored outer leaves and cut a cross in the stalk. Cook in boiling salted water for 8–10 minutes or until tender. Drain well and serve buttered with a grind of fresh pepper.
1 pound makes 2–3 servings.

## CABBAGE
Remove the coarse outer leaves, cut the cabbage in wedges and remove the hard center core, leaving just enough core to retain shape. Cook rapidly in about 1 in. boiling salted water for 10–12 minutes or until tender. Do not overcook. Drain well, chop roughly if desired and toss with butter, a grind of fresh pepper and a pinch of grated nutmeg, if wished. Serve at once.
Cabbage may be cut into quarters and cut into medium shred with a sharp knife. Cook in boiling salted water for 5–7 minutes or

*Sauté zucchini and tomatoes, finished au gratin*

until just tender.
1 pound makes 3–4 servings.

## RED CABBAGE WITH APPLES
*6 servings*

**1 head (2½ pound) red cabbage, shredded**
**¾ cup boiling water**
**3 large cooking apples, pared, cored and sliced**
**3 tablespoons butter or margarine**
**¼ cup vinegar**
**1½ teaspoons flour**
**¼ cup brown sugar**
**2 teaspoons salt**
**Pinch of pepper**

Put the cabbage in a kettle. Add water and cook, covered, for 10 minutes. Add the apples and cook for 10 minutes or until apples are tender. Add the remaining ingredients. Heat thoroughly, toss lightly and serve.

## CARROTS
Trim the tops and any root from new carrots. Scrub with a brush or scrape very lightly. Cook the carrots whole in boiling salted water for about 15 minutes or until tender. Serve tossed with a little butter and parsley.

Peel old carrots with a vegetable peeler and cut into strips lengthwise, or into cubes or into thin rounds. Cook in boiling salted water for 15–20 minutes or until tender.
1 pound makes 3–4 servings.

## CAULIFLOWER
Buy a compact, crisp white head, as free from blemishes as possible, with fresh, green outer leaves. Remove the outside leaves and cut off any blemishes. Wash well. Leave whole, removing as much of the core as possible without altering the shape. Boil, stem side down, in salted water for 20–30 minutes, depending on size. Drain well and serve with cheese sauce. The cauliflower can be broken into flowerets and cooked in boiling salted water for 8–12 minutes. Drain well and toss with butter or margarine.
1 medium cauliflower makes 4 servings.

## CELERIAC
Cut away leaves and root fibres. Do not peel. Cook in boiling salted water for 40–60 minutes or until tender. Drain, peel and slice. Toss in the pan with butter, salt, pepper and chopped parsley.

Serve hot.
Celeriac may also be served raw, peeled and cut into julienne strips, and mixed with other salad vegetables.
1 pound makes 4 servings.

## CELERY
Remove leaves and trim roots. Wash well. With a knife, scrape off any discolorations. Cut into slivers or half moons. Cook in boiling salted water for 15–20 minutes or until tender. Drain well and serve with a white or cheese sauce.
2–3 stalks make 1 serving.

## CORN ON THE COB
Buy young corn that spurts milk when kernels are pressed. Just before cooking remove husks, silk and any blemishes. Cook at one time only enough ears of corn to serve every one once. Drop into plenty of boiling salted water. Boil, covered, for 5–6 minutes. Serve at once with butter or margarine.
Allow 1 ear per serving.

## EGGPLANT
Egg plant should be of uniform purple color, free from blemishes. Wash. Pare if desired when ready to use. Eggplant discolors on standing.
Cut eggplant into ¼ in. crosswise slices. Sprinkle with salt, pepper and a little flour. Or dip into beaten egg, then into cracker crumbs. Sauté in hot oil in a skillet until golden brown on both sides.
Allow about ⅓ pound per serving.

## ENDIVE
Buy fresh-looking, well bleached heads from 4–6 in. long. Endive is generally eaten raw in a salad but it may also be cooked. Wash quickly in water and pat dry. Cut a thin slice from the base and pull away any damaged outer leaves. To cook, plunge the whole heads in boiling water and blanch for 5 minutes. Drain well. Cook in a small amount of boiling water with a tablespoon of butter, lemon juice and seasoning, for 10–15 minutes or until tender. Serve sprinkled with chopped parsley or a little paprika.
Allow 1 or 2 heads per serving.

## GREEN OR WAXED BEANS
Buy crisp, slender green pods that snap. Wash, remove ends and strings, if any. Beans may be

49

snapped or cut into pieces, cut crosswise into thin slanted slices or cut lengthwise into strips. Cook in a small amount of boiling salted water for 10–15 minutes or until tender.

Beans may be cooked and served cold with a vinaigrette dressing.

1 pound makes 3–4 servings.

## MUSHROOMS

Buy firm, plump, cream-colored mushrooms with short stems. Wash well. Do not peel if fresh and tender. Cut thin slice off stem and use whole, or cut in slices parallel to stem.

1 pound makes 4 servings.

## SAUTE MUSHROOMS
*4 servings*

**1 pound mushrooms**
**¼ cup butter or margarine**
**2 tablespoons ground onion**
**1 teaspoon lemon juice**
**½ teaspoon salt**
**Grind of fresh pepper**

Cut washed whole mushrooms into thick slices. Melt butter or margarine in a large skillet and sauté the onion until tender. Add the mushrooms. Sauté over medium heat for about 10 minutes, stirring occasionally. Turn off heat, cover, and let stand 4–5 minutes. Sprinkle with lemon juice, salt and pepper. Serve over toast or with meat or chicken.

## ONIONS

Onions vary considerably in both size and flavor from the small white 'cocktail' onions to the large, mild Spanish onion. Both the leaves and the bulbs of the young plants, known as scallions, may be eaten in salads or whole. In the case of the ordinary mature onions, the stems and skins are discarded. Chopped onions are included in many savory dishes as flavoring. As a separate vegetable they are best braised, fried or stuffed and baked.

## BAKED STUFFED ONIONS
*4 servings*

**4 medium sized onions**
**2½ tablespoons fresh white breadcrumbs**
**Salt and pepper**
**½ cup grated Cheddar cheese**
**Butter**

Cook the onions in boiling salted water for 15–20 minutes, removing them before they are quite soft. Drain and cool. Scoop out the centers, using a pointed knife to cut the onion top and a small

*Onions, stuffed with cheesy crumbs, baked and served with tomato sauce*

spoon to remove the centers. Chop the centers finely, mix with the crumbs, seasoning and ¼ cup cheese. Fill the onions and place them in a greased ovenproof baking dish. Put a small lump of butter on top and sprinkle with the remaining cheese. Bake in the center of a fairly hot oven (400°F.) for 20–30 minutes or until the onions are cooked and brown. Serve with tomato sauce.

## PARSNIPS

Wash the parsnips, peel and cut up. Remove the hard center cores if the parsnips are at all woody. Cut up or slice and cook in boiling salted water for 15–20 minutes or until soft. Drain and toss in butter, salt and pepper and a little grated nutmeg.

To roast parsnips, par-boil them (halved or quartered) for 5 minutes in boiling salted water. Drain and cook as for roast potatoes for about 1 hour.

1 pound makes 2–3 servings.

## PEAS

Buy well-filled, fresh, green pods. Shell by pressing between thumbs to open, remove peas. Discard any with shoots. Place in boiling water with about 1 level teaspoon sugar and a sprig of mint and cook for 10–20 minutes or until tender. Drain, remove mint and toss with butter before serving.

1 pound makes 2 servings.

## SAUTE OF PEAS
*4 servings*

**4 scallions, trimmed**
**2 tablespoons butter**
**2 pounds peas, shelled**
**Salt**
**Freshly ground black pepper**
**1 cup white stock**
**1 teaspoon chopped parsley**

Lightly sauté the onions in the hot butter for about 2 minutes. Add the peas, salt and pepper and just enough stock to cover peas. Cover tightly and cook gently for 10–20 minutes or until the peas are tender. Remove the lid 5 minutes before peas are cooked to allow the cooking liquid to evaporate. Sprinkle with chopped parsley just before serving.

## POTATOES

Pare old potatoes as thinly as possible; new potatoes are scraped, or scrubbed and cooked with the skins on and peeled before serving. Cook the potatoes as soon as possible after peeling.

1 pound makes 2–3 servings.

## BAKED POTATOES

Choose even sized old potatoes, free from eyes or blemishes. Scrub well, dry and prick all over with a fork. Bake near the top of a fairly hot oven (400°F.) for ¾–1 hour for small potatoes, 1–1¼ hours for large potatoes, or until

soft when pinched. Cut a cross in the top of each potato and add butter or dairy sour cream. Serve immediately.

## BOILED POTATOES

Cut the pared potatoes into even sized pieces (leave new potatoes whole), put into cold water, add ½ teaspoon salt per pound of potatoes, bring to a boil and simmer until tender – 15–20 minutes for new potatoes, 20–30 minutes for old.

Drain well, add butter and serve sprinkled with parsley.

## MASHED POTATOES

Boil old potatoes until tender. Drain well. Mash with a potato masher or hand-held electric mixer with butter, salt, pepper and hot milk. Beat well until light and fluffy. Serve in a heated dish sprinkled with chopped parsley.

## ROAST POTATOES

Using old potatoes, pare and cut into even sized pieces. Cook in boiling salted water for about 7 minutes. Drain well. Transfer to a roasting pan containing ½ cup hot lard or dripping, baste well and cook near the top of a hot oven (425°F.) for about 20 minutes. Turn them and continue cooking until soft inside and crisp and brown outside, about 40 minutes altogether. Alternatively, place potatoes in the pan around a roast. Cook until brown and crisp. Drain well on paper towels and serve sprinkled with salt.

## LYONNAISE POTATOES
*4 servings*

**½ pound onions, sliced**
**2½ tablespoons salad oil**
**1 pound potatoes, sauté**
**Chopped parsley**

Fry the onions slowly in the oil until golden brown, about 10 minutes. Serve in layers with the potatoes and sprinkle with chopped parsley.

## SCALLOPED POTATOES
*4 servings*

**4 cups thinly sliced, pared**
**potatoes**
**⅔ cup ground onions**
**2 tablespoons flour**
**1 teaspoon salt**
**⅛ teaspoon pepper**
**2 tablespoons butter or**
**margarine**
**1½ cups scalded milk**
**Paprika**

Arrange a layer of potatoes in a greased 2-quart casserole. Cover with some of the onions. Sprinkle with some of the combined flour, salt and pepper. Dot with some of the butter. Repeat layers until all are used, ending with butter. Pour the milk over the top and sprinkle with paprika. Cover and bake in a fairly hot oven (375°F.) for 45 minutes. Remove cover and bake 15 minutes longer or until tender and lightly browned.

## SPINACH
Wash several times in water to remove all grit and strip off any coarse stalks. Pack into a saucepan with only the water that clings to the leaves after washing. Heat gently, turning the spinach occasionally, then bring to a boil and cook gently for 6–10 minutes or until tender. Drain thoroughly. Chop roughly or purée and reheat with butter and a sprinkling of salt and pepper.
1 pound makes 2 servings.

## SQUASH
**Acorn.** Buy ridged squash that are green, firm and oval or round. Scrub well. Cut in half lengthwise. Remove seeds and stringy portion. Brush cut sides with melted butter or margarine. Arrange cut side down in a baking pan. Bake in a fairly hot oven (400°F.) for 30 minutes. Turn cut sides up. Brush with melted but-

ter. Fill each half with 1 tablespoon brown sugar. Bake for 30 minutes or until tender.

**Hubbard.** Scrub well. Cut into serving pieces; remove seeds and stringy portion. Brush with melted butter and sprinkle with salt and pepper. Arrange squash pieces, side by side, cut side down in a greased baking pan. Bake in a fairly hot oven (400°F.) for 30 minutes. Turn cut sides up. Brush with melted butter. Bake for 30 minutes or until tender, brushing often with melted butter.

## SWEET PEPPERS
Both red and green peppers can be sliced or chopped and eaten raw in salad. Small amounts of raw or blanched peppers may be included in savory dishes made with rice and macaroni. Peppers may be fried or stuffed and baked. To prepare them, remove stalk, seeds and membrane. For stuffing and baking, leave whole, par-boil for 5 minutes and bake in a moderate oven (350°F.) for 25–30 minutes. Or cut in rings and sauté in butter for 5 minutes. Allow 1 pepper per serving for stuffed or fried peppers.

## SWEET PEPPERS WITH TOMATOES
*4 servings*

**2½ tablespoons salad oil**
**½ onion, chopped**
**1 clove garlic, crushed**
**4 tomatoes, peeled and sliced**
**2½ tablespoons tomato paste**
**⅝ cup dry white wine**
**4 medium sized peppers, seeded**
**and thinly sliced**
**Salt and pepper**

Heat the oil and lightly fry the onion and garlic for 5 minutes without browning. Add the tomatoes, tomato paste and wine and simmer for 5 minutes. Add the peppers, cover and simmer for 25–30 minutes. Adjust seasoning before serving.

## TURNIPS
Buy white turnips with fresh green tops. Turnips should be firm and heavy. Avoid those that are light-weight for size; they may be woody and pithy. Scrub and pare. Cut into strips or cubes. Cook in boiling salted water for 15–20 minutes. Toss in butter or a little light cream, season with salt and pepper. Or mash with salt, pepper, nutmeg and butter. Yellow turnips, often called

*Vegetables in season make a good hot curry*

rutabagas, should be heavy and firm, not light-weight and pithy. Pare and cut into strips or cubes. Cook in boiling salted water for 20–25 minutes or until tender. Drain well and mash with salt, pepper, a little nutmeg and butter. 1 pound makes 2–3 servings.

## ZUCCHINI
Cut away the stalk end and ¼ in. from the rounded end. Do not pare. If small, blanch whole, otherwise slice thickly; blanch in salted water for 5 minutes. Drain, then sauté in a little butter, lemon juice and chopped parsley for a few minutes. Season and serve. 1 pound makes 4 servings.

## ZUCCHINI WITH TOMATOES
*4 servings*

**1 pound zucchini, cut into ¼ in.**
**slices**
**Salt**
**5 tablespoons butter**
**½ pound tomatoes, peeled and**
**chopped**
**1 tablespoon chopped parsley**
**1 small clove garlic, crushed**
**Pepper**
**½ teaspoon sugar**
**½ cup grated cheese**
**½ cup fresh white breadcrumbs**

Put the zucchini slices into a colander, sprinkle with salt and allow to drain for about an hour; dry them well. Melt 4 tablespoons

butter in a skillet and put in the zucchini. Cook gently until soft and slightly transparent and put them in a shallow baking dish. Melt the remaining butter and cook the tomatoes, parsley, garlic, pepper and sugar until a thickish purée forms.

Re-season the mixture if necessary and pour over the zucchini. Sprinkle with the cheese and breadcrumbs. Broil under a hot broiler until cheese has melted and crumbs are golden brown.

## VEGETABLE CURRY
*4 servings*

**1 cauliflower, cut in large sprigs**
**6 tomatoes, peeled and sliced**
**6–8 small potatoes, cut up**
**¼ pound shelled peas**
**¼ pound green beans, sliced**
**1 tablespoon turmeric**
**1½ tablespoons curry powder**
**½ teaspoon salt**
**¼ cup butter**
**6 small onions**
**1 clove garlic, crushed**
**1¼ cups stock**

Place the vegetables on a large plate and sprinkle with the mixed spices and salt. Melt the butter in a heavy pan and sauté the onions and garlic. Add the spiced vegetables and the stock. Cover, bring to a boil and simmer for about 20 minutes until all the vegetables are tender. Serve with hot cooked rice.

# SALADS

Serve crisp, cool salads for main courses, starters and accompaniments. Full of vitamins and minerals for your family, quick and easy to prepare for guests – salads are the answer to many a 'what shall we eat?' situation. Above: Dutch salad, based on cheese, apples and spinach.

## MAIN COURSE SALADS

### PORK AND BEAN SALAD
*4 servings*

2½ tablespoons chopped parsley
1 small onion, very finely chopped
1¼ teaspoons dry mustard
1¼ teaspoons French mustard
1 teaspoon paprika
1 teaspoon salt
Freshly ground black pepper
¼ teaspoon grated nutmeg
2½ teaspoons sugar
Juice of 1 orange
5 tablespoons salad oil
2½ tablespoons tarragon vinegar
½ can (16 ounces) red kidney beans, drained
2 large cooked potatoes, diced
1 pound cold, cooked pork sausages
2 eating apples, cored and diced
2 tomatoes, peeled and seeded

Put the parsley, onion, seasonings, spices, sugar, orange juice, oil and vinegar in a bottle with a lid. Shake well to make dressing.

In a bowl, lightly toss together the beans, potatoes, sausages (cut into ¼ in. slices), apples and chopped tomatoes. Add the dressing and toss lightly. Let stand 30 minutes to let the mixture blend through, stirring occasionally. Turn into a salad bowl to serve.

### CHICKEN SALAD
*6 servings*

1 stewing fowl, about 3½ pound
1 small onion
2–3 strips lemon rind
2½ tablespoons lemon juice
Blade of mace
2 sprigs parsley
6 peppercorns
2 whole cloves
Salt
½ cup long grain rice
½ cup white raisins
2 tablespoons seedless raisins
½ pound white and black grapes, peeled and seeded
⅝ cup mayonaise
1 tomato, sliced
1 egg, hard-cooked and sliced
Watercress

Put the fowl in a heavy Dutch oven with the onion, lemon rind, lemon juice, herbs and spices, tied in a small square of muslin, salt to taste and sufficient water to cover. Simmer slowly over medium heat until tender, about 3 hours.
Remove all bones and skin from the fowl and dice the meat. Boil

the rice in the strained chicken stock until tender. Drain if necessary and chill rice. Mix the diced fowl, rice, dried fruit and half the grapes. Toss lightly with the mayonnaise.
Pile high in a deep dish and garnish with a border of alternating black and white grapes. Garnish top of salad with tomato slices, egg slices and watercress.

### SWEDISH CHICKEN SALAD
*6 servings*

3½ pound cooked chicken
¾ cup long grain rice
1 green eating apple
1 red eating apple
2 bananas
Lemon juice
⅝ cup heavy cream
⅞ cup mayonnaise
1¼ teaspoons curry powder
Salt and pepper
Watercress

Carve the chicken into slices and cut into thin strips. Cook the rice in boiling salted water until tender, drain if necessary and cool. Halve and core the apples and cut into thin slices. Peel the bananas and slice thickly. Sprinkle the apples and bananas with lemon juice.
Whip the cream to the same consistency as the mayonnaise and fold into mayonnaise. Add the curry powder. Fold in the chicken, apple and banana. Add more

lemon juice and adjust seasoning, if necessary. Pile on a bed of rice or mix together with the rice. Garnish with watercress.

### BEEF SALAD
*4 servings*

1 cup long grain rice
2–3 tomatoes, peeled and sliced
½ pound cold, cooked beef, thinly sliced and cut into strips
1¼ tablespoons finely chopped onion
1¼ teaspoons prepared mustard
4 tablespoons French dressing
1 head lettuce, washed and separated into leaves
4 tomatoes, sliced, to garnish

Cook the rice in boiling, salted water until tender. Let cool. Mix with tomatoes, beef and onion. Add the mustard to the French dressing. Toss lightly with the beef mixture. Serve with lettuce and tomatoes.

### CHEESE SALAD BOWL
*4 servings*

Lettuce cups
Bunch watercress, washed and trimmed
½ pound tomatoes, peeled and sliced
¼ pound small, new potatoes, cooked and diced
½ pound Cheddar cheese, diced
⅝ cup mayonnaise
¼ teaspoon prepared mustard
Chopped chives

Line a salad bowl with lettuce cups and watercress.

Combine the tomatoes, potatoes and cheese. Mix the mayonnaise with the mustard and toss lightly with the potato mixture. Pile in the center of the salad bowl and sprinkle with chives.

## SALAMI SALAD
*4 servings*

¼ pound salami, thinly sliced
¼ pound Swiss or Cheddar cheese, diced
French dressing
Small bunch radishes, trimmed and sliced
1 clove garlic, cut
1 head lettuce, washed and broken into chunks
½ cucumber, thinly sliced
Bunch watercress, washed and trimmed
¼ pound Gruyère cheese, thinly sliced

Put 8 slices of the salami to one side and cut the rest into strips, using scissors. Toss the cheese in 2 tablespoons French dressing, mix in a bowl with the cut salami and radishes. Add the garlic. Let stand a while for flavors to blend. Cut half-way through each slice of the reserved salami and curl into cones.

To serve, remove the garlic, lightly toss the lettuce, cucumber and half the watercress in a little French dressing. Arrange the greens in a shallow flat dish. Tuck in the slices of Gruyère around the edge and pile the cheese and salami mixture in the center. Surround with salami cones and watercress sprigs.

## PIQUANT EGG SALAD WITH YOGURT DRESSING
*4 servings*

*For dressing:*
1¼ cups low fat unflavored yogurt
1¼ teaspoons paprika
1¼ teaspoons sugar
1¼ tablespoons lemon juice
1¼ tablespoons orange juice
Pepper
1 tablespoon finely chopped parsley

1 bunch celery, finely sliced
4 eggs, hard-cooked and sliced
4 carrots, grated
Few radishes, sliced
½ cucumber

For the dressing, combine the yogurt with the paprika, sugar, lemon and orange juices, a little pepper and the parsley. Blend

*Salami salad, served continental style on a wooden board*

thoroughly.

Fold the celery through half the dressing and spoon into a salad bowl. Arrange the eggs on top. Cover with the grated carrot and surround with sliced radishes and cucumber.

Spoon the remaining dressing over the top. Chill well before serving.

## TIVOLI SALAD
*8 servings*

1 head lettuce
1½ pound thickly sliced, cooked ham
½ pound Swiss cheese
1 can (12 ounces) whole kernel corn
4 teaspoons finely chopped onion
Chopped chives

*For dressing:*
5 tablespoons mayonnaise
2½ tablespoons light cream
1½–2½ tablespoons lemon juice
Freshly ground black pepper

Wash and separate the lettuce into cups. Cut the meat and cheese into thick slices, then into small cubes. Drain the corn and add to the meat and cheese. Toss together and toss in the onion. Blend the mayonnaise and cream with lemon juice, just enough to sharpen. Season with pepper. Fold the mayonnaise mixture through the meat and cheese. Arrange a bed of lettuce in a salad bowl. Pile the ham and cheese mixture on top. Garnish with chopped chives.

## SIDE SALADS

## TUNA-FILLED TOMATOES
*4 servings*

4 large tomatoes
¼ cup butter
1 onion, chopped
¼ pound button mushrooms, sliced
1 can (7 ounces) tuna, drained and flaked
2½ tablespoons chopped parsley

Remove the top from each tomato, cutting in a zig-zag fashion with a small, sharp-pointed knife. Using a teaspoon, scoop out the soft core and seeds and discard. Put the tomato cases on a cookie tray.

Heat the butter in a skillet. Add the onion and cook until soft, but not browned. Add the mushrooms and continue cooking for a few minutes. Add the flaked tuna and parsley. Toss lightly. Divide the filling between the tomatoes. Cover with foil and bake in a moderate oven (350°F.) for 20–30 minutes.

## DUTCH SALAD
*6 servings*

2 tablespoons lemon juice
3 green eating apples
½ pound Edam cheese, rinded
1 jar (7 ounces) pimiento, drained
¾ pound spinach

*For dressing:*
1½ tablespoons cider vinegar
2 tablespoons corn oil
Salt
Freshly ground black pepper
½ teaspoon dry mustard
½ teaspoon sugar

Put the lemon juice in a bowl. Dice the apples, discarding the core. Toss with the lemon juice. Cut the cheese into small cubes the same size as the apples. Cut the pimiento into small strips. Carefully wash the spinach and remove all the coarse stems. Roughly break the well drained leaves into small pieces.

Beat together the dressing ingredients and toss the spinach in the dressing until it glistens. Drain and arrange around the edge of a salad bowl. Toss the apple, cheese and pimiento in the remaining dressing and pile in the center of the spinach.

## TOMATO AND ANCHOVY SALAD
*6 servings*

Rind of ½ lemon
3¾ tablespoons lemon juice
3¾ tablespoons salad oil
½ teaspoon sugar
Salt
Freshly ground black pepper
1 can (2 ounces) anchovy fillets, drained and finely chopped
3 shallots, chopped
1½ pound tomatoes, peeled and sliced

Using a potato peeler, thinly pare the lemon rind, free of the white part, and chop in tiny pieces. Beat together the chopped rind, juice, oil, sugar and seasoning. Add the anchovies and shallots. Pour this dressing over the tomato slices and let stand in a cool place for 1–2 hours, turning carefully once or twice.

## RED CABBAGE AND SWEET CORN SALAD
*8 servings*

1½ pound red cabbage
⅓ cup French dressing
½ cucumber, peeled and diced
Salt
Freshly ground black pepper
1 can (12 ounces) whole kernel corn, drained
¼ teaspoon grated lemon rind
2½ teaspoons honey

Quarter the cabbage, discarding any coarse stems. Shred the leaves very finely. Place in a large bowl with the French dressing, toss lightly and let stand for 2 hours.

Put the cucumber in a bowl, season and let stand for 2 hours. Drain off any excess moisture. Add the cucumber, corn, lemon rind and honey to the cabbage and toss lightly.

## SPINACH SLAW
*4 servings*

½ pound fresh spinach
⅓ pound cabbage, washed and trimmed
¼ cup seedless raisins
5 tablespoons lemon juice
3¾ tablespoons salad oil
Salt
Freshly ground black pepper
Sugar
1 eating apple, cored and chopped

Remove any coarse stems from the spinach. Wash thoroughly in cold water. Pat the leaves dry on a clean cloth. Finely shred the spinach and cabbage. Soak the raisins in half the lemon juice until soft and swollen, then add to the spinach and cabbage.

Beat together the oil, remaining lemon juice, salt, pepper and sugar to taste. Add the apple and pour over the spinach and cabbage. Toss lightly until the vegetables glisten with the dressing.

## RICE SALAD, GREEK STYLE
*12 servings*

2 cups long grain rice
⅓ cup French dressing
¼ pound onions, ground
½ green pepper, chopped
½ red pepper, chopped
2 stalks celery, thinly sliced
1 can (7 ounces) pimiento, drained and chopped
Pitted black olives

Cook the rice in boiling salted water until tender. Drain if necessary. While the rice is still hot, pour the dressing over and mix well. Add the onion, peppers, celery and pimiento. Brush a 1½-quart plain ring mold with oil, carefully spoon in the rice mixture and pat down. Cool. Turn out on a flat plate just before serving. Garnish with olives.

## SALADE BASQUE
*4 servings*

6 eggs, hard-cooked and sliced
1 can (7 ounces) tuna, drained and flaked
2 small cucumbers, finely sliced
8 tomatoes, peeled and sliced
1 can (2 ounces) anchovy fillets, drained
3–4 tablespoons salad oil
1¼ tablespoons wine vinegar
1 teaspoon French mustard
2½ tablespoons catsup
1 teaspoon dried mixed herbs

Layer the sliced eggs, flaked tuna, cucumber and tomatoes in a salad

bowl. Split the anchovy fillets in half lengthwise and arrange in a lattice on the tomatoes.

Beat together the remaining ingredients to make a dressing. Pour over the salad. Chill well before serving.

## BEAN AND CELERY SALAD
*4 servings*

½ pound green beans, trimmed and slivered
1 celery heart, thinly sliced
¼ cup chopped dill pickle
1 can (8 ounces) lima beans, drained.
3–4 tablespoons French dressing
Chopped chives

Cook the green beans in boiling salted water for about 5 minutes. Drain and cool. Toss the celery, dill pickle, lima beans and green beans in enough French dressing to moisten. Chill slightly. Serve sprinkled with chopped chives.

## SALAD DRESSINGS

## FRENCH DRESSING

¼ teaspoon salt
⅛ teaspoon pepper
¼ teaspoon dry mustard
¼ teaspoon sugar
1 tablespoon vinegar or lemon juice
2–3 tablespoons salad oil

Put the salt, pepper, mustard and sugar in a bowl, add the vinegar and stir until well blended. Beat in the oil gradually with a fork. The oil separates out on standing, so if necessary beat the dressing again immediately before using. Alternatively, make a large quantity and store in a bottle with a screw top, shaking it up vigorously just before serving.
*Note:* The proportion of oil to vinegar varies with individual taste, but use vinegar sparingly. Wine, tarragon or other herb flavored vinegar may be used.

## MAYONNAISE

1 egg yolk
½ teaspoon dry mustard
½ teaspoon salt
¼ teaspoon pepper
½ teaspoon sugar
⅝ cup salad oil
1 tablespoon vinegar or lemon juice

Put the egg yolk in a small bowl with the seasonings and sugar. Beat with a wire whisk. Add the oil drop by drop, beating briskly the whole time, until the sauce is thick and smooth. If it becomes

*Celery and beans make a sophisticated side salad*

too thick, add a little vinegar. When all the oil has been beaten in, add the vinegar gradually and mix thoroughly.

## THOUSAND ISLANDS MAYONNAISE

⅝ cup mayonnaise
1¼ tablespoons finely chopped stuffed olives
1 teaspoon ground onion
1 egg, hard-cooked and chopped
1¼ tablespoons ground green pepper
1 teaspoon chopped parsley
1¼ teaspoons tomato paste

Mix all the ingredients together until evenly combined. This is popular served over lettuce.

## GREEN MAYONNAISE

12 spinach leaves
12 watercress leaves
8 sprigs parsley
9 sprigs fresh chervil
9 sprigs fresh tarragon
1 tablespoon chopped green onions or scallions
1 cup mayonnaise

Blanch fresh greens in boiling water for 2 minutes. Drain, reserving 2 tablespoons liquid. Purée the blanched greens, onion and liquid in electric blender for 30 seconds at high speed. Stir into the mayonnaise. Chill. Serve with chilled fish.
*Note:* 1 teaspoon each dried chervil leaves and dried tarragon leaves may be substituted for fresh herbs. Stir into the mayonnaise with the blanched greens.

## FOAMY MAYONNAISE

2 egg yolks
Salt and pepper
⅝ cup salad oil
2½ tablespoons lemon juice
1 egg white, stiffly beaten

Beat the egg yolks and seasonings together. Add the oil drop by drop, beating with a wire whisk all the time, until the mayonnaise is thick and smooth. Stir in the lemon juice.

Put mayonnaise in a cool place. Just before serving, fold in the stiffly beaten egg white.

*A molded rice salad, with onion, peppers, celery and olives*

*Pork and bean salad*

# SAVORY SAUCES

A good sauce can make a dish. It enhances the flavor of the food and adds new dimensions of texture and moisture. A sauce is not difficult to make, either, once the basic principles are mastered – the right amount of flour to liquid and careful regulation of the heat while blending are probably the two factors that have the greatest bearing on the texture of the finished sauce.

Most savory sauces are thickened with either flour or egg. Flour sauces are based on a roux, made by melting the butter (or other fat), adding the flour, mixing thoroughly and cooking until they are well combined. For a brown sauce the roux is cooked until it is an even golden brown color; the roux for a white sauce is not allowed to color. The liquid is then added gradually and the sauce is stirred and cooked after each addition until it reaches the required consistency. (Beginners will find it easier if they take the pan off the heat to add the liquid.) For white sauces, the liquid used is usually milk or milk and white stock. For brown sauces, meat stock or vegetable water give a good flavor (stock made from a bouillon cube is adequate for most

but beware of over-seasoning) and for fish sauces you can use the bones from the fish to make a stock, combining this with milk for a sauce.

If you are entertaining, it helps the last-minute rush if you can make the sauce earlier in the day – but the one thing worse than a lumpy sauce is one with a skin on top. If you make a sauce well in advance, press a piece of damp waxed paper on to its surface to stop this happening, and reheat it when needed. The basic white sauce recipes given here show how to vary the proportion of flour and fat to liquid to give sauces of different consistencies for different purposes.

## WHITE SAUCES

### 1 Pouring consistency

**1½ tablespoons butter**
**2½ tablespoons flour**
**1¼ cups milk or milk and stock**
**Salt and pepper**

Melt the fat, add the flour and stir with a wooden spoon until smooth. Cook over a gentle heat for 2–3 minutes, stirring until the mixture begins to bubble. Remove from the heat and add the liquid gradually, beating and stirring rapidly after each addition to prevent lumps forming. Bring the sauce to a boil, stirring continuously, and when it has thickened, cook for a further 1–2 minutes. Add salt and pepper to taste.

### 2 Coating consistency

**2 tablespoons butter**
**¼ cup flour**
**1¼ cups milk or milk and stock**
**Salt and pepper**

Make the sauce as for pouring consistency.

### 3 Binding (panada) consistency

**¼ cup butter**
**½ cup flour**
**1¼ cups milk or milk and stock**
**Salt and pepper**

Melt the fat, add the flour and stir well. Cook gently for 2–3 minutes, stirring. Add the liquid gradually, beating well. Bring to a boil, stirring all the time, and cook for 1–2 minutes after it has thickened. Add salt and pepper to taste.

This thick sauce is used for binding mixtures such as croquettes. There are many variations on a basic white sauce – those given here are perhaps the most popular. These may also be made with béchamel.

**MUSHROOM SAUCE** Wash and slice 4–5 button mushrooms. Fry in 2 tablespoons butter until soft but not colored and fold into 1¼ cups white sauce. Season to taste.
Serve with fish, meat and eggs.

**PARSLEY SAUCE** Make 1¼ cups white sauce, using half milk and half stock, if available. When the sauce thickens, stir in 2 tablespoons chopped parsley and a little salt and pepper. Don't reboil

or the parsley may turn the sauce green.
Serve with fish, boiled or braised ham, or vegetables.

**SHRIMP SAUCE** Simmer the rind of 1 lemon and a bay leaf for 5 minutes in 1¼ cups liquid from which the sauce is to be made (milk or milk and fish stock). Strain and use to make the white sauce. When it thickens, stir in ½ cup frozen, canned or potted shrimp, season to taste and reheat for 1–2 minutes.
Serve with fish.

**ANCHOVY SAUCE** Make 1¼ cups white sauce with half milk and half fish stock. When it thickens, remove it from the heat and stir in 1–2 teaspoons anchovy paste (to taste), then a squeeze of lemon juice. (Anchovy paste is very salty and you will not need extra seasoning.) If you wish to tint the sauce a dull pink, add a few drops of red coloring.
Serve with fish.

**CAPER SAUCE** Make a white sauce using 1¼ cups milk, or ⅝ cup milk and ⅝ cup cooking liquid from the meat. When the sauce thickens, stir in 1 tablespoon capers, and 1–2 teaspoons vinegar from the capers or lemon juice. Season well. Reheat for 1–2 minutes.
Serve with boiled mutton or lamb.

## BÉCHAMEL SAUCE
*A classic, rich white sauce*

1¼ cups milk
1 shallot, sliced (or a small piece of onion)
Small piece of carrot, cut up
½ stalk celery, cut up
½ a bay leaf
3 peppercorns
2 tablespoons butter
¼ cup flour
Salt and pepper

Put the milk, vegetables and flavorings in a saucepan and bring slowly to a boil. Remove from the heat, cover and leave to infuse for about 15 minutes. Strain the liquid and use this with the butter and flour to make a white sauce. Season to taste before serving.

## AURORE SAUCE

1¼ cups béchamel sauce
1–2 tablespoons tomato paste
2 tablespoons butter
Salt and pepper

*Chicken chaudfroid, garnished with radishes, angelica and lemon rind*

*White sauce, made to a pouring consistency*

Make the sauce and when it has thickened stir in the tomato paste. Add the butter a little at a time and season to taste.
Serve with egg dishes, chicken or fish.

## MORNAY SAUCE

1¼ cups béchamel sauce
½ cup Parmesan, Gruyère or mature Cheddar cheese, grated
Paprika
Salt and pepper

Make the béchamel or plain white sauce and when it thickens, remove from the heat and stir in the cheese and seasonings. Do not reheat or the cheese will become overcooked and stringy.
Serve with eggs, chicken or fish.

## WHITE CHAUDFROID SAUCE

1 cup chicken bouillon
2 envelopes unflavored gelatin
1¼ cups béchamel sauce
⅝ cup light cream
Salt and pepper

Soften the gelatin in chicken bouillon in a bowl. Place the bowl over hot water and heat until gelatin is dissolved. Cool slightly and stir in the warm béchamel sauce.

Beat well and stir in the cream. Adjust the seasoning.
Strain the sauce and let stand to cool, stirring frequently so that it remains smooth and glossy. When the consistency of heavy cream or egg whites, use for coating chicken, fish or eggs.

## SOUBISE SAUCE

½ pound onions, chopped
2 tablespoons butter
Little stock or water
1¼ cups béchamel sauce
Salt and pepper

Cook the onions gently in the butter and a small amount of stock or water until soft – about 10–15 minutes. Sieve and stir the purée into the sauce, with seasoning to taste; reheat for 1–2 minutes.
Serve with lamb or veal.

## VELOUTE SAUCE

1½ tablespoons butter
about 2 tablespoons flour
1⅞ cups chicken or other light stock
2–3 tablespoons light cream
Few drops of lemon juice
Salt and pepper

Melt the butter, stir in the flour and cook gently, stirring well,

until the mixture is a pale fawn color. Stir in the stock gradually, bring to a boil, stirring all the time. Simmer until slightly reduced and syrupy. Remove from the heat and add the cream, lemon juice and seasoning.
Serve with poultry, fish and veal.

## TOMATO SAUCE
*(made from fresh tomatoes)*

2 tablespoons butter
1 small onion, chopped
1 small carrot, chopped
2 tablespoons flour
1 pound cooking tomatoes, cut up
1¼ cups chicken stock (made from a cube)
½ a bay leaf
1 clove
1 teaspoon sugar
Salt and pepper
2 teaspoons tomato paste, optional
1–4 tablespoons white wine or sherry, optional

Melt the butter in a skillet and lightly fry the onion and carrot for 5 minutes. Stir in the flour and add the tomatoes, stock and flavorings. Bring to a boil, cover and simmer for about 30 minutes, or until the vegetables are cooked. Sieve, reheat and reseason if necessary.
Tomato paste may be added to give a fuller flavor and a better color. The wine or sherry may be added just before serving. Adjust seasoning after adding these optional ingredients.
Serve with croquettes, cutlets, réchauffés or any savory dish.

## TOMATO SAUCE
*(made from canned tomatoes)*

1 tablespoon butter
½ onion, chopped
2 slices bacon, chopped
1 tablespoon flour
1 can (15 ounces) tomatoes
1 clove
½ a bay leaf
Few sprigs of rosemary (or 1 teaspoon mixed dried herbs)
Salt and pepper
Pinch of sugar, optional

Melt the butter in a skillet and fry the onion and the bacon for 5 minutes. Stir in the flour and gradually add the tomatoes, flavorings and seasonings. Simmer gently for 15 minutes, then sieve and re-season if necessary. Add sugar if the flavor is too acid. Serve with made-up meat dishes such as rissoles or stuffed peppers, and with cutlets.

## HOLLANDAISE SAUCE

2½ tablespoons wine or tarragon
   vinegar
1¼ tablespoons water
2 egg yolks
¼ cup butter
Salt and pepper

Put the vinegar and water in a small pan and boil until reduced to about 1 tablespoon. Cool slightly.

Put the egg yolks in a small bowl and stir in the vinegar. Put over a pan of hot water and heat gently, stirring all the time, until the egg mixture thickens (never let the water go above simmering point or the sauce will curdle). Divide the butter into small pieces and gradually beat into the sauce; season to taste.

If the sauce is too sharp add a little more butter – it should be slightly piquant, almost thick enough to hold its shape and warm rather than hot when served.

Serve with salmon and other fish dishes, asparagus or broccoli. (The vinegar may be replaced by lemon juice – this tends to give a slightly blander sauce.)

## MAYONNAISE
*makes about ¾ cup*

1 egg yolk
½ teaspoon dry mustard
½ teaspoon salt
¼ teaspoon pepper
½ teaspoon sugar
⅝ cup oil
1 tablespoon white vinegar

Make sure that all ingredients are at room temperature. Put the egg yolk in a bowl with the seasonings and sugar. Mix thoroughly, then add the oil drop by drop, beating briskly with a wooden spoon the whole time, or use a whisk. Continue adding oil until the sauce is thick and smooth – if it becomes too thick too quickly, add a little of the vinegar. When all the oil has been added, add the vinegar gradually and mix thoroughly.

## TARTAR SAUCE

⅝ cup mayonnaise
1 teaspoon chopped tarragon or
   chives
2 teaspoons chopped capers
2 teaspoons chopped gherkins
2 teaspoons chopped celery
1¼ tablespoons lemon juice or
   tarragon vinegar

Mix all the ingredients well, then leave the sauce to stand at least 1

*Add oil very gradually for a mayonnaise, beating all the time*

hour before serving, to allow the flavors to mellow.
Serve with fish.

# BROWN SAUCES

## GRAVY

A rich, brown gravy is served with all roast meats – thin with roast beef and thick with other meats. If the gravy is properly made in the roasting pan, there should be no need to use extra coloring. Remove the roast from the pan and keep it hot while making the gravy.

## THIN GRAVY

Pour the fat very slowly from the pan, draining it off carefully from one corner and leaving the sediment behind. Season well with salt and pepper and add 1¼ cups hot vegetable water or stock (stock made from a bouillon cube is adequate but extra seasoning will not be required). Stir thoroughly with a wooden spoon until all the sediment is scraped from the pan and the gravy is a rich brown. Return the pan to the heat and boil for 2–3 minutes.

Serve very hot.

This is the 'correct' way of making thin gravy, but some people prefer to make a version of the thick gravy given below, using half the amount of flour.

## THICK GRAVY

Leave 2½ tablespoons of fat in the pan, stir in 1 tablespoon flour (preferably shaking it from a flour sifter, to give a smoother result). Blend well and cook over the heat until it turns brown, stirring continuously. Carefully mix in 1¼ cups hot vegetable water or stock and boil for 2–3 minutes. Season well, strain and serve very hot.

## ESPAGNOLE SAUCE
*This classic brown sauce is used as a base for many savory sauces*

2 tablespoons butter
2 slices bacon, chopped
1 shallot, chopped (or a small
   piece of onion, chopped)
3 mushroom stalks, chopped
1 small carrot, chopped
2–3 tablespoons flour
1¼ cups beef stock
Bouquet garni
2 tablespoons tomato paste
Salt and pepper
1 tablespoon sherry, optional

Melt the butter in a skillet and fry the bacon for 2–3 minutes. Add the vegetables and fry for a further 3–5 minutes, or until lightly browned. Stir in the flour, mix well and continue frying very slowly until it turns brown. Remove from the heat and gradually add the stock (which if necessary can be made from a bouillon cube). Stir after each addition. Return the pan to the heat and stir until the sauce thickens. Add the bouquet garni, tomato paste, salt and pepper. Reduce the heat, cover and allow to simmer very gently for 1 hour, stirring from time to time to prevent it sticking (an asbestos mat under the pan is a good idea). Alternatively, cook in the center of the oven at 300°F. for 1½–2 hours. Strain, reheat and skim off any fat, using a metal spoon. Reseason if necessary.

If required, add the sherry just before the sauce is served, to give extra flavor.

Serve with beef dishes.

## DEMI-GLACE SAUCE

⅝ cup clear beef gravy or jellied
   stock from under beef
   dripping
1¼ cups espagnole sauce

Add the gravy to the sauce and boil (uncovered) until the sauce has a glossy appearance and will coat the back of the spoon with a shiny glaze.

Serve with dishes made from beef.

## BROWN CHAUDFROID SAUCE

2 envelopes unflavored gelatin
1 cup beef bouillon
2 cups espagnole sauce
Madeira, sherry or port to taste
Salt and pepper

Soften the gelatin in the beef bouillon in a bowl. Let stand over hot water until gelatin has dissolved. Warm the espagnole sauce and beat in the gelatin mixture. Add Madeira, sherry or port to taste and extra salt and pepper if necessary.

Strain the sauce and allow to cool, beating it from time to time so that it remains smooth and glossy. When it reaches the consistency of heavy cream or egg whites, use to coat game, duck or cutlets. (See illustration for chicken chaudfroid on page 57.)

# SWEET SAUCES

*Add a delicious sweet sauce to your dessert, to give it new dimensions. Whether you are serving a hot, steamy pudding or a smooth, icy sherbert a sauce will provide added flavor and texture. For a quick dessert, nothing can beat a bought ice cream with a helping of your own favorite sauce.*

*A true custard sauce, made with eggs, for fruit sweets*

## CUSTARD SAUCE
*makes 2½–3 cups*

**1 package (3¼ ounces) vanilla pudding and pie filling mix**
**2½–3 cups milk**

Blend together the pudding mix and milk in a heavy saucepan. Cook over medium heat, stirring constantly, until the mixture comes to a boil and thickens slightly.
Serve warm with puddings or fruit.

## EGG CUSTARD SAUCE
*makes about 1¼ cups*

**1¼ cups milk**
**Few strips of thinly pared lemon rind**
**3 egg yolks**
**1 tablespoon sugar**

Warm the milk and lemon rind and let stand 10 minutes to blend flavors. Beat together the egg yolks and sugar. Pour the milk on to the eggs and beat lightly. Strain the mixture into a very heavy bottomed saucepan. Cook over a very low heat, stirring constantly, until the sauce thickens and lightly coats the back of the spoon.
Serve hot or cold with fruit sweets.

## CHOCOLATE CUSTARD SAUCE
*makes 1¼ cups*

**1 tablespoon cornstarch**
**1 tablespoon cocoa**
**2 tablespoons sugar**
**1¼ cups milk**
**1 teaspoon butter**

Blend the cornstarch, cocoa and sugar with 1 tablespoon of the milk. Heat the remaining milk with the butter until boiling and

pour on to the blended mixture, stirring all the time to prevent lumps forming. Return the mixture to the pan and bring to a boil, stirring until it thickens; cook for a further 1–2 minutes.
Serve with steamed or baked sponge puddings.
*Note:* The cornstarch and cocoa may be replaced by 2 tablespoons chocolate blancmange powder.

## JAM SAUCE
*makes ⅝ cup*

**4 tablespoons jam**
**⅝ cup water or fruit juice**
**2½ teaspoons arrowroot**
**2½ tablespoons cold water**
**Squeeze of lemon juice, optional**

Warm the jam and water or fruit juice. Simmer for 5 minutes. Blend the arrowroot and cold water to a smooth paste and stir into the jam mixture. Return the sauce to the heat, stirring, until it thickens and clears. Add the lemon juice and put through a sieve into a sauce boat.
Serve hot with steamed or baked puddings or cold over ice cream.
*Note:* A thicker sauce is made by just melting the jam on its own over a gentle heat and adding a little lemon juice.

## SYRUP SAUCE
*makes about ⅝ cup*

**3–4 tablespoons maple syrup**
**3 tablespoons water**
**Juice of ½ lemon**

Warm the syrup and water, stir well and simmer, uncovered, for 2–3 minutes; add the lemon juice. Serve with steamed or baked sponge puddings.

## APRICOT SAUCE
*makes about 1¼ cups*

**1 can (16 ounces) apricot halves, drained**
**2½ teaspoons arrowroot**
**Squeeze of lemon juice or 1 tablespoon rum, sherry or fruit liqueur**

Purée the strained fruit in an electric blender. Make up to 1¼ cups with the juice. Place in a saucepan and heat until boiling. Blend the arrowroot with a little more juice until it is smooth. Stir into the puréed fruit. Return the mixture to the pan and heat gently, continuing to stir, until the sauce thickens and clears. A squeeze of lemon juice or the rum, sherry or fruit liqueur may be added just before the sauce is served.
Good with meringue sweets, cold soufflés, hot baked pudding, steamed puddings and ice cream.

## LEMON OR ORANGE SAUCE
*makes 1¼ cups*

**Grated rind and juice of 1 large lemon or orange**
**1¼ tablespoons cornstarch**
**2½ tablespoons sugar**
**1 egg yolk, optional**

Make up the fruit rind and juice with water to give 1¼ cups. Blend the cornstarch and sugar with a little of the liquid to a smooth paste. Boil the remaining liquid and stir into the mixture. Return it to the pan and bring to a boil, stirring, until the sauce thickens and clears. Cool. Add the egg yolk (if used) and reheat, stirring, but do not boil.
Serve hot or cold, as for apricot sauce.

## BUTTERSCOTCH NUT SAUCE
*makes 2½ cups*

**1 package (3¼ ounces) butter-scotch pudding and pie filling mix**
**2½–3 cups milk**
**1 tablespoon butter**
**¼ cup chopped nuts**

Combine the pudding mix and milk in a heavy saucepan. Cook over medium heat, stirring constantly, until the mixture comes to a boil and thickens slightly. Stir in the butter. Cool slightly and stir in the chopped nuts.
Serve hot or cold with baked or steamed puddings.

## MOUSSELINE SAUCE
*makes about ⅝ cup*

**1 egg**
**1 egg yolk**
**3 tablespoons sugar**
**1¼ tablespoons sherry**
**5 tablespoons light cream**

Place all the ingredients in a bowl over a pan of boiling water and beat with a rotary whisk or electric blender until pale and frothy and a thick creamy consistency. Serve at once, over light steamed or baked puddings, fruit, fruit desserts or Christmas pudding.

## SABAYON SAUCE
*makes about ⅝ cup*

**¼ cup sugar**
**5 tablespoons water**
**2 egg yolks**
**Rind of ½ lemon, grated**
**Juice of 1 lemon**
**2¼ tablespoons rum or sherry**
**2½ tablespoons light cream**

Dissolve the sugar in the water over gentle heat and boil for 2–3 minutes, until syrupy. Pour on to the beaten yolks and beat until pale and thick. Add the lemon rind, lemon juice and rum or sherry, and beat for a further few minutes. Fold in the cream and chill well.
Serve with cold fruit desserts.

## BRANDY BUTTER

**6 tablespoons butter**
**⅜ cup confectioners' sugar**
**2½–4 tablespoons brandy**

Cream the butter until pale and soft. Beat in the sugar gradually and add the brandy a few drops at a time, taking care not to allow the mixture to curdle. The finished sauce should be pale and frothy. Pile it up in a small dish and leave in a cool place to harden before serving.

Traditionally served with Christmas pudding and mince pies.

## RUM BUTTER

**6 tablespoons butter**
**½ cup soft brown sugar**
**3 tablespoons rum**
**Grated rind of ½ lemon**
**1 teaspoon lemon juice**

Cream the butter and beat in the other ingredients carefully, as for brandy butter.

Serve with Christmas pudding and mince pies.

## CHOCOLATE SAUCE

**2 squares semi-sweet chocolate**
**1 tablespoon butter**
**1¼ tablespoons milk**
**1 teaspoon vanilla extract**

Melt the chocolate and butter in a bowl standing in a pan of hot water. Stir in the milk and vanilla and serve straight away, over ice cream.

## COFFEE SAUCE

**⅔ cup sugar**
**2 tablespoons water**
**1¼ cups strong black coffee**

Put the sugar and water in a heavy-based pan and dissolve over a gentle heat, without stirring. Bring to a boil and boil rapidly until the syrup becomes golden in color. Add the coffee and stir until the caramel has dissolved. Boil for a few minutes, until syrupy. Allow to cool, and serve poured over ice cream.

## PECAN RUM SAUCE
*makes 1⅞ cups*

**1 cup soft brown sugar**
**2½ teaspoons instant coffee**
**7½ tablespoons light cream or evaporated milk**
**2 tablespoons butter**
**1¼ tablespoons maple syrup**
**1¼ tablespoons rum**
**¼ cup shelled pecans (or walnuts)**

Combine in a saucepan the sugar, coffee, cream or evaporated milk, butter and maple syrup. Cook over a low heat to dissolve the sugar, bring to a boil and boil gently, stirring, for 2–3 minutes, or until thickened. Stir in the rum and nuts.

Serve either cold or warm, with vanilla ice cream.

*Add a little extra to ice cream with a rich, home-made sauce*

*Brandy butter is a traditional 'hard' sauce for mince pies*

This sauce may be bottled and stored for a short time.

## CHERRY SAUCE
*makes about 1⅞ cups*

**½ pound black or dark red cherries**
**¼ cup sugar**
**2 teaspoons arrowroot**
**Almond extract**
**2 teaspoons cherry brandy**

Pit the cherries and cook in a little water with the sugar until fairly tender. Drain the fruit; make the juice up to 1¼ cups with water if necessary. Blend the arrowroot with a little juice, return it with the rest of the measured juice to the pan, and cook until transparent. Pour over the cherries and add a little almond extract and the cherry

brandy.

Allow to cool. Serve with ice cream.

## MELBA SAUCE

**5 tablespoons red-currant jelly**
**⅜ cup sugar**
**⅝ cup raspberry purée (from ½ pound raspberries or a 15 ounce can)**
**2½ teaspoons arrowroot**
**1¼ tablespoons cold water**

Mix the jelly, sugar and raspberry purée and bring to a boil. Blend the arrowroot with the cold water to a smooth cream, stir in a little of the raspberry mixture, return the sauce to the pan and bring to a boil, stirring with a wooden spoon until it thickens and clears. Strain and cool.

This sauce is traditionally served over fresh peaches and ice cream.

## APRICOT SAUCE

Mix some sieved apricot jam with a little lemon juice and 2 teaspoons sherry; pour it over ice cream and sprinkle with flaked coconut or other decoration.

## BUTTERSCOTCH SAUCE

**2 tablespoons butter**
**2 tablespoons soft light brown sugar**
**1 tablespoon maple syrup**
**¼ cup nuts, chopped**
**Squeeze of lemon juice, optional**

Warm the butter, sugar and syrup until well blended. Boil for 1 minute and stir in the nuts and lemon juice.

Serve at once, over ice cream.

## FLAMBE SAUCE
*makes about 1 cup*

**1 can (8 ounces) fruit cocktail**
**Grated rind of ½ lemon**
**6 tablespoons sugar**
**3 tablespoons butter**
**3¾ teaspoons cornstarch**
**2½ tablespoons brandy**

Gently heat the fruit cocktail with the grated lemon rind, sugar, butter and cornstarch, stirring until the mixture thickens. Add the brandy carefully, but do not stir. Ignite the brandy and spoon into the sauce. Pour the sauce at once over vanilla ice cream.

## MARSHMALLOW SAUCE
*makes 1¼ cups*

**½ cup sugar**
**3¾ tablespoons water**
**8 marshmallows, cut up in little pieces**
**1 egg white**
**½ teaspoon vanilla extract**
**Red coloring, optional**

Dissolve the sugar in the water and boil for 5 minutes. Add the marshmallows and stir the mixture until marshmallows are melted. Beat the egg white until stiff. Gradually fold in the marshmallow mixture. Flavor with vanilla and if liked, add a drop or two of coloring to tint it pink. Serve at once over coffee or chocolate ice cream.

## HONEY SAUCE

**¼ cup butter**
**2 teaspoons cornstarch**
**4–6 ounces honey**

Melt the butter in a pan and stir in the cornstarch. Gradually add the honey. Bring to a boil and cook for a minute or two.

# HOT DESSERTS

*Brown sugared peaches with dairy sour cream*

## APPLE DUMPLINGS WITH WALNUT SAUCE

*4 servings*

**Double recipe Shortcrust Pastry, page 75**
**4 large cooking apples, washed and cored**
**6 tablespoons mincemeat**
**1 egg, beaten**

*For sauce:*
**¼ cup butter**
**¼ cup sugar**
**2 tablespoons cream**
**½ cup coarsely chopped walnuts**

Divide the pastry into 4 parts. Knead lightly and roll each piece out into a large enough circle to wrap around an apple. Place each apple on to a pastry round and fill the centers with mincemeat.
Brush the pastry edges with egg and completely enclose the apples with the pastry, sealing the edges. Place the dumplings in a baking pan, seam side down, and brush all over with beaten egg. Bake in a fairly hot oven (400°F.) for 35 minutes or until golden. Meanwhile, make the walnut sauce by melting the butter and stirring in the sugar. When dissolved, add the cream and nuts and bring to a boil. Serve the sauce separately in a jug to pour over the dumplings.

## BROWN-SUGARED PEACHES WITH SOUR CREAM

*4 servings*

**4 large fresh peaches**
**2½ tablespoons brown sugar**
**½ teaspoon cinnamon**
**1¼ cups dairy sour cream**
**5 tablespoons sugar**

Preheat broiling compartment and pan. Dip the peaches in boiling water, count 10, then plunge them into cold water. Skin, pit and slice them. Arrange the slices evenly in individual soufflé dishes or ramekins.
Blend the brown sugar with the cinnamon and sprinkle the mixture over the peaches.
Spoon the sour cream over the peaches. Sprinkle top with sugar. Place under the broiler and broil until the sugar melts and caramelizes. It is important that the broiler is very hot, otherwise the cream will melt before the sugar forms a crust.
If practical, chill before serving; otherwise, serve straight from the broiler.

## APPLE AND GRAPE PLATE PIE

*6 servings*

**2 pound cooking apples, pared and cored**
**7½ tablespoons water**
**½ teaspoon dried grated orange rind**
**6 tablespoons sugar**
**Double recipe Shortcrust Pastry, page 75**
**4 tablespoons grape preserves, or any desired flavor**
**Milk**
**Sugar**

Slice the apples fairly thickly and place in a shallow layer in the bottom of a large saucepan. Cover with the water and bring gently to a boil. Reduce heat and cook for a few minutes until some of the fruit begins to break up – most of it should remain in slices and there should not be any extra juice. Stir in the orange rind and sugar. Let stand to cool.
Divide the pastry in half. Roll out one part on a lightly floured board into a circle large enough to line an 8-in. pie pan. Fit pastry into pie pan. Spread the bottom of the pastry with the preserves. Spoon the part-cooked apples on top. Roll out the remaining pastry into a circle. Dampen the edges of the pastry with a little water and place the circle of pastry on top of the apples. Seal edges together. Make a slit in the top. Brush top of crust with milk and dredge with sugar.
Bake in the center of a fairly hot oven (400°F.) for 35–40 minutes or until the pastry is cooked and lightly browned. Serve warm with heavy cream.

## HOT GINGER SOUFFLE

*4 servings*

**3 tablespoons butter**
**6 tablespoons flour**
**1¼ cups milk**
**6 tablespoons sugar**
**1 tablespoon brandy, optional**
**⅛ teaspoon ginger**
**¼ cup chopped preserved ginger**
**4 large eggs, separated**

Butter a 1½-quart soufflé dish. Preheat oven to 350°F. Melt the butter in a saucepan. Stir in the flour. Remove from heat and stir in the milk. Cook over a moderate heat, stirring constantly, until mixture thickens. Cook over very low heat for 2 minutes. Stir in the sugar, brandy and ginger. Beat in the egg yolks, one at a time. Beat egg whites until stiff and fold into the yolk mixture.

Turn the mixture into the prepared soufflé dish. Bake for 40–45 minutes or until well risen and just firm to the touch.

Serve at once with ginger syrup and cream.

## ALMOND FRUIT PUFF
*6 servings*

*For filling:*
¼ **cup butter**
¼ **cup sugar**
½ **teaspoon almond extract**
1 **egg, beaten**
1½ **tablespoons flour**
½ **cup ground almonds**
6–8 **maraschino cherries, halved**
1 **can (8 ounces) plums, drained**
1 **can (8 ounces) sliced peaches, drained**
1 **can (8 ounces) apricot halves, drained**
1 **small apple, pared and chopped**
2 **packages (10 ounces each) frozen patty shells**
1 **egg, beaten**

Cream the butter and sugar until light and fluffy. Beat in the almond extract, egg, flour and almonds and then lightly fold in the cherries, canned fruits and apple. Set aside.

Remove the patty shells from package and let thaw. Place 4 patty shells close together on a lightly floured board and press firmly together. Roll out into an 8-in. circle. Place on a cookie tray and prick well all over with a fork. Brush around the edge with beaten egg. Take 4 more patty shells and press together in a row. Roll out into a strip about 1 in. wide and 14 in. long. Divide this strip in half and lay the strips over the egg-glazed edge of the circle to form a 'wall'. Let pastry stand in a cool place for 30 minutes. Roll the remaining 4 patty shells into a 9-in. circle.

Pile the fruit mixture inside the 'wall'. Brush the 'wall' with beaten egg. Place the 9-in. circle of pastry on top and press the edges together lightly. Roll out remaining pastry trimmings thinly and cut into thin, narrow strips. Arrange on top like spokes of a wheel. Glaze the pastry with the beaten egg.

Bake in a very hot over (450°F.) for 15 minutes. Cover the top of the pastry with a square of aluminum fol. Lower oven temperature to 350°F. Cook for 45 minutes. Serve warm in wedges with whipped cream.

*Golden apple dumpling, served with hot walnut sauce*

## APPLE FLAN
*6 servings*

*For pastry case:*
¾ **cup all-purpose flour**
¾ **cup self-rising flour**
¼ **cup butter**
¼ **cup margarine**
¼ **cup confectioners' sugar, sifted**
**Water**

*For filling:*
5 **tablespoons apricot preserves**
2½ **tablespoons water**
**Juice of 1 small lemon**
1¼ **pound eating apples**
2 **tablespoons sugar**

Place the flours in a bowl. Cut in the fats with a pastry blender or two knives to the consistency of fine breadcrumbs. Stir in the sugar. Mix to a firm but pliable dough with cold water. Turn out of the bowl and knead lightly on a lightly floured board. Roll out into a circle and use to line a 9-in. loose-bottomed French fluted flan tin or a 9-in. pie plate. Boil together the preserves and water for 2–3 minutes, stirring. Put the cooked preserves through a sieve into a small bowl. Cool. Spread half the preserves over the bottom of the flan. Squeeze the

lemon juice into a medium sized bowl. Pare, core and thinly slice the apples into the bowl. Turn them in the juice to prevent discoloration. Spoon the apples into the flan case, keeping the surface level. Sprinkle with sugar. Place the flan pan on a cookie tray and bake in a fairly hot oven (400°F.) for 35 minutes or until apples are tender and the crust is baked. While flan is hot, brush with the rest of the apricot glaze to which any excess lemon juice has been added. Serve warm, rather than hot, with heavy cream.

## RICE AND FRUIT TART
*8 servings*

⅞ **cup long grain rice**
3 **cups milk**
¾ **cup sugar**
2 **eggs, beaten**
3 **firm pears, pared and cored**
12 **apricots, halved and pitted**
3 **peaches, halved and pitted**
½ **pound apricot preserves**

Simmer the rice in boiling water for 3 minutes. Drain well. Put the milk and ⅓ cup of the sugar on to boil and when boiling add the rice. Stir well and simmer gently until rice is tender and most of the liquid has been absorbed.

Meanwhile, using a shallow pan, dissolve the remaining sugar in ⅞ cup water. Bring to a boil and boil for 2 minutes.

Beat the eggs into the rice, then mold the mixture into a well-buttered 10-in. shallow ovenproof dish, covering the base and sides. Place the dish in the center of a moderate oven (350°F.) for 10 minutes.

Remove the dish from the oven, remold the sides if necessary and return it to the oven for a further 20 minutes or until the rice is firm and set.

Quarter the pears and simmer gently in the sugar syrup for about 10 minutes. Add the apricots and peaches and continue to simmer for 5 minutes until all the fruits are tender but not soft. Drain them well. Arrange them in the rice case. Keep everything warm.

Melt the apricot preserves in the remaining syrup and boil until reduced by one-third. Strain and spoon a little over the fruits just enough to glaze them.

Put the rest in a sauce boat and serve as an accompaniment to the hot tart.

## CHERRY-WALNUT UPSIDE DOWN PUDDING
*6 servings*

*For topping:*
2 **tablespoons butter**
4 **tablespoons light brown sugar**
6 **glacé cherries, halved**
½ **cup coarsely chopped walnuts**
1 **tablespoon extra strong coffee**

*For sponge base:*
½ **cup butter or margarine**
½ **cup sugar**
2 **eggs, lightly beaten**
2½ **tablespoons extra strong coffee**
1½ **cups self-rising flour**

Lightly grease a 6-in. round cake pan. Melt the butter and brown sugar for the topping and stir in the cherries, walnuts and coffee. Spread the mixture evenly over the base of the cake pan.

Cream the butter and sugar until light and fluffy. Beat in the eggs and blend well. Stir in the coffee. Fold in the sifted flour and stir to make a smooth dough. Turn batter into prepared pan. Bake in a moderate oven (350°F.) for 50–55 minutes or until the cake is firm but springy to the touch and shrinks slightly from the pan.

Turn out the pudding on to a heated serving platter and serve hot with whipped cream.

## PEACH COBBLER
*4 servings*

1½ cups dried peaches
½ cup sugar

*For topping:*
½ cup butter
2 cups self-rising flour
2 tablespoons sugar
⅝ cup milk, approximately
1 egg, beaten
Brown sugar

Soak the peaches for 2–3 hours in 2½ cups water. Put the peaches, sugar and water in a saucepan. Bring to a boil and simmer for about 30 minutes or until the peaches are tender. Arrange in a 9-in. pie dish.

Cut the butter into the flour with a pastry blender or two knives until the mixture resembles fine breadcrumbs. Stir in the sugar and enough milk to give a soft but manageable dough. Knead the dough lightly on a floured board and roll out to approximately ½-in. thickness. Cut out 1½ in. rounds with a floured, fluted cutter. Arrange over the peaches. Brush the rounds with beaten egg and sprinkle with brown sugar. Bake in a very hot oven (450°F.) for 15 minutes or until well risen and golden brown.

## LEMON LAYER SPONGE
*4 Servings*

2 eggs, separated
¾ cup sugar
¼ cup butter, softened
½ cup flour
1¼ cups milk
3¾ tablespoons lemon juice
Grated rind of 1 lemon

Beat the egg yolks with the sugar and the softened butter in a large bowl. Stir in the flour, milk, lemon juice and rind. Beat until smooth. Beat the egg whites until stiff. Fold evenly into the mixture. Turn into a buttered 1½ quart shallow casserole. Place in a baking pan half-filled with hot water. Bake in a moderate oven (350°F.) for 40–50 minutes or until lightly set.

## LEMON CANDY ALASKA
*4 servings*

6 tablespoons butter
⅞ cup sugar, divided
1 cup crushed cornflakes
1½ cups vanilla ice cream
9 sour lemon drops, finely crushed
2 egg whites
Juice of ½ lemon

Melt the butter in a saucepan, stir in half the sugar. Heat gently until sugar is dissolved and then add the cornflakes. Press the cornflake mixture on to the bottom and sides of an 8-in. pie plate. Soften the ice cream in a bowl and beat in the lemon drops. Refreeze the ice cream. Beat the egg whites until stiff. Gradually add half the remaining sugar and beat again until stiff. Fold in the remaining sugar. Scoop the lemon ice cream into the chilled pie shell. Sprinkle lemon juice over the top.

Pile the meringue over the ice cream, covering it completely. Cook on the top shelf of a very hot oven (450°F.) for 5 minutes or until light brown. Serve at once.

## BAKED ALASKA
*4 servings*

An 8-in. round cake layer
1 can (8 ounces) fruit, drained (raspberries or other berries)
1 quart ice cream
3–4 egg whites
½–¾ cup sugar

Preheat the oven to 450°F. Place the cake on a flat, ovenproof dish and spoon just enough of the canned fruit juice over the cake to moisten it. Scoop out the ice cream and pack it in a pile in the center of the cake, leaving a border of ½ in. of the cake. Pile the fruit on top and place the plate in the freezer.

Beat the egg whites until stiff. Gradually beat in the sugar and continue beating until the egg whites stand in stiff peaks. Remove cake from freezer and pile meringue mixture over cake, completely covering the cake, ice cream and fruit. Be sure to take the meringue right down to the dish, sealing the sides completely. Place in the oven, near the top, and cook for 2–3 minutes or until the outside of the meringue just begins to brown. Serve at once.

## BANANES EN CROUTE
*4 servings*

4 large bananas, peeled
Grated rind and juice of 1 lemon
1¼ tablespoons sugar
½ teaspoon cinnamon
8 slices brown bread
3 tablespoons butter
¼ cup chopped walnuts

Halve the bananas lengthwise and leave to soak in lemon juice for 1 hour. Blend together the sugar, lemon rind and cinnamon.

*Crêpes with a difference – filled with pear and almond*

Remove crusts from the bread. Melt 1 tablespoon butter in a skillet and fry bananas on both sides until golden. Toast and butter the bread. Sprinkle with cinnamon-sugar mixture. Lay banana on top and sprinkle with the chopped nuts.

## PEAR AND ALMOND CREPES

*For batter:*
1 cup all purpose-flour
Pinch of salt
1 egg
1¼ cups milk
1 tablespoon brandy
1 tablespoon butter, melted

*For filling:*
½ cup butter
⅜ cup confectioners' sugar
½ cup ground almonds
¼ teaspoon almond extract
Grated rind of 1 lemon
1 can (16 ounces) pears, drained and diced
Melted butter
Lemon wedges

Sift the flour and salt into a bowl. Break the egg into the center, add 2 tablespoons of milk and stir well. Gradually add the rest of the milk, stirring. Beat until the batter has the consistency of light cream. Then add the brandy and melted butter. Let stand 30 minutes.

Heat a 7-in. skillet and brush the surface with a little butter. Raise the handle side of the pan slightly and pour in the batter from the raised side so that a very thin skin of batter flows over the pan. Place pan over a moderate heat and leave until the pancake is golden brown; turn over and brown lightly. Turn the pancake out on to a plate and keep warm. Make 8 pancakes, stacking them up as you go, separated with sheets of waxed paper.

Cream the butter and sugar until light and fluffy. Stir in the ground almonds, almond extract, lemon rind and diced pears. Spread a little of the filling over one half of each pancake; fold the other half over and then in half again to form a triangle.

Arrange the pancakes in an ovenproof baking dish, overlapping each other. Brush lightly with melted butter. Place under a preheated broiler just long enough to heat quickly. Serve with lemon wedges.

*A simple apple flan, served warm, is always popular*

# PARTY DESSERTS

## PISTACHIO APPLE FLAN
*6 servings*

*For flan case:*
**2 large eggs**
**¼ cup sugar**
**½ cup all-purpose flour**

*For filling:*
**1¼ cups milk**
**¼ cup sugar**
**¼ cup flour**
**1 tablespoon cornstarch**
**1 large egg**
**2 tablespoons butter**

*For decoration:*
**2 sharp eating apples**
**1¼ cups water**
**Juice of ½ lemon**
**¼ cup sugar**
**6 tablespoons apricot preserves**
**¼ cup pistachio nuts, peeled and chopped**

Grease an 8-in. spring-form pan very well. Place a circle of waxed paper on the bottom and grease again. Set aside. Preheat oven to 425°F.
Put the eggs and sugar in a large deep bowl. Stand bowl over a pan of hot water and beat with a wire whisk until light and creamy. The whisk should leave a trail when lifted from the mixture. Remove from the heat and beat until cool. Sift half the flour over the mixture and fold in lightly with a rubber scraper. Add the remaining flour and fold in carefully. Turn the mixture into the prepared pan. Bake towards the top of the oven for 12–15 minutes or until well risen and golden

brown. Let stand 5 minutes then carefully remove from the pan and cool on a wire rack.
Meanwhile, heat the milk in a pan. Mix the sugar, flour, cornstarch, egg and a little milk together and mix until smooth. Stir in the hot milk. Return to saucepan and cook over a low heat, stirring, just until mixture comes to a boil. Add the butter and beat well. Cover and let cool. Pare, core and slice the apples in rings. Poach until soft but not broken in a light syrup made from the water, lemon juice and sugar. Drain the apple rings and let cool. Brush the outside and top rim of the flan case with warm, sieved apricot preserves to which a little water has been added. Coat the outer edges with pistachio nuts. Fill the flan case with the custard and arrange the apple rings on top. Glaze with more apricot preserves and chill before serving.

## STRAWBERRY PALMIERS
*Makes 6 pairs*

**1 package (10 ounces) frozen patty shells**
**Sugar**
**1½ cups heavy cream**
**1 tablespoon orange liqueur**
**2½ teaspoons confectioners' sugar**
**1 pint strawberries, cleaned and halved**

Remove patty shells and let thaw. Place on a lightly floured surface and press edges together. Roll out into a rectangle 12 in. by 10 in.

Sprinkle heavily with sugar. Fold the long sides to meet in the center. Sprinkle heavily with sugar. Fold in half lengthwise. Press lightly with a rolling pin. Cut into 12 equal slices, place well apart on a cookie tray, cut side down. Open the tip of each.
Bake near the top of a hot oven (425°F.) for about 8 minutes, until the sugar is light caramel color. Turn each one over and bake for another 4 minutes. Cool on a wire rack.
Whip the cream until light and fluffy. Add the liqueur and confectioners' sugar. Use the cream to sandwich the palmiers in pairs. Tuck halved strawberries into each pair.

## MELON AND PINEAPPLE SALAD
*6 servings*

**1 honeydew melon**
**2 cans (16 ounces each) pineapple chunks, drained**
**5 tablespoons Cointreau or curaçao**
**Sugar, optional**
**Few glacé cherries**

Slice the melon in half lengthwise, scoop out and discard the seeds. Scoop out the flesh in large pieces and put on one side. Using scissors or a sharp knife, serrate the edge of one of the melon halves.
Cut the melon flesh into chunks and pile with the pineapple chunks in the decorated melon. Sprinkle over the liqueur and

sugar, if needed. Decorate with glacé cherries.

## MANDARIN LIQUEUR GATEAU
*8 servings*

**3 large eggs**
**6 tablespoons sugar**
**¾ cup all-purpose flour**
**2 cans (11 ounces each) mandarin oranges, drained**
**2½ tablespoons maraschino liqueur**
**1 can (8 ounces) red cherries, drained**
**Apricot glaze**
**1¼ cups heavy cream, lightly whipped**
**Confectioners' sugar**
**Angelica**

Grease and line the bottom of a 10-in. deep cake pan with waxed paper and grease again. Put eggs and sugar in a bowl over a pan of hot water and beat with a whisk until thick and pale in color. Sift the flour over the whisked eggs and fold in lightly and quickly with a rubber spatula. Turn the mixture into the prepared cake pan. Bake in a fairly hot oven (375°F.) for 30 minutes. Cool on a wire rack.
Combine the mandarins and maraschino liqueur and let stand for 30 minutes. Check cherries to see that all of the pits are removed. Split the cooled cake in half and place one half, cut side up, on a serving platter. Strain the liqueur from the mandarin oranges and spoon over the cake

on the platter. Spread with a little apricot glaze.

From the center of the second half, cut out three 2-in. circles, close to each other. Brush remaining cake surface with apricot glaze. Arrange groups of mandarins around the edge, chop the remainder. Spread most of the cream over the first half and top with chopped mandarins and most of the cherries.

Carefully lift the second half on top of the first. Fill the holes with the remaining cream and top with the cut-out cake circles, covered with confectioners' sugar. Finish with a cluster of cherries and angelica leaves.

## TRANCHE AUX FRUITS
*6 servings*

*For pastry case*
- 1¼ cups all-purpose flour
- 6 tablespoons butter or margarine
- 2 teaspoons sugar
- 1 egg yolk
- 5 teaspoons cold water, approximately

*For filling:*
- 1 small eating apple, pared, cored and thinly sliced
- 1 medium orange, pared and sliced
- 1 banana, sliced
- 1 can (8 ounces) plums, drained and pitted
- 4 tablespoons Grand Marnier

*For confectioners' custard:*
- 1¼ cups milk
- ¼ cup sugar
- ¼ cup flour
- ½ tablespoon cornstarch
- 1 large egg
- Confectioners' sugar
- 2½ tablespoons apricot preserves

Put the flour in a bowl. Cut in the butter with a pastry blender or two knives until well blended. Blend in sugar. Beat together the egg yolk and water. Stir into flour mixture. Add a little more water if necessary to make a firm dough. Knead the dough lightly on a lightly floured board.

Roll the dough out and use to line a 14 in. by 4½ in. tranche frame, or a 9-in. loose-bottomed French fluted flan pan. Line the case carefully with aluminum foil and fill with dried beans. Bake in a fairly hot oven (400°F.) for about 20 minutes. Remove foil and beans and bake for 5 minutes or until fully baked and lightly browned. Cool on a wire rack.

Meanwhile, prepare the apple, orange, banana and plums. Place them in separate bowls and add ½ tablespoon Grand Marnier to each fruit.

Prepare the custard by bringing the milk to a boil. Beat together the sugar, flour, cornstarch and egg. Stir half the hot milk into the ingredients, then return the mixture to pan. Bring to a boil over low heat, stirring constantly.

Remove from the heat and stir in the remaining Grand Marnier. Cool the custard slightly and pour into the pastry shell. Dust with confectioners' sugar to prevent a skin forming.

When completely cold, arrange the fruits in alternate rows over the surface.

Heat the apricot preserves and left-over fruit juices in a small pan. Bubble until thickened. Put through a sieve and brush the glaze over the fruit. Serve with heavy cream, if desired.

## BLACKBERRY AND PINEAPPLE BRIOCHE
*6-8 servings*

- 2 cups all-purpose flour
- ¼ teaspoon salt
- 1 tablespoon sugar
- 2 packages active dry yeast
- 2 tablespoons warm water
- 2 eggs, beaten
- ¼ cup butter, melted and cooled
- 1 egg, beaten with 1 teaspoon water for glaze

*For filling:*
- 1 can (16 ounces) pineapple chunks
- 4 tablespoons Kirsch
- 1¼ cups heavy cream
- 1 tablespoon confectioners' sugar
- 1 pint blackberries or raspberries

Sift together the flour, salt and sugar. Combine the yeast and the warm water and let stand a few minutes. Add yeast to the dry ingredients with the eggs and butter. Work into a soft dough. Turn out on a lightly floured board and knead well for 5 minutes. Oil the bottom of a large bowl. Place dough in bowl and turn over so that the top is lightly oiled. Cover and let rise at room temperature for 1–1½ hours or until dough has doubled in size. Brush a 1½-quart fluted brioche mold or other mold with oil. On a lightly floured board, thoroughly knead the brioche dough. Make a ball with three-quarters of it and place in the bottom of the mold. Press a hollow in the center and place the remaining piece of

*A brioche loaf filled with pineapple and blackberries*

dough in the middle. Cover the dough and let stand in a warm place until it has risen up light and fluffy, about 1 hour.

Brush the top carefully with the egg glaze. Bake in a very hot oven (450°F.) for 15–20 minutes or until brown. When cooked, the brioche should sound hollow when tapped on the bottom. Allow to cool, then cut a thin slice from the top and scoop out some of the crumbs. Drain the pineapple and mix 3 tablespoons of the juice with the Kirsch; spoon the liquid over the inside of the brioche and let it soak for 5 minutes. Whip the cream just until it holds its shape, then beat in the confectioners' sugar. Reserve part of the cream and a few pineapple pieces for decoration. Fold remaining pineapple, into remaining cream.

Spoon layers of the cream mixture and most of the blackberries into the brioche. Decorate with whirls of cream, blackberries and pineapple. If liked, top with the lid of the brioche.

## NUTTY CARAMEL PIES
*4 servings*

- ⅝ cup sugar
- ⅝ cup milk
- 1 egg
- 1 egg yolk
- ⅝ cup heavy cream, lightly whipped

*For base:*
- ¾ cup all-purpose flour
- ¼ cup butter
- 2 squares semi-sweet chocolate

*For decoration:*
- ⅝ cup honey sauce, page 60
- ½ cup roughly broken walnuts

*Caramel ice cream on a pastry base, with nuts and a honey sauce*

*Strawberry galette and whipped cream*

Dissolve ¼ cup sugar in a heavy-bottomed pan over low heat and allow to caramelize to a pale golden. Remove from the heat and add 3 tablespoons of boiling water, very, very slowly. Return to the heat and simmer to dissolve the caramel. Add the milk and stir well. Remove from heat.

Beat the whole egg and yolk with 3 tablespoons sugar. Beat in the caramel-milk and strain back into the saucepan. Cook over very low heat, stirring, until the custard coats the back of a spoon. Pour the custard into a bowl and let cool. When it is cold, transfer the custard to an ice cube tray and freeze it to a slush in the freezer. Remove slush to a bowl, beat well. Fold in the whipped cream. Return mixture to the ice cube tray and freeze until firm.

Knead the flour, butter and remaining 2 tablespoons sugar into a manageable dough. Roll out thinly on a lightly floured board and use to line four 3½-in. shallow patty pans. Line carefully with foil and fill with beans. Bake in a fairly hot oven (375°F.) for 15 minutes. Remove beans and foil and return to the oven for 2 minutes. Allow to cool.

Melt the chocolate in a bowl over hot water. Dip the edges of the pies into the soft chocolate. Allow to cool and set.

To serve, pile ice cream into the pastry shells and spoon over honey sauce and walnuts.

## PUDDING GLACE

*8-10 servings*

*For coffee ice:*
**10 egg yolks**
**1½ cups sugar**
**1¼ cups water**
**2½ cups heavy cream, whipped**
**3¾ tablespoons instant coffee powder**
**5 teaspoons water**

*For whisked sponge:*
**2 large eggs**
**¼ cup sugar**
**½ cup all-purpose flour**
**3¾ tablespoons rum**
**Juice of 1 small orange**

*For decoration:*
**Glacé fruits, e.g. cherries, angelica**
**⅝ cup heavy cream, whipped**

*For coffee sauce:*
**1¼ cups water**
**1 cup sugar**
**5 tablespoons instant coffee powder**
**2½ tablespoons cornstarch**

First make the ice cream. Beat the yolks thoroughly in a deep bowl. Dissolve the sugar in the water in a small saucepan and boil to 217°F., about 5 minutes. Cool slightly, then slowly pour on to the egg yolks in a thin stream, beating constantly. Place the bowl over a pan of hot water and continue to beat until thick. Cool. When cold, fold in the whipped cream and the coffee blended with the water. Pour into ice cube trays and freeze until slushy.

Meanwhile, grease and line the bottom of an 8-in. cake pan with waxed paper. Beat together the whole eggs and sugar until pale and fluffy and the beaters leave a trail. Sift the flour over the mixture and fold in with a rubber spatula. Pour the mixture into the prepared cake pan and bake in a fairly hot oven (375°F.) for about 15 minutes or until done. Turn out and cool on a wire rack; remove the paper.

Split the cake in half. Blend together the rum and orange juice and spoon over the sponge halves. Line an 8-in. spring pan with waxed paper. If necessary, trim half the sponge cake to fit the base of the pan and ease into place. Spoon the slushy ice cream over this half of the sponge.

Top with the remaining sponge cake half and return to the freezer until firmly set – about 2 hours. Unmold on a serving platter and decorate with whipped cream and glacé fruits.

To make the coffee sauce, dissolve the sugar in the water in a saucepan over gentle heat. Stir in the coffee. Blend the cornstarch with a little cold water. Pour on some of the coffee syrup, stirring. Return to the pan. Cook over low heat, stirring, until mixture is clean and thickened. Serve the sauce separately with the cake.

## ICED CHARLOTTE RUSSE

*12 servings*

*For ice cream layers:*
**1¼ cups milk**
**1⅞ cup sugar**
**1 vanilla bean pod**
**2 eggs, beaten**
**1¼ cups heavy cream**
**2½ cups water**
**1 quart raspberries**
**10 tablespoons lemon juice**
**1¼ cups raspberry yogurt**

*For sponge case:*
**3¾ tablespoons sugar**
**5 tablespoons water**
**5 tablespoons sherry**
**28 lady fingers**

Heat the milk with 6 tablespoons sugar and the vanilla pod. Pour over the beaten eggs and stir. Return mixture to the saucepan. Cook over low heat, stirring constantly, until the custard thickens. Strain and remove the vanilla pod. Cool.

Beat the cream lightly, but not stiff. Fold into the cold custard. Pour the mixture into an ice cube tray and freeze until slushy. Turn into a chilled bowl and beat thoroughly. Return to ice cube tray and freeze again until slushy.

For the raspberry layers, dissolve 1½ cups sugar in the water. Bring to a boil and reduce by boiling to 2½ cups. Cool. Sieve the berries to remove the seeds and make a purée. Stir in the lemon juice, yogurt and sugar syrup. Turn mixture into an ice cube tray and freeze to a slush.

Fold up some aluminum foil and make it into a collar to fit in the bottom of an 8-in. spring-form pan, leaving a small gap between the tin side and foil to support the lady fingers.

Dissolve the 3¾ tablespoons of sugar in the water in a small saucepan and simmer for 5 minutes. Combine with the sherry in a flat dish, then dip the lady fingers briefly in the mixture,

removing them before they become soggy. Place the lady fingers side by side in the gap made by the foil. Chill.

Layer the vanilla and raspberry ice cream, starting with half the vanilla. Lift the foil collar as the vanilla layer is spooned in, but return it to position above the vanilla layer to give support to the lady fingers. Freeze the vanilla layer until solid; remove the foil. Continue by adding half the raspberry ice cream, freezing, then repeating with the remaining vanilla and raspberry. Leave in the freezer until serving time. Turn out on to a serving platter, leave in a cool place to soften a little, then cut with a knife dipped in warm water.

*Note:* This large iced charlotte is best made in a home freezer; if you are using the freezing compartment of a refrigerator, make the mixture in 2 lots.

## STRAWBERRY GALETTE

*8 servings*

**2½ cups all-purpose flour**
**¾ cup butter**
**6 tablespoons sugar**
**1 quart strawberries, hulled**
**1 cup red-currant jelly**
**3¾ teaspoons arrowroot**

Stand a 9-in. plain flan ring on a cookie tray. Sift the flour. Cut in the butter with a pastry blender or two knives until the consistency of breadcrumbs. Add the sugar. Lightly knead the mixture until it forms a ball.

Roll out the dough and use to line the flan ring, drawing the sides up to make a wall. Press into shape with the fingertips and crimp the edge with finger and thumb. Prick the bottom with a fork and bake in a moderate oven (350°F.) for about 30 minutes or until lightly browned.

Allow to cool for 15 minutes on the cookie tray. Then remove the ring and with a spatula lift on to a wire rack. Leave until cold.

Cut the strawberries in half. Brush the base of the galette with red-currant jelly and arrange the strawberries, cut side uppermost, on top.

Make up a glaze by heating ½ cup red-currant jelly with ½ cup water. Bring to a boil. Put through a sieve and blend in the arrowroot mixed with a little water. Return to the pan and cook until it is clear and thickened. Coat the strawberries with the warm glaze and let stand until set. Serve with whipped cream.

# Homemade Ice creams and Ices

*Although bought ices are very good, the variety achieved by making your own is well worth the little extra trouble.*

*The only equipment necessary is an ordinary domestic refrigerator with a frozen food compartment, or a home freezer, and a rotary whisk. An electric ice cream machine makes the process easier still, but is not essential. There are several varieties of both cream and water ices. The most common types are:*

**Cream ices** *These are seldom made entirely of cream, but any of the following mixtures give good results: equal parts cream and custard (egg custard, made with yolks only); cream and fruit purée; cream and egg whites. The cream may be replaced by unsweetened evaporated milk and flavoring and coloring ingredients are added as required.*

**Water ices** *The foundation is a sugar and water syrup, usually flavored with fruit juice or purée; wine or liqueur is frequently added.*

**Sherbets** *A true sherbet is a water ice with whipped egg white added, to give a fluffy texture.*

**Sorbets** *Semi-frozen ices, sometimes flavored with liqueur. Because they are soft, they are not molded but served in tall glasses or goblets.*

**Bombes** *Iced puddings frozen in a special bomb-shaped mold; bombes may be made of a single ice cream mixture known as a parfait or of two or more. They are often elaborately decorated after unmolding.*

## MAKING ICE CREAM

To obtain the best results, use a rich mixture, with plenty of flavoring. A flavor that tastes quite strong at room temperature will become much less so when frozen. See that the mixture is well sweetened, too, as this helps to accentuate the flavor of the frozen ice. But don't go to the other extreme and over-sweeten, as too much sugar will prevent the mixture freezing properly (too much alcohol used as flavoring will also prevent freezing). Coloring is not affected by freezing, so use sparingly, a drop at a time.

## FREEZING

If you are using the frozen food compartment of a refrigerator, set the dial at the lowest setting about 1 hour before the mixture is ready. Put the mixture into a plastic ice cube tray and place in the frozen food compartment. To improve the texture, either stir the mixture at 20-minute intervals until it is half frozen and then leave it undisturbed until frozen, or allow it to half-freeze, turn it into a cool bowl and beat thoroughly with a rotary beater, then replace it in the freezing compartment and leave until

hard. The time required will vary with the refrigerator, but usually it takes several hours. Once the mixture is frozen the temperature may be returned to normal storage temperature. The ice cream develops a better, more mellow flavor if left for a while. If you have a home freezer, use the same method, but the mixture will of course freeze much more quickly.

## FRENCH VANILLA ICE CREAM

*makes 3 quarts*

**1 quart milk**
**6 egg yolks, beaten**
**1 cup sugar**
**¼ teaspoon salt**
**3 cups heavy cream**
**2 tablespoons vanilla extract**

In a 3-quart heavy saucepan, combine the milk, egg yolks, sugar and salt; blend thoroughly. Cook over a medium heat, stirring constantly, until the mixture coats a spoon, about 15 minutes. *Do not boil.* Cool. Add the cream and vanilla. Chill. Freeze in ice cream maker according to manufacturer's instructions.

## GERMAN CHOCOLATE ICE CREAM

*makes about 1 gallon*

**1 cup sugar**
**¼ cup all-purpose flour**
**¼ teaspoon salt**
**¼ teaspoon cinnamon**
**1 quart milk**
**2 bars (4 ounces each) sweet cooking chocolate, melted**
**3 eggs, beaten**
**1 can (3⅓ ounces) shredded coconut**
**1 quart light cream**
**1 cup chopped pecans**

In a heavy 3-quart saucepan, combine the sugar, flour, salt and cinnamon. Gradually add the milk. Cook over a medium heat, stirring constantly, until thickened. Cook for 2 additional minutes. Remove from heat. Blend in the melted chocolate. Blend a small amount of hot mixture into the eggs; return to pan. Cook for 1 minute. *Do not boil.* Remove from heat and add the coconut. Cool. Blend in the cream. Chill. Stir in the nuts. Freeze in ice cream maker according to manufacturer's directions.

*Serve strawberry liqueur ice cream with luscious strawberry sauce*

*Pear sorbet with meringue is light and refreshing*

## EGG NOG ICE CREAM
*makes about 1 gallon*

1½ cups sugar
½ teaspoon nutmeg
5 eggs, separated
3 cups milk
3 cups heavy cream
½ cup rum
1 teaspoon vanilla extract
¼ teaspoon salt

Blend ¼ cup sugar with the nutmeg. Add to the egg yolks in a small mixing bowl and beat until thick. In a large mixing bowl beat the egg whites until soft peaks form. Gradually add ¼ cup sugar and beat until stiff peaks form. Gently fold the egg yolks into the egg whites. Blend in the milk, cream, remaining 1 cup sugar, rum, vanilla and salt. Chill. Stir to blend. Freeze in ice cream maker using a slightly greater proportion of salt to ice than for other ice creams.

## TOASTED ALMOND ICE
*4 servings*

1¼ cups milk
6 tablespoons sugar
Pinch of salt
4 egg yolks
⅝ cup heavy cream
Vanilla extract
½ cup crushed praline (recipe below)
2 egg whites
3¾ tablespoons confectioners' sugar
1 tablespoon chopped toasted almonds

Boil the milk. Mix the sugar, salt and egg yolks and stir in the hot milk. Cook over very low heat, stirring constantly, until thick. Remove from heat and cool. Pour into an ice cube tray and freeze for 20–30 minutes.
Turn the mixture out into a chilled bowl. Whip with a rotary beater until creamy. Add the cream, a little vanilla and the crushed praline. Pour the mixture back into the freezing tray and freeze until firm. Stir after the first 30 minutes of freezing.
Serve with a sauce made by beating the egg whites and confectioners' sugar together just until stiff enough to drop from a spoon. Fold in the chopped nuts.

## PRALINE

¼ cup sugar
¼ cup chopped toasted almonds

Heat the sugar in a pan until it is a deep amber color. Stir in the almonds and pour the mixture on to a greased pan or slab. When cool, pound in a mortar or crush with a rolling pin.

## STRAWBERRY LIQUEUR ICE CREAM
*4 servings*

⅝ cup heavy cream, lightly whipped
1 cup fresh strawberry purée
½ teaspoon vanilla extract
1¼ tablespoons rum
¼ cup sugar

Mix the cream with the remaining ingredients. Pour into an ice cube tray and freeze for ¾–1 hour. Turn out and beat until smooth. Return mixture to the ice cube tray and freeze until firm.

## BERRY ICE CREAM
*8 servings*

2½ teaspoons unflavored gelatin
2½ tablespoons water
1 can (16 ounces) strawberries or raspberries, puréed
¼ cup brown sugar
2 tablespoons lemon juice
⅝ cup light cream
½ cup cookie crumbs
1¼ cups heavy cream, whipped

Soften the gelatin in the water in a small glass cup. Put in a small pan of hot water and heat gently until gelatin is dissolved. Pour the fruit pulp into a bowl, add sugar to taste and the lemon juice. Stir in the dissolved gelatin, light cream and cookie crumbs. Pour into an ice cube tray and freeze until fairly stiff. Turn mixture into a chilled bowl and beat with a rotary beater. Fold in the whipped cream. Return to ice cube trays and freeze.

## HONEY ICE CREAM
*8 servings*

1 quart raspberries
⅝ cup heavy cream
⅝ cup unflavored yogurt
2½ tablespoons lemon juice
¾ cup honey
Pinch of salt
3 egg whites

Put the raspberries through a sieve to give 1¼ cups raspberry purée. In a bowl, blend together the raspberry purée, cream, yogurt, lemon juice, honey and salt. Turn the mixture into an ice cube tray and freeze until firm. Turn the mixture out into a chilled bowl and beat with a rotary beater until smooth.
Beat the egg whites until stiff and fold carefully into the ice cream. Return the mixture to the ice cube tray and freeze.

## LEMON ICE CREAM

*6 servings*

1¼ cups heavy cream
2 eggs
Grated rind and juice of 2
  lemons
1¼ cups sugar
1¼ cups milk

Beat together the cream and eggs until smooth. Add the lemon rind, lemon juice, sugar and milk and mix thoroughly. Pour into an ice cube tray and freeze for about 2 hours. Do not stir while mixture is freezing.

## ORANGE SHERBET

*4 servings*

½ cup sugar
1¼ cups water
1¼ tablespoons lemon juice
Rind of 1 orange, grated
Rind of 1 lemon, grated
Juice of 3 oranges and 1 lemon
1 egg white

Dissolve the sugar in the water over a low heat, bring to a boil and boil gently for 10 minutes. Add 1¼ tablespoons lemon juice. Put the grated fruit rinds in a bowl, pour the boiling syrup over and let stand until cold. Add the mixed fruit juices. Strain mixture into an ice cube tray.
Half-freeze the mixture then turn it into a chilled bowl. Beat the egg white until stiff and fold it into the chilled mixture. Return to the tray and freeze.
Other flavors of sherbet may be made by adding 1¼ cups fruit purée and the juice of ½ a lemon to 1¼ cups syrup.

## APRICOT SHERBET

*4 servings*

2 eggs, separated
2 tablespoons sugar
1 can (16 ounces) apricots,
  puréed
Pinch of nutmeg
5 tablespoons light cream

Beat the egg whites until stiff. Add 1 tablespoon sugar and continue beating. Fold in remaining sugar. Mix the puréed fruit, egg yolks, nutmeg and cream. Fold carefully into the egg whites. Pour immediately into an ice cube tray and freeze 3–4 hours.

## LEMON SHERBET

*4 servings*

1 cup sugar
2½ cups water
Rind and juice of 3 lemons
1 egg white

*A crunchy cornflake crust coats this lemon freeze*

Dissolve the sugar in the water over a low heat. Add the thinly-pared lemon rind and boil gently for 10 minutes. Let stand to cool. Add the lemon juice and strain the mixture into an ice cube tray. Half-freeze, then turn into a chilled bowl. Beat the egg white until stiff and fold into chilled mixture, blending thoroughly. Return to tray and freeze.

## FRUIT SORBET

Follow the recipe for lemon sherbet, but add 2 egg whites, which will give a much softer consistency. Freeze the mixture only until it is stiff enough to serve. Spoon into glasses.

## LEMON FREEZE

*8 servings*

1 cup crushed cornflakes
6¼ tablespoons sugar
2 tablespoons butter, melted
2 eggs, separated
1 can (14 ounces) sweetened
  condensed milk
5 tablespoons lemon juice

Blend together the cornflake crumbs, 2½ tablespoons sugar and the butter until well mixed. Press all but 5 tablespoons of the mixture into the bottom of an ice cube tray.
Beat the egg yolks in a deep bowl until thick and creamy. Combine with the condensed milk. Add the lemon juice and stir until thickened. Beat the egg whites until stiff but not dry. Gradually beat in remaining sugar. Fold into the lemon mixture. Spoon into the ice cube tray and sprinkle with remaining crumbs. Freeze. Cut into wedges or triangles to serve.

## APRICOT BOMBE

*4 servings*

1 recipe French vanilla ice
  cream, page 67
2 tablespoons finely chopped
  blanched almonds
1 can (8 ounces) apricots,
  drained
2½ tablespoons brandy

Allow the ice cream to soften a little, stir in the almonds.
Spoon two-thirds into a chilled 1¼-cup bowl and press it against the sides to form a shell. Freeze until firm. Pile the well drained apricots with a tablespoon of the juice and the brandy into the center. Cover with remaining ice cream. Cover with foil and freeze until firm. Unmold to serve.

## PINEAPPLE SORBET

*6 servings*

A 2¾ pound pineapple
7½ tablespoons lemon juice
5 tablespoons orange juice
⅝ cup water
1⅜ cup sugar
Whipped cream

Skin the pineapple, remove the core and discard. Cut the pineapple into chunks and purée in an electric blender. Put the pineapple pulp through a sieve to give 2 cups purée. Mix the purée with the lemon and orange juice, water and sugar, stirring until the sugar is completely dissolved. Pour into ice cube trays and freeze without stirring until crystals have formed but the spoon still goes in. Serve accompanied by whipped cream, either in dessert dishes or returned to the empty pineapple shell.

## PEAR SORBET MERINGUE

*6 servings*

1 can (16 ounces) pear halves,
  drained
1½ cups sugar
1¼ cups water
3¾ tablespoons lemon juice
3 egg whites
1 fresh pear, sliced and cored
Melted chocolate

Place the pears in a measure and make up to 1¼ cups with some of the juice. Purée in a blender or put through a sieve. Dissolve half the sugar in the water, bring to a boil and reduce to 1¼ cups syrup. Pour on to the pear purée, add the lemon juice and stir well. Pour into an ice cube tray and freeze until firm.
Meanwhile, draw a 9 in. circle on a sheet of waxed paper and mark into 6 sections. Beat the egg whites until stiff. Add 6 tablespoons of the sugar gradually and beat until stiff. Fold in the remaining 6 tablespoons sugar.
Spoon the meringue into a pastry bag fitted with a large star nozzle. Following pencil lines as a guide, pipe a scalloped edge around the circle, indenting each section. Fill in the base with more meringue, then build up the scalloped edge and outline each section. Dry out in a very cool oven (250°F.) for 3–4 hours or until crisp and firm. Cool and remove the paper.
To serve, spoon the sorbet into the meringue nests. Arrange slices of fresh pear, dipped in lemon juice, between them and drizzle with melted chocolate.

*Gâteau Nougatine*

# Gâteaux and Pâtisserie

*Continental gâteaux and pâtisserie are made from traditional basic mixtures. Many of the decorations are also traditional. If you long for the lovely things that fill the windows of French and Viennese pastry shops, try your hand at some of these.*

## BASIC GENOESE SPONGE
*This sponge is used as a base for many gâteaux (cakes)*

**3 tablespoons butter**
**⅝ cup all-purpose flour**
**1 tablespoon cornstarch**
**3 large eggs**
**6 tablespoons sugar**

Grease the bottom of a 9-in. cake pan. Cover the bottom of the pan with a circle of waxed paper. Grease again. Preheat the oven to 375°F.
Heat the butter gently until it is melted, remove it from the heat and let it stand for a few minutes. Sift together the flour and cornstarch. Place the eggs in a large deep bowl over a saucepan of hot water, beat for a few seconds. Add the sugar and continue beating with a whisk over the heat until the mixture is very pale in color and a trail forms when the whisk is lifted.
Remove from the heat and whisk for a few seconds longer. Resift

half the flour over the egg mixture and carefully fold it in, using a rubber spatula. Then pour in the melted butter (cooled until it just flows) folding it in alternately with the remaining flour. Turn the mixture into the prepared pan. Bake near the top of the oven for 30 minutes or until well risen and just firm to the touch. Turn out carefully and let cool on a wire rack.

## CREME AU BEURRE

**6 tablespoons sugar**
**5 tablespoons water**
**2 egg yolks, beaten**
**½–¾ cup unsalted butter**

Place the sugar in a heavy bottomed saucepan. Add the water and let stand over very low heat to dissolve the sugar, without boiling. When the sugar is completely dissolved, bring to a boiling point and boil steadily for 2–3 minutes, to 225°F. Pour the syrup in a thin stream on to the egg yolks, beating with a rotary beater or whisk all the time. Continue to beat until the mixture is thick and cold.
Gradually beat the egg yolk mixture into the creamed butter and flavor as desired.
**Chocolate:** Put ¼ cup chocolate morsels in a small bowl with 1¼ tablespoons hot water. Let stand

70

over hot water until the mixture is smooth and the chocolate is melted. Cool slightly and beat into the basic crème au beurre.
**Coffee:** Beat in 1–2½ tablespoons coffee flavoring to taste.

## GATEAU CENDRILLON

**9 in. Genoese sponge**
**1¼ tablespoons coffee flavoring**
**Coffee crème au beurre**
**Apricot glaze, page 85**
**Coffee fondant icing or glacé icing, page 84**
**12 hazel nuts, lightly toasted**

To the basic recipe for Genoese, add the coffee flavoring at the whisking stage. Bake in the usual way and cool.

Split the cold sponge in half and sandwich the halves together with two-thirds of the crème au beurre. Brush the top with apricot glaze, coat with icing and leave to set.

To decorate, pipe with whirls of crème au beurre and top each whirl with a hazel nut.

## GATEAU MONT BLANC

*For sponge base:*
**¼ cup sugar**
**2 large eggs**
**½ cup all-purpose flour**

*For filling:*
**1 can (8½ ounces) sweetened chestnut purée**
**1¼ cups heavy cream, lightly whipped**
**Confectioners' sugar**

Grease the bottom of a 9-in. deep cake pan. Line the bottom with a circle of waxed paper and grease again. Preheat oven to 425°F. Beat together the sugar and eggs with a rotary beater until thick and creamy – the beater should leave a trail when lifted. Sift the flour over the surface and lightly fold it in with a rubber spatula. Turn the mixture into the prepared pan. Level with a spatula and tap the pan once or twice on the table top. Bake above the center of the oven for about 15 minutes. Turn out carefully on to a wire rack to cool.
Spread a little whipped cream over the base of the flan. Using a pastry bag with a plain icing nozzle, pipe the chestnut purée in a net over the cream, gradually working it into a dome shape. Using a pastry bag and a large star nozzle, pipe the remainder of the whipped cream in a shell pattern round the edge. Lightly dust the whole with confectioners' sugar.

*Gâteau Mont Blanc, with piped chestnut purée*

## GATEAU ROXALANNE

**1¼ cups self-rising flour**
**¼ cup cornstarch**
**½ cup sugar**
**1¼ teaspoons baking powder**
**½ teaspoon salt**
**¼ cup corn oil**
**⅝ cup cold water**
**1 teaspoon grated lemon rind**
**1¼ teaspoons lemon juice**
**2 egg yolks**
**4 egg whites**
**¼ teaspoon cream of tartar**

*For icing and decoration:*
**½ pound semi-sweet chocolate**
**¾ cup butter**
**2⅝ cup confectioners' sugar**
**2 egg yolks**
**Flaked almonds**

Lightly grease a 7-in. round cake pan. Sift all the dry ingredients into a mixing bowl. Beat together the corn oil, water, lemon rind, lemon juice and egg yolks. Add to the dry ingredients and beat with a rotary beater or hand electric mixer to a smooth, slack batter.
Beat the egg whites and cream of tartar until stiff and dry. Fold carefully into batter mixture. Turn into the prepared pan and bake in the center of a moderate oven (350°F.) for about 1 hour. When the cake is cooked, invert it on to a wire rack until the cake slips out of the pan.
Melt the chocolate in a bowl over hot, not boiling, water. Cream the butter and sugar together until light and creamy. Beat in the egg yolks and melted chocolate. When the cake is cold, spread the sides with this chocolate icing. Coat the edges in flaked almonds. Cover the top with more icing and pipe on a decoration.

## GATEAU CARAQUE

**½ cup sugar**
**4 large eggs**
**1 cup all-purpose flour**

*For filling and decoration:*
**Apricot glaze, page 85**
**Chocolate crème au beurre**
**Grated semi-sweet chocolate**
**Chocolate caraque (see below)**
**Confectioners' sugar**

Grease a 13 in. by 9 in. shallow baking pan. Line the bottom with a sheet of waxed paper and grease again. Preheat oven to 425°F.
In a deep bowl, beat together the sugar and eggs with a rotary beater or electric mixer until really thick and creamy – the beater should leave a trail when lifted from the mixture. Sift the flour over the surface and lightly fold in, using a rubber spatula. Turn the mixture into the prepared pan. Level the surface with a spatula. Bake for 25–35 minutes or until well risen, golden and spongy to the touch. Let stand in pan for 5 minutes. Turn out very carefully and cool on a wire rack. Remove paper from bottom.
Carefully cut the cake lengthwise, giving two strips 13 in. by 4½ in. long. Sandwich the two together with apricot glaze and brush the top with apricot glaze. Spread the chocolate crème au beurre around the sides and coat with coarsely grated chocolate. Arrange the chocolate caraque pieces side by side over the apricot glaze. Dust the center with sifted confectioners' sugar.
**Chocolate Caraque:** Shred or grate 4 squares semi-sweet chocolate on to a plate and place over a pan of hot, not boiling,

water. When melted, spread thinly over a marble slab or other cool surface. When just on the point of setting, run the edge of a sharp knife across the surface of the chocolate, so that it forms curls.

## LINZER TORTE

**1½ cups all-purpose flour**
**1¼ teaspoons cinnamon**
**Pinch of ground cloves**
**2 teaspoons cocoa**
**½ teaspoon baking powder**
**¾ cup finely chopped blanched almonds**
**¾ cup butter**
**⅝ cup sugar**
**2 eggs, beaten**
**Raspberry preserves**
**Confectioners' sugar**

Grease a 9-in. spring-form or loose-bottomed cake pan.
Sift together the flour, spices, cocoa and baking powder. Put the almonds in a bowl, add the butter (straight from the refrigerator and coarsely grated). Stir in the sugar, eggs and flour mixture, in that order. Work together and shape into a roll with the hands. Wrap in waxed paper and chill for about 1 hour.
Roll out about two-thirds of the dough to line the bottom of the pan; press the dough up the sides to form a ½ in. thick wall. Fill with a thick layer of preserves. Roll out the remainder of the dough, cut into strips and use to cover the preserves in an open lattice. Bake in the center of a moderate oven (350°F.) for 1 hour.
Let the torte cool in the pan, then remove the sides of the pan. Mature for 1–2 days before cutting. Fill in the lattice with fresh preserves and serve dusted with confectioners' sugar.

## GATEAU AMANDINE

**⅝ cup sugar**
**3 large eggs**
**¾ cup all-purpose flour**

*For filling and decoration:*
**Apricot glaze, page 85**
**½ cup whole blanched almonds**
**1¼ cups heavy cream**
**Confectioners' sugar**

Grease a 9-in. loose-bottomed cake pan. Cover the bottom with a circle of waxed paper and grease again.
With a rotary beater or electric mixer, beat together the sugar and eggs until thick and creamy –the beaters should leave a trail when lifted. Sift the flour over the

surface and lightly fold in with a rubber spatula. Turn the mixture into the prepared pan and bake just above the center of a fairly hot oven (375°F.) for 30 minutes, until well risen and golden brown. Cool on a wire rack.

When the cake is cold, split and sandwich with apricot glaze. Using a sharp knife, split the nuts in half and cut into thin strips. Whip the cream and lightly sweeten with confectioners' sugar. Completely mask the cake with cream and cover with sliced nuts. Dust lightly with confectioners' sugar and chill. Eat the same day.

## GATEAU NOUGATINE

*For Genoese sponge:*
**6 tablespoons butter**
**1 cup all-purpose flour**
**½ cup cornstarch**
**6 large eggs**
**¾ cup sugar**

*For nougat:*
**11 tablespoons sugar**
**1 cup finely chopped, blanched almonds**
**1 lemon**

*For filling and topping:*
**Crème au beurre**
**2½ teaspoons Tia Maria**
**2½ tablespoons apricot glaze, page 85**
**6 squares semi-sweet chocolate**

Grease and line the bottoms of two 9-in. round cake pans with waxed paper.

Heat the butter gently until it is melted, remove it from the heat and let stand a few minutes. Sift together the flour and cornstarch. Place the eggs in a large deep bowl. Add the sugar and beat with an electric mixer or rotary beater until the mixture is very pale in color and a trail forms when the beater is lifted. Sift half the flour mixture over the egg and fold it in, using a rubber spatula. Pour in the melted butter and fold it in alternately with the remaining flour. Turn the batter into the prepared cake pans. Bake in a hot oven (425°F.) for 10 minutes. Reduce the temperature to 375°F. and bake for a further 15 minutes. Turn out and cool on a wire rack.

For the nougat, put the sugar in a heavy bottomed pan and dissolve a little at a time, stirring gently with a rubber spatula. Turn quickly on to an oiled surface and use the lemon to roll it out thinly. Using a warmed cutter, quickly stamp out 12–14 leaf shapes. Leave the remainder of the

*Profiteroles, filled with cream and served with chocolate sauce*

nougat to set, then roughly crush it. (Should the nougat become too set before all the leaf shapes are cut, put it in a warm oven for a few minutes.)

To finish the cake, make up the crème au beurre, adding the Tia Maria. Sandwich the cake layers together with it. Spread the remainder around the edges and coat evenly with the crushed nougat. Brush the cake top with apricot glaze.

Shred or break up the chocolate into a shallow bowl. Place over hot, not boiling water, and melt. Spread the melted chocolate carefully over the top of the cake with a spatula. When it is nearly set, mark the chocolate into serving pieces with a warmed knife. Arrange the nougat leaves before the chocolate sets, or fix with a little crème au beurre.

## DOBOS TORTE

**4 eggs**
**¾ cup sugar**
**1¼ cups all-purpose flour**
**½ cup sugar for caramel**
**Toasted hazel nuts**

*For chocolate butter cream:*
**10 tablespoons butter or margarine**
**1¾ cup confectioners' sugar, sifted**
**2 squares semi-sweet chocolate, melted**

Draw 5–6 rectangles, 10 in. by 4½ in., on non-stick paper. Place the papers on cookie trays.

Combine the eggs and sugar in a bowl over a pan of hot water and beat with a whisk until very thick and fluffy. Remove from heat, sift the flour very carefully over the top and fold it in with a rubber spatula. Divide the mixture between the rectangles in thin, even layers. Bake towards the top of a fairly hot oven (375°F.) for about 10 minutes or until golden brown.

Peel off the papers and if necessary trim the edges of the rectangles with a sharp knife to make even sides. Cool on wire racks.

Select the layer with the best surface and lay it on an oiled cookie tray or non-stick paper. Put the ½ cup sugar for the caramel in a heavy skillet and place over very low heat to dissolve without stirring. Shake the pan occasionally. When it is completely dissolved, cook gently to a golden brown. Pour the caramel evenly over the selected cake layer, so that the surface is completely covered. Quickly mark it into 8 sections with the back of an oiled knife. Cream the butter and gradually beat in the confectioners' sugar. Beat in the cool but still soft chocolate. Sandwich together the layers of cake with butter cream and place the caramel covered

layer on top.

Cover the sides with butter cream and mark decoratively with a fork. Pipe the remainder in whirls on the caramel surface and top each whirl with a toasted hazel nut.

## PROFITEROLES
*Makes about 20*

**1 recipe Choux Pastry, page 78**
**⅝ cup heavy cream**
**1 egg white**
**Confectioners' sugar**

*For chocolate sauce:*
**½ cup chocolate morsels**
**1 tablespoon butter**
**2½ tablespoons water**
**2½ tablespoons corn syrup**
**Vanilla extract**

Lightly grease 2 cookie trays. Spoon the choux pastry into a pastry bag fitted with a ½ in. plain nozzle. Pipe out about 20 small bun shapes on the cookie trays; hold the nozzle upright while piping and lift it away with a sharp pull to release the mixture.

Bake the choux buns just above the center of a hot oven (425°F.) for about 25 minutes until well risen and golden brown. If correctly cooked, the insides should be hollow and fairly dry. Make a hole in the base of each bun with a skewer or knife and cool them on a wire rack.

Shortly before the profiteroles are to be served, make the chocolate sauce. Melt the chocolate morsels with the butter in a small pan over a very low heat. Add the water, syrup and 2–3 drops of vanilla. Stir well until smooth and well blended.

Put the heavy cream and egg white in a bowl and beat with a rotary beater until thick and standing in peaks. Spoon into a pastry bag fitted with a small plain nozzle and pipe into the center of each bun, through the hole in the bottom.

Dust with confectioners' sugar and serve with the chocolate sauce spooned over or served separately.

## BELGIAN TORTE

**1 cup butter**
**¼ cup sugar**
**2½ tablespoons corn oil**
**Vanilla flavoring**
**1 large egg, beaten**
**4 cups all-purpose flour**
**2½ teaspoons baking powder**
**Pinch of salt**
**½ pound stiff apricot preserves**
**Confectioners' sugar**

Grease an 8-in. round spring-form pan. Beat the butter until creamy, add the sugar and beat again. Add the oil, a few drops of vanilla and the egg. Beat well. Sift the flour with the baking powder and salt. Gradually work it into the creamed mixture. Then, using the fingertips, knead the dough together as for a shortbread dough.

Divide the dough into 2 pieces and knead lightly until smooth. Coarsely grate half the dough into the cake pan in an even layer. Cover with warm preserves nearly to the edge. Coarsely grate the remainder of the dough on top.

Bake the cake just above the center of a cool oven (300°F.) for about 1½ hours or until the surface is lightly browned. While hot, cover heavily with confectioners' sugar. Cool in the pan. When cold, remove ring very carefully.

## PETITES FEUILLETEES

**1 recipe Flaky Pastry, page 76**
**1 egg white, lightly broken with a fork**
**Apricot preserves**
**Heavy cream, whipped**
**Chopped nuts**

Roll out the pastry very thinly and cut into 3 in. squares. Fold the corners of each square to the center and join them with a tiny cut-out of pastry. Brush with egg white. Bake in the center of a very hot oven (450°F.) for 10–15 minutes.

Cool on wire racks. Sieve the apricot preserves and brush over each pastry to glaze. Decorate with whipped cream and nuts.

## CREAM PUFFS
*Makes about 16*

**1 recipe Choux Pastry, page 78**
**1¼ cups heavy cream**
**Confectioners' sugar**

The characteristic light, crisp texture and crazy-paving tops of cream puffs are achieved by baking the pastry in its own steam. For this you will need large, shallow pans with tightly fitting lids, or heavy, flat cookie trays with roasting pans inverted over them, sealing the base with a flour and water paste if necessary.

Spoon the choux pastry into a pastry bag fitted with a ½ in. plain nozzle and pipe into small rounds on the pans or trays. Leave plenty of space between them.

Cover the cream puffs with lids or pans and bake just above the center of a fairly hot oven (400°F.)

for 40–50 minutes. It is important that the puffs are left undisturbed during cooking, or the steam will escape and cause the buns to collapse. Estimate the end of the cooking time by giving the pan a gentle shake – if the buns are cooked they will rattle on the base. Remove and cool on a wire rack.

Just before the puffs are served, make a hole in the base of each. Whip the cream and fill the puffs, piping with a small plain nozzle. Dust with confectioners' sugar.

## BASIC PATE SUCREE
*This French flan pastry is traditionally used in pâtisserie and larger gâteaux*

**1 cup all-purpose flour**
**Pinch of salt**
**¼ cup sugar**
**¼ cup butter at room temperature**
**2 egg yolks**

Sift together the flour and salt on to a pastry board or marble slab. Make a well in the center and into it put the sugar, butter and egg yolks. Using the fingertips of one hand, pinch and work the sugar, butter and egg yolks together until well blended.

Gradually work in all the flour and knead lightly until smooth. Put the pastry in a cool place for at least 1 hour to relax, then roll out and use according to individual recipe.

## BATEAUX SAINT ANDRE
*Makes 6*

**⅓ of the basic pâte sucrée recipe**
**½ pound cooking apples, pared and cored**
**2 tablespoons sugar**
**1¼ tablespoons water**
**½ an egg white**
**⅞ cup confectioners' sugar**

Roll out the pastry and use to line six 4½ in. boat-shaped patty pans, pressing it lightly into shape.

Slice the apples into a pan and stew with the sugar and water until pulpy, then continue to cook until the purée is thick enough to hold its shape. Let stand until cold.

Divide the purée between the uncooked pastry boats and spread it out evenly.

Beat the egg white and the sugar until stiff. Spread a thin layer over the top of each boat. Roll out the pastry trimmings and cut into short strips; place two across each boat. Bake in the center of a fairly hot oven (375°F.) for about 10

*Make petites feuilletées from flaky pastry*

minutes or until the pastry has set and the topping is tinged brown. Let cool in the molds for a few minutes, then turn out carefully and cool on a wire rack.

## BATEAUX AUX FRUITS
*For this and following recipes, make up the basic recipe of pâte sucrée given above and use one third of the dough for each variation*
*Makes 6*

**⅓ of the basic pâte sucrée recipe**
**Apricot glaze, page 85**
**1 can (11 ounces) mandarin oranges, drained**
**6 glacé cherries**

Roll out the pastry thinly and use to line six 4½ in. boat-shaped patty pans, pressing it lightly into shape. Prick well with a fork. Bake towards the top of a fairly hot oven (375°F.) for 5–7 minutes or until just tinged brown. Turn out and cool on a wire rack.

Warm the apricot glaze slightly and brush it over the insides of the pastry boats.

Arrange the fruit neatly in the

boats and brush with more warm apricot glaze.

## BATEAUX DE MIEL
*Makes 6*

**⅓ of the basic pâte sucrée recipe**
**½ cup butter**
**½ cup sugar**
**½ cup ground almonds**
**3¾ tablespoons thick honey**
**Coffee extract**
**Coffee glacé icing, page 84**

Roll out the pastry thinly and use to line six 4½ in. boat-shaped patty pans, pressing it lightly into shape. Prick well with a fork. Bake towards the top of a fairly hot oven (375°F.) for 5–7 minutes until just tinged brown. Turn out and cool on a wire rack.

Cream the butter and sugar until light and fluffy. Beat in the almonds, honey and 2 teaspoons coffee extract.

Divide the creamed mixture between the boats, piling it up to a ridge and smoothing the surface on either side. Chill. When firm, coat with icing and decorate with a wavy line of stiffer piped icing.

*Bateaux aux fruits, on a base of pâte sucrée*

# PERFECT PASTRY

Many people consider good pastry the mark of a good cook – so make sure of your results by checking a few general rules before you start. The first requirements for success are cool working conditions and a hot oven – and the richer the pastry, the hotter the oven. To help keep the pastry cool, handle it as little as possible and use only your fingertips for rubbing in the fat. Always use cold water for mixing (except for choux pastry and hot water crust). The rich pastries– flaky and puff – will be improved if left in a cool place between rollings and again before baking. The proportion of ingredients is vital to the texture of the finished pastry, so add the water cautiously, using only enough to make the mixture bind without becoming sticky – sticky dough leads to hard pastry. Use the barest minimum of flour on the rolling pin and working surface, or you will alter the proportions, giving you dry pastry.

Always roll pastry lightly and as little as possible. Avoid stretching it when you are lining a flan case or covering a pie, or it will shrink back during cooking and spoil the finished shape.

## INGREDIENTS

Pastry ingredients are simple, basic foodstuffs, so make sure you use good quality brands for the best results.

**Flour** All-purpose flour is best, though for shortcrust pastry you can use self-rising with quite good results.

**Fat** Butter, margarine and lard are generally used, though now-adays proprietary vegetable shortenings (both blended and whipped) and pure vegetable oils are often used as well, with excellent results. If you are using one of these, remember to follow the directions on the package, as the proportion of fat to flour may vary slightly.

**Liquid** As a rule, allow 1 teaspoon of liquid per ¼ cup of flour for shortcrust pastry and 1 tablespoon per ¼ cup to bind suet or flaky pastries to an elastic dough.

## BAKING BLIND

Flans and tarts are often 'baked blind' when they are to be filled with a cold or soft uncooked filling, as with lemon meringue pie. To do this, line the pie dish or flan ring with the pastry. Cut out a round of greased waxed paper slightly larger than the pastry case and fit this, greased side down, inside the pastry. Half-fill the paper with uncooked dried beans or rice or with stale bread crusts. Bake the pastry as directed in the recipe for 10–15 minutes, until it has set. Remove the paper and beans, rice or crusts from the pastry case and return it to the oven for another 5 minutes or so to dry out. It is now ready to use. Alternatively, line the pastry case with aluminum foil.

Small tartlet cases can be baked blind without lining. Line the tartlet pans with pastry, prick well with a fork and bake as directed in the recipe.

## SHORTCRUST PASTRY

*Quick and simple, it forms the basis of a wide range of sweet and savory dishes.*
*Makes one 6–7 in. flan ring*

1½ cups all-purpose flour
Pinch of salt
3 tablespoons lard
3 tablespoons margarine
7½ teaspoons water
(approximately)

Sift the flour and salt into a wide, shallow bowl. Cut the fat into small lumps and add to bowl. With a pastry blender or two knives, cut in the fat until the mixture looks like cornmeal. Add the water, a little at a time, tossing lightly with a fork until the particles stick together. Dough should not be wet or slippery. With the hands, lightly form the dough into a ball. The pastry can be used immediately, but it is better to let it 'rest' for 15 minutes. It keeps well in the refrigerator, wrapped tightly in plastic wrap, for a day or two. Allow dough to return to room temperature before rolling it out.
Sprinkle a small amount of flour on a board and roll out the dough evenly, turning occasionally. The usual thickness is about ⅛ in.; do not pull or stretch. Use as required.

### FLAN PASTRY

*Slightly richer than the shortcrust. It is usually sweetened and ideal for flan cases, tarts and other sweet pastries.*
*Makes one 6–7 in. flan ring.*

1¼ cups all-purpose flour
6 tablespoons butter or
   margarine and lard, mixed
2 teaspoons sugar
1 egg, beaten
5 teaspoons water

Sift the flour and salt together into a bowl. Cut in the fat as for shortcrust pastry, until the mixture resembles cornmeal. Mix in the sugar. Add the egg and water, stirring until the ingredients begin to stick together. With one hand collect the mixture together and knead very lightly to give a firm, smooth dough. Roll out as for shortcrust pastry and use as required.

### CHEESE PASTRY

*A savory pastry, suitable for pies, tarts and flans.*

*Almonds and fruit for a frangipan flan*

*Makes 8 boat molds, 12 patty pans or one 7 in. flan ring.*

1 cup all-purpose flour
Pinch of salt
¼ cup butter or margarine and
   lard, mixed
½ cup finely grated Cheddar
   cheese
A little beaten egg or water

Sift the flour and salt together into a bowl and cut in the fat, as for shortcrust pastry, until the mixture resembles fine crumbs. Mix in the cheese. Add the egg or water, stirring until the ingredients begin to stick together. With one hand collect the dough together and knead very lightly to give a smooth dough. Roll out as for shortcrust pastry and use as required.

### RICH CHEESE PASTRY

*Suitable for party and cocktail 'nibblers', not suitable for flan cases.*

6 tablespoons butter or
   margarine and lard mixed
¾ cup finely grated Cheddar
   cheese
1 cup all-purpose flour
Pinch of salt

Cream the fat and cheese together until soft. Gradually work in the flour and salt with a wooden spoon until the mixture sticks together. With one hand collect it together and knead very lightly until smooth. Cover with waxed paper and leave in a cool place. Use as required. Cook at 400°F.

### SUETCRUST PASTRY

*A traditional pastry, quick and*

*To line pastry into small molds, ease the pastry to the shape of the molds and then roll the rolling pin over the top*

*easy to make. It can be baked, but steaming and boiling give much more satisfactory results.*
*Makes enough for a 1-quart steak and kidney pudding.*

2 cups self-rising flour
½ teaspoon salt
½ cup shredded suet
10 tablespoons cold water
   (approximately)

Sift together the flour and salt into a bowl. Add suet and enough cold water to give a light elastic dough. Knead very lightly until smooth. Roll out to ¼ in. thickness and use as required.

### FORK MIX PASTRY

*Made with oil, this is more suitable for savory dishes than sweet.*
*Makes one 8 in. pie crust.*

3 tablespoons corn oil
1¼ tablespoons cold water
1 cup all-purpose flour
Pinch of salt

Put the oil and water into a bowl and beat well with a fork to form an emulsion. Add the sifted flour and salt gradually to the mixture to make a dough. Roll out between two sheets of waxed paper.

### STRAWBERRY FLAN

*8 servings*

⅓ cup sugar
¼ cup cornstarch
¼ teaspoon salt
1¾ cups milk
2 eggs, slightly beaten
¼ teaspoon grated lemon rind
¼ teaspoon vanilla extract
A 9-in. baked flan case
2 pints fresh strawberries
⅓ cup red-currant jelly

Mix together the sugar, cornstarch and salt in a heavy saucepan. Slowly blend in milk. Cook over medium heat, stirring constantly, until mixture thickens and boils for 30 seconds. Stir a small amount of the hot mixture into beaten eggs. Return egg mixture to saucepan. Cook over low heat, stirring constantly until very thick and smooth. Remove from heat and stir in lemon rind and vanilla. Press a piece of waxed paper directly on surface of custard to prevent skin forming. Cool. Chill in refrigerator. Spread chilled custard filling in baked flan case. Clean and hull berries. Place berries as close together as possible on surface of custard. Put jelly in a small saucepan and heat over low heat until melted. Spoon over strawberries. Chill flan before serving.

## CORNISH PASTIES
*Makes 4*

¾ pound boneless chuck steak
¼ pound potatoes, peeled
   and diced
1 small onion, chopped
Salt and pepper
1 double recipe Shortcrust
   Pastry

Cut the steak into small pieces, add the potato and onion and season well. Divide the pastry into four and roll each piece into an 8 in. round.

Divide the meat mixture between the pastry rounds, dampen the edges and draw them together to form a seam across the top. Flute with the fingers.

Put in a large, shallow baking pan. Bake in a hot oven (425°F.) for 15 minutes to start browning the pastry. Reduce heat to 325°F. and cook for about 1 hour or until meat is tender. Serve hot or cold.

## FRANGIPAN FLAN
*4 servings*

1 recipe Shortcrust Pastry

*For frangipan cream:*

3 tablespoons cornstarch
2 cups milk
4 egg yolks
2 tablespoons sugar
¾ cup ground almonds
Vanilla extract

*For fruit layer:*

¼ pound white grapes, peeled
   and halved
2 oranges, pared
1 banana, sliced

*For topping:*

Sugar
½ cup flaked, toasted almonds

Roll out the pastry and use to line a 7½-in. plain flan case or an 8-in. removable-bottomed cake pan. Line the case with foil and fill with dried beans. Bake in a hot oven (425°F.) for 15 minutes. Remove foil and beans and bake 5 minutes or until cooked and lightly browned. Cool.

Mix the cornstarch with a little cold milk. Blend in remaining milk. Cook over moderate heat, stirring constantly, until mixture comes to a boil. Remove from heat and beat in the egg yolks, one at a time. Add the sugar, almonds and few drops of vanilla. Cook for about 1 minute until the sauce thickens. Stir well. Cover and let stand until cold.

Meanwhile, remove the seeds from the grape halves and cut the oranges into sections. Arrange the grapes, oranges and banana

*Place the butter on the dough in small pieces, using a spatula*

slices in the pastry case. Spread the cool frangipan cream over the fruit, piling it into a pyramid shape. Dust heavily with sugar. Stand the flan on a serving platter. With a red-hot skewer (held in a cloth) brand the sugar until it caramellizes. Reheat skewer between brandings. Sprinkle the sugar with almonds. Serve within a few hours.

## CREAM CHEESE BOATS
*Makes 16*

1 recipe Cheese Pastry
1 package (3 ounces) cream
   cheese
1 slice boiled ham, finely
   chopped
2½ teaspoons milk
Salt and pepper
4 slices processed American
   cheese

Line sixteen 3½ in. boat-shaped molds with pastry. Prick the bottom of the pastry all over with a fork. Bake in a fairly hot oven (400°F.) for about 10 minutes or until golden brown.

When cool, remove from the molds. Beat the cream cheese until smooth, add the ham and milk. Season well. Put the mixture into a pastry bag and pipe into the pastry boats. Decorate with triangular 'sails' cut from the sliced cheese. Use within a few hours of making.

## STEAK AND KIDNEY PUDDING
*4 servings*

1 recipe Suetcrust Pastry
¼ pound kidney, skinned and
   cored
½–¾ pound boneless chuck or
   round steak, cut into ½ in.
   cubes
2½ tablespoons seasoned flour
1 onion, chopped

Half-fill a steamer or large saucepan with water and bring to a boil.

Grease a 1-quart mixing bowl. Roll out three-quarters of the pastry and use to line the bowl. Slice the kidney and coat both the steak and the kidney with seasoned flour. Fill the basin with the meat and onion. Add 2–3 tablespoons water. Roll out the remaining pastry to around the size of the top of the bowl. Dampen the edge of the bowl. Place the pastry 'lid' on top of the meat and seal the edges securely.

Cover with greased foil. Steam over rapidly boiling water for about 4 hours, refilling the pan as necessary with boiling water.

The meat can be prepared and stewed with the onion for about 2 hours earlier in the day before being used for the filling. In this case, reduce the steaming time to 1½–2 hours.

## RICH PASTRIES
Always handle flaked pastries lightly and as little as possible.

The fat to be used should be worked on a plate with a spatula before you start to make the pastry. This softens it, as it needs to be about the same consistency as the dough with which it is going to be combined.

Remember to allow these richer pastries to 'rest' during the making as well as after shaping and before baking. Cover the pastry and leave in a cool place for 15 minutes or so. This prevents the fat becoming oily and spoiling the flaked texture of the finished pastry.

Roll out the pastry lightly, evenly and as quickly as possible.

## FLAKY PASTRY
*The commonest of the flaked pastries, used for both savory and sweet dishes.*
*Makes 16 eccles cakes or cream horns, or lines 2 pie pans.*

2 cups all-purpose flour
Pinch of salt
¾ cup butter or butter and
   shortening
10 tablespoons cold water to mix
   (approximately)
Squeeze of lemon juice

Mix together the flour and salt. Soften the fat by working it with a small spatula on a plate; divide into 4 equal parts. Rub one quarter of the softened fat into the flour with the fingertips and mix to a soft, elastic dough with the water and lemon juice. On a floured board, roll the pastry into an oblong 3 times as long as it is wide.

Put another quarter of the fat over the top two-thirds of the dough in small flakes, so that it looks like buttons on a card. Fold the bottom third up and the top third down and give the pastry half a turn, so that the folds are now at the sides. Seal the edges of the pastry by pressing with the rolling pin. (On a warm day, refrigerate at this stage for a while before continuing.) Re-roll into the same oblong shape as before. Continue with the remaining two quarters of fat in the same way. When all the fat is used, wrap the pastry loosely in plastic wrap and refrigerate for at least 30 minutes before using.

Sprinkle a board or marble slab with a very little flour. Roll out the pastry ¼–⅛ in. thick and use as required.

## ROUGH PUFF PASTRY
*Similar in appearance and texture to flaky pastry, though generally not so even. Quicker and easier to make and can be used as an alternative for flaky in most recipes.*

2 cups all-purpose flour
Pinch of salt
¾ cup butter or margarine and
   shortening mixed
10 tablespoons cold water to mix
   (approximately)
Squeeze of lemon juice

Sift the flour and salt into a bowl. Cut the fat (which should be quite firm but not hard) into cubes about ¾ in. across. Stir the fat into the flour without breaking up the pieces and mix to a fairly stiff dough with the water and lemon juice. Turn out on to a lightly floured board and roll into a strip 3 times as long as it is wide, using firm, sharp movements. Fold the bottom third up and the top third down, then give the pastry a half-turn so that the folds are at the sides. Seal the edges of the pastry by pressing lightly with the rolling pin.

Continue to roll and fold in this fashion 4 times altogether. Wrap in plastic wrap and let stand in refrigerator for about 30 minutes before using. Roll out and use as for flaky pastry.

## PUFF PASTRY

*The richest of all pastries, giving the most even rising, the most flaky effect and the crispest texture. Requires very careful handling, allowing plenty of time to rest before the final rolling and shaping.*

**2 cups all-purpose flour**
**Pinch of salt**
**1 cup butter, preferably unsalted**
**10 tablespoons cold water to mix (approximately)**
**Squeeze of lemon juice**
**Beaten egg to glaze**

Sift the flour and salt into a bowl. Work the fat with a small spatula on a plate until it is soft, then rub about 1 tablespoon of it into the flour.

Mix to a fairly soft, elastic dough with the water and lemon juice and knead lightly on a floured board or marble slab until smooth.

Form the rest of the fat into an oblong and roll the pastry out into a square.

Place the fat on one half of the pastry and enclose it by folding the remaining pastry over and sealing the edges firmly with the rolling pin.

Turn the pastry so that the fold is to the side, then roll out into a strip 3 times as long as it is wide.

Fold the bottom third up and the top third down and seal the edges with the rolling pin. Cover the pastry and let it rest in the refrigerator for about 20 minutes. Turn the pastry so that the folds are to the side and continue rolling, folding and resting until the sequence has been completed 6 times altogether.

After the final resting, shape the pastry as required. Always brush the top surfaces with beaten egg before cooking, to give the characteristic glaze of puff pastry; – add a pinch of salt if a really rich glaze is required.

## BAKEWELL TART
*4 servings*

**½ recipe Flaky or Rough Puff Pastry**
**2 tablespoons raspberry preserves**
**¼ cup butter or margarine**
**¼ cup sugar**
**Grated rind and juice of ½ lemon**
**1 egg, beaten**
**1 cup sieved cake crumbs**
**¾ cup ground almonds**

Roll out the pastry thinly and line a deep 8-in. pie pan. Spread the bottom of the pastry case with the preserves.

Cream the butter, sugar and lemon rind together until light and fluffy. Add the egg and beat thoroughly. Combine the cake crumbs and almonds. Fold half into the mixture with a spoon, then fold in the rest, with a little lemon juice if necessary to give a good consistency.

Put the mixture into the pie pan and smooth the surface with a spatula. Bake near the top of a hot

oven (425°F.) for about 15 minutes until the tart begins to brown. Reduce temperature to 350°F. and continue baking for 20–30 minutes or until the filling is firm to the touch.
Serve hot or cold.

## HOT CHICKEN PIE
*6 servings*

**A 4 pound chicken, cut in pieces**
**1 onion, cut up**
**1 carrot**
**1 leek, well cleaned**
**6 peppercorns**
**Salt**

*For the sauce:*
**¼ cup butter**
**¾ cup chopped onion**
**2 sweet red peppers, finely chopped**
**2–3 green chillies, halved and seeded**
**5 tablespoons flour**
**2½ cups chicken stock**
**1 cup grated Cheddar cheese**
**Salt**
**Freshly ground black pepper**

**1 package (10 ounces) frozen patty shells**
**1 egg, beaten**

Simmer the chicken in sufficient water to cover with the onion, carrot, leek, peppercorns and salt, for about 2 hours. Remove the chicken and let cool. Reduce the liquid in the pan to 2½ cups by boiling rapidly. Strain and discard the vegetables.

Melt the butter in a saucepan. Add the chopped onion, peppers and chillies. Fry for about 10 minutes; if desired, the chillies can be removed at this stage.

Remove the chicken from the bones, discard the skin. Cut the chicken meat into bite-sized pieces and place in a 2-quart casserole.

Stir the flour into the fried vegetables and cook for 1 minute. Remove from the heat and stir in the strained stock. Cook, stirring constantly, until the mixture comes to a boil. When it has thickened, remove from the heat and stir in the cheese. Adjust the seasoning. Spoon over the chicken and let cool.

Remove the patty shells from package and allow to thaw. Place very close together on a lightly floured board and pinch edges together to make a sheet of dough. Roll out into a shape to fit the top of the casserole. Seal the edges and brush the top with beaten egg. Place on a cookie tray and cook in a very hot oven (450°F.) for 30 minutes. Reduce temperature to 325°F. and cook for 30 minutes longer.

## MILLE-FEUILLES SLICES
*Makes 4*

**½ recipe Puff or Rough Puff Pastry**
**Raspberry preserves**
**Whipped cream**
**Glacé icing**
**Chopped nuts**

Roll the pastry into a strip ½ in. thick, 4 in. wide and 12 in. long. Brush a cookie tray with water and lay the pastry on it. Cut it from side to side in strips 2 in. wide, but don't separate the slices. Bake near the top of a very hot oven (450°F.) for 10 minutes. Separate the strips and cool.
Split each strip into two and sandwich them together in threes or fours with preserves and cream. Cover the tops with glacé icing and a few chopped nuts.

## CHOUX PASTRY

*A rich pastry that swells in cooking to a crisp, airy texture.*
*Makes 10–12 éclairs or 20 profiteroles.*

**3 tablespoons butter or margarine**
**⅝ cup water**
**⅝ cup sifted all-purpose flour**
**2 eggs, lightly beaten**

Melt the fat in the water in a saucepan and bring to a boil. Remove from the heat and quickly add the flour all at once. Return the pan to the heat and beat with a spoon until it is smooth and forms a ball in the

*Puff pastry, cream, preserves and glacé icing for a mille-feuilles slice*

center of the pan. (Take care not to over-beat or the mixture becomes fatty.) Allow to cool slightly. Beat in the eggs gradually, adding just enough to give a smooth, glossy mixture of piping consistency. Use dough as required.

## CHOCOLATE ECLAIRS
*Makes 10–12*

**1 recipe Choux Pastry**
**Whipped cream or crème pâtissière**
**Chocolate glacé icing (page 84) or melted chocolate**

Spoon the choux pastry into a pastry bag fitted with a ½ in. plain round nozzle. Pipe fingers 3½–4 in. long on to a cookie tray. Keep the lengths even and cut the paste off with a wet knife against the edge of the nozzle. Bake near the top of a fairly hot oven (400°F.) for 30–35 minutes or until well risen, crisp and of a golden brown color. Remove from the tray, make a slit in the side to allow the steam to escape and leave on a wire rack to cool.
When the éclairs are cold, fill with the whipped cream or crème pâtissière, then ice the tops with a little chocolate glacé icing or dip them in melted chocolate.

## HOT WATER CRUST PASTRY
*Use for raised pies, as the hot water used to mix the pastry makes it pliable enough to mold easily.*

**4 cups all-purpose flour**
**2½ teaspoons salt**
**½ cup lard**
**14 tablespoons milk or milk and water**

Sift the flour and salt together. Melt the fat in the liquid and then bring to a boil. Pour the boiling liquid into the flour. Working quickly, beat with a wooden spoon to form a fairly soft dough. Turn out on to a lightly floured board and knead until smooth. Use as required, keeping the part of the dough not actually being used covered with a cloth or an upturned bowl to prevent it hardening.

## SHAPING A RAISED PIE BY HAND

Roll out two-thirds of the dough to a 12 in. round. Take a straight-sided 4 in. round container (e.g. a large preserves jar), dredge well with flour and turn

*Fill each éclair with cream and dip in melted chocolate*

upside down. Lift the round of dough with the rolling pin and place over the base of the container. Mold dough round the container by pressing firmly to the sides, keeping the edge even. Cut a double thickness of waxed paper or foil to fit round the pie. Wrap the paper round the pastry and tie with string. Leave in a cool place until the pastry is firm enough to stand in the 'raised' position without a mold.
Turn the container the right way up and gently ease it out of the pastry case, twisting it gently to loosen. Leave the paper in position. Place the pastry case on a cookie tray, and fill with the prepared meat mixture. Pack the filling well down at the sides to hold the shape of the pie. Brush the edge with water. Roll out the remaining pastry to make a lid. Place on top of the pie and press the edges together to seal. Trim away the surplus pastry and paper with scissors.
Make a hole in the center of the lid and decorate the top with pastry leaves cut from the trimmings. Brush with beaten egg white or water and bake as directed.

## MAKING A RAISED PIE IN A CAKE PAN OR MOLD

Grease a 6-in. round cake pan – preferably one with a loose bottom, which makes it easier to remove the pie after baking. Roll out two-thirds of the dough and line the sides and bottom of the pan making sure that the pastry is free of creases and splits. Add the filling, cover with the remaining

dough, rolled out to form a lid, and decorate.
Bake as directed in the recipe.

## RICH RAISED PIE
*6–8 servings*

**1 pound veal bones**
**A 2½ pound chicken, boned**
**Salt and pepper**
**½ pound lean pork**
**½ pound sliced bacon**
**½ pound lean veal**
**2½ tablespoons chopped parsley**
**1 pound pork sausage meat**
**1 recipe Hot Water Crust Pastry**
**Beaten egg**

Chop the veal bones and use them, together with the chicken bones, skin and giblets, to make a well-seasoned, concentrated jellied stock. Leave to cool in the refrigerator.
Separate the chicken breasts and cut into pieces.
Put the rest of the chicken meat through a grinder with the pork and half the bacon slices. Cut the veal into tiny cubes. Blend the parsley into the sausage meat. Cut the remaining bacon slices in half, stretch each piece with the back of a knife, spread a thin layer of sausage meat on each bacon slice and roll up.
Use two-thirds of the pastry to line an 8-in. oval fancy pie mold or an oval shallow casserole. Place the mold on a cookie tray. Press the pastry well into the base and the pattern. Use three-quarters of the remaining sausage meat to make a lining over the pastry. Fill the center alternately with the bacon rolls, ground chicken mixture, veal and chic-

ken breast pieces, piled well up. Season well and cover with the remaining sausage meat.
Dampen the edges of the pastry. Roll out the remaining piece and use for a lid. Trim the edges and seal. Decorate with pastry trimmings and make a hole in the center of the pie. Brush well with beaten egg.
Bake in a fairly hot oven (400°F.) for 30 minutes. Reduce oven temperature to 350°F. and cook for 2 hours. Cover with foil once the pastry is a good golden brown. When the pie is quite cold, fill with the cool but not cold liquid stock through the hole in the center of the lid. Leave for several hours before serving.

### Handy hint

If you use a glass or earthenware flan case rather than a metal ring and cookie tray, the pastry on the bottom will take longer to cook. To overcome this, put a cookie tray in the oven when you light it and put the flan case on to the hot tray. This helps to cook the underside of the pastry.

# CAKES FOR THE FAMILY

Most cakes are straightforward to make if you follow the recipe carefully. Always use the ingredients specified. Always make sure eggs are at room temperature when you use them and don't use butter or margarine straight from the refrigerator either; let them soften a little first, unless you are using one of the 'soft' margarines. Oven temperature is critical in cake baking, so always pre-heat the oven before you start and don't open the door until two-thirds of the cooking time given in the recipe has elapsed. If the cake seems to be browning too quickly, lower the temperature towards the end of the time. To test whether a light textured cake is cooked, press it lightly with the tip of a finger – it should be spongy, give only very slightly to the pressure, then rise again immediately. With a fruit cake, lift it gently from the oven and listen to it carefully; if there is a sizzling sound, the cake is not yet cooked through. Alternatively, insert a warm skewer (never a cold knife) into the center of the cake. It should come out perfectly clean; if any mixture is sticking to it, the cake requires longer cooking.

## WHISKED SPONGE

**2 eggs**
**½ cup sugar**
**1 cup sifted all-purpose flour**

Grease an 8-in. cake pan, line the bottom with a circle of waxed paper and grease again.
Beat the eggs and sugar with a wire whisk in a bowl over hot water until thick, with the whisk leaving a trail across the surface when it is raised. Remove from the heat. Sprinkle the sifted flour over the egg mixture and carefully fold in with a rubber spatula until the flour is evenly distributed. Pour into the prepared pan. Bake just above the center of a moderate oven (350°F.) for 25–30 minutes.
Let stand a few minutes on a wire rack. Turn out of pan, remove waxed paper and let cool on rack. Use as required.

## VICTORIA SANDWICH CAKE

**½ cup butter or margarine**
**½ cup sugar**
**2 large eggs**
**Grated rind of 1 lemon**
**1 cup self-rising flour**

Grease a 9-in. cake pan, line the bottom with a circle of waxed paper and grease again.
In a bowl, cream together the butter and sugar until light and fluffy. Add the eggs, one at a time, beating well after each addition. Add the lemon rind.
Lightly beat in the flour. When well mixed, pour into the prepared pan and level off the surface. Bake in a moderate oven (350°F.) for about 30 minutes or until a cake tester, inserted in the cake, comes out clean.
Let stand for a few minutes on a wire rack. Turn out of pan, remove the waxed paper and cool. Split the cake in half and sandwich together with preserves or butter cream. Ice the top or dust with confectioners' sugar.

## COFFEE NUT CAKE

**¾ cup butter or margarine**
**¾ cup sugar**
**3 large eggs**
**1½ cups all-purpose flour**
**1 teaspoon baking powder**
**Pinch of salt**
**Coffee butter cream**
**Chopped and whole walnuts to decorate**
**Coffee glacé icing, page 84**

Grease two 7-in. cake pans, cover with a circle of waxed paper and grease again. (You may use 8-in. cake pans, but the baking time will be less and the layers will be thin.)

Cream the butter and sugar until light and fluffy, then beat in the eggs one at a time. Sift together the flour, baking powder and salt. Fold into the mixture a little at a time.

Divide the mixture equally between the prepared pans and bake in a moderate oven (350°F.) for about 30 minutes or until golden brown and firm to the touch. (For 8-in. pans, start checking cooking time at 20 minutes.) Remove to wire rack to cool a little. Turn cakes out, remove paper and cool on wire rack.

Make some butter cream with 6 tablespoons butter and 1 cup sifted confectioners' sugar; add sufficient coffee extract to give a good flavor.

Sandwich the layers together with the butter cream and use the remainder to coat the sides of the cake. Roll the sides in chopped walnuts and coat the top with coffee glacé icing. Decorate with whole walnuts.

## SPICY DATE AND NUT CAKE

**3 cups all-purpose flour**
**¾ cup butter or margarine**
**¾ cup sugar**
**2½ teaspoons cinnamon**
**1½ cups chopped nuts**
**1 cup pitted dates, chopped**
**1 can (16 ounces) apple sauce**
**1¾ teaspoons baking soda**
**1 tablespoon milk**
**(approximately)**

*For topping:*
**2½ tablespoons chopped dates**
**2½ tablespoons chopped nuts**
**2½ teaspoons sugar**
**½ teaspoon cinnamon**

Grease an 11 in. by 5 in. loaf pan. Line the bottom with waxed paper and grease again.

Sift the flour into a bowl. Cut in the fat with a pastry blender or two knives. Add the sugar, cinnamon, nuts and dates. Make a well in the center and add the apple sauce. Dissolve the soda in the milk and add to the mixture. Mix well and turn into the pan. Mix together the topping ingredients, sprinkle over the cake and bake in a fairly hot oven (375°F.) for about 1¼ hours. Cool slightly, turn out and cool on a wire rack.

*Grasmere cake to cut and keep*

## FARMHOUSE CAKE

**1 cup wholewheat flour**
**1 cup self-rising flour**
**¼ teaspoon cinnamon**
**¼ teaspoon nutmeg**
**½ teaspoon baking soda**
**6 tablespoons lard**
**½ cup sugar**
**¼ cup seedless raisins**
**¼ cup white raisins**
**2 tablespoons chopped mixed peel**
**1 egg, beaten**
**½ cup milk (approximately)**

Grease an 8 in. by 4 in. loaf pan. Line the bottom with waxed paper and grease again.

Sift together the flours, spices and soda. With a pastry blender or two knives, cut in the fat to a coarse consistency. Add the sugar, fruit and peel. Stir in the beaten egg and enough milk to give a soft dough.

Pour into the prepared pan and bake in a moderate oven (350°F.) for about 1 hour. Turn out and cool on a wire rack.

## FROSTED APPLE CAKE

**½ cup butter or margarine**
**½ cup sugar**
**2 large eggs**
**1 cup self-rising flour**
**Vanilla extract**

*For topping*
**1¼ tablespoons sugar**
**2½ teaspoons cinnamon**
**¼ cup flaked almonds**
**1 large cooking apple**
**Confectioners' sugar**

Grease and line the bottom of an 8-in. square cake pan with waxed paper.

Cream together the butter and sugar until light. Beat in the eggs, one at a time. Lightly beat in the flour with a few drops of vanilla. Turn the mixture into the prepared pan.

Toss together the sugar, cinnamon and nuts. Cover the surface of the cake evenly with pared, cored and very thinly sliced apple. Sprinkle with the nut mixture. Bake in a moderate oven (350°F.) for about 30 minutes.

Cool slightly, then turn out carefully or serve squares of cake from the pan.

## GRASMERE CAKE

**3 cups all-purpose flour**
**½ teaspoon cinnamon**
**½ teaspoon nutmeg**
**1¾ teaspoons baking soda**
**¾ cup butter or margarine**
**1¼ cups milk plus 1 tablespoon**
**1¼ tablespoons lemon juice**
**1 cup sugar**
**¾ cup currants**
**⅓ cup white raisins**

Line the bottom of an 11 in. by 5 in. loaf pan with greased waxed paper.

Sift together the flour, spices and baking soda into a mixing bowl. Cut in the butter with a pastry blender or two knives until the mixture resembles fine breadcrumbs.

Add the lemon juice to the milk (the milk will clot and turn sour). Add the sugar, currants and raisins to the dry ingredients and mix well. Gradually add the soured milk, stirring with a wooden spoon, until the batter is smooth.

Leave the mixture covered for several hours or overnight.

Turn the mixture into the prepared pan. Level off the surface with a spatula. Place the pan on a cookie tray and bake in a warm oven (325°F.) for about 2 hours or until a cake tester inserted in the center of the cake comes out clean.

The Grasmere cake should have risen evenly and have a smooth surface. Let stand in the pan for a few minutes. Turn out on to a wire rack, remove paper and let stand until cold.

Grasmere cake can be stored satisfactorily for about a week. Wrap it in aluminum foil when cold and store in an airtight tin. *Note:* If you prefer, omit the milk and lemon juice and use an equal amount of buttermilk.

## RICH FRUIT CAKE
*Suitable for Christmas and birthday cakes*

**2 cups all-purpose flour**
**½ teaspoon ground ginger**
**½ teaspoon ground mace**
**1 cup butter**
**1½ cups dark brown sugar, firmly packed**
**4 large eggs, beaten**
**2 tablespoons brandy**
**Grated rind of 1 lemon**
**1 cup currants**
**1 cup seeded raisins, roughly chopped**
**1 cup white raisins**
**½ cup glacé cherries, halved**
**½ cup mixed chopped candied peel**
**¼ cup chopped almonds**

Cut a double strip of waxed paper long enough to line the sides of an 8-in. spring-form pan, and 2 in. deep. Make a 1 in. fold lengthwise and snip at intervals. Cut out 2 paper rounds for the base.

Grease the pan. Fit 1 paper round into the bottom of the pan. Line the sides with the long strip, fitting the snipped pieces so that they overlap in bottom of the pan. Fit in the second round and grease the lining. Either tie a band of brown paper around the outside of the pan or place it inside a slightly larger pan.

Sift the flour with the spices. Cream the butter and sugar together in a bowl until light and fluffy. Continue beating with a wooden spoon until the mixture is about twice its original volume. Add 1 tablespoon egg at a time, beating well. If the mixture shows signs of curdling, beat in 1–2 tablespoons sifted flour.

With a rubber spatula, lightly fold in the flour, alternately with the brandy, followed by the lemon rind, fruits and nuts. Mix thoroughly to distribute the fruit evenly, then spoon it into the prepared pan, pushing well into the corners. Use a rubber spatula to get all the mixture from bowl. With the back of a spoon, make a slight hollow in the center of the mixture to prevent uneven rising. Put the tin on a newspaper-lined cookie tray. Bake in a cool oven (300°F.) for about 3¾ hours. If the cake shows signs of browning too quickly, cover with waxed paper and reduce the heat to 275°F. for the last hour of cooking time. Test by sticking a warmed skewer into the center of the cake. Allow it to cool for a few minutes in the pan, then turn out on to a wire rack. When cold, remove the papers.

## DEVIL'S FOOD CAKE

2½ cups all-purpose flour
2½ teaspoons baking soda
½ teaspoon salt
6 tablespoons butter or margarine
1½ cups light brown sugar, firmly packed
2 large eggs
4 squares unsweetened chocolate, melted
1 cup milk
1¼ teaspoons vanilla extract

*For butter filling:*
6 tablespoons butter
1 cup confectioners' sugar
1¼ tablespoons milk

*For frosting:*
1 package (6 ounces) semi-sweet chocolate morsels
3⅓ cups confectioners' sugar
2½ tablespoons hot water
2 egg yolks
6 tablespoons butter, melted

Grease two 9-in. cake pans. Line with a circle of waxed paper and grease again.
Sift together the flour, baking soda and salt. Set aside. Cream together the butter and sugar until pale and fluffy, then gradually add the eggs, one at a time, beating well after each addition. Add the melted chocolate and beat well. Add the flour alternately with the milk and vanilla, beating thoroughly after each addition. Turn the mixture into the prepared pans. Bake in a moderate oven (350°F.) for about 40 minutes or until top of cake springs back when touched with fingers. Cool the cakes in pans for a few minutes. Turn out, remove paper and cool on wire racks.

*A light, fluffy gâteau for tea-time*

Cream the butter until soft, then gradually beat in the confectioners' sugar with the milk for the butter filling. Use this to sandwich the two layers together. For the frosting, melt the chocolate morsels in a bowl over hot, not boiling, water. Remove from heat and stir in the sifted confectioners' sugar and hot water. Gradually beat in the egg yolks, one at a time, followed by the melted butter, a little at a time. Continue to beat until of spreading consistency and use to cover the top and sides of the cake. Let stand, preferably until the next day, before slicing.

## GATEAU A L'ORANGE

4 eggs, separated
½ cup sugar
Grated rind of 1 orange
5 tablespoons orange juice
⅞ cup all-purpose flour

*For filling and decoration:*
9 tablespoons butter
⅝ cup sugar
1 egg
1 egg yolk
Grated rind of 1 orange
5 tablespoons orange juice
1 tablespoon orange liqueur
¼ cup almonds, flaked and toasted
1 whole orange

Grease a 9-in. cake pan. Line with a circle of waxed paper and grease again.
Place the egg yolks and sugar in a bowl and beat with a rotary beater until light in color and very thick. Beat in the orange rind and juice. Fold in the flour with a rubber spatula. Beat the egg whites stiffly and fold into the mixture. Turn into the pan and bake in a moderate oven (350°F.) for about 30 minutes. Let stand a few minutes. Turn out, remove paper and cool on a wire rack.
Meanwhile, prepare the filling.

Put 3 tablespoons butter in a bowl with the sugar, egg, egg yolk, orange rind, juice and liqueur. Place over a pan of hot water and beat with a whisk until smooth and thick. Let stand until completely cold. Split the cake in 2 layers and sandwich together with a little of the filling mixture. Cream the remaining butter and beat it into the rest of the filling. Use this thickened butter cream to cover the top and sides of the cake. Press the toasted almonds into the cream around the sides of the cake. Section the orange and use to garnish top of cake.

## FRUIT AND ALMOND SLICES
*Makes 12*

¾ cup all-purpose flour
2 tablespoons sugar
¼ cup butter
¼ cup currants
12 glacé cherries, halved

*For topping:*
¼ cup butter
¼ cup sugar
1 large egg, beaten
½ cup ground almonds
Almond extract
Confectioners' sugar

Shape a shallow oblong pan 12 in. by 4 in. from heavy duty aluminum foil. Grease the pan thoroughly and place on a small cookie tray.
In a bowl, mix together the flour and sugar. Lightly work in the butter, using the fingertips, until the mixture begins to stick together. Turn the mixture into the foil pan and press it into an even layer, using a small spatula. Scatter the currants over the top and arrange the cherries on top. For the topping, cream the butter and sugar together until light and fluffy. Add the egg and beat thoroughly. Stir in the ground almonds and 1–2 drops almond

extract. Spread mixture carefully over the fruit layer and bake in a fairly hot oven (375°F.) for about 40 minutes or until just set and golden brown.
Loosen the edges, turn out and cool on a wire rack. Dredge with confectioners' sugar, cut into bars.

## MADEIRA CAKE

¾ cup butter
¾ cup sugar
3 large eggs
1¼ cups self-rising flour
1 cup all-purpose flour
Juice and grated rind of ½ lemon
Citron peel

Grease an 8-in. round cake pan. Cream together the butter and sugar until light and fluffy. Add the eggs, one at a time, beating well after each addition.
Sift the flours and fold in alternately with the lemon juice and rind. Turn the mixture into pan. Top with a few slices of thinly cut citron peel. Bake in a warm oven (325°F.) for 1 hour and 10 minutes.
Cool for a few minutes in the pan, then turn out on a wire rack.

## UNCOOKED CHOCOLATE CAKE

1½ cups coarse vanilla cookie crumbs
¼ cup chopped walnuts or seedless raisins
7 tablespoons butter or margarine
2 tablespoons sugar
½ cup light corn syrup
½ cup cocoa, sifted

*For icing:*
2 squares unsweetened chocolate
1 tablespoon hot water
½ cup confectioners' sugar
Lump of butter

Place an 8-in. flan ring on a flat serving platter or use an 8-in. lightly greased cake pan.
Combine the cookie crumbs with walnuts or raisins. Cream together the butter, sugar and syrup. Beat in the cocoa and work in the cookie crumb mixture. When the ingredients are well mixed, press evenly into the flan ring or cake pan. Leave in the refrigerator overnight.
The next day, put the icing ingredients in a small saucepan and stir together over very low heat until the chocolate has melted and is of a coating consistency. Remove the flan ring from the cake, spread the icing over the top and leave to set.

*Devil's food cake*

# CAKE DECORATING

Many of the nicest cakes are also the simplest to make, but they often require a little filling or decoration with a simple icing to turn them into something special. A sponge or Victoria sandwich would be nothing without its touch of glacé icing, preserves filling or butter cream. None of these is a specialist decoration, anyone can make an attractive finish with a very little practice, and even beginners' mistakes are not too expensive!

Icings are not merely decoration, of course. They add moisture and a contrast of texture and flavor to the cake itself. So ring the changes and add to your repertoire. There is very little special equipment you need. For piped decorations you will want a pastry bag and a few nozzles, but even if you don't possess a piping set, that needn't deter you. Butter cream, glacé icing and fondant icing can all be poured over the top of the cake or spread on with a spatula. There are just a few simple rules to follow in order to achieve a perfect result.

First, allow the cake to cool thoroughly before you start. While it is cooling, prepare any decorations you plan to use – chop walnuts, cut glacé cherries or angelica into small pieces, grate chocolate, cut up crystallized fruit, etc. When you are ready to start, brush any crumbs off the top of the cake. If you are planning to ice the top, it must be level, so if necessary level the top, turn the cake over and use the flat underside. Most cakes can be left on the wire cooling rack while you are icing, but a soft sponge should be placed on a flat plate, as moving it would crack a soft icing. Do the filling first, then decorate the sides and finally the top.

If you are going to pipe some icing on to the cake, you may find the large fabric pastry bags are rather large for icing nozzles – so here's how to make your own paper icing bag.

Fold a 10 in. square of waxed paper in half to form a triangle and then roll it up along the longest edge, so that it looks like an ice cream cone. Snip off the tip of the bag, drop in the icing nozzle (preferably one without a screw band) and fill with the required amount of icing. Be careful to avoid overfilling. Fold the top flap down, enclosing the front edge until the bag is sealed and quite firm.

To decorate the sides of a cake with preserves, coconut, nuts and so on, first brush apricot glaze around the sides of the prepared cake, or spread it on with a spatula. Either put the chosen decoration on waxed paper and, holding the cake carefully on its side, roll it through the decoration, or press the nuts etc. a little at a time on to the cake with a spatula. Continue until the sides are evenly and completely coated. Do this before icing the top.

## BUTTER CREAM OR ICING
*This amount will coat the sides and top of an 8 in. cake or give a topping and a filling.*

½ cup butter
1½–1¾ cups confectioners' sugar, sifted
Few drops of vanilla extract or other flavoring
1–2½ tablespoons milk

Cream the butter until soft and gradually beat in the sugar, adding a few drops of vanilla and the milk.

**As a filling** Spread the butter cream evenly over the lower half of the cake with a spatula, taking it right to the edges, then put the top half of the cake neatly in place.

**As a side covering** Spread the butter cream evenly around the sides of the cake, using a spatula and making sure all the cake is coated. Then, using a spatula, pat chopped nuts or chocolate vermicelli on to the sides.

*Many attractive decorations can be made using only a spatula*

**As a topping** Pile the butter cream on top of the cake and spread it out smoothly and evenly to the edges until it completely covers the surface. To give a more interesting effect, the surface of the butter cream can be patterned by using a fork or knife before being decorated with crystallized fruits, nuts, glacé cherries, chocolate morsels, or extra butter cream piped in whirls, etc.

### ALMOND BUTTER CREAM
Substitute almond extract for vanilla and add 2½ tablespoons very finely chopped toasted almonds; mix well. This is not suitable for piping.

### APRICOT BUTTER CREAM
Omit the vanilla extract and milk. Add 3¾ tablespoons sieved apricot preserves and a squeeze of lemon juice.

### BUTTERSCOTCH BUTTER CREAM
Omit the vanilla extract. Melt 1¼ tablespoons light brown sugar and 2 tablespoons butter together and heat for a few minutes. Cool slightly and beat well into the basic butter cream.

### CHOCOLATE BUTTER CREAM
Add either ¼ cup melted but not hot chocolate or chocolate morsels, or 1 tablespoon cocoa blended to a paste with a little hot water.

### COFFEE BUTTER CREAM
Omit the vanilla extract and flavor instead with 2 tablespoons instant coffee powder or 1¼ tablespoons coffee extract.

### COFFEE AND WALNUT BUTTER CREAM
Omit the vanilla extract. Add 1–2 teaspoons coffee extract and 1 tablespoon chopped walnuts. This is not suitable for piping as the nuts will block the nozzle.

### GINGER BUTTER CREAM
Omit the vanilla extract. Add 3 ounces preserved ginger, very finely chopped. This is not suitable for piping.

### LIQUEUR BUTTER CREAM
Omit the vanilla extract and milk. Add 1–2 teaspoons liqueur, and coloring according to the flavor of the liqueur.

### MOCHA BUTTER CREAM
Omit vanilla extract and milk.

Blend 1 teaspoon cocoa and 2 teaspoons instant coffee powder with a little warm water; cool before adding to the mixture.

### ORANGE BUTTER CREAM
Omit vanilla extract and milk. Beat in 2½ tablespoons orange juice, the grated rind of 1 orange and 1 tablespoon Angostura bitters.

### RASPBERRY BUTTER CREAM
Omit the milk. Beat in 2½ tablespoons raspberry purée or sieved preserves.

### WALNUT BUTTER CREAM
Add 2–3 tablespoons , very finely chopped walnuts. This is not suitable for piping.

### CREAM CHEESE FROSTING
*Makes 1½ cups*

1 package (3 ounces) cream cheese
1 tablespoon warm water
1 teaspoon vanilla extract
3 cups sifted confectioners' sugar

Mash cream cheese until softened. Add water and vanilla. Gradually add sugar, beating until smooth and of good spreading consistency.

### GLACE ICING
*This amount is sufficient to cover the top of an 8 in. cake or 18 small buns. If the sides are also to be iced, make twice the amount.*

⅞ cup confectioners' sugar, sifted
1–2½ tablespoons warm water
Coloring and flavoring (see below)

Put the confectioners' sugar in a bowl and gradually add the warm water. The icing should be thick enough to coat the back of a spoon quite thickly. Add a few drops of coloring or flavoring as required and use immediately. For icing of a finer texture, put the sugar, water and flavoring into a small pan and heat, stirring, until the mixture is warm – don't make it too hot. The icing should coat the back of a wooden spoon and look smooth and glossy.
If the sides of the cake are to be decorated, other than with glacé icing, do this before icing the top. To coat the whole cake, place the filled or plain cake on a wire rack over a large sheet of waxed paper. Pour the icing evenly from the

*Feather icing–simple but pretty*

bowl on to the center of the cake and allow to run down the sides, guiding the flow with a spatula. Keep a little icing in reserve in the bowl to fill any gaps.
If only the top of the cake is to be coated, pour the icing on to the center of the cake and spread it, using a spatula and stopping just inside the actual edge to prevent the icing dripping down the sides. Decorate with cherries, angelica and so on and leave to set, or leave the plain icing to set and add piped decoration later.
**Added decorations** Put these in place quickly before the icing sets – this holds them firmly and prevents the icing from cracking, as it would do if they were added later. Allow the icing to set firmly before attempting to do any piped decoration.
**Small cakes** These can be iced either by pouring the icing over them as above, or by holding them lightly in the fingers and

dipping them into it.
*Note:* Glacé icing should not be runny, but should coat the back of a spoon quite thickly.

### CHOCOLATE GLACE ICING
Dissolve 2 teaspoons cocoa in the measured water.

### COFFEE GLACE ICING
Blend 1 teaspoon coffee extract or 2 teaspoons instant coffee in a little water.

### LEMON GLACE ICING
Substitute 1–2½ tablespoons strained lemon juice for the water.

### LIQUEUR GLACE ICING
Replace 2–3 teaspoons of the water by the required liqueur.

### MOCHA GLACE ICING
Add 1 teaspoon cocoa and 2 teaspoons instant coffee to a little water.

*Butter cream and walnuts turn a plain cake into a glorious gâteau*

## FEATHER ICING

Before you start, make up a small amount of icing in a contrasting color (e.g. chocolate on plain or lemon glacé icing); it should be of a slightly thicker consistency than the basic icing. Ice the cake with glacé icing in the usual way. Immediately, while the original icing is still wet, using a writing nozzle or a paper piping bag with the tip cut off, pipe parallel lines ½–¾ in. apart across the cake. Quickly draw a skewer or the sharp point of a knife through the icing at right angles to the piping, in alternate directions. Wipe the point after drawing each line.

## FONDANT ICING

*Makes sufficient icing to give a thick coating to an 8 in. cake.*

**⅝ cup water**
**2 cups sugar**
**Good pinch of cream of tartar**

Choose a strong, heavy pan large enough to avoid the syrup boiling over. Put the water into the pan, add the sugar and let it dissolve slowly without stirring. When the sugar has dissolved, bring the syrup to a boil. Add the cream of tartar and boil to 240°F. Pour into a heat-resistant bowl and leave to cool until a skin forms on top. Beat the icing until it thickens, then work the fondant with a knife and finally knead with the hands until it is smooth. Coloring and/or flavoring (e.g. lemon, coffee, chocolate) may be worked in at this stage. The icing may now be used at once, or stored.

**To use** Place the icing in a bowl over hot water and heat until it is the consistency of heavy cream (don't over-heat or the texture will be spoilt). If necessary, dilute with sugar syrup or water.

**To ice small cakes or pastries** Spear them on a fork or skewer and dip them in the fondant.

**To ice a large cake** Put the cake on a wire rack with a plate below and pour the icing quickly all over the cake. Don't touch the icing with a knife, or the gloss finish will be spoilt. Add any decoration and leave the icing to set.

**To give a thick topping** Pin a band of double waxed paper closely around the cake so that it comes 1 in. above the top. Prepare the fondant from 1 cup sugar and the thinning syrup from ½ cup sugar. Pour the fondant over the top of the cake. When the icing has set, ease off the paper collar, using the back of a knife

*Marzipan shapes like these teddy bears are favorites with children*

blade dipped frequently in hot water. This method can also be used with glacé icing.

*Note:* Cakes to be coated with fondant icing should first be coated completely with apricot glaze and then covered with almond paste.

## APRICOT GLAZE

Place ½ pound apricot preserves and 2 tablespoons water in a saucepan over a low heat and stir until the preserves soften. Sieve the mixture, return it to the pan, bring it to a boil and boil gently until the glaze is of a suitable coating consistency. This glaze can be potted, as for preserves, and kept for future use.

## ALMOND PASTE

**(Marzipan)**
*Makes 1 pound*

**⅞ cup confectioners' sugar, sifted**
**½ cup sugar**
**2 cups ground almonds**
**1 teaspoon lemon juice**
**Almond extract**
**Beaten egg**

Blend together the sugars and ground almonds, add the lemon juice, a few drops of almond extract and enough beaten egg to stick the mixture together to give a firm but manageable dough. Turn it out on to a sugared board and knead lightly until smooth. Almond paste can be used to make many simple yet attractive decorations for a cake. There are two basic methods to achieve this.

**1** For flat decorations, roll out the paste on a sugared board and cut out the required shapes. This can be done either with a pastry cutter, if this will give the shape you want; or with a sharp knife drawn carefully round a pattern of stiff card. Don't choose anything too complicated to begin with – stars, candles, engines or boats all have straight sides and clear, simple outlines.

**2** For animal figures, roll the paste in the hands to form small balls or sausage shapes and use these to make up the animal. It is a good idea to draw the figure first to give you an idea of the proportions. Make the body first, then stick on the arms, head, legs, etc. Paint on a face with food coloring, using a very fine brush. Simple shapes to start with are cats, teddy bears, Santa Claus (colored red where appropriate) and snails (made from one long 'sausage' wound round and round).

To give more variety, almond paste may be colored if wished – Santa Claus, as we've already suggested, can be a nice bright red, and holly or ivy leaves to decorate a Christmas cake could be a good, strong green. But be careful to color only as much paste as you need, or the rest will be wasted.

As you gain more confidence, you will find the ideas are almost inexhaustible. Almond paste shapes and figures are particularly good for children's party cakes – a clown, rocket ships, a 'magic roundabout', trains and houses can all be made from a basic cake shape and imaginative use of almond paste. Color some paste with a very little molasses or

caramel coloring and cut out witches and broom sticks for a Hallowe'en cake.

Leaves – particularly good for decorating a Christmas cake – can be made by drawing round a real leaf on to a piece of white card and using that as a pattern for cutting the shape from the almond paste. Draw in the veins with the point of a skewer and leave the paste to dry lying over a piece of crumpled foil, to give it a natural curve. To make holly leaves, cut strips of thinly rolled green almond paste, ½ in. wide and 1–1¾ in. long. Using a tiny round cutter (the reverse end of a piping nozzle may be suitable), cut curves out of the sides to make the holly leaf shape. And, of course, almond paste is the traditional decoration for an Easter-time simnel cake. You can make miniature colored Easter eggs for the top of the cake and cut out little chick shapes to go around the edge.

## AMERICAN FROSTING

*Makes sufficient frosting for an 8 in. cake. This is the traditional finish for a walnut cake.*

**1 cup sugar**
**5 tablespoons water**
**1 egg white**

Gently heat the sugar in the water, stirring until dissolved. Then, without stirring, heat to 240°F. Beat the egg white stiffly in a deep bowl. Remove the sugar syrup from the heat and when the bubbles subside, pour it on to the egg white, beating continuously. When the mixture thickens, is almost cold and starts to look opaque, pour it quickly over the cake. With a spatula, quickly swirl the frosting into peaks. Add any required decorations.

*Note:* To make this frosting properly, it is necessary to use a sugar-boiling thermometer.

## CARAMEL FROSTING

Substitute brown sugar for the white sugar.

## COFFEE FROSTING

Add 1 teaspoon coffee extract to the mixture while beating.

## LEMON FROSTING

Add a little lemon juice while beating the mixture.

## ORANGE FROSTING

Add a few drops of orange extract and a little orange coloring to the mixture while it is being beaten.

# MORE ADVANCED CAKE DECORATING

*Most rich fruit cakes for celebration occasions are decorated with almond paste and royal icing. Royal icing is not so easy to handle as glacé or fondant, but the results can be so delightful that it is well worth a little practice. It makes economic sense too, since most confectioners charge quite highly to ice even a birthday cake. Practise on family birthday cakes, before you tackle something for a big party; or try out one or two designs on paper (it's cheaper than cake!).*

## QUANTITIES OF ICINGS FOR A FORMAL CAKE

| Cake size | | Almond Paste | Royal Icing |
|---|---|---|---|
| | 6in. ● | ¾ pound | 1 pound |
| 6in. ■ | 7in. ● | 1 pound | 1¼ pound |
| 7in. ■ | 8in. ● | 1¼ pound | 1½ pound |
| 8in. ■ | 9in. ● | 1¾ pound | 2 pound |
| 9in. ■ | 10in. ● | 2 pound | 2¼ pound |
| 10in. ■ | 11in. ● | 2¼ pound | 2¾ pound |
| 11in. ■ | 12in. ● | 2½ pound | 3 pound |
| 12in. ■ | 13in. ● | 3 pound | 3½ pound |

## ALMOND PASTE

Make up a quantity of paste, according to the size of your cake. With a piece of string, measure round the outside of the cake. Take two-thirds of the almond paste and roll it out on a surface dredged with confectioners' sugar to a rectangle half the length of the string and in width twice the depth of the cake. Trim with a knife and cut in half lengthwise. Knead the trimmings into the remaining paste and roll out to fit the top of the cake. Check at this stage that the surface of the cake is absolutely level.

Brush the sides of the cake with apricot glaze. Put the 2 strips of almond paste round the cake and smooth the joins with a spatula, keeping the top and bottom edges square. Brush the top with apricot glaze, place the rolled-out top paste in position and roll lightly with a sugar-dusted rolling pin. Make sure the joins adhere well. Run a straight-sided preserves jar round the edge to smooth the paste and stick it firmly to the

*Break up a spray of artificial flowers to make a delicate decoration*

cake. Leave the almond paste for a week before icing, loosely covered.

## ROYAL ICING

**4 egg whites**
**7 cups confectioners' sugar, sifted**
**1¼ tablespoons lemon juice**
**2 teaspoons glycerin**

Whisk the egg whites until slightly frothy. Stir in the sugar a spoonful at a time with a wooden spoon. When half the sugar is incorporated, add the lemon juice. Continue adding more sugar, beating well after each addition until you reach the right consistency.

It is this initial beating that gives it a light texture; skip it and the result will be disappointing, often heavy and difficult to use. The mixture is right for coating if it forms soft peaks when pulled up with a wooden spoon; it should be a little stiffer for piping and thinner for flooding.

Lastly stir in the glycerin, which prevents the icing becoming too hard. If you use an electric mixer, take care not to overbeat. If royal icing becomes too fluffy, it gives a rough surface and breaks when piped. It helps to allow it to stand for 24 hours in a covered container before using. Gently beat by hand and if necessary adjust the consistency before using.

## EQUIPMENT

Before starting to decorate with icing you will need the following equipment:

1. A turntable – this enables you to get a smooth finish all over and

around the sides of the cake. It is possible to work without a turntable, using an upturned bowl instead, but it makes it much more difficult to obtain a good finish.

2. An icing ruler, or a long, straight bladed knife longer than the diameter of the cake – this is for flat icing.

3. An icing nail or a cork fixed to a skewer. This serves the same function as a turntable, in miniature, for piping flowers and other small designs.

4. Plain writing nozzles in 3 sizes, to make lines, dots or words.

5. Star nozzles for rosettes, zig-zags and ropes.

6. Shell nozzles.

7. Petal and leaf nozzles.

8. A pastry bag. Preferably make one yourself from waxed paper and use with icing nozzles without a screw band. If you use a fabric bag, attach a screw adjustment and use nozzles with a screw band.

## FLAT ICING

To ice the cake, place it on a silver cake board 2–3 in. larger than the cake. With the cake and board on a turntable, spoon on an ample quantity of icing and use a spatula to work it evenly over the top, using a paddling motion to remove any air bubbles. Roughly level the surface.

Draw an icing ruler (or a knife longer than the width of the cake) steadily across the cake top at an angle of 30° to smooth the surface. Be careful not to press too heavily. Neaten the edges, removing surplus icing by holding the

knife parallel with the side of the cake. Leave to dry for about 24 hours.

Cover the sides the same way, still using a paddling motion. Hold a small spatula or plain-edged icing comb in one hand to the side of the cake and at a slight angle towards it. Pass the other hand under and round the turntable so that a little more than a complete revolution can be made. Keeping the knife quite still in one hand, revolve the turntable with the other, smoothly and fairly quickly. Towards the end, draw the knife or comb away without leaving a mark. Remove any surplus from the edge with a knife. If you prefer, ice the sides before the top.

To achieve a really professional looking finish (and this is a must with a tiered wedding cake), give the cake a second coating with slightly thinner icing, about 2 days after the first. Trim off any rough edges from the first coat with a sharp knife or fine clean sandpaper and brush off the loose icing before starting the second coat.

## PIPING TECHNIQUES

**When using a pastry bag,** avoid overfilling. Small sized bags are easier to handle especially when using a writing nozzle – it is much better to refill frequently. Insert the appropriate nozzle in the end of the bag, spoon the icing in and fold the top flap down, enclosing the front edge, until the bag is sealed and quite firm. Hold the bag in one hand with the thumb on top, the first finger resting down on the side of the bag and the second finger curved underneath. Use your other hand to steady the bag while piping.

**To pipe lines** use a writing nozzle. Make contact with the surface of the iced cake and squeeze out just enough icing to stick to the surface. Continue squeezing and at the same time raise the bag and pull towards you; hold the bag at an angle of about 45°. Lift the nozzle and the line of piped icing from the surface to keep a sagging line. The icing can then be guided and lowered into the required design.

**To pipe stars and scrolls** use a star nozzle. For stars, hold the nozzle almost upright to the flat iced surface, pipe out a blob of icing and withdraw nozzle with a quick up and down movement.

*Piping random lacework to fill in the scallops*

For scrolls, hold the bag at an angle, as for a straight line. With the nozzle almost on the iced surface, pipe out a good head and then gradually release the pressure on the bag. Pull away with a double or single curve; the whole operation is one movement.

**Trellis** work can be very effective. Use a writing nozzle to pipe parallel lines across the space to be covered; when these are dry pipe more lines on top of them in the opposite direction. For a really good finish, pipe a third layer, using a very fine nozzle. If any 'tails' are left at the ends of lines, trim them off while still soft.

**Flowers and leaves** Leaves are piped with a special leaf nozzle directly on to the surface of the cake. Flowers are made up in advance on paper and fixed to the cake after they have dried out. Stick a 2 in. square of non-stick paper to an icing nail with a small blob of icing (or to a cork fixed to a skewer). Work on this surface and leave the flowers to dry on the paper. When dry, peel away the paper and fix the flowers to the cake with a small blob of icing.

**'Run out' designs** may either be piped directly on to the cake and flooded, or on to non-stick paper and fixed on the cake when dry. For separate 'run outs', draw out the design first on card, quite clearly. Cut a piece of non-stick paper to cover it and fix it with a spot of icing at each corner. Trace the outline of the design with a medium-fine writing nozzle; thin the icing to a 'just-flowing' consistency with unbeaten egg white and pour it into a small paper pastry bag. Cut the top off the bag and flood the icing into the outline; if it is the correct consistency it will run smoothly into place. Leave flat for several days before peeling off the paper.

To pipe a 'run-out' directly on to the cake, prick the design out first with a fine pin and work as above.

## TO DECORATE OUR WEDDING CAKE

Before starting any piping, place the pillars in position and prick round them with a pin. This will ensure that there is still room for them when everything else is done!

## SCALLOPS

For each cake in turn, cut a circle of waxed paper the diameter of the cake. Fold the large one into 8, the middle one into 8 and the small one into 6, then for each cake proceed as follows.

Either free-hand or with compasses mark in the scallops (about 1 in. deep at the widest point) between the folds in the paper. Place the paper on the cake and secure with pins. Prick the outline of the scallops on to the flat iced surface. Remove and, using the prick marks as a guide, pipe the scallops in with a No. 2 writing nozzle. Pipe a second scallop ¼ in. outside the first, using a No. 3 writing nozzle, and a third line using the No. 2 nozzle again.

To make the scallops on the side of the cake, measure the depth of the cake and cut a band of waxed paper to size. Place it around the cake and secure with a pin at a point where one of the top scallops comes to the edge of the cake. Mark the points of the scallops right around the cake, remove the paper and draw in the scallops as for the top. At the same time draw corresponding scallops ½ in. deep at the base. Secure the paper around the cake and prick out the design. Tilt the cake slightly and rest it on a firmly wedged, shallow pan, so that you can work on the sides. A damp cloth under the pan helps to prevent movement. Pipe in the scallops round the top and base, as for the flat surface.

## LACE

Fill in the scallops –top, sides and base – with 'lace'. This is done with a No. 2 writing nozzle, almost resting on the surface. Pipe a wriggly line with no obvious set pattern, but keep it looking neat.

## FLOWERS

The easiest flowers to pipe are daisies. Fix a square of paper to an icing nail or cork and use a medium petal nozzle. Pipe one petal at a time by squeezing out a small amount of icing, withdrawing the nozzle with a quick down and up movement. Pipe 5 petals, almost touching in the center. Fill in the center of each daisy either with a silver ball or with a small dot or several tiny dots from a No. 2 nozzle.

## FERN SHAPED LINES

The fern shaped lines have to be piped on the side of the cake freehand. Tilt the cake as for the scallops and pipe the lines ¼ in. from the side scallop, using a No. 3 nozzle. Repeat with a No. 2 nozzle ¼ in. below the first line. The vertical line is done with a No. 2 nozzle. Finish with a bold dot from a No. 3 nozzle at the apex of the lines. This pattern may be piped as a fine line or as a series of small dots, which are easier to control.

## FINISHING

Neaten the base of each cake with a series of dots in the angle between the cake and the board; for the large cake using a No. 3 nozzle, for the smaller cakes a No. 2 nozzle. Where the scallops meet at the base, bring a line of 3 dots up the side of the cake, with a No. 2 nozzle, using varying degrees of pressure to obtain different sizes. Position the pillars within the guide lines previously pricked out. Check that they are level, to ensure that the tiers stand level when positioned. Ideally use a spirit level for this. Fix each pillar in position with icing, using a little extra if the height needs adjusting at all. Ensure that none of the icing creeps out from under the base of the pillars. Allow to dry.

Mount the tiers carefully on the pillars to make sure that everything fits together properly, and decide on the decoration for the top. Then dismantle the cake again and keep the tiers separately until the day.

*Making daisies separately to be fixed on the cake later*

# BREAD MAKING AT HOME

For centuries bread has been a symbol of all that is good in life. Even today, when commercially baked bread is so readily available, there is something peculiarly satisfying about baking your own. Perhaps it is the special flavor and smell of bread that has just come out of the oven, perhaps it is working with live yeast that causes it – either way it is a joy not to be missed.

There is nothing unduly difficult about yeast cookery, provided you realize that yeast, unlike other rising agents, is a living plant, requiring gentle warmth in order to grow. Like any other plant, yeast also requires food and water; it obtains these from the flour itself and from the moisture used in mixing the dough. Given these conditions, yeast grows rapidly and as it grows carbon dioxide is formed. The bubbles of this gas are responsible for the spongy texture of the bread. The growing yeast also gives the characteristic smell of bread. Not all breads use yeast as the rising agent; baking powder and baking soda are also used. Breads made with these rising agents, except for soda bread, are usually slightly sweetened and are used as tea breads rather than as general purpose breads.

### YEAST
Dried yeast can be stored for up to 6 months if kept in a tightly sealed container. It comes in the form of small, hard, light brown granules and instructions for activating it are usually given on the package.

Compressed yeast looks rather like putty and has a faint 'winey' smell. To keep it fresh, store it in the refrigerator; it can also be frozen, in which case it will keep for up to 6 months if tightly wrapped.

### FLOUR
For the best results when making a basic white bread, use 'strong' bread flour. This has a higher

*Home-made traditional breads – so satisfying*

gluten content than all-purpose flour, so it absorbs more water, giving a larger volume and a lighter texture. However, all-purpose flour works well.

## ONE BOWL WHITE BREAD
*Makes 2 loaves*

6–7 cups unsifted all-purpose flour
2 tablespoons sugar
1 tablespoon salt
2 packages active dry yeast
½ cup softened margarine
2 cups very hot tap water
Salad oil

In a large bowl, thoroughly mix 2 cups flour, the sugar, salt and active dry yeast. Add the margarine. Gradually add very hot tap water to dry ingredients and beat for 2 minutes at medium speed with an electric mixer, scraping the bowl occasionally. Add 1 cup flour or enough to make a thick batter. Beat at high speed for 2 minutes, scraping the bowl occasionally. Stir in enough additional flour to make a soft dough. Turn out on to a lightly floured board; knead until smooth and elastic, about 8–10 minutes. Cover with plastic wrap then a towel; let rest 20 minutes.

Punch dough down; divide in half on a lightly-floured board and shape into loaves. Place in 2 greased 8½ in. by 4½ in. by 2½ in. loaf pans. Brush with oil. Cover pans loosely with plastic wrap. Refrigerate 2–24 hours.

When ready to bake, uncover the dough and let stand 10 minutes at room temperature. Puncture any gas bubbles with a greased toothpick or metal skewer. Bake in a fairly hot oven (400°F.) for 30–40 minutes or until done. Remove from pans and cool on wire racks.

## SEEDED WHITE BREAD
*Makes a 10-in. ring*

5½–6½ cups unsifted all-purpose flour
3 tablespoons sugar
2 teaspoons salt
1 package active dry yeast
1½ cups water
½ cup milk
3 tablespoons margarine
1 egg white, beaten
1 tablespoon poppy seeds

In a large bowl, thoroughly mix 2 cups flour, the sugar, salt and active dry yeast. Combine the water, milk and margarine in a saucepan. Heat over a low heat until the liquids are warm. (Margarine does not need to melt.)

Gradually add to the dry ingredients and beat for 2 minutes at medium speed with an electric mixer, scraping the bowl occasionally. Add ¾ cup flour or enough to make a thick batter. Beat at high speed for 2 minutes, scraping the bowl occasionally. Stir in enough additional flour to make a soft dough. Turn out on to a lightly floured board and knead until smooth and elastic, about 8–10 minutes. Place in a greased bowl, turning to grease top. Cover and let rise in a warm place, free from draft, until doubled in bulk, about 1 hour.

Punch dough down and turn out onto a lightly floured board. Cover and let rest 15 minutes. Roll dough into a 16 in. by 9 in. rectangle. Roll up dough, starting from the 16 in. side, as for a jelly roll. Pinch seam to seal. Place the dough into a greased 10-in. tube pan, so that it fully covers the bottom of the pan. Cover and let rise in a warm place, free from draft, until doubled in bulk, about 1 hour.

Brush ring lightly with beaten egg white and sprinkle with poppy seeds. Bake in a fairly hot oven (400°F.) for about 40 minutes or until done. Remove from pan and cool on wire rack.

## AMERICANIZED SALLY LUNN
*Makes 2 small loaves*

3½ cups sifted all-purpose flour
1 package active dry yeast
½ cup milk
½ cup water
½ cup salad oil
¼ cup sugar
1 teaspoon salt
2 eggs

Measure 1½ cups flour into the large bowl of an electric mixer. Add the yeast and blend lightly. Combine the milk, water, oil, sugar and salt in a saucepan. Heat over a low heat until the mixture is just warm. Add to the dry ingredients and beat on low speed just until mixture is smooth. Add the eggs and beat until well blended. Turn to lowest speed and gradually add 1 cup flour. Beat until smooth. Scrape down beaters and bowl. Remove the bowl and stir in 1 cup flour with a spoon to make a soft dough. Spoon the batter into two well-greased 1–pound coffee cans. Cover with the plastic lids or plastic wrap and let stand in a warm place, free from draft. When the dough has risen almost to the top

*Sally Lunn is a traditional tea bread from Bath*

of the cans, remove the lids. Bake in a fairly hot oven (375°F.) for 30–35 minutes or until browned. Let cool about 10 minutes in cans before removing to wire racks.

## SALTED RYE BRAIDS
*Makes 2 braids*

**5 cups unsifted all-purpose flour**
**2 cups unsifted rye flour**
**1 tablespoon salt**
**1 tablespoon caraway seeds**
**2 packages active dry yeast**
**1 tablespoon soft margarine**
**2½ cups very hot tap water**
**Corn meal**
**1 egg white, beaten**
**1 tablespoon cold water**
**Caraway seeds**
**1 teaspoon coarse salt**

Combine the flours. In a large bowl, thoroughly mix 3 cups of the flour mixture, the salt, caraway seeds and active dry yeast. Add the margarine.

Gradually add very hot tap water to dry ingredients and beat for 2 minutes at medium speed with an electric mixer, scraping the bowl occasionally. Add ½ cup flour mixture or enough to make a thick batter. Beat at high speed for 2 minutes, scraping the bowl occasionally. Stir in enough additional flour mixture to make a soft dough. Turn out on to a lightly floured board and knead until smooth and elastic, about 8–10 minutes. Place in a greased bowl,

turning to grease top. Cover and let rise in a warm place, free from draft, until doubled in bulk, about 45 minutes.

Punch dough down; turn out on to a lightly floured board. Divide the dough in half; divide each half into 3 equal pieces. Roll each piece into a rope 18 in. long. Braid 3 ropes together. Seal ends and tuck underneath. Place on greased cookie tray which has been sprinkled with corn meal. Repeat with remaining ropes. Cover and let rise in a warm place, free from draft, until doubled in bulk, about 30 minutes. Bake in a very hot oven (450°F.) for 20 minutes. Remove braids from oven. Brush with combined beaten egg white and water. Sprinkle with caraway seeds and coarse salt. Return the braids to the oven; bake for 5 minutes longer. Remove from cookie trays and cool on wire racks.

## OLD FASHIONED WHOLE WHEAT LOAVES
*Makes 4 small loaves*

**4½ cups unsifted whole wheat flour**
**2¾ cups unsifted all-purpose flour**
**3 tablespoons sugar**
**4 teaspoons salt**
**2 packages active dry yeast**
**1½ cups water**
**¾ cup milk**
**⅓ cup molasses**
**⅓ cup margarine**

Combine the flours. In a large bowl, thoroughly mix 2½ cups of the flour mixture, the sugar, salt and active dry yeast.

Combine the water, milk, molasses and margarine in a saucepan. Heat over a low heat until the liquids are warm. (Margarine does not need to melt.) Gradually add to the dry ingredients and beat for 2 minutes at medium speed with an electric mixer, scraping the sides of the bowl occasionally. Add ½ cup of the flour mixture or enough to make a thick batter. Beat at high speed for 2 minutes, scraping the bowl occasionally. Stir in enough additional flour mixture to make a soft dough. (If necessary, add additional white flour to obtain desired dough.) Turn out on to a lightly floured board. Knead until smooth and elastic, about 8–10 minutes. Place in a greased bowl, turning to grease top. Cover and let rise in a warm place, free from draft, until doubled in bulk, about 1 hour.

Punch dough down; turn out on to a lightly floured board. Divide into four equal pieces. Form each piece into a round ball and place on a greased cookie tray. Cover and let rise in a warm place, free from draft, until doubled in bulk, about 1 hour. Bake in a fairly hot oven (400°F.) for about 25 minutes or until done. Remove from cookie trays and cook on wire racks.

## MAPLE PECAN RING
*Makes 2 coffee cakes*

**5½–6½ cups unsifted all-purpose flour**
**½ cup sugar**
**1½ teaspoons salt**
**2 packages active dry yeast**
**½ cup softened margarine**
**1½ cups very hot tap water**
**2 eggs, at room temperature**
**¾ cup chopped pecans**
**⅓ cup firmly packed brown sugar**
**1 teaspoon maple flavoring**
**Melted margarine**
**Salad oil**
**Confectioners' sugar frosting**

In a large bowl, thoroughly mix 2 cups flour, the sugar, salt and yeast. Add the margarine.

Gradually add very hot tap water to the dry ingredients and beat for 2 minutes at medium speed with an electric mixer, scraping the bowl occasionally. Add the eggs and ½ cup flour, or enough flour to make a thick batter. Beat at high speed for 2 minutes, scrap-

ing the bowl occasionally. Stir in enough additional flour to make a soft dough. Turn out on to a lightly floured board and knead until smooth and elastic, about 8–10 minutes. Cover with plastic wrap, then a towel and let rest 20 minutes.

Combine the pecans, brown sugar and maple flavoring. Punch the dough down and divide in half. On a lightly floured board, roll half the dough into a 16 in. by 8 in. rectangle. Brush with melted margarine. Sprinkle half the sugar mixture over dough. Roll up from the long side to form a 16 in. roll. Pinch the seam to seal. Place the sealed edge down in a circle on a greased cookie tray. Seal ends together firmly. Cut two-thirds into the ring with scissors at 1 in. intervals; turn each section on its side. Repeat with the remaining dough and sugar mixture.

Brush the rings with oil and cover loosely with plastic wrap. Refrigerate for 2–24 hours. When ready to bake, uncover the dough and let stand for 10 minutes at room temperature.

Bake in a fairly hot oven (375°F.) for about 20–25 minutes, or until done. Remove immediately from cookie trays and cool on wire racks. When cool, frost with confectioners' sugar frosting and sprinkle with additional pecans if desired.

## CHEESE BREAD
*Makes 2 loaves*

**7–8 cups unsifted all-purpose flour**
**⅓ cup sugar**
**1 tablespoon salt**
**2 packages active dry yeast**
**2 cups water**
**⅔ cup milk**
**3 cups grated sharp Cheddar cheese**
**Melted margarine**

In a large bowl, thoroughly mix 2½ cups flour, the sugar, salt and active dry yeast.

Combine the water and milk in a saucepan. Heat over a low heat until the liquids are very warm (120–130°F.). Gradually add to the dry ingredients and beat for 2 minutes at medium speed with an electric mixer, scraping the bowl occasionally. Add the cheese and ½ cup flour. Beat at high speed for 2 minutes, scraping the bowl occasionally. Stir in enough additional flour to make a stiff dough. Turn out on to a lightly floured board and knead until smooth and elastic, about 8–10 minutes. Place in a greased bowl, turning to grease top. Cover and let rise in a warm place, free from draft, until doubled in bulk, about 1 hour. Punch dough down; turn out on to a board. Cover and let rest 15 minutes.

Divide the dough in half. Roll each half to a 14 in. by 9 in. rectangle. Beginning with upper short side, roll dough towards you, like a jelly roll. Seal with thumbs or heel of hand. Seal ends and fold under. Place seam side down in 2 greased 9 in. by 5 in. by 3 in. loaf pans. Cover and let rise in a warm place, free from draft, until doubled in bulk, about 1 hour.

Bake on lowest rack position in a fairly hot oven (375°F.) for about 40 minutes, or until done. Remove from pans and cool on wire racks. Brush tops with melted margarine.

## CORN BUBBLE LOAF
*Makes 1 large loaf*

**5–6 cups unsifted all-purpose flour**
**2 tablespoons sugar**
**1 tablespoon salt**
**1 cup yellow corn meal**
**2 packages active dry yeast**
**1¾ cups milk**
**½ cup water**
**3 tablespoons margarine**
**Salad oil**
**Melted margarine**

In a large bowl, thoroughly mix 1¾ cups flour, the sugar, salt, corn meal and yeast.

Combine the milk, water and 3 tablespoons margarine in a saucepan. Heat over a low heat until the liquids are warm. (Margarine does not need to melt.) Gradually add to the dry ingredients and beat for 2 minutes at medium speed with an electric mixer, scraping the bowl occasionally. Stir in enough additional flour to make a soft dough. Turn out on to a lightly floured board and knead until smooth and elastic, about 8–10 minutes. Cover with plastic wrap, then a towel, and let rest for 20 minutes. Punch dough down, divide into 32 equal pieces and shape into balls on a lightly floured board. Arrange the balls in a greased 10-in. tube pan, making 2 layers. Brush the loaf with oil and cover loosely with plastic wrap. Refrigerate for 2–24 hours.

When ready to bake, uncover the dough and let stand 10 minutes at room temperature. Puncture any

*Teatime bakery looks as good as it tastes*

gas bubbles with a greased toothpick or metal skewer. Bake in a fairly hot oven (375°F.) for about 55–60 minutes or until done. Remove from the pan and cool on a wire rack. Brush with melted margarine.

## SWEET APPLE BREAD

**1¾–2½ cups unsifted all-purpose flour**
**½ cup sugar**
**½ teaspoon salt**
**1 package active dry yeast**
**¼ cup milk**
**¼ cup water**
**⅓ cup butter or margarine**
**2 eggs, at room temperature**

*Topping:*
**2 large apples, cored and sliced**
**⅔ cup sugar**
**½ cup all-purpose flour**
**2 teaspoons ground cinnamon**
**6 tablespoons butter or margarine**

In a small bowl, thoroughly mix 1 cup flour, ½ cup sugar, the salt and yeast. Combine the milk, water and butter in a saucepan. Heat over low heat until liquids are very warm (120–130°F.). (The butter does not need to melt.) Gradually add to the dry ingredients and beat for 2 minutes at medium speed with electric mixer, scraping the bowl occasionally. Add the eggs and ½ cup flour, or enough flour to make a thick dough. Beat at high speed for 2 minutes, scraping the bowl occasionally. Stir in enough additional flour to make a stiff batter. Spread evenly in a well-greased 9-in. square pan. Arrange the apple slices evenly over batter. Combine the sugar, flour, cinnamon and butter and mix until crumbly. Sprinkle over apples. Cover; let rise in a warm place, free from draft, until doubled in bulk, about 1 hour. Bake in a fairly hot oven (375°F.) for 35–40 minutes or until done. Cool for 10 minutes in pan, then remove to wire rack.

## CROISSANTS
*Makes 24*

**1 cup margarine, cut into pieces**
**1¼ cups milk**
**4 teaspoons sugar**
**1 teaspoon salt**
**3–4 cups unsifted all-purpose flour**
**⅓ cup cornstarch**
**⅓ cup warm water (105–115°F.)**
**1 package active dry yeast**
**¼ cup corn or peanut oil**
**1 egg, beaten**
**1 teaspoon water**

Place the margarine in a large bowl of ice water. Squeeze the margarine through fingers about 20 times. Remove and wipe off excess water. Divide into 3 equal portions. Wrap each in plastic wrap and chill while preparing dough.

Scald the milk; add the sugar and salt. Cool to lukewarm. Combine the flour and cornstarch; set aside. Measure the warm water into a large warm bowl. Sprinkle in the yeast and stir until dissolved. Add the lukewarm milk mixture, oil and enough flour mixture to make a soft dough. Turn out on to a lightly floured board, knead lightly until smooth and elastic, about 5 minutes. Place in a greased bowl, turning to grease top. Cover and let rise in a warm place, free from draft, until doubled in bulk, about 45 minutes. Punch dough down; turn out on to a lightly floured board. Roll into a 16 in. by 12 in. rectangle, long side towards you. Dot center third with one portion chilled margarine. Cover the margarine with right-hand third of dough. Fold the left-hand piece under the margarine section. Seal edges. Wrap in plastic wrap and chill for 30 minutes.

Place chilled dough on a lightly floured board with the margarine layer near top, long side toward you. Repeat the procedure of rolling, dotting with margarine, folding, sealing and chilling, with second portion of margarine, then with third.

Cut the chilled dough in half. On a lightly floured board roll and stretch each half to a 16-in. circle. Cut each into 12 pie-shaped wedges. Roll up each wedge, beginning at the wide end. Place on greased cookie trays with the points underneath. Curve to form crescents. Cover and let rise in a warm place, free from draft, until doubled in bulk, about 1 hour. Combine the egg and 1 teaspoon water. Brush mixture gently on rolls. Bake in a hot oven (425°F.) for about 15 minutes or until golden brown. Remove from cookie trays and cool on wire racks. Best served warm.

These rolls freeze beautifully.

Lobster is the most delicious of shellfish, and is popular even in parts of the world where it is comparatively commonplace. Lobster thermidor is a classic way of preparing it as a hot main dish for two.

When buying lobster, choose one that weighs heavy in proportion to its size. If you are buying a live one, make sure it is lively, too, as one that seems tired may have been around for a day or two and grown thin inside its shell. A good 2 pound lobster should yield about 12 ounces of meat.

The smaller, hen lobsters are the more tender and delicate and the coral, or spawn, from the hen is an extra delicacy. If you are making a dish such as lobster thermidor, which does not require the coral, save it for a sauce or soup the next day. (You could add it to the thermidor sauce, but the subtle flavor would be lost with the cheese.)

Most people buy lobsters ready boiled, but if you have a live one, wash it, place in cold salted water, bring slowly to a boil and boil fairly quickly for 15–25 minutes, according to size. When the water is brought slowly to a boil like this, the warmth penetrates the central nervous system gradually and the lobster apparently experiences no discomfort.

Do not overcook it as the meat tends to become hard and thready. An alternative method of killing a lobster for this dish, so that you don't cook it twice, is to pierce the brain with the sharp point of a knife. To do this, lay the lobster out flat on a wooden board, hard shell uppermost. Have the head toward your right hand and cover the tail with a cloth. Hold it behind the head and pierce through the little cross marking on the head—this is the brain and the lobster will be killed instantly.

*2 servings*

**A 2-pound lobster, cooked**
**¼ cup butter**
**1 small onion, finely chopped**
**¼ cup all-purpose flour**
**⅝ cup milk**
**¼ cup grated Cheddar cheese**
**1¼ tablespoons dry white wine**
**Pinch of paprika**
**Salt and pepper**
**Grated Parmesan cheese**
**Lettuce**
**Watercress**
**Lemon slices**

*Cut the cooked lobster down the center back, and open out*

*Crack the claws with a rolling pin and take out the meat*

Using a large, sharp-pointed knife, cut the lobster carefully down the center back; open out the two halves and remove the meat. Discard the intestine, which looks like a small vein running through the center of the tail, the stomach, which lies near the head, and the spongy gills, which are not edible. Clean the shells thoroughly and rub with oil to make them shiny. Twist the large and small claws from the shells. Using a rolling pin or other heavy object, crack the large claws and carefully remove all the meat.

Cut the lobster meat into pieces about ½ in. long (you may find it easier to cut the meat at an angle). Heat half the butter in a small skillet. Add the lobster and sauté gently, turning occasionally. Meanwhile, in a small pan heat the remaining butter. Add the

*Sauté the lobster and start to make the thermidor sauce*

onion and sauté until soft. Stir in the flour and cook over low heat for about 30 seconds. Remove from the heat and stir in the milk. Cook over medium heat, stirring constantly, until mixture comes to a boil. Simmer gently for about 2 minutes. Remove from the heat and stir in the cheese, wine and paprika. Season. Cook over low heat, stirring, for about 1 minute. Pour the cheese sauce over the hot lobster in the skillet. Cook over low heat for a few minutes. Remove from heat. Place the cleaned lobster shells on a broiler rack and fill them with the lobster

*Add grated cheese, wine, paprika and seasoning to the sauce*

*Pour the sauce over the lobster and cook over gentle heat*

*Fill the mixture into the shells, sprinkle with Parmesan and broil*

mixture. Sprinkle heavily with grated Parmesan cheese. Broil in a pre-heated broiling compartment, about 4 in. from the source of heat, until sauce is bubbling and cheese topping is golden brown. Place lobster halves on a platter on a bed of lettuce. Garnish with watercress and lemon.

*6–8 servings*

**3½–4 pound roasting chicken**
**1 onion, coarsely chopped**
**1 carrot, cut up**
**3 stalks parsley**
**1 bay leaf**
**6 peppercorns**
**½ pound pork sausage meat**
**½ pound lean pork, ground**
**2 shallots, chopped**
**Salt and pepper**
**5 tablespoons Madeira**
**¼ pound thickly sliced boiled
 ham**
**¼ pound thickly sliced tongue**
**⅛ pound pork fat**
**2 tablespoons pistachio nuts,
 blanched and peeled**
**6 pitted black olives**

*For finishing:*
**¼ cup butter**
**¼ cup flour**
**2 cups milk**
**Salt**
**White pepper**
**2 envelopes unflavored gelatin**
**Chicken stock**
**Cucumber, radishes and black
 olives for garnish**

94

Lay the chicken on a board, breast side up. Using a sharp boning knife, cut off the wings at the second joint and the legs at the first joint. Turn the chicken breast side down and make an incision down the center of the back. Keeping the knife close to the carcass and slightly flat to avoid damaging the meat, carefully work the meat off the rib cage – scrape far enough to expose both of the wing joints. Take hold of the severed end of 1 wing joint. Scrape the knife over the bone, backwards and for-

wards, working the meat away from the bone. Continue until both wing and socket are exposed. Sever all the ligaments and draw out the bone. Repeat for second wing.

Continue cutting the meat off the carcass until the leg and socket are reached. Cut the ligaments attaching the bone to the body and break the leg joint by twisting it firmly. Hold the exposed joint firmly in one hand and scrape away all the meat down to the broken leg joint. Working from the opposite end of the leg, ease

out the bone, scraping off the meat until the bone is completely exposed. Pull the leg bone free; repeat for the other leg. Continue working the meat cleanly off the body and breast, being careful not to break the skin. Lay the boned chicken, skin side down, on the board and turn the legs and wings inside out.

Place the chicken bones, giblets, onion, carrot, parsley, bay leaf and peppercorns in a large kettle. Add enough water to cover. Bring to a boil, reduce heat and simmer for about 1 hour to make a stock. Combine the sausage meat, pork, shallots, salt and pepper in a bowl. Blend in the Madeira. Cut the ham, tongue and pork fat into long strips about ¼ in. wide. Spread half the sausage mixture over the boned chicken. Cover the mixture with alternate strips of ham, tongue, pork fat, pistachio nuts and olives. Cover with remaining pork sausage mixture. Draw the sides of the chicken together and sew up, using a trussing needle and fine string.

Wrap the stuffed boned chicken in a double thickness of muslin and tie the ends to make a neat shape. Strain the chicken stock into a heavy Dutch oven or large heavy kettle. Place chicken in

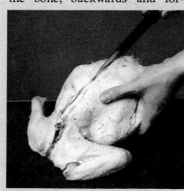

*Turn the chicken on its breast and
cut down the center back*

*Scrape the meat off the leg bone,
down to the broken joint*

stock. Cover tightly and simmer for about 2¼ hours. Remove chicken and reserve stock.

Place the chicken, still wrapped in muslin, on a plate. Cover with another plate and put a heavy weight on top. When almost cold, remove the muslin. When thoroughly cold remove the trussing string. Keep chicken cold while preparing the glazes.

Melt the butter in a small saucepan. Stir in the flour and cook over low heat for 1 minute. Remove from heat and stir in the milk. Cook over a medium heat, stirring constantly, until the mixture comes to a boil and is smooth and thick. Remove from heat and season to taste with salt and white pepper. Cover top of sauce with a piece of waxed paper and set aside to cool. Strain enough of the chicken stock to make 2 cups liquid. Soften 1 envelope gelatin in ½ cup of the stock. Heat the remaining stock and dissolve softened gelatin in it. Soften the remaining envelope of gelatin in 2 tablespoons cold water. Dissolve in ½ cup of the hot prepared gelatin stock. Stir the ½ cup double strength gelatin mixture into the cold white sauce. Put mixture through a strainer and beat thoroughly.

Place the chicken on a wire rack with a board or cookie tray underneath. When the white sauce is just on the point of setting, pour it carefully over the chicken to coat it thoroughly. Let stand until set. Decorate the top in desired pattern or design with cucumber, radishes and black olives. Carefully spoon the clear gelatin stock over top of garnish to cover completely. Put in a cool place until set.

*Work the meat cleanly off the carcass without breaking the skin*

*Flatten the chicken and arrange the stuffing ingredients on it*

*Sew up the chicken carefully, using a trussing needle*

*Coat the cooked chicken in a rich white sauce*

95

Creamy white chicken breasts, filled with rich garlic butter, coated in breadcrumbs and crisp fried in deep fat – chicken Kiev is another perfect choice for a special dinner for two, and relatively easy for four, as it can be kept hot for a short while. Warn your guests what is in the middle of the golden ball on their plates – if they attack it too ferociously the butter will spurt! As you want the breasts only of two chickens for this dish, why not use packaged chicken portions? Or if you prefer to use whole birds, save the legs for a delicious casserole for the family. Use freshly made breadcrumbs to give a real soft-and-crispy outside to the chicken. If you use ready-made crumbs (your own or bought) you will find that they brown long before the chicken is cooked and in the full cooking time will become unpleasantly brown and hard. For the best results, use a day-old sandwich loaf and either grate it or crumb in a blender.

# CHICKEN KIEV

A frying thermometer is essential for chicken Kiev, as the temperature of the oil is critical. If it is too hot, the outside will brown before the inside is cooked. If it is not hot enough, the oil will soak right through coating and chicken before the outside is brown, making it soggy and oily.

4 servings

**4 chicken breasts, about ½ pound each**
**½ cup butter**
**Grated rind of ½ a lemon**
**5 teaspoons lemon juice**
**Salt and pepper**
**1 large clove garlic**
**2½ tablespoons chopped parsley**
**¼ cup seasoned flour**
**4 eggs, beaten**
**6 cups fresh white breadcrumbs**
**Oil for deep fat frying**

If the chicken breasts are frozen, allow to thaw completely. Using a small sharp knife, carefully work the meat off the bone. Be careful

*Beat out the chicken breasts with a heavy cleaver*

not to split the chicken meat. Remove skin. Place each chicken breast between 2 sheets of waxed paper. Beat until very thin with the side of a cleaver or other heavy object. Refrigerate.

Soften the butter in a small bowl. Beat in the lemon rind. When well blended, slowly beat in the lemon juice. Season with salt and pepper and mix well. Crush the garlic clove, stir into the butter

*Cream the butter with lemon juice*

with the parsley and blend well. Put the butter on a piece of waxed paper and shape into a roll about 1 in. diameter. Wrap tightly and chill well in the refrigerator. When the butter is firm, divide it into 4 pieces. Place one piece in the center of each chicken breast. Fold the chicken tightly around the butter making sure that the butter is completely enclosed. Secure with toothpicks. Dip each piece in seasoned flour. Brush

*Coat well with egg and fresh white breadcrumbs*

*Fry the chicken Kiev 2 at a time in deep fat, and keep hot*

*Crush the garlic before adding it*

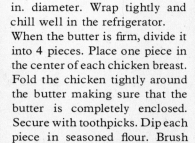

*Roll a portion of butter in each*

with beaten egg and cover with breadcrumbs. Repeat, making sure the entire piece of chicken is well covered. Refrigerate for 1–2 hours until thoroughly chilled. Put oil in a deep saucepan or deep fat fryer to a depth of about 3 in. or deep enough completely to cover the chicken. Heat the oil to 350°F. on a deep fat thermometer. Place 2 pieces of chicken in the

frying basket and lower into the oil. Fry for 12–15 minutes or until the chicken is golden brown. Remove from the fat and drain on paper toweling. Keep warm in a moderate oven (350°F.) while frying the remaining pieces of chicken. Remove toothpicks and serve immediately.

# Veal à la Crème Flambé

*This is a dinner party dish using a choice cut of veal. With a delicious creamy flavor, and a light hint of herbs, you'll find it a treat by any standard.*

*Serve it with a white Burgundy and your guests will remember your cooking with pleasure.*

*Just a hint before you start – you will need a really sharp knife to skin the veal neatly and economically; if you don't have one that you think will be up to the job, it is better to ask the butcher to do it for you.*

*6 servings*

**2 pound leg of veal, boned**
**¾ cup butter, divided into 3**
**1 onion**
**Bouquet garni**
**1 clove garlic, crushed**
**1¼ cups veal or chicken stock**
**1¼ cups white wine**
**Salt and pepper**
**½ pound button mushrooms**
**1 tablespoon lemon juice**
**½ pound tiny white onions**
**1 teaspoon sugar**
**6 tablespoons all-purpose flour**
**5 tablespoons heavy cream**
**3 tablespoons brandy**
**Watercress**

With a very sharp knife, remove the skin from the veal. Cut into 1 in. cubes.

Melt ¼ cup of the butter in a pan. Allow it to sizzle, then sauté the veal cubes quickly on all sides just long enough to seal. Sauté the meat in 2 batches, so that all of the meat in the pan can rest on

*Cut the skin and fatty tissue away from the meat*

*Fry the cubes of veal a few at a time to brown them all over*

the bottom. When it is sealed, remove and place in a casserole. Add the whole onion, bouquet garni and crushed garlic. Put the stock and wine in the pan that the meat was fried in and bring to a boil. Pour over the veal. Season well with salt and pepper. Cover casserole and cook in a warm oven (325°F.) for about 1 hour or until veal is tender.

While meat is cooking, wipe the mushrooms with damp paper towels, but do not peel. Using a small knife, 'turn' the mushrooms by removing tapering strips from the caps, all the way around: insert the blade of the knife into the top of the mushroom cap and draw the knife in a spiral, turning the mushrooms towards you until the knife rests horizontally.

Put the mushrooms in a small saucepan and cover with water. Add the lemon juice and 2 tablespoons butter. Cook over moderate heat until the water has evaporated. Keep warm.

Soak the onions in warm water for 5 minutes, remove skins. Place in a small saucepan. Cover

*Make a bouquet garni by tying the herbs in a piece of muslin*

*Pour boiling stock over the meat and seasoning in the casserole*

with water, add a pinch of salt, the sugar and 2 tablespoons butter. Simmer for 5 minutes. Raise the heat and boil rapidly to evaporate all the water. Watch carefully so that onions do not burn. Keep warm with the mushrooms.

When the veal is cooked, remove the bouquet garni and onion from casserole. Strain liquid from veal

*'Turn' the button mushrooms to make an attractive garnish*

*Button onions soaked in warm water are easy to peel*

into a saucepan. Keep veal warm. Reduce the liquid in the saucepan to 2 cups by boiling quickly over high heat. Cream together the flour and remaining ¼ cup butter to make a smooth paste. Beat the flour-butter mixture (beurre-manié) into the boiling liquid with a whisk. Simmer for about 5 minutes, stirring constantly. Remove from heat and stir a small amount of the sauce into the heavy cream. Return to the mixture in the saucepan. Heat very gently. Adjust the seasoning. Warm the brandy in a soup ladle or small pan. Ignite with a kitchen match and pour over the warm veal cubes. Add the sauce to the meat. Turn mixture into a heated serving platter. Add the mushrooms and onions and garnish with watercress.

*Add beurre manié a little at a time and beat into the liquid*

COLONIAL
GOOSE

*Colonial goose is a New Zealand classic, stemming presumably from a time when goose was hard to come by, but lamb was plentiful. The apricot and honey stuffing is delicious and the flavor of the meat itself is enhanced by marinating. Of course, you don't have to bone the meat yourself if you order it from the butcher in advance. If you do attempt it yourself, use a really sharp knife and keep the blade close to the bone. That way it is comparatively easy.*

*For the marinade, a plastic bag is not essential but it is a convenient way of keeping the wine and vegetables close to the meat so that the flavor penetrates thoroughly.*

*6–8 servings*

**4½ pound leg of lamb**

*For stuffing:*
**2 tablespoons butter**
**1 tablespoon honey**
**1 large onion, grated**
**2 cups fresh white breadcrumbs**
**¼ teaspoon dried thyme**
**1 egg, beaten**
**½ cup dried apricots**
**¼ teaspoon salt**
**Freshly ground black pepper**

*For marinade:*
**3 carrots, sliced**
**2 large onions, sliced**
**1 bay leaf**
**3 stalks parsley, coarsely chopped**
**1 cup dry red wine**

*Next, cut along the bone from the opposite end of the leg*

Place the leg of lamb on a wooden board. Using a small, sharp knife, work the meat away from the bone, from the top of the leg down to the first joint. Cut along the line of the bone from the opposite end of the leg, just enough to release the bone. Work the meat away from the bone, being careful not to puncture the skin in any other place. Sever the bone from all the meat and ligaments. Draw out the bone, working from the top of the leg.

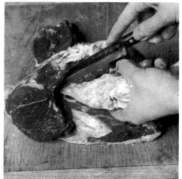

*Draw out the bone, carefully severing all the ligaments*

Put the butter and honey in a small saucepan. Melt over a low heat. Combine the melted butter-honey mixture with the onion, breadcrumbs, thyme and egg. Snip the apricots into small pieces with kitchen scissors. Add to breadcrumb mixture and toss well. Season with salt and pepper to taste. Add a small amount of hot water for a moist stuffing.

Wipe the lamb with a damp paper

*Apricots and honey make this stuffing pleasantly unusual*

towel. Trim off the excess fat from top of the leg. Spoon the stuffing mixture into the cavity from which bone was removed. Force the stuffing well down into the leg with the back of the spoon. Sew up with a trussing needle and fine string. Do not sew it too tightly or the skin may split while the meat is roasting.

Place the meat in a large plastic bag and place in a large deep bowl. Add the carrots, onions, bay

*Fill the lamb with as much stuffing as it will hold*

*Sew up the joint with a trussing needle, but not too tightly*

leaf, parsley and red wine. Secure the top of the bag and refrigerate for 6 hours, turning occasionally. Remove lamb from marinade and place on a rack in a roasting pan. Roast in a moderate oven (350°F.) for 25 minutes per pound. If meat becomes too brown, cover with foil. Remove lamb from oven and place on a serving platter. Remove the string and keep meat hot.

Pour off the fat from roasting pan. Stir a little flour into the juices. Cook, stirring, for a few minutes. Add 2–3 tablespoons of strained marinade and a little water. Season to taste. Bring to a boil, stirring, and simmer for about 2 minutes. Serve gravy separately.

*A large plastic bag helps when marinating the joint*

Tourne
Prove

These delicious steaks are served on slices of fried eggplant and accompanied by a rich sauce of tomatoes, onions and herbs. Serve them with creamed potato and sauté mushrooms.
Tournedos are thick slices of beef cut from the heart of the fillet and tied into rounds. In England they are lean, but in France the butchers make them up with a small piece of fat tied round each steak. We show you how to add the fat for this classic dish from southern France.
For a more economical recipe you could substitute noisettes of lamb, in which case there is no need to wrap the meat in fat.

*4 servings*

**⅓ pound pork fat in one piece**
**4 tournedos (beef fillet), cut 1½ in. thick**
**2 medium eggplants**
**Salt**
**1 pound ripe tomatoes**
**2 medium onions**
**3 tablespoons butter**
**Water**
**Bay leaf**
**¼ teaspoon dried basil**
**1 clove garlic**
**1 tablespoon salad oil**
**Freshly ground black pepper**
**Sauté mushrooms**
**Watercress**

Cut the pork fat into strips as wide as the tournedos are thick. Flatten each strip of fat by drawing the blade of a knife along each slice. Trim edges to make neat slices. Wrap a strip of fat around each steak and secure with string. Do not tie fat too tightly.
Cut the eggplant into 4 thick slices at an angle; each slice should be roughly the same diameter as the tournedos, so that each steak can just about cover each slice of eggplant. Place the eggplant in a single layer on a plate and sprinkle with salt. Cover tomatoes with boiling water and pour off at once. Cover with cold water. Slip skins from tomatoes, reserving skins. Cut the tomatoes in half and scoop out seeds. Combine the tomato seeds and skins and tie loosely in a double thickness of muslin or

*Peel the tomatoes and scoop out the seeds with a spoon*

*Cut strips of pork fat and flatten with a knife*

*Tie the tomato seeds and skin in muslin and add to the pan*

*Wrap a strip around each steak and tie with string*

cheesecloth. Cut the tomatoes in chunks and place in a saucepan with the cheesecloth bag. Cut the onions in thin slices and sauté in hot butter until tender but not browned. Pour into a saucepan with the tomatoes, about ¾ cup water, bay leaf and basil. Bring to a boil, reduce heat, cover and simmer for about 15 minutes or until reduced to a thick pulp. Season to taste and keep hot.
Skin the garlic. Cut off 1 end and push garlic on to the prongs of a fork. Rub the cut surface over a

heavy skillet. Pour in the oil and heat gently. Add the remaining butter and when it is almost brown, add the tournedos, using tongs. Cook over a medium heat about 14 minutes (see chart below) turning the meat half-way through cooking time. When the meat is turned, dry the eggplant slices on paper towels. Fry the eggplant on both sides in the same skillet for remaining time. Arrange eggplant on a hot platter, snip the string from each tournedos and place each steak on a slice of eggplant. Garnish with sauté mushrooms and watercress. Remove the muslin bag from stewed tomatoes, squeeze the bag to extract all the juice. Serve tomato sauce in a separate bowl.

*Cook the provençal sauce until it is thick and pulpy*

*Rub the frying pan with a cut clove of garlic*

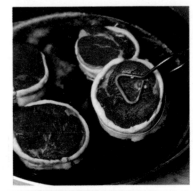
*Fry the steaks in oil and butter, handling them with tongs*

# FILET DE BOEUF EN CROUTE

This succulent, rich French way with fillet of beef is a delectable main course for a special occasion dinner party. The finest, tenderest cut of beef is coated with a rich pâté de foie and encased in crisp puff pastry. The contrasting textures and flavors will delight any palate. Be sure to choose your best Burgundy to go with it! When buying the beef for this dish it is essential to ask for the best quality. Ask the butcher to cut a 2 pound fillet about 8–9 in. long – this will be the right thickness for the cooking times given in this recipe. The pâté used must also be a good one – firm and fine textured. Beat it well with a wooden spoon to make it soft and easy to spread. We start by tying the fillet with string to keep its shape – fillet tends to shrink and curl when cooked

and this is the only way to keep it in a long narrow roll – so whatever you do, don't try to take short cuts. Filet de boeuf en croûte is at its best served piping hot straight from the oven. Make sure the vegetables match the standard of the meat – asparagus and broccoli are a suitable choice in season, and creamed potatoes offer a better contrast of texture with the pastry than roast. Any left-over beef will still be good served cold, with a tossed green salad and new potatoes.

*6 servings*

**2 pound fillet of beef**
**Salt and pepper**
**¼ cup butter**
**1 tablespoon salad oil**
**1 can (6–8 ounces) liver pâté**
**1 package (10 ounces) frozen patty shells, defrosted**
**1 egg, beaten**
**Watercress**
**Tomato**

Place the meat on a board. Trim off all excess fat and sinewy parts with a sharp knife. Sprinkle meat

*Brown the fillet in hot oil and butter to seal*

*Soften the pâté and spread it all over the meat*

with salt and pepper.
Tie fine string around the meat at intervals to form it into a neat shape 8–9 in. long. Carry the string around the ends and across to the other side as for a parcel. Tie firmly.
Heat half the butter with the oil in a heavy skillet. Brown the meat on all sides. Place the beef in a roasting pan and dot with the remaining butter. Roast in a hot oven (400°F.) for 10 minutes. Remove and let stand until cold. Cut off the string.
Place the pâté in a small bowl and beat until smooth. Season to taste. Spread the pâté over top and

*Brush the edge of the pastry with egg to help it seal*

sides of cooked fillet. Remove patty shells from box and place close together on a lightly floured

*Trim the ends at an angle and cut off close to the meat*

*Brush the trimmed ends with egg and fold diagonally across*

*Decorate the croûte with leaves cut from pastry trimmings*

surface. Press rounds together. Roll out into an oblong, about ⅛ in. thick, large enough to cover meat completely. Place the meat, pâté side down, in the center of the pastry. Spread the remaining pâté over top of meat. Brush one long side of the pastry with the beaten egg. Fold the unbrushed side over the meat, fold up the second side and press together. Trim the ends of the pastry at an

angle, cutting it straight off close to the meat. Reserve trimmings for decoration. Brush the upper surfaces of the trimmed ends with beaten egg and fold diagonally across the ends of the parcel. Roll out the pastry trimmings and cut into leaf shapes. Brush the top of

the roll with beaten egg, arrange the leaves down the center and brush with beaten egg.
Raise oven temperature to 425°F. Bake the meat for 40 minutes until the pastry is golden brown in color.
Serve on a heated platter with watercress and tomato.

# Crème Caramel

Rich and creamy, smooth and delicately flavored – that is our vanilla flavored custard. Topped with the burnt flavor of caramel it becomes the most delicious sweet ever, a favorite from nursery to adult dinner parties.

The recipe is basically simple, but it is not always easy to turn out successfully, so follow our step by step instructions and pictures for perfect results every time.

The traditional molds to use are individual custard cups, for which you can substitute tea cups so long as they will withstand the heat of the caramel (boiling sugar is much hotter than boiling water). Alternatively, you can make it in a single 1½-quart capacity mold (in this case, extend the cooking time to about 1 hour).

This is one of the best examples of the use of a bain marie for cooking;

it is vital that the custards should not get too hot in the oven or they will curdle, so a bain marie is used to ensure an even, low temperature.

Crème caramel is an ideal recipe for the busy hostess to prepare – it can be made well in advance and kept in a cool place.

8 servings

For caramel:
**2½ tablespoons cold water**
**⅝ cup sugar**
**3¾ tablespoons boiling water**

For custard:
**2½ cups milk**
**1 vanilla pod**
**4 large eggs**
**2 egg yolks**
**3 tablespoons sugar**

Pour the cold water into a small, thick-bottomed skillet. Stir in the sugar, using a wooden spoon. Place over a low heat to dissolve the sugar, stirring occasionally. When the sugar has dissolved, bring to a boil and boil without stirring until the sugar turns a dark, golden brown. Remove at

*Dissolve the sugar in the water, then bring to a boil*

*The caramel is ready when it is a rich, golden brown*

once from the heat and slowly spoon in the boiling water, stirring constantly. Lightly oil eight 6-ounce custard cups and divide the caramel syrup mixture evenly between them. Cool.

Combine the milk and vanilla pod in a saucepan and bring

*Strain the custard before pouring into the custard cups*

*Spoon a little caramel into each cup before filling with custard*

*Cook the crèmes caramels au bain marie to prevent them boiling*

*Ease the custard away from the custard cup with a knife*

milk. Rinse the pod, dry and store for further use. Pour the milk over the egg mixture and blend well. Strain the milk mixture into the custard cups. Place the custard cups in a large baking pan. Pour about ½ in. cold water into baking pan. Cover top with a sheet of aluminum foil.

Cook in the center of a moderate oven (325°F.) for about 45 minutes or until set. To test, insert a skewer about two-thirds of the way through each custard; if it comes out clean the custard is cooked. Remove the custard cups from the pan and place on a wire rack to cool. While molds are still

slowly to a boil. Remove from heat and let stand for about 10 minutes. Combine the eggs, egg yolks and sugar in a mixing bowl. Beat with a rotary beater or electric blender until pale yellow in color.
Remove the vanilla pod from the

warm, ease the custard away from the sides of the cups with a small, sharp knife. Shake once and invert each one into an individual serving dish.
Cool completely before serving.

# Bavarois
# au Chocol

*Cool, rich bavarois is the smoothest dessert you can offer. Make it in an old-fashioned mold like the copper one we have used to make it even more interesting. A bavarois (or Bavarian cream as it is sometimes called) is a rich custard mixture set with gelatin and flavored either with chocolate, as here, or with coffee, or just vanilla.*

*Don't try to hurry the making, or you are likely to curdle the custard or to get a stringy gelatin mixture. Work at it gently and slowly, stirring all the time when necessary, until it is setting. As a change from this molded dessert, make the cream in individual soufflé dishes and flavor individual portions differently, say 2 chocolate, 2 coffee and 2 vanilla. For another variation – a favorite for parties and exceptionally rich – split lady fingers in half, dip quickly in brandy or sherry and stand upright around the sides of an 8-in. spring-form pan. Prepare the bavarois in either vanilla or chocolate flavor. Carefully pour bavarois into prepared pan. Chill until firm. To unmold release spring and remove sides of mold carefully. Place on a serving platter and garnish with additional whipped cream, flavored with brandy or sherry.*

*Ladle some of the warmed milk on to the creamy yolks and sugar*

*Stir custard over gentle heat, without boiling, until it thickens*

*6–8 servings*

**3 large eggs, separated**
**1⅞ cup milk**
**1 vanilla pod**
**⅜ cup sugar**
**½ package (6 ounces) semi-sweet chocolate morsels**
**6¼ tablespoons water**
**2 envelopes unflavored gelatin**
**1¼ cups heavy cream**

*Dissolve the gelatin in a small bowl over a pan of warm water*

*Pour the gelatin steadily into the custard, stirring constantly*

Let the egg whites stand at room temperature while preparing the custard.

Combine the milk and vanilla pod in a saucepan. Heat gently, just until it reaches boiling point. Beat together the egg yolks and sugar in a mixing bowl until the mixture is pale and fluffy. Pour about one-third of the hot milk over beaten yolks and beat well. Remove the vanilla pod from the milk. Rinse under cold water, dry well and store for future use. Stir the yolk mixture into the hot milk in the saucepan. Cook over low heat, stirring constantly, until mixture thickens. This will take some time so be patient. Do not allow the mixture to boil. This can be done in the top of a double boiler over hot water.

Add the chocolate morsels to the hot custard and stir until the chocolate is melted. Remove from heat.

Measure the water into a small bowl. Add the gelatin and let stand to soften. Place the softened gelatin over a pan of hot water and dissolve gelatin. Remove from heat and let stand a few minutes. Stir 1–2 tablespoons of the chocolate custard into the dissolved gelatin and stir well. Return to the cooked custard and blend well. Turn the chocolate custard mixture into a mixing bowl. Place the mixing bowl in a bowl of iced water and stir the custard constantly until thick but still flowing.

Beat ¾ cup cream until stiff. Beat egg whites until stiff but not dry. Fold the cream into the custard. Pour the custard over the beaten egg whites and fold in the whites quickly and lightly until no pockets of egg whites are visible. Do not fold in too much as this will beat out some of the air in the mixture, and the bavarois will be small and solid.

Pour the mixture into a lightly oiled 6-cup mold or bowl. Chill in the refrigerator until set.

*In a bowl over ice water, stir cream and custard together until blended*

To serve, remove the mold from the refrigerator and let stand 15 minutes. Ease the bavarois away from the side of the mold by tilting at a slight angle and rotating the mold. Unmold on to a serving platter. Whip the remaining cream and use to garnish the bavarois. Garnish with chocolate curls, if desired.

*When almost setting, pour mixture into a mold and leave to set*

# CREPES SUZETTE

*If you have a chafing dish, let your guests enjoy watching you finish this delicious flambé dish of pancakes in orange butter sauce. If you don't have a pan pretty enough for public scrutiny (or if you're not sufficiently extrovert to want to display your skills), simply heat the pancakes and sauce in the oven and pour the flaming brandy over when you take it to the table. Either way you can do the main preparation the day before if you wish.*

*4 servings*

*Pancakes:*
**1 cup sifted all-purpose flour**
**Pinch of salt**
**Grated rind of ½ lemon**
**1 egg**
**1¼ cups milk**
**1 tablespoon butter, melted**
**Butter for frying**

*For orange butter sauce:*
**5–6 sugar cubes**
**2 large oranges**
**6 tablespoons butter**
**¼ cup sugar**
**1¼ tablespoons orange juice**
**1¼ tablespoons cointreau**
**3 tablespoons brandy**

*Beat in the liquid gradually to obtain a smooth batter*

Sift the flour and salt together. Mix in the lemon rind. Make a well in the center and add the egg. Add half the milk and beat thoroughly until the batter is smooth. Add the remaining liquid and melted butter. Beat until well mixed. Let batter stand for about 30 minutes. Heat a little butter in a 7 in. heavy-bottomed skillet or a crêpe pan. When the pan is very hot, tilt it so that the butter runs round and completely coats the sides of the pan; pour off any surplus butter. Pour in just enough batter to cover the bottom of the pan thinly and cook quickly until golden brown underneath. Turn with a small spatula and cook the second side until gol-

den. The pancakes should be very thin and lacy.

As the pancakes are cooked, stack them flat on a plate with a sheet of waxed paper between each and cover. If you are preparing them in advance, keep in a cool place until required.

Rub the cubes of sugar all over the oranges until they are soaked with oil. Crush the sugar cubes and add to the butter with the sugar. Beat mixture until soft and creamy. Stir in orange juice and cointreau. Blend well. Refrigerate until needed.

If you are serving from a chafing dish put it on a tray with the brandy, some kitchen matches, a serv-

*The pancakes should be thin and lacy for this dish*

*Remove the zest from the oranges by rubbing with cube sugar*

ing spoon and a fork. Cover the plate of pancakes with a sheet of aluminum foil and heat in a cool oven (300°F.) for about 10 minutes. Place the heated pancakes and orange butter mixture on serving tray.

To serve, place half the orange butter in the chafing dish. Light the flame underneath and when the mixture is melted, take one pancake at a time, place it in the dish, spoon over the hot sauce, fold the pancake in half and in half again. Push to one side of the dish while you repeat with more pancakes, until the pan is full. (You will have to do this in two lots.) Make sure that all the pancakes are well soaked with sauce.

*Work the butter and sugar with a wooden spoon until soft*

Pour some brandy into the serving spoon, heat the bowl of the spoon with a lighted match. Pour warm brandy over the pancakes and ignite. Serve at once. Repeat with remaining sauce and pancakes.

To prepare without using a chafing dish, place a little of the orange butter in the middle of each pancake, fold the pancakes into four and arrange them in a shallow, ovenproof serving dish. Melt the remaining orange butter in a pan on top of the stove and pour over the pancakes. Cover the dish with a sheet of aluminum foil and warm in a cool oven (300°F.) for 30 minutes.

*Add orange juice and cointreau to the orange butter*

*Fold the pancakes and soak in the warm butter sauce*

To serve, remove cover. At the table, warm the brandy as before, pour it over the pancakes and ignite. Serve immediately.

111

This is a classic French sweet made of mouth-watering meringues and cream flavored with chestnut purée. Although it looks and tastes so luscious it is quite easy to make and because of its exotic appearance it is sure to gain you many compliments from your guests at a dinner party or buffet.

For a party, make the meringue rounds and shells well in advance and store them in airtight tins until you require them.

To whip the maximum amount of air into meringues, the egg whites must be at room temperature and they should be whisked by hand with a balloon or rotary beater. It will help if you use a really large, deep bowl.

An electric mixer works too fast and tends to produce a flat, close-textured meringue.

**8–10 servings**

**6 large egg whites**
**1½ cups sugar**
**1¼ cups heavy cream**
**1 can (8¾ ounces) sweetened chestnut purée**
**1¼ tablespoons dry sherry**
**3 marrons glacés**
**¼ cup semi-sweet chocolate morsels**

Cover 3 cookie trays with waxed paper. Invert a 9-in. cake pan on each one and draw a line around the pan.

Ensure that the eggs are at room temperature by removing them from the refrigerator at least 1 hour before starting to cook. Place the whites in a large mixing bowl. Beat with a rotary beater until they stand in soft peaks.

*Beat the egg whites in a large bowl until stiff and frothy*

Gradually beat in the sugar, a spoonful at a time, sprinkling it over the entire surface of the beaten egg whites. Continue beating until all the sugar is well beaten in and the whites are glossy. Put the egg whites in a large pastry bag fitted with a large star

nozzle. Pipe meringue circles to fill the pencil circles on the paper, starting from the center and working out. Use slightly less than a third of the meringue for each circle. With the remaining meringue, pipe 6 shell shapes on the paper in the corners of the cookie trays.

Pre-heat the oven to the lowest possible setting. Put the cookie trays in the oven and let them dry out for 4 hours. Half-way through the cooking time reverse the top and bottom cookie trays in the

*Pipe out three 9-in. circles of meringue on to waxed paper*

oven so that one meringue does not color more than either of the others. When they are dry, remove from the oven and cool slightly. Then turn the meringue discs over on to the palm of your hand and peel away the paper. Cool on wire racks.

Beat the cream just until it holds its shape. Remove about ½ cup of the cream and reserve for later use. Fold the chestnut purée and sherry into the remaining cream. Place one meringue disc on a flat serving platter. Spoon half of the

*When the meringue is cooked the paper should peel off easily*

chestnut cream on to the meringue base. Spread the mixture to the edges with a small spatula. Place the second meringue disc on top. Repeat process with the remaining chestnut cream. Place third meringue disc on top. Position the meringue shells evenly

*Layer the meringue discs with chestnut flavored cream*

*Fix the meringue shells in position with plain whipped cream*

around the top of the vacherin. Removing one shell at a time, dab a little of the reserved plain whipped cream under each and press back into position. Drop the remaining cream from a spoon between the meringue shells. Place the marrons glacés on the meringue in the center.

Melt the chocolate morsels in a small bowl over a pan of hot water. Make a small paper cone from a square of waxed paper. Snip off the end. Put the chocolate into the cone. Drizzle the

*Spoon cream between the shells and drizzle with melted chocolate*

melted chocolate over each spoonful of cream, drawing the chocolate from side to side. Chill the vacherin for 1–2 hours before serving.

Gâte...
St. H...

# au onoré

8 servings

*For pastry base:*
**1 cup sifted all-purpose flour**
**Salt**
**¼ cup butter**
**2 tablespoons sugar**
**1 egg yolk**
**¼ teaspoon vanilla**

*For choux pastry:*
**¼ cup butter**
**⅝ cup water**
**⅝ cup sifted all-purpose flour**
**Pinch of salt**
**2 eggs, beaten**

*For filling:*
**⅝ cup heavy cream, whipped, optional**

*For glaze:*
**1 cup sugar**
**10 tablespoons water**

*For pastry cream:*
**2½ cups milk**
**½ cup sugar**
**½ cup all-purpose flour**
**2 tablespoons cornstarch**
**2 large eggs**
**¼ cup butter**

*For decoration:*
**1 can (1 pound, 13 ounces) apricot halves, drained**
**Angelica**

For the pastry base, sift the flour and a pinch of salt on to a working surface such as a marble slab or pastry board. Make a well in the center, add the butter and sugar and work them together with the fingertips of 1 hand. Add the egg

*Mix the pastry on a flat surface with the fingers of one hand*

yolk and vanilla and mix to a soft dough with 1 hand; knead slightly with the heel of 1 hand. Wrap the dough in waxed paper and chill for 30 minutes. Roll the dough out to an 8½-in. round. Place on a cookie tray and prick the surface with a fork. Crimp the edges with the fingers. Bake in a moderate oven (350°F.) for 20 minutes. Cool on the cookie tray until the crust begins to get firm. Lift on to a wire rack.

Place the butter and water in a pan and melt over low heat. Sift the flour and salt together. Bring

the butter and water to a boil. Add the flour all at once and continue cooking, over low heat, stirring constantly until the mixture leaves the sides of the pan and becomes a paste. Remove from heat. Add the eggs slowly, beating hard between each addition

*Crimp the edge of the pastry base with the fingers*

until mixture is smooth and shiny.

Grease a cookie tray. Press the edge of an 8-in. cake pan in flour. Invert the pan and place it on the cookie tray to make a floured imprint. Spoon the choux dough into a pastry bag fitted with a large plain nozzle. Using the floured ring as a guide, pipe two-thirds of the pastry in a circle on the outside edge of the ring to make the circle the same size as the pastry base. Pipe out the remaining dough on to another greased cookie tray into 16 small puffs.

*Pipe out a choux ring, using the flour circle as a guide*

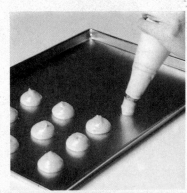

*Pipe 16 small puffs, taking care to keep them all the same size*

Bake the puffs and ring in a very hot oven (450°F.) for 15 minutes. Reduce heat to 375°F. and cook for about 20 more minutes. When cooked, pierce the bases of the puffs and ring to release the steam. Leave to cool on wire racks.

If desired, split the puffs when cold and fill with whipped cream. For the glaze, dissolve the sugar in the water over low heat. Bring to a boil and boil rapidly to 260°F. or until a drop of syrup will harden when dropped into cold water. Using tongs, dip the tops and sides of the puffs into the syrup. Set on a rack to drain.

Place the pastry base on a flat plate, position the ring on top and arrange the glazed puffs around the ring, dipping your fingers in iced water as you do so so that the hot syrup does not stick.

To make the pastry cream, heat

*Use tongs to dip the choux puffs in hot sugar glaze*

the milk in a saucepan. Mix together the sugar, flour, cornstarch and eggs and blend well. Stir in a little of the hot milk. Return the mixture to the milk in saucepan. Cook over low heat, stirring constantly, until mixture thickens and just comes to a boil. Add butter and beat thoroughly. Arrange all but 6 apricot halves in the center of the pastry base. Spoon over the warm, not hot, pastry cream. Brush with apricot juice. Decorate the top with the remaining apricots and the angelica. Serve cold the same day that it is made.

*Arrange the choux ring and puffs on the flat pastry base*

# Baba au Rhum

*Rum babas are favorites both at tea-time and as a dessert. Traditional French pâtisserie, the dough is light and fluffy because of the yeast used to raise it. Spoon over it the warm honey and rum syrup and the result is delicious indeed. French pastry shops sell them heavily glazed with apricot to give a really rich, glowing appearance.*

*Babas are difficult to serve if you pour over too much syrup initially,*

*Blend together yeast, milk and ½ cup flour until smooth*

*as they become wet while standing, but if you serve a small jug of syrup separately, the extra syrup is good added just before eating. Alternatively, some people will appreciate an extra spoonful of rum spooned over at the last minute.*

*8–10 servings*

**1 envelope active dry yeast**
**7½ tablespoons lukewarm milk**
**2 cups sifted all-purpose flour**
**½ teaspoon salt**
**2 tablespoons sugar**
**4 eggs, beaten**
**½ cup soft butter**
**1 cup currants**

*For honey and rum syrup:*
**5 tablespoons honey**
**5 tablespoons water**
**Rum**

*For glaze:*
**4 tablespoons apricot preserves**
**2½ tablespoons water**
**Whipped cream**
**Glacé cherries**

Combine the yeast and lukewarm milk in a large mixing bowl. Let stand 3–4 minutes. Add ½ cup of the flour and stir until smooth. Cover bowl and let stand in a warm place for about 30 minutes or until batter is frothy. During this period the yeast is growing and as it does so it forms carbon dioxide. The bubbles of this gas

*Leave the yeast mixture in a warm place until frothy*

*Add all the ingredients to the original dough*

*Beat thoroughly with a wooden spoon for 3–4 minutes*

are responsible for the spongy texture of the finished cake.
Add the remaining flour, salt, sugar, eggs, butter and currants and beat thoroughly for 3–4 minutes. This develops the dough so that it will rise.
Grease eight–ten 3½-in. ring molds with shortening. Half fill the molds with the dough. Cover with oiled plastic wrap and allow to rise until the molds are two-thirds full.
Bake near the top of a fairly hot

oven (400°F.) for 15–20 minutes. Cool for a few minutes and turn out on to a wire rack, placed over a tray to catch the drips of syrup. Warm the honey and water together. Add rum to taste. While the babas are still hot, spoon over sufficient warm honey and rum syrup to soak each baba well.
Heat the preserves and water

*Half fill the baba molds and cover with oiled plastic*

*Spoon honey and rum syrup over the babas while they are hot*

together. Put mixture through a sieve. Brush each baba with apricot glaze and let cool.
Pipe a whirl of whipped cream into each baba with a pastry bag fitted with a large star nozzle. Top each baba with a cherry. Transfer to serving platters and serve with extra syrup and/or whipped cream if desired.

*When cold, fill the center of each with piped cream*

# For the Hostess

*A hot, puff-topped chicken pie (page 77)*

# THE WINE TO GO WITH IT

If you are serving good food you owe it the justice of a good wine. Precisely which wine you serve with which food is largely a matter of personal taste and pocket; the suggestions we give with our dinner party menus are by no means the ultimate and some connoisseurs would doubtless have quite different ideas. There are, however, certain guidelines that it is as well to follow; just as some foods don't mix well, so some wines are better than others with certain foods.

Fish is always better with a white wine; for some reason, when fish is eaten with red wine both tend to take on a metallic taste which ruins them. Very oily fish can do this even to white wine and the only answer then is to stick to beer. Meats will take red, white or rosé. Beef and lamb tend to have the most pronounced flavors and do justice to the finest of clarets and Burgundies – but if mint sauce, garlic or other strong herbs are in the dish you are wasting your money if you drink anything too expensive, as the flavor will be drowned. A vinegary salad dressing will also kill any wine; if you wish to serve a dish accompanied by salad and wine, make the dressing with white wine or lemon juice in place of vinegar. Pork, veal and chicken are good with white wines (though not with a light red or rosé). The really sweet, heavy wines are best with desserts, especially cakes and pastries. Any dish cooked in wine should of course be accompanied by the same type of wine.

Most of our recommendations refer to French or the better known European wines and/or many of the outstanding American wines. However, these are only suggestions and you are free to do your own experimenting.

**Serving wine**

There is a lot of nonsense talked about different glasses for different types of wine. To enjoy wine, your glass should be large enough to hold a generous helping without being more than half full, and the bowl should be roundish, cupping in towards the top so that the bouquet of the wine doesn't escape the instant it is poured out (that is also why you don't fill it more than half full). It should be stemmed so that the temperature of your hand does not affect the temperature of the wine, and it should be clear so that you can see the true color of the wine. Tall stemmed hock

*Draw the cork firmly but gently*

## FOOD AND WINE

| | |
|---|---|
| Clear soup, consommé, oxtail soup, smoked salmon or eel | Dry or medium dry sherry |
| Meaty and savory hors d'oeuvre | Red Burgundy or Bordeaux or rosé |
| Other soups and most starters | Dry sherry or the wine chosen for the main course |
| Oysters, shellfish, fine fish plainly cooked | Chablis, Muscadet |
| Turbot, trout, bass, sole, salmon | White Burgundy, Moselle, Hock |
| Fish with sauces, cold meat | White Alsace |
| Pasta and pizza | Red Chianti Valpolicella, Bardolino |
| Paella | White Italian (eg. Soave) or Spanish |
| Chicken, veal, pork | Red or white Bordeaux (dry) Alsace, Hock, Graves or rosé |
| Lamb, beef, roast chicken, ham, game pork, duck | Red Bordeaux or Burgundy, Côtes du Rhône (choose a fine wine for, say, a plain roast sirloin; something less demanding if there is a rich sauce with the meat). |
| Light sweets, gâteaux, ices | Sweet White Bordeaux |
| Cheese, nuts and dessert fruit | Port, Madeira, Marsala or cream sherry |
| | Champagne or a sparkling hock or Moselle can be served throughout a meal |

glasses are very good for a chilled wine as they keep your hand well away from the bowl, and a long flute encourages Champagne bubbles to rise. But a glass that is right for one wine is just as right for any other and the range shown are all a good shape; 2–3 sizes could see you through from sherry to port, whatever you serve in between.

The temperature at which wine is served is most important, as a fine wine can be ruined if it is over-heated; equally if it is too cold you will not be able to appreciate the full flavor. Red wine should be drunk at room temperature and should be left standing in a warm room for several hours before serving. It should be opened an hour or so before serving to give it time to breathe. If you have left it too late for that, pour it into a warmed decanter, or warm the glass with your hands, but never stand it in front of the fire, on a radiator, or hold it under a warm tap – sudden warmth ruins the wine and it will never recover. When red wine has been brought to room temperature it is better to drink it all as it will probably spoil if allowed to go cold again. White wine is rather less sensitive – you just lay it down in the refrigerator for half an hour or so, or if the refrigerator is full stand it in a bucket of cold water and ice cubes for 20 minutes, until it is just chilled but not iced.

It may be a good idea to decant a red wine if it is more than 5–6 years old. Wine gradually forms a sediment which makes it cloudy if the bottle is shaken at all. A bottle that has lain on its side for a while will have all the sediment lying along the one side of the bottle, so when you take it out of the rack, either keep it on its side in a cradle while you bring it to room temperature and open it, or stand it upright for a few *days* so that the sediment can settle to the bottom of the bottle or decant it carefully, leaving the sediment behind.

*Choose stackable racks to store your wines so that you can add to them as your cellar grows. A dozen or so bottles will meet the demands of most occasions if you choose a wide selection of wines. Our selection includes a light, sparkling French wine, red and white Burgundies, a good red Chianti, a lighter white from Alsace and 2–3 cheap, lesser known wines to experiment with* ▶

Drawing the cork is not difficult. The easiest way is to use a levered cork-screw. This will enable you to do it without jerking the bottle – particularly useful if you are trying to keep the bottle on its side in a cradle. If you use a traditional cork-screw you will certainly have to raise the neck of the bottle a little, but if you keep it tilted as our expert has, the sediment will remain together and just slide gently down the side of the bottle. Don't panic if the cork breaks and you cannot get it out – just push it in and strain the wine if necessary.

### Starting a cellar

People who do much entertaining, or like to open a bottle fairly regularly for family gatherings, will find it worth starting their own small cellars. If bottles are bought by the dozen they are, like most things, cheaper. You will also find that somehow the wine tastes better if you have kept it a while.

'Cellar' may sound a very grand word, but that closet in the spare room may be an ideal place

*Use glasses with a rounded bowl and a longish stem; 2–3 sizes will serve most occasions*

for storing wine. Anywhere that is dark, has an even temperature (preferably on the cool side) and is not subject to vibration, will do. It needs to be deep enough to take the bottles lying down, and a store of a dozen will see most families through most occasions. Wine needs to be kept lying on its side, otherwise the cork will dry out and shrink, and there are many types of rack available. It is probably best to buy stackable racks, that you can add to as your stock increases; the traditional wood and galvanized metal racks as shown in our picture are as good as any.

If you are used to buying wine in single bottles, when required, you will have had some pleasant experiences and some nasty surprises. This is because very few wines are at their best when newly lugged home from the corner store; they need time to settle again before you drink them. Another reason is that many wines are sold when freshly bottled and the merchant *intends* that you should keep them for 2–3 months at the very least before

opening them – the trouble is unless you know him he probably won't tell you that! Merchants like to sell quickly because storage space is expensive and short term storing cannot affect the price they can charge to the customer; but wines suffer a sort of shock when transferred from barrel to bottle, almost like a bruising, which only time will heal.

If you have to buy in a hurry you are as well off with a brand-name wine; these are blended wines whose characters do not alter much with time and which will go down much the same as vin ordinaire does in France – enjoyable but not exactly select. Try several until you find one you like. Being less subtle in the first place, these wines also suffer less noticeably from being moved around. They are not meant for long term keeping.

When it comes to choosing wine, the novice often looks a bit blankly at the label. There is no need to be put off, though, if you are willing to admit your ignorance and let the wine merchant help you. The first thing you can tell from the label is whether you have a wine from a particular area, blended and bottled on the estate or by an established shipper; whether it is an out and out mix-up, aimed simply at producing an acceptable drink with no pretensions (this usually applies to branded wines, which often are blends not only from different areas, but even from different countries); or whether it is a wine from a single vineyard and a single year's growth – in which case the grower will have put his own name on it because he believes it is something to be proud of.

Nobody drinks fine wines every day, just as nobody eats fillet steak every day. Blended wines are often very good and are definitely not to be sneezed at (all except the most exceptional vintages of Champagne are blended, and nobody queries the quality then). If you decide to go for something better, though, ask your merchant for help.

The French laws of Appellation Controllée mean that French wine labels must tell you

exactly what you're getting – which vineyard, what year and whether home bottled. Though not obliged to by law, the Germans often go into even more detail about whether they were early or late grapes, first pressing or second – all sorts of information which does mean something to an expert. Unfortunately other countries are less scrupulous and labels tend to be less helpful – you have to feel your way around and get to know those that are good from those that are not so good. From the label on a single vineyard French or German wine bottle, an experienced merchant can tell you whether the wine will be a full flavored Burgundy or a lighter one, whether the white you are buying will be smooth, heavy and rich flavored, or fresh and young tasting, and what degree of dryness or sweetness to expect. With these carefully labelled wines, it's not a question of good or bad, but a question of what you're after. At the other end of the scale, if you buy something labelled 'Spanish Chablis' or 'Australian Burgundy' you still know what you are getting – something that doesn't deserve a name of its own, but which vaguely resembles something else. Australian and Californian vineyards are now beginning to label their wines more carefully, to tell the customer in more detail what he is getting.

The date on the bottle is not necessarily an indication of a good or bad vintage, but of the age of the wine. Wines of really poor vintages are rarely exported anyway, and many growers will sell off their poorer wine for blending rather than put their own label on it. There *are* special vintages for certain wines, but only a connoisseur could be expected to remember, or pay for, these.

What you need to know is how old a particular type of wine should be before it is likely to reach its best. Most white wines are very good after as little as 3 or 4 years – some people will lay them down for longer but it is debatable whether it is worth the trouble. Rosés and a very few red wines are similar (the more recent the date on a Beaujolais bottle the better it should be; outside France it is rarely sold less than 2 years old, but beware of any that has more than 4 years under its belt).

The wines that are usually better for age are the red table wines (and port of course, but that's a subject in itself). No claret or red Burgundy will ever be bottled at much less than two years old. The best are then probably worth keeping in the bottle for 10 years to mature – if you pay a high price for a good single vineyard claret and then drink it while it is only 3–4 years old, you are wasting money; these are made to be kept and if drunk sooner are no better than a cheaper wine.

Financially it is sound to buy some young wines to lay down for a few years, as when they are ready to drink they be much more expensive to buy – but do buy some for drinking sooner as well or you'll be miserable while you wait! Whatever you buy it will be a good investment in terms of enjoyment for yourself and your friends.

An apéritif is the liquid equivalent of an appetizer. It stimulates the appetite and livens the palate; it also serves a social function of 'breaking the ice' during the first half hour of a gathering before a meal (in the last century, when they hadn't caught on to the idea of before-dinner drinks, they used to call this the black half hour). Many people at this stage of the evening will drink their favorite form of refreshment regardless of what is to follow – which often means a spirit or spirit-based mix. But a real food lover shuns spirits, for nothing deadens the palate more quickly.

The best apéritifs are wine-based and on the dry side. Often a glass of the wine to be drunk with the meal is a perfectly good start, particularly if it is a light white wine or perhaps a Beaujolais; a full claret is rather heavy going without food, though. Champagne is the perfect apéritif, as it is perfect at any other stage of the meal.

Sweet drinks of any sort are to be avoided since sweetness tends to dull the appetite. (Having said that, one should add that many people nevertheless do take sweet sherry before a meal and you should always have it available to offer.) The most common and acceptable apéritifs, though, are the dry or medium dry sherries, vermouths and certain patent apéritifs which usually have a wine base and some bitter additive such as herbs or quinine, or both. The French particularly specialize in patent apéritifs, though they hardly know what sherry is.

# SHERRIES & APERITIFS

## SHERRY

'Sherry' is an anglicization of the name Jerez de la Frontera, a small, triangular, coastal area of Spain. Situated on the far western coast, just south of the southern tip of Portugal, it is bounded on two sides by the great rivers Guadalquivir and Guadalete, on the third by the Atlantic dunes. The vineyards are no more than 20½ miles long and less than 15 miles wide; from this area comes the world's entire supply of genuine sherry. The English are the great sherry drinkers of the world and have been since the 16th century; the celebrated 'sack' of Elizabethan days was the same type of wine as today's sherry, though sweeter than most. Seventy per cent of the entire produce of Jerez is today exported to England.

There are no 'vintage' sherries, as there are wines. The produce of different years is slowly blended together and fortified with brandy, until in time certain characteristics develop which determine the type of sherry in a particular cask. There are two main divisions of type: *fino,* the drier sherries, and *oloroso,* the fuller or sweeter types.

As a general rule, the drier the taste of a sherry, the paler the color.

*Finos* are pale, delicate and dry.

*Manzanillas* come from an area on the coast, which is said to account for their sharp, almost salty flavor. These are the palest of all sherries. When a manzanilla is taken away from its home district it tends to lose its characteristic flavor and become just a very good fino – it is therefore rare for sherry to be exported under a manzanilla label.

*Amontillados* develop a darker color and a distinctive 'nutty' flavor early in the maturing process and the wine is then left to mature, with no more blending. Amontillados are usually stronger than other sherries, containing up to 25 per cent alcohol. They need to age in the wood for at least 8 years, and there is always the chance that the wine will go off instead of maturing properly. This is the reason that amontillados are more expensive than other sherries. An amontillado is often known as a 'medium' sherry, indicating that its flavor is somewhere between a fino and an oloroso – but it should never be 'medium' in quality.

The *cream* and *golden* sherries based on *oloroso* wine are darker in color and considerably sweeter than the finos. The term 'oloroso' means fragrant, and the wine starts its life just as dry as the finos; the sweetness comes in the blending with other wines.

*Amoroso* is particularly rich and usually slightly darker than the cream sherries.

The sweetest, darkest sherry of all is *East India Brown* – so called from the 17th century habit of sending barrels of sherry on a round trip to India in the hold of sailing ships to speed the maturing process.

These brown sherries, because of their full, rich flavor, are essentially dessert wines as their sweetness defeats the object of an apéritif. They are more suitable as an alternative to liqueurs or port at the end of a meal. There are certain characteristics of sherry that make it very different from other wines. One is that the new wine is totally unpredictable. When 2 lots of a table wine are made from the same type of grape, grown on the same slopes, it will be possible for the grower to predict certain characteristics long before the wine is tasted. 2 casks of sherry made from exactly the same harvest of grapes, picked in neighbouring rows of vines, can be entirely different; not until the taster opens the cask can he tell whether it is going to develop into fino, amontillado, oloroso or a 'raya', which will never be anything much and may either serve as a blending wine or may even be turned into vinegar if it is really mediocre.

The distinguishing mark of a fino in the making is its tendency to grow a thick 'flor'. This is caused by a wild yeast carried in the air, which when it settles on the wine produces a thick, white scum which totally excludes all other yeasts and bacteria that normally attack wine. Whereas growers of other wines try to exclude air from the new wines to avoid contact with these bacteria, sherry growers leave several inches space at the top of their casks to allow the flor to take hold. A good fino has a delicacy and freshness of taste that is largely imparted by this bacteriological action.

All sherries are blends, the newer wines readily taking on the flavor and characteristics of the more mature. Sherry growers have elaborate systems of barrels called 'solera', which enable them to add newer wine progressively to older and to top up the first barrel with a newer one still. Apart from their own special blends they will also make up blends for a shipper who asks for a wine with certain characteristics. This is why many sherries are known by the name of the shipper rather than the grower.

Each shipper has his own system of classifying the sherries within the broad categories, so it is possible to give only general guidelines on how to choose sherries for your own use. The best method is to find one or two sherries that suit your personal taste and stick to them. When you are giving a party you can always widen the selection so as to be able to offer your guests a choice – and by buying from

*Left to right: very pale dry fino; pale dry fino; amontillado; golden doroso; pale cream*

the same shipper's range you will have a very good idea of what to expect by way of dryness and richness.

Many other parts of the world produce a fortified wine known as sherry, notably South Africa, Australia and Cyprus. Most of these wines are poor substitutes for true sherry; the soil and climate of the Jerez area have indisputably marked its produce as unique. South African sherries are the closest to the original since they are made from the same type of grape and with the same solera system of blending; the climate of the vineyards and their closeness to the sea are also similar to Jerez. The result is a range of extremely good sherries, particularly on the medium-to-sweet

side, which tend to sell more cheaply.

The traditional sherry glass is smaller than an ordinary wine glass, but proportionally rather taller; it should never be more than half filled or the scent of the wine is lost. Dry sherry is often drunk very slightly chilled.

## OTHER APERITIFS

Of apéritifs other than sherry, the best known is vermouth. This is another fortified wine, this time blended with herbs and spices, the principal flavoring agent being wormwood (German 'Wermut'). Although still often referred to merely as 'French' (dry) or 'Italian' (sweet), both kinds are made in either country. There are three different types of Italian vermouth – dry white, sweet white and sweet red – the best known brand names being Cinzano and Martini. French vermouths are generally drier than the Italian, the best known being Noilly Prat. One particularly good French vermouth is Chambéryzette – a light, slightly pink drink made from wild strawberries.

Vermouth may be served either neat over ice or diluted with soda; a twist of lemon is usually added to dry vermouth, a cherry to sweet. In addition, vermouths are often mixed with spirits: dry vermouth with dry gin to make a dry martini; sweet red vermouth with rye whisky to make a manhattan; sweet white vermouth also mixes well with gin or vodka. There are many other well known wine-based apéritifs, such as Dubonnet, St. Raphael, Byrrh and Punt e Mes. In addition to a blend of herbs, all of these drinks contain a little quinine which gives them a distinctive flavor. They are usually served in a similar way to vermouth – over ice, with soda and with a twist of lemon or lime.

*A slice of lime, a twist of lemon rind or a cherry on a stick can garnish most apéritifs*

Although hard spirit does not make a good apéritif, there is available a variety of spirit-based apéritifs, generally known as 'bitters'. The best known of these is Angostura Bitters, which should be used literally in drips. When added to gin, this makes a pink gin; it can also be added to the water in your ice trays, to make pink ice. A popular Italian bitters is Campari, usually served with ice and soda and a twist of lemon. The equivalent French drink is Amer Picon, which is dark and has a very bitter flavor; it is usually mixed with Grenadine and soda and served over ice. Fernet Branca and Underberg, also quinine-flavored apéritifs, are medicinal and said to be good for clearing the head as well as clearing the palate!

The last category is the aniseed based apéritifs, which come from all around the Mediterranean, and there are several brands available. Pernod and Ricard are probably the best known, and they should all be served well diluted with water and ice. They taste quite gentle but are much stronger than brandy.

# RED WINES

The most and the best of the world's red wines are made in France. The Bordeaux and Burgundy areas alone produce something like 2,500 different red wines and several other, smaller, wine areas of France also produce quite large quantities. Italy and Spain are the only other European red wine producers of any consequence. Portuguese red wines, though very good, are little known; in Germany, Hungary and Yugoslavia what few are made are not very good. California, Australia and one or two of the South American countries are the only other areas that export much, and these are not yet well known.

Red wine is always made from black grapes, and from grapes that have been ripened in really hot sun so that they have lost all trace of acidity. To give the wine the 'lift' it needs (that made from the juice of totally sweet grapes can be rather flat and dull), the skins and sometimes the pips and stalks are used as well as the juice. The skins, pips and stalks contain tannin which by itself is harsh tasting but which is a vital ingredient in red wine. White wine is made from the juice only of rather less fully ripened grapes.

### Bordeaux Wines

Almost half the production of the vast Bordeaux wine area is red. These are the wines that in Britain are known as claret, and have been the favorite table wines for centuries. Many clarets are the finest possible wines, and there is at present a speculative market in them, so expensive have they become.

The chief geographical areas within Bordeaux are Médoc, Pomerol, St. Emilion and Graves. The finest of these wines are traditionally classified into 'growths' (e.g. premier cru, etc.); the not-so-great are expressed in different ways. There are several hundred 'bourgeois' growths, more 'artisan' growths and even 'paysan' growths. It is the bourgeois growths that most of us drink most of the time, and they are considerably better than their rather derogatory sounding name implies – extremely good wines at generally very reasonable prices.

Wines which carry the district names on their label will be either a blend of wines from that area, or a wine from the local co-operative, from a specific village or from a specific vineyard. You can be sure with Bordeaux that wine with any pretensions at all will claim on its label the highest level to which it is legally entitled, indicated at the lower levels by the words Bordeaux and Bordeaux Supérieur (blends, the latter with a minimum 10·5 per cent alcohol content), then a district name

*Burgundy, bread and cheese – what could be better for a quick lunch?*

(Médoc, Pomerol, St. Emilion), then at the top a commune or village name. These all fall within the laws of appellation controllée. Beyond this are some 2,000 estates, all of which sell under their own château name – on the labels of these the appellation controllée is usually in small type.

The Medoc area supplies a large number of good clarets, usually at a sensible price; they are comparatively light and are usually ready to drink after 3–4 years. Haut-Médoc wines are rather better and include those from the communes of St. Estèphe, Pauillac, Margaux and St. Julien, all of which are appellations controllées. The number of excellent châteaux wines from this area makes it impossible to list them. All you can do is to try some of them and remember the names of those that particularly appeal. As for age, none of these is ready to drink at less than 6 years old and many, depending on the particular château and vintage, will go on improving the longer they are kept –10 years is not too

long for most, 15 is not unusual and longer can produce the most exquisite drinks if you have the patience to wait.

Pomerol is a small area containing dozens of very small châteaux, from which come some of the finest first growth wines. They are on the whole lightish, almost slightly sweet wines compared with the rest of Bordeaux and are good at about 4–5 years old. A lesser vintage may even be ready to drink at 3 years old, yet no Pomerol will spoil for keeping longer. By contrast, the neighboring area of St. Emilion, one of the largest districts in the Bordeaux area, is usually better represented on wine lists than the others. These are full, savory, strong wines, often ready to drink at only 4 years old. Again the number of châteaux makes it impossible to list them.

It comes as a surprise to many people to know that Graves produces any red wine at all, for the name never in fact appears on the bottles – the area is much better known for its white wines which do carry the name. Reds from the covering many names; nearly all will need something like 10 years in the bottle before they are ready for drinking.

The Côte de Beaune, which includes Beaune, Pommard and Volnay, produces wines that are marginally less good than those from the Côte de Nuits; but it does produce, in far greater quantities, wines that need only 6–7 years in the bottle – they therefore tend to appear on the wine list more frequently.

It is worth remembering that the simple label Beaune is rather more specific, and therefore better, than Côte de Beaune, and Hospices de Beaune (the wines made at the the hospital, whose proceeds support the hospital) are better still. Otherwise the names to look for are Corton (preferably on its own but also in combination with other names), Pommard (Epenots and Rugiens) and Volnay (especially Caillerets or Santenots), Chassagne-Montrachet and Santenay.

### Beaujolais

In the southern tip of the Burgundy area are 3 districts that produce wines rather different from the rest of Burgundy. These are the Côte Chalonnaise, a small area, Mâcon, producing many reasonable wines but nothing great, and Beaujolais. Beaujolais produces large quantities of lightish, lively wine. It is cheap both because there is lots of it and because it is best drunk young – locally and in Paris it is drunk as 'vin de l'année', when it is very light indeed. Outside France it tends to be 2–4 years old and therefore slightly heavier, but it should still not be a strong wine – if it is, it has probably been doctored.

### Rhône

Most Rhône wines are rather dark colored and strong tasting unless they are kept for a long time to mature (10–15 years), and few are honored with this treatment. Probably only Hermitage and Côte-Rôtie come into this category. Much better known is Châteauneuf-du-Pape. This is a strong, warm tasting wine that needs only 2–3 years in the bottle and is often cheaper than Burgundy.

### Red Wines from Italy and Spain

The red wines most exported from Italy are Chianti, Valpolicella, Soave and Barolo. There are many other good ones grown, but unfortunately very few of the rest are exported. To appreciate fully how good they can be, one has to drink them in Italy. The best are matured in cask rather than the bottle, sometimes for as long as 7–8 years, and are ready to drink as soon as they are bottled.

One of the best red wines made in Spain is Rioja, which is frequently exported. Young Rioja is an excellent, cheap vin ordinaire much better than its French equivalents. Rioja that has been allowed to mature is smooth and velvety; it may become light and slightly sweet, or be stronger yet still somewhat fresh tasting. These mature wines are known as Rioja Reservas; they may be 15 or more years old and are certainly very good indeed. They deserve to be better acknowledged on the world's wine lists.

*Claret in an attractive decanter to complement rich roast pork*

Graves area bear the name of a château or village rather than area. The best known of all, one that has been classed as a first growth for over a century, is Château Haut-Brion; this wine needs a really long time in the bottle to bring out the best in it. Following that are some 20 or so wines of classed growths, all of which are extraordinarily good. They have a strong, full flavor excellent with plain roast meat or game.

### Burgundy

Burgundy wines tend to be rather more robust than clarets, without becoming in any measure strong or coarse. In fact the two are much more similar than most people make out – it is the stronger wines of Italy, Spain and the southern hemisphere that really stand out as different. There is no system of classification in Burgundy such as that used in the Bordeaux area, each wine is sold purely on the reputation of the village or vineyard name it bears; it therefore becomes possible to buy rather inferior wines because they seem to bear the right name, which is a trap for the unknowing. What in fact happens is that village, vineyard and market town names become hyphenated to each other in a mammoth effort at identification, and it is a question of knowing precisely which combination is the best of several which sound similar – unfortunately a task for the merchant or connoisseur rather than the ordinary consumer. The finest Burgundies are grown on the hills known as the Côte de Nuits. The names to watch for here are Fixin, Chambertin (notably Gevrey-Chambertin and Chambertin Clos de Bèze), Morey-St.-Denis, Chambolle-Musigny (if you find something labelled just Musigny it is the best from here), Clos de Vougeot, Vosne-Romanée and Nuits-St.-Georges. The last named village produces more wine than most in Burgundy but is also particularly subject to blending with cheaper wines, so should be approached with circumspection. These are very broad categories,

Supreme amongst white wines is Champagne. It is a party drink; its bubbles and fine golden color make it look gay, its delicate balance of tart and sweet flavors, its delicious bouquet and the speed with which its alcohol takes effect (also the gentleness with which it lets you down again) make it ideal for celebrations of all kinds. All Champagnes are blends and it is therefore the shipper's name that appears on the bottle. There are 12–20 of these, all of whom are well known and whose non-vintage Champagne (wine blended from different years as well as different vineyards) will always be good. The Champagne that is sometimes not so good is that sold by the retailer under his own brand name. This is often recommended for parties, but unless it is one you know it may be a rather unexciting drink and may disappoint many newcomers to Champagne. On the other hand, a good one is the best value for money, so shop around.

Vintage Champagne is an animal rarely seen at large parties – it needs reserving for quiet celebrations amongst a few friends, for the price tends to be prohibitive. This is still a blended wine from several different vineyards, but all from the same year's grapes. The growers declare a special vintage only occasionally, usually a hot year when the grapes have come early to a full, sweet ripeness. French law prevents shippers selling as 'Vintage' more Champagne than was made in a particular year, so it is virtually impossible to be fooled.

Before we go on to other white wines, the table wines that we drink more often, it would perhaps be as well to be technical for a moment and point out how white wine is made. It is basically a simpler process than red wine. Only the juice of the grapes is used, the skins being discarded, so both black and white grapes can be made into white wine (very few black grapes have dark flesh as well and all have clear juice). The grapes are lightly pressed, instead of being squeezed as for red, and left to ferment until the required amount of sugar is converted into alcohol. If a sweeter wine is required, fermentation is stopped sooner than for a medium or dry wine – this is done by various methods, the most common being filtering off the yeast or adding sulphur dioxide. For the very sweet white wines, such as those of Sauternes, the grapes need to be really sweet and ripe before they are picked;

for the dryer wines this is not so important. Once the fermentation stops, white wines are usually ready to drink. They may improve with a little time in the bottle but there is rarely any point in laying down white wines as you would red. Their quality often lies in their freshness of flavor.

### German wines

Whereas France undoubtedly takes first place for red wines, first place for white is a contest between France and Germany. More French wines are drunk because they are cheaper than the good German wines, but it would be impossible to judge which are actually best. The reason German white wines are so good, and so expensive, is that the growers are meticulous about not mixing wines from different casks, even if they are from the same vintage and vineyard. Whereas a French grower harvests all his grapes virtually at once, presses them, then the following year blends wines from different casks to make what he thinks will be the best wine he can achieve, a German grower picks his grapes in several different stages, from when they are just ripe enough right up to the time when they are shrivelling on the stem. All the wines made from these are kept separately throughout their development, and labeled on the bottle to show exactly what they are. Thus 'Spätlese' means late-gathered grapes; 'Auslese' means selected picking of the best and the ripest bunch of grapes; 'Beerenauslesen' means individually selected ripe grapes off the best bunches; 'Trockenbeerenauslesen' means the grapes have been left so

long that they have shrivelled and the juice has concentrated to a rich syrup – the wine produced from these is virtually a liqueur. There is no wonder with this elaboration that the product is expensive – one should perhaps point out that even the Germans drink these wines only on special occasions and can get cheap branded wines for everyday drinking. The main wine producing areas in Germany are the Moselle and the Rhine. Moselle wines are fresh tasting and light colored, with a tendency to an almost 'hard' taste that is characteristic. The best are made in the villages of the middle Moselle – Piesport, Brauneberg, Bernkastel, Graach, Wehlen, Zeltingen, Uerzig and Erden; all are made from the Riesling grape. So labels on a fine Moselle wine will give first the name of the village (or exceptionally the name of a very famous vineyard), then the name of the vineyard – e.g. Bernkastler Doktor – finally come the words or phrases describing quality and when the grapes were gathered. The later the grapes were gathered, and therefore the sweeter the wine, the better the quality expected.

Also on the label will be the name of the grower and where the wine was bottled ('original-abfüllung' or 'orig.-abf.' indicates that it was bottled on the estate). To a connoisseur the grower's name is important, for some can be utterly relied upon to produce the best wines possible from the grapes of a given year.

To return to the humbler, blended wines that are more readily available, there are a number available that are first class blends, for example the one known as Moselblümchen. The standard usually depends on the shipper and is also indicated in the comparative prices.

Rhine wines (hock) are a richer, more golden color than those from the Moselle and tend to be fuller and softer. The two wines can be distinguished easily without even opening the bottle, as Moselle wine is in tall elegant green bottles, while Rhine wines go into similarly shaped brown bottles. On the Rhine the Riesling grape is again the most commonly grown, for it is very hardy as well as producing good wine, but other grapes are also grown. On hock bottles the label therefore bears the name of the grape between the vineyard name and the description of quality. More often than not a commercial blend of Rhine wines is labeled Liebfraumilch – the name on its

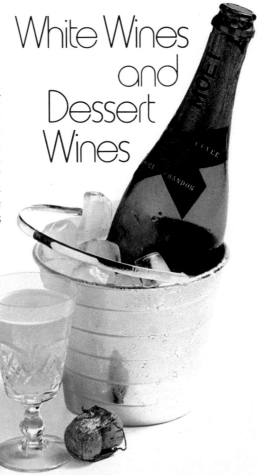

White Wines and Dessert Wines

own meaning simply Rhine wine. The quality of the blend depends on the shipper's name (Sichel, Deinhard, Langenbach and Hallgarten are among the best known).

The Rhine includes 4 main areas which produce excellent wines – the Rheingau, the Nahe, Rheinhessen, and the Palatinate. Wines from these areas are all known as hock and are broadly better or worse, usually depending on the amount of Riesling grape used in the blend.

## French white wines

Among the French white wines the Burgundies are considered by many to take first place. Typically, a white Burgundy is still and dry. Burgundy includes a number of the names that are familiar to all wine drinkers. Perhaps the most famous, not only because of its own wine but because it is much imitated, is Chablis. Chablis wines are very dry, delicately scented, slightly stony flavored wines with a fresh, crisp taste. The cheap Chablis that are very popular tend to be young, very fresh and rather hard, and there are about 30 vineyards that produce wines under their own names. The better known, because they are the largest, are Les Fourchaumes, Vaillons and Montée de Tonnerre. Wines from all these vineyards can be found labeled with the vineyard name, or simply the terms Chablis Grand Cru or Chablis Premier Cru.

The next most important part of Burgundy is Côte de Beaune, from where come Corton-Charlemagne, Montrachet and Meursault. Different as these wines are, they are similar when compared together against Chablis. In different degrees they are soft, smooth, full wines with a delicate scent. Montrachet, if good, can be equal to the best white wine Burgundy produces.

The last of the well known areas is Mâcon, producing Mâcon Blanc, the white Burgundy equivalent of Beaujolais, cheap and drunk young, Mâcon Supérieur, the next cheapest and a yellowish, general purpose carafe wine, and Pouilly Fuissé. This last has the virtue of producing in quantity a wine of great character that is excellent with fish and chicken. Burgundy of course produces many other white wines, too numerous to cover here. From Bordeaux, the great claret area, come Sauternes, Barsac, Graves and Médoc. Ordinary Sauternes is a sweet table wine, very popular in Britain as it is lightish and not too expensive. But the great châteaux of Sauternes – Yquem and others close by – produce a wine that comes into an altogether different category. Château wines from Sauternes are made from what the Germans would call Spätlese or Auslese – selected bunches of grapes that have ripened until they are almost rotten, so that the juice is so sweet and concentrated that it will go on and on fermenting and when it can ferment no more there will still be sugar left in the wine, leaving it so sweet and rich that it is really only suitable as an after dinner wine (the ordinary Sauternes have to be stopped fermenting artificially in order that there should be some sugar remaining). Compared with the Ger-

*A selection of dessert wines*

man wines of this type, though, Sauternes is very good value. While the better Sauternes are perhaps only twice the price of the lesser ones, the best German wines are ten times the price of their lesser brethren. Barsac is similar to Sauternes, but perhaps less sweet.

The best known dry white wine from Bordeaux is Graves. Unlike the red wines from this area, the white does not bear any distinguishing village names but simply calls itself Graves or Graves Supérieur. At its best, Graves is dry, full and mellow; the lesser ones tend to be a little sweeter. Graves is classed with Sauternes as being one of the most popular basic white table wines in Britain. There are half a dozen châteaux in Graves that export under their own names and whose produce is superb. The other main area is Entre-deux-Mers which produces large quantities of a medium wine that is very popular locally, served with oysters and other seafoods.

One of the links between Burgundy and Bordeaux is the river Loire. The six hundred miles of this valley naturally produce some very diverse wines, some much akin to white Burgundies, others more like those from Bordeaux, yet others with a character all of their own. The names to watch for particularly are Muscadet, Pouilly-Fumé and Sancerre. These are all likely to be reasonably priced and pleasant.

The other well known white wine comes from the border between France and Germany – Alsace. Though thoroughly French now, Alsace has many German traditions from the days when it belonged to the German empire. This shows to some extent in the typical bottles of Alsace wines – long thin green bottles, taller still than the German bottles.

The wines from this area are dry and full flavored. They are similar to German wines in some ways, usually fresh and young tasting, occasionally sparkling, but on the whole they are fuller. Identified by grape variety, the Riesling, Sylvaner and Traminer (a spicy, aromatic wine) are the best and the most common; Muscat is rather sweeter and more

flowery scented, while Sylvaner grapes give the local carafe wine.

## Dessert wines

We have already covered some of the best wines for serving after dinner when talking about hock and Sauternes. Although these are generally drunk as table wines throughout the meal, the best, and the sweetest, are good only with the dessert. At their best they need to be drunk alone, when all the food is finished. They are so sweet that they take the edge off the appetite and both wine and food would lose their pleasure if consumed together. These wines are extremely expensive, though, and most people will turn instead to port, Madeira or Marsala to drink with their cheese and fruit. Not that these fortified wines are of a lesser breed than the first but they are made differently. Port starts as a dark red, strong wine from the Oporto district of Portugal. It is a blended wine made from sweet grapes and in the old days these were allowed to go on fermenting until all the sugar was converted to alcohol, giving a very strong, dry wine. Then somebody thought of stopping the fermentation by adding a little brandy (the extra alcohol is what does the trick) – and the result was a rich, strong wine but a sweet one. The wine improves enormously by ageing in cask or bottle.

Ordinary, cheap port is called Ruby Port. It is aged in barrels and bottled only when it is ready to drink. It is then sold quite cheaply for drinking young. Tawny Port is also kept in barrels, but for a much longer time. It spends perhaps 10–15 years in the barrel, until its color lightens from red to tawny, and the flavor is correspondingly mellower. This is the most popular of ports, combining smoothness of flavor with a more reasonable price.

Vintage port is a little like Champagne – it only happens in special years. When a shipper declares a 'vintage' he bottles the wine 2 years after the vintage and leaves it to age in the bottle, where it forms a considerable deposit and finally a crust which means it has to be treated with the greatest respect. Usually only merchants, clubs and large restaurants have the facilities for laying down vintage port and leaving it undisturbed for the appropriate length of time.

Madeira is made on a similar principle, the difference being the grapes from which it is made. The sweetest Madeira and the best for after dinner are Malmsey and Bual. Others are not quite so sweet and are often drunk, chilled, as apéritifs. Equally, because they are not so sweet, they are sometimes more acceptable to the unaccustomed palate.

Marsala unfortunately rarely appears except in zabaglione. It is nevertheless an extremely good fortified wine not unlike a cream sherry, but with the rather more burnt, caramelly taste of Madeira. Coming from the flat area on the west coast of Sicily it is of course drunk more in Italy than anywhere, but there have been periods when it has been fashionable in all parts of the world. Certainly it is good enough for all but the grandest meals.

# MIXING DRINKS

*All mixed drinks are greatly improved by being really cold, so use plenty of ice, or chill the bottles thoroughly in the refrigerator beforehand. The correct garnish makes all the difference to the appearance of a drink and adds a really professional finishing touch to a cocktail. Many of the cocktail recipes given in our chart can be made with other spirits — in particular, gin and vodka are virtually interchangeable, a vodka martini being a very popular drink. Try making a gimlet with gin or vodka — you'll find it very refreshing. A Collins can be made with any of the spirits as a base and a Rickey or a Manhattan can also be mixed using any of the spirits.*

## GIN

Perhaps the most popular of all bases for mixed drinks. Don't use Dutch gin — this is not really suitable.

**Martini**
5—6 ice cubes
1 part dry vermouth
3 parts gin
1 large olive

Put the ice cubes in a glass jug, pour in the vermouth and gin and stir vigorously. Strain the drink into a martini glass and decorate with an olive.

**Pink gin**
2—3 drops Angostura bitters
1 part gin
2—3 parts ice water

Put the bitters into a glass and turn it until the sides are well coated. Add the gin and top up with iced water to taste.

**Gibson**
5—6 ice cubes
1 part very dry sherry
5 parts gin
1 pearl cocktail onion

Put the ice cubes in a glass jug, pour in the sherry and gin and stir well. Strain the drink into a chilled martini glass and add the onion on a stick.

**Negroni**
2—3 ice cubes
½ part Campari
1 part sweet vermouth
2 parts gin
1 slice orange
Soda water

Put the ice cubes into a tumbler and pour over them the Campari, vermouth and gin. Float the slice of orange on top and then top up with soda water to taste.

## VODKA

An increasingly popular drink which can be successfully used as an alternative to gin in many recipes

**Moscow mule**
3 ice cubes
2 parts vodka
Ginger beer or lemonade
Lemon and cucumber slices

Put the ice into a mug or tall glass and add the vodka. Top up with ginger beer or lemonade and garnish with lemon and cucumber. Stir lightly.

**Bronx**
1 part dry vermouth
1 part sweet vermouth
Juice of ½ orange
3 parts vodka

Put 4—5 ice cubes into a shaker and pour in the vermouths, orange juice and vodka. Shake well till a frost forms and strain into a chilled martini glass.

**Bloody Mary**
1 part vodka
2 parts tomato juice
Squeeze of lemon juice
Dash of Worcestershire sauce

Put some ice into a shaker with vodka, tomato juice, lemon and sauce. Shake and strain into a tumbler. Tabasco, salt and pepper may be added.

**Screwdriver**
1 part vodka
Juice of 1 orange
Angostura bitters (optional)

Put some ice cubes into a tall glass and pour in the vodka and orange juice. Add the bitters and stir lightly.

## WHISKY

Scotch, Irish, Canadian, rye or Bourbon all have different tastes. Where necessary we have specified which type should be used.

**Old fashioned**
1 sugar cube
1—2 dashes Angostura bitters
1—2 ice cubes
1 part whisky
½ slice orange

Put the sugar cube in a glass and shake the bitters onto it; mix around the glass to dissolve the sugar. Put in the ice, pour over the whisky and float the orange on top.

**Whisky sour**
Juice of ½ lemon
1 teaspoon sugar
1 teaspoon egg white
1 part rye whisky

Put all the ingredients in a shaker and stir together, then add cracked ice and shake well. Strain into a chilled glass and decorate with a twist of lemon.

**Virginia mint julep**
9 sprigs of mint
1 teaspoon sugar or sugar
  syrup
Crushed ice
3 parts Bourbon whisky

Put 6 sprigs of mint into a cold glass. Add the sugar and crush the 2 together. Fill the glass with crushed ice and pour in the whisky, stirring well.

**Tom Collins**
Juice of 1 lemon
1 tablespoon sugar or sugar
  syrup
3 parts whisky
Soda water

In a shaker, mix 6 ice cubes, lemon, sugar and whisky until a frost forms. Pour into a glass and add a slice of orange. Top with soda water and stir.

## RUM

A sugar-based drink with a wide range of flavors. There are three basic colourings — dark, golden and white.

**Cuba libré**
2 parts golden or dark rum
3 parts Coca Cola
Juice and peel of ½ lime
  or lemon

Put 3—4 ice cubes into a tall glass and pour in the rum, Coca Cola and fruit juice. Stir gently and drop in the lemon or lime peel.

### Gimlet
3–4 ice cubes
1 part lime juice
3 parts white or golden rum

Put the ice into a jug and pour in the lime juice and rum. Stir well and strain into a chilled martini glass.

### Manhattan
4–5 ice cubes
1 part sweet vermouth
3 parts white or golden rum
1 maraschino cherry

Put the ice cubes into a glass jug and pour in the vermouth and rum. Stir vigorously and strain into a chilled martini glass. Drop in the cherry.

### Daiquiri
Cracked ice
Juice of 2 limes
1 teaspoon sugar or sugar
 syrup
3 parts white rum

Put lots of cracked ice in a shaker and add the lime juice, sugar and rum. Shake well till a frost forms and then strain into a chilled martini glass.

# BRANDY

Don't use your best brandy for mixed drinks — it should be drunk on its own. Use a younger, cheaper one instead.

### Brandy Rickey
1 lime
½ teaspoon sugar
3 parts brandy
Maraschino cherry
Soda water

Put 4–5 ice cubes in a shaker and add the lime juice, sugar and brandy. Shake well and pour into a tall glass. Drop in the cherry and lime peel and top up with soda water.

### Brandy fizz
4–5 ice cubes
Juice of 1 lemon
1 teaspoon sugar or sugar
 syrup
1 part yellow Chartreuse
2 parts brandy
Soda water

Put the ice cubes in a shaker and pour in the lemon, sugar, Chartreuse and brandy and shake until a frost forms. Pour without straining into a tall glass, top with soda and stir lightly.

### Brandy Alexander
4–5 ice cubes
1 part cream
1 part crème de cacao
3 parts brandy

Put the ice cubes into a shaker and add the cream, crème de cacao and brandy. Shake until a frost forms and strain into a glass.

# SHERRY

The classic before-dinner drink in a new, exciting guise — these recipes may shock the purists but they're delicious.

### Sherry cobbler (makes 2)
Ice
10 tablespoons sherry
1 teaspoon sugar
2 teaspoons fresh orange
 juice
Slices of orange
Few strawberries

Put a few pieces of ice in a glass jug and add the sherry, sugar and orange juice. Stir well. Pour without straining into 2 chilled tumblers and decorate with the fruit. Serve with a drinking straw.

### Sherry refresher (makes
 4–6)
3 grapefruit
7½ tablespoons sweet sherry
Soda water
Ice

Squeeze the juice from the grapefruit and strain into a jug. Add the sherry and chill. Serve in goblets with a little ice and soda water to taste.

### Sherry cocktail
4–5 ice cubes
1 part dry vermouth
3 parts very dry sherry
1 slice lemon rind

Put the ice in a glass jug and pour in the vermouth and sherry. Stir well and strain into a chilled martini glass. Drop in the twisted lemon rind.

# WINE

Ideal for warm days, a wine cocktail, whether based on Champagne or a cheap rosé, is light and refreshing.

### Spritze (approx. 2 quarts)
1 bottle white wine
2 pints soda water

Chill the wine and soda water thoroughly. Just before serving, combine in a large glass jug.

### Sangria (approx. 1½ quarts)
1 bottle red wine, chilled
1 pint fizzy lemonade, chilled
1 slice of lemon
1 liqueur glass brandy
Slices of apple and orange
Sugar

Shortly before serving, mix the chilled wine and lemonade in a large bowl and add the lemon slice and brandy (optional). Float the apple and orange slices on top and add sugar to taste.

### Alfonso
1 sugar cube
2 dashes Angostura bitters
1 tablespoon Dubonnet
Champagne, well chilled

Put the sugar in the base of a champagne glass and drop on the bitters. Add the Dubonnet and, if liked, an ice cube as well. Top up with champagne.

### Vin blanc cassis
4 parts dry white wine
1 part crème de cassis

Chill the wine. Pour the crème de cassis into a claret glass and top up with wine.

# PORT

Not your favorite vintage port, of course, but a good ruby or tawny one — and white port looks especially refreshing.

### Port flip
1 egg
1 teaspoon confectioners'
 sugar
1 wineglass port
2–3 ice cubes
Nutmeg

Break the egg into a shaker or an electric blender and add the sugar, port and ice. Shake or blend well. Strain into a goblet and sprinkle with a little nutmeg before serving.

### Tawny sparkler (2 quarts)
Juice of 1 lemon
1 whole lemon
1 bottle tawny port
5 tablespoons curaçao
Soda water

Put the lemon juice in a bowl and add the port and curaçao. Slice the whole lemon, float it on top and leave for 20 minutes. Fill glasses two-thirds full and top up with chilled soda water.

### Port cocktail
4–5 ice cubes
2 drops Angostura bitters
1 teaspoon curaçao
3 parts port

Put 4–5 ice cubes in a jug and pour in the bitters, curaçao and port. Stir vigorously and strain into a chilled martini glass.

*Note:* Whatever you use as a measure, be sure to use the same measure for all the ingredients in a drink, so that the proportion of one ingredient to another is accurate.

# AMERICAN Wines

Wines produced in the United States are not to be regarded as step-children of European wines but should be judged on their own merits. This country produces a large quantity of inexpensive wines, similar to the 'Vin Ordinaire' of France, and a smaller quantity of very good wines which can certainly hold their own in any contest.

Wines of the United States can be recognized and judged in several different ways. Many of the generic names of American wines – such as Burgundy, Rhine Wine and Sauternes – came into use centuries ago as the names of the wines of Old World Viticultural districts famed for these particular types. As the wine types became known throughout the world, the same names were applied to all wines having similar characteristics, wherever they were grown. Claret, which is not a place name, thus has no geographic significance. This was the name applied by the British to the 'vin Clairette', or lighter wine of Bordeaux and eventually to any red dinner wine with similar characteristics.

Probably the best way to distinguish or compare American wines is by the name of the principal grape used to make the wine. To bear a varietal name a wine must derive at least 51 per cent of its volume from the grape for which it is named and must have the flavor and aroma of that grape.

Some varietal wines are made 100 per cent from the grape for which they are named. Others are made from blends of various grapes, once the required 51 per cent or more of the wine's volume is assured from the grape whose name appears on the label. Many wines produced in the United States are sold without any of the name types discussed, but are simply labeled red dinner wine, white dinner wine, red dessert wine or sparkling wines. They are usually sold simply by brand name and often can be purchased in gallon or half gallon jugs. When buying wine thus labeled it is important to remember that dinner wines have not more than 14 per cent alcoholic content and can be referred to as table wines, dry wines, light wines and natural wines. Dessert wines, including appetizer wines, are those which have between 14 and 21 per cent alcoholic content.

Completing the wine name picture, most wines are labeled not only with the type or class name, but with the name of the state or the viticultural area within the state in which the wine was grown. For example, sherry may be labeled California Sherry or New York State Sherry.

## Red dinner wines

Red dinner wines usually are dry, suited to accompany main course dishes. Burgundy is the generic name used to describe generous, full bodied, dry red wine, traditionally heavier in flavor, body and bouquet and of a deeper red color than Claret. California Burgundy is made from one or more of a number of grape varieties including Gamay, Pinot Noir and Petite Sirah. Pinot Noir is the classic grape of red Burgundy-type wines and the California wine made from it has a velvety-soft body and deep rich bouquet.

Barbera may be said to fit within the broad Burgundy group because it is full-bodied, but it is far heavier bodied and more tart than most Burgundies.

Claret is the name popularly applied to any dry, pleasantly tart, light or medium bodied wine of ruby-red color. Wines of this type are the most widely used mealtime wines in almost every wine drinking country in the world. California wines marketed under the broad title of Claret are made from one or more of a number of grape varieties such as Cabernet Sauvignon, Ruby Cabernet and Zinfandel. Cabernet Sauvignon is stronger in flavor and bouquet than most other Clarets and is fast becoming the premier wine of California. The production of wine from this grape is small and usually very good, therefore the price is usually rather high.

Zinfandel with its distinctive fruity taste and aroma is produced from a grape that is grown only in California. It is well worth trying, especially from one of the smaller vineyards.

Gamay Beaujolais is a red wine that is meant to be drunk young. A spin-off of the Beaujolais wine of France, the California varieties are rich in fruity taste and are normally a pleasant, inexpensive table wine.

In color and body, the red dinner wine known as Chianti may resemble either Claret or Burgundy, but it differs from them in its strong, characteristic Italian flavor. Chianti is dry, fruity, slightly tart and ruby red in color.

## White dinner wines

White dinner wines vary from extremely dry and tart to sweet and full bodied with the delicate flavor that blends best with white meat, fowl and seafood. They range from pale straw to deep gold in color and in alcoholic content from 10 to 14 per cent. The most popular white dinner wines are Chablis, Rhine Wine and Sauternes.

Chablis is very dry, with a fruity flavor and a delicate pale gold color. It is slightly fuller-bodied and less tart than a Rhine wine. Traditionally it is made from a number of white Burgundy grape varieties, notably the aristocratic Pinot Blanc and Chardonnay, which produces a very special California wine. This grape makes a wonderful, distinguished wine, full bodied and strong in character.

Rhine wine is the generic name popularly applied to any thoroughly dry, pleasantly tart, light bodied white dinner wine, pale golden or slightly green-gold. The original Rhine wines were made from only a few special grapes, notably the Riesling varieties, but wines of many other grapes are classed as Rhine wines in this country.

Riesling is Rhine wine made from one of the Riesling variety grapes and having its particular flavor and aroma. The best known California Riesling is produced from the true Johannesberg Riesling grape and is a refreshing wine, fruity and satisfying. Hock and Moselle are other American names for Rhine-type wines. They have separate geographic significance in European wines but none in America. The name Hock is used in English-speaking countries as a synonym for Rhine wine.

Sauternes are golden-hued, fragrant, full bodied wines ranging from dry to sweet. California Sauternes are generally drier than those of France.

Other white dinner wines, produced in the East and Midwest of the United States, have the typical flavors, aromas and tartness of the grapes for which they are named. Catawba is produced both dry and semi-sweet, like Sauternes, while Delaware and Elvira have more Rhine Wine characteristics.

However, reading the words and discussing the different varieties and names of wines, is not really the true test. Try drinking California and New York State wines to find which kinds appeal to you the most. You may like to start with various jug wines which are inexpensive and very pleasant. When you have decided whether you like dry wines or sweet, or red wines or white, you should try some of the varietal wines to discover that great wines can be produced in this country.

# Brandy and Liqueurs

When the eating is over, when all the wine has gone and the dishes have been cleared away, then is the time to serve coffee and to offer brandy and liqueurs. This habit probably started as a precaution against the ill effects of overeating, for many spirit-based drinks, especially those that include herbs, act as aids to digestion. But medicine is forgotten now and we enjoy a wide range of after-dinner drinks for the pleasure of their flavors alone. Liqueurs are expensive but are served in very small glasses, so they need not be extravagant.

## BRANDY

Brandy is the most widely known and widely made of these drinks. A spirit distilled from wine, it is made in every country that grows wine, the character of the wine being reflected in the brandy. It is not, however, the 'best' wines that provide the most palatable brandy. This is illustrated by the history of Cognac. This comes from a region in the west of France which used to produce a rather poor grade wine. Yet the grape grown and the type of soil in that region yield a brandy recognized as the finest in the world.

The grapes for brandy are picked before they are fully ripe, so that they retain a certain degree of acidity. The wine is made in the early autumn and distilled as soon as fermentation stops, before the winter is over.

The wine is heated in a still, the alcoholic vapor is driven off, recaptured and condensed into liquid spirit. In the Cognac region the stills used are old-fashioned pot-stills, operated by craftsmen. Different constituents of the wine vaporize at different temperatures, and pot-stills give a very fine control over just which part of the vapor, containing the desirable amount of alcohol and flavor, is retained. The wine is distilled twice to give a high alcohol content. Other areas use different types of still which give varying, usually less fine, control.

The spirit obtained is, of course, clear and colorless. Much of the color is drawn from the oak barrels in which the brandy is left to mature, and the flavor is affected by the wood too. Freshly distilled Cognac is about 70 per cent alcohol; for sale it is normally diluted to about 40 per cent, and the sweetness and color are adjusted with sugar and caramel – different shippers using different amounts of both but usually keeping to a constant style.

Brandy is as much affected by the treatment it receives after distillation as by the wines from which it is made. This can be seen if Cognac is compared with Armagnac – another very fine brandy coming from an area in western France not far from the Cognac country.

In Armagnac a different type of still is used, in which the wine is distilled only once; the alcohol content is therefore lower (53 per cent) but the flavor and smell are correspondingly stronger. The brandy is then matured in barrels made of black oak, a rather soft, moist wood which gives the brandy a darker color and stronger flavor than the lighter oak used for Cognac. Sugar is not normally added, so the final product is much dryer. Cognac and

crème de menthe, crème de cacao), others such as Bénédictine or Chartreuse are sold under a brand name and the ingredients are kept secret.

The most common liqueur bases are brandy, whisky, gin and rum, but some are based on a spirit with very little flavor, distilled from potatoes or a grain; this provides the alcohol content, the other ingredients providing all the flavor. Many liqueurs are not colored by their ingredients, others are deliberately given brilliant or rich colors which add to their appeal – crème de menthe is an obvious example. (Where the word 'crème' occurs in the name, this usually indicates that the liqueur is particularly sweet.) Below is a list of

made in that area. It is very sweet and highly aromatic, suggesting that its main flavoring ingredients are spices and herbs.

### Calvados
An apple brandy, made in Normandy from cider. The best comes from the Vallée d'Auge. Old Calvados can be magnificent.

### Cassis
A blackcurrent liqueur mainly drunk in France, where it is sometimes diluted and served as a long drink. The base is brandy.

### Chartreuse
Another of the secret recipes, again originating from a monastery in France, this time in the 17th century at a Carthusian monastery near Grenoble. There are 2 types of Chartreuse, one is green and has a very high alcohol content; the other yellow, much sweeter and not so strong.

### Cherry brandy
The best is made from a base of distilled cherries. Cherries are then macerated in the brandy to give it color and flavor. Cheaper cherry brandies are made by macerating cherries in a neutral spirit.

### Crème de cacao
A very sweet, colorless liqueur, flavored with cocoa.

### Crème de menthe
A very sweet liqueur flavored with fresh mint. It is available both colorless and colored.

### Crème de moka
A very sweet, coffee-flavored liqueur.

### Curaçao
A colorless liqueur flavored with oranges and based on either brandy or gin. There are many different brands of curaçao, the best known being Grand Marnier and Cointreau.

### Drambuie
A whisky-based liqueur flavored with honey.

### Fruit brandies
There are many brandies distilled directly from fruits and berries other than grapes. The prime example is Kirsch, made from cherries, but popular liqueurs are also made from raspberries (crème de framboise, Himbeergeist), plums (quetsch, Zwetschenwasser), apricots (abricot, Aprikosengeist), gentiane (Enzian) and many others.

### Kirsch
A colorless liqueur distilled from the small black cherries native to Switzerland, Germany and Alsace.

### Kummel
A liqueur with definite medicinal properties. It is based on a highly distilled spirit made from grain or potatoes, and flavored with cumin and caraway seeds. Some brands are sweeter than others. It is always colorless.

### Maraschino
A cherry liqueur distilled from marasca cherries, on the Dalmatian coast of Yugoslavia.

### Van der Hum
A South African liqueur based on Cape Brandy. The main flavoring ingredient is naartje, the South African tangerine, with other fruits and spices.

*Rich, sweet, spirit-based liqueurs for after dinner*

Armagnac are always matured for at least 2 years, usually up to 5. If kept for as much as 20 years the flavor becomes increasingly fine, but the alcohol content decreases as it evaporates through the porous wood. The letters VSOP on the label stand for Very Special Old Pale that has been kept for at least 5 years.

## LIQUEURS
Liqueurs are all based on a spirit of some sort, many on brandy. They are flavored with all kinds of different fruits, herbs, nuts, roots, seeds, leaves and flowers, sometimes a combination of these, and are nearly all heavily sweetened with sugar. Many are known by their chief ingredient (such as cherry brandy,

the commonest liqueurs, their characteristics and ingredients (where known).

### Advocaat
A thick, yellow liquid, the texture of double cream. Made from brandy and egg yolks.

### Anisette
Colorless, very sweet liqueur flavored with aniseed.

### Apricot brandy
A brandy base, flavored with dried apricots; the very best may be distilled from fresh apricots and their kernels (see fruit brandies).

### Bénédictine
This is one of the secret recipes. It originated with the Benedictine monks at Fécamp in Normandy, in the 16th century, and is still

# COFFEE

Devoted coffee drinkers tend to be fanatical about their favorite blend and their favorite method of preparing it. However, it is all a matter of personal taste and what is right for one can well be quite wrong for another. There are three basic secrets for success without which you cannot hope to produce a good, refreshing brew.
1. Use a sparkling clean coffeemaker.
2. Use accurate measure of coffee and freshly drawn cold water.
3. Discard coffee grounds as soon as coffee has been brewed and *never* let coffee boil.

Now relax and enjoy a cup of fragrant, flavorful, steaming coffee.

Start with a sparkling clean coffeemaker. Coffee oils and stains tend to collect inside coffeemakers, so a coffeemaker needs to be scrubbed and rinsed clean every time it is used (otherwise the sediment will affect the flavor of the coffee). Heavily chlorinated or very hard water also tends to give coffee an off-flavor. Coffeemakers should be used at their full capacity to obtain the best flavor – never less than ¾ capacity.

You should always use fresh coffee. If you have a grinder, buy the coffee beans freshly roasted and store them in an airtight container. Do not buy too large a quantity and use them up as soon as possible. Be sure to set the grinder to the grind that is specified by the manufacturer of your coffeemaker.

Buy ground coffee in small amounts, unless it is used in a large quantity. The sooner the coffee is used after it is ground, or after a vacuum-packed can of ground coffee is opened, the better the coffee. For a rich, full-bodied coffee start with 2 level tablespoons coffee and ¾ measuring cup (6 ounces) freshly drawn cold water. (Never use water which has been kept in a teakettle as it has lost oxygen and will taste flat.)

Experiment with the amount of coffee until you find the strength of coffee you like best. When you find this amount, use the same measure of coffee and water every time for consistently good results.

Remove coffee grounds and serve coffee as soon as possible after brewing – never make a bigger quantity than you need and save it for

later. Stale coffee becomes bitter-tasting and is unpleasant to drink. If it must be kept hot, do so over low heat. *Never* boil coffee.

## TOP-OF-RANGE PERCOLATOR

Measure cold, fresh water into percolator (water level should always be below the bottom of the basket). Insert the basket and measure in the required amount of regular grind coffee. When the water boils it is forced up the center tube and filters down through the ground coffee. As soon as the water begins to turn amber, reduce heat at once so perking is slow and gentle (otherwise coffee will be bitter). Percolate gently for 5–8 minutes (overperking causes bitterness). Remove the coffee basket as soon as perking stops as used coffee grounds absorb aroma and give coffee an unpleasant flavor. Serve at once.

## DRIP METHOD

Preheat pot by rinsing with very hot water. Measure drip-grind coffee into the filter section. Put the upper container over the filter section. Measure briskly boiling water into the upper container and cover. Let water drip through only once. When dripping is completed, remove the upper section and basket. Serve immediately.

## VACUUM METHOD

Put cold fresh water into the lower bowl and put on heat. Put filter in the upper bowl and add vacuum-grind or extra fine ground coffee. When the water boils, reduce the heat and insert the upper bowl with a slight twist. Let most of the water rise into upper bowl. Lower the heat, stir gently once or twice and allow the coffee to infuse for 1–3 minutes. Remove from the heat. The coffee will then filter back into the lower container. Remove the upper bowl and serve at once.

The particular advantage of this method is that the coffee itself is never in direct contact with the heat and therefore cannot boil, however careless you may be. Many people also like the result obtained using a glass container in preference to metal.

## ESPRESSO METHOD

Espresso machines make a strong brew of coffee which should be served in small cups. Allow 2 tablespoons of special espresso-roast finely ground coffee for 2 cups water. Put the cold water in the machine and the coffee in the special container. When the water boils it is forced under steam pressure through the grounds into a separate jug.

Alternatively, there is another special pot similar to a drip coffee pot. Put special espresso-roast finely ground coffee in the basket; put over boiling water in the bottom of the pot. Put the top part of the pot in place and turn the entire coffeepot upside down so water runs through coffee. Process may be repeated if very strong coffee is desired.

## ELECTRIC PERCOLATOR

Follow manufacturer's directions. If no amounts are given, start with 1 or 2 level tablespoons of special electric coffee pot grind coffee and ¾ measuring cup (6 ounces) of water for each cup of brewed coffee. Brew the full capacity of the percolator – never less than ¾ capacity, unless it has been especially designed to make less. The strength of the coffee can be adjusted to suit your taste by using more or less coffee, or changing the brewing time, or using milk, medium or strong setting on the coffeemaker.

# HOW DO

*Some of the most delicious foods are difficult to eat tidily, but you can at least present your guests with the right equipment or prepare the food as helpfully as possible. If you are in doubt about the best things to provide, here is a brief check list for the foods that can cause most embarrassment to the uninitiated.*

**Globe artichokes** The outer leaves are pulled away with the fingers, and the fleshy base of each leaf dipped in melted butter or dressing and sucked. When setting the table, provide individual small plates or bowls for the discarded leaves. Finger bowls are a help (use small glass or pottery fruit bowls if you don't have special bowls). A small knife and fork are needed for the 'choke'.

**Asparagus** If served as a separate course, asparagus is eaten in the fingers, each spear being dipped in melted butter, sauce or dressing, which is poured on the side of the plate. It helps if you leave part of the firm stalk on

when you trim the asparagus for cooking, to serve as a 'handle'. Lay a small knife and fork to be used to retrieve any of the tips which may break off. Finger bowls are a help, or thick napkins may be provided.

**Avocados** Serve on a small plate (or special avocado dish), with a teaspoon. You use your spare hand to steady the avocado while eating.

**Corn on the cob** It is easier to eat this vegetable tidily with special holders to spear into each end of the cob, instead of grasping it with the fingers. If you do not have special holders, use your smallest skewers. A small knife and fork should also be laid, the knife to spread the butter and the fork to help gather up the last bits of corn. Bear in mind that it is difficult to eat this elegantly, even with the proper equipment!

**Melon** Your guests will find it much easier to eat melon if it has been cut beforehand into bite-size pieces and arranged back on the skin. Provide a fruit knife and fork, which is also the best equipment if you have not pre-cut the melon. For small Charentais or Ogen melons,

served cut in halves, provide a teaspoon.

**Chicken in the basket** This is eaten with fingers only, so have plenty of thick paper napkins and finger bowls.

**Gulls' and quails' eggs** Serve hard-cooked and in their shells, for your guests to peel the eggs themselves. Dip them in salt or celery salt and eat in the fingers.

**Spaghetti** Lay a spoon, fork and a knife, so that guests can choose whether they twist the strands around the fork in the bowl of the spoon, Italian style, or cut it up more conventionally; even those who cut it up will probably want a spoon for the last pieces of spaghetti and sauce. For other pasta (cannelloni, lasagne) a spoon and fork are sufficient.

**Lobster** It is sensible to serve lobster already removed from its shell, in a salad. If you do leave it in the shell, you must provide lobster picks, and there is no good substitute for the specially designed implement. If you dress the lobster and return it to its shell for serving, provide a fish knife and fork.

**Mediterranean shrimp** It is easier to pull the

134

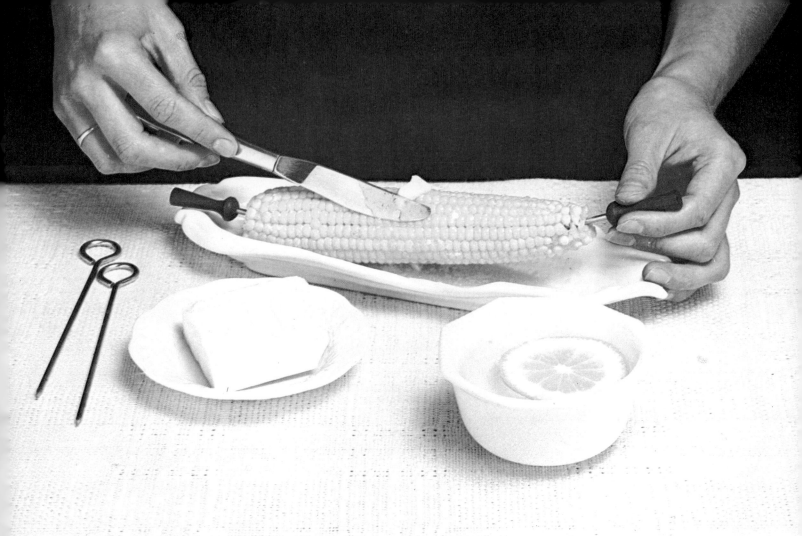

# I SERVE IT?

shell off the shrimp in the fingers and then eat the meat with the help of a small fish fork, but provide a fish knife as well, to meet all preferences. Provide finger bowls.

**Mussels (Moules marinières)** These are best eaten from a bowl or soup plate, with a fork to get the mussel out of the shell (holding the shell in your fingers) and a spoon for the liquid. Provide a plate for discarded shells. Finger bowls are a help.

**Oysters** A small fork is all that is needed.

**Shrimp or lobster cocktail** Put a teaspoon on the plate under the cocktail glass – this is the easiest implement to eat it with.

**Soups** Most soups of course are simply served in an open soup plate or double handled cup, with a soup spoon. Some of the more substantial soups – bouillabaisse, cock-a-leekie, etc. – contain more solid foods. If you wish, drain off the liquid, serve it separately in a soup cup with a spoon, and serve the meat or more solid foods with a knife and fork.

**Snails** Serve the snails in their shells, preferably in a special snail dish which will hold the shells upright and prevent the butter running out. Provide long, thin snail forks for extracting the snails from the shells and special tongs to hold the shell.

**Whelks and winkles** Serve in the shells, like snails. Unfortunately there are few forks made that are thin enough to go into these shells, and the usual alternative is to provide your guests with sterilized hat pins with which to prize out the fish. Sturdy, plastic cocktail sticks might serve as a substitute if elegant pins are not to be found.

**Grapefruit** Cut the fruit in half and carefully cut around between the flesh and the skin with a curved, serrated knife. Then cut either side of each membrane, so that the segments can be lifted out completely free of membrane. Provide long, tapering grapefruit spoons. Serrated spoons for grapefruit are available; if you have these, the halved grapefruit do not need any preparation.

**Smoked trout** Remove the skin from the body of the fish but leave the head and tail intact. Provide fish knives and forks.

**Smoked salmon** Just cut as thinly as possible. If it is really tender it should be possible to cut and eat it with a fork only, but check this first and provide a knife as well, if in doubt.

**Swiss cheese fondue** Provide a basket full of cubes of crusty bread and long-handled forks. Each guest spears a cube of bread on a fork and dips it into the fondue.

**Chinese food** The Chinese traditionally do not serve separate courses. All the food is set out at once in serving dishes in the centre of the table, with the exception of rice – each person has an individual bowl of rice. The hot dishes are usually kept on a hot plate. Each person takes a mouthful of food from one dish (using chopsticks, or a fork) and either eats it direct or puts it in his rice bowl; he may dip it in one of the sauces on the way. A mouthful of rice is taken between each helping from the central dishes. The diners go to each dish in turn, to mingle the flavors and textures. Apart from the rice bowl and chopsticks, provide each person with a plate for discarded bones, shells and so on.

# Setting the Table

Setting the table is a gracious art that should not be allowed to die. Whatever anybody says about looks not counting, they most definitely do count when it comes to food. The look of the food itself somehow affects the way it tastes and an elegant or pretty table-setting, depending on the mood of the meal, will help your party off to a good start and maintain the atmosphere right through to the dessert.

If you are slightly nervous about the forthcoming meal (though you have no need to be if you follow our timetables!) a carefully planned table-setting can reassure you. This is the one place where nothing can go wrong at the last minute. You can set the table hours in advance if you wish and, provided you can keep the children out, it will still be perfect when guests arrive – leaving you free to give all your last minute attention to the food.

The basis for your table-setting will be the linen or mats you choose. Individual place mats can be right even for a formal occasion if you have a really super table to show off. A word of warning, though, to those with temperamental table surfaces –if you are going to supply enough mats to protect the table thoroughly from heat and scratches from all possible sources, the effect will be lost; you need to be able to leave large areas of wood exposed to achieve an uncluttered look.

Both to protect your table and set off your best china and cutlery, the answer is an efficient heat-proof covering and a lovely linen tablecloth. It is possible to buy to order protective cork mats that will exactly fit your table and fold away when not in use. However, many of the newer dining-tables have a protective finish, making the use of a heat-proof covering unnecessary.

The traditional white damask cloth is still used for special occasions. However, for a background for fine table accessories, something more unusual will give you more opportunity to use your imagination to co-ordinate a color scheme for total effect. There are many other white cloths, from sheerest organdy type 'burn outs' to plains with lace edge or embroidery trim, to fine Belgian or Irish linen with color appliqué or special edging. If mats are of high count linen Madeira, hand-embroidered or all lace, they are as formal as any cloth.

Print mats or cloths are popular today for both family use and for entertaining. Wipe-off vinyl mats are often amusing, colorful and easy to care for. Synthetic no-iron cloths should be selected with the less formal china in mind. As in other decorating, caution should be taken in mixing patterns and colors. The mood of a table changes quickly with a change from vibrant tones to subdued sophisticated ones.

In general, keep your setting as simple as possible. Use colors sparingly and base them on the tones predominant in the china, bearing in mind that when the food arrives it should take the center of attention. Silver, glass, candles (white or to match the china) and a few flowers will complete the picture. It would be so nice if we could all have a

*Mix and match your tableware in style*

choice of china for different occasions. To have fine china for formal dinners and chunky earthenware for less formal occasions would be ideal (as would a choice of silver or stainless steel cutlery) –but of course we have to make do with what is available. The rule, though, is not to try to make your tableware do something for which it is not designed. If all you have is studio pottery, don't try to be formal with it.

Glasses go to the right of the place setting, above the knives. If you are putting out more than one glass, arrange them so that the one to be used first is on the right, and work inwards. Although it looks attractive to set out different shaped glasses, don't worry too much about having the correct glasses for each wine as the rules are much less strict now than they used to be. A large, stemmed glass with a rounded bowl, cupping in towards the top, is suitable for all wines.

The rules for the arrangement of silver are very simple. Knives, blades pointing towards the plate, and spoons always go on the right. Forks go on the left side of the plates. All items should be as close together as possible without actually touching. This produces a tidy result, especially if all the handles are lined up a consistent ½ in. from the edge of the table. A menu of soup, then meat and finally dessert, should have a left to right place setting as follows; meat fork, space for plate, meat knife and soup spoon. The butter knife is placed vertically across the butter plate. Spoons or forks for dessert can be brought in with the dessert. If you wish to serve salad as a separate course, the salad fork should be on the table next to the meat fork.

Once the table covering and accessories are decided upon, attention should turn to the centerpieces. Flowers or greens give the table 'life'. They are often effective as an accent to many other objects such as fresh or artificial fruit or vegetables, china figures, animals or even children's toys. A centerpiece is the means of making a good impression with very little, if it is just right. A hostess is free to follow her whims and be praised for it.

The mellow glow of candles suggests the warmth of hospitality and creates an atmosphere of mystery and festivity which not even dimmed artificial candles can equal. They are a tradition dating back to the times when castles and cottages were lit by them. Fortunately, today the sizes, colors and shapes of candles are limitless, so it is suggested that a collection of them be started, keeping a supply in the colors which tie in with the household's china and decor.

For a buffet, even a formal one, the rules for positioning the tableware are thrown totally to the winds. The prevailing need at a buffet is to display the food to advantage and to put plates, cutlery and napkins where they will least hinder people coming to the table for serving. This usually means grouping them at one end of the table, where guests can collect them before moving on to gather their first course without getting in each other's way. Another solution, ideal if your room space will allow it, is a side table or rolling cart for these things. Positioning of utensils aside, the rules for setting a buffet table remain similar to those for any other table. Simplicity is again the key, the more so here as the display of all the food together at once imparts its own festive atmosphere. A plain cloth is the perfect background for elaborate trays of salads, cold meats and sumptuous desserts, and one big centerpiece of flowers, set well back where it can't be knocked over by reaching hands, will complete the scene.

For all the delights of displaying all the foods at once, it is better not to over-crowd the table. If you have a large number of guests and only an average-size table, it may be worth leaving the desserts elsewhere until most people have eaten their main course. You can then whisk away the empties and refurnish the table with desserts, refreshing the eye as well as tempting the palate.

Feel free to mix formal and informal styles. Any style followed through too precisely becomes stiff, and it is the unexpected touches that give individual flair. A formal table setting should logically have formal flowers, but simple garden flowers, like daisies or sweet peas, arranged casually in a pottery jug, may just bring the table to life. Conversely, an informal setting with pottery and multi-colored linen could become magnificent with the help of a silver candelabra. 'Mix and match' is therefore the key. Bear this in mind when you are buying tableware and it will be much easier when you actually come to set the table. A little planning and imagination go a long way!

# Informal Table Settings

To make the best of informal occasions, go for natural finishes – wood, earthenware, chunky glasses, coarse linen napkins and cloth or mats. Straw mats are attractive, inexpensive and protect the table well. Use of colors in the green/brown range helps to accentuate the casual feeling and these tones will always complement wooden and earthenware dishes; they are also good colors to put beside food. If your casual tableware is of the decorated earthenware type, maybe white with a brightly colored pattern, follow through the colors of the dishes into the cloth and napkins, but choose coarse linen or cotton; wooden bowls and stainless steel cutlery fit the mood better than silver and fine glass.

This is the ideal time, too, to bring out odd bits and pieces of pottery and glass that you

more than one plate, and choose a lightweight material so that it is easy to handle. Tray cloths have gone rather out of style now, and with easy-clean surfaces it is probably easier to do without. But a pleasant arrangement of dishes, a fresh, bright napkin and perhaps a single flower in a small jug or an egg cup will add savour to any meal. If your tray does not clean too easily or if the surface is smooth and slippery, use a linen table mat or tray cloth that matches the napkin.

The secret of setting a tray is two-fold; never over-load it so that it looks overcrowded or precarious; but do include on it everything that is needed for the meal – cruet, side plate, cream jug, depending on what you are serving. This means of course that you have to plan the right sort of meal for a tray. This

several variations on straight-sided cups in plain pastel colors can mix very well, or curvy cups in different flower patterns, perhaps some with scalloped edges. Serving plates can also be pretty pieces of china that you have collected over the years – often you can find single dishes that are a better shape for sandwiches than the conventional, round plates usually supplied with a tea service. The teapot can match the cups or not, as you please, though it is nicer if the teapot, milk jug and sugar basin match. All that you need otherwise are napkins, teaspoons, tea knives and perhaps cake forks if you are serving a squashy gâteau. Knives must be small, otherwise they overbalance off the small tea plates and become an embarrassment. If you don't have special cake forks, small fruit forks will serve the purpose and are better than leaving people to fight the cream with their bare fingers. The napkins for tea should be small – they are really only for wiping fingers, since tea-time food is usually cut to small sizes.

For most carts, cloths are essential. The glass cart in our picture is an exception, since the surfaces clean easily with a damp cloth and look much better with no covering, but a wooden cart should be protected. Use pretty or plain cloths to match the napkins and the style of the china.

*Set the afternoon tea cart with fine china and linen*

have collected just because you liked them – they don't have to match anything else so long as the mood is right. Be flexible about the purpose of certain utensils. If you have only one set of bowls and want to use these for the sweet course, bring out some pottery mugs for the soup; or if you're not serving soup but need the bowls for a side salad, serve the sweet in wine glasses – or on the pottery side plates if they are most suitable. Bring out your odd jugs for sauces and salad dressings, and a really old fashioned, chunky glass jug looks just right for holding celery sticks alongside the cheese.

### MEALS ON A TRAY

Whatever the reason for a meal on a tray, it is a luxury for most of us. An invalid tray in bed, when you are starting to recover from 'flu, or just tea by the fire, either way it is really rather pleasant. To make it even more pleasant it is worth setting the tray properly.

Use a large tray if possible, to give room for

should preferably be a 1-dish meal, and only a single course. It rather detracts from the luxury if you have to get up in the middle to take out the dirty dishes and fetch another course. (For an invalid of course it's different; there's somebody else to see to such details!)

### AFTERNOON TEA

It is rather sad that afternoon tea is disappearing from the social scene. For one thing, it is a far less expensive way of offering hospitality than a dinner party. Nevertheless the opportunity to indulge does still arise and it is worth making an occasion of it.

This is without doubt the time to bring out the wedding-gift china tea service. Although tea doesn't really taste any different out of a mug or an earthenware cup, somehow a fine china cup is one of the niceties. If you haven't a complete service of matching plates, cups and saucers, a harlequin set made up from different services is just as pretty, so long as the pieces are all of a similar style. For instance,

### COFFEE MORNINGS

Coffee mornings fall into 2 groups. Some are large gatherings, perhaps in aid of a charity or local association, in which case the table should be set on much the same lines as for a buffet. Cups and saucers should be laid at one end of the table, with space for the coffee pot. A good supply of coffee is the central point of the occasion, and for this you must have several coffee pots at the ready, hot milk or cream and 2–3 bowls of sugar on the table for people to help themselves. Serving plates and teaspoons are usually the only other equipment needed; if you are serving fruit breads or open sandwiches you will need to put out small plates, but if it is biscuits only, most people will find it easier to use their saucers.

A casual coffee morning for a few friends is a much different affair. Again the cart comes into its own, but it would be a mistake mid-morning to use the fine china that is suitable for tea. Chunky earthenware cups and plates are the best at this time of day, and the coffee cups should of course be full size – tiny coffee cups are for after dinner only.

It is unlikely that you will serve anything for which knives will be needed, but your guests will almost certainly be sitting down, so provide plates, and small napkins may be a help. Again, have at least 2 pots of coffee available, with a choice of cream or warm milk. Use plain cart cloths in the morning, to encourage the informal atmosphere. There is not usually room for flowers on a loaded cart so put 1–2 bowls around the room instead.

The rules for any occasion may of course be bent to suit your own taste. Nevertheless any hostess will feel more relaxed if the setting is right, and designed to complement the food.

# FLOWERS FOR THE TABLE

Flowers bring any table setting to life. Before the meal, when all the linen and tableware are set out but there is no food, the table seems dead until flowers help to distract from the bare table mats.

Arranging flowers for the table is a special art, something over and above the normal skills of producing an artistic arrangement. In this context, the choice of flowers is crucial to the success of the arrangement – you can't necessarily just make use of the flowers you have available, as you would in a normal room setting. Just as linen and china are chosen to tone together and to match the mood of the food, the flowers must do the same. Their colors must also tone with or complement the colors of the tableware.

Other considerations also come into your choice of flowers. At a dinner party, or any sit-down meal, the flowers should never be so tall that they obscure one guest's face from another, or that they run the risk of being knocked over as dishes are passed around. Strong-smelling flowers should be avoided as these distract from the pleasure of the food smells and can even conflict with them unpleasantly. On the other hand, flowers for the buffet table benefit from height as the guests are usually standing anyway and the height of a flower arrangement can give shape to an otherwise flat arrangement of foods.

Choose your containers for table flowers carefully. Keep them low, fairly flat and if they have any height at all, be sure they are heavy based and therefore stable. Collect together old pottery dishes, copper or brass pans, large glass ashtrays even – all these are ideal containers for table flowers.

The arrangement shown at the head of this page was made in a copper gratin dish, the handles showing to break up an otherwise rather formal arrangement of red roses, dahlias and briony berries. This particular arrangement is designed for a formal dinner table setting on a white cloth or dark, polished wood surface – the color is strong, the arrangement low and the shape very compact, the outline merely broken by a few straying dahlia buds. This red on a colored cloth could be quite wrong unless it tied in very closely with the colors of the cloth and china.

Try fixing a small pin holder to one side of a large glass ashtray, using plasticine or florist's clay; make a posy of 2–3 cabbage roses, clematis heads or other wide flowers to cover the pin holder only, leaving the gleaming glass and water exposed alongside. This is an elegant small arrangement that cannot obstruct the dinner table conversation.

Alternatively, twine a few trailing flowers and leaves around the holder of a tall candle – the candle will be firmly enough wedged not to tip, and the flowers will serve to soften the shape of the holder. (Please don't let the wax drip on them though – there's nothing more dismal than scorched, drying flowers.) If you particularly like candles, you may like to buy a special candle holder with a flower holder in the base – these make it much easier to provide the flowers with water.

It is rarely advisable to go for a strictly formal arrangement at the table, even if the setting is a formal dinner. Fine china and silver can become somehow sterile if a stark arrangement of flowers is used, and something soft and casual, added as if an afterthought (but a planned afterthought) will be more pleasing. When it comes to choosing flowers, your choice does of course depend largely on what grows in your garden or what you can afford to buy from the florist. Roses are nearly always suitable – either arranged with other flowers as here, or casually placed in a small pottery jug for the supper table. Daisies of all sorts, marigolds and any small flowers lend themselves well to table arrangements. Don't neglect scabious, Christmas roses or the little early gladioli and even the common nasturtium, with its pretty, round leaves. Large flowers are difficult unless you have a table like a football pitch – guests sit so close to the blooms that the arrangement disappears behind one single flower head. And do be careful to shake dahlias well before you bring them to the table – they are rather prone to hiding earwigs within their curly petals and it is not very appetizing to see an insect emerge and wander across the dinner table.

*Arctotis, early gladioli, dianthus and chincherinchees will stay fresh for days*

*Use height and width for a buffet table arrangement*

It is, of course, possible to use large flower heads by simply floating a single head in a dish of water – take this a stage further and place a small finger bowl by the side of each place, with a flower head floating in it. Big tea roses are ideal for floating in a bowl, though they do need to be fully out to look effective. Hydrangeas also look well in this way and can be used quite late in the year when they are fading to lovely tapestry reds, blues and greens.

Failing finger bowls, use oyster or scallop shells with 1–2 small flower heads fastened with plasticine.

To present a striking splash of color in the center of the table, arrange a mass of tulip heads in a shallow white, or glass, bowl – cut the heads really short and be generous with the quantity so that they are packed tightly in. Another attractive mass arrangement can be made simply with 4–5 pots of African violets in full bloom, grouped in a shallow, square casserole or similar container. This is not as extravagant as it sounds because the violets will go on as pot plants.

At times when flowers are short, use wild berries, hips, spindle, old man's beard, or leaves from variegated plants like peperomia, tradescantia or begonia. Alternatively, use an arrangement of fruit and leaves. Make a base of wide leaves in a dish – ivy, rhododendron, even rhubarb well polished with oil – and make an arrangement of different shapes and colors. Aubergines and grapes go together well, or polished apples and copper beach leaves. Gourds are particularly helpful in this context and it is well worth trying to cultivate an ornamental gourd plant in your garden or on a balcony; they make an extremely attractive base for a table arrangement. Failing this a common marrow makes a good color base, as long as you cover part of it with something more interesting.

For a buffet table, long stems and an abundance of flowers become an advantage. Tone the colors with the china and linen again but for a buffet you can be much freer with shape. Use either a single, large display or several tiny posies. All the flowers shown in the two biggest arrangements are good buys from the florist as they last well. In the white bowl, spray chrysanthemums, day lilies and chincherinchees with moluccella (bells of Ireland) should keep fresh looking for days. The pink and white arrangement of arctotis (South African daisies), early gladioli, dianthus and chincherinchees should keep similarly well. Remember even for a buffet table to stick with delicately scented flowers.

If you want an arrangement which does not take up too much room on a buffet table, use tall candlesticks with a special holder that fits where the candle normally goes. The flowers are arranged in the holder, secured in plastic foam and wire, so that they stand above the food while the candlestick itself takes up very little table space. This is a good arrangement for a wedding buffet where the cake takes pride of place. Choose delicate flowers like dianthus, white early gladioli and trails of stephanotis.

China, glass, silver and table linen can turn a meal into a banquet. They can transform the atmosphere of something quite ordinary into a really special occasion. Perhaps this is why people so love to give them as wedding presents. But to keep them in good condition does require just a little effort.

The easiest to care for is china. Most china and earthenware will keep its good looks with simple washing in hot water and detergent. It is best rinsed in very hot water after washing and left to drain in a plastic covered rack, then put away as soon as it is dry – drying on a tea towel is a miserable job and not terribly hygienic unless you use a clean cloth every time.

Glasses take a little more effort. These really do need polishing with a soft, dry, fluff-free cloth while they are still hot, otherwise they will not have that lovely shine that sets off your table. If your glassware does develop a film – in the bottom of a decanter, for instance – it can be removed with a solution of 1 tablespoon salt in ⅝ cup vinegar. When shaken, this acts as a gentle abrasive that will not harm the surface. Stubborn, stuck-on food should be removed from china or glass first by soaking in cold water then, if necessary, rubbing gently with a nylon scourer. Never use a metal scourer, as this will damage the surface.

A dish washer is still regarded as something of a luxury in some households, despite the acceptance of clothes washing machines. But if you have a large family or do a lot of entertaining – or even if you have a small family but are out at work all day – it can save more time than almost any other appliance. The important things to remember if you have a dish washer are to use the correct amount of powder and to stack things carefully in the machine. And don't use it for non-stick pans, or for knives that have bone, wooden or plastic handles that might come loose or warp and discolor in very hot water. If you have any difficulties, such as film forming on the china, try adjusting the amount of powder – this is usually the reason for the film. If the trouble persists contact the supplier of your dish washer, who will usually be able to give you a simple answer depending on the model and type of powder you are using.

Silver is very important. Nothing is less inviting than a fork that does not look thoroughly clean – however sure you are that it has actually been washed. Stainless steel is by far the easiest to keep good-looking. All it requires is careful washing in hot water with an ordinary dish washing liquid, and drying and polishing to retain its shine. If you leave silver to drain you will find it retains the water spots and these cannot be removed once it is dry. Treat stainless steel bowls and vegetable dishes the same way.

If your stainless steel does become marked, perhaps because you have inadvertently left a dish with something in it for too long, use one of the patent stainless steel cleaners, which are usually either a powder or a paste. Never touch it with a tarnish remover

# Caring for tableware and linen

*There are several cleaners for silver*

*Crisp, home-laundered linen*

intended for silver – this will severely damage the surface. The second common enemy of stainless steel is salt – if allowed to come into contact with stainless steel in hot water it may very quickly cause pitting. Another is electrolysis – if food is left in a stainless steel dish with a silver or nickel plated spoon in it, or covered with aluminum foil, the two metals set up an electrolytic action and subsequent corrosion that is extremely difficult to remove – and the food is contaminated.

Silver is much more tedious to keep in good condition, though most people think the result is worth any amount of trouble. Ordinary, everyday silver doesn't tarnish as readily as one might think, as the constant washing and drying up polishes it. It will want a thorough clean from time to time though. For any silver there are many proprietary cleaners on the market. Liquid dips are extremely useful in an emergency, particu-

larly for items with a difficult shape like a fork, but silver cleaned this way tarnishes again fairly quickly. Paste or semi-liquid polish or an impregnated pad is more effective for long-term cleaning, and there are some preparations that give a truly long-lasting shine. Whatever preparations you choose, do use a very soft cloth – cheese cloth is ideal – or you will risk scratching the silver. For decorative ware a soft brush is useful, to remove the polish from the cracks. After cleaning always wrap any silver that is not on display in tissue paper and a plastic bag as excluding air delays the tarnishing action (specially treated tarnish preventing cloths are available). Silver cared for like this may need thorough cleaning perhaps only twice a year. Copper, brass and pewter are the same in this respect, and there are special cleaners for all of them.

When it comes to special table cloths and napkins, there is a lot to be said for sending them to a professional laundry. The finish your linen will receive there is much better than you can give at home unless you enjoy ironing and are prepared to spend a lot of time and effort achieving a good finish. Laundries are also experienced in stain removal and are much less likely to damage a badly stained article than you are if you tackle it yourself.

But for everyday cloths and some made from easy-care fabrics, home laundering is just as effective. Polyester and Dacron are particularly good as they need only light ironing; cotton seersucker is pretty for a breakfast or supper cloth and even looks better for not being ironed! Rayon is difficult to keep looking good however you treat it — it needs as much ironing as linen but will not take starch and loses its 'body' very quickly. The only real disadvantage of synthetic fibres for the table is that stain removal can be difficult, though some do have a special stain-resistant finish. Most synthetics do not react well to very hot water and some will not withstand the use of chemical solvents. Wherever possible, take some corrective action over a stain as soon as possible, though not at the expense of your guests' comfort and peace of mind! Rinse or sponge any stain with cold water first (hot water will often set a stain like a dye), then soak in a washing powder solution for several hours before washing.

White linen is usually not much of a problem; normal washing will remove most stains, and a mild solution of bleach can be used for anything that is particularly stubborn. Coloreds are more difficult as the colors may not be fast – whatever treatment you intend using, do test a small corner first. For grease marks use a grease solvent before normal washing – and failing all else send the article to the laundry! Try to keep your tablecloths flat – a special linen cupboard or drawer helps. Nothing is more frustrating than to find that a beautifully laundered cloth has been pushed up to a corner and needs ironing all over again. It helps to preserve the color of linen that is not used often if you cover it with tissue paper or sheeting.

# COOK AHEAD FOR YOUR PARTY

*Dinner party menus that can be prepared in advance. These are menus for working wives, or for the day when you are expected to be out with your guests all day and return in the evening to provide a splendid feast.*

## MENU *serves 4*

**TOMATO JUICE**
**BEEF OLIVES**
**BUTTERED RICE, GREEN SALAD**
**SHERRY TRIFLE**

**Timetable** *for dinner at 8.00 p.m.*
**Day before:** *Cook beef olives, cool and store in refrigerator. Cook and drain rice. Cool and cover. Store in refrigerator. Wash and dry salad ingredients. Prepare French dressing.*
**In the morning:** *Prepare sherry trifle, cover and store in refrigerator.*
**7.00** *Put tomato juice in refrigerator. Put beef olives to warm in oven at 325°F., turning after 20 minutes.*
**7.45** *Sauté mushrooms. Toss rice in melted butter until hot. Dish up beef olives and keep warm. Toss salad. Remove trifle from refrigerator.*
**8.00** *serve tomato juice.*

## BEEF OLIVES

**8 small pieces round steak cut about ¼ in. thick and measuring 2½ in. by 3 in.**
**¼ pound button mushrooms**
**1 large tomato, peeled and seeded**
**1 small onion, ground**
**1 cup fresh white breadcrumbs**
**2½ teaspoons chopped parsley**
**1 teaspoon mixed fresh herbs**
**Salt and pepper**
**1 egg yolk**
**Fat for frying**
**2 cups beef stock or tomato juice**
**1¼ tablespoons flour**
**Parsley**

Remove all the fat from the steak. Flatten each piece as thin as possible by pounding with a rolling pin or a wooden mallet. Reserve fat and set steak pieces aside.

*Sherry trifle is a traditional dessert*

Wipe and peel the mushrooms. Trim the stalks level with the caps. Chop the mushroom skins and stalks. Chop the tomato finely. Combine chopped mushrooms, tomato, onion, breadcrumbs, parsley and herbs. Season with salt and pepper and mix in the egg yolk. Grind any fat that was cut off the steak and stir into mixture. Divide the stuffing into 8 portions and place one portion in the center of each piece of steak. Roll up carefully and secure tightly with cord. Brown the olives (meat rolls) in a little melted fat. Remove and place in a casserole. Pour over the hot stock and cook in a warm oven (325°F.) for about 2 hours or until meat is tender.
While the meat is cooking, sauté the mushrooms in a little hot butter. Keep warm. Remove the string from the olives and place on a hot serving platter. Keep warm. Strain the gravy from the casserole into a saucepan. Make a paste from the flour and a little water. Stir into the gravy and cook, stirring, until the mixture boils and thickens. Garnish the olives with mushrooms and parsley sprigs. Serve with hot gravy, buttered rice and a green salad.

## SHERRY TRIFLE

**1 package (3½ ounces) vanilla pudding mix**
**2½ cups milk**
**An 8 in. sponge cake layer**
**Strawberry preserves**
**1 can (16 ounces) sliced peaches**
**2 tablespoons syrup from canned peaches**
**2½ tablespoons sherry**
**1¼ tablespoons finely chopped, blanched almonds**
**¾ cup heavy cream**
**1 egg white**
**Small macaroons**
**Toasted almonds**

Prepare the vanilla pudding mix according to package directions, using 2½ cups milk for a thin pudding. Cover the top with a piece of waxed paper and set aside to cool.
Split the sponge layer in half and spread the bottom half with strawberry preserves. Reassemble layer and cut it into fingers about 2 in. long by 1 in. wide. Place the fingers in the bottom and part way up the sides of a shallow glass serving dish. Drain the peach slices and arrange in pairs, alternating with sponge cake so that the peach slices stand above the sponge cake. Reserve a

few for decoration. Combine the syrup and sherry and sprinkle over the cake and peaches. Scatter the chopped almonds over the peaches. Pour the cool custard over the top.
Beat together the cream and egg white just until thick enough to hold its shape. Spoon over the custard and shape into swirls with a knife.
Decorate with small macaroons, chopped toasted almonds and remaining peach slices. Chill before serving.

## MENU *serves 4*

**CHILLED MELON (CANTALOUP)**
**VEAL FRICASSEE**
**BAKED TOMATOES AND DUCHESSE POTATOES**
**CHEESE BOARD**
**FRESH FRUIT**

**Timetable** *for dinner at 8.00 p.m.*
**Day before:** *Prepare veal fricassee, except for garnish. Cool and keep in refrigerator.*
**7.15** *Cut melon and chill. Set oven at 350°F. and put veal to reheat, adjusting sauce consistency if necessary. Bake tomatoes and fill. Boil and cream potatoes, add ½ a beaten egg and 1 tablespoon cream. Season well and pipe out in rosettes on a cookie tray. Glaze with remaining beaten egg and brown in the oven.*
**7.30** *Prepare croûtes to garnish veal.*
**8.00** *Serve first course.*

## VEAL FRICASSEE

**1½ pound stewing veal**
**½ pound thick sliced bacon**
**Butter or margarine**
**1¼ tablespoons oil**
**½ small onion, finely chopped**
**1¼ cups water**
**Salt and pepper**
**3 tablespoons flour**
**2 tablespoons lemon juice**
**2 slices white bread**
**Parsley**

Cut the veal and bacon into 1 in. cubes. Melt 2 tablespoons butter and the oil in a skillet. Add the veal and bacon and sauté until pale brown. Remove the meat and bacon with a slotted spoon and place in a casserole. Add onion to hot fat and fry until tender. Add the onion, water and salt and pepper to the casserole. Cover and cook in a moderate oven (350°F.) for 1½ hours until meat is tender. Strain off the liquid from the meat into a small saucepan. Keep the meat in the casserole. Knead together 2 tablespoons butter with the flour to make a smooth mixture. Drop small pieces of kneaded butter-flour mixture into the warm liquid. Stir well, bring to a boil and boil for 2–3 minutes or until thickened. Add the lemon juice and additional seasoning, if necessary. Pour the sauce over the veal in the casserole. Toast the bread and cut each slice into 4 triangles. Use the triangles to garnish veal. Top with parsley.

## BAKED TOMATOES

**8 large, firm tomatoes**
**2 tablespoons butter or**
  **margarine**
**¼ cup long grain rice**
**Salt and pepper**
**½ cup cooked peas**

Cut a thin slice from the rounded end of each tomato. Scoop out a little of the seed and core. Divide butter into each tomato center. Bake in a moderate oven (350°F.) for 10 minutes. Meanwhile, cook the rice according to package directions. Season rice with salt and pepper and spoon into the tomatoes. Top each with a few cooked peas.

## MENU *serves 4*

### MARINATED MUSHROOMS
### GLAZED BAKED SALMON GARNI
### FRENCH BEANS, TOMATOES, ASPARAGUS
### LEMON MERINGUE PIE

**Timetable** *for dinner at 8.00 p.m.*
**Day before:** *Prepare mushrooms and leave in refrigerator to marinate. Prepare salmon, but not vegetable garnish.*
*Bake flan case.*
**In the morning:** *Finish lemon meringue pie if to be served cold.*
*5.30 Garnish salmon.*
*6.30 Finish pie if serving warm.*
*7.00 Take mushrooms out of refrigerator.*
*8.00 Serve first course.*

## MARINATED MUSHROOMS

**1½ pound button mushrooms**
**Juice of 1 large lemon**
**1½ cups wine vinegar**
**1 small clove garlic, crushed**
**2 medium onions, chopped**
**1 bouquet garni**
**1 teaspoon salt**
**Freshly ground black pepper**
**1¼ cups olive oil**
**2 tablespoons catsup**
**Chopped parsley**

*A glazed baked salmon has a really festive air about it*

Wipe the mushrooms with damp paper toweling. Put in a saucepan with the lemon juice and enough water to cover. Bring to a boil and boil for 5 minutes. Remove from heat and let stand until cold. Combine the wine vinegar, garlic, onion, bouquet garni, salt and pepper in a saucepan. Bring to a boil and boil, uncovered, for 5 minutes. Cool. Add the olive oil and catsup to the cooled liquid. Drain the mushrooms and place in a deep bowl. Pour the marinade over the mushrooms. Chill in the refrigerator, tossing occasionally.
To serve, lift out the mushrooms, place in a shallow dish and sprinkle with chopped parsley. Strain marinade through a sieve and pour over mushrooms.

## GLAZED BAKED SALMON GARNI

**1½ pound fresh salmon, cut from**
  **middle**
**Butter or margarine**
**½ envelope unflavored gelatin**
**1 cup weak chicken bouillon**
**Black olives**
**Cucumber slices**
**12 cherry tomatoes**
**½ pound French beans, cooked**
  **and cooled**
**1 can (1 pound) asparagus tips,**
  **drained**
**1 cup French dressing**

*Veal fricassee can be prepared well in advance and reheated*

Generously butter a large piece of aluminum foil. Lay the salmon in the center, make a drug store fold of foil over top of fish and tuck in the edges to form a loose package. Place on a cookie tray and bake in a cool oven (300°F.) for about 1 hour or until fish flakes easily when tested with a fork. Remove from the oven, unwrap the fish and carefully remove the skin from the salmon. Let stand to cool.
When completely cold, place on a serving platter. Soften the gelatin in chicken bouillon. Place in a pan of hot water and let dissolve. Cool slightly. Spoon over the top of the fish to make a thin layer of aspic. Chill. Add more chilled mixture to make a smooth, shiny covering on fish. Pour the remaining aspic into a flat pan to set. Garnish the top of the salmon with halved olives and cucumber slices. Chop the aspic in the pan and place around the salmon. Surround with tomatoes, beans and asparagus tips. Spoon the French dressing over vegetables.

## LEMON MERINGUE PIE

*For pie shell:*
**1 cup all-purpose flour**
**Pinch of salt**
**6 tablespoons butter or**
  **margarine**
**1 teaspoon superfine sugar**
**1 egg, beaten**

*For lemon filling:*
**1¼ cups water**
**Grated rind and juice of 1 lemon**
**¼ cup sugar**
**2½ tablespoons cornstarch**
**2 egg yolks**
**1 tablespoon butter or margarine**

*For meringue topping*
**2 egg whites**
**½ cup superfine sugar**

Sift flour and salt together. Cut in the butter with a pastry blender or two knives until the mixture resembles fine crumbs. Mix in the sugar. Add the egg, stirring with a fork, until the ingredients begin to stick together. Turn out on a lightly floured board and knead very lightly to give a firm, smooth dough. Roll out into a circle larger than an 8-in. pie plate. Fit the dough into the pie plate. Turn under the edges and flute. Prick all over with a fork. Line with aluminum foil and fill with dried beans. Bake in a fairly hot oven (400°F.) for 15 minutes or until lightly browned. Remove foil and beans and cool.
Place the water, grated lemon

rind and sugar in a saucepan. Heat gently until the sugar is dissolved. Combine the cornstarch and lemon juice, pour in the hot syrup and stir well. Return to the pan and bring to a boil. Cook, stirring, until mixture clears and is bubbling and thick. Remove from heat and beat in the egg yolks and butter. Set aside.

Beat the egg whites until stiff. Gradually add the sugar and beat until smooth glossy peaks are formed.

Pour the lemon filling into the pie shell. Pile the meringue on top, making sure the meringue covers the edge of the pastry. Bake in a cool oven (300°F.) for 30 minutes or until meringue is crisp and lightly browned. Serve warm or cold.

## MENU serves 4

### SPRING VEGETABLE SOUP
### PORK-STUFFED PEPPERS
### ORANGES A LA TURQUE

**Timetable** *for dinner at 8.00 p.m.*
**Day before:** *Blanch peppers, make stuffing and sauce. Keep separately, covered, in refrigerator. Prepare oranges and refrigerate.*
**In the morning:** *Prepare soup from a package.*
**7.30** *Fill peppers, pour over sauce and heat in oven at 375°F. for about 30 minutes.*
*Take oranges out of refrigerator. Reheat soup.*
**8.00** *Serve first course.*

### PORK-STUFFED PEPPERS

**4 large or 6 small green peppers**
**2 onions, chopped**
**2 tablespoons shortening**
**¼ cup long grain rice**
**2 cups beef stock**
**1 pound smoked pork sausage**
**2 tablespoons chopped parsley**
**Salt and pepper**
**1 pound tomatoes, peeled and seeded**
**1 tablespoon all-purpose flour**
**½ teaspoon sugar**

Remove a thin slice from the stalk end of each pepper. Scoop out the seeds and white membrane. Blanch the peppers and tops in boiling water for 2 minutes. Drain and cool.
Fry the onion in half the shortening in a saucepan. Add the rice and cook gently, stirring constantly, until the rice is opaque. Stir in 1 cup stock. Cover and simmer for 12–15 minutes or until the rice is tender and the

*Whole oranges in caramel sauce – what could be more delicious?*

liquid completely absorbed. Skin and coarsely grind the sausage. Stir into rice. Add the parsley and season to taste with salt and pepper. If the mixture looks dry, stir in 1–2 tablespoons water. Stuff the peppers with the mixture and replace tops on peppers. Put in a casserole that has a cover. Fry the remaining onion in the remaining shortening until soft but not browned. Chop the tomatoes and add to onion. Simmer until tomatoes are cooked down. Sprinkle the flour on top and stir well. Pour on the remaining stock and simmer until the sauce is thick. Season to taste and stir in sugar. Pour the sauce over the peppers in the casserole. Cover and cook in a fairly hot oven (375°F.) for about 30 minutes.

### ORANGES A LA TURQUE

**4 large juicy oranges**
**⅝ cup water**
**1 cup superfine sugar**
**1 clove**

Thinly pare the rind from 2 of the oranges, making sure that you do not peel any of the white part. Cut into very thin strips with a sharp knife or scissors. Put strips into a small pan. Cover with water and cook until peel is tender. Drain thoroughly. Cut away all the white part from the oranges and

the rind and white from the remaining 2 oranges. Hold the oranges over a bowl to catch any juice and cut carefully into slices, crosswise. Reassemble oranges and secure with toothpicks.
Place water, sugar and clove in a saucepan. Bring to a boil and boil until caramel-colored. Remove from heat and stir in 3 tablespoons water. Return to very low heat to dissolve the caramel. Stir in any orange juice from cutting the oranges. Arrange the oranges in a serving dish, top with shredded orange rind and pour the caramel syrup over the top. Chill, turning occasionally.

## MENU serves 4

### MELON COCKTAIL
### CHICKEN BEAUJOLAIS
### GREEN SALAD,
### FRENCH BREAD
### SYLLABUB

**Timetable** *for dinner at 8.00 p.m.*
**Day before:** *Cook chicken Beaujolais but do not add tomato quarters, cool and store in refrigerator. Wash and dry salad ingredients. Prepare French dressing. Make syllabub and store in a cool place, but not the refrigerator.*
**7.30** *Put chicken to reheat with tomatoes in oven at 350°F. Toss*

*salad. Prepare melon cocktail and chill briefly.*
**8.00** *Serve first course.*

### CHICKEN BEAUJOLAIS

**4 slices bacon, cut up**
**Salad oil**
**1 broiler-fryer chicken, quartered and skinned**
**1 onion, sliced**
**3 tablespoons flour**
**⅝ cup Beaujolais wine (or dry red wine)**
**⅝ cup water**
**1 chicken bouillon cube**
**Salt and pepper**
**4 tomatoes, peeled and cut up**
**Chopped parsley**

In a shallow, flameproof casserole or large skillet (large enough to take the chicken in a single layer), gently fry the bacon until lightly brown. Remove with a slotted spoon. Add just enough oil to the casserole to cover the bottom. Brown the chicken pieces on all sides. Remove chicken and pour off all but 1 tablespoon of remaining fat. Add the onion and cook until very lightly browned. Stir in flour and cook for 1–2 minutes. Slowly stir in wine, water and bouillon cube. Stir up the residue from bottom of the casserole or skillet and bring the mixture to a boil, stirring constantly. Season to taste. Replace the bacon and chicken pieces, meat side down. Tuck the tomato quarters into the corners between the chicken pieces. Cover and simmer for 1¼ hours or until the chicken is tender. Serve chicken with sauce spooned over top and garnished with chopped parsley.

### SYLLABUB

**Thinly pared rind of 1 lemon**
**5 tablespoons lemon juice**
**7½ tablespoons white wine or sherry**
**2½ tablespoons brandy**
**¼ cup superfine sugar**
**1¼ cups heavy cream**
**Grated nutmeg**

Place the lemon rind, juice, wine and brandy in a bowl and let stand several hours or overnight. Strain into a large bowl. Add the sugar and stir until sugar is dissolved. Slowly add the cream, stirring all the time. Beat with a wire whisk until the mixture forms soft peaks. Spoon into serving glasses and sprinkle tops with nutmeg. Store in a cool place, but do not refrigerate. Serve with lady fingers, if desired.

# COOK AHEAD - WITH A FREEZER

Freezing is fast superseding bottling, canning and drying as the most important means of preserving food. Unlike other forms of preserving, freezing does not destroy or alter anything contained in the food. The natural cycle of life is not destroyed, but held in 'suspended animation'; equally, enzymes and micro-organisms in the food (which cause normal deterioration) are not destroyed. The food will therefore come out of the freezer as good (or as bad) as it went in. There is only one proviso – that it is wrapped and sealed correctly.

Frozen food, then, is as fresh as fruit and vegetables from the greengrocer. Indeed, it is often fresher and in better condition, as stock at the shop has probably been in transit for several days, whereas fruit and vegetables from your own garden (and commercially frozen) are frozen within hours of picking – with the result that they will have lost far fewer vitamins. Almost any food can be frozen, but whatever it is, it should, of course, be in first-class condition. Fruit and vegetables should be ripe, firm and freshly picked; meat and poultry must be good quality and suitably hung. Cooked foods need to be cooled as rapidly as possible before going into the freezer. Everything should be clean and done as quickly as possible – food deteriorates quickly if it is left lying around and may become contaminated.

## USING THE FREEZER

To freeze food successfully, retaining its appearance, taste and food value, it must be frozen quickly so that the ice particles that form are tiny. If you freeze slowly, the ice particles are large and damage the cell structure of the food. This means choosing a freezer with a special low freezing temperature and freezing in smallish quantities so that the fresh food going in doesn't raise the temperature in the cabinet too much and slow the freezing process (a maximum of 1/10 the freezer's capacity in any 24 hours is recommended by most manufacturers). Once the food is frozen, raise the temperature to the normal 0°F. (−18°C.) for storage.

## PACKAGING

Packaging food for your freezer is all-important. Solids should be packed as tightly as possible, excluding all the air. Aluminum foil is best for molding difficult shaped objects, like chickens or roasts, but it tears easily on jagged bones, so it is safest to overwrap afterwards with plastic wrap (again squeezing out as much air as you can).

Fruit and vegetables can either be packed in rigid containers (imperative for delicate whole fruits) or simply in sealed plastic bags. In this case, if you are having problems removing the air, dip the bag into a bowl of water – this pushes all the air out and molds the bag snugly around the vegetables. Alternatively, suck the air out through a straw. Seal the bag immediately, and don't forget to dry the outside before putting it

*Frozen fruit salad in a solid block*

147

into your freezer.

If you can't fill a rigid container completely, use crumpled waxed paper to fill up the remaining space. Liquids expand when frozen, so always allow at least ½ in. headspace when sealing a plastic bag or a container with a lid. Alternatively, leave the container open until the liquid is frozen – but don't forget to seal it when it *is* frozen, or it will dehydrate rapidly. If you are using a plastic bag for liquids, it helps to fit the bag into a preformer – any straight-sided carton or plastic box – before pouring in the liquid. Freeze the liquid in the preformer and when it is solid just slip it out and store it – and your carton is ready for re-use.

If you're freezing a combination of solids and liquids – such as fruit in syrup, or a casserole – do be sure the solid pieces are all below the level of the liquid. A piece of crumpled waxed paper over the top will generally be sufficient to keep the pieces down. Aluminum foil is the best material in which to freeze casseroles, again because it molds so closely; you can freeze them in a casserole dish, but this slows the freezing and thawing processes and also puts one of your dishes out of action. The best way is to cook and cool the casserole; line an ovenproof dish with foil and spoon the meat and sauce into it, making sure the meat is completely covered. Put it in the freezer and when it is solid lift the foil out of the dish, wrap it over the top and overwrap in plastic wrap. To use the casserole, simply remove the plastic wrap and foil and pop the food into the same ovenproof dish to reheat.

There are available foil dishes in various shapes and sizes which are invaluable for use in freezing, as they can go straight from the freezer to the oven. With care they can be used more than once, which needn't make them an extravagance. Many small containers used for commercial products, such as ice cream and yogurt, can be re-used in home freezing and are a great help for freezing small quantities of sauces, herbs and breadcrumbs.

Remember to package food in the quantities you will want to use. It's no good freezing a pâté for 10 if you are going to need only 4 slices from it; so slice it *before* you freeze it, put a sheet of waxed paper or plastic wrap between each piece and then wrap the whole thing in foil. The same applies to cakes, meat, or anything that you freeze in quantity but use only in small amounts. If you make up a sauce, freeze it in 1¼-cup or 2-cup containers, not in 1 solid block.

Another idea is to freeze stock and sauces in an ice-cube tray. When solid, turn out the cubes and put them in a plastic bag. A little soda water squirted into the bag will prevent the cubes sticking together. This is also an ideal way to freeze a variety of foods used in small quantities – concentrated mint sauce, tomato sauce, chopped herbs in a little water and so on. Finally, do label everything you put in the freezer. You may think that you'll remember what each package is, but after a while you may find it a problem – especially if you have a number of packages all much the same shape. Serving a dish of mashed potato instead of shepherd's pie, or a second course of chicken pie instead of blackberry and apple could be embarrassing! So tie or stick a label on to each package as it goes into your freezer and put on the date as well as the contents. A list of everything you freeze, kept handy inside the door of the freezer, will ensure a steady rotation of stock.

## PREPARING FOOD FOR THE FREEZER

**FRUIT** should be just ready for eating; over-ripe fruit can be puréed and frozen for use in fools, mousses, etc. Rinse all but soft fruits (such as raspberries) in ice-cold water and drain very thoroughly. To prevent discoloration, keep fruits such as apples and pears covered in water and lemon juice or vitamin C during preparation.

Fruit may be frozen in 3 ways – as a dry pack, in sugar, or in syrup.

**Dry packing** is suitable for fruit that is to be used for pies or preserves and for small whole fruit, so long as the skin is undamaged. Pick over, wash, dry on paper towels and use a rigid container to prevent damage during handling and storage.

**Free-flow dry packing** is suitable for small fruit or pieces of fruit such as strawberries or grapefruit segments. Pick the fruit over and prepare as necessary; spread it out on a cookie tray and freeze until firm. Then pack (preferably in a rigid container) for storage.

**Dry sugar packing** is particularly suitable for soft fruits. Pick over

*Freeze small quantities of stock or sauces in ice-cube trays*

the fruit but don't wash it unless really necessary. The sugar and fruit can either be put into rigid containers in layers, or else mixed together before being packed. The fruit is more likely to retain its shape if layered, because when it is mixed with sugar the juice is drawn out and leaves the fruit almost in purée form. Use superfine sugar.

**Syrup** is the best for non-juicy fruits or for those which discolor during preparation and storage. The strength of the syrup varies according to the particular fruit being frozen – refer to the chart for the correct strength.

*20% syrup is ½ cup sugar dissolved in 2½ cups water*
*30% syrup is 1 cup sugar dissolved in 2½ cups water*
*40% syrup is 1¼ cups sugar dissolved in 2½ cups water*
*50% syrup is 2 cups sugar dissolved in 2½ cups of water*

Dissolve the sugar in the water by heating gently and bringing to a boil; cover and allow the syrup to become quite cold before using. Normally you will find 1¼ cups syrup is enough to cover 1 pound fruit. Leave about ½ in. space at the top of the container to allow for expansion during freezing. If the fruit tends to float above the level of the syrup, hold it down with crumpled waxed paper.

## VEGETABLES

Speed is particularly important when dealing with vegetables. These should be frozen as soon as possible after picking. They need to be blanched before freezing, to kill some of the micro-organisms which cause discoloration and 'off' flavours. Of course, this also drives off some of the vitamins, but don't think it ruins the nutritional value of the vegetables – after all, when you cook them fresh, some of the vitamins are still lost.

For blanching you need a very large pan and a wire basket. Place the vegetables in the basket and immerse in boiling water (approximately 15 cups to 1 pound of vegetables). When the water re-boils, cook for the recommended blanching time (see chart), then plunge the vegetables into ice-cold water. Drain and pack immediately. Don't try to do too large a quantity – 1 or 2 pounds at a time is about right, in successive batches. Pack the vegetables in rigid containers or plastic bags, allowing a little space for

*Extracting air from the package is essential for successful freezing*

expansion for vegetables which pack tightly, such as peas.

## MEAT

If you are going to home-freeze meat, do be absolutely sure the meat is fresh. Many butchers provide meat ready-packed for the home freezer and this is probably a better bet than trying to butcher half a carcass yourself. If you buy jointed fresh meat to freeze yourself there are 1 or 2 points to watch for. Very lean meat tends to dry out during freezing, so look for a good 'marbling' of fat, which helps to prevent this. On the other hand, too much fat tends to go rancid after a while, so trim some of it off if you think it's excessive.

It is generally better to freeze meat off the bone whenever possible – the bones slow down freezing and thawing and take up a lot of space in your freezer. If, however, you leave the bone in place – such as in a leg of lamb or pork chops – pad it well to avoid puncturing the wrapping. Separate steaks and chops with waxed paper or plastic wrap so that you can remove just one or two.

## POULTRY AND GAME

Truss the bird as for the table, but *do not* stuff it. Pad the protruding bones before you wrap it. Game must be hung before freezing, for the same length of time as if you were going to eat it immediately. Then proceed as for poultry.

## FISH

Fish should be frozen only if you can get it to your freezer within 12 hours of the catch. Clean the fish as usual, leaving small fish whole but removing the heads and tails of larger ones. Skin and fillet flat fish. Salmon, trout and similar fish can be frozen whole in a sheet of ice; dip them in cold water, leave them uncovered in the freezer until frozen and then repeat the process several times until the ice glaze is about ⅛ in. thick. Wrap individual fish in plastic wrap and pack in cartons or overwrap with heavy-duty plastic wrap.

## COOKED DISHES

One of the great advantages of a freezer is that you can cook when you feel like it and store whole meals for future use. You can make 3 or 4 pies at once (particularly useful if you have a glut of fruit in your garden), eat 1 now and freeze the rest; or make up a

*A well-stocked freezer, with each package clearly labelled*

casserole using double your normal quantity – eat half and freeze the rest.

In general the foods can be prepared and cooked as if they were to be served immediately, but it is wise to reduce the amount of seasoning. Take care not to over-cook the food, particularly if it is to be reheated for serving. Chill food quickly after cooking and wrap and freeze it carefully. When you are freezing stock or soups, remember that liquid expands when frozen, so allow some space for this.

## THAWING AND REHEATING

Ideally, food should be thawed very gently in the refrigerator – but this can take up to 6 hours a pound, and most people simply don't have that amount of time in hand. There are some foods, though, that *must* be thawed right through before they are cooked – in particular poultry. Whole fish retain their flavor and texture better if thawed out slowly and whole fruit that is to be eaten with no further preparation will retain its shape more readily. Leave the food in its original wrapping while thawing.

If you don't have quite so much time in hand, thaw at room temperature, but don't let it stand too long. Once food thaws out, the micro-organisms start working again and it will deteriorate much more quickly.

Luckily, a lot of the real standbys you keep in the freezer can be cooked straight from frozen. Stews, casseroles, cooked meat in gravy, fruit pies will all reheat

appetizingly from frozen – but if the dish the food is in isn't one of the freezer-to-oven type, do allow it at least 30 minutes at room temperature. Anything in a foil container, of course, can go straight into the oven.

Chops, steaks, small fish and other small items can be cooked without thawing. The only point to watch is that the food is thoroughly hot right through – and not burnt to a cinder on the outside at the same time. A roast can equally well be thawed or cooked straight from the freezer – either way is quite satisfactory. Again, you must ensure that it is cooked through to the center.

Soups and sauces are best thawed slowly, though if you're in a hurry you can turn the frozen lump into a saucepan and heat it very gently. Cakes, pâtés, sweets and so on also need slow, gentle thawing (though, of course, if you've followed our advice and sliced them before freezing they won't take more than an hour).

Finally, vegetables should never be thawed. Pop them straight into a little boiling water, or toss gently in butter in a heavy lidded pan.

Microwave ovens are ideal for defrosting frozen foods.

## DO NOT FREEZE...

**Eggs** in their shells (they crack) or hardcooked (they turn rubbery). The solution is simple – freeze the whites and yolks separately.

**Boiled old potatoes** (they go leathery); mash them with butter – but not milk.

**Fully-cooked chips** (they go sog-

gy); the answer is to part-cook them, freeze, and just crisp them up in deep hot fat straight from the freezer.

**Salad stuffs** – lettuce, watercress, celery, chicory – all go limp, soggy and unattractive. If you have a glut in the garden you can freeze a soup made from one of these ingredients.

**Light cream** – of less than 40% butterfat (it separates). Heavy cream is fine.

**Mayonnaise** (it curdles).

**Custards** (they tend to separate) – so freeze them *before* cooking.

**Molds** – anything containing a high proportion of gelatin.

**Anything flavored with garlic** (it develops an unpleasant, musty flavor) – if possible, add garlic at point of reheating or use it very sparingly.

## GOLDEN RULES

1. Always start with good-quality foods and freeze them at peak freshness.
2. Keep handling to a minimum and see everything is clean.
3. Pay special attention to packaging and sealing. Exposure to air and moisture will damage frozen foods.
4. Cool food rapidly if it's been cooked or blanched; never put anything hot – or even warm – into your freezer.
5. Freeze as quickly as possible, and in small quantities.
6. Freeze in the coldest part of the freezer, and don't pack the food to be frozen too closely.
7. Transfer newly added items to the main part of the cabinet once they've been frozen.
8. Remember to return the switch from 'accelerated to 'normal' once newly added foods have been frozen – i.e. after 24 hours.
9. Maintain a steady storage temperature of 0°F. and don't do anything that will cause temperature fluctuations within the freezer.
10. Label and date food to ensure a good rotation of stock.
11. Defrost the freezer at a time when stocks are low.
12. Be prepared for emergencies. Know what to do in case of breakdown or powercuts.

**And for freezing cooked foods**
1. Go lightly with the herbs and spices and preferably omit garlic.
2. Use shallow rather than deep dishes.
3. Cool everything as rapidly as possible and freeze at once.
*Note:* Plastic bags or film *must* be removed before food is put into the oven.

| | |
|---|---|
| **Raw meat** (do not stuff): | lamb, veal, pork—6 months; beef—8 months |
| **Cooked meat:** | roasts (whole or sliced)—2—4 weeks; meat loaves, pâtés—1 month; casseroles, curries, etc.—2 months |
| **Poultry and game:** | giblets—3 months; duck, goose—4—6 months; turkey, game birds—6—8 months; chicken, venison—12 months |
| **Raw fish and shellfish:** | salmon—4 months; white fish—6 months. *Not advisable unless within 12 hours of catch* |
| **Cooked fish:** | pies, fish cakes, croquettes, kedgeree, mousse, paellas—2 months |
| **Liquids:** | highly seasoned sauces, etc.—2 weeks; other sauces, stocks, soups—2—3 months; fruit juices—6—8 months |
| **Pizza:** | baked—2 months; unbaked—3 months |
| **Pastry, uncooked:** | pies—3 months; shortcrust—3 months; flaky and puff—3—4 months |
| **Pastry, cooked:** | meat pies—3—4 months; fruit pies—6 months; empty cases—6 months |
| **Pancakes:** | filled—1—2 months; unfilled—2 months |
| **Desserts:** | mousses, fruit creams—2—3 months; home-made ice cream, cooked sponge puddings—3 months; heavy cream—4—6 months |
| **Cakes:** | uncooked—2 months; cooked, iced—2 months; sponge flans, jelly rolls, layer cakes—6 months |
| **Scones and cookies:** | unbaked Danish pastries—6 weeks; baked and unbaked cookies, baked scones and teabreads—6 months |
| **Bread:** | baked—1 month; sandwiches—1—2 months; bought part-baked bread and rolls—4 months |
| **Butter:** | salted—3 months; unsalted—6 months |
| **Commercially-frozen:** | ice cream—1 month; other—3 months |
| **Fruit and vegetables:** | 10—12 months |

## Freezing fruit

| Fruit | Preparation | Pack |
|---|---|---|
| **Apples;** raw sliced purée | Blanch slices 2—3 min., cool in ice-cold water. Pack. Peel, core and stew in minimum amount of water—sweetened or not. Sieve or liquidize. Cool before packing | Mix ½ cup sugar with 1 pound fruit or mix with 30% syrup. Pack in rigid containers |
| **Apricots** (and Nectarines) | Plunge into boiling water for 30 secs. to loosen skins. Peel, leave whole, or cut in half or slice into syrup | Mix with 30% syrup plus ascorbic acid |
| **Blackberries** (and Blueberries) | Wash in chilled water, drain. Dry pack or dry sugar pack—lightly crush and mix with sugar until dissolved. Can also be frozen in cold syrup—leave headspace | Dry sugar pack—½ cup sugar to 1 pound fruit. Syrup—50% |
| **Cherries** (*best used for pie filling*) | Remove stalks, wash and dry. Dry pack or dry sugar pack *pitted* cherries or cover with cold syrup—leave headspace | Dry sugar pack—½ cup sugar to 1 pound fruit. Syrup—30% |
| **Citrus fruits** (Grapefruit, Orange, Lemon and Lime) | (a) Squeeze out juice and freeze, sweetened or not, in ice cube trays. Remove when frozen and pack for storage. (b) Peel, section and pack in cold syrup (including juice from fruit) or dry sugar pack—sprinkle sugar over fruit until juices start to run. (c) Mix grated peel with a little sugar for pancakes, etc. (d) Freeze slivers of peel, free of white part, to add to drinks. (e) Slice peel into julienne strips, blanch for 1 min., cool and pack. Use for garnish | (a) Pack cubes in plastic bags. (b) Syrup—50%. Dry sugar pack—mix 1 cup sugar to 1 pound fruit. In rigid containers. (c—e) Wrap in foil. |
| **Currants** (Black, red) | Wash and trim. Either dry pack for whole fruit or cook to a purée with very little water and brown sugar | Pack whole in rigid containers or plastic bags |
| **Figs** | Wash gently, remove stems. Freeze unsweetened, whole or peeled; or peel and pack in cold syrup; or leave whole and wrap in foil—suitable for dessert figs | Syrup—30%. Pack whole in plastic bags or in rigid containers |
| **Gooseberries** | Wash and dry. Dry pack whole fruit for pie filling, or pack in syrup; purée, sweetened to taste, for fools, etc. | Pack in plastic bags or rigid containers. Syrup—45% |
| **Grapes** | Seedless grapes can be packed whole; others should be peeled, pitted and halved. Pack in cold syrup | Syrup 30%. Use rigid containers |
| **Greengages** (*skins tend to toughen during freezing*) | Wash and remove stones. Pack in syrup with ascorbic acid. Don't open till required, as fruit discolors rapidly | Syrup—30% plus ascorbic acid. Use rigid containers |
| **Melon** (Cantaloup and honeydew) | Halve, seed, and cut into balls, cubes or slices. Put straight into syrup. Or use dry pack—sprinkle over a little sugar | Syrup—30%. Pack in plastic bags |
| **Peaches** | Peel, pit, brush with lemon juice. Pack halves or slices in cold syrup. Or purée with 1¼ tablespoons lemon juice and ½ cup sugar to 1 pound fruit—use for sorbets, soufflés, etc. | Syrup—30% plus ascorbic acid Use a rigid container |
| **Pineapple** | Peel and core. Pack unsweetened slices in boxes, separated by waxed paper. Pack cubes in syrup (including any juice). Pack crushed pineapple with sugar | Syrup—30%. Sugar pack—½ cup sugar to ¾ pound fruit. Use rigid containers. |
| **Plums** (and Damsons) | Wash, halve and pit. Stew with a little sugar and pack as a purée, or pack whole fruit uncooked in syrup (stew later) | Syrup—30% plus ascorbic acid. Use plastic bags |
| **Raspberries** (and Loganberries) | Choose firm, clean, dry fruit. Use dry method, dry sugar method, or purée—sweetened to taste | Dry sugar pack—½ cup sugar to 1 pound fruit. Freeze in small quantities |
| **Rhubarb** | Wash, trim, slice. Blanch for 1 min., cool quickly. Pack in syrup, or dry pack, to use for pies, crumbles, etc. | Syrup—50%. Use rigid containers |
| **Strawberries** | Choose firm, clean, dry fruit; remove stalks. Pack by dry method, dry sugar method, or as purée—sweeten to taste | Dry sugar pack—½ cup sugar to 1 pound fruit. Use small containers |
| *Unsuitable for freezing:* | Bananas. Pears discolor and go mushy—not very satisfactory | |

## Freezing vegetables

| Vegetable | Preparation | Blanching time |
|---|---|---|
| **Artichokes** (Globe) | Trim, wash in cold water, add a little lemon juice to blanching water. Cool and drain upside-down. Pack in rigid containers | Blanch a few at a time in a large pan for 7—10 min. |
| **Asparagus** | Grade into thick and thin stems (for asparagus tips, cut off stalks). Wash, blanch, cool and drain. Tie into *small* bundles, separated with waxed paper. Pack in rigid containers | Thin stem—2 min. Thick stem—4 min. |
| **Avocados** | Peel; mash with $1\frac{1}{4}$ tablespoons lemon juice per avocado and pack | — |
| **Beans**—Green | Select young, tender beans; wash thoroughly trim ends and blanch; cool, drain and pack | 3 min. |
| **Beets** (*short blanching and long storage can make beets rubbery*) | Choose small beets. Wash well, blanch and rub off skin. Beets under 1 in. diameter may be frozen whole; large ones should be sliced or diced. Pack in cartons | Small whole—5—10 min. Large—cook until tender (45—50 min.) |
| **Broccoli** | Trim off any woody parts and large leaves. Wash in salted water, and cut into small sprigs. Blanch, cool and drain well. Pack in boxes in 1 or 2 layers, tips to stalks | Thin stem—3 min. Medium stem—4 min. Thick stem—5 min. |
| **Brussels sprouts** (*pack those of equal size together*) | Use small compact heads. Remove outer leaves and wash thoroughly. Blanch, cool and drain well before packing | Small—3 min. Medium—4 min. |
| **Cabbage** (red and green) | Use only young, crisp cabbage. Wash thoroughly, shred finely. Blanch, cool and drain. Pack in small quantities | $1\frac{1}{2}$ min. |
| **Carrots** | Scrape and dice. Blanch, cool, drain and pack | 3—5 min. |
| **Cauliflower** | Heads should be firm, compact and white. Wash, break into small sprigs Add lemon juice to the blanching water. Blanch, cool, drain and pack | 3 min. |
| **Celery** (*goes soft when thawed*) | Trim, scrub well. Cut into 1 in. lengths. Use in cooked dishes | 3 min. |
| **Celeriac** (Celery root) | Wash and trim. Cook until almost tender, peel and slice | — |
| **Corn on the cob** (*there may be loss of flavor and tenderness after freezing*) | Select young yellow kernels, not starchy, over-ripe or shrunken. Remove husks and 'silks'. Blanch, cool and dry. Pack individually in freezer paper or foil | Small—4 min. Medium—6 min. Large—8 min. |
| **Eggplant** | Peel and slice roughly. Blanch, chill and dry on paper towels. Pack in layers, separated by waxed paper | 4 min. |
| **Fennel** | Cut into short lengths. Blanch, cool, drain and pack | 3 min. |
| **Kohlrabi** | Use small roots, 2—3 in. diameter. Cut off tops, peel and dice. Blanch, cool, drain and pack | $1\frac{1}{2}$ min. |
| **Mushrooms,** small button large | Leave whole; wipe clean and sauté in butter. Cool and pack in plastic bags. Slice and use only in cooked dishes | Sauté in butter 1 min. |
| **Onions,** large | Peel, finely chop and blanch. Pack in small plastic containers and overwrap to prevent the smell filtering out | 2 min. |
| small | Blanch whole to use later in casseroles | 4 min. |
| **Parsnips** (*young*) | Peel and cut into narrow strips. Blanch, cool and dry | 2 min. |
| **Peas** (*young, sweet ones*) | Shell and blanch. Cool, drain and pack in plastic bags | 1 min. |
| **Peppers, sweet** | Freeze red and green separately. Wash well, remove stems, seeds and membranes. Blanch as halves for stuffed peppers, or in thin slices for stews and casseroles | 3 min. |
| **Potatoes,** old | Fry French fries in deep fat, cool and freeze in plastic bags for final frying. Or freeze as croquettes or duchesse potatoes | Fry for 2 min. |
| new | Scrape, cook fully with mint and cool | |
| **Spinach** | Select young leaves. Wash very thoroughly; drain. Blanch in small amounts, cool quickly, press out excess moisture. Pack, allowing $\frac{1}{2}$ in. headspace | 2 min. |
| **Tomatoes,** purée or juice | Peel, core and quarter. Simmer in their own juice 5—10 min. until soft. Push through a nylon sieve or purée in a blender and season with salt. Cool and pack in small quantities | — |
| **Turnips** (*small, young ones*) | Peel, cut into $\frac{1}{2}$ in. dice. Blanch, cool, drain and pack. Can be fully cooked and mashed before freezing—allow headspace | $2\frac{1}{2}$ min. |
| **Zucchini** | Choose young ones. Wash, cut into $\frac{1}{2}$ in. slices. Blanch, or sauté in a little butter. Cool, drain and pack | 1 min. |
| *Unsuitable for freezing* | Chicory, endive, kale, lettuce, radishes, watercress. Jerusalem artichokes are suitable only as purées and soups | |

*Packing a selection of foods for the freezer*

*Scallops and duchesse potato – a good starter from the freezer*

*Borsch – Russian beet soup served with a swirl of dairy sour cream*

## COQUILLES ST. JACQUES
*6 servings*

½ pound fresh scallops, shelled
⅝ cup dry white wine
¼ small onion
1 sprig parsley
1 bay leaf
2 tablespoons butter or
  margarine
4–6 mushrooms, sliced
Duchesse Potatoes (made with
  1½ pounds potatoes, page 155)
Beaten egg
*For sauce:*
¼ cup butter or margarine
½ cup all-purpose flour
1⅞ cup milk
½ cup grated Parmesan cheese
Salt and pepper

Rinse and slice the scallops into 4 if they are large, 2 if they are small. Place in a stainless steel or enamel saucepan with the wine, onion, parsley and bay leaf. Bring to a boil, lower heat and simmer for 5 minutes. Strain, reserving the liquid and scallops. Melt the butter and sauté the mushrooms for 5 minutes.

Melt the butter for the sauce in a pan. Stir in flour and cook, without browning, for 1 minute. Remove from heat and stir in the strained wine and milk. Cook over medium heat, stirring constantly, until the mixture thickens and comes to a boil. Cool lightly. Fold in the scallops, mushrooms and cheese. Season to taste. Chill mixture in a pan of ice water.
**To pack and freeze:** Divide the mixture between 6 scallop shells or 6 small individual ovenproof dishes. Place on a cookie tray and freeze. Shells can be placed inside heavy freezer plastic bags and fastened securely, or put in a cardboard box and wrapped with moisture-vapor proof wrapping.
**To use:** Remove coquilles and place on a cookie tray. Let stand in refrigerator for about 8 hours. Pipe Duchesse Potato (page 155) round the edges of shells. Brush with beaten egg. Cover loosely with aluminum foil. Bake in a hot oven (425°F.) for 15 minutes. Remove foil and bake for 10–15 minutes or until piping hot and golden brown.
Or, place frozen coquilles on a cookie tray. Pipe Duchesse Potato mixture around the edges. Brush with beaten egg. Cover loosely with foil. Bake in a hot oven for 50–60 minutes. Remove foil and bake just until golden. Serve piping hot garnished with a wedge of lemon.

## BORSCH
*6 servings*

6 small beets, peeled
2 medium onions, chopped
10 cups beef bouillon

Grate beets coarsely. Put in a large soup pot with the onions and beef bouillon. Bring to a boil. Lower heat and simmer, uncovered, for 45 minutes. Strain. Chill in a pan of ice water.
**To freeze and pack:** Pour into freezer containers, leaving at least ½ in. head space. Label and seal. Freeze.
**To use:** Defrost overnight in the refrigerator or allow 8 hours at room temperature. When it is fully defrosted, stir thoroughly and add 2½ tablespoons lemon juice and 7½ tablespoons dry sherry. Season to taste. Serve chilled with a whirl of dairy sour cream and a few chopped chives floating on top of soup.

## QUICHE LORRAINE
*4 to 6 servings as an appetizer*
*3 servings for a buffet party*

1 recipe shortcrust pastry, page
  75
6 slices bacon, chopped
2 medium onions, chopped
2 tablespoons butter or
  margarine
½ cup grated Gruyère cheese
⅝ cup half milk, half cream
2 large eggs
Salt and pepper

Stand an 8 in. flan ring on a cookie tray and line it with the pastry. Or line an 8 in. pie pan with pastry, turn under edges and flute. Put in refrigerator to chill. Fry the bacon and onion in hot melted butter until the onion is transparent and the bacon cooked through. Cool. Place the cheese in the base of pastry shell. Spoon the onion and bacon mixture over the top. Whisk together the milk and cream, eggs and seasoning. Pour over the filling.
**To pack and freeze:** Put the uncooked and unwrapped quiche on a level area of the freezer until very firm. When frozen, cover the top of the flan with a circle of wax paper. Remove the flan ring, if desired. (Don't forget to replace the ring before the flan is cooked.) Lift the frozen flan from the cookie tray. Wrap in moisture-vapor proof material. Seal and label.
**To cook:** Unwrap and place on a cookie tray, replacing flan ring if necessary. Cover loosely with foil. Bake in center of a fairly hot oven (375°F.) for 45 minutes. Remove foil and cook for 15 minutes or until golden brown on top. Serve hot or cold.

## ZUCCHINI A LA GRECQUE
*4 servings*

2 small onions, thinly sliced
3¾ tablespoons olive oil
1 clove garlic, crushed
⅝ cup dry white wine
Salt and pepper
1½ pound zucchini
½ pound tomatoes
Pinch of dried chervil, optional

Sauté the onions in the hot oil until soft but not browned. Add the garlic, wine and a little seasoning. Wipe the zucchini and cut a small slice off each end. Slice into rings. Peel and cut up the tomatoes and remove seeds. Add the zucchini and tomatoes to the pan and cook gently, uncovered, for 10 minutes. Cool quickly in a pan of ice water. Add a little chervil if desired.
**To pack and freeze:** Spoon into plastic container, leaving at least 1 in. head space for expansion. Seal, label and freeze.
**To use:** Defrost for 12–14 hours in the refrigerator or 6–8 hours at room temperature. Turn into a serving platter. Add another ½ pound peeled, quartered and seeded tomatoes. Season to taste. Sprinkle with chopped parsley.

## UPSIDE-DOWN BEEF AND POTATO PIE
*4 servings*

**6 tablespoons butter or margarine**
**2 cups fresh white breadcrumbs**
**2 pound potatoes, cut up**
**Salt and pepper**
**1 large onion, chopped**
**1 clove garlic, crushed**
**6 gherkins, chopped**
**½ pound button mushrooms, sliced**
**1 pound lean ground chuck**
**1 tablespoon mild curry powder**
**1¼ tablespoons flour**

Line a 1½-quart casserole with aluminum foil, leaving enough foil to enclose the contents when filled. Brush lightly with butter. Heat 4 tablespoons of the butter in a skillet, add the breadcrumbs and fry, stirring, until golden. Place in the lined dish. Cook the potatoes in boiling, salted water until just tender. Drain, mash and season with salt and pepper. Set aside. Heat the remaining butter and fry the onion until golden. Add the garlic, gherkins, mushrooms, chuck and curry powder. Fry for 10 minutes, stirring frequently. Stir in the flour and mix well.

Arrange half the mashed potatoes over the crumbs in the prepared casserole. Cover with the meat mixture and remaining potatoes. Press down well and cool quickly.

**To pack and freeze:** Seal foil over the top potato layer. Freeze. Ease the foil pack from the dish. Overwrap with moisture-vapor proof material. Seal, label and freeze.

**To use:** Remove the overwrap. Return the foil-wrapped food to the original casserole. Open up the foil. Bake in a fairly hot oven (375°F.) for about 1½ hours. To serve, invert on to a serving platter and garnish with tomato and parsley.

## BEEF EL DORADO
*4 servings*

**2 small onions**
**4 young carrots, pared**
**3 tablespoons salad oil**
**1 pound lean chuck, cubed**
**Seasoned flour**
**1¼ cups light ale**
**½ tablespoon molasses**
**½ cup white raisins**
**Salt and pepper**

Thickly slice the onions; cut the carrots into thin rings. Heat the oil and fry the onions and carrots for about 2 minutes; remove from the pan. Toss the meat in sea-

*These date scone bars keep especially well in the freezer*

soned flour and fry it until lightly colored. Return the vegetables to the pan, pour in the light ale, bring to a boil and add the molasses and white raisins. Place in an ovenproof dish, cover and cook at 325°F. for 1½ hours. Check seasoning. Cool quickly.

**To pack and freeze:** Spoon into a rigid foil container. Cover with lid and label. Freeze rapidly until solid.

**To use:** Remove the lid and cover loosely with foil. Reheat in the oven at 350°F. for about 1½ hours, until bubbling. Serve accompanied by natural yogurt sprinkled with chopped parsley.

## BEEF CURRY
*6 servings*

**2 pound thick round steak**
**¼ cup seasoned flour**
**¼ cup butter or margarine**
**1¼ cups beef stock**
**1 teaspoon tomato paste**
**Salt and pepper**

Trim the fat from the steak and cut into even-sized cubes. Toss cubes in seasoned flour. Fry in melted, hot butter until lightly brown on all sides. Stir in the stock and tomato paste. Add a little more salt and pepper. Bring mixture to a boil, then pour into a casserole. Cover tightly and cook in a warm oven (325°F.) for 1½ hours or until fork-tender. Cool casserole quickly in a pan of ice water.

**To pack and freeze:** Turn mixture into 2 shallow aluminum foil

pans or into a foil-lined casserole. Wrap pans in moisture-vapor proof material. Seal, label and freeze. If frozen in a foil-lined casserole, freeze in casserole. Removed foil-wrapped food and overwrap in moisture-vapor proof material. Seal, label and freeze.

**To use:** Thaw for 14 hours in the refrigerator. Place the meat in a saucepan containing 5 cups thawed curry sauce and heat gently. Test seasoning and adjust if necessary. Serve with traditional side dishes and boiled rice.

## CURRY SAUCE
*Makes 1½ quarts*

**½ cup butter or margarine**
**1¼ tablespoons salad oil**
**2 Spanish onions, chopped**
**2 cooking apples, pared and chopped**
**¾ cup curry powder**
**½ cup flour**
**5 cups meat stock**
**3¾ tablespoons sweet chutney**
**2½ tablespoons tomato paste**
**Juice of ½ lemon**

Melt the butter and oil in a saucepan. Add the onions and apples and cook gently without browning for 5–8 minutes. Stir in the curry powder and cook for 5 minutes, stirring occasionally, to bring out the full flavor. Add the flour and cook for 1 minute, stirring constantly. Remove from heat. Stir in the stock. Cook, stirring constantly, until the mixture comes to a boil and thickens. Add the chutney, tomato paste and

lemon juice. Cover and simmer for about 45 minutes. Cool quickly in a pan of ice water.

**To pack and freeze:** Pack into 2½-cup freezer containers leaving ½ in. headspace for expansion. Seal, label and freeze.

**To use:** Turn the sauce into a very heavy saucepan. Break up with a wooden spoon as sauce thaws. Heat gently until completely thawed. Check the seasoning. Use with chicken, meat, fish, or as desired.

## CHICKEN TETRAZZINI
*5 servings*

**¼ pound mushrooms, sliced**
**5 tablespoons butter or margarine, divided**
**5 tablespoons flour**
**2 cups chicken broth**
**1 cup light cream**
**Salt and pepper**
**2 cups diced or slivered cooked chicken**
**1 package (8 ounces) thin spaghetti**
**½ cup grated Parmesan cheese**

Cook the mushrooms in 1 tablespoon of the butter in a skillet until lightly browned. Set aside. Melt the remaining butter in a saucepan. Stir in the flour and cook for 1 minute. Remove from heat and blend in the chicken broth. Cook over medium heat, stirring constantly, until smooth and thickened. Stir in the cream. Season to taste with salt and pepper. Divide the sauce in half. Add the chicken to one half of the sauce and set aside.

Meanwhile, cook the spaghetti according to package directions, but cook to the firm stage, do not overcook. Drain the spaghetti and stir into the other half of the cream sauce.

Line a 2-quart casserole with aluminum foil. Allow enough foil to lap over and cover top of casserole. Put the spaghetti mixture into casserole. Make a hole in the center of the spaghetti and pour in the cooled chicken mixture. Lap foil over top.

**To pack and freeze:** Freeze casserole until firm. Remove foil-lined food from casserole. Wrap in moisture-vapor proof material. Seal, label and return to freezer.

**To use:** Unwrap casserole and place frozen food back in original casserole. Sprinkle Parmesan cheese over the top. Cover casserole and bake in a fairly hot oven (375°F.) for 1½ hours. Remove cover and continue baking 15 more minutes or until mixture is piping hot.

## DUCHESSE POTATOES
*10 servings*

**6 pound old potatoes, cooked**
**¼ cup butter or margarine**
**1 large egg**
**1 teaspoon salt**
**Freshly ground black pepper**
**¼ teaspoon nutmeg**

Mash the potatoes, add remaining ingredients and beat well. Line a cookie tray with waxed paper. Fill a pastry bag fitted with a large star nozzle. Pipe on to the tray about 20 raised pyramids of potato, with a base of about 2 in.

**To pack and freeze:** Place the cookie tray in the freezer and freeze until the potatoes are firm. Remove from freezer. Place in plastic freezer bags, remove as much air as possible and seal. Label and freeze.

**To use:** Lightly grease a cookie tray. Place the frozen potato portions on the tray. Brush lightly with beaten egg and place in a cold oven. Heat at 400°F. for 20–30 minutes or until heated through and lightly browned.

## LEMON CRUMB PIE
*4–6 servings*

**½ pound gingersnap cookies**
**½ cup unsalted butter**
**3¾ tablespoons cornstarch**
**⅝ cup water**
**Grated rind and juice of 2 lemons**
**½ cup superfine sugar**
**2 eggs, separated**

Place the cookies in a bag. Crush with a rolling pin to make fine crumbs. Pour into a mixing bowl. Melt the butter and mix with the crumbs. Press the crumb mixture into an 8½-in. loose-bottomed French fluted flan pan to line the bottom and sides. Or press the crumbs into an 8-in. pie pan. Chill until firm. Combine cornstarch and water in a saucepan. Add the lemon rind and juice. Bring slowly to a boil, stirring, until the mixture thickens and becomes clear, then stir in the sugar and cook until it is dissolved. Remove from heat. Beat the egg yolks slightly. Stir some of hot mixture into the yolks. Return the mixture to the saucepan and mix thoroughly. Return to very low heat and cook, stirring constantly, for 1–2 minutes. Cool slightly. Pour into the chilled crust and let stand until cold.

**To pack and freeze:** Remove the flan pan from around the crust.

*Cakes can be frozen complete with icing and decoration*

Place on a cookie tray and freeze until firm. Wrap in moisture-vapor proof material. Pack the egg whites in a small plastic container. Cover, label and freeze.

**To use:** Replace flan pan. Let the egg whites thaw in the container for about 2½ hours at room temperature, together with the lemon pie. Beat the egg whites until stiff. Beat in ¼ cup sugar until stiff, shiny peaks are formed. Fold in ¼ cup more sugar. Pile the meringue on top of the lemon filling, making sure that it covers the edge of pie. Bake in the center of a fairly hot oven (400°F.) for 5–7 minutes. Reduce heat to 300°F. and bake for 10 minutes. Remove from oven and cool. Remove flan pan and serve.

## ICED STRAWBERRY MOUSSE
*4 servings*

**Strawberries, enough for ⅝ cup strawberry purée**
**2 tablespoons sugar**
**4 egg yolks**
**⅝ cups heavy cream**
**Lemon juice, optional**
**2 egg whites**

Hull the strawberries and put through a sieve or purée in a blender. Make ⅝ cup purée. Put the purée in the top of a double boiler with the sugar and egg yolks. Cook, beating occasionally, until the mixture is thick. Remove from heat, place over cold water and beat from time to time while mixture is cooling. Beat the cream just until it holds its shape; lightly fold into the strawberry mixture. Add more sugar to taste, or sharpen the taste with lemon juice. Beat the egg whites until stiff and fold into the strawberry mixture.

**To pack and freeze:** Spoon the mixture into individual soufflé dishes or one large dish. Cover

tightly with foil. Freeze until firm. Overwrap with heavy duty aluminum foil or moisture-vapor proof wrap. Seal, label and return to freezer.

**To use:** Unwrap and put in the refrigerator 30 minutes before serving time.

## HAZELNUT GATEAU

**¾ cup butter**
**¾ cup sugar**
**3 large eggs**
**1¼ cups self-rising flour**
**¼ cup hazelnuts, ground**

*For icing:*

**2⅜ cup confectioners' sugar, sifted**
**3–4 tablespoons water**

*For decoration:*

**2 tablespoons butter**
**⅝ cup confectioners' sugar, sifted**
**Milk**
**24 whole hazelnuts**

Preheat the oven to 350°F. Lightly grease a 9-in. spring form pan. Line the bottom of the pan with a circle of waxed paper. Grease again.

Cream together the butter and sugar until light and fluffy. Beat in the eggs, one at a time, stirring well after each addition. Sift the flour over the surface and stir into the creamed ingredients, together with the ground hazelnuts. Turn the mixture into the prepared pan and level off. Bake in the center of the oven for about 40 minutes or until a cake tester inserted in center of cake comes out clean. Cool on a wire rack for 5 minutes. Carefully remove ring from outside of cake and cool.

Blend the confectioners' sugar with enough water to make a smooth, medium paste. Spread the mixture over the top of the cooled cake to coat the surface

evenly. Let stand to set.
Cream together the butter and confectioners' sugar. Gradually beat in enough milk to make a stiff frosting. Place the frosting in a pastry bag with a star nozzle. Pipe the frosting around the top of the cake. Top with whole hazelnuts.

**To pack and freeze:** Place the cake on a cookie tray and freeze until firm. Place cake carefully in a rigid container to protect the frosting. Overwrap with moisture-vapor proof material. If desired, cut the cake into portions before freezing and separate with waxed paper. Reassemble into cake form and freeze. Seal, label and return to freezer.

**To use:** Remove the wrapping and allow to thaw for 3–4 hours at room temperature if whole, 2–2½ hours if sliced.

## DATE SCONE BARS
*Makes 8 bars*

**2 cups sifted all-purpose flour**
**½ teaspoon baking soda**
**1 teaspoon cream of tartar**
**Pinch of salt**
**¼ cup butter or margarine**
**2 tablespoons sugar**
**⅝ cup cut up dates**
**⅝ cup milk**

Preheat oven to 450°F. Sift together the flour, baking soda, cream of tartar and salt. Cut in the butter with a pastry blender or 2 knives to the consistency of coarse cornmeal. Stir in the sugar and add the dates. Add just enough milk to make a soft light dough. Roll out on a lightly floured board into an oblong about 14 in. by 4 in. Brush with milk and place on a lightly greased cookie tray. Mark through into 8 bars, using the back of a knife. Bake near the top of the oven for 15 minutes or until cooked and lightly browned. Break apart and cool on a wire rack.

**To pack and freeze:** Wrap immediately after cooling in moisture-vapor proof material. Seal, label and freeze. Or freeze on a cookie tray and pack in plastic bags, removing as much air as possible. Seal, label and return to freezer.

**To use:** Leave in wrappings at room temperature for 1–1½ hours. Or, if wrapped in aluminum foil, bars may be heated in a fairly hot oven (400°F.) for 10 minutes. Remove from foil and cool on wire rack or serve warm.

*Packing beef curry for the freezer*

# COOKING IN A HURRY

### SHRIMP CELESTE
*4 servings*

1 can (7½ ounces) button
   mushrooms, drained
¼ cup butter or margarine
½ cup all-purpose flour
1¼ cups milk
¾ cup light cream
Salt and pepper
1 can (6 ounces) shrimp
2 teaspoons dry sherry
Chopped parsley
Fried bread cubes

Cook the mushrooms in hot butter for 2–3 minutes. Stir in the
flour and cook for 2 minutes.
Remove from heat and stir in the
milk and cream. Cook over
moderate heat, stirring constantly, until the sauce has thickened and come to a boil. Season
to taste. Rinse the shrimp in cold
water. Drain and add to hot sauce
with the sherry. Heat thoroughly.
Sprinkle on the chopped parsley
and serve with fried bread cubes.

### LIVER PATE DIP
*8–12 servings*

¾ pound liverwurst
Dash of brandy or dry sherry
¼ cup softened butter or
   margarine
Grind of fresh black pepper
Large pinch of mixed spices
Heavy cream

Put all the ingredients, except the
heavy cream, into a bowl and beat
with a fork until smooth and
creamy. Or place in a blender and
whirl until smooth. Add sufficient cream to make the pâté soft
but not runny. Spoon into a serving bowl. Place on a platter and
surround with crackers, potato
chips, and raw vegetables for
dunking. This makes a good
'filler' for an impromptu party.

### CREME ANDALOUSE
*3–4 servings*

1 can (10¾ ounces) condensed
   tomato soup
4 medium onions, thinly sliced
¼ cup butter or margarine
1 can (6½ ounces) pimiento,
   drained
½ cup cooked rice
Stock or water, optional

Dilute the soup according to
directions on the can in a saucepan. Fry the onions in hot butter
until well browned. Stir into the
soup. Bring to a boil. Reduce
heat, cover and simmer for 5
minutes. Remove half the
pimientos and put through a sieve
or whirl in a blender. Add to soup.
Cover and simmer for 5 minutes.
Dice the remaining pimiento.
Just before serving, stir the diced
pimiento and cooked rice into the
soup. Add more water or stock if
necessary. Serve piping hot.

### SHERRIED CONSOMME
*3 servings*

1 can (15 ounces) consommé
¼ cup dry sherry
Lemon slices

Combine the consommé and
sherry in a saucepan. Heat slowly
over low heat until piping hot.
Serve in warmed wine goblets
with a spoon in each. Garnish
with lemon slices.
*Note:* This is an elegant start to a
dinner party.

## TOMATO AND TUNA EN GELEE

*4 servings*

½ envelope (½ tablespoon)
  unflavored gelatin
1¼ cups tomato juice
2 cans (7 ounces each) tuna
4 hard-cooked eggs, sliced
Lemon juice
Salt and pepper
Watercress

Sprinkle the gelatin over the tomato juice to soften. Heat over low heat until gelatin dissolves. Cool. Flake the tuna with a fork. Add to the tomato juice with 2 of the hard-cooked eggs, a squeeze of lemon juice and seasoning. Pour into a 2½-cup ring mold. Refrigerate until set.

Dip the mold in hot water quickly and turn out on to a serving platter. Fill the center of the ring with watercress. Surround with remaining hard-cooked eggs which have been chopped. Serve as a first course or as a light lunch.

## DEEP FRIED STEAK EN CROUTE

*4 servings*

¼ cup butter or margarine,
  divided
4 small minute steaks, about ¼
  pound each
1 or 2 packages (10 ounces each)
  frozen patty shells
1 can (5 ounces) liver pâté
1 egg, beaten
All-purpose flour
Oil for deep fat frying
2 cans (16 ounces each) small
  whole carrots
Chopped parsley
Watercress

Melt 2 tablespoons of the butter in a skillet until hot. Fry the steaks for about 3 minutes, turning half-way through cooking time. Set aside. Defrost the patty shells and push together. Roll out to ⅛ in. thickness on a lightly floured board. Spread a quarter of the pâté on one side of each steak. Position the meat on the pastry, leaving sufficient pastry between to cover each steak completely. With a sharp knife, cut a large circle of pastry around each steak. Brush pastry edge with beaten egg, dust lightly with flour and wrap pastry around the meat, securing it with a little more beaten egg. Pinch edges firmly together. Turn the parcels over and brush with egg. Roll out pastry trimmings, cut into strips and then

into leaves and use to decorate each parcel. Refrigerate. Half fill a deep skillet or kettle with oil and heat to about 350°F.

While oil is heating, melt the remaining butter in a small saucepan. Drain and cut up the carrots. Place in pan and heat, covered, for about 6 minutes. Lower the pastry parcels into the hot oil and cook for about 4 minutes or until lightly browned and puffy. Drain on paper towels. Sprinkle parsley over heated carrots and serve with steaks garnished with watercress.

## CHICKEN AND ASPARAGUS SAUTE

*2 servings*

3 chicken legs
All-purpose flour
2 tablespoons butter or
  margarine
1 tablespoon salad oil
1 can (10¾ ounces) asparagus
  soup
⅔ cup water
2 tomatoes, peeled and chopped
Soy sauce
1 can (3 ounces) button
  mushrooms, drained
Potato chips

Cut each chicken leg in 2 parts, discarding skin if wished. Dust with flour. Heat the butter and oil in a skillet. Brown chicken pieces quickly and evenly. Remove from skillet and reserve. Pour off most of the fat. Stir in the soup, water and tomatoes. Return the chicken to the pan. Cover and simmer for about 30 minutes or until the chicken is tender. Remove the chicken and keep warm. Add a few drops of soy sauce and the drained mushrooms to the saucepan. Stir well and bring to a boil. Pour the sauce over the chicken legs. Serve with potato chips.

## BEEFEATER PIE

*6 servings*

1 package (1⅔ ounces) beef stew
  seasoning mix
1¼ cups water
2½ tablespoons dehydrated
  onion flakes
1¼ tablespoons marjoram
2 cans (12 ounces each) corned
  beef
2 cans (1 pound each) baked
  beans in tomato sauce
2 packages (3¼ ounces each)
  instant mashed potatoes
¼ cup butter or margarine
Salt and pepper
Chopped chives

*Tomato and tuna en gelée – a starter or light lunch dish*

Combine the seasoning mix and water in a saucepan until smooth. Add the onions and marjoram. Bring to a boil, lower heat and simmer. Cut the corned beef into 1-in. cubes and add to the sauce with the baked beans. Mix well, cover and simmer gently until piping hot.

Meanwhile, make up the potatoes with water as directed on the package. Beat the butter and seasoning into the mashed potatoes. Turn the hot meat mixture into a shallow casserole. Spoon the potatoes over the top in rough mounds. Place under a hot broiler and broil until lightly browned and piping hot. Sprinkle with chopped chives.

## PAELLA

*4 servings*

Water
½ teaspoon turmeric
½ cup instant rice
1 chicken bouillon cube
¼ cup butter or margarine
2 onions, chopped
1 cup cooked diced chicken
½ cup cooked shrimp
1 jar (5 ounces) mussels, drained
1 package (10 ounces) frozen
  peas
Salt and pepper
4 tomatoes, peeled and cut up

Bring 1¼ cups salted water to a boil in a saucepan. Remove from heat. Add turmeric and rice, mix well. Cover tightly and let stand.

*An instant dinner party – delicious steaks, pâté and puff pastry*

158

Dissolve the bouillon cube in 1¼ cups water.

Melt the butter in a skillet and gently sauté the onion. Add the chicken, shrimp and bouillon. Bring to a boil and simmer for 2–3 minutes. Add the mussels and peas. Season well and simmer for 2–3 minutes. Add tomatoes and simmer lightly until the peas are tender. Fluff up the rice with a fork and fold into the mixture in skillet. Heat and serve piping hot. *Note:* If mussels are not available, use a can of whole clams.

## CURRIED CHICKEN CORNETS
*4 servings*

**1 package (10 ounces) frozen patty shells**
**1 egg, beaten**
**1 cup curry sauce, page 154**
**¾ cup finely diced cooked chicken**
**1¼ tablespoons currants**
**1¼ tablespoons chopped almonds**

Preheat oven to 450°F. Let patty shells defrost. Push together to make one piece. Roll out the pastry to a rectangle approximately 16 in. by 6 in. Cut into strips ½ in. wide by 16 in. long. Brush strips with beaten egg. Wind around cream horn cases, slightly overlapping, with the egg side outside. Place on cookie trays and bake near the top of the oven for about 10 minutes. Remove from oven. Carefully remove the horn cases by giving them a little twist and return the cases to the cookie tray. Lower oven heat to 400°F. and bake 5 minutes more or until golden brown and crisp.

Meanwhile, in a saucepan heat together the curry sauce, chicken, currants and almonds. When piping hot, fill the warm pastry cornets and serve.

## CHOCOLATE NUT SUNDAE
*4 servings*

**2 squares (2 ounces) unsweetened chocolate**
**1 tablespoon butter or margarine**
**1¼ tablespoons milk**
**1 teaspoon vanilla extract**
**Vanilla ice cream**
**Heavy cream**
**Chopped nuts**

Melt the chocolate and butter in top part of double boiler over hot water. Stir in the milk and vanilla to make a creamy sauce. Put a

*Chocolate nut sundae is a treat for all ages*

*Abricots à la crème, quick but delicious*

scoop of ice cream in each dessert glass and pour over the chocolate sauce. Top with whipped cream and chopped nuts if desired.

## LIQUEUR ICE CREAM

**Vanilla ice cream**
**Liqueur such as crème de menthe, cherry brandy, apricot brandy or Tia Maria**

Spoon the ice cream into sundae dishes. Trickle over it a little of your favorite liqueur.

## APRICOTS A LA CREME
*4 servings*

**1 can (16 ounces) apricot halves**
**2½ teaspoons cornstarch**
**5 tablespoons Cointreau**
**⅝ cup heavy cream**
**Pistachio nuts**

Drain the apricots, reserving syrup. Divide apricots between 4 dessert dishes, reserving 4 halves for garnish. Combine syrup with the cornstarch in a small saucepan. Stir in the Cointreau and ¼ cup cream. Bring to a boil over medium heat, stirring constantly, until smooth and thick. Pour over the apricots. Cool. Beat remaining cream until stiff. Spoon into dishes and top with an apricot half and pistachios.

## PEACH AND ALMOND UPSIDE-DOWN
*4 servings*

**Butter or margarine**
**Sugar**
**1 can (1 pound) peach halves**
**½ cup whole almonds, blanched and toasted.**
**1 package (9 ounces) white or yellow cake mix**
**1 teaspoon cornstarch**

Preheat oven to 375°F. Butter an 8 in. round deep cake pan. Sprinkle a thin layer of sugar over the bottom of the pan. Drain the peaches, reserving the syrup. Cut each peach half in quarters and arrange in the pan with the almonds. Prepare the cake mix according to directions on package. Spoon the mixture over the top of the peaches. Bake for 35–40 minutes or until a tester inserted in center of cake comes out clean. Remove from oven and immediately invert on a serving plate. Combine the cornstarch with the reserved peach syrup. Cook over medium heat, stirring constantly, until mixture boils and is clear. Pour the hot glaze over the cake.

# COOKING IN A HURRY

### FISH RAMEKINS
*3 servings*

**7½ tablespoons light cream**
**1 can (5½ ounces) pilchards or**
  **sardines in tomato sauce**
**1½ tablespoons lemon juice**
**Salt and pepper**
**3 large eggs**

Spoon 1 tablespoon cream into 3 ramekin dishes. Mash the pilchards and divide between the dishes. Sprinkle with lemon juice. Season to taste. Break an egg into each ramekin. Top with remaining cream. Bake in a moderate oven (350°F.) for about

160

15 minutes or until eggs are set. Serve piping hot.

### BRISLING FRIED PASTRIES
*Makes about 24*

**1 package (10 ounces) frozen**
  **patty shells, thawed**
**2 cans (3¾ ounces each) smoked**
  **brisling (sardines)**
**Mango chutney**
**2 eggs, beaten**
**1¼ cups chopped almonds**
**Oil for deep frying**

Push the patty shells together and roll out into a rectangle 19 in. by

12 in. Cut in half lengthways. Drain the brisling and lay in pairs side by side down the center of each pastry strip. Dot each pair with a little chutney. Brush one long edge of each piece of pastry with egg, fold over and press edges together tightly. Cut into pieces about 1½ in. long. Brush each roll with beaten egg then roll in chopped almonds. Heat oil in a deep kettle to 375°F. on a fat thermometer. Fry pastries in hot oil for about 3 minutes or until crisp and brown. Drain on paper towels and serve at once.
*Note:* These pastries are at their

best served straight from the hot oil, but if this is not convenient, keep them warm in a hot oven.

### VICHYSSOISE
*4 servings*

**1 package (5½ ounces) instant**
  **mashed potatoes**
**Chicken bouillon**
**1 teaspoon onion salt**
**Cold milk**
**⅝ cup heavy cream**
**Salt and pepper**
**Chopped chives**

Put the potatoes in a large bowl. Gradually beat in enough hot chicken bouillon to make a fairly thick mush. Beat in the onion salt. Still beating, add enough cold milk to thin the mixture to the consistency of thick cream soup. Gently stir in the cream. Season to taste. Serve very cold, garnished with chives.

## AVOCADOS WITH CRAB DRESSING
*4 servings*

½ cup mayonnaise
2½ teaspoons lemon juice
½ small clove garlic, crushed
Black pepper
½ pound crab meat, picked over
2 ripe avocados
1 lemon

Mix together the mayonnaise, 1 teaspoon lemon juice, garlic and a little freshly ground black pepper. Flake the crab meat and fold into mayonnaise. Cut the avocados in half lengthways. Rub inside of avocados with a little lemon juice to prevent discoloration. Fill the hollows with the crab mixture. Serve with lemon quarters and brown bread and butter sandwiches.

# QUICK SOUPS

# (CANNED AND PACKAGE SOUP VARIATIONS)

### Oxtail and tomato
Combine 1 can oxtail soup and 1 can cream of tomato soup, diluted according to directions. Stir in a little lemon juice or sherry. Heat. Serve piping hot with grated cheese.

### Crab and asparagus
Drain and flake 1 small can crab meat. Stir into 1 can asparagus soup, diluted according to directions. Heat. Serve piping hot with chopped parsley.

### Quick mulligatawny
Combine 1 can onion soup with 1 can oxtail soup, diluted according to directions. Heat with 1 bay leaf, a pinch of dried mixed herbs and 2 teaspoons curry powder. Simmer for 10 minutes. Serve.

### Chicken and almond
Fry 1 tablespoon ground onion, 1 tablespoon finely chopped parsley and 1 tablespoon chopped blanched almonds in 1 tablespoon butter until soft but not browned. Add 1 can cream of chicken soup, diluted according to directions. Simmer for 10 minutes. Serve piping hot.

## OYSTER FRITTERS
*2 servings*

*Fritter batter:*
1 cup all-purpose flour
Salt
⅝ cup warm water
1¼ tablespoons salad oil
1 egg white

*Filling:*
1 can (3½ ounces) smoked oysters
8 slices lean bacon
Oil for deep fat frying
Chopped parsley

Sift the flour and a pinch of salt into a bowl. Combine the water and oil and pour into the flour. Beat with a rotary beater until well blended. Set aside.
Drain the oysters. Place the separated bacon slices on a board. Draw the back of a knife blade the length of each slice to stretch it longer. Place an oyster on each bacon slice and roll up. Secure with a toothpick. Heat the oil for frying to 350°F. on a fat thermometer. Beat the egg white until stiff. Beat the batter again and pour into egg white. Fold in with a rubber spatula. Coat each oyster roll with batter. Fry in oil for 5 minutes, turn occasionally. Drain on paper towels. Sprinkle with parsley and serve piping hot.

## CANNED PHEASANT EN CASSEROLE
*4 servings*

½ package (7 ounce package) herb-seasoned bread-cube stuffing
¼ pound sliced bacon, cooked and chopped
¼ cup shortening
1 can (3 pound) whole roast pheasant in Burgundy jelly, or duck
3¾ tablespoons cornstarch
1 tablespoon red-currant jelly
Lemon juice
1 can (1 pound) small whole white onions
2 tablespoons butter or margarine
Chopped parsley

*Halving an avocado*

Prepare the stuffing mix according to package directions. Stir in the bacon. Shape into 20 balls. Melt the shortening in a small baking dish and add the stuffing balls. Drain and joint the pheasant or duck. Arrange in a large ovenproof casserole, cover and place in the center of a hot oven (425°F.). Place the stuffing balls on the top shelf. Bake both for 15–20 minutes. Combine the cornstarch with the stock from the can. Cook, stirring constantly, until the mixture comes to a boil and is clear and thick. Add the red-currant jelly and lemon juice to taste. Drain the onions and brown in the hot melted butter just until golden. Add to the pheasant in the casserole, pour over the sauce and top with stuffing balls. Sprinkle with chopped parsley and serve.

## FRANKFURTER ROKA SALAD
*4 servings*

1 package (12 ounces) frankfurters
1 can (1 pound) small whole potatoes, drained
½ cup bottled blue cheese dressing
1 teaspoon chopped parsley
½ cup halved stuffed green olives
Lettuce cups
Paprika

*Frankfurter Roka salad*

161

*An unusual mixture of canned fruits goes into this salad*

*Flaming brandy and cherry pie filling make this special ice cream dish*

*Use canned pears to make this delicious dessert*

Cut the frankfurters into ½ in. slices. Drop in a small pan of boiling water. Cook for 2 minutes, drain. Cut the potatoes in to small chunks and toss in a bowl with the frankfurters and dressing. Add the parsley and olives and toss lightly. Arrange lettuce in a serving platter. Fill with the mixture and sprinkle with paprika. Chill before serving.

## ESCALOPES WITH MARSALA AND CHEESE
*4 servings*

**4 veal scallops**
**Seasoned flour**
**¼ cup butter or margarine**
**3 tablespoons Marsala, sherry or Madeira**
**5 tablespoons grated Parmesan cheese**

Coat each scallop with seasoned flour. Heat butter in a skillet. Fry gently until just tender and golden, about 3 minutes on each side. Stir in Marsala and sprinkle each scallop with cheese. Spoon some of the butter-wine mixture over the top. Cover the pan and simmer gently for 2–3 minutes or until cheese is melted.

## PINEAPPLE CORN CRUNCH
*4 servings*

**1 can (8¼ ounces) crushed pineapple**
**1 cup sweetened apple sauce**
**⅝ cup dairy sour cream**
**1–1½ cups sugar-coated cornflakes**

Drain excess juice from the pineapple. Combine with the apple sauce and blend well. Divide between 4 dessert dishes. Divide the sour cream between dishes and spread over the top of the mixture. Top with sugar-coated cornflakes just before serving.

## TROPICAL FRUIT SALAD
*6 servings*

**1 can (20 ounces) lychees**
**1 can (15½ ounces) guava halves**
**1 can (14½ ounces) crushed pineapple**
**3 bananas**
**Juice of 1 small lemon**
**¾ cup ginger ale**

Drain the canned fruit. Slice the bananas diagonally and mix all the fruit together in a large glass bowl with lemon juice. Pour over the ginger ale. Chill. Serve with cream and cookies if desired.

## FRUIT VELVET
*4–6 servings*

**2 cups cold custard, made from a mix**
**1 can (21 ounces) pie filling – cherry, blueberry or apple**
**Grated rind of 1 orange**
**Whipped cream**

Combine the custard, pie filling mix and orange rind and blend well. Spoon into dessert dishes and chill. Top with whipped cream just before serving.

## CHERRIES JUBILEE
*6 servings*

**1 can (21 ounces) cherry pie filling**
**Grated rind of 1 orange**
**Brandy**
**6 portions vanilla ice cream**

Heat the pie filling in a saucepan with the grated orange rind. Warm some brandy in a small pan. Carefully add to the cherry mixture and ignite with a kitchen match. Spoon the flaming cherry mixture over the ice cream and serve immediately.

## STUFFED PEARS
*6 servings*

**1¼ cups heavy cream**
**4 small pieces crystallized ginger**
**8 candied cherries**
**½ cup chopped nuts**
**6 drained canned pear halves**
**1 small bakery jelly roll**

Beat the cream until it holds its shape. Chop the ginger and cherries into small pieces. Combine ginger, cherries and nuts with just enough of the cream to hold the mixture together. Divide mixture between the pear halves. Cut the jelly roll into 6 and place each slice in a dessert dish. Place 1 pear half on each slice. Coat entire top of pear and jelly roll with remaining cream.

## CREME MARRON
*4 servings*

**1½ cups heavy cream**
**1 can (8½ ounces) sweetened chestnut purée**
**1¼ tablespoons coffee liqueur**
**3 tablespoons chopped marron glacé**
**2 gg whites, stiffly beaten**

Whip the cream until stiff peaks are formed. Combine the chestnut purée, coffee liqueur and 2 tablespoons chopped marron glacé. Fold in the cream and egg whites. Pile mixture into dessert dishes and top with remaining marron glacé. Chill well.

### DRESSED ARTICHOKE HEARTS
*3 servings*

**1 can (14 ounces) artichoke hearts**
**¾ cup French dressing**
**12 black olives**
**Chopped parsley**

Drain the artichoke hearts. Cover with French dressing and let stand for 15 minutes, tossing occasionally. Remove the artichoke hearts from dressing and arrange on individual plates. Garnish with olives and parsley. Serve with brown bread and butter.

### FRIED WHITEBAIT
*4 servings*

**2 pound whitebait or fresh smelts**
**5 tablespoons seasoned all-purpose flour**
**Deep fat for frying**
**1 lemon, sliced**

Wash the whitebait in a colander under cold running water. Drain thoroughly and dry on paper towels. Toss half the fish in the seasoned flour. Heat deep fat to 375°F. on a fat thermometer. Place the fish in frying basket, lower into the hot fat and fry until crisp but still pale. Drain well on paper towels. Flour remaining fish and repeat the process. Reheat the fat and fry the fish until crisp and golden brown. Drain well on paper towels and serve at once with lemon slices.

### STEAK DIANE
*2 servings*

**2 thin minute steaks**
**Salt and pepper**
**2 tomatoes, cut up**
**3½ teaspoons Worcestershire sauce, divided**
**3 tablespoons butter, divided**
**1 small onion, chopped**
**2 teaspoons chopped parsley**

Season the steaks with salt and pepper. Place the tomato halves under a hot broiler and cook while steak is cooking. Put 2 teaspoons Worcestershire sauce in a skillet. Place over low heat and cook until sauce has evaporated. Add 2 tablespoons butter and increase heat. Add the onion and fry for 1 minute. Add seasoned steaks and fry for 1 minute on each side. Remove steaks to hot serving platter. Sprinkle with parsley. Melt the remaining butter in skillet. Add the remaining Worcestershire sauce and blend well. Pour the sauce over the hot steaks and serve with the broiled tomato halves.

### SANDWICH STEAKS
*4 servings*

**1 pound finely ground chuck**
**4 thin slices cooked ham**
**French mustard**
**Salt and pepper**

*Anchovy butter:*
**¼ cup butter or margarine**
**2 teaspoons anchovy paste**

Divide the ground chuck into 8 equal portions. Flatten each portion on a floured board to ¼ in. thick. Trim the ham to fit the patties. Spread ham with mustard and sprinkle with salt and pepper. Place a slice of ham on one patty and cover with another patty to make a sandwich. Repeat to make 4 sandwiches. Preheat broiling compartment. Place the sandwiches on broiler pan and broil, about 4 in. from source of heat, for about 3 minutes on each side. Cream together butter and anchovy paste. Serve the steaks with a pat of anchovy butter on each sandwich.

*Dressed artichoke hearts*

# COOKING IN A HURRY

## CANADIAN BACON DINNER
*4 servings*

**8 slices Canadian bacon, cut about ½ in. thick**
**1 small cooking apple**
**½ cup walnuts, chopped**
**½ cup seedless raisins, chopped**
**Juice of ½ lemon**
**1 tablespoon butter or margarine**

Pan-fry the bacon until heated through and lightly browned. Cut the apple in quarters and remove core but do not peel, then grate. Combine the apple, walnuts, raisins and lemon juice. Heat butter in a small skillet. Cook the mixture in hot butter just until heated through. Serve the nut mixture topped with bacon.

## CHINESE CHICKEN
*2 servings*

**¾ cup long grain rice**
**¼ cup butter or margarine, divided**
**1 can (8 ounces) pineapple slices**
**1¼ tablespoons brown sugar**
**1¼ tablespoons cornstarch**
**7½ tablespoons water**
**2½ tablespoons wine vinegar**
**2½ teaspoons soy sauce**
**1 cup thin strips cooked chicken**
**3 small tomatoes, peeled and cut up**
**1 small green pepper, seeded and thinly sliced**
**Salt and pepper**
**1 can (1 pound) bean sprouts**
**2 teaspoons chopped parsley**

Cook the rice in boiling, salted water according to package directions. Add 2 tablespoons butter and keep warm.
Drain the pineapple syrup into a saucepan. Cut pineapple slices in wedges and set aside. Stir sugar and cornstarch into the syrup. Add the water, vinegar and soy sauce. Cook, stirring constantly, until clear and thickened. Add

chicken, tomatoes, sliced pepper and pineapple. Cover and simmer for 5 minutes or until piping hot. Melt the remaining butter in a saucepan. Drain the bean sprouts and heat in butter for 2–3 minutes.
Make a ring of hot rice on a serving platter. Spoon the chicken mixture into the center. Serve the bean sprouts separately, garnished with chopped parsley.

## COD PROVENCALE
*4 servings*

**4 cod steaks, about ⅓ pound each**
**½ cup butter or margarine**
**Salt and pepper**
**2 onions, chopped**
**1 green pepper, seeded and chopped**
**2½ tablespoons tomato paste**
**2½ tablespoons all-purpose flour**
**1 can (1 pound) peeled tomatoes**
**Dash Worcestershire sauce**
**1¼ teaspoons sugar**
**1 pound potatoes, cooked and mashed**
**Milk**

Place fish on broiler pan. Dot with butter and season with salt and pepper. Broil, about 4 in. from source of heat, for 6 minutes. Turn, season with salt and pepper and broil 6 more minutes or until fish flakes easily when tested with a fork. While fish is cooking melt half the butter in a saucepan. Add the onion and pepper and fry gently for about 5 minutes or until the onion is tender but not browned. Stir in the tomato paste, flour and canned tomatoes. Bring to a boil, stirring constantly. Add the Worcestershire sauce and sugar. Lower heat and simmer while cooking fish. Prepare the potatoes, beating in remaining butter and adding enough milk to make them light and fluffy. Spoon the potatoes into a pastry

bag with a large star nozzle and pipe the potatoes around the edge of a heatproof serving dish. Place the fish in center, carefully spoon over sauce, place in broiler and reheat for 1 minute.

## HERRINGS WITH LEMON CRUMBLE
*2 servings*

**2 herrings**
**2½ tablespoons salad oil**
**2 thin slices dry bread**
**2 tablespoons butter or margarine**
**Grated rind and juice of ½ lemon**
**2 tablespoons chopped parsley**
**Lemon wedges**

Clean the herrings, cut off the heads and fins, but leave the tails on. Brush the fish with oil and place on broiler pan. Broil, about 6 in. from source of heat, for 8 minutes, turning once during cooking time.
Meanwhile, make breadcrumbs from the bread. Melt butter in a small saucepan, stir in breadcrumbs and cook over medium heat until golden brown. Remove from heat and stir in the lemon rind, juice and parsley. Put the breadcrumb mixture in a serving platter and place the herrings on top. Garnish with lemon wedges.

## PEACH CONDE
*4 servings*

**1 can (16 ounces) rice pudding**
**1 can (16 ounces) peach halves, drained**
**1 cup red-currant jelly**
**1 tablespoon water**
**1 tablespoon lemon juice**

Divide the rice pudding between 4 dessert dishes. Arrange peach halves on top, cut side down. Combine the red-currant jelly, water and lemon juice in a small saucepan. Heat, stirring constantly, until smooth and some-

what thickened. Pour carefully over top of peaches. Chill before serving.

## APRICOT RICE MERINGUE
*4 servings*

**1 can (16 ounces) rice pudding**
**1 can (16 ounces) apricot halves, drained**
**2 egg whites**
**5 tablespoons sugar, divided**

Preheat oven to 350°F. Turn the rice pudding into a small glass casserole or pie dish. Place the drained apricot halves on top. Beat the egg whites until stiff. Gradually add 4 tablespoons of the sugar, beating until egg whites stand in stiff peaks. Spoon the meringue over the apricots. Sprinkle the remaining sugar on top of the meringue. Bake in the center of the hot oven for about 15 minutes, or until the meringue is cooked and lightly browned. Serve warm or cold.

## BRANDIED APRICOTS
*4 servings*

**1 pound fresh apricots**
**1¼ cups water**
**½ cup sugar**
**Thinly pared rind of 1 lemon, with no white part**
**3¾ tablespoons brandy**

Put the apricots into boiling water, drain and remove skins. Halve and remove pits. Put 1¼ cups water, sugar and lemon rind in a pan. Cook over medium heat until mixture comes to a boil. Add the apricots and simmer gently for 5–10 minutes or just until soft. Remove the apricots with a slotted spoon. Place in a serving platter. Boil syrup rapidly to reduce it to about one-third the amount. Strain it and stir in the brandy. Pour over apricots and chill. Serve with whipped cream, if desired.

*Whitebait are very popular as a starter – quick to cook, too*

*Apricot rice meringue is a real quickie*

# COOKING IN A HURRY

*Eggs are invaluable for a multitude of quick snacks. They are rich in protein, are always available and remain cheap compared with meat and fish. Except in the case of hard-cooked eggs, the more lightly an egg dish is cooked, the better, especially with fried and baked egg dishes and omelets, where cooking for too long makes the eggs tough.*

## SCRAMBLED EGG NESTS
*4 servings*

½ cup mashed potatoes
Flour
Bacon fat
3 eggs
Salt and pepper
Milk
1 teaspoon butter or margarine
Parsley

Shape the mashed potatoes into 4 flat cakes and flour them lightly. Fry in hot bacon fat until golden brown on the underside. Turn the cakes over and hollow the center of each slightly with the bowl of a spoon. Leave over very low heat to brown underneath. Beat the eggs lightly with salt, pepper and a little milk. Melt the butter in a skillet. Cook the eggs over a low heat, stirring gently until lightly set. Fill the potato nests with the scrambled eggs and garnish with parsley.

## STUFFED ROLLS
*4 servings*

4 dinner rolls
2 tablespoons butter or margarine
4 large mushrooms, chopped
3 tomatoes, peeled and chopped
1 small onion, grated
3 eggs
Salt and pepper

Cut a slice from the top of each roll and scoop out some of the soft center. Set aside. Melt the butter in a skillet. Add the mushrooms, tomatoes and onion. Fry lightly for about 5 minutes or until tender but not browned. Beat the eggs with salt and pepper. Add to the mixture in the skillet and cook, stirring, over a low heat until thickened. Pile into the dinner rolls, replacing the lids. Place on a cookie tray. Cook in the center of a hot oven (400°F.) until the rolls are crisp and the filling thoroughly heated.

## SCRAMBLED EGGS ARCHIDUCHESSE
*4 servings*

¼ cup butter or margarine
6 eggs, beaten
Salt
Paprika
3 tablespoons light cream
½ cup chopped cooked ham
2 mushrooms, sliced and lightly sautéd
4 slices fried bread
1 can (10 ounces) asparagus spears, heated

Melt the butter in a skillet. Combine the eggs, salt, paprika and cream. Pour into the skillet and cook very slowly. As the mixture starts to thicken, add the ham and mushrooms. Serve on fried bread, topped with asparagus.

## HOT STUFFED EGGS
*4 servings*

4 eggs, hard-cooked
3 tablespoons butter or margarine
4 large mushrooms, finely chopped
1 onion, chopped
1¼ cups tomato juice
1 teaspoon sugar
Salt and pepper
2½ teaspoons cornstarch

Cut the eggs in half lengthways and remove the yolks. Melt the butter in a small skillet and cook the mushrooms and onions until tender and lightly browned. Divide the mixture in half and put one half in a small bowl. To the remaining mixture in skillet, add the tomato juice, sugar and seasoning. Simmer for 5 minutes. Blend the cornstarch into a little water to make a smooth paste.

Stir into the hot tomato juice mixture. Bring to a boil, stirring constantly, until the mixture thickens and becomes clear. Keep hot over low heat.

Mash the egg yolks, mix with the mushroom and onion mixture and use to stuff the egg white halves. Arrange in a serving platter and pour over the hot sauce. Serve immediately.

## SHRIMP OMELET
*1 serving*

**2 eggs**
**Salt and pepper**
**1 tablespoon water**
**Butter or margarine**
**4 or 5 peeled shrimp, fresh or frozen and thawed**
**Lemon juice**

Beat the eggs lightly with salt, pepper and water. Heat about 1 teaspoon butter in a skillet. Pour the beaten eggs into the skillet. Stir gently with the back of a fork, drawing the mixture from the sides to the center as it sets and letting the liquid egg from the center run to the sides. When the egg has set, stop stirring and cook for another minute until it is golden underneath.

Meanwhile, sauté the shrimp in a little hot butter with a squeeze of lemon. Place in the center of the cooked omelet. Fold over a third of the omelet to the center, then fold over the other side. Turn onto a warmed plate with the fold underneath.

## EGGS FRITURA
*4 servings*

**1 green pepper, seeded, chopped and blanched**
**½ onion, chopped**
**¼ cup butter or margarine**
**4 tomatoes, peeled and chopped**
**Salt**
**Freshly ground black pepper**
**4 eggs**
**4 slices buttered toast**
**½ cup grated Cheddar cheese**
**Parsley**

Cook the green pepper and onion in the melted butter for about 2 minutes. Add the tomatoes, plenty of salt and a grind of pepper. Cook for 15 minutes.

Poach the eggs. Spoon the tomato mixture on to buttered toast. Place a poached egg on each portion. Sprinkle with grated cheese. Put under a hot

broiler just long enough to melt the cheese. Serve immediately garnished with a sprig of parsley.

## BRAINS WITH EGGS
*2 servings*

**2 sets of brains (lambs' or calves')**
**¼ cup butter or margarine**
**Chopped parsley**
**2–4 eggs, lightly beaten**
**Salt**
**Freshly ground black pepper**

Wash the brains and soak for an hour in cold water. Remove as much of the skin and membrane as possible. Melt the butter in a skillet and fry the brains until they look white and stiff. Sprinkle with a little chopped parsley. Pour the beaten eggs into the pan, season well and leave over gentle heat until they are lightly set. Serve immediately.

## EGGS A LA FLORENTINE
*4 servings*

**1 pound fresh spinach**
**Salt and pepper**
**3 tablespoons butter or margarine**
**¼ cup all-purpose flour**
**1¼ cups milk**
**½ cup grated Parmesan or Cheddar cheese**
**4 eggs**
**3 tablespoons light cream, optional**
**Tomato slices**

Wash the spinach in cold running water, removing tough stem parts. Shake to drain and place in a large pan. Add a little salt. Cook, with just the water that clings to the leaves, until tender. Melt 2 tablespoons butter in a small saucepan. Blend in the flour and cook for 1 minute. Remove from heat and stir in the milk. Cook over medium heat, stirring constantly, until mixture comes to a boil and is thick. Simmer for 1 to 2 minutes. Stir in the cheese, reserving about 2 tablespoons for later use.

Drain the spinach thoroughly and chop roughly. Toss with remaining butter and season to taste. Spread spinach out in an ovenproof baking dish. Poach eggs lightly and place side by side on the spinach. Pour over the cheese sauce and sprinkle with remaining cheese. Place in the center of a fairly hot oven (375°F.) and bake for 10–15 minutes or until golden brown. Garnish with tomato slices.

## CHINESE OMELET
*4 servings*

**½ pound onions, finely chopped**
**4 bamboo shoots or stalks celery, finely chopped**
**4 large mushrooms, chopped**
**1 clove garlic, finely chopped**
**1 slice fresh ginger, finely chopped (if available)**
**2 tablespoons long grain rice**
**1¼ tablespoons oil**
**Salt**
**1 teaspoon cider vinegar**
**2 teaspoons soy sauce**
**1¼ cups stock or water**
**¼ pound peeled shrimp, fresh or frozen and thawed**
**4 eggs**

Fry the vegetables, garlic, ginger and rice in hot oil for a few minutes. Add salt, cider vinegar, soy sauce and stock. Cover and cook for 10–15 minutes or until the rice and vegetables are tender. Stir in shrimp and heat well.

Beat the eggs with 5 tablespoons water and salt to taste. Cook half the mixture as an omelet. Pile half the shrimp mixture along the center of the omelet and fold in half. Repeat with remaining egg and shrimp mixture. Serve any left-over filling separately. Each omelet serves 2.

## SHIRRED EGGS WITH CHICKEN LIVERS
*4 servings*

**¼ pound chicken livers, sliced**
**Butter or margarine**
**5 tablespoons tomato juice**
**4 eggs**
**Salt and pepper**
**Chopped parsley**

Sauté the chicken livers lightly in a little butter. Divide between 4 ramekins and pour 1¼ tablespoons tomato juice into each.

*Chinese omelet, with bamboo shoots, mushrooms and shrimp*

Slide 1 egg on top of livers. Sprinkle with salt and pepper. Bake in a moderate oven (350°F.) until eggs are done to your liking. Sprinkle with chopped parsley and serve.

## CHEESY EGGS
*4–6 servings*

**2 tablespoons butter or margarine**
**¼ pound mushrooms, sliced**
**Salt**
**Freshly ground black pepper**
**6 eggs**
**½ pound mild Cheddar cheese, thinly sliced or grated**

Melt the butter in a skillet, sauté the mushrooms until barely cooked. Season with salt and freshly ground black pepper. Put the eggs into boiling water and cook for 5 minutes. Peel carefully, holding the hot egg with a clean cloth or paper towel. Place eggs in an oven-proof baking dish. Spoon mushrooms over top. Smother with cheese.

Broil in a hot broiler until cheese melts and starts to bubble.

*Eggs à la florentine is a classic dish*

# COOKING IN A HURRY

## USING A PRESSURE COOKER

*A pressure cooker is an invaluable help, both when you need to produce a meal in a hurry and for other time-consuming cooking processes such as making stock or 'boiling' a fowl.*
*This versatile piece of equipment will cook almost any meal in substantially less than the normal cooking time.*

If you are buying a new pressure cooker, there are various models to choose from. If you generally cook for only 2–3 people, then a 4-quart is big enough; for 6–8 people, you will need a larger, 6-quart size. Cookers are available with a simple, deadweight regulator that maintains 15 pounds pressure to cook all foods except steamed puddings; for these and for small quantity canning, a variable three pressure control model is needed. Whichever you have, do study the maker's instructions.

There are certain rules which have to be followed when using all makes of pressure cookers. First, don't over-fill the cooker; it should never be more than two-thirds full with solid foods or half-full with liquids, rice or dried beans. Over-filling reduces the space for steam within the cooker and can cause the safety plug to blow. (This plug is designed to blow if pressure reaches 25 pounds; for instance, if the center vent pipe becomes clogged, or the cooker boils dry. If this happens, clean the vent – a pipe cleaner is excellent for this job – and check that there is the correct amount of liquid in the cooker before replacing the plug and closing the cover securely.)
*Do not* pressure-cook apple sauce, cranberries, rhubarb, pearl bar-ley, split peas, cereals or foods such as noodles, macaroni or spaghetti. These foods tend to foam, froth and sputter and may block the vent pipe.

When cooking time is completed, it is very important to let the pressure reduce before opening the cooker – and whether you do this quickly or slowly depends on what you have been cooking. To reduce pressure quickly, hold the cooker under cold running water. In models with an automatic air vent (which also acts as the safety plug), the small metal plunger in the vent will drop when pressure has been completely reduced and no steam escapes when the regulator is tilted. Only then should the regulator be removed and the cover opened. To reduce pressure slowly, set the cooker aside to cool at room temperature.

Keep the cooker thoroughly clean, paying particular attention to the vent pipe and sealing ring.

**Stock** Remove the rack. Break up the bones as small as possible, add to the cooker with enough water just to cover the bones (e.g. 2 pounds bones, 7–8 cups water). Add the required vegetables, herbs and seasonings. Bring to a boil without the lid, skim. Close the cover securely, place the pressure regulator on the vent pipe and cook for 40–45 minutes; if using marrow bones, pressure cook for 2 hours. Let pressure drop of its own accord.

**Soup** Follow any favorite recipe and cook for the time given in your instruction book. If you wish to make a larger quantity than can be made by half-filling the pressure cooker, make a strong soup and dilute with stock or milk after cooking. Don't over-season as pressure cooking concentrates flavor.

**Stews and casseroles** Again you can use any favorite recipe, Decrease the length of cooking time by two-thirds and, if necessary, decrease the amount of liquid, using about ½ cup more liquid than is desired in the finished product. Toss the meat in seasoned flour and brown it lightly in a little fat in the cooker before adding the liquid. Any additional thickening agent is best added after cooking.

To pressure cook a rather tough boiling fowl, rub the skin well with seasoning and place on the rack. Add 2 cups water and cook for 10–12 minutes per pound. More tender broiler-fryers should be cooked only about 10 minutes. When it is cooked, placing the chicken in a hot oven for about 15 minutes gives a delicious crisp, brown finish to the bird. Or, brown the bird before cooking in hot fat with a selection of vegetables; cover the bottom of the cooker with the cut vegetables, just cover them with water and lay the chicken on top; cook for 20 minutes per pound.

**Pot roasting** is a suitable method for less expensive cuts that are inclined to dry out when roasted in the oven. Rub some pepper (not salt) into the meat and brown it lightly all over in a little hot fat. Strain off excess fat and add 1 cup liquid for a cut of meat up to 4 pounds. Place the meat on the rack. Cook for 12–15 minutes per pound, depending on the thickness of the cut. For **braising**, prepare the meat and vegetables in the usual way, add the amount of liquid stated in the recipe and cook for 12–15 minutes per pound, depending on thickness.

**Vegetables** When you are preparing vegetables for pressure-cooking, make sure they are approximately the same size, or cut them into even-sized pieces. Always use the rack when cooking vegetables. Sprinkle salt sparingly onto the vegetables, rather than in the water. Use ½ cup water in a 4-quart cooker (1 cup in a 6-quart) except for potatoes and corn on the cob which require 1 cup (1 ½ cups in a 6-quart cooker). Follow manufacturer's directions for cooking time and cool the cooker at once. You can cook several kinds of vegetables together as there is no transfer of flavor. Be sure to check the cooking times given in your instruction booklet before you do this or else you will have some vegetables over-cooked and pulpy while others aren't cooked at all. First put in those that require the longest cooking; after the necessary time has elapsed, cool cooker and add the remaining vegetables. Bring the cooker up to pressure once more and cook until all the vegetables are done.

## CELERY SOUP
*4 servings*

1 large bunch celery
2 tablespoons butter
2 medium onions, finely chopped
2½ cups chicken stock or bouillon
Salt and pepper
1 bay leaf
1¼ cups milk
1¼ tablespoons cornstarch
½ cup cream

Chop the celery and reserve a few of the leaves for garnish. Melt the butter in the pressure cooker, sauté the celery and onion gently for 2 minutes. Add the stock and seasonings. Close cover securely and cook for 10 minutes (15 pound pressure). Let pressure

*Burgundy beef with ratatouille – both made in a pressure cooker*

drop of its own accord. Remove bay leaf. Purée in a blender or work through a coarse sieve and return to pressure cooker. Blend together the milk and cornstarch and stir into the mixture. Bring to a boil, without cover, stirring. Remove cooker from heat and stir in the cream. Adjust seasoning if necessary. Serve garnished with a few celery leaves.

## CHICKEN LIVER PATE
*4–6 servings*

2 tablespoons butter
3–4 slices lean bacon, coarsely chopped
1 small onion, chopped
½ pound chicken livers, washed and dried
¼ pound cooked chicken, chopped
1 chicken bouillon cube
5 tablespoons boiling water
Salt and pepper
2 large eggs, beaten

Grease a 1-quart mold or bowl that will fit loosely in the cooker. Melt the butter in a pan. Add the bacon and onion and sauté gently for 4 minutes. Add the livers and sauté for 3 minutes. Remove pan from heat and add the chicken. Dissolve the bouillon cube in the boiling water. Either finely grind the liver mixture separately or purée it in a blender with the stock. If ground, add the stock afterwards. Season with salt and pepper and mix in the beaten egg. Put the mixture in the mold and cover with foil. Place on rack in the pressure cooker and pour 4 cups water around the mold. Cook for 20 minutes (15 pound pressure). Cool cooker quickly and let stand to cool.

## BARBECUED PORK CHOPS
*4 servings*

4 lean rib pork chops, cut ½ in. thick, trimmed of fat
Salt and pepper
2½ tablespoons honey
2½ tablespoons soy sauce
1½ tablespoons catsup
1 small clove garlic, crushed
¼ teaspoon dry mustard
Juice of 1 large orange
Juice of ½ small lemon
5 tablespoons vinegar
1¼ tablespoons salad oil
1 small onion, chopped

Season the chops well. In a bowl combine the honey, soy sauce, catsup, garlic, mustard, fruit juices and vinegar.

Without the rack, heat the oil in the pressure cooker. Sauté the chops quickly on both sides until brown. Remove chops from cooker and drain off excess fat. Return chops to the cooker, pour on the sauce mixture and top with onion. Close cover securely and cook for 8 minutes (15 pound pressure). Cool cooker at once and serve chops.

## BURGUNDY BEEF
*4 servings*

**2½ tablespoons salad oil**
**1 large onion, sliced**
**2 green peppers, seeded and diced**
**1½ pound boneless chuck steak, trimmed and diced**
**¼ pound button mushrooms, cleaned and halved**
**1 cup dry red wine**
**3⅓ tablespoons tomato paste**
**Bouquet garni**
**Salt and pepper**

Heat pressure cooker, add oil and sauté the onion and peppers gently for 4 minutes. Add the meat cubes and brown lightly on all sides. Add the mushrooms, wine, tomato paste, herbs and seasoning. Close cover securely and cook for 12 minutes (15 pound pressure). Cool cooker at once. Remove the bouquet garni and serve accompanied by ratatouille.

## CHICKEN FRICASSEE
*4–6 servings*

**3 pound stewing chicken, cut in pieces**
**Seasoned flour**
**3 tablespoons salad oil**
**1 small onion, chopped**
**⅛ teaspoon rosemary**
**Salt and pepper**
**Few peppercorns**
**1 cup water**
**5–6 carrots, cut in chunks**
**1 cup light cream**
**2 egg yolks**
**3 tablespoons flour**

Roll the chicken pieces in seasoned flour. Heat pressure cooker. Add the oil and fry the chicken pieces until golden. Drain off excess oil. Add the onion, rosemary, salt, peppercorns and water. Close cover and cook for 15–20 minutes (15 pound pressure). Cool cooker at once. Add the carrots. Close cover and cook 3 minutes. Cool cooker at once. Remove the chicken from cooker and keep warm. Combine the cream, egg yolks and flour. Stir the mixture into liquid in cooker and cook until thickened. Add salt and pepper to

*The pressure cooker is useful for desserts like this*

taste; return the chicken to the gravy. Serve with rice or noodles or split baking powder biscuits.

## RATATOUILLE
*4 servings*

**2½ tablespoons salad oil**
**2 tablespoons butter**
**4 tomatoes, peeled and chopped**
**1 large eggplant, washed and chopped**
**4 zucchini, sliced**
**1 green pepper, seeded and sliced**
**2 large onions, thinly sliced**
**1 clove garlic, crushed**
**2½ tablespoons tomato paste**
**¼ cup water**
**Salt and pepper**

Remove rack and heat the oil and butter in the pressure cooker. Add the remaining ingredients and

stir well. Close cover securely and cook for 4 minutes (15 pound pressure). Cool cooker at once. Serve hot or cold.

## 'BOILED' DINNER
*4–6 servings*

**3⅓–4 pounds corned beef**
**2 cups water**
**1 bay leaf**
**½ teaspoon peppercorns**
**4 potatoes, cut up**
**4 carrots**
**8 small white onions**
**1 small yellow turnip, cut in 4 slices**
**1 small head cabbage, cut up**

Place the corned beef, water and spices in pressure cooker. Close cover securely and cook for 45 minutes (15 pound pressure). Let pressure reduce of its own accord.

*Corned beef and vegetables – easy with a pressure cooker*

Open cooker and add the vegetables, tucking them in close together in layers around and on top of meat. *Do not* fill cooker over two-thirds full. Replace cover securely. Cook for 5 minutes. Cool cooker at once.

## WINTER FRUIT SALAD
*4 servings*

**1 pound mixed dried fruit**
**2½ cups boiling water**
**6¼ tablespoons sugar**
**¼ cup seedless raisins**
**4 slices thinly pared orange rind**

Wash and drain the fruit well. Put into a bowl and pour on boiling water; cover and allow to stand 10 minutes. Turn fruit and water into pressure cooker. Add the sugar, raisins and rind. Close cover securely and cook for 10 minutes (15 pound pressure). Cool cooker at once. Before serving, the juices may be thickened with cornstarch or arrowroot.

## APRICOT CARAMEL CUSTARD
*4 servings*

**5 tablespoons apricot jam**
**4 large eggs**
**2½ tablespoons sugar**
**2½ cups milk**
**½ cup sugar**
**1 cup heavy cream**
**1 egg white**
**Few drops vanilla extract**

Butter a deep soufflé dish or bowl that will fit loosely in pressure cooker. Spoon jam into bottom of dish. Beat together the whole eggs, 2½ tablespoons sugar and milk; strain mixture on top of the jam. Cover top of dish with a sheet of aluminum foil. Place on rack in cooker, pour around 4 cups water and add a slice of lemon (this prevents the cooker discoloring). Close cover securely and cook for 10 minutes (15 pound pressure). Cool cooker at once and when custard is cool, refrigerate it.

Meanwhile, dissolve the remaining sugar and 10 tablespoons water in a pan over low heat, stirring constantly. Bring to a boil and boil until golden in color, then pour the caramel onto an oiled cookie tray to cool.

Beat the cream and egg white together until stiff. Beat in a little vanilla. Spread half the cream mixture on top of the chilled custard. Break up the caramel with a rolling pin and sprinkle on top. Pipe remaining cream around edge.

# QUICK CAKES AND COOKIES

### CHOCOLATE CRACKLES
*makes 12*

**1 package (6 ounces) semi-sweet
  chocolate morsels**
**2 tablespoons corn syrup**
**¼ cup butter or margarine**
**2 cups cornflakes or rice crispies**

Combine the chocolate morsels, syrup and butter in the top part of a double boiler. Heat over hot water until the chocolate melts. Stir to make a smooth mixture. Fold in the cornflakes or rice crispies. Divide the mixture between 12 paper cake cups. Let stand until cold.

### TRUFFLE CAKES
*makes 16–18*

**1 cup dry cake crumbs**
**½ cup superfine sugar**
**1 cup ground almonds**
**Apricot preserves**
**Sherry or rum**
**Chocolate shot**

Combine the crumbs, sugar, almonds and enough preserves to bind the mixture together. Flavor as desired with either sherry or rum. Shape the mixture into small balls. Let stand until balls are firm. Force some of the apricot jam through a sieve. Dip each ball into jam and roll in chocolate shot. When firm, serve in small paper cake cups.

### SHELL CAKES
*makes 12–14*

**6 tablespoons butter or
  margarine**
**⅓ cup superfine sugar**
**1 small egg, beaten**
**1¼ cups all-purpose flour**
**Preserves**
**Confectioners' sugar**

Preheat oven to 400°F. Lightly grease 2 cookie trays. Cream the butter and sugar together until very light and fluffy. Beat in the egg. Fold in the flour and mix well. Place the mixture into a pastry bag with a large star nozzle and pipe the mixture out in small shell shapes on the cookie trays. Bake in the center of the oven for 10–15 minutes or just until colored. Remove from tray and cool on wire racks.

To serve, sandwich two cookies together with preserves and dredge with confectioners' sugar.

### TUTTI FRUTTI CUPS
*makes 20*

**½ cup butter or margarine**
**½ cup superfine sugar**
**2 eggs, beaten**
**1 cup self-rising flour**
**Grated rind of ½ lemon**
**2 tablespoons chopped candied
  cherries**
**2 tablespoons chopped almonds**
**2 tablespoons currants**
**⅓ cup light brown sugar**

Preheat oven to 375°F. Place paper cup cake liners in muffin pans. Cream the butter and sugar until light and fluffy. Beat in the eggs. Gently stir in the flour and lemon rind. Divide the mixture between about 20 cup cake liners. Combine remaining ingredients. Top each bun with a spoonful of the mixture. Bake for 15–20 minutes or until done. Let cool on wire racks before serving.

### ONE-TWO-THREE COOKIES
*makes about 9*

**¼ cup butter or margarine**
**2 tablespoons sugar**
**¾ cup all-purpose flour**
**Confectioners' sugar**

Preheat oven to 300°F. Lightly grease a cookie tray. Cream together the butter and sugar until light. Work in the flour and knead with fingers to form a ball. Roll out carefully on a lightly floured board. The mixture will be crumbly and will have to be pressed with fingers to stay together. Cut the dough into

170

strips, about 2 in. by 3 in. Mark lines in cookies with a fork. Bake in center of the oven for about 25 minutes or just until lightly browned. Remove from cookie tray and cool. Dust with confectioners' sugar before serving.

## MELTING MOMENTS
*makes about 24*

½ cup butter or margarine
⅓ cup sugar
Vanilla extract or grated lemon rind
1 egg yolk
1¼ cups self-rising flour
Crushed cornflakes

Preheat oven to 375°F. Lightly grease 2 cookie trays. Cream together the butter and sugar until light. Beat in a little vanilla or lemon rind and egg yolk. Work in the flour and mix to a smooth dough. Wet the hands and divide into small balls. Roll in cornflakes and place on cookie trays. Bake in the center of the oven for 15–20 minutes. Cool on a wire rack.

## GINGER NUTS
*makes about 24*

1 cup self-rising flour
½ teaspoon baking soda
2 teaspoons ground ginger
1 teaspoon cinnamon
2 teaspoons sugar
¼ cup butter or margarine
⅓ cup corn syrup

Preheat oven to 375°F. Lightly grease 2 cookie trays. Sift together the flour, soda, ginger, cinnamon and sugar. Combine the butter and syrup. Stir this mixture into the dry ingredients and mix well. Roll the mixture into small balls, place well apart on the cookie trays and flatten slightly. Bake in the center of the oven for 15–20 minutes. Cool for a few minutes. Remove from cookie trays on to a wire rack. Store in an airtight container.

## LACE COOKIES
*makes 6 dozen*

¼ cup butter or margarine
¼ cup vegetable shortening
½ cup light corn syrup
⅔ cup firmly packed brown sugar
1 cup sifted all-purpose flour
1 cup finely chopped nuts
1 cup semi-sweet chocolate pieces

Preheat oven to 325°F. Place the butter, shortening, syrup and sugar in a saucepan. Bring to a

*1–2–3 cookies, ginger nuts, shell cakes and lace cookies*

boil and remove from heat immediately. Blend in the flour. Stir in the nuts. Drop by rounded measuring teaspoonfuls, 3 in. apart, on to greased cookie trays. Bake for 8–10 minutes or until set and lightly browned. Cool 1 minute on cookie trays. Remove immediately to a wire rack. Place chocolate over hot water and stir. When partially melted, remove from hot water and stir until melted. Brush some of the chocolate on the bottom of each cooled cookie. Brush tops of some and leave some plain.

## STRAWBERRY SHORTCAKES
*makes 6*

2 cups all-purpose flour
2½ teaspoons baking powder
¼ cup butter or margarine
2 tablespoons sugar
1 egg, beaten
Milk
2 pints strawberries, hulled
Sugar for berries
1 cup heavy cream, whipped

Preheat oven to 450°F. Lightly grease a cookie tray. Sift together the flour and baking powder. Cut in butter with two knives to the consistency of cornmeal. Stir in the sugar and beaten egg. Add just enough milk to make a stiff dough. Pat dough together and roll out on a lightly floured board ½–¾ in. thick. Cut into 6 rounds with a 3-in. cookie cutter. Place the rounds on the cookie tray, place near the top of the oven and bake for 7–10 minutes or until golden brown. Remove from oven. Reserve 6 of the perfect strawberries for garnish. Lightly crush remaining berries and sweeten to taste. While shortcakes are still warm, split each in half and spread with crushed berries. Top with whipped cream and whole berries.

## OVEN SCONES
*makes 10–12*

2 cups self-rising flour
1¼ teaspoons baking powder
¼ teaspoon salt
3 tablespoons butter or margarine
3 tablespoons sugar
¼ cup currants
⅝ cup milk

Preheat oven to 450°F. Sift together the flour, baking powder and salt into a mixing bowl. Cut in butter with a pastry blender or two knives until mixture looks like fine breadcrumbs. Stir in the sugar and currants. Add the milk, a small amount at a time, stirring with a fork until the mixture begins to hold together, making a light dough. With one hand, make a ball of mixture and knead lightly to form a smooth, fairly soft dough. Turn it out on to a lightly floured board. Form into a flat round and roll out to 1 in. thick. Cut into 2 in. rounds and place on a cookie tray. Brush tops with milk. Place in the top part of the oven and bake for 10 minutes or until well risen and golden brown. Cool on a wire rack. Serve split and buttered the same day that they are made.

## DROP SCONES (SCOTCH PANCAKES)
*makes 15–18*

1 cup self-rising flour
1–2 tablespoons sugar
1 egg
⅝ cup milk

Prepare a special griddle or a heavy skillet by rubbing the surface with salt on a pad of paper toweling, wiping clean and then greasing it very lightly. Just before cooking the scones, heat the griddle until the fat is very lightly smoking, wipe the surface with paper toweling.

Put the flour and sugar in a bowl, add the egg and half the milk and beat until smooth. Add the remaining milk and beat until bubbles rise to the surface. Spoon the batter on to the heated griddle, spacing some distance apart. When bubbles rise to the surface, turn the scones with a spatula and cook for ½–1 minute, or until golden brown. Place on a wire rack and cover with a clean tea-towel until all the scones are cooked. Serve well buttered.

## GINGER AND DATE CAKES
*makes 15–18*

1½ cups self-rising flour
Pinch of salt
6 tablespoons butter or margarine
6 tablespoons sugar
¼ cup chopped dates
2 tablespoons chopped crystalized ginger
1 egg, beaten
Milk

Preheat oven to 375°F. Lightly butter 15–18 muffin cups.
Sift the flour and salt into a bowl. Cut in fat lightly. Stir in the sugar, dates and ginger. Mix in the egg and enough milk to form a soft dough. Place in spoonfuls in the muffin pans. Bake in top part of the oven for 15 minutes. Let stand until almost cool then remove from pans.

## ROCK CAKES
*makes 12*

2 cups unsifted all-purpose flour
Pinch of salt
2½ teaspoons baking powder
½ teaspoon cinnamon
½ teaspoon nutmeg
¼ cup butter or margarine
¼ cup shortening
½ cup currants or seedless raisins
⅔ cup Demerara (raw) sugar
1 large egg, beaten
Milk

Preheat oven to 400°F. Lightly grease 2 cookie trays.
Sift together the flour, salt, baking powder and spice. Cut in the butter and shortening with a pastry blender or two knives to the consistency of coarse meal. Add the fruit and sugar and mix well. Add the egg and sufficient milk to give a stiff dough. Using 2 forks, place the mixture in small rough piles on the trays and place towards the top of the oven. Bake for 15–20 minutes. Cool on a wire rack.

Mixers take the arm ache out of food preparation. The most tiring processes – beating, whisking and mashing vegetables – become nothing more than a flick of the switch once your mixer is installed. Whether you have a small hand-held model or a full size one keep it out on the work surface, or hanging on the wall nearby, where it can become almost an extension of your own hands, to use automatically without thinking, at every possible opportunity. A large mixer particularly is cumbersome to lift and fit together and if it is tucked away out of sight in a cupboard you will tend not to use it as much as you might. If your hand model has a stand, keep that handy too. You need no special recipes for a mixer, though you may have to adapt the method. A hand-held model will beat or cream small quantities for any cake mixture, beat the lumps out of sauces, whip cream, beat up an omelet or mash potatoes without any effort at all. Follow the manufacturer's instructions regarding speeds but make sure that you do not over-beat, especially when adding flour to a cake mixture, or whipping small quantities of cream. Also make sure that you do not overload the machine – some of the beaters are light-weight and cannot handle heavy fruit cake mixtures in large quantities. The large models usually have a variety of basic fitments (apart from the range of extra attachments) and a much wider variety of speeds, making it possible to mix small or large quantities for cakes, pastries and even bread. Cooking for a large family or for freezing, you can handle jumbo-size mixtures in a large mixer that would be hard work by hand.

Whatever type of mixer you have, study the manufacturer's instructions before you use it, and do use the right type of beater at the correct speed. Never run a small mixer for more than 2 minutes without a break, or a large one for more than 5 minutes – this isn't as limiting as it sounds for everything is quicker with a mixer and it is only too easy to over-beat, over-whisk or rub-in for too long. As a general rule, for beating light mixtures such as meringues and sponges, use the top speed. Creaming fat and sugar or whipping cream is better done on a medium speed, or the mixture will splatter everywhere. If you're using the mixer instead of cutting

# MIXER COOKING

in by hand, as with pastry use a very low speed.

Cake making is one of the main uses of a mixer. To give the best results, ingredients should be at room temperature, so remove eggs and butter from the refrigerator an hour or so before they are required (except in very hot weather or if you are using one of the luxury margarines). If the fat is too firm, cream it a little alone before incorporating the sugar, or warm the bowl and beaters before you start – but take care not to make the fat oily.

If the mixer has only one speed, it is better not to use it for folding in the flour; you can do this quite easily and quickly with a spatula and it really needs a very slow speed to do it successfully with the machine.

To judge the degree of beating, always test your mixture with a spoon if you are using a fine whisk. Mixer whisks are often so fine that the mixture tends to fall away too easily – giving the impression that more beating is required. Sometimes a creamed mixture or dough will climb too far up the side of the bowl; if this happens, stop the mixer and scrape the mixture back into the bottom of the bowl with a spatula. If the head of a stand-held mixer is not adjustable, this may be necessary once or twice during creaming. With a hand-held

mixer this is avoided by moving the whisk round the bowl slowly, much as you would a spoon. Choose a fairly straight sided bowl if possible.

Mixers can be pretty fierce, and it is often as well to start working for a moment or two at a low speed before switching to a higher one. Otherwise there is a tendency for the mixture to be thrown out of the bowl – this applies particularly to liquids such as cream, or to powders such as confectioners' sugar. Another trick with confectioners' sugar, when adding it to butter cream icing, is to cover the head of the mixer and/or the bowl with a cloth, to stop spillage.

All your favorite baking recipes can be adapted to making in the mixer, but until you are used to using it, it will probably help to use recipes such as the following, that have been specially tested for suitability for mixers.

## WHISKED SPONGES

These marvellously light sponge cakes are ideal to make with the help of your mixer. With no raising agent added, they rely on the amount of air you can beat into the mixture to give them that airy texture and it is essential to beat the eggs and sugar until they are really thick and creamy.

Here is a good basic recipe, followed by flavoring variations

which will help you to ring the changes – delicious cakes for weekend teas, a plain sponge to accompany ice cream for family supper, or an elaborate – yet not heavy – gâteau when you have guests for dinner.

The basic sponge will keep fresh for several days in an airtight tin or wrapped in foil, and this will be helped by the addition of some glycerine to the ingredients – 2 teaspoons to a 3-egg mixture.

## PLAIN SPONGE

**2 eggs**
**½ cup superfine sugar**
**1 cup sifted all-purpose flour**

Preheat oven to 350°F. Grease an 8 in. square cake pan. Coat with equal amounts of flour and sugar. Shake out excess.

Warm the bowl and beaters with hot water. Dry out bowl. Put the eggs and sugar in bowl and beat at high speed until thick and light in color. If you move the beaters across the bowl they should leave a definite trail. Sift the flour over egg mixture and carefully fold it in with a rubber spatula. Continue folding until the flour is evenly distributed. Turn into the prepared pan. Place in the center of the oven and bake for 25–30 minutes. When cooked, the sides of the cake should shrink slightly from the edge of the pan and when you lightly press the top it should leave no impression.

## PINEAPPLE SPONGE

**1 plain sponge (recipe above)**
**1 can (8 ounces) pineapple slices**
**1¼ cups heavy cream, whipped**
**3¾ tablespoons apricot preserves**
**½ cup chopped walnuts**
**Walnut halves, optional**

Prepare the plain sponge cake and remove from pan. Drain the pineapple slices, reserving syrup. Split the cake in half and sprinkle each half with 2 tablespoons of syrup. Put the bottom half of the cake on a serving platter. Beat the cream until stiff. Chop 2 pineapple rings and combine with 4 tablespoons of the whipped cream. Spread over bottom half of cake. Put remaining half on top.

Combine apricot preserves and 2 tablespoons pineapple syrup in a saucepan. Bring to a boil, reduce heat and simmer for 2 minutes. Brush this glaze over the top and sides of the cake. Press chopped nuts around the sides of the cake. Spread remaining cream on top.

Decorate with remaining pineapple slices cut in pieces and walnut halves, if desired.

### CHOCOLATE SPONGE
Sift 2 tablespoons cocoa with the flour. Sprinkle cake heavily with confectioners' sugar when cool.

### LEMON SPONGE
Add the grated rind of 1 lemon with the flour.

### ORANGE SPONGE
Add the grated rind of 1 orange with the flour.

### CREAM SCONES
*makes 16*

2 cups sifted all-purpose flour
¾ teaspoon salt
1 teaspoon sugar
1 teaspoon baking powder
1 teaspoon soda
1 cup dairy sour cream
5 tablespoons butter or
    margarine
1 cup currants

Sift together the flour, salt, sugar and baking powder into a large mixing bowl. Combine the soda, 2 tablespoons water and sour cream in small bowl of mixer. Beat just until smooth. Add the butter to the flour mixture. Beat at low speed just until mixture resembles cornmeal. Add the sour cream mixture and beat only until blended. Remove the beaters. Stir in the currants. Turn the mixture on to a lightly floured board and knead a few times. Divide the dough into 4 parts. Pat each part into a circle 1 in. thick. Cut each circle into quarters. Heat a pancake griddle or large skillet over medium heat until very warm but not too hot. Grease lightly. Put quarters of scones on griddle and cook for about 20 minutes, turning frequently for even browning on both sides. Be sure to cook long enough to cook interior of scones.

### DUNDEE CAKE

2 cups all-purpose flour
1¼ teaspoons baking powder
Pinch of salt
1 cup butter or margarine
1 cup sugar
4 large eggs
2 cups seedless raisins
2 cups currants
1 cup chopped mixed candied
    fruit
½ cup halved glaće cherries
Grated rind of ½ lemon
½ cup whole blanched almonds

Preheat oven to 300°F. Grease the bottom of an 8 in. spring form pan. Sift together the flour, baking powder and salt and set aside. Cream together the butter and sugar on low speed until light and fluffy, about 3 minutes. Break in the eggs, one at a time, beating well after each addition. Add the flour and beat in on low speed. Remove beaters and stir in the candied fruit, cherries and lemon rind. Chop ¼ cup almonds and stir into the batter. Turn the mixture into the prepared cake pan. Level surface with a spatula. Split the remaining almonds in half and arrange neatly on top of the cake, rounded side up. Place cake just below center of oven and bake for 2½ hours or until a cake tester inserted in center of cake comes out clean.

### SWEET SOUFFLE OMELET
*1 serving*

2 eggs
1 teaspoon sugar
2 tablespoons water
1 tablespoon butter or margarine

Separate the eggs, putting the whites into small bowl of electric mixer. Add the sugar and water to the egg yolks and beat lightly with a fork. Beat the egg whites at high speed until very stiff. Melt the butter in an omelet pan over low heat. Turn the yolks into the egg whites and fold in carefully with a rubber spatula. Make sure the pan is covered with melted butter. Pour in the egg mixture. Cook for 1–2 minutes over moderate heat until the omelet is golden brown on the underside. Place pan, about 4 in. from source of heat, in hot broiling compartment. Cook just until the omelet is lightly browned and puffy. Do not over-cook as this will make it tough. Loosen the omelet around the sides, make a mark across the center, add the required filling and double the omelet over. Turn it gently on to a hot plate and serve at once.

### SOUFFLE OMELET FILLINGS

**Preserves** Spread the cooked omelet with warmed preserves, fold it over and sprinkle with sugar.

**Rum** Add 1 tablespoon rum to the egg yolks before cooking. Put the cooked omelet on a warm plate, pour 3–4 tablespoons warmed rum around and over it, ignite and serve immediately.

**Apricot** Add the grated rind of an orange to the egg yolks. Spread thick apricot preserves over the omelet before folding. Sprinkle with confectioners' sugar.

### COFFEE CREAM
*4 servings*

4 teaspoons unflavored gelatin
3¾ tablespoons water
1⅞ cups heavy cream
⅝ cup light cream
⅜ cup superfine sugar
4 teaspoons instant coffee,
    dissolved in 2 teaspoons hot
    water

Soften the gelatin in water in a bowl. Place the bowl in a pan of hot water and heat until the gelatin is dissolved. Put both creams in the large bowl of electric mixer. Beat at medium speed until stiff. Fold the sugar and coffee into the cream. With the mixer at medium speed, pour the gelatin into the bowl in a thin, steady stream, taking care to avoid the mixture setting in lumps. Keep beating until the mixture is just on the point of setting. Pour quickly into 4 individual molds or dessert dishes. Chill in refrigerator until set. This can be unmolded before serving or left in dessert dishes.

# BLENDER COOKERY

*The electric blender deserves to be the most widely used of all kitchen gadgets. It cuts the time spent mixing and blending ingredients to a tiny fraction of that needed for traditional methods; in addition it will do most of the time-consuming chopping and grinding that are essential to good home cooking.*

**Breadcrumbs** Cut off the crusts and drop the bread into the container, a piece at a time, through the feeder hole in the lid. For buttered crumbs, butter the bread slices first.

**Cookie crumbs** Break the cookies into 3–4 pieces each and feed them into the goblet through the feeder hole.

**Nuts** A blender will chop or grind nuts – add butter to make peanut, cashew or other nut butter.

**Vegetables** To chop cabbage, carrot and raw onion, half fill the container with water, cut the vegetable into manageable-sized pieces and add to the container. Blend until it is chopped as finely as you require. Drain off the water. (Some blenders will chop vegetables without added water, but follow the manufacturer's instructions and chop only a small amount at a time.)

**Sauces** For a white sauce, put all the ingredients in the blender and switch on to high speed. When blended, turn into a saucepan and cook gently to thicken.

**Soups** Cook vegetables until soft, then purée in the blender. Add extra liquid and seasoning after blending. Be careful not to overcook the vegetables.

**Fruit purées** Soft fruits will purée without prior cooking, but harder fruits should be pitted, and cooked gently beforehand. Some fruit purées, e.g. raspberry, may need sieving through a fine sieve afterwards to remove the seeds.

### REMEMBER!

**Do** read the manufacturer's instructions carefully.

**Do** place the lid in position before switching on.

**Do** cut solid foods small.

**Do** begin with small quantities of heavy and solid foods.

**Do** put liquids in before solids.

**Do** use the highest recommended speed for the smoothest results.

**Don't** overfill your blender. Most perform best when they are no more than half-full.

**Don't** let it run for more than the recommended time (2–3 short bursts are better than 1 long one).

**Don't** let the motor race. If the mixture creeps up the side of the container, stop the motor and scrape the mixture down on to the blades.

**Don't** try to whip cream in your blender – it won't do it; nor will it extract juice or crush ice (unless this is specifically stated by the manufacturer).

**Don't** try to chop raw meat unless you have a high-powered blender, beat egg white, mash potato or cream fat and sugar.

### CREAM OF VEGETABLE SOUP
*6 servings*

**1 pound vegetables, such as onions, tomatoes, carrots, celery or leeks**
**¼ cup butter or margarine**
**1¼ cups white stock or chicken bouillon**
**Salt and pepper**
**¼ cup all-purpose flour**
**2½ cups milk**

Wash and trim the vegetables and cut into rough pieces. Melt 2 tablespoons of the butter in a saucepan and cook the vegetables for about 5 minutes, without browning. Add the stock and simmer for 10–15 minutes or until tender. Season with salt and pepper. While vegetables are cooking, melt the remaining butter in a saucepan. Stir in the flour and cook for 1 minute. Remove from heat and stir in milk. Cook over

medium heat, stirring constantly, until mixture comes to a boil and thickens. Pour the vegetables and stock into the container and blend on low speed until vegetables are blended. Add the white sauce and blend on low speed a few seconds. Switch to high and blend until smooth and creamy. Return mixture to saucepan and reheat, but *do not boil.* Taste and add salt and pepper, if needed.
*Note:* If using onions or tomatoes, use only ⅝ cup liquid to cook.

## COD ROE PATE
*6 servings*

1 thin slice white bread
1 can (8 ounces) cod roe
1 small cooked potato
1 clove garlic
Few sprigs parsley
Juice of ½ lemon
1½ teaspoons salad oil
Salt and pepper
Black olives
Cucumber slices
Lemon slices

Break up the bread and place in the container of electric blender. Use medium speed to make crumbs of bread. Add the cod roe and blend on high speed until mixed. Add the potato, garlic and parsley and blend on medium for a few seconds. Add the lemon juice, oil and seasoning and blend on high until smooth. Spoon the mixture into a shallow dish. Garnish with olive slices, cucumber slices and lemon slices. Serve with melba toast or hot toast fingers.

## STUFFED TOMATOES
*6 servings*

2 slices bread without crusts
6 large tomatoes
2 slices bacon, cooked crisp
½ small onion, sliced
Small sprig parsley
¼ cup cubed Cheddar cheese
Salt and pepper

Make breadcrumbs in blender and turn them into a bowl. Cut a small round from each tomato at the end opposite to the stalk. Scoop out the centers and put in blender container with the bacon, onion, parsley, cheese and seasoning. Blend until smooth. Spoon out of container and stir into breadcrumbs. Fill each tomato shell with the crumb mixture and place in a baking dish. Bake in a fairly hot oven (375°F.) for 15–20 minutes or until the tomato cases begin to soften and the mixture is piping hot.

## FAMILY MEAT LOAF
*6–8 servings*

2 thin slices white bread, crusts removed
1 onion, halved
1 clove garlic
Rind of ½ lemon, with no white part
2 large eggs
1¼ cups red wine
½ teaspoon dried sage
1½ teaspoons salt
¼ teaspoon pepper
½ teaspoon dry mustard
1 teaspoon Worcestershire sauce
Few sprigs parsley
1 pound ground lean beef
½ pound ground lean pork
½ pound ground lean veal

Make breadcrumbs in blender and turn them into a bowl. Put the onion, garlic, lemon rind, eggs, red wine, sage, salt, pepper, mustard and Worcestershire sauce in container of blender. Blend until onion and garlic are finely chopped. Add the parsley sprigs and blend until roughly chopped. Add the beef, pork and veal to the crumbs and blend together. Gradually add the mixture from blender container and blend thoroughly. Turn meat into an 8 or 9 in. baking pan. Cover with foil and bake in a moderate oven (325°F.) for 1½ hours. Remove the foil and cook, uncovered, for 30 minutes. Drain off the juices and thicken with a little cornstarch, if desired. Serve with meat loaf.

## JELLIED CHICKEN CREAM
*6 servings*

2 envelopes (2 tablespoons) unflavored gelatin
1⅞ cups chicken stock or bouillon
1 small onion, cut up
¾ pound cooked chicken
2 stalks celery, chopped
6 stuffed olives
⅝ cup heavy cream
⅝ cup mayonnaise
Salt and pepper
Sliced cucumber
Watercress
Sliced tomatoes
1 onion, very thinly sliced

Soften the gelatin in a small amount of chicken stock. Dissolve over hot water. Stir in the remaining stock and leave to cool. Put the onion and part of the chicken in container of blender. Turn on high speed for a few seconds until roughly chopped. Scrape the mixture into a bowl. Repeat until all the chicken is

*Cod roe pâté is so simple in a blender*

chopped. Place the celery and olives in the container, blend on high until roughly chopped. Add to chopped chicken. Put the cream and mayonnaise in the container and blend for a few seconds. Spoon the mixture into the chicken. Mix together and season to taste, if necessary. Pour a little of the cooled chicken stock in the bottom of a 1-quart ring mold. Arrange the sliced cucumber in the stock. Add just enough cooled stock to cover cucumber and chill to set. Stir the remaining stock into the chicken mixture. Spoon into ring mold on top of the cucumber. Let stand until mixture sets, but do not chill. Unmold on a serving platter. Fill the center with watercress. Surround with tomato and onion slices.

## BURGERBRAISE
*4 servings*

3 thin slices white bread
¾ pound lean chuck, ground
1 onion, cut up
Pinch of mixed herbs
Salt and pepper
Flour
2 tablespoons shortening
1 can (16 ounces) tomatoes, broken up with a fork

Make breadcrumbs in blender. Turn into a mixing bowl and add the meat. Put the onion in the container and blend on high speed until finely chopped. Add to the meat with the herbs and seasoning. Shape the mixture into 4 round flat cakes. Toss them lightly in flour. Melt the shortening in a skillet. Add the burgers

*Jellied chicken cream for a summer salad party*

and brown well on both sides. Add the tomatoes, cover and simmer for 25–30 minutes or until thoroughly cooked.

## PORK AND BACON LOAF
*8 servings*

**1 pound lean pork**
**1 pound slab bacon, rind removed**
**1 large carrot, sliced**
**1 onion, cut up**
**⅝ cup water or stock**
**1 teaspoon Italian seasoning**
**1 bay leaf**
**Pepper**
**3 slices white bread**
**1 egg, beaten**

Cut the pork and bacon in pieces. Put in a casserole with the carrot, onion, water, seasoning, bay leaf and pepper. Cover and cook in a fairly hot oven (400°F.) for 1½ hours or until the meat is tender. Make breadcrumbs in blender. Empty into a mixing bowl. Put half the contents of the casserole into container, switch to low and then to high and process until meat is finely ground. Add to the breadcrumbs. Process remaining mixture in casserole. Mix together and stir in the egg. Check seasoning and add more if desired.

Turn the mixture into a 9 in. by 5 in. by 3 in. loaf pan. Cover with foil and bake in a hot oven (400°F.) for 1½ hours. Cool slightly before turning out onto a serving platter. This is excellent served hot or cold.

## FEATHER SPONGE

**1¼ cups unsifted all-purpose flour**
**¼ cup cornstarch**
**¾ cup sugar, divided**
**2½ teaspoons baking powder**
**½ teaspoon salt**
**7 tablespoons salad oil**
**7 tablespoons water**
**2 eggs, separated**
**Preserves**
**Whipped cream**

Preheat oven to 375°F. Grease the bottom of two 8-in. cake pans. Cover with a circle of waxed paper and grease again.

Sifted together the flour, cornstarch, ½ cup of the sugar, baking powder and salt. Spoon into container of the blender. Add the oil, water and egg yolks. Blend just enough to make a smooth batter. Beat the egg whites until foamy. Add the remaining sugar and beat with a rotary beater until egg

whites are stiff. Pour the batter into the egg whites and fold in lightly and evenly with a rubber scraper. Divide the mixture between the prepared cake pans. Bake for 18–20 minutes or until a cake tester inserted in center of cake comes out clean. Let stand in pans 5 minutes. Turn out on to a wire rack. remove waxed paper and cool thoroughly. Put layers together with preserves and spread cream over top of cake.

## LEMON LAYER SPONGE

**1 large juicy lemon**
**2 large eggs, separated**
**¾ cup sugar**
**¼ cup soft butter or margarine**
**½ cup all-purpose flour**
**1¼ cups milk**

Preheat oven to 350°F. With a potato peeler thinly pare lemon rind, free from all white part. Put the peel in container of blender. Squeeze the lemon and add 3 tablespoons lemon juice to rind. Add the egg yolks, sugar, butter, flour and milk. Blend just until mixture is smooth and rind is finely chopped. Beat the egg whites in a large bowl until stiff. Pour in blender mixture and fold in just until smooth. Turn into a buttered 1½-quart shallow casserole. Set casserole in a pan of hot water. Bake for 40–50 minutes or until golden brown and lightly set. Serve hot or warm.

## BANANA NUT BREAD

**2½ cups sifted all-purpose flour**
**3 teaspoons baking powder**
**½ teaspoon salt**
**¾ cup walnut meats**
**1 cup sugar**
**⅓ cup soft butter or margarine**
**1 egg**
**3 small bananas, cut up**
**½ cup milk**

Preheat oven to 350°F. Grease a 9 in. by 5 in. by 3 in. loaf pan. Mix together the flour, baking powder and salt in a medium sized mixing bowl. Set aside. Put walnut meats into blender container. Process for about 10 seconds or until chopped. Turn out of container and mix with the flour. Put the sugar, butter, egg, bananas and milk into container. Process for about 15 seconds or until mixture is smooth. Stop the motor and push the bananas down with a rubber spatula, if necessary. Pour over the dry ingredients and stir just until they are well moistened. Pour the batter into the prepared pan. Bake for about 1

hour or until a cake tester inserted in center of loaf comes out clean. Remove from pan and cool on a wire rack.

## OATMEAL NUT BREAD

**1½ cups sifted all-purpose flour**
**½ teaspoon salt**
**½ teaspoon baking powder**
**1 teaspoon baking soda**
**¾ cup quick-cooking oatmeal**
**1 egg**
**½ cup sugar**
**1 cup dairy sour cream**
**⅓ cup dark molasses**
**½ cup pitted dates**
**1 cup nuts**

Preheat oven to 350°F. Line a greased 8½ in. by 4½ in. loaf pan with waxed paper; grease again. Sift the flour, salt, baking powder and soda into a mixing bowl. Stir in the oatmeal. Put the egg, sugar, sour cream and molasses into container of blender; cover and process until smooth and well blended. Add the dates and nuts and process just until dates are chopped. Empty the mixture into the dry ingredients and stir well. Pour batter into the prepared pan. Bake for 45–55 minutes or until bread is done. Let stand in pan 5 minutes, turn out on a rack and cool thoroughly before cutting.

## MAYONNAISE
*makes 1¼ cups*

**1 egg**
**2 tablespoons lemon juice or vinegar**
**¼ teaspoon salt**
**¼ teaspoon dry mustard**
**1 cup salad oil**

Put the egg, lemon juice, salt and mustard in container of blender. Process on high speed for about 10 seconds. With speed at medium, gradually pour in the oil in a steady stream through opening in lid of container. Be sure to use all of the oil and continue beating just long enough so that mixture is smooth and slightly thickened.

## SUPERB CHOCOLATE MOUSSE
*4 servings*

**1 package (6 ounces) semi-sweet chocolate pieces**
**2 eggs**
**3 tablespoons strong, hot coffee**
**1–2 tablespoons rum, brandy, or Grand Marnier**
**¾ cup milk, scalded**

Combine the ingredients in container of blender. Cover and pro-

cess on medium speed for 2 minutes. Pour into dessert dishes and refrigerate for at least 4 hours before serving.

## SPIRITED CREAM
*8 servings*

**½ cup cold milk**
**2 envelopes unflavored gelatin**
**½ cup hot milk**
**2 eggs**
**⅓ cup sugar**
**⅛ teaspoon salt**
**2 tablespoons coffee liqueur or fruit liqueur**
**1 cup heavy cream**
**1½ cups crushed ice**

Put the cold milk and gelatin in container of blender. Cover and process at low speed to soften the gelatin. Remove feeder cap and add the hot milk to dissolve the gelatin. Process just until gelatin is dissolved. If gelatin granules cling to container, use a rubber spatula to push them down. Add the eggs, sugar, salt and liqueur. Process until smooth. Add the cream and ice and process until ice is liquefied. Pour into individual dishes or a 5-cup mold. Chill until firm.

## FROZEN FRUIT SHERBET
*4 servings*

**1 can (6 ounces) frozen orange juice**
**¼ cup sugar**
**3 heaped cups crushed ice**

Put the ingredients in container of blender. Cover. Blend for 15–20 seconds. As the mixture freezes around blades, stop motor and stir down with a rubber spatula. Start motor again and continue to blend till desired consistency. Spoon into dessert dishes and serve immediately.

---

**Handy hint**

For deep fat frying, the temperature of the oil should be 350–375°F. If you do not have a frying thermometer, the only way to test the temperature is to drop a cube of bread into the fat. At 350–375°F. it should brown in 1 minute.

# Entertaining

*Chicken Marsala (page 210)*

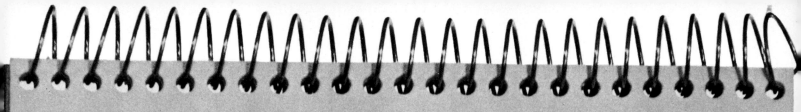

# PLANNING A MENU

Planning daily menus for the family presents quite a problem for most people, without the extra thought of guests. There are the nutritional considerations to take into account, the personal likes and dislikes of the children, and the need for variety. You have to think of the time available for shopping and cooking, too. Cooking for guests takes just that little extra effort of planning. If anyone finds it no effort it is because her mind has learned to cope automatically with the groundwork, usually after much practice.

For a beginner it is important to accept your limitations, with regard to both cooking ability and circumstances. Unless you are lucky enough to have competent help for your dinner party, include only one course that is going to need serious on-the-spot concentration. Try to start with something that can either be bought or made a day or two in advance, like pâté. This will mean you can enjoy a pre-dinner drink with your guests and need vanish only at the last minute to prepare the toast. If the weather is cold, serve a hot soup made the day before and heated up at the last moment. (A chilled soup in summer avoids even that!) Plan for a sweet that's simple too. There is no knowing how long the main course of a meal is going to take, and it is a pity to spoil it with worry about whether the next course is burning or boiling dry. Obvious dishes to avoid, unless you are quite confident of your skills and timing, are anything hit-or-miss like a hot soufflé, or anything fried. Mysterious pauses will have your guests every bit as worried as you are, wondering if they ought to offer to help.

For the inexperienced cook, the simplest solution is to choose as the main course a casserole that can be prepared entirely in advance. Potatoes baked in their jackets make a fool-proof accompaniment, and you could offer a simple salad as a separate course. It is always best to choose vegetables that can wait happily for a few minutes while your guests catch up with them. Why sit wondering if the sprouts have gone soggy and yellow, when French beans, peas or carrots would have done equally well? And never risk trying out something new on an important occasion. If you want to branch into more exciting dishes, have a full 'dress rehearsal' with your family or some close friends who won't mind, the week before.

A good menu is a varied one. Give your guests cream of artichoke soup, veal à la crème and soufflé milanese and you'll have them all struggling to the sofa and falling asleep afterwards – the combined effect of a major assault on their digestive capacity and a certain boredom induced by cream in every course and a pale beigey color predominating throughout. But if you serve a tomato salad before the veal and a tasty strawberry water ice with shortbread after, the effect will be quite different. If soufflé milanese remains your favorite dessert, serve steak and a fresh, green salad as the main course. The general principle is that a 'wet' course should follow a 'dry' one or vice versa and the same major ingredient should not feature in two courses. Texture is important and a menu that seems to be heading towards imbalance can often be redeemed by a simple touch, such as crisp croûtons with the soup or a salad instead of a cooked vegetable with the main course. A biscuit or a tiny helping of fresh fruit with a creamy dessert will often help. Flavor obviously needs considering because too much bland food is dull, whereas too much that is piquant is just impossible to eat. This is why a sharp hollandaise sauce is served with turbot, and a lemon sauce with a steamed sponge. In reverse, it's why cream goes with a sharp flavored apple pie, or rice with curry.

Appearance, another vital factor, is one that is often overlooked. This can easily be improved by the moderate use of garnishes. A steak with chipped potatoes looks much more appetizing if set off with watercress and a grilled tomato, and avoid any really anaemic-looking combination – creamed fish with marrow and potatoes for instance; serve carrots instead of marrow and use chopped parsley and perhaps some paprika pepper to make it look more attractive. Consider the individual tastes of your guests and don't serve curry, tripe or any other fairly specialized taste without first checking that they're going to like it. Be considerate in less obvious ways too – if you know one of your guests is shy, don't serve something that needs to be eaten with blasé defiance of conventional table manners (like corn-on-the-cob and spaghetti).

Having planned the menu, spend a little time working out a rough timetable. Give yourself time the day before to do any preparation that can be done in advance – however simple the menu, if you leave everything till 2 hours before the meal you will be rushed and flustered by the time the guests arrive. If you have chosen a simple menu, give yourself a treat by doing the absolute minimum of cooking on the day so you can enjoy the meal.

Plan the shopping, too. Order anything like fresh fruit that you cannot buy in advance, to avoid disappointment, and let your butcher know if you want any special cut or boning out done for you. He will appreciate not having to tackle a whole side of beef when the shop is full on a Saturday morning.

All this planning is practical, and it has an additional psychological effect. A hostess who knows she has all the details under control and that the work is progressing to schedule will be calm and relaxed on the day, able to take a little more time over her own appearance. In the end she will win compliments from all angles!

# EASY BUFFETS

Buffets for 12, 20, or 30 need be no effort
if you plan your menus carefully. Follow
our timetables for a really easy passage.

### Timetable

*The ham and tongue may be prepared 2–3 days before. The meringue layers and mayonnaise may also be made well in advance. Prepare the salmon, salad dressings and dip the day before and also the pineapple chiffon flans. On the day, finish off the sweets and make up the salads.*

### CHEDDAR DIP

*makes 1½ cups*

**1 tablespoon Worcestershire sauce**
**½ teaspoon dry mustard**
**2 ounces Gruyère cheese, cubed**
**1 bottle (7 ounces) beer**
**Dash cayenne pepper**
**½ pound mild Cheddar cheese, cubed**

Put all the ingredients except Cheddar cheese into container of blender. Cover and process at medium speed until smooth. Remove circle in top of cover and add the Cheddar cheese cubes gradually. Continue to process until mixture is smooth. Serve with potato chips or crackers.

### CLAM DIP

**1 can (6 ounces) ground clams**
**6 drops Tabasco sauce**
**½ teaspoon Worcestershire sauce**
**¼ teaspoon salt**
**½ teaspoon onion salt**
**1 cup creamed cottage cheese**

Drain the clams, reserving 1 tablespoon clam juice. Put the clams, juice and remaining ingredients into container of electric blender. Cover and process until the mixture is smooth.

180

Chill well before serving with raw vegetables or crackers.

### GLAZED BAKED HAM

**½ fully-cooked ham, about 5–6 pound**
**Cloves**
**¾ cup brown sugar**
**2 teaspoons dry mustard**

Preheat oven to 325°F. Place the ham, fat side up, on a rack in an open roasting pan. Bake for 18–24 minutes per pound or until a meat thermometer inserted in ham registers 130°F. About 45 minutes before ham is done, remove from the oven. Score the top in a diamond pattern and stud with cloves. Combine the sugar and mustard and spread over top of ham. Return to oven and continue cooking until heated through and nicely browned.

### PRESSED TONGUE

**1 salted tongue, about 2½–3 pound**
**8 peppercorns**
**1 carrot, sliced**
**1 onion, studded with 3 cloves**
**1 bay leaf**

Wash tongue well. Cover with water and let stand overnight if highly salted. Pour off water and put tongue in a large kettle. Cover with cold water and bring just to a boil. Skim off any scum with a spoon. Add the remaining ingredients. Bring to a boil again. Reduce heat, cover and simmer until the tongue is thoroughly tender. Allow at least 1 hour per pound for cooking. When the tongue is cooked, remove from the liquid and cool slightly in cold water. Remove from water and skin while tongue is still warm. Remove the small bones from the back of the tongue.

Return the meat to the cooking liquid and let stand until cool. When cold, curl the tongue into a round soufflé dish or deep cake pan lined with aluminum foil. The container used should be large enough to take the tongue, leaving a few gaps.
Check to see that the cooking liquid will set when cold. If it does not set to a firm jelly, either reduce by boiling very fast or add a small amount of softened plain gelatin to hot liquid. Strain the liquid and pour over tongue. Place a heavy weight on top of dish to hold tongue down firmly.

Chill until thoroughly chilled and set. Turn out of pan and garnish as desired.

### SALMON CUTLETS IN ASPIC

**10 salmon cutlets or steaks, 6–8 ounces each**
**Butter or margarine**
**2 lemons**
**5 bay leaves**
**Salt and white pepper**
**1 envelope (1 tablespoon) unflavored gelatin**
**2 cups chicken bouillon**
**Cucumber and lemon slices**
**Mayonnaise**

*Strawberry meringue slice is a delicious way of making a little fruit go a long way*

If salmon steaks are used, cut each one in half and carefully remove all bones. Liberally butter 10 pieces of aluminum foil large enough to envelop each cutlet. Place 1 cutlet or 1 steak (both halves) on each piece of foil. Lay a thin slice of lemon and half a bay leaf on each cutlet. Season with salt and pepper and fold up foil around fish. Place on a cookie tray. Cook in a moderate oven (325°F.) for about 20 minutes or until fish is tender. Chill in foil. Unwrap the packages and discard the bay leaves and lemon slices. Turn the cutlets upside down on a wire rack placed over a cookie tray. Soften the gelatin in the chicken bouillon. Heat over moderate heat until the gelatin is dissolved. Cool until the mixture is the consistency of egg whites. Spoon over the cutlets, making a thin layer over the top and sides. Chill. Serve on a platter, garnished with cucumber and lemon slices, and serve with mayonnaise.

## TOMATO AND ONION SALAD

Skin and slice 30 tomatoes and arrange in dishes. Sprinkle with finely chopped onion, and salt and pepper. Pour over about 1 cup French dressing. Sprinkle with chopped fresh parsley and marjoram. Chill well before serving.

## STRAWBERRY MERINGUE SLICE

*make 2 for the party*

**6 egg whites from large eggs**
**1½ cups sugar**
**2 cups heavy cream**
**1 quart strawberries, hulled**

Preheat oven to 250°F. On each of 3 pieces of unglazed brown paper, mark with a pencil a rectangle 12 in. by 4 in. Place on cookie trays. Place the egg whites in a deep bowl and beat until they are stiff. Gradually add the sugar, 1 tablespoonful at a time, beating constantly until no grains of sugar can be felt in the bottom of the bowl. Spread a thin film of meringue over one of the rectangles to cover well. With part of the meringue in a pastry bag, using a ½ in. nozzle, pipe a trellis pattern across the meringue. Divide the remainder of the meringue between the other rectangles and level off smoothly. Sprinkle a little sugar lightly over top of all meringues. Bake in the oven until

dried out and hard to the touch, at least 1½ hours. Turn off oven heat and let stand in oven until cool. Remove from the oven and peel off the brown paper. When cold, store in an airtight container until day of party.

Beat the cream until stiff enough to hold its shape. Slice half the strawberries. Put meringue layers together with about two-thirds of the cream and the sliced strawberries. Press the top lightly then pipe rosettes of cream over the top and sides and decorate with the remaining strawberries.

## PINEAPPLE CHIFFON FLAN

*make 2 for the party*

**2 cups vanilla cookie crumbs**
**½ cup butter or margarine, melted**
**Sugar**
**5 tablespoons water**
**1 envelope (1 tablespoon) unflavored gelatin**
**3 large eggs, separated**
**1 can (16 ounces) crushed pineapple, drained**
**Grated rind and juice of 1 lemon**
**1 package (8 ounces) cream cheese, softened**
**Whipped cream**

Combine the cookie crumbs, butter and 2 tablespoons sugar and blend well. Pat on to the bottom and sides of a 10-in. loose-bottomed French fluted flan pan or into a 10-in. pie plate.

Combine the water and gelatin and let stand. Beat the egg yolks with ¼ cup sugar until thick and light colored. Stir in the pineapple, lemon rind and juice. Turn into a saucepan and cook over low heat, stirring constantly, until thickened. Remove from heat and stir in the gelatin until dissolved. Stir in the cream cheese and stir until well blended. Cool until mixture just

*A cookie crumb case and a cheesy filling make this unusual flan*

begins to set. Beat the egg whites until stiff. Beat in ½ cup sugar gradually until mixture stands in firm peaks. Fold in the pineapple mixture. Let stand just until it begins to set. Pile immediately into the cookie shell. Chill in refrigerator until set. To serve, remove flan ring and garnish with whipped cream.

---

## MENU *serves 12*

**CHICKEN MILLE FEUILLES**
**HAM ROYALE**
**GALA SALAD WHEEL**
**JACKET POTATOES**
**ALMOND-ORANGE MOUSSE**

### Timetable

*Make the pastry layers and the chicken mixture for the mille feuilles the day before, also stuffing for ham royale. Finish off the savories and salads on the day. The mousse is also best made the same day, but may be made early in the morning.*

---

## CHICKEN MILLE FEUILLES

*make 2 for the party*

**1 package (10 ounces) frozen patty shells**
**1 package (8 ounces) cream cheese**
**2½ teaspoons lemon juice**
**5 tablespoons mayonnaise**
**¼ teaspoon salt**
**Freshly ground black pepper**
**2 cups finely cubed cooked chicken**
**4 lettuce leaves, finely shredded**
**2 medium tomatoes, thinly sliced**

Let pastry stand at room temperature until defrosted. Remove from package, arrange side by side on a pastry board and press

edges together. Roll out into a 12 in. square. Prick top all over with a fork. Cut into 3 parts, making 3 rectangles about 4 in. by 12 in. Place on cookie tray. Bake in a fairly hot oven (400°F.) for 20–25 minutes or until puffy and lightly browned. Remove and cool on a wire rack.

In a bowl combine the cream cheese, lemon juice, mayonnaise, salt and pepper. Beat with an electric mixer until smooth. Fold in 1½ cups of the chicken. Spread the mixture lightly over the tops of the 3 pastry layers. Sprinkle with shredded lettuce. Slice tomatoes thinly and arrange most of the slices over the top of the lettuce. Pile layers on top of each other, sandwich fashion. Sprinkle remaining chicken on top and garnish with remaining tomato slices. To serve, cut into thick slices with a sharp knife.

*Ham royale – thinly sliced ham with curry flavored rice*

**Handy hint**

When using the juice only of lemons or oranges, save the rind. Grate it finely and either dry in the oven and store in an airtight jar, or blend it with sugar and store in an airtight jar or keep in a tiny container in the freezer.

*Serve this asparagus quiche warm*

*Salads are a favorite at any buffet party. Try zucchini and rice*

## HAM ROYALE

**¾ cup uncooked rice**
**Pinch of saffron**
**1 bay leaf**
**Olive oil**
**1 large cooking apple, pared**
**3 tablespoons butter or**
    **margarine**
**1 onion, finely chopped**
**2½ teaspoons curry powder**
**¾ cup light cream**
**1 lemon**
**Salt**
**Freshly ground black pepper**
**15 slices boiled ham**
**1 jar (4 ounces) pimientos**
**Pitted black olives**
**Parsley**

Cook the rice in boiling salted water, to which the saffron and bay leaf have been added. Remove bay leaf. Stir in olive oil so that each grain of rice is well coated with oil. Chop apple in tiny pieces. Melt the butter in a saucepan and add apple and onion. Cover and cook gently for about 5 minutes. Sprinkle in the curry powder and cook for 1 minute longer. Add to the rice with the cream and toss lightly. Grate the rind from lemon and squeeze out 3 tablespoons juice. Add to rice and season well. Dice 3 slices of the ham. Cut the pimientos in small pieces. Add the ham and pimientos to the rice and toss lightly with a fork. Let mixture stand in refrigerator several hours to blend the flavors. Divide the mixture between 12 slices of ham. Roll up and secure with toothpicks. Garnish platter with olives, parsley and extra pimientos if liked.

## GALA SALAD WHEEL

*For tomato cups:*
**12 medium tomatoes**
**⅝ cup dairy sour cream**
**⅝ cup mayonnaise**
**1 small cabbage, finely shredded**
**12 pitted black olives**

*For devilled eggs:*
**12 hard-cooked eggs**
**¼ cup mayonnaise**
**2 teaspoons curry powder**

*For mixed salad:*
**1 small bunch celery, finely chopped**
**2 eating apples, pared and finely chopped**
**1 onion very thinly sliced**
**1¼ cups French dressing**
**2 medium heads lettuce**
**2 pound cold cuts**
**Watercress**
**Cucumber slices**

Cut a thin slice from each of the tomatoes at the end opposite the flower. With a teaspoon, carefully scoop out the pulp and discard. Drain the tomato cases upside down. Combine the sour cream and mayonnaise. Toss lightly with the cabbage. Pile the coleslaw mixture into the tomatoes and top each with an olive. Refrigerate until serving time. Cut the eggs in half lengthwise and remove the yolks. Mash the yolks and combine with the mayonnaise and curry powder. Pile yolk mixture back into egg whites. Cover and refrigerate until serving time. Combine the celery, apples and onion with French dressing. Just before serving, break lettuce up into chunks and toss with the vegetable and French dressing mixture.

To serve, pile the celery and apple mixture in the center of a large flat serving platter. Twist or fold the cold cuts and arrange on top of the salad. Arrange tomato cups and devilled eggs around edges of platter. Garnish in between eggs and tomatoes with watercress and cucumber slices. Serve with extra French dressing, if desired.

## ALMOND-ORANGE MOUSSE

**1 cup sugar**
**3 tablespoons grated orange rind**
**1 tablespoon unflavored gelatin**
**1 cup orange juice**
**¼ cup lemon juice**
**¾ cup heavy cream**
**1 cup slivered toasted almonds**

Put the sugar, orange rind and ½ cup boiling water in a small saucepan and boil for 1 minute. Soften the gelatin in ¼ cup cold water. Dissolve in hot syrup. Add the orange and lemon juice and refrigerate until the mixture begins to thicken. Whip the cream until stiff. Fold in the orange mixture, then the almonds. Pour into a serving dish. Refrigerate until firm. Serve extra whipped cream if desired.

**MENU** *serves 12*

**TUNAFISH CREAMS**
**ASPARAGUS QUICHE**
**COLD ROAST CHICKEN**
**CABBAGE AND PINEAPPLE SALAD**
**ZUCCHINI AND RICE SALAD**
**STRAWBERRIES WITH MACAROONS**

### Timetable

*Prepare pâté and quiches the day before and roast the chicken. (Do not put the quiches in the refrigerator – just keep in a cool place.) Carve the chicken, cover until ready to serve with plastic wrap. Prepare the salads and sweet on the day. To heat up the quiches, put them on cookie trays in the oven at 400°F. for about 15 minutes.*

## TUNAFISH CREAMS

2 cups dairy sour cream
¼ cup mayonnaise
Salt and pepper
Dash of Worcestershire sauce
1 tablespoon chopped chives
1 tablespoon chopped capers
1 teaspoon finely grated onion
2 envelopes unflavored gelatin
5 tablespoons water
2 cans (7 ounces each) tuna,
    drained and flaked
4 hard-cooked eggs, chopped
3 firm tomatoes
Parsley

Combine the sour cream, mayonnaise, seasonings, herbs and onion. Set aside. Soften the gelatin in cold water. Set over a pan of hot water to dissolve. Cool slightly and stir into the sour cream mixture. Add the flaked tuna and eggs and mix well.
Spoon into individual soufflé dishes and chill until set. To serve, garnish with tomato wedges and parsley.

## ASPARAGUS QUICHE
*make 2 for the party*

*For pastry:*
2½ cups sifted all-purpose flour
Pinch salt
6 tablespoons butter or
    margarine
¼ cup shortening
½ cup grated Cheddar cheese

*For filling:*
2 packages (10 ounces each)
    frozen asparagus spears,
    cooked
⅝ cup heavy cream
1¼ cups light cream
Salt
Freshly ground black pepper
8 eggs, beaten
6 tablespoons grated Parmesan
    cheese

Preheat oven to 400°F. Sift together the flour and salt. Cut in the butter and shortening with a pastry blender or two knives to consistency of cornmeal. Stir in the cheese. With the fingers work the dough into a ball. Turn out on a lightly floured board and knead lightly. Divide the pastry in half. Roll out each half into a circle and use to line two 8- or 9-in. flan rings placed on cookie trays. Or line two 9-in. pie plates with pastry. Trim the asparagus from the base end to fit the pastry cases. Cut up remaining pieces and place in the bottom of each flan case. Arrange the trimmed spears as the spokes of a wheel. Combine the creams, salt, pepper, eggs and Parmesan cheese.

*Sherry-soaked macaroons, cream and strawberries – delicious*

Pour over asparagus. Bake for about 40 minutes or until filling is set and pastry golden brown. Serve warm.
*Note:* If this flan is stored in a refrigerator, the pastry will become soft, so cover and store in a cool place. Reheat in a fairly hot oven (400°F.) for 15 minutes.

## CABBAGE AND PINEAPPLE SALAD

1 firm head cabbage
4 eating apples, pared and cored
1 can (16 ounces) pineapple
    chunks, drained
4 stalks celery, chopped
1¼ cups mayonnaise
Salt and pepper

Wash the cabbage. Shred and soak in ice water for about 15 minutes. Dice the apples. Drain the cabbage thoroughly. Mix with the pineapple chunks, apples and celery. Season the mayonnaise to taste with salt and pepper. Pour over the cabbage and toss well. Serve chilled.

## FRENCH DRESSING
*makes about 1 cup*

Put 1 teaspoon salt, 1 teaspoon dry mustard, 1 teaspoon sugar and ½ teaspoon pepper in a bowl with 5 tablespoons vinegar. Stir until blended. With a fork, beat in 10 tablespoons salad oil. Beat again just before using.

## ZUCCHINI AND RICE SALAD

8 zucchini
1 cup long grain rice
4 tomatoes
16 black olives, pitted
French dressing
Fresh mint
4 teaspoons chopped basil

Slice the zucchini, discarding a thin slice from the top and bottom. Cook, without paring, in boiling salted water just until tender, but still crisp. Drain well. Cook the rice according to package directions. Fluff with a fork to dry out a little. Slice the tomatoes and halve the olives. Combine zucchini, olives and rice. Add French dressing to taste. Pile into a serving platter and surround with sliced tomatoes. Garnish with basil.

## STRAWBERRIES WITH MACAROONS

*This dessert is reminiscent of the traditional English trifle, but less substantial. It can be made in one large dish, but is more attractive in individual portions*

3 dozen small macaroons
½ cup sherry
½ cup orange juice
2 quarts strawberries
Confectioners' sugar
2 cups heavy cream

Crumble 2 dozen macaroons in large crumbs and divide between 12 small dessert glasses. Combine the sherry and orange juice and spoon over the crumbs. Let stand about 1 hour.
Reserve 12 of the largest and best strawberries. Hull the rest and slice. Divide between the glasses. Dust lightly with confectioners' sugar. Whip the cream until stiff. Take the 12 reserved berries, split almost down to the stem end. Open out and fill with a dab of whipped cream. Top the berries in the glass with the remaining cream. Top each glass with a split strawberry and a macaroon. Chill before serving.

## MENU *serves 20*

**QUICHE LORRAINE**
**RARE ROAST BEEF**
**PATE STUFFED CHICKEN**
**LES CRUDITES**
**WALDORF SALAD**
**GARLIC BREAD**
**CHOCOLATE RUM MOUSSE**
**WINTER FRUIT SALAD**

**Timetable**
*Roast beef, stuff chicken but do not coat with crumbs, and make quiches the day before. Also prepare sweets. Coat and bake chicken, prepare salads and garlic bread on the day. Heat up quiches and garlic bread together just before serving.*

## QUICHE LORRAINE
*make 2 for the party*

1 package (10 ounces) frozen
    patty shells
½ pound lean bacon, chopped
½ pound Gruyère cheese, thinly
    sliced
4 eggs, beaten
1¼ cups light cream
Salt and pepper

Preheat oven to 400°F. Remove patty shells and let stand until almost defrosted. Place side by side and press edges together. Roll out on a lightly floured board into a large circle, about 11 in. Use to line a 10 in. flan ring or 10 in. cake pan. Make a fluted edge at top of ring or pan. Cook the bacon in a skillet until about half done. Drain on paper towels. Put into the bottom of the pastry ring with the cheese. Combine the eggs and cream, season well, and pour into the pastry ring. Bake towards the top of the oven for about 40 minutes until the filling is set and the pastry golden.

## PATE STUFFED CHICKEN

**20 chicken legs**
**2 pound liverwurst**
**Salt and pepper**
**6 eggs**
**7½ tablespoons water**
**Fresh breadcrumbs**
**1 cup butter or margarine**

Remove the skin from chicken legs. Using a small, sharp knife, carefully work the meat off the bone from the thigh end downwards, taking care not to split the meat. Twist out the bone. Mash liverwurst and season well. Stuff each chicken with part of the liverwurst, pushing the filling in from the thigh end. Reshape the meat and fasten together with toothpicks. Chill at least 1 hour in the refrigerator.

Remove the toothpicks. Beat the eggs and water together. Dip the chicken pieces one at a time in the egg mixture, coating them evenly. Season the breadcrumbs and roll chicken pieces in crumbs, putting on well on all sides. Recoat with egg and crumbs on top of the first coating. Place the legs in a single layer in 2 roasting pans. Melt the butter and pour over top of chicken. Bake in a moderate oven (350°F.)

*Pâté stuffed chicken – a soft, rich filling and a crisp outside*

for 30 minutes. Carefully turn the chicken legs over and bake for another 30 minutes. Raise the temperature to 400°F. and cook for 20 minutes until crisp and golden brown. Serve hot or cold.

## LES CRUDITES

**1¼ cups salad oil**
**5 tablespoons wine vinegar**
**5 tablespoons lemon juice**
**1 teaspoon sugar**
**1 teaspoon salt**
**1 teaspoon dry mustard**
**Freshly ground black pepper**
**1 pound tomatoes, peeled**
**1 small head cauliflower**
**1 red pepper**
**1 green pepper**
**1 bunch carrots**
**1 bunch radishes**
**10–12 stalks celery**
**½ pound thinly sliced salami**
**Black olives**
**Chopped parsley**

Beat together the oil, vinegar, lemon juice, sugar and seasonings. Cut the tomatoes in wedges. Clean and break the cauliflower into flowerets. Cut the peppers in half lengthwise, remove the seeds and cut into thin slices. Cut the carrots into very thin strips.

Clean the radishes. Cut the celery into sticks. Marinate each vegetable separately in a little of the dressing for about 30 minutes. Arrange the vegetables separately in mounds, on 2 large platters, adding the sliced salami and black olives. Garnish with a little chopped parsley.

## WALDORF SALAD

**2 pound crisp eating apples**
**Lemon juice**
**2 teaspoons sugar**
**1¼ cups mayonnaise**
**1 bunch celery, chopped**
**1 cup walnuts, coarsely chopped**
**1 head lettuce**
**Walnut halves**

Pare and core the apples, slice 2 and dice the rest. Dip slices in lemon juice to prevent discoloration. Toss the diced apples with 4 tablespoons lemon juice, the sugar and 2 tablespoons mayonnaise. Let stand about 30 minutes. Just before serving, add the celery, chopped nuts and remaining mayonnaise. Toss lightly. Serve in a large bowl lined with lettuce leaves. Garnish with apple slices and a few walnut halves.

*Hot French bread with garlic butter is a tasty buffet filler*

## GARLIC BREAD

For each loaf of French bread allow ½ pound butter or margarine and 2 cloves garlic, crushed. Cut the loaves into thick slices, without completely separating the slices, so that the loaf appears to be hinged. Cream the butter with the garlic and spread between the slices. Wrap each loaf loosely in aluminum foil and place in a warm oven (325°F.) for 15 minutes. Raise the temperature to 450°F. Take out the loaves, fold back the foil and return to the oven for 10 minutes to crisp.

## CHOCOLATE RUM MOUSSE
*makes 2 for the party*

**¼ cup cold milk**
**1 envelope unflavored gelatin**
**¾ cup milk, heated to boiling**
**6 tablespoons dark rum**
**1 egg**
**¼ cup sugar**
**⅛ teaspoon salt**
**1 package (6 ounces) semi-sweet chocolate pieces**
**1 cup heavy cream**
**2 ice cubes**

Put the cold milk and gelatin in container of electric blender. Cover and process until mixed and softened. Remove the feeder cap from top of container and add the hot milk. Blend until gelatin is dissolved. If gelatin granules cling to sides of container, stop blender and use a rubber spatula to push down gelatin. When the gelatin is dissolved add the rum, egg, sugar, salt and chocolate pieces. Process until mixture is very smooth. Add the cream and ice cubes and process until the ice is liquefied. Pour into 8–10 small dessert glasses. Chill until firm. Serve with whipped cream, if desired.

## WINTER FRUIT SALAD

**1½ cups sugar**
**3¾ cups water**
**Rind and juice of 3 lemons**
**¾ pound prunes, stewed**
**¾ pound dried apricots, stewed**
**3 bananas, sliced**
**6 oranges, pared and sectioned**
**3 grapefruit, pared and sectioned**

Make a syrup by dissolving the sugar in the water over gentle heat. Add the lemon rind, heat gently and boil for 5 minutes. Stir in the lemon juice. Strain the syrup over the prepared fruit and let stand to cool before serving.

# Formal Buffets

**Enjoy entertaining at home—there's no need to worry if you follow our menus and timetables**

PRAWN COCKTAIL
CHEDDAR-OLIVE BITES
COLD ROAST TURKEY
PORK AND HAM
GALANTINE
SALAD ROMANA
MUSHROOM SALAD
SLICED TOMATOES WITH
DAIRY SOUR CREAM
AND LEMON DRESSING
BAKED POTATOES
FRUITS IN SYRUP
FLORENTINE CORNETS
RASPBERRY SHORTCAKE
GATEAUX

**Several days before:** *Make florentine cornets and shortcake; store in airtight tins.*
**Day before:** *Stuff and roast turkey. Make galantine. Prepare salad vegetables. Make mayonnaise and salad dressings.*
**In the morning:** *Carve turkey. Make fruit salad.*
**2 hours before:** *Put potatoes to cook. Finish shortcake gâteaux. Make up prawn cocktails. Finish and dress salads.*

## PRAWN COCKTAIL

2 heads lettuce, shredded
1¼ pound peeled shrimp
Cucumber slices
Capers
Lemon wedges

*For dressing:*
1¼ cups mayonnaise
1¼ cups tomato catsup
1¼ cups light cream
Salt and pepper
Juice of 1 lemon

Line 20 small cocktail glasses with the shredded lettuce. Mix together the dressing ingredients and combine with the shrimp. Pile into the glasses on top of lettuce. Garnish as desired with cucumber slices, capers or lemon wedges.

## CHEDDAR-OLIVE BITES
*makes 40 appetizers*

1 can (7½ ounces) extra-large pitted ripe olives
Sharp Cheddar cheese
1 cup prepared biscuit mix
¼ teaspoon thyme
¼ teaspoon oregano
2 tablespoons melted butter
3 tablespoons milk

Drain the olives. Cut the cheese in small cubes and use to stuff the olives. Combine the biscuit mix and herbs. Stir in the butter and

*Prawn cocktail – a popular and refreshing start to a buffet meal*

milk to make a smooth dough. Mold a teaspoon of dough around each olive, covering it competely. Place on a cookie tray. Bake in a fairly hot oven (400°F.) for 10–12 minutes or until lightly browned. Serve piping hot.

## COLD ROAST TURKEY

15 pound turkey, dressed weight

*For stuffing:*
4 slices bacon, chopped
3 cups fresh white breadcrumbs
2 teaspoons chopped parsley
3 tablespoons melted butter
Grated rind of 1 large lemon
1½ cups chestnut purée (see below)
Salt
Freshly ground black pepper
1–2 eggs, beaten

Rinse out turkey with cold water. Pat dry with paper towels. Fry the bacon gently in a skillet for 3–5 minutes, or until crisp. Drain thoroughly. Combine the bacon with the breadcrumbs, parsley, butter, lemon rind and chestnut purée. Season to taste. Add just enough beaten egg to hold mixture together.
Stuff the neck cavity of the turkey with the mixture. Wrap the bird

in aluminum foil. Place on a rack in a shallow roasting pan and roast in a very hot oven (450°F.) for 4–4¼ hours. Open the foil for the last 30 minutes of cooking time to allow turkey to brown. Alternatively, wrap the bird in a large plastic roasting bag or plastic wrap and cook according to manufacturer's directions. Serve turkey cold. The breast meat can be sliced and replaced on carcass.

**To make chestnut purée:** Boil 1 pound chestnuts for 2 minutes to soften the skins. Remove from heat and peel quickly while hot. Simmer the peeled chestnuts in just enough milk to cover for about 40 minutes or until very soft. Push through a sieve or purée in a blender.
If you use canned chestnut purée, be sure that it is not sweetened.

## PORK AND HAM GALANTINE

1½ pound lean raw pork
1½ pound lean cooked ham
2 tablespoons finely chopped onion
1 cup thick white sauce
2 eggs
Salt and pepper
½ teaspoon dried rosemary
½ teaspoon dried savory
Thin slices of lean bacon
1 carrot, cut up
1 small onion
Vinegar
½ envelope unflavored gelatin
1 cup chicken bouillon

Put the pork, ham and onion through the food chopper twice. Blend in with the white sauce, beaten eggs and seasonings. Blend well and shape into a roll about 3 in. diameter.
Scald a clean white dish-towel in boiling water. Dredge cloth with flour. Lay slices of bacon over lapping each other on the cloth wide and long enough to cove roll. Lay the roll on the bacon and roll up the cloth so that the bacon covers the roll. Tie the ends of the cloth tightly with fine string o coarse thread. In a kettle larg

*A crisp shortcake forms the basis of this attractive raspberry gâteau*

Preheat oven to 350°F. Melt the butter in a saucepan. Add the sugar and boil together for 1 minute, stirring. Stir in the remaining ingredients. Cool the mixture for a few minutes. Drop by small teaspoonfuls on to a cookie tray lined with unglazed brown paper. Keep mixture well apart, allowing only about 4 or 5 to each tray.

Bake towards the top of the oven for about 10 minutes or until golden and bubbling. Let stand to cool enough until it is possible to handle. Remove carefully with a spatula and roll around a cream horn pan. When cold, remove the pan by twisting.

These cornets will store in an airtight tin for 2–3 days. Separate the layers with waxed paper.

## RASPBERRY SHORTCAKE GATEAU
*make 2 for the party*

**2½ cups sifted all-purpose flour**
**1 cup butter**
**½ cup sugar**
**Finely grated rind of 1 lemon**
**½ cup walnuts, finely chopped**
**1 egg yolk**
**1 cup heavy cream**
**1 pint fresh raspberries**
**Confectioners' sugar**

Preheat the oven to 350°F. Place flour, butter, sugar and lemon rind in a bowl and cut in with a pastry blender or two knives until the mixture resembles fine breadcrumbs. Add the walnuts and egg yolk and knead together to give a soft dough. Wrap in a plastic bag and chill for 30 minutes. Roll two-thirds of the dough into a rectangle 12 in. by 6 in. and place carefully on a cookie tray. Roll out the remainder of the dough and cut into six 3 in. rounds. Cut each round in half and place on a cookie tray.

Bake for about 30 minutes for the rectangle and about 20 minutes for the half circles, or until light brown and firm. While still warm on the cookie tray, cut the rectangle in half with a very sharp knife. Cool. Wrap in foil to store. To serve, whip the cream until stiff. Pipe two-thirds of the cream in a thick line down the center of 1 walnut shortbread. Spoon most of the fruit over the cream. Put on the second piece of shortbread and press down lightly. Pipe the remaining cream on top. Arrange the semi-circles along the top of the cream and put a whole berry in between each.

enough to lay roll flat, place a saucer or small plate. Half fill with water. Add the carrot, onion, a little vinegar and salt. Bring to a boil. Add the pork roll and simmer for about 2½ hours. Remove the roll from water and place on a flat board. Cover with another board and place weights, such as cans of fruit, on top. When it is thoroughly cold, remove the cloth and place the galantine on a wire rack over a plate. Soften the gelatin in the chicken bouillon, then heat gently to dissolve it. Cool the gelatin to the consistency of unbeaten egg white. Spoon over the meat. Repeat until the galantine is well glazed. Chill before serving.

## SALAD ROMANA

**2 packages (6 ounces each) Italian dressing mix**
**5 tablespoons water**
**10 tablespoons cider vinegar**
**1¼ cups dairy sour cream**
**1 firm cabbage, finely shredded**
**1 cup salted nuts, chopped**
**24 dates, pitted and chopped**
**2 apples, cored and chopped**
**2 teaspoons celery seeds**
**Paprika**

Put the Italian dressing mix in a screw-top jar. Add the water and shake. Add the vinegar and sour cream and shake very thoroughly. In a large bowl, toss together the cabbage, nuts, dates, apples and celery seeds. Pour the dressing over and toss thoroughly. Sprinkle with paprika.

## MUSHROOM SALAD

**1 pound mushrooms**
**3¾ tablespoons lemon juice or vinegar**
**⅝ cup salad oil**
**3¾ tablespoons finely chopped parsley**
**Freshly ground black pepper**
**Salt**

Wash and dry the mushrooms, remove the stalks. Slice the mushrooms very thinly into a serving platter. Add the lemon juice, oil, parsley and pepper. Marinate in the dressing for at least 30 minutes before serving. Salt lightly just before serving.

## FRUITS IN SYRUP

**2 cups sugar**
**2½ cups water**
**5 tablespoons orange liqueur**
**2½ tablespoons lemon juice**
**8–12 fresh peaches**
**1½ pounds white seedless grapes**
**1½ pound raspberries**

Dissolve the sugar in the water. Bring to a boil and boil for 5 minutes. Turn into a bowl and stir in the liqueur and lemon juice. Cool.

Peel and halve the peaches, and remove the pits. Keep the grapes whole. Arrange the peach halves in a shallow dish. Pile grapes and raspberries in the center. Spoon over the sugar syrup and let stand 2–3 hours before serving, spooning the juice over the fruit occasionally.

## FLORENTINE CORNETS
*makes about 15*

**7 tablespoons butter**
**½ cup sugar**
**1 cup almonds, finely chopped**
**¼ cup raisins, finely chopped**
**¼ cup chopped glacé cherries**
**¼ cup mixed candied peel, finely chopped**
**1¼ tablespoons light cream**

**Day before:** *Mix dry ingredients for pastry. Roast beef. Make ham cornets, cover and refrigerate. Make salad dressings and soufflé.*
**In the morning:** *Prepare salad vegetables but not apples. Prepare filling for quiches; add water and roll out pastry and line patty pans. Cut melon, cover and keep in a cool place, not refrigerator. Carve beef, arrange on serving platters; cover with plastic wrap and keep cool. Make ginger cream trifles.*
**Before serving:** *Fill and start to cook quiches 1 hour ahead. Arrange the salad platter and dress salads 1 hour before. Remove soufflé and ham cornets from refrigerator 30 minutes before serving.*

## SEAFOOD QUICHES

**2 packages (10 ounces each) frozen patty shells, thawed**

*For filling:*
**¼ pound shelled shrimp**
**¼ pound smoked salmon**
**2½ cups light cream**
**8 egg yolks, beaten**
**Salt**
**Freshly ground black pepper**
**2 tablespoons chopped parsley**

Push the patty shells together to form one piece. Roll out and use to line twelve 4 in. fluted patty pans or tart shells. Chop the shrimp and cut the salmon into narrow strips. Divide the fish equally between the uncooked pastry cases. Beat together the cream and egg yolks and season to taste. (Remember that salmon is on the salt side.) Add the chopped parsley. Place the pastry cases on cookie trays and spoon in the filling. Bake in a fairly hot oven (400°F.) for 10 minutes. Reduce heat to 350°F. and cook for 20–25 minutes or until the filling is lightly set and the crust is beginning to become light brown. Serve warm.

*Spicy ginger cream trifles are simple to make*

## COLD ROAST BEEF

**5 pound sirloin of beef, boned and rolled**

Place meat on a rack in a shallow roasting pan. Insert a meat thermometer in center of meat. Roast in a warm oven (325°F.) for 25–30 minutes to the pound until the meat thermometer registers 160°F. for medium doneness. Allow to cool.
To serve, slice thinly. Fold each slice in half and arrange neatly on a serving platter.

## PATE STUFFED HAM CORNETS

**6 slices boiled ham**
**½ cup butter or margarine**
**1 can (8 ounces) pâté**
**2 black olives, pitted**
**½ envelope unflavored gelatin**
**1 cup chicken bouillon**
**Watercress**

Cut each slice of ham in half. Wrap each piece around a 4 in. long cream horn pan and place seam side down on a cookie tray. Refrigerate until firm.
Cream together the butter and pâté until smooth and well blended. Spoon into a pastry bag fitted with a star nozzle. Carefully remove the cream horn pans from inside the ham, one at a time, and pipe in the pâté mixture. Place the cornets on a wire rack. Press a few slices of black olive on top of the pâté. Refrigerate.
Combine the gelatin and bouillon and let stand 5 minutes to soften. Then heat gently until the gelatin is dissolved. Chill until it is the consistency of unbeaten egg whites. Remove the cornets

from the refrigerator and spoon the gelatin mixture over the ham. Chill thoroughly. Serve garnished with watercress.

## DRESSED LEEKS

**2½ pound leeks**
**½ cup salad oil**
**2½ tablespoons cider vinegar**
**1 teaspoon French mustard**
**2 tablespoons finely chopped onion**
**1½ teaspoons sugar**
**½ teaspoon salt**
**Freshly ground black pepper**

Trim about half the green part from the leeks. Cut the remainder of the leeks into ⅛ in. slices and wash thoroughly in cold water. Drain. Blanch in boiling salted water for 3–4 minutes. Cool quickly with cold water. Drain thoroughly. Combine the remaining ingredients and blend well. Pour over the leeks and toss lightly. Chill before serving.

## DRESSED MACARONI AND MUSHROOMS

**1 pound macaroni**
**½ pound button mushrooms**
**1 clove garlic, crushed**
**5 tablespoons lemon juice**
**2½ tablespoons wine vinegar**
**Salt and black pepper**
**1 large red pepper, chopped**
**1 large green pepper, chopped**
**⅝ cup mayonnaise**
**½ cup plain yogurt**
**Chopped parsley**

Cook the macaroni in boiling salted water until tender. Drain and rinse under cold running water. Thinly slice the mushrooms and place in a bowl with

the garlic, lemon juice, vinegar, salt and pepper. Let stand 30 minutes, stirring frequently. Blanch the peppers for 1 minute, rinse in cold water and drain. Blend together the mayonnaise and yogurt. Pour over the mushrooms and mix well. Stir in the peppers. Toss with the macaroni until well coated in dressing. Turn into a serving platter and chill before serving.

## PLATTER SALAD

**½ pound red eating apples, diced**
**½ pound green eating apples, diced**
**½ cup chopped walnuts**
**1 small bunch celery, chopped**
**⅝ cup lemon dressing (see below)**
**Watercress**
**1 cucumber, sliced**
**1 bunch radishes, trimmed**
**1 pound chicory, sliced (optional)**
**Chopped parsley**
**Chopped chives**

Combine the apples, walnuts and celery. Add the lemon dressing and toss well. Arrange down the center of a flat platter.
Wash and trim the watercress and arrange down either side of the apple salad. Add the cucumber slices, sliced radishes and finally the chicory. Sprinkle with chopped parsley and chives.
**Lemon Dressing:** Thoroughly season 2–3 tablespoons salad oil with salt and pepper. Blend well with a fork and whisk in 1 tablespoon lemon juice.

## PEACH AND APPLE SOUFFLE

**1¼ pound cooking apples, pared and cored**
**1 can (16 ounces) sliced peaches**
**6 eggs, separated**
**1¼ cups sugar**
**2½ tablespoons lemon juice**
**2 envelopes unflavored gelatin**
**3¾ tablespoons water**
**2½ tablespoons orange liqueur**
**2 cups heavy cream**
**Frosted black grapes (see below)**

Prepare a 2-quart soufflé dish by tying a double band of lightly buttered aluminum foil around the outside of the dish to stand 3 in. above the rim. Slice the apples into a pan and stew in ½ cup of the syrup from the peaches. Cook until soft. Cool. Sieve or purée in a blender with the drained peaches until smooth. Place the egg yolks, sugar and lemon juice in a bowl over a pan of hot water and beat with a whisk until very thick and creamy. When finished the whisk should leave a trail through the mixture. Remove from heat and beat until cool. Soften the gelatin in 3 tablespoons water. Place over low heat and heat until dissolved. Cool slightly. Beat the fruit purée into the egg mixture. Stir in the gelatin mixture and beat. Add the orange liqueur. Beat the cream until thick but not stiff and fold into the mixture. Beat the egg whites until stiff and fold into mixture. Turn into the prepared soufflé dish and chill until set. Carefully remove the collar from the soufflé and decorate with frosted grapes.

**To frost grapes:** Dip the wiped grapes in egg white then coat thoroughly with sugar and leave to dry.

## GINGER CREAM TRIFLES
*makes 12*

**2 packages lady fingers**
**Apricot preserves**
**½ pound candied ginger**
**Sherry**
**4 cups heavy cream, lightly whipped**
**¼ cup almonds, blanched and halved**

Halve the lady fingers and spread thickly with preserves. Sandwich together and cut into 1 in. pieces. Divide between 12 dessert glasses. Finely chop the ginger, set aside one-third and mix the remainder with the sponge pieces. Pour about 2 tablespoons sherry into each glass and let stand. Just before serving, spoon the cream over lady fingers and garnish with halved blanched almonds and remaining ginger.

## WEDDING MENU *serves 30*

CONSOMME INDIENNE
ROQUEFORT TOMATOES
SALMON AND
MAYONNAISE VERTE
CUCUMBER CHARTREUSE
GREEN SALAD
POTATO SALAD LOAF
FRENCH BREAD AND
BUTTER
STRAWBERRY NUT
MERINGUES
WEDDING CAKE

**In advance:** *Make and ice cake (see recipe).*
**Several days before:** *Make consommé and chill. Make meringues and store in airtight tin. Make mayonnaise and French*

*Poached salmon is an impressive central display for a buffet*

*dressing; store in a screw-top jar.*
**Day before:** *Poach salmon. Make cucumber chartreuse and potato salad loaf. Make curry cream for consommé. Prepare salad vegetables. Hull strawberries and whip cream. Prepare the table, except for the food.*
**In the morning:** *Prepare Roquefort tomatoes. Dish up consommé and add topping. Unmold cucumber chartreuse and potato salad loaf, but keep covered. Finish strawberry nut meringues. Set foods out at last possible minute.*

## CONSOMME INDIENNE
*make double this quantity*

**12½ cups brown stock, cold**
**½ pound lean round steak**
**1½ cups water**
**2 large carrots, cut up**
**Bouquet garni**
**2 egg whites**
**Salt**
**2 tablespoons sherry, optional**
**½ cup chopped fresh herbs (chives, parsley and tarragon)**
**1 teaspoon curry powder**
**1¼ cups heavy cream, whipped**
**2 tablespoons flaked toasted almonds**

Remove any fat from the stock. Shred the meat in very thin strips and soak it in the water for 15 minutes. Put the meat, water, vegetables, stock and bouquet garni into a large soup kettle. Add the egg whites. Heat gently and whisk continuously with a balloon whisk until a thick froth

starts to form. Stop whisking and bring to a boil. Immediately reduce the heat and simmer for 2 hours. If the liquid boils too rapidly, the froth will break and cloud the consommé

Scald a large piece of cheese cloth. Place a double layer of cheese cloth in a collander and place the collander over a large bowl. Pour the soup through the cheese cloth very carefully, keeping the froth back with a spoon, then let it slide out on to the cloth. Again pour the soup through the cheese cloth and the filter of egg white. Adjust the seasoning in the strained broth and add a little sherry, if desired, to improve the flavor. Stir in the fresh chopped herbs and let the consommé cool and set.

To serve, break up the jellied consommé and serve in individual bowls. Stir the curry powder into the cream, spoon a little over each serving and sprinkle with almonds.

## ROQUEFORT TOMATOES

**30 large, firm tomatoes, peeled**
**2 packages (8 ounces each) cream cheese, softened**
**¾ pound Roquefort or Stilton cheese, softened**
**6 stalks celery, finely chopped**
**½ pound walnuts, finely chopped**
**2½ cups heavy cream**
**Salt and pepper**
**Chopped parsley**

Remove a slice from the round end of each tomato. Carefully scoop out the core and seeds with the bowl of a teaspoon. Turn tomatoes upside down to drain.

Beat together the cheeses and stir in the celery and nuts. Lightly whip the cream, stir into the cheese mixture and adjust the seasoning. Pile the cheese filling into the tomato cases and replace the lids. Garnish with parsley.

## COLD POACHED SALMON

**1 large salmon, scaled and cleaned, about 12 pounds**
**Court bouillon (see below)**

Clean and scale the fish. Fill a fish kettle with just enough court bouillon to cover the salmon. Bring to a boil, lower in the salmon and boil gently for 10 minutes. Remove the fish kettle from the heat, remove the lid and let stand until fish is cold. To serve, arrange the fish whole on a long dish. Garnish with radishes and cucumber slices and serve with mayonnaise verte.

## COURT BOUILLON

**3¾ cups water**
**1¼ cups dry white wine**
**1 small carrot, sliced**
**1 small onion, sliced**
**1 small stalk celery, chopped**
**1 tablespoon vinegar**
**Few sprigs parsley**
**½ bay leaf**
**3–4 peppercorns**
**2½ teaspoons salt**

Place all the ingredients in a pan. Bring to a boil and simmer for about 30 minutes. Allow the liquid to cool and strain before using to poach salmon.

## MAYONNAISE VERTE

**1 bunch watercress**
**1–2 sprigs fresh tarragon or chervil**
**Few sprigs parsley**
**2½ cups mayonnaise**
**1 tablespoon heavy cream**

Chop the watercress leaves and herbs very finely. Just before serving stir into the mayonnaise and cream. Blend well. Serve with Cold Poached Salmon.

## CUCUMBER CHARTREUSE
*make 2 for the party*

**1 package (6 ounces) lime flavor gelatin**
**3 cups boiling water**
**1 cup cider vinegar**
**1 tablespoon sugar**
**Green coloring**
**1 pound cucumbers, peeled and diced**
**Small tomatoes, peeled**

Dissolve the gelatin in the boiling water and stir until dissolved. Stir in the vinegar, sugar and a few drops of green coloring and let cool until the consistency of unbeaten egg whites. Fold in the diced cucumbers. When partially set pour into a 2-quart ring mold. Refrigerate until thoroughly set. To serve, unmold and fill the center with tomatoes.

## POTATO SALAD LOAF

*make 3 for the party*

1½ pounds potatoes, peeled and
   diced
⅓ pound sliced boiled ham
1 envelope unflavored gelatin
3 tablespoons salad dressing
1 small onion, grated
3 olives, chopped
1 teaspoon chopped chives
Salt and pepper
1 hard-cooked egg

Line an 8 in. by 4 in. loaf pan with waxed paper, letting the paper extend about 2 in. above the rim. Cook the potatoes in boiling salted water for about 10 minutes or until tender but not mushy. Drain. Rinse in cold water. Line the sides of the baking pan with slices of ham. Dice remainder of the ham.
Soften the gelatin in 2 tablespoons water in a small bowl. Place in a pan of hot water and stir until dissolved. Immediately stir in the salad dressing and pour over the cooked potatoes. Add the onion, olives, chives and seasoning. Mix well.
Place half the potato mixture in the ham-lined pan. Cover with diced ham. Add remaining potato mixture. Level the top and fold the paper over. Chill thoroughly. Just before serving, unfold the paper and invert the loaf on to a serving platter. Remove the paper. Decorate with sliced hard-cooked egg.

## STRAWBERRY NUT MERINGUES

*makes 36*

3 cups confectioners' sugar,
   sifted
6 egg whites
2¼ cups almonds, blanched and
   very finely chopped
Almond flavoring
2½ cups heavy cream, whipped
36 large whole strawberries,
   hulled

*A loaf-shaped mold adds interest to a potato salad*

Preheat oven to 300°F. Lightly butter 2 cookie trays.
Put the confectioners' sugar in a bowl with the egg whites and place over a saucepan of hot water. Beat steadily with an electric beater until the mixture forms stiff peaks. Remove the bowl from the heat and stir in the nuts and few drops of almond flavoring. Drop by spoonfuls on to the prepared trays and flatten with a spatula into small discs about 2 in. across. Bake for about 30 minutes or until the meringue is crisp on the outside and creamy in color. Remove from the cookie trays and cool on a wire rack.
To serve, pipe a border of cream around each and place a large strawberry in the center.

### Handy hint

When using unflavored gelatin, always soak it in a little cold water for a few minutes to allow it to swell, then place the basin over a pan of hot water to dissolve the gelatin completely.

## WEDDING CAKE

*This recipe is for a 3-tier cake which will serve approximately 150 people.*

*For the bottom tier:*
3 pound plus ½ cup currants
1 pound plus ¾ cup white raisins
1 pound plus ¾ cup seedless
   raisins
¾ pound glacé cherries
7¼ cups all-purpose flour
1¼ tablespoons ground
   cinnamon
1¾ teaspoons ground mace
Grated rind of 1 lemon
1¾ pound butter
4½ cups light brown sugar
14 eggs, beaten
½ pound mixed chopped
   candied peel
1½ cups chopped almonds
6 tablespoons brandy

*For the upper two tiers:*
1½ pound currants
1¾ cups white raisins
1¾ cups seedless raisins
½ pound glacé cherries
4½ cups all-purpose flour
1¾ teaspoons ground cinnamon
1 teaspoon ground mace
Grated rind of ¼ lemon
1⅞ cups butter
2½ cups light brown sugar
8 eggs, beaten
¼ pound mixed chopped
   candied peel
⅔ cup chopped almonds
3 tablespoons brandy

*For finishing:*
Brandy
Almond paste
Decorations
Icing

Make up and cook the bottom tier first, using a 12-in. round pan; prepare the mixture for the 2 upper tiers, divide between an 8-in. and a 6-in. round pan. Cook the two smaller cakes together. Grease the cake pans and line with a double layer of waxed paper. Tie a double band of brown paper around the outside edge or put each pan into a slightly larger pan. Stand pans on brown paper for cooking.
Wash and thoroughly dry the currants and white raisins, unless you are using pre-washed packaged fruit, in which case simply check it carefully. Chop the raisins, quarter the cherries.
Sift together the flour and spices. Add the grated lemon rind. Cream the butter and sugar together until very light and fluffy. Beat in the eggs a little at a time. If the mixture shows signs of curdling, beat in 1–2 tablespoons flour. Fold in the rest of the flour and then the fruit, peel, nuts and brandy.
Spoon the mixture into the prepared pans and level the surface. Using the back of a spoon, hollow out the center of the cakes slightly so they will be level when cooked. At this stage the mixture may be left overnight; cover lightly with a cloth. Leave in a cool place, not the refrigerator. Bake on the lowest shelf in the oven at 300°F. Cook the 12 in. cake for about 8 hours, the 8 in. cake for about 3½ hours and the 6 in. cake for about 2½–3 hours. Look at the cakes half-way through the cooking time. If they seem to be browning too quickly, cover the top with a double thickness of waxed paper. With a large cake it is often wise to reduce the oven temperature to 275°F. after two-thirds of the cooking time. Cool the cakes for a short time in the pans and then turn on to wire racks. When cold prick at intervals with a fine skewer and spoon some brandy evenly over the surface. Wrap completely in foil. Store for at least 1 month, preferably 2–3 months, in a cool, dry place before icing. After icing, wrap and store similarly, but for not longer than 2 months as a mold may form between the cake and the almond paste.
If one tier of the cake is kept for a later occasion, such as a christening, remove the icing and almond paste and redecorate it for the second occasion.
Directions for almond paste and icing are on page 86.

# SIT-DOWN LUNCHES

Lunch for 6-8 people is a tall order
if you are not prepared. Try some of
our planned menus, then branch out with
ideas of your own.

*This page: Chilled prawn soup*

**TOMATO APPETIZERS**
**PORK CHOP BRAISE**
**VARIETY RICE**
**FRESH FRUITS AND**
**CHEESE**
Wine – Riesling

**Timetable** *for lunch at 1.00 p.m.*
**Early:** *Assemble ingredients and equipment.*
*Peel and halve the tomatoes and arrange in dishes on a cookie tray, ready for baking. Divide 2 oranges into sections. Set out the fruit and cheese board.*
**11.30** *Start to cook pork.*
**12.00** *Prepare rice and sauté mushrooms, keep hot. When chops are cooked, keep hot. Do not add mushrooms and orange sections.*
**12.45** *Bake first course.*
**1.00** *Stir mushrooms and orange sections into pork. Serve first course.*

### TOMATO APPETIZERS

**16 firm red tomatoes, peeled and halved**
**1 cup freshly grated Parmesan cheese**
**Salt**
**Freshly ground black pepper**
**Dried basil**
**⅝ cup cream**

*Pork chop braise with variety rice*

Arrange the tomato halves in 8 individual baking dishes. Sprinkle with cheese, salt and pepper. Sprinkle with a little basil. Divide the cream between the dishes. Place on a cookie tray, towards the top of a moderate oven (375°F.) for about 15 minutes. Serve hot.

### PORK CHOP BRAISE

**8 pork chops, about ¾ in. thick**
**2½ tablespoons all-purpose flour**
**2½ tablespoons salad oil**
**5 tablespoons honey**
**1¼ cups boiling water**
**¼ teaspoon ground cloves**
**4 oranges**
**2 onions, chopped**
**½ pound mushrooms, sliced**
**¼ cup butter or margarine**

Remove any excess fat from the pork chops. Dust with the flour. Heat the oil in a large saucepan and fry the chops, 2 at a time, until golden brown on both sides. As each one is browned, remove from the pan, drain on absorbent paper towels and keep warm. Dissolve the honey in the water, stir in the cloves and juice of 2 of

the oranges.
When the chops are all browned, fry the onions in the oil until soft, drain off as much fat as possible. Stir in any remaining flour. Add the honey mixture and stir. Replace the chops, bring to a boil, cover and simmer for 45 minutes or until chops are tender. Arrange chops on a serving plate and keep warm. While chops are cooking, sauté the mushrooms in the butter. Peel the remaining oranges and divide into sections, free of white part. Stir into the mushrooms and add to the pork chop sauce. Bring to a boil and boil briskly for about 3 minutes. Pour over chops.

### VARIETY RICE

**1½ cups rice**
**Salt**
**¾ cup frozen peas**
**¾ cup frozen kernel corn**
**Freshly ground black pepper**

Cook the rice in boiling salted water until tender. Cook vegetables according to package directions. Combine the rice with vegetables and season with freshly ground black pepper.

**SMOKED SALMON WITH**
**BROWN BREAD AND**
**BUTTER**
**ESCALOPES DE VEAU AU**
**POIVRE ROSE**
**BOILED RICE AND**
**MUSHROOMS**
**GRAPEFRUIT SORBET**
Wine — Alsace Sylvaner

**Timetable** *for lunch at 1.00 p.m.*
**Day before:** *Make the grapefruit sorbet.*
**Early:** *Assemble ingredients and equipment.*
**11.00** *Slice smoked salmon and garnish with lemon wedges; leave covered with plastic wrap. Cut brown bread and butter. Leave covered.*
*Beat the veal and leave covered.*
**12.00** *Scoop sorbet into individual dishes and return to coldest part of refrigerator.*
**12.30** *Start to cook veal (do not add cream); keep hot. Stir in the cream and reheat just before serving.*
*Cok rice, drain and keep hot.*
*Sauté mushrooms in butter and keep hot.*
**1.00** *Serve first course.*

### ESCALOPES DE VEAU AU POIVRE ROSE

**6 veal escalopes (about 5 ounces each)**
**1¾ tablespoons salad oil**
**3 tablespoons butter or margarine**
**1¾ tablespoons flour**
**1½ teaspoons paprika**
**3 bay leaves**
**1½ lemons**
**Salt**
**Freshly ground black pepper**
**½ cup heavy cream**
**Watercress**

Place each veal escalope between 2 sheets of waxed paper and beat with a heavy knife or meat cleaver until very thin. Cut the edges slightly to prevent the meat from contracting during cooking. Heat the oil in a wide shallow skillet. When hot add the butter. Coat the escalopes with the flour mixed with the paprika. When the butter is sizzling, add the escalopes and quickly cook on 1 side only until golden brown. Remove the escalopes and drain off the fat, retaining the meat juices in the pan. Add to the pan the bay leaves, the thinly pared rind of ½ a lemon, 1½ tablespoons lemon juice, salt and pepper. Replace

*Pecan stuffing for a party-roast chicken*

the escalopes, browned side uppermost, in the pan. Cover tightly and simmer for about 20 minutes. Remove the escalopes and keep hot. Boil the pan juices fast to reduce the liquid to about 3 tablespoonfuls. Stir in the cream and gently reheat. *Do not boil.* Serve the escalopes with the sauce and garnish with watercress and lemon wedges.

## GRAPEFRUIT SORBET

**¾ cup sugar**
**1⅛ cups water**
**1 can (6 ounces) frozen grapefruit juice**
**2 egg whites**
**Mint sprigs**

Dissolve the sugar in the water. Bring to a boil and boil, uncovered, for 10 minutes. Turn the frozen juice into a bowl and pour on the sugar syrup; leave to cool. When cold pour into a 2½ cup ice-cube tray and place in freezing compartment. Freeze until slushy. Beat the egg whites until thick and foamy but not dry. Fold into the grapefruit mixture. Return to the ice tray and freeze until firm. Just before serving, scoop into chilled glasses and garnish with mint.

---

**MENU** *serves 6*

**CHILLED SHRIMP SOUP**
**MELBA TOAST**
**ROAST CHICKEN WITH PECAN STUFFING**
**BUTTERED ZUCCHINI AND ROAST POTATOES**
**RED-CURRANT COMPOTE**
**Wine – White Burgundy (Pouilly Fuissé – Chardonnay)**

**Timetable** *for lunch at 1.00 p.m.*
**Day before:** *Make stuffing and compote. Store both in refrigerator.*
**Early:** *Assemble ingredients and equipment.*
*Make soup, store in refrigerator. Stuff and truss chicken. Prepare vegetables.*
*Remove crusts from bread and slice as thinly as possible for Melba toast.*
**11.00** *Put chicken to roast. When cooked, keep warm.*
**12.00** *Start to roast potatoes. Whip and flavor cream. Take soup and compote out of refrigerator.*
**12.30** *Cook zucchini. Make gravy for chicken.*
**12.45** *Toast the bread.*
**1.00** *Serve first course.*

---

## CHILLED SHRIMP SOUP

**1 can (14½ ounces) evaporated milk, chilled**
**5 tablespoons lemon juice**
**2½ teaspoons finely grated onion**
**1 teaspoon prepared mustard**
**2½ tablespoons heavy cream**
**Salt**
**¾ cup finely chopped cooked shrimp**
**4 tablespoons finely chopped parsley**
**Paprika**

Combine the evaporated milk with the lemon juice, onion, mustard, cream and salt to taste.

### Handy hint

Instead of greasing cake pans, line them with non-stick paper. This has a special silicone finish which prevents sticking. You can also use it to wrap frozen food to help keep it moist.

---

Blend well. Gently stir in the prawns and parsley. Pour into glasses or cups. Sprinkle the tops lightly with paprika. Chill for at least 1 hour before serving. Serve with Melba toast.

## ROAST CHICKEN WITH PECAN STUFFING

**4 pound roasting chicken**
**Melted butter or oil**
**Salt and pepper**

*For stuffing:*
**Heart and liver from chicken**
**1 cup fresh white breadcrumbs**
**½ cup chopped pecans**
**1 egg, hard-cooked and chopped**
**Pinch of ground nutmeg**
**Pinch of ground mace**
**Pinch of dried thyme**
**1 tablespoon chopped parsley**
**Pinch of celery salt**
**½ cup mushrooms, chopped**
**3 tablespoons butter**
**1 small onion, chopped**
**2½ tablespoons sherry**
**Freshly ground black pepper**

Place the heart and liver in a small saucepan. Cover with water and simmer for 10 minutes. Drain. Chop finely and cool. Add this to the breadcrumbs with the nuts, egg, spices, herbs and celery salt. Sauté the mushrooms in half the butter for 3–4 minutes. Stir into the breadcrumb mixture. Fry the onion in the remaining butter and add to breadcrumb mixture with the sherry. Season with pepper and toss thoroughly.
Rinse the chicken with cold water and pat dry with paper towels. Stuff and truss the chicken. Brush with melted butter or oil and season with salt and pepper. Place on a rack in a shallow roasting pan. Roast in a fairly hot oven (375°F.) for 20 minutes per pound plus 20 minutes. Serve with roast potatoes, buttered zucchini and gravy made with chicken stock.

## RED-CURRANT COMPOTE

**1½ pound ripe red-currants**
**1⅓ cups sugar**
**3¾ tablespoons water**

Remove any stalks from the fruit. Wash and drain thoroughly. Put in a pan with the sugar and water. Shake the pan over gentle heat until the sugar is all dissolved, stirring gently. Cool. Divide the fruit between 6 individual dishes and let stand 2–3 hours, by which time the juice should have jelled. Serve with whipped cream flavored with brandy.

*Individual seafood quiches make a tasty lunch*

**MENU** *Serves 6*

**CUCUMBER SWEET AND SOUR**
**SEAFOOD QUICHES**
**ENDIVE AND TOMATO SALAD**
**APPLE AND ORANGE BRISTOL**
**Wine – Rosé**

**Timetable** *for lunch at 1.00 p.m.*
**Day before:** *Make pastry cases (do not bake), cover with plastic wrap and keep in a cool place.*
**Early:** *Assemble ingredients and equipment. Prepare apple and orange Bristol, but do not decorate (prepare caramel). Slice cucumber and layer with salt. Prepare salmon and shrimp, leave to marinate in the lemon juice in a covered bowl, in a cool place.*

*Prepare salad and dressing.*
**12.00** *Finish dessert.*
**12.15** *Fill flans and cook. When ready, keep warm.*
**12.30** *Combine cucumber and dressing. Toss salad.*
**1.00** *Serve first course.*

## CUCUMBER SWEET AND SOUR

1 large cucumber
Salt
1 onion
2 gherkins
6 tablespoons white raisins
1 cup dairy sour cream
2 tablespoons lemon juice
¾ teaspoon sugar
Dash of Tabasco
Freshly ground black pepper

Peel the cucumber and slice very, very thin. Layer in a dish and sprinkle salt between the layers. Leave for a few hours. Chop the onion, gherkins and raisins and blend into the sour cream with the lemon juice, sugar, Tabasco and pepper. Drain the cucumber slices and dry on paper towelling. Fold the cream mixture through the cucumber. Serve in individual dishes.

## SEAFOOD QUICHES

*For flan cases:*
3 cups all-purpose flour
Pinch of salt
1 cup butter
1 egg yolk
⅝ cup water

*For filling:*
⅓ pound smoked salmon
½ pound cooked shrimp, shelled
1¼ tablespoons lemon juice
4 large eggs, beaten
⅝ cup light cream
1⅞ cups milk
Salt
Freshly ground black pepper
Chopped parsley

Sift the flour and salt into a bowl. Rub in the butter with a pastry blender until the mixture resembles fine breadcrumbs. Blend the egg yolk and water together. Stir into the dry ingredients. Form into a ball. Knead the dough on a lightly-floured board. Divide into 6 parts and roll into pieces large enough to line six 5 in. shallow flan or tart cases. Prick the bottom of each with a fork and crimp the edges.
Using scissors, snip the salmon into 1 in. pieces. Add the shrimps and sprinkle with the lemon juice. Divide the salmon and shrimps between the pastry cases. Beat the eggs and whip in the cream and milk. Season well.

Pour over fish. Bake in a fairly hot oven (400°F.) for 15 minutes. Reduce heat to 325°F. and cook for about 20 minutes or until set and pastry lightly browned. Sprinkle with chopped parsley before serving.

## ENDIVE AND TOMATO SALAD

1 endive
3 tomatoes, peeled and cut up
Bunch of watercress, washed and trimmed
½ small onion, chopped

*For dressing:*
1¼ tablespoons lemon juice
2½ tablespoons salad oil
Salt
Freshly ground black pepper
Pinch of dry mustard
Pinch of sugar

Wash and roughly break up the endive. Toss together with the tomatoes, watercress and onion. Beat together the ingredients for the dressing and pour over the salad. Toss lightly until the salad is evenly coated.

## APPLE AND ORANGE BRISTOL

⅞ cup sugar
1¼ cups water
6 cooking apples, pared and cored
3 oranges
1¼ cups heavy cream, whipped

Put ½ cup of the sugar in a heavy pan and heat gently until it becomes a light brown color, taking care not to let it burn. Pour the syrup on to a greased tray, spreading it as thinly as possible, and leave to set. When cold, crush with a rolling pin.
Put the water and remaining sugar in a thick skillet and bring to a boil. Cut the apples up and put into the boiling syrup. Cover and poach gently until just tender. Remove from heat and let apples stand in the syrup until they become transparent.
Pare 5–6 very fine strips of rind, free of white part, from 1 of the oranges, cut into fine shreds and put into cold water. Bring to a boil and cook for 5–10 minutes, or until tender. Drain and rinse in cold water. Pare the oranges and divide into sections free of membrane. Arrange the apple and orange pieces in a dish and pour a little of the apple syrup over the top. Just before serving, sprinkle with strips of orange rind and the broken caramel. Serve topped with whipped cream.

*Peaches stuffed with cheese, as a first course for lunch*

> **Handy hint**
>
> Buttercream will keep for up to 3 weeks in a covered container in the refrigerator. Make up a large quantity at a time, without flavorings, and add the flavoring when required.

*Apple and orange Bristol, with a caramel decoration*

## MENU *serves 8*

### PECHES FROMAGE
### MIXED GRILL MAITRE D'HOTEL
### SOUFFLE MONTE CRISTO
Wine – Claret

*Timetable for lunch at 1.00 p.m.*
**Day before:** *Prepare soufflé but do not decorate (do not soak ratafias yet). Make savory butter.*
**Early:** *Assemble ingredients and equipment. Finish soufflé and leave out of refrigerator. Prepare pêches fromage and chill. Prepare ingredients for grill. Cut savory butter into pats.*
**11.30** *Cook matchstick potatoes, keep hot.*
**12.00** *Cook mixed grill, keep hot. Remove pêches fromage from refrigerator.*
**1.00** *Serve first course.*

### PECHES FROMAGE

¾ **cup grated Cheddar cheese**
¼ **cup grated Parmesan cheese**
2 **tablespoons soft butter or margarine**
**Salt**
**Cayenne pepper**
1 **can (1 pound 13 ounces) peach halves, drained**
1 **head lettuce**
8 **tomatoes, cut up**
1 **package (3 ounces) cream cheese, softened**
⅝ **cup light cream**
**Paprika**

Blend together the Cheddar cheese, Parmesan cheese and butter. Season with salt and cayenne and mix until light. Fill the cheese mixture into the hollows in the peach halves.
Arrange a lettuce leaf and a quartered tomato on each plate with an upturned, stuffed peach half. Beat the cream cheese in a small bowl. Gradually add the cream to give a smooth, coating consistency. Spoon over the peach halves. Dust with a little paprika and chill before serving.

### MIXED GRILL MAITRE D'HOTEL

*For maître d'hôtel butter:*
½ **cup butter**
2½ **tablespoons finely chopped parsley**
**Lemon juice**
**Salt and cayenne pepper**

8 **lamb chops**
4 **lambs kidneys**
8 **tomatoes, cut up**
8 **mushrooms, trimmed**
**Salt**
**Freshly ground black pepper**
**Melted butter or margarine**
**Basil**
1 **pound small sausages**
8 **slices bacon**
**Watercress**

First blend together the butter, parsley, lemon juice, salt and cayenne pepper for the butter. Pat out between 2 sheets of waxed paper into a patty about ¼ in. thick. Chill until firm. When firm, cut out into 8 small rounds with a 1 in. cutter.
Heat the broiling compartment of the range. Trim the chops and halve and core the kidneys. Season the chops, kidneys, tomatoes and mushrooms and brush with melted butter. Remove rack from broiler pan. Place the tomatoes, cut side up, on the broiler pan and sprinkle with basil. Add the mushrooms. Place the broiler rack over the tomatoes and mushrooms and put on chops. Broil the chops for 10–12 minutes, turning frequently. Remove chops and keep hot. The juices from the meat will baste the tomatoes and mushrooms without need of further attention.
Prick the sausages, and place on the rack with the kidneys. Cook several inches away from source of heat for 14–16 minutes, turning the food frequently. The kidneys will probably be cooked first, in which case remove them and keep them hot. Add the bacon slices and cook for 3–5 minutes or until bacon is cooked to taste. Serve on two large platters, garnished with watercress. Top each chop with maître d'hôtel butter.

### SOUFFLE MONTE CRISTO

6 **eggs, separated**
⅜ **cup sugar**
1 **teaspoon vanilla flavoring**
3 **envelopes unflavored gelatin**
3¾ **tablespoons water**
2½ **cups heavy cream**
4 **plain chocolate candy bars**
8–10 **small almond cookies or lady fingers**
¼ **cup Kirsch or maraschino**

Tie a lightly buttered band of aluminum foil around the top of a 1½ quart soufflé dish to stand 3 in. above the rim of the dish.
Beat the egg yolks, sugar and vanilla in a bowl over a pan of hot water until thick and creamy and the whisk leaves a thick trail. Soften the gelatin in the water in a small bowl. Place the bowl over hot water and dissolve the gelatin. Stir into the egg mixture. Cool until the mixture begins to set. Lightly whip about three-quarters of the cream. Beat the egg whites until stiff. Fold cream and egg whites into the egg yolk mixture. Lightly crush the chocolate candy bars.
Place a straight sided tumbler or glass in the center of the prepared soufflé dish and spoon the mixture around the outside of the glass, alternating it with layers of crushed candy bar, using three-quarters of the candy bars. Chill in refrigerator until set.
Soak the cookies or lady fingers briefly in the Kirsch. To serve, remove the paper from around the soufflé. Fill the glass with warm water to loosen it and remove it, gently but quickly. Fill the hole with the Kirsch-soaked cookies. Whip the remaining cream and decorate the top of the soufflé. Decorate with the remaining chocolate candy bars.

## MENU *serves 6*

### WATERCRESS SOUP or FRESH GRAPEFRUIT
### BEEF GALANTINE
### POTATO SALAD AND MIXED SALADS
### APPLE AND BRANDY POTS
Wine – Burgundy (Morey-St. Denis – Pinot Noir)

**Timetable** *for lunch at 1.00 p.m.*
**Day before:** *Make soup and savory butter. Make beef galantine (leave in mold).*
**Early:** *Assemble ingredients and equipment.*
*Prepare salads, unmold galantine.*
**11.00** *Prepare apple and brandy pots and cook. Sprinkle with cinnamon and keep warm. (Cut grapefruit and sprinkle with sugar.)*
**12.50** *Reheat soup.*
**1.00** *Serve first course.*

### WATERCRESS SOUP:

*For savory butter:*
2 **tablespoons butter**
**Paprika**
**Chopped chives**

½ **cup butter or margarine**
½ **cup all-purpose flour**
3 **cups chicken bouillon**
1¼ **cups milk**
**Salt**
**Freshly ground black pepper**
¾ **cup chopped onion**
2 **bunches watercress**

Beat together the 2 tablespoons butter, a little paprika and a few chopped chives. Pat out between waxed paper. Chill.
Melt 6 tablespoons of the butter or margarine in a saucepan. Stir in the flour and cook gently for 1–2 minutes. Remove from heat and stir in the bouillon and milk. Cook over medium heat, stirring constantly, until smooth and thick. Simmer gently for about 2 minutes. Season well.
Cook the onion in the remaining 2 tablespoons butter until soft. Wash the watercress and trim, leaving a little of the stem. Chop roughly and add to the onion. Cover and cook for 4 minutes. Stir the vegetables into the white sauce. Purée in an electric blender or put through a sieve. Reheat gently. Season to taste and ladle

into hot bowls. Stamp the savory butter into fancy shapes with small decorative cutters and float 1 pat in each bowl of soup.

## BEEF GALANTINE

**1 pound beef chuck**
**¾ pound pig's knuckle**
**1 pig's foot**
**½ onion**
**2 carrots**
**1 tomato**
**Sprigs of parsley**
**1–2 slivers of lemon rind**
**3–4 peppercorns**
**1 stalk celery**
**Pinch of dried thyme**
**½ clove garlic**
**1 tablespoon chopped parsley**
**Salt and pepper**

*For garnish:*
**2 tomatoes, peeled and cut up**
**½ envelope unflavored gelatin**
**1 cup chicken bouillon**
**2 hard-cooked eggs, cut up**

Trim the beef of excess fat. Leave in large chunks. Wash and split the pig's knuckle and pig's foot. Place the beef, knuckle and foot in a pan with the onion, carrots, tomato, parsley, lemon rind, peppercorns, celery, thyme and garlic. Cover with cold water. Bring to a boil. Skim off top of liquid. Cover and simmer for 2 hours or until the meats are fork tender. Remove the meats. Boil the cooking liquid, vegetables and bones, uncovered, until reduced to 1½ cups liquid. Strain and discard bones and vegetables.
Grind or finely chop the meats. Stir in the reduced liquid and chopped parsley. Season to taste. Seed the tomatoes and remove the cores. Chop in large chunks and season to taste. Soften the gelatin in bouillon. Heat over low heat until the gelatin is dissolved. Let stand until the consistency of uncooked egg whites. Arrange the tomatoes and hard-cooked eggs in the bottom of a 1-quart ring mold. Pour over the gelatin and let chill until firm. When firm, spoon the beef mixture over the top. Chill until firm. Unmold and garnish as desired.

## APPLE AND BRANDY POTS

**1¼ tablespoons finely grated orange rind**
**¾ cup fresh orange juice**
**3¾ tablespoons brandy**
**3 pound cooking apples, pared and finely sliced**
**2½ tablespoons sugar**
**Cinnamon**
**1¼ cups heavy cream, whipped**

*Serve this sorbet in frosted orange cups*

Blend together the orange rind, juice and brandy. Tightly pack the sliced apples into 6 individual soufflé dishes or ramekins and sprinkle with 1 teaspoon sugar over each dish. Pour over the orange juice and brandy. Cover each dish with buttered aluminum foil. Top each with a small weight and place on a cookie tray. Bake in a cool oven (300°F.) for 1½ hours. Serve warm, sprinkled with cinnamon and topped with whipped cream.

**MENU** *serves 6*

**GLOBE ARTICHOKES**
**WITH BUTTER**
**POT ROAST VEAL**
**BROCCOLI SPEARS AND**
**CREAMED POTATOES**
**ORANGE SORBET CUPS**
**CREAM CHEESE COOKIES**
Wine – White Burgundy
(Mâcon blanc – Chardonnay)

**Timetable** *for lunch at 1.00 p.m.*
**Day before:** *Prepare the orange sorbet and chill the orange shells. (If you do not have a separate ice making compartment or freezer, buy a good brand of sorbet on the day). Make cookies and store in airtight tins.*
**10.30** *Assemble ingredients and*

*equipment.*
*Start to cook veal. When ready, keep hot.*
*Trim artichokes, prepare potatoes and broccoli.*
**12.00** *Pile sorbet into chilled shells and return to the coldest part of the refrigerator.*
**12.15** *Cook artichokes. Put potatoes on to boil.*
*Gently melt butter.*
**12.45** *Carve veal, thicken sauce and keep warm.*
*Cook broccoli and keep vegetables warm.*
**1.00** *Serve first course.*

## POT ROAST VEAL

**3 pound shoulder of veal, boned and rolled**
**Salt and pepper**
**¼ cup butter or margarine**
**1 tablespoon salad oil**
**1 small onion, sliced**
**6 small carrots, sliced**
**1¼ cups water**
**Pinch dried thyme**
**Cornstarch**

Wipe the meat with damp paper towels and season well with salt and pepper. Melt the butter with the oil in a skillet. Lightly brown the meat on all sides. Remove

meat and place in a casserole. Cook the onion and carrots in the skillet until lightly brown. Add the water and bring to a boil. Pour over the meat in the casserole. Add thyme. Cover and cook in a moderate oven (350°F.) for 2½ hours or until the meat is tender. Slice the meat and arrange on a serving platter. Thicken the gravy with a little cornstarch mixed in cold water. When thick and hot, pour gravy over the meat.

## ORANGE SORBET CUPS

**6–7 large oranges**
**¾ cup sugar**
**1⅞ cups water**
**3 tablespoons lemon juice**
**3 egg whites**

Using a small, sharp, pointed knife, cut the tops off 6 oranges with a zig-zag pattern. Scoop out the flesh and membrane. Work over a bowl to catch all of the juice. Discard membrane. Wash the empty shells and set them with their tops in the freezing compartment.
Dissolve the sugar in the water. Bring to a boil and boil for 5 minutes. Remove and cool.
Purée the orange pulp in an electric blender or put through a sieve. Make up to 1⅞ cups with juice from the extra orange if necessary. Combine with the syrup and lemon juice. Pour into an ice tray and freeze until nearly firm. Beat the egg whites until stiff but not dry. Turn the frozen fruit mixture into a chilled bowl, stir with a spoon and fold in the egg whites. Return to freezer and freeze until firm, but still slightly soft in texture. Pack small spoonfuls of the orange sorbet into the chilled shells and fill high. Replace lids on top and chill for at least 1 hour before serving.

## CREAM CHEESE COOKIES
*makes about 2 dozen*

**1 package (3 ounces) softened cream cheese**
**½ cup butter**
**1 cup all-purpose flour**
**Preserves**

Combine the cheese, butter and flour and blend thoroughly. Chill. Roll out the dough, half at a time, to about ¼ in. thick. Cut into small rounds. Make a small depression in center of each cookie. Place ½ teaspoon preserves on each. Bake on an ungreased cookie tray in a moderate oven (350°F.) for about 20 minutes. Cool.

*Red-currant compote*

# INFORMAL BUFFET LUNCHES

## MENU *serves 12*

**LEMON CONSOMME**
**HOSPITALITY WAFERS**
**JELLIED CHICKEN PIE**
**HAM AND ASPARAGUS ROLLS**
**CUCUMBER SALAD**
**NEW POTATOES**
**GINGER MERINGUE CREAMS**

**Timetable** *for lunch at 1.00 p.m.*
**Day before:** *Prepare consommé and chill.*
*Make meringue cases and wafers and store in airtight tins.*
*Prepare salad dressings. Scrape potatoes; keep under water.*
*Assemble chicken pie ingredients.*
**Early:** *Assemble ingredients and equipment. Bake chicken pie, leave to cool. Combine yogurt and flavorings and refrigerate.*
**11.00** *Make up ham and asparagus rolls. Fill meringue.*
**12.00** *Make cucumber salad. Cook potatoes, drain and cool.*
*Set out foods on table.*
**12.45** *Spoon yogurt over consommé and garnish.*

## LEMON CONSOMME

**3 cans (10½ ounces each) consommé**
**1½ tablespoons dry sherry**
**Grated rind and juice of 1 lemon**
**2½ cups plain yogurt**
**Fresh mint**

Warm the consommé, sherry and lemon juice together. Pour into individual soup bowls and chill. Combine the lemon rind with the yogurt and add a few mint leaves. Just before serving, remove the mint from the yogurt and spoon it over the consommé. Garnish each bowl of soup with mint.

## HOSPITALITY WAFERS
*makes 3 dozen*

**¾ cup butter or margarine, softened**
**½ cup grated Cheddar cheese**
**½ cup crumbled Bleu cheese**
**2 cups all-purpose flour**
**½ clove garlic, finely chopped**
**1 teaspoon chopped parsley**
**1 teaspoon chopped chives**

*Ham and asparagus rolls, jellied chicken pie and cucumber salad*

Cream together the butter and cheeses. Mix in flour, garlic, parsley and chives. With the hands, shape into rolls 1½ in. in diameter. Wrap in aluminum foil or plastic wrap and chill. Slice in ¼ in. thick slices. Bake in a fairly hot oven (375°F.) 8–10 minutes, until lightly browned.

## JELLIED CHICKEN PIE

**Two 3 pound roasting chickens**
**½ pound lean bacon, chopped**
**½ pound onions, thinly sliced**
**½ pound mushrooms, sliced**
**2½ tablespoons chopped parsley**
**½ teaspoon mixed, dried herbs**
**Salt and pepper**
**5 tablespoons water**
**1 recipe Shortcrust Pastry (page 75)**
**1 egg, beaten**

Remove the skin from the chicken, carve off all the meat and cut into pieces. Layer the chicken, bacon, onions and mushrooms in a shallow ovenproof dish about 12 in. by 9 in. by 2 in. Sprinkle the layers with parsley, herbs and seasoning. Add the water.
Roll out the pastry on a lightly-floured board into a shape that will fit over the top of the baking dish. Place on top of baking dish

and crimp the edges. Roll out any pastry trimmings, cut into leaves and use to decorate the top of the pie. Brush with beaten egg. Cut a slit in the top of the pastry. Place on a cookie tray and bake in a moderate oven (350°F.) for 1½ hours or until chicken is tender and crust browned. Allow pie to cool before serving.

## HAM AND ASPARAGUS ROLLS

**½ pound fresh or frozen asparagus spears, cooked**
**1½ pounds boiled ham, thinly sliced**
**⅝ cup mayonnaise**
**Watercress**
**Paprika**

Divide the cooled asparagus spears between the slices of ham. Roll up and arrange side by side on a serving dish. Spoon the mayonnaise down the center, sprinkle with paprika and garnish with watercress.

## CUCUMBER SALAD

**1 cucumber**
**French dressing**
**Paprika**
**½ green pepper, chopped**

Wipe the cucumber or peel it. Slice thinly. Place in a dish and cover with dressing. Let stand in a cool place for about 15 minutes. Sprinkle lightly with paprika and garnish with chopped pepper.

## GINGER MERINGUE CREAMS

**6 large egg whites**
**1½ cups sugar**
**2 cups heavy cream**
**7½ tablespoons finely chopped candied ginger**

Line 2 cookie trays with lightly buttered unglazed brown paper. Preheat oven to 250°F.
Beat the egg whites until stiff. Beat in the sugar gradually until the mixture stands in stiff peaks. Spoon the meringue into 12 heaps on the prepared trays, keeping well apart. Make each mound into a flan shape by hollowing out the centers with the back of a spoon. Bake for about 2½–3 hours or until dry and set. Place the brown paper on a damp surface and peel off the meringues with a very thin spatula. Cool on a wire rack.
Beat the cream until slightly stiff. Fold in half the ginger. Divide cream between meringue shells and top with reserved ginger.

## MENU *serves 12*

**MELON AND PROSCIUTTO**
**DEEP FRIED CHICKEN DRUMSTICKS**
**TARTARE SAUCE**
**BURGUNDY BEEF GALANTINE**
**TOMATO AND WATERCRESS SALAD**
**FRENCH BREAD AND BUTTER**
**ROLLA TORTE**

**Timetable** *for lunch at 1.00 p.m.*
**Day before:** *Make the Burgundy beef galantine.*
*Egg and crumb the drumsticks, leave in a cool place. Prepare tartare sauce.*
*Make Rolla Torten and leave, covered, in a cool place.*
**Early:** *Fry chicken joints, drain well, cover and leave in a cool place.*
*Make up the salad and French dressing.*
*Slice the galantine.*
**11.00** *Cut the melons and chill.*
**12.00** *Remove melons from the refrigerator, add ham and lemon wedges. Set food on the table.*

## MELON AND PROSCIUTTO

**2 large melons**
**1 pound thinly sliced Prosciutto**
**Lemon wedges**

Cut each melon into 6 portions and remove the seeds. Chill slightly. Place a slice of Prosciutto on each portion. Serve with a lemon wedge.

## DEEP FRIED CHICKEN DRUMSTICKS

**12 chicken drumsticks**
**Salt and pepper**
**2 eggs, beaten**
**Breadcrumbs**
**Oil for deep frying**

Season the drumsticks with salt and pepper. Dip in beaten egg and coat in breadcrumbs. Refrigerate before frying to give the crumbs a chance to set.

Heat the frying oil to 375°F. on a deep fat thermometer. Fry the chicken legs 2 or 3 at a time. When golden brown drain on paper toweling. Cool. Trim the drumsticks with paper frills.

## TARTARE SAUCE

**⅝ cup mayonnaise**
**1 teaspoon chopped tarragon**
**1 teaspoon chopped chives**
**2½ teaspoons chopped capers**
**2½ teaspoons chopped sweet pickles**
**2½ teaspoons chopped parsley**
**1¼ tablespoons lemon juice or tarragon vinegar.**

Combine all ingredients and blend well. Let stand for at least 1 hour to blend flavors.

## BURGUNDY BEEF GALANTINE

*make 2*

**One 3 pound boneless chuck steak**
**¼ pound sliced bacon**
**Salt and pepper**
**¼ cup butter or margarine**
**1¼ tablespoons salad oil**
**1 large onion, sliced**
**1 large carrot, sliced**
**1 bay leaf**
**1 teaspoon dried herbs**
**1¼ cups dry red wine**
**½ pound button mushrooms, sliced**
**2 tablespoons unflavored gelatin**

Trim excess fat from the chuck steak. Lay the bacon slices over meat to cover it completely and tie meat and bacon into a long roll

*A delicious spread for a buffet lunch*

with white string. Sprinkle the roll with salt and pepper. Heat 2 tablespoons of the butter with the oil in a large Dutch oven or heavy kettle. Add the meat and fry, turning until well browned on all sides. Add the onion, carrot, herbs, wine and 1¼ cups water. Bring to a boil. Cover and bake in a moderate oven (350°F.) for 3 hours or until meat is tender.
Remove the meat from the Dutch oven and let stand until cold. Chill the stock. When it is cold, skim off the fat and discard. Add enough water, if necessary, to make 2½ cups of stock. Strain and discard vegetables.
Melt the remaining butter in a small skillet. Sauté the mushrooms. Let stand until cold.
Cut the meat into thin slices and arrange half of them in a 2–2½ quart loaf pan, cover with the mushrooms and then the remaining sliced meat.
Soften the gelatin in 2 tablespoons water in a small bowl placed over hot water to dissolve the gelatin. Stir into the stock and blend well. Let stand until it just begins to set. Pour carefully over meat and mushrooms. Chill until thoroughly set. To serve, unmold and slice.

## ROLLA TORTE
*make 3 for the party*

**⅛ teaspoon cream of tartar**
**Pinch of salt**
**3 egg whites**
**⅝ cup sugar**
**¼ cup ground almonds**
**¼ cup cornstarch**

*For filling and decoration:*
**6 tablespoons sugar**
**5 tablespoons water**
**2 egg yolks, lightly beaten**
**½–¾ cup unsalted butter**
**¼ cup chocolate morsels**
**¼ cup toasted, sliced almonds**
**Confectioners' sugar**

Grease and lightly flour 3 cookie trays (shake off excess flour), or cover trays with heavy baking paper. Draw three 7 in. circles on the trays or paper. Preheat oven to 325°F.
Add the cream of tartar and salt to the egg whites and beat until very stiff. Beat in two-thirds of the sugar, 1 tablespoonful at a time. Combine the remaining sugar with the almonds and cornstarch. Fold into the stiffly beaten egg white mixture.
Put the meringue in a pastry bag with a ¼ in. nozzle. Pipe the mixture on to the papers, starting at

the center of the circles and working out to fill the marked area. If you do not have a pastry bag, spread the meringue in smooth layers on each circle. Bake just below the center of the oven for 30 minutes or until dry and just beginning to brown. Remove from the cookie trays and peel off paper if used. Cool on a wire rack. Place the sugar for filling in a large, heavy saucepan. Add the water and dissolve the sugar over a very low heat without boiling. When completely dissolved, bring to boiling point and boil steadily for 2–3 minutes or until a little of the cooled syrup will form a thread when pulled between your wetted finger and thumb. Place the egg yolks in a deep bowl and pour on the syrup in a thin stream, beating all the time. Continue to beat until the mixture is thick and cold. Cream the butter and gradually add the syrup mixture, beating constantly.
Melt the chocolate morsels with 1 tablespoon water. Cool slightly and stir until smooth. Beat into the butter mixture. Put the layers of meringue together with the chocolate mixture. Spread the coating around sides to cover layers completely. Sprinkle flaked almonds on sides of torte. Dredge top of cake with confectioners' sugar.
Let torte stand in a cool place for at least 24 hours before cutting; the meringue layers should soften a little.

---

**MENU** *serves 12*

**SMOKED HADDOCK AND CHEESE FLAN**
**CHICKEN AND ALMOND SALAD**
**AVOCADO AND TOMATO SALAD**
**GREEN SALAD**
**BAKED POTATOES**
**ORANGE PRALINE MOUSSE**

**Timetable** *for lunch at 1.00 p.m.*
**Day before:** *Bake flans; store, covered, in a cool place but not the refrigerator. Prepare ingredients and dressings for salads (except avocados); refrigerate separately. Scrub the potatoes.*
*Prepare the mousse but do not turn out (when preparing a mousse so far in advance, line the tin with non-stick paper or plastic wrap to prevent discoloration).*
**Early:** *Turn out mousse and decorate.*
**11.30** *Prick potatoes and put to*

*An orange mousse, flavored and decorated with praline*

bake in the oven at 400°F. When cooked keep hot.

**12.00** *Cut avocados and dress salads. Refresh the flans in the oven for a short time to re-crisp the pastry. Set out the food on the table.*

---

## SMOKED HADDOCK AND CHEESE FLAN

*make 2 for the party*

*For flan case:*

**1¼ cups all-purpose flour**
**Pinch of salt**
**6 tablespoons butter or margarine**
**1 egg yolk**
**5 teaspoons water**

*For filling:*

**½ pound smoked haddock**
**⅝ cup water**
**Juice of ½ lemon**
**2 tablespoons butter or margarine**
**1 small onion, finely chopped**
**4–5 mushrooms, chopped**
**2 eggs**
**3¾ tablespoons light cream**
**½ cup cottage cheese**
**Salt**
**Freshly ground black pepper**
**Chopped parsley**

Sift together the flour and salt. Cut in the butter with a pastry blender or 2 knives until the mix-

ture looks like fine breadcrumbs. Add the egg yolk beaten with 2 teaspoons water. Add more water if needed to make a dough that will stick together. Knead lightly for a few seconds to give a firm, smooth dough. Let rest in a cool place for 15 minutes.

Roll out on a lightly floured board into a circle ⅛ in. thick and large enough to line an 8-in. flan ring or cake pan. Crimp top of dough and prick the base all over with a fork. Gently press in a piece of foil and fill with dried beans. Bake in a fairly hot oven (400°F.) for 15 minutes. Remove the foil and beans and cook for 5–10 minutes or until pastry is lightly browned. Cool.

Poach the haddock in a pan with the water and half the lemon juice. Drain the fish, discard the skin and bones and flake the fish. Melt the butter in a pan, cook the onion for a few minutes, add the mushrooms and continue to cook for 3–4 minutes.

Combine the fish and vegetables and spread over the base of the flan case. Beat the eggs, add the cream, cheese and remaining lemon juice. Season to taste and pour over the fish mixture.

Bake in a fairly hot oven (375°F.) for about 35 minutes or until set and golden. Garnish with chopped parsley before serving, either hot or cold.

## CHICKEN AND ALMOND SALAD

**½ pound seedless raisins**
**2¼ pound cooked chicken**
**1½ cups almonds, blanched**
**½ onion, grated**
**⅝ cup light cream**
**⅝ cup mayonnaise**
**1¼ tablespoons lemon juice**
**3¾ tablespoons chopped parsley**
**Salt and pepper**
**Lettuce cups**

Cover the raisins with boiling water. Let stand 5 minutes, drain. Cut the chicken into chunks. Chop the almonds roughly and brown lightly in the oven. Combine the onion, cream, mayonnaise, lemon juice and parsley. Season to taste. Toss lightly with the raisins, chicken and almonds. Serve in a salad bowl lined with lettuce cups.

## AVOCADO AND TOMATO SALAD

**3 avocados**
**Juice of 1 lemon**
**2 small green peppers, thinly sliced**
**6 tomatoes, peeled and sliced**
**2 onions, very thinly sliced**
**French dressing**
**1 tablespoon chopped parsley**

Cut the avocados in half lengthwise. Remove the pits. Peel and slice the avocados and toss lightly in lemon juice to prevent discoloration. Arrange on a large platter with the peppers, tomatoes, and onion. Moisten lightly with French dressing and garnish with chopped parsley.

## ORANGE PRALINE MOUSSE

*make 2 for the party*

**¼ pound lump sugar**
**2 large juicy oranges**
**6 egg yolks**
**2½ teaspoons cornstarch**
**3¾ cups milk**
**4 envelopes unflavored gelatin**
**6 egg whites**

*For praline:*
**½ cup sugar**

*Garnish:*
**Orange sections**
**Whipped cream**
**Small cookies**

Rub 2–3 lumps of sugar over the skins of the oranges to extract some of the zest. Squeeze the oranges and if necessary add a little water to make 7½ tablespoons orange juice.

Beat the egg yolks and blend with the cornstarch. Put the sugar lumps in the milk and place over low heat. Bring to just below boiling point. Pour hot milk over egg yolks, stirring constantly. Return the egg mixture to the pan and cook gently, stirring constantly, until mixture thickens.

Soften gelatin in the orange juice in a small bowl. Place over hot water until the gelatin is dissolved. Stir into the egg yolk mixture, blending well. Let stand until almost set.

Beat the egg whites until stiff but not dry. Quickly and evenly fold into the custard mixture with half of the praline (see below). Turn into an 8-in. spring-form cake pan with a loose base. Chill in the refrigerator.

To serve, turn out of spring-form pan on to a flat plate. Decorate with orange sections, whipped cream, small cookies and the remainder of the praline.

**Praline**
Place the sugar in a heavy pan. Dissolve very carefully over low heat. Continue cooking until the sugar becomes golden brown. Quickly turn out on to a greased cookie tray. When cold, crush finely with a rolling pin.

200

# HOT SUPPERS

Whether your supper is an after theatre meal or a casual alternative to dinner, dream up some hot, tasty snacks to fill your hungry family and guests. Start with our ideas and build your repertoire from there.

*This page: Lasagne and jumbo prawn risotto*

## LASAGNE
*4 servings*

2 cans (16 ounces each) tomatoes, drained
1 tablespoon tomato paste
1 teaspoon marjoram
Salt
Freshly ground black pepper
1 pound ground beef
½ package (8 ounces) lasagne
2 tablespoons butter
¼ cup flour
1¼ cups milk
1½ cups grated Cheddar cheese
Oil
¼ pound sliced Mozzarella

Combine the canned tomatoes, tomato paste, marjoram, salt and pepper in a large kettle. Simmer, uncovered, for 30 minutes. Add the beef and simmer, uncovered for 25 minutes.

Cook the lasagne in boiling salted water according to package directions. Drain.

In a small saucepan, melt the butter. Stir in the flour and cook for 1 minute. Remove from heat and stir in the milk. Cook, stirring constantly, until smooth and thickened. Remove from heat, stir in the Cheddar cheese and season to taste.

Cover the bottom of a shallow baking dish with strips of the lasagne. Add alternate layers of meat and cheese sauce. Finish the final layer with strips of pasta placed diagonally across, with the sauces spooned between. Lightly oil the pasta to prevent it from drying out. Bake in a fairly hot oven (375°F.) for 30 minutes. Remove from oven and top with the Mozzarella. Raise oven temperature to 425°F. Bake until the lasagne is golden brown and bubbling.

## VEGETABLE FRICASSEE
*2 servings*

½ pound zucchini
½ pound tomatoes, peeled and sliced
7 tablespoons butter or margarine
1 large onion, sliced
½ teaspoon thyme
2½ tablespoons flour
1⅞ cups milk
1 cup grated Cheddar cheese
Salt and pepper
1 cup breadcrumbs

Slice the zucchini and cook in boiling salted water for 3 minutes. Drain. Arrange all but a few slices of the zucchini and tomato in the bottom of a 1½-quart shallow casserole. Dot with

1 tablespoon of the butter. Cover casserole with foil. Keep warm in a slow oven (325°F.) while making the sauce.

Melt 4 tablespoons of the butter in a pan. Add the onion and cook until tender. Stir in the thyme and flour. Remove from heat and stir in the milk. Cook over moderate heat, stirring constantly, until the mixture comes to a boil and thickens. Stir in the cheese and season to taste.

Melt the remaining 2 tablespoons butter in a skillet and add the breadcrumbs. Cook until well browned, stirring. Remove the foil from the vegetables, cover with cheese sauce and top with the browned crumbs. Garnish with the remaining slices of zucchini and tomato.

*Top a vegetable fricassee with crisp fried crumbs*

## CHICKEN RAMEKINS
*2–4 servings*

1 cup ground cooked chicken
2 mushrooms, chopped
2 eggs, separated
2½ tablespoons light cream
Salt and pepper
1 tablespoon butter or margarine

Combine the chicken, mushrooms, egg yolks and cream and blend well. Season to taste. Beat the egg whites until stiff. Fold

into the chicken mixture. Divide the mixture between 4 buttered ramekins or small baking dishes. Place on a cookie tray and cook in a moderate oven (350°F.) for 15–20 minutes.

## OEUFS A LA MAISON
*2–4 servings*

¾ cup frozen peas
1 onion, finely chopped
4 tomatoes, peeled and chopped
⅛ teaspoon garlic salt
Salt
Freshly ground black pepper
3 large eggs
1¼ cups milk
Parsley

Cook the peas according to package directions. Just before the end of the cooking time add the chopped onion and cook for 1–2 minutes. Drain.

Divide the peas, onion and tomatoes between 4 individual ovenproof soup bowls or soufflé dishes. Sprinkle garlic salt, salt and pepper on top.

Beat together the eggs and milk and pour over vegetables. Place the dishes in a baking pan. Add hot water to come halfway up the sides of the dishes. Cook in a fairly hot oven (375°F.) for about

40 minutes. Garnish with parsley before serving.

## ROQUEFORT QUICHE
*4–6 servings*

An 8 in. partially baked pastry shell
½ cup Roquefort cheese or other blue cheese
2 packages (3 ounces each) cream cheese
2 eggs, beaten
⅝ cup light cream
1 tablespoon chopped chives
Salt and pepper

Precook the pastry shell for about 10 minutes or until just set. Cream together the cheeses until smooth. Stir in the eggs, cream, chives and seasoning. Pour into the pastry shell. Bake in a fairly hot oven (375°F.) for about 30 minutes or until well risen and golden brown. Serve warm.

## GREEN BEAN AND BACON FLAN
*4 servings*

*For cheese pastry:*
1 cup self-rising flour
Pinch of salt
¼ cup butter, margarine or shortening
½ cup grated Cheddar cheese
Water

*For filling:*
5 tablespoons milk
½ cup grated Cheddar cheese
4 eggs, beaten
Salt and pepper
4 slices bacon
¾ cup cooked green breans

Sift together the flour and salt. Cut in the fat with a pastry blender or two knives until the mixture resembles fine crumbs. Stir in the cheese. Add just enough water to make a firm dough. Roll dough out on a lightly floured board into a circle large enough to line an 8-in. flan ring or pie dish and crimp the edges. Fit a piece of aluminum foil close to crust and fill with dry beans. Bake in a fairly hot oven (400°F.) 10 minutes. Remove from oven. Remove foil and beans and reduce temperature to 375°F.

Stir together the milk, cheese and eggs. Adjust seasoning. Cook the bacon until crisp, then break up in small pieces. Arrange half the bacon in the flan case. Pour on a little of the egg mixture. Add the green beans, rest of the bacon and pour on remainder of the egg mixture. Bake for about 30 minutes or until just set. Serve hot or cold.

## STUFFED ARTICHOKES
*2–4 servings*

**4 artichokes, trimmed**
**½ small onion, finely chopped**
**2 mushrooms, finely chopped**
**1 tablespoon butter or margarine**
**¼ cup chopped ham**
**2 teaspoons fresh white**
**breadcrumbs**
**1 egg, beaten**
**Salt and pepper**

Cook the artichokes in boiling salted water for 20–40 minutes, depending on the size, until the leaves will pull off easily. Drain upside down. Remove the inner leaves and the choke.

Lightly fry the onion and mushrooms in the hot melted butter for about 5 minutes. Stir in the ham and breadcrumbs. Use enough beaten egg to hold the mixture together. Season to taste. Spoon the mixture into the centers of the artichokes. Place in a greased baking dish. Cover with waxed paper. Bake in a fairly hot oven (375°F.) for 10–15 minutes or until piping hot.

## TUNA AND SPAGHETTI CRISP
*4 servings*

**¼ pound spaghetti**
**1 can (7 ounces) tuna, drained**
**and flaked**
**1¼ cups white sauce**
**¾ cup grated Cheddar cheese**
**Salt and pepper**
**1 cup crushed potato chips**

Cook the spaghetti in boiling salted water according to package directions. Drain well and turn into a mixing bowl.

Add the tuna, white sauce, cheese and seasoning. Mix thoroughly. Turn mixture into a 1½ quart casserole. Top with crushed potato chips. Bake in a moderate oven (350°F.) for 20–30 minutes.

**Handy hint**

If your eyes run when you are peeling onions, soak the onions in cold water for 30 minutes first. Alternatively hold them under cold water while peeling.

## JUMBO SHRIMP RISOTTO
*4 servings*

**1 tablespoon dried onion flakes**
**¼ cup butter or margarine**
**¾ cup raw rice**
**¼ teaspoon dried basil**
**1⅞ cups stock**
**1 can (7–8 ounces) shrimp**
**3 large eggs, hard-cooked and**
**chopped**
**2 tablespoons chopped parsley**
**Salt and pepper**

Soak the onion flakes in a little water for several minutes. Drain. Melt the butter in a saucepan, add the onion and fry gently for about 3 minutes. Stir in the rice and cook, stirring occasionally, for several minutes or until the rice appears opaque.

Add the basil, stock and any liquid from the shrimp. Bring to a boil, cover and simmer for 20–25 minutes or until the rice is cooked and the liquid absorbed. Stir in the shrimp, eggs, 1 tablespoon parsley and seasoning. Turn into a serving platter and garnish with remaining parsley.

## STUFFED EGGS AU GRATIN
*4 servings*

**1 can (15 ounces) celery hearts,**
**drained**
**4 slices lean bacon**
**4 hard-cooked eggs**
**1 cup grated mild Cheddar**
**cheese**
**2 cups white sauce**
**Prepared mustard**
**4 slices white bread, crusts**
**removed**
**Melted butter**

Cut the celery hearts in thick slices and place in the bottom of a 1½-quart broiler-proof shallow casserole. Cook the bacon until crisp, then crumble it. Halve the eggs lengthwise and remove the yolks. Mix together the bacon and egg yolks. Fill the mixture into the egg white halves and pair up the halves again. Place them on the bed of celery.

Mix most of the cheese into the white sauce, adding mustard to taste. Pour the sauce over the eggs. Dice the bread, dip in a little melted butter and spoon in a ring around the outer edge of the dish. Sprinkle the remaining cheese in the center.

Place the dish in the broiling compartment, 6–8 in. from the source of heat. Broil carefully until the bread cubes are brown and the sauce is bubbling.

*Stuffed artichokes are a luxury supper dish*

## KROMESKI
*8 servings*

*For fritter batter:*
**1 cup all-purpose flour**
**Pinch of salt**
**1¼ tablespoons salad oil**
**⅝ cup warm water**
**1 egg white**

*For filling:*
**¼ cup butter**
**½ cup all-purpose flour**
**1¼ cups milk**
**1 egg yolk**
**1¼ tablespoons fruit table sauce**
**Salt and pepper**
**2 green peppers, chopped**
**½ pound cooked chicken,**
**chopped**
**8 thin slices bacon**
**Deep fat for frying**

Sift together the flour and salt into a bowl. Make a well in the center and pour in the oil and warm water; beat well. Let stand for 1 hour.

Melt butter in a saucepan. Stir in the flour and cook for 1 minute. Remove from heat and stir in the milk. Cook over moderate heat, stirring constantly, until smooth and thickened. Remove from heat and beat in the egg yolk and fruit sauce and season to taste.

Blanch the green peppers in boiling water for 1–2 minutes. Drain and plunge in cold water. Drain well. Add to the sauce with the chopped chicken. Cool.

Divide the mixture into 8 portions. Shape into cork shapes on a lightly-floured board. Wrap each portion in a slice of bacon, securing the end with a toothpick.

Beat the egg white until stiff. Fold the batter into the beaten

*Supper Russian style, with kromeski*

203

*Use up left-over vegetables in a Spanish omelet*

egg white.

Heat the deep fat to about 375°F. on a deep fat thermometer. Dip the kromeski into the batter and deep fry for 5 minutes or until crisp and golden brown. Drain well on paper towels. Remove the toothpicks. Serve piping hot, garnished with lemon slices.

## SAVORY MERINGUE SLICES
*4 servings*

**4 eggs, separated**
**4 rounds buttered toast**
**Salt and pepper**
**¼ cup grated Parmesan cheese**

Place an egg yolk on each round of toast. Beat the egg whites until stiff. Season lightly with salt and pepper and fold in the cheese. Pile the mixture on top of the toast. Place on a broiler pan and broil several inches from source of heat until firm and golden brown. Serve immediately.

## PICK OF THE PANTRY PIZZA
*4 servings*

**1 tablespoon dried onion flakes**
**Boiling water**
**2 cups self-rising flour**
**1 teaspoon baking powder**
**¼ cup butter or margarine**
**Milk or water, or milk and water**
**1 can (15 ounces) pilchards in tomato sauce**
**1 can (8 ounces) tomatoes, drained**
**¾ cup grated Parmesan cheese**
**Freshly ground black pepper**

Soak the dried onion in a small amount of boiling water for 5 minutes. Drain.
Sift together the flour and baking powder. Cut in the butter with a pastry blender or 2 knives until the consistency of corn meal. Add enough milk or water, or both, to make a firm dough. Turn out on to a lightly floured board and knead lightly. Roll out into a 9 in. circle and place on a cookie tray. Spread the onions over top of dough. Arrange the pilchards on top with the drained tomatoes. Sprinkle with cheese. Season with pepper.
Bake in a hot oven (425°F.) for 45 minutes. Cover with foil, if necessary, to prevent excessive browning. Cut in wedges and serve immediately.

## CHAKCHOUKA
*4 servings*

**2 tablespoons shortening**
**1 pound tomatoes, peeled and sliced**
**¾ pound potatoes, sliced**
**1 green pepper, finely chopped**
**1 clove garlic, crushed**
**Salt**
**Freshly ground black pepper**
**4 eggs**

Melt the shortening in a saucepan and fry the tomatoes and potatoes slowly for 20 minutes. Add the peppers and garlic. Season and simmer for 15 minutes. Poach the eggs in gently simmering water for 3–4 minutes.
Turn the vegetables into a hot serving platter. Drain the eggs and arrange on top.

## STUFFED MUSHROOMS ON TOAST
*4 servings*

**8 medium mushrooms, wiped with a damp paper towel**
**1 small onion, finely chopped**
**1 tablespoon butter**
**4 tablespoons finely chopped cooked ham or bacon**
**6 tablespoons fresh white breadcrumbs**
**¼ cup grated mild Cheddar cheese**
**1 teaspoon chopped parsley**
**Salt and pepper**
**1 egg, beaten**
**Salad oil**
**4 rounds buttered toast**

Remove and chop the stalks from the mushrooms. Lightly fry the stalks and onion in the butter until soft but not browned. Add the ham, breadcrumbs, cheese, parsley and seasoning to taste. Stir in enough of the beaten egg to hold the mixture together.

Brush the mushrooms with a little oil and place in a greased baking pan. Pile the filling in the mushroom caps. Cover with foil and bake in the center of a fairly hot oven (375°F.) for about 20 minutes. Serve on buttered toast.

## CRAB TOASTS
*4 servings*

**Butter**
**½ cup fresh white breadcrumbs**
**1 can (6 ounces) crab meat**
**3⅓ tablespoons milk**
**Salt and pepper**
**1 tablespoon sherry**
**4 slices toast**

Melt 2 tablespoons butter in a saucepan. Add the breadcrumbs and flaked crab meat and mix well. Stir in the milk. Stir for a few minutes over moderate heat. Season well and stir in the sherry. Cut the toast into triangles, removing the crusts. Butter lightly. Pile high with crab mixture.

## CURRIED SCRAMBLE
*2 servings*

**1 small onion, chopped**
**Fat for frying**
**2 teaspoons curry powder**
**4 eggs**
**1 teaspoon chopped parsley**
**3¾ tablespoons milk**
**Salt**
**Freshly ground black pepper**
**2 slices buttered toast**

Fry the onion in a little fat until soft but not browned. Add the curry powder and cook, stirring, for 5 minutes.
Beat together the eggs, parsley, milk and seasoning. Add to pan and cook gently, stirring constantly and lifting the egg from the bottom of the pan.
Serve immediately on hot buttered toast.

**Handy hint**

To keep a sauce warm without allowing a skin to form, place a circle of buttered or damp waxed paper over it in the pan. Sprinkle a sweet custard sauce with superfine sugar to prevent a skin forming.

*Toast snacks are popular at supper time*

## SPANISH OMELET
*2 servings*

**Butter or oil**
**1 small onion, chopped**
**3 mushrooms, sliced**
**1 cooked potato, diced**
**1 pimiento, chopped**
**½ cup cooked peas**
**4 eggs**
**Salt**
**Freshly ground black pepper**
**Chopped parsley**

Put enough butter or oil in an 8 in. skillet just to cover the bottom. Add the onion and cook until soft but not browned. Add the mushrooms and cook until tender. Add the potato, pimiento and peas. Heat gently but thoroughly.

Lightly mix the eggs. Season with salt and pepper and pour over the vegetable mixture, which should be hot and bubbling. When eggs are just set, turn upside down on to a heated serving dish. Garnish with chopped parsley and serve at once.

## MUSHROOMS IN PORT WINE
*2 servings*

**3 tablespoons butter or**
**    margarine**
**¾ pound button mushrooms,**
**    wiped clean and trimmed**
**4 thick slices bread**
**2½ tablespoons port wine**
**Salt**
**Freshly ground black pepper**
**½ cup instant potato flakes**
**2½ tablespoons milk**
**⅝ cup heavy cream**
**1½ tablespoons grated Parmesan**
**    cheese**

Melt 2 tablespoons butter in a saucepan. Add the mushrooms and shake well to coat with butter. Cook gently.
Toast 2 slices of the bread. Grate the remaining slices into breadcrumbs. Cut the crusts from the toast and slice each piece in 2. Add the port to the mushrooms, season and continue to simmer.
Make up the instant potato with boiling water according to package directions. Stir in the milk and remaining butter. Spoon into a pastry bag and pipe with a large star nozzle around the edge of a heatproof serving platter.
Stir the cream into the mushrooms and continue to cook gently, stirring until the sauce thickens slightly.
Place the potato dish in a heated broiling compartment, several inches from source of heat, and

brown lightly. Remove and spoon the mushroom mixture into the center. Sprinkle with breadcrumbs and Parmesan cheese. Return to broiler and cook until cheese is golden brown. Garnish with toast triangles and serve immediately.

## SAUSAGE IN WINE
*4 servings*

**1½ pound pork sausage**
**¼ cup water**
**¾ cup dry white wine**
**1 tablespoon butter or margarine**
**1 tablespoon flour**
**1 cup beef bouillon**
**1 egg yolk, beaten**
**1 tablespoon lemon juice**
**Salt and pepper**

Place the sausage in a large skillet. Add the water, cover and simmer for 5 minutes. Drain off water and continue cooking for 10 minutes or until sausage is well browned on all sides. Pour the fat from the skillet. Add the wine and cook until it is reduced to half the original volume.
Meanwhile, melt the butter in a small saucepan. Stir in the flour and cook for 1 minute. Remove from heat and stir in the bouillon. Cook over moderate heat, stirring constantly, until smooth and thickened.
Remove the sausage to a heated serving platter and keep warm. Stir the reduced wine into the bouillon, then stir a little into the beaten egg yolk. Return to the saucepan and stir in the lemon juice. Cook over very low heat, stirring constantly, for 1 minute. Season to taste.

Pour over hot sausage and serve immediately.

## SHRIMP PANCAKES
*2 servings*

*For filling:*
**1 small green pepper, diced**
**1 tablespoon butter**
**¼ pound cooked shrimp,**
**    coarsely chopped**
**2 tablespoons flour**
**⅝ cup light cream**
**5 tablespoons milk**
**Grated Parmesan cheese**

*For pancakes:*
**¾ cup all-purpose flour**
**1 egg, beaten**
**⅝ cup milk and water mixed**
**Salt**
**Freshly ground black pepper**
**Shortening for frying**

Blanch the pepper in boiling

*Use shrimp, peppers and cheese as a luxury pancake filling*

water for 3 minutes. Drain. Melt the butter in a skillet. Add the shrimp and heat gently. Stir in the flour and cook for 1 minute. Remove from heat and stir in two-thirds of the cream, the milk and green pepper. Cook over moderate heat, stirring constantly, until thickened. Keep hot.
Sift the flour into a bowl. Beat in the egg, milk and water and seasoning. Beat until smooth.
Heat some shortening in a large skillet. Spoon in ¼ of the batter, swirl around to coat the bottom of the skillet. Cook until golden brown. Turn and brown the other side. Turn out on to a hot tea towel and keep warm. Repeat with remaining batter three times.
Divide the filling between the pancakes and roll up each one

carefully. Arrange on a hot heatproof platter. Pour the remaining cream over the pancakes and sprinkle with cheese. Brown lightly under a heated broiler.

## KIDNEY TOASTS
*2 servings*

**½ pound veal kidney or 4 lamb**
**    kidneys**
**8–10 mushrooms**
**¼ cup butter or margarine**
**¼ cup flour**
**1¼ cups stock**
**5 tablespoons light cream**
**1¼ tablespoons dry sherry**
**Salt and pepper**
**2 large slices white bread**
**Butter**
**Chopped parsley**

Remove the fat and skin from the kidneys and cut away the core. Cut the kidney into small pieces. Slice the mushrooms.
Melt the butter in a pan and sauté the mushrooms and kidney for 5 minutes. Stir in the flour and mix well. Remove from heat and stir in stock. Cook over low heat, stirring constantly, until thickened. Bring to a boil, reduce the heat, cover and simmer for about 20 minutes or until kidneys are cooked.
Stir in the cream and sherry. Heat carefully but *do not boil*. Season to taste.
Prepare 2 slices of hot toast and spread generously with butter. Stir some parsley into kidney mixture and spoon over toast.

## QUICHE LYONNAISE
*4 servings*

**1 recipe Shortcrust Pastry, page**
**    75**
**1 large onion, chopped**
**2½ tablespoons salad oil**
**2 tablespoons butter**
**2 tablespoons all-purpose flour**
**1¼ cups milk**
**¼ pound Cheddar cheese, grated**
**Salt**
**Freshly ground black pepper**
**4 eggs**

Roll out the pastry on a lightly-floured board into a 9 in. circle. Fit pastry into an 8-in. flan ring or cake pan. Carefully press in a piece of aluminum foil and fill foil with dried beans. Bake in a fairly hot oven (400°F.) for 15 minutes. Remove foil and beans. If the crust is not cooked, return to oven until baked and lightly browned.
Fry the onion in hot oil until soft and lightly browned. Drain off the fat and spread the onion over

the bottom of baked flan case. Melt the butter in a small pan. Stir in the flour and cook for 1 minute. Remove from heat and stir in the milk. Cook over moderate heat, stirring constantly, until mixture comes to a boil and is thickened. Stir in almost all of the cheese. Season to taste. Keep the sauce warm over hot water or very low heat.

Poach the eggs in gently simmering water for 3–4 minutes. Drain well on paper towels, patting tops dry. Arrange in the flan case on top of the onion. Pour over the cheese sauce and sprinkle with remaining cheese.

Place the flan in a pre-heated broiling compartment. Brown quickly. Serve at once.

### CREAMED HAM AND ASPARAGUS
*6 servings*

**2 cans (10¾ ounces each) cream of chicken soup**
**1 medium onion, finely chopped**
**2½ tablespoons dry sherry**
**Salt**
**Freshly ground black pepper**
**¾ pound lean cooked ham, diced**
**1 can (16 ounces) asparagus tips, drained**
**4 or 5 thin slices Emmenthal or Gruyère cheese**

Blend together the soup, onion and sherry. Adjust seasoning. Layer the ham and asparagus in a 1½-quart casserole. Pour the soup mixture over the top. Top with cheese slices. Cook in a fairly hot oven (400°F.) for about 30 minutes or until piping hot.

### BUCK RAREBIT
*4 servings*

**½ pound Cheddar cheese, grated**
**2 tablespoons butter**
**1 teaspoon dry mustard**
**Salt**
**Freshly ground black pepper**
**4–5 tablespoons ale**
**4 eggs**
**4 large slices hot buttered toast**

Place the cheese, butter, mustard, seasoning and ale in a heavy pan. Heat very gently until a creamy mixture is obtained, stirring occasionally. Meanwhile poach the eggs.

*Supper-time drinks are best served hot*

# HOT DRINKS FOR SUPPER TIME

### HOT SPICED TEA
*6 servings*

**3 whole cloves**
**½ in. cinnamon stick**
**5 cups water**
**2 tablespoons tea leaves**
**¼ cup sugar**
**⅓ cup orange juice**
**Juice of 1 lemon**
**Cinnamon sticks for serving**

In a saucepan add the spices to the water and bring to a boil. Pour over the tea in a bowl and let stand 5 minutes. Add the sugar and stir until dissolved. Stir in orange and lemon juice. Return to saucepan and reheat over low heat, but do not boil or simmer. Strain and serve with cinnamon sticks.

### CHINESE ORANGE TEA
*makes about 6 cups*

**3 oranges**
**½ cup all-purpose flour**
**½ cup sugar**
**5 cups water**

Cut the oranges in half, scoop out the pulp and juice and place in a bowl. Gradually add a small amount of water to the flour to form a stiff dough. Roll into balls the size of tiny marbles and set aside. Dissolve the sugar in 5 cups water in a large pan and bring to a boil. Drop in the flour balls and continue to boil until they float to the surface.

Add the orange pulp and juice and boil for 30 seconds. Serve the tea very hot.

### BORGIA COFFEE
*3 servings*

**Pared rind of 1 orange**
**2 tablespoons espresso coffee**
**1¼ cups water**
**1¼ cups milk**
**2½ tablespoons cocoa**
**Whipped cream**

Shred the orange rind into fine julienne strips and blanch in boiling water for a few minutes until tender. Drain.

Use the coffee and water in an espresso machine to make strong coffee, or use special espresso powdered coffee, and make 1¼ cups strong coffee. Heat the milk in a small saucepan. Beat in the cocoa.

Combine the black coffee and the hot cocoa. Divide between 3 mugs and top with plenty of whipped cream. Decorate with shreds of orange rind.

### EGG NOG
*1 serving*

**1 egg**
**1 tablespoon sugar**
**2–3 tablespoons sherry or brandy**
**⅞ cup milk**

Beat the egg and sugar together. Add the sherry or brandy. Heat the milk without boiling and pour it over the egg mixture. Stir well and serve in a heated glass.

### HOT SPICED PINEAPPLE CUP
*makes about 4 cups*

**4 cups pineapple juice**
**5 tablespoons sugar**
**2½ tablespoons lemon juice**
**A 4 in. cinnamon stick**

Simmer all ingredients together for 10 minutes. Remove the cinnamon and serve in warm heatproof glasses.

### HUCKLE-MY-BUFF
*6 servings*

**5 cups draft beer**
**6 eggs, beaten**
**¼ cup sugar**
**Grated nutmeg**
**Brandy to taste**

Heat 2½ cups beer with the eggs and sugar but *do not boil*. Remove from heat and add the remaining beer, a generous amount of nutmeg and brandy to taste. Serve in heatproof glasses.

**Handy hint**

To prevent dark rings forming round the yolks of hard-cooked eggs, cool the eggs quickly by cracking the shells and holding under cold running water until completely cold.

# HOT SUPPER MENUS

**SUPPER MENU** *serves 6*
*after the theatre*

**BEEF AND PEPPER
CASSEROLE**
**GREEN SALAD**
**CRUSTY BREAD AND
BUTTER**
**GRAPE FLAN**

**Timetable** *for supper at 11.15
p.m.*

**Early in the day:** *Prepare the
salad ingredients and dressing but
do not mix. Store salads in the
refrigerator.*
*Make the grape flan, cool and
cover. Leave in a cool place (not
the refrigerator.)*
*Prepare and cook the beef
casserole, discard bouquet garni
but do not add the reserved slices of
pepper. Cool quickly and leave in
a cool place.*
*If available, use automatic oven
timer to reheat casserole.*
**10.45** *(on returning from theatre).
Add reserved pepper to casserole.
If automatic timer was not used,
put casserole in the oven at 400°F.
to reheat.*
*Serve drinks, crisps, nuts etc.
Slice bread and toss salad.*
**11.15** *Serve supper.*

## BEEF AND PEPPER
## CASSEROLE

**2 pound chuck steak**
**2 tablespoons fat or oil**
**2 large onions, sliced**
**2 green peppers, sliced**
**⅛ cup flour**
**3¾ cups brown stock**
**2½ tablespoons tomato paste**
**Salt**
**Freshly ground black pepper**
**Bouquet garni**

Cut the meat into 1 in. cubes.
Heat the fat or oil in a skillet. Fry
the onions until golden brown.
Remove with a slotted spoon and
place in a casserole. Reserve a few
slices of the pepper and fry the
rest lightly. Add to the casserole.
Brown the meat in the remaining
fat, adding only a few pieces at a
time to the pan, so that the fat
remains really hot. When the
meat is well browned, transfer to
the casserole with the vegetables.
Stir the flour into the fat in the

*A hot casserole and fresh salad make a good choice for supper after the theatre*

*A cold flan looks delicious and is easily prepared in advance*

skillet. Stir and cook for 1 minute. Remove from heat and stir in the stock and tomato paste. Cook over moderate heat, stirring constantly, until mixture comes to a boil. Season. Pour over meat. Add the bouquet garni.

Cover the casserole and cook in a moderate oven (350°F.) for 1–1½ hours; 20 minutes before serving add the reserved slices of green pepper and return to oven. Remove the bouquet garni.

## GREEN SALAD

For 6 people you will need 1 large head lettuce, 1 bunch watercress, 1 head of endive and 1 green pepper. Wash and trim salad greens. Slice the pepper. Toss in French dressing (page 54) to taste.

## GRAPE FLAN

*For pastry:*
**1 cup all-purpose flour**
**Pinch of salt**
**6 tablespoons butter or margarine and shortening, mixed**
**1 teaspoon sugar**
**1 egg, beaten**

*For filling:*
**1¼ cups milk**
**¼ cup sugar**
**¼ cup all-purpose flour**
**2½ teaspoons cornstarch**
**1 large egg**
**1¼ teaspoons grated orange rind**
**2½ teaspoons orange liqueur**
**¾ pound grapes, black and green**
**Juice of 1 orange, strained**
**1 teaspoon cornstarch**

Sift together the flour and salt. Cut in fat with a pastry blender or two knives until the mixture resembles fine crumbs. Mix in the sugar. Add the egg, stirring until the ingredients begin to stick together. Knead into a ball with the fingers to make a firm smooth dough. Roll out on a lightly floured board into a circle. Fit the dough into an 8½-in. flan ring or an 8-in. cake pan. Carefully fit in a piece of aluminum foil and fill with dried beans. Bake in a fairly hot oven (400°F.) for 20 minutes. If the shell is not quite browned enough, return to oven for just a few minutes. Cool. Heat the milk but do not boil. In a bowl blend together the sugar, flour, cornstarch and egg. Stir in a little hot milk to give a smooth paste. Return the mixture to the pan and cook over low heat, stirring constantly, until the mixture thickens and just comes to a boil. Stir in the grated orange rind and

*Soup and a warm quiche for a casual supper party*

liqueur. Cool the custard. Spoon into the pastry shell. Cover the surface with buttered waxed paper to prevent a skin from forming on top. Let stand until cold. Halve and remove seeds from grapes. Arrange in a pattern on top of custard. Combine the orange juice with cornstarch and bring to a boil until mixture is clear. Brush carefully over top of grapes for a glaze.

**SUPPER MENU** *serves 10*
*for an informal evening at home*

**CREAM OF
MUSHROOM SOUP
OR CHILLED TOMATO
JUICE
ONION QUICHE
PINEAPPLE AND
PEPPER SALAD
FRENCH BREAD AND
BUTTER
CHEESE BOARD**

**Timetable** *for supper at 10.00 p.m.*
**Day before:** *Make the soup and refrigerate.*
*Fry the croûtons, cool and store in an airtight container.*
*Bake the shortcrust flan cases.*
**Same day:** *Slice the onions, sauté and keep in a covered bowl. Beat together the egg mixture and keep in a cool place. Prepare anchovies and cheese board and keep covered.*
**Early evening:** *Prepare salad.*
**9.30** *Fill the flan cases, decorate*

*and bake.*
*Put the soup to reheat.*
*Refresh croûtons in oven for a short time. Toss the salad.*
**10.00** *Serve supper.*

---

## CREAM OF MUSHROOM SOUP

**¾ cup butter**
**¾ pound onions, finely chopped**
**1 pound button mushrooms, chopped**
**¾ cup all-purpose flour**
**7½ cups chicken bouillon**
**2½ cups milk**
**Salt**
**Freshly ground black pepper**
**¼ teaspoon garlic salt**
**Lemon juice**
**Fried croûtons**

Melt the butter in a large soup pan or Dutch oven. Add the onions and sauté for 10 minutes, until soft but not browned. Add the mushrooms. Cover and cook for 5 minutes.
Stir in the flour and cook for 3 minutes, stirring. Remove from heat and stir in the bouillon. Cook over medium heat, stirring, until mixture comes to a boil. Lower heat and simmer gently for 20 minutes.
Stir in the milk, seasonings and lemon juice. Simmer for 10 minutes. *Do not boil.* Serve in heated soup bowls, topped with fried croûtons.

## ONION QUICHE

**2½ cups all-purpose flour**
**¼ teaspoon salt**
**¾ cup butter or margarine**
**2 egg yolks**
**3 tablespoons water**

*For filling:*
**½ cup butter**
**2 pound onions, sliced**
**4 eggs**
**½ cup all-purpose flour**
**1⅞ cup milk**
**Salt and pepper**
**2 cans (2 ounces each) anchovy fillets, drained**
**Pitted black olives**

Sift the flour and salt together. Cut in the butter with a pastry blender or two knives until the mixture looks like fine breadcrumbs. Add the egg yolks blended with 2 tablespoons water. Add more water if needed to make the dough stick together. Knead lightly for a few seconds to give a firm, smooth dough. Let rest 15 minutes. Divide the dough in half and roll out into circles on a lightly floured board. Fit into two 8-in. flan rings. Lightly press aluminum foil into pastry and fill with dried beans. Bake in a fairly hot oven (400°F.) for 15 minutes. Remove the foil and continue baking for 5 minutes until cooked and lightly browned. Cool.
Melt the butter in a skillet. Cook the onions until soft, but not browned. Divide the onions between the two flan shells. Beat together the eggs, flour, milk, salt and pepper. Pour over the onions. Arrange the anchovy fillets in a criss-cross pattern on top of each flan. Place a black olive in each space. Bake in a moderate oven (350°F.) for 20–30 minutes or until set and lightly browned. Serve warm or hot.

## PINEAPPLE AND PEPPER SALAD

**1 can (20 ounces) pineapple chunks**
**1 green pepper, seeded, sliced and blanched**
**¼ cucumber, diced**
**¼ cup white raisins**
**1 head lettuce, cleaned and shredded**
**5 tablespoons French dressing**

Drain the pineapple and reserve juice. Mix the pineapple pieces with the green pepper, cucumber, raisins and lettuce. Combine French dressing with 2½ tablespoons pineapple juice. Pour over the salad and toss.

# Perfect Dinner Parties

Perfect dinner parties need planning. The menus here have been selected carefully to please the most discerning palate, without over-taxing the energies of the cook-hostess. Follow the timetables and there will be no last minute flusters!

*This page: A classic Boeuf Stroganoff*

## HARICOTS VERTS A LA TOMATE
## BOEUF STROGANOFF
## LEAF SPINACH AND BOILED RICE
## TRANCHE AUX FRUITS

Wine – Claret
(Haut Médoc – St. Emilion or Cabernet Sauvignon)

**Timetable** *for dinner at 8.00 p.m.*
**Day before:** *Make flan case.*
**5.00** *Collect ingredients and equipment. Fill flan.*
*Beat and cut the steak and coat with seasoned flour. Prepare onions and mushrooms. Cook rice, drain and leave to cool. Wash and pick over spinach.*
**7.30** *Prepare first course. Put drained rice in a buttered casserole, cover tightly with a lid and place in warm oven to heat through. Boil spinach, drain and refresh.*
**7.45** *Cook beef (add dairy sour cream between courses); keep warm. Place roughly chopped spinach over a low heat with a little butter.*
**8.00** *Serve first course.*

## HARICOTS VERTS A LA TOMATE

1 pound green beans
½ pound firm tomatoes
3 tablespoons butter
1 bay leaf
Sprig of thyme
Salt
Freshly ground black pepper

Clean beans and remove tips. Plunge into boiling salted water, cover and cook for 5 minutes. Peel the tomatoes and cut in quarters. Drain the beans in a colander. Melt the butter in the cooking pan over low heat. Return beans to pan with the tomatoes, bay leaf and thyme. Season with salt and pepper. Cover tightly and simmer very gently for about 15 minutes, shaking the pan occasionally so that mixture does not stick. Remove bay leaf and thyme before serving.

## BOEUF STROGANOFF

1½ pound round steak
3¾ tablespoons seasoned flour
¼ cup butter
1 onion, thinly sliced
½ pound mushrooms, sliced
Salt and pepper
1¼ cups dairy sour cream

Beat the steak with the side of a cleaver. Trim away all fat and cut into strips ¼ in. by 2 in. Coat with seasoned flour. Melt half the butter. Fry the meat until golden brown, about 5–7 minutes. Cook the onion and mushrooms in remaining butter for 3–4 minutes. Season to taste and add the beef. Stir in the sour cream and heat gently but *do not boil.* Serve with hot cooked rice and spinach.

*Tranche aux fruits, concealing a deliciously smooth pastry cream*

## TRANCHE AUX FRUITS

*For pâte sucrée:*
1½ cups all-purpose flour
Pinch of salt
3 tablespoons sugar
6 tablespoons butter
2½ tablespoons beaten egg

*For pastry cream:*
2½ cups milk
½ cup sugar
½ cup flour
2 tablespoons cornstarch
2 large eggs
¼ cup butter
Confectioners' sugar

*For filling:*
1 can (14½ ounces) pineapple chunks
1 can (11 ounces) mandarin oranges
1 jar (8 ounces) maraschino cherries

*For fruit glaze:*
2½ tablespoons apricot preserves
1 tablespoon water

Sift the flour and salt on to a pastry board or marble slab. Make a well in the center and put into it the sugar, butter and egg. Using the fingertips of one hand, pinch and work the ingredients together until blended. Gradually work in all the flour and knead lightly until smooth. Put pastry in a cool place for 1 hour. Roll out on a lightly floured board or marble slab into a rectangle and use to line a 14 in. by 4½ in. by 1 in. flan frame placed on a cookie tray. If you do not have a flan frame, fit the pastry carefully into an 8-in. square cake pan. Line the flan with aluminum foil and fill with dried beans. Bake in a fairly hot oven (400°F.) for about 25 minutes. Remove the foil and bake for 5 minutes or until shell is cooked and lightly browned. Cool.

Heat the milk. Blend together the sugar, flour, cornstarch and beaten eggs. Stir in the milk. Return to pan and cook over low heat, stirring constantly, until the mixture thickens and just comes to a boil. Stir in the butter. Cool. When nearly cold spoon into the pastry case. (If baked in an 8-in. pan carefully remove case before filling.) Dust with confectioners' sugar to prevent a skin from forming on top.

Drain the canned fruit thoroughly and arrange over the pastry cream in tight panels. Combine the preserves and water and bring to a boil. Bubble gently for 1 minute. Put through a sieve and brush over top of fruit while still warm. Chill before serving.

## PATE MAISON, FRENCH BREAD
## CASSEROLE OF GAME
## BRAISED CELERY AND GAME CHIPS
## PINEAPPLE AND MARASCHINO GRANITO

Wine –Red Burgundy
(Côte de Beaune-Villages – Pinot Noir)

**Timetable** *for dinner at 8.00 p.m.*
**Day before:** *Make pâté and pineapple granito.*
**5.30** *Collect ingredients and equipment. Start birds cooking. Prepare potatoes for game chips. Slice pâté and put on individual plates.*
**7.00** *Scoop granito into pineapple shell and leave in coldest part of refrigerator.*
*Cook game chips (or heat packet chips) and celery; keep warm.*
**7.30** *Carve birds and complete casserole.*
**8.00** *Serve first course.*

## PATE MAISON

½ pound chicken livers
¼ pound lean pork or veal
1 cup fresh white breadcrumbs
½ cup milk
Salt and pepper
Pinch of nutmeg
Sliced bacon
Sprig of thyme
1 bay leaf
1 tablespoon brandy

Put the liver through a food chopper one time and the pork or veal two times. Combine the breadcrumbs and milk and let stand a few minutes. Season the liver and pork with salt, pepper and nutmeg. Stir in the breadcrumbs very gently, otherwise the liver will lose its color.

Line a 2½–3 cup terrine or loaf pan with bacon slices. Put the liver mixture into the terrine. Top with more bacon slices and add the thyme and bay leaf. Cover with a lid or a piece of aluminum foil and place in a roasting pan. Add water to a depth of 1 in. Cook in a warm oven (325°F.) for 1½ hours.

About 15 minutes before cooking time is up, pour the brandy over the meat. When cooked, remove from the oven and cool slightly. When just a little cool, discard lid and place a plate and a weight on top. Allow to cool completely. To serve, turn out on a serving platter and slice.

## CASEROLE OF GAME

2 partridges or pheasants,
   dressed
2 tablespoons butter
2½ tablespoons oil
1 small onion, chopped
¼ pound chopped lean veal
¼ pound chopped lean ham
1 small cooking apple, pared and
   sliced
1 clove garlic, crushed
Salt and pepper
1 bay leaf
5 tablespoons stock
⅝ cup light cream
2½ tablespoons brandy
Lemon juice, optional
¼ pound button mushrooms
Butter
Watercress

Truss the birds and fry in the combined butter and oil until well browned on all sides. Remove from pan and reserve. Cook the onion, veal, ham, apple and garlic in the hot fat for 5 minutes, stirring. Turn the mixture into a casserole large enough for the two birds. Season and add the bay leaf. Place the birds on top, breast side down, and add the stock. Roast in a warm oven (325°F.) for about 1 hour. Remove casserole from oven and discard bay leaf. Turn birds breast side up. Pour in the cream. Warm the brandy, ignite with a kitchen match and pour over birds. Cover casserole tightly and cook for 45 minutes or until birds are tender.

To serve, carve the birds and keep hot. Adjust the seasoning in the sauce and add a little lemon juice, if desired. Sauté the mushrooms in a little hot butter and add to the sauce. Reheat, but do not boil. Spoon over the carved birds. Garnish with watercress.

*Note:* This method is also suitable for duck. Use a 3½ pound roasting duck, cut into 4 pieces. Fry skin side down until brown and drain well on paper towels. Pour off nearly all the drippings from the pan and then continue as for game birds. Before adding the cream, again skim off as much fat as possible.

## PINEAPPLE AND MARASCHINO GRANITO

1 medium ripe pineapple
Sugar to dredge
⅝ cup water
1 cup sugar
Rind and juice of 1 lemon
2½ tablespoons Maraschino
   liqueur
10 Maraschino cherries

*Dressed endive spears make a refreshing starter*

Split the pineapple down the middle and scrape the flesh and juice into a bowl. Discard center core. Sprinkle the inside of the pineapple with sugar and chill. Purée the pineapple pulp and juice in an electric blender. Turn the purée into a saucepan. Add the water, sugar, lemon rind and juice and bring to a boil. Boil for 5 minutes. Cool. Turn the mixture into a freezing tray. Freeze until mushy. Turn the pineapple mush into a bowl, beat well with a rotary beater and add the liqueur and cherries. Return to freezer and freeze until firm.

To serve, scoop the pineapple mixture out of the tray and pile into the chilled shell. This dish looks particularly attractive if served in a bed of crushed ice.

**MENU** *serves 6*

**DRESSED ENDIVE
SPEARS**
**CHICKEN MARSALA**
**MUSHROOMS, GREEN
BEANS AND NEW
POTATOES**
**APPLE BRULEE**
Wine – Hock (Sichel's Blue
Nun or Deinhard's Hanns
Christoff Wein)

**Timetable** *for dinner at 8.00 p.m.*
**Day before:** *Make apple sauce.*
*5.00 Collect ingredients and equipment. Prepare endive and dressing. Prepare dessert and chill. Prepare vegetables.*
*6.30 Start to cook chicken. When ready, transfer to flameproof dish and keep warm. Prepare cheese topping.*
*7.30 Cook mushrooms and keep warm.*
*7.45 Cook beans and potatoes. Spoon cheese topping over chicken and place under hot broiler. When ready return to oven to keep warm. Combine endive and dressing.*
*8.00 Serve first course. Leave broiler alight to finish off dessert between courses.*

## DRESSED ENDIVE SPEARS

1 pound endive
Juice of 1 large lemon
1 egg yolk
Salt and pepper
⅝ cup salad oil
2 medium peppers, 1 green and 1
   red

Cut the base off each head of endive. Separate the leaves under cold running water. Drain and dry thoroughly. Toss in 3 tablespoons lemon juice. Beat the egg yolks with a pinch of salt and some freshly ground pepper. Add the oil, a little at a time, beating with a wire whisk continuously. When thick, stir in the lemon juice drained from the endive. Adjust the thickness to a stiff pouring consistency by adding a little warm water.

Divide the endive between 6 large goblet or balloon glasses. Just before serving, spoon over the dressing. Sprinkle with finely chopped red and green peppers.

## CHICKEN MARSALA

3 broiler-fryer chickens, halved
¼ cup butter
⅝ cup Marsala or sherry
⅝ cup heavy cream
¼ teaspoon paprika
1 clove garlic, crushed
1 cup grated Cheddar cheese
Salt and pepper
Chopped parsley

Fry the chicken halves in butter for about 5 minutes or until golden brown. Remove from the pan and drain off excess fat. Replace chicken meat side down. Pour over the Marsala or sherry. Cover tightly and simmer gently for about 40 minutes or until chicken is tender.

Meanwhile, whip the cream. Fold in the paprika, garlic and cheese. Season to taste. Transfer the chicken halves and juices to a flameproof casserole. Spoon over the cheese topping. Broil quickly under a very hot broiler until the cheese melts and is brown. Serve sprinkled with parsley.

## APPLE BRULEE

2½ cups thick apple sauce
1¼ cups heavy cream
Grated rind of 1 orange
Soft light brown sugar

Turn cold apple sauce into 6 individual soufflé dishes, about 1 in. in depth. Beat the cream until light and fluffy, but not too stiff. Fold in the orange rind. Spread over the apple mixture. Chill until serving time.

Before serving, cover with a thick layer of sugar, about ¼–½ in. in depth. Place under a hot broiler and broil just long enough to melt the sugar. Be careful that the sugar does not burn. Serve immediately.

## CHILLED CUCUMBER SOUP
## BARBECUED LAMB
## LEEKS, CARROTS AND CREAMED POTATOES
## RASPBERRY CHEESE FLAN

**Wine — Vin ordinaire**

**Timetable** *for dinner at 8.00.*
**Day before:** *Make soup and chill.*
**In the morning:** *Make raspberry cheese flan.*
**6.00** *Prepare barbecue sauce and put lamb to cook.*
**6.30** *Whip cream, decorate flan.*
**6.45** *Cook vegetables and keep warm.*
**7.15** *Dish up meat and keep warm.*
**8.00** *Serve first course.*

### CHILLED CUCUMBER SOUP

1 small onion, sliced
3¾ cups white stock
1 large cucumber
Sprig of mint
1¼ tablespoons cornstarch
3 tablespoons cream
Salt and pepper
Green coloring

Simmer the onion in a pan with the stock for 15 minutes. Peel and chop the cucumber, saving a little for garnish. Add the cucumber and mint to the stock and simmer for about 20 minutes or until cucumber is tender. Purée the mixture in an electric blender. Return to the pan and reheat. Combine the cornstarch with a little cold water to make a smooth paste. Stir a little of the hot soup into the mixture, return the mix-

**Handy hint**

To chop an onion, peel it keeping the root intact. Cut in half through the root. Holding the root end away from the knife, and using a sharp, pointed knife, cut down in even slices about ½ in. apart. Make a similar number of horizontal cuts, stopping just short of the root. Holding the onion firmly, cut down at rightangles to the previous cuts: the onion will then fall away in neat dice.

*A chilled cucumber soup makes a good start to a warm evening*

ture to the pan. Bring to a boil, stirring constantly, until soup thickens and is clear. Simmer gently for 2–3 minutes. Stir in the cream and season, if necessary. Tint the soup very delicately with green coloring, pour it into a large bowl and chill thoroughly. Serve with 2 or 3 slices of cucumber floating on top.

### BARBECUED LAMB

1 shoulder of lamb, about 3½ pound
1 teaspoon dry mustard
1 teaspoon ground ginger
Salt and pepper
2 cloves garlic, crushed
Flour

*For barbecue sauce:*

5 tablespoons Worcestershire sauce
5 tablespoons catsup
2½ teaspoons sugar
1¼ tablespoons vinegar
2 tablespoons butter or margarine, melted
Cayenne pepper and salt
⅝ cup water
1 small onion, thinly sliced

Trim off any excess fat from the lamb. Combine the mustard, ginger, salt, pepper and garlic, blend

well. Rub into the meat and sprinkle with flour. Place on a rack in a shallow roasting pan. Blend together the ingredients for the sauce, adding the sliced onion last. Pour over the meat. Roast in the center of a hot oven (425°F.) for 30 minutes; lower heat to moderate (350°F.) and cook, allowing 27 minutes to the pound. Baste the meat with the sauce 2–3 times during cooking, adding a little more water to the sauce if needed.

### RASPBERRY CHEESE FLAN

*For rich flan pastry:*

1½ cups all-purpose flour
Salt, optional
½ cup butter or margarine
2½ teaspoons sugar
1–2 egg yolks, according to size
3–5 teaspoons water

*For filling:*

1 package (3 ounces) cream cheese, softened
1¼ tablespoons milk
1 cup boiling water
½ package (3 ounces) raspberry flavored gelatin
1 pint raspberries
Whipped cream

Sift the flour with a pinch of salt. Cut in the butter with a pastry blender or two knives until the consistency of cornmeal. Add the sugar. Blend the egg yolks with 2–3 teaspoons water and add to flour with additional water to make a firm, pliable dough. Roll out into a circle ⅛ in. thick. Use to line a 9 in. flan ring placed on a cookie tray or a 9 in. cake pan. Flute the top edge. Prick case with a fork. Carefully fit in a piece of aluminum foil and fill with dried beans. Bake in a fairly hot oven (400°F.) for 15 minutes. Remove from oven and remove foil and beans. Return to oven and bake until pastry is lightly browned and cooked, 5–10 minutes. Cool.
Beat together the cream cheese and milk until smooth. Spread over the bottom of the cooked flan case. Combine the boiling water and gelatin and stir until the gelatin is dissolved. Cool before stirring in the raspberries. When the gelatin has begun to set, pour into the flan case. Chill until firm and well set. Just before serving, top with whipped cream.

## AVOCADO WITH CHEESE DRESSING
## ROAST CHICKEN ITALIENNE
## BROCCOLI SPEARS AND NEW POTATOES
## MALAKOFF TORTE

**Wine – Red or White Chianti**

**Timetable** *for dinner at 8.00 p.m.*
**Day before:** *Bone and stuff chicken. Prepare torte but do not decorate; keep in refrigerator. Make chocolate squares.*
**5.45** *Collect ingredients and equipment. Put chicken to roast.*
**6.30** *Decorate Malakoff Torte and return to refrigerator.*
**7.30** *Prepare avocados. Cook vegetables and keep warm.*
**7.45** *Dish up chicken and keep warm.*
**8.00** *Serve first course.*

### AVOCADO WITH CHEESE DRESSING

3 ripe avocados
Lemon juice
1 package (1¼ ounces) Roquefort cheese
½ cup cottage cheese

Halve each avocado lengthwise with a stainless steel knife, making a deep cut through the flesh up to the pit and encircling the fruit. Separate the halves by gently twisting them in opposite ways and discard pits. Brush cut surface with lemon juice.

Dice the Roquefort cheese and mix lightly with the cottage cheese. Carefully scoop out all of the flesh from the avocado skins. Dice it and toss with cheese mixture. Pile the mixture back into the shells to serve.

## ROAST CHICKEN ITALIENNE

**A 4 pound roasting chicken, oven ready**
**1 large orange**
**½ pound lean pork**
**½ pound unsliced lean bacon, rinded**
**1 large clove garlic**
**Liver from chicken**
**1 large onion, chopped**
**½ pound pork sausage meat**
**½ teaspoon salt**
**Freshly ground black pepper**
**½ teaspoon dried thyme**
**4 small sweet gherkins**
**2 tablespoons butter**
**2 tablespoons honey**
**¼ teaspoon cinnamon**

To bone the chicken, first cut off the wings at the second joint and the legs at the first. Then, using a small sharp knife, slit down the center of the back and work the meat from the bones, gradually turning it inside out and being careful not to break the skin. The ligaments of the wing and leg joints need to be severed and the leg joints broken before the meat can be scraped off. Work round to the breast bone and, after separating the meat from it, remove the carcass. (If this sounds too difficult, ask your butcher to bone the chicken. Boned, it should weigh about 2½ pound.)

Finely grate the rind of the orange. Put the pork, bacon, garlic, liver and onion through a food chopper. Blend in the sausage meat, salt, black pepper, thyme and ½ teaspoon of the grated orange rind. Lay the boned chicken, skin side down, on a board. Turn the wings inside out. Spread half the stuffing over the chicken and place the gherkins down the center. Force a little stuffing into both legs and cover the gherkins with the remaining stuffing. Bring the sides together and sew them up, using a trussing needle threaded with fine string. Sew legs flat against body and pat chicken back into shape.

Place the chicken in a small

*A shoulder of lamb and a tasty glaze for an economical party dish*

roasting pan. Melt the butter in a small pan. Stir in remaining orange rind. Brush the mixture over chicken and season with salt and pepper. Roast in a fairly hot oven (400°F.) for about 1½ hours. Meanwhile, squeeze 7½ tablespoons juice from the orange. Put this in a pan with the honey and cinnamon. Bring to a boil and bubble for 2 minutes. Pour juices from the chicken into the pan with the honey. Spoon this mixture over the chicken and return to oven on the lowest shelf. Cool for 25 minutes, basting every 10 minutes so that the chicken acquires a pretty glaze.

## MALAKOFF TORTE

**½ pound unsalted butter**
**¾ cup sugar**
**1 egg yolk**
**1¼ tablespoons instant coffee powder**
**¼ cup finely chopped candied peel**
**¼ cup chopped almonds**
**½ cup ground almonds**
**½ cup rum**
**½ cup water**
**3 packages lady fingers**
**⅝ cup heavy cream**

Lightly oil an 8-in. cake pan with a removable bottom, or use an 8-in. spring form pan or malakoff mold. Line the base and sides of the pan with waxed paper.

Cream together the butter and sugar until light and fluffy. Beat in the egg yolk and coffee powder. Fold in the candied peel and nuts. Combine the rum and water in a flat saucer. Dip the lady fingers, one at a time, quickly in the rum and water; do not let them soften. Place side by side around the edge of the pan, putting them very close together so that they are wedged in tightly and will stand up, and line the bottom of the pan. Spoon half the creamed mixture over the lady fingers. Spread in an even layer. Dip more lady fingers in the rum mixture and layer over the filling. Spoon remaining filling over the biscuit layer and place remaining lady fingers, dipped in rum, over the top. Cut the tips off the lady fingers where they extend above the top of the cake. Place pieces on top and press in lightly. Chill for at least 3 hours before serving.

Ease the torte away from the pan by gently pulling on the paper or by loosening the spring form outer ring. Invert the torte on to a serving platter. Whip cream just until slightly thick, place in a pastry bag with a large star nozzle and pipe large whirls of cream over top of cake.

**Handy hint**

When buying endive, be careful to pick the whitest you can find. If there are traces of green at the tips, this indicates the endive has been exposed to the light and will be excessively bitter.

213

**TOMATO JELLY RINGS**
**PORK RAGOUT**
**FRESH GARDEN SALAD**
**CHOCOLATE SOUFFLE**
**& TUILES D'AMANDES**
Wine – Alsace
Gewürztraminer
Emerald Dry Riesling

**Timetable** *for dinner at 8.00 p.m.*
**In advance:** *Make the tuiles d'amandes and store in an airtight tin.*

**In the morning:** *Make tomato jelly rings and leave in a cool place to set.*
*Make soufflé but do not decorate with cream yet.*
**5.30** *Collect ingredients and equipment. Start pork cooking.*
*Make stuffing balls.*
*Prepare garnish for first course.*
*Decorate soufflé.*
**7.00** *Fry stuffing balls and keep warm.*
*Turn out jelly rings and garnish.*
**8.00** *Serve first course.*

## TOMATO JELLY RINGS

1 pound firm ripe tomatoes
2 small onions
1 small clove garlic
1 teaspoon sugar
½ teaspoon salt
Pinch celery salt
Pinch grated nutmeg
1 bay leaf
1 teaspoon peppercorns
1 envelope unflavored gelatin
1 tablespoon tarragon vinegar
3¾ tablespoons lemon juice
Watercress

Scald the tomatoes, remove the skins and cut in quarters. Remove the centers if they are tough. Chop the onions and crush the garlic. Put the tomatoes, onions, garlic, sugar, salts and nutmeg in a saucepan. Add the bay leaf and peppercorns tied in muslin. Cook over low heat until the onion is tender. Remove muslin bag. Soften the gelatin in 2 table-spoons cold water in a small bowl. Set the bowl in a pan of hot water and let stand until gelatin is dissolved. Purée the tomato mixture in an electric blender. Rub through a sieve and put purée into a 1-quart measure. Add the vinegar and lemon juice and if necessary make up to 2½ cups with extra water. Stir in dissolved gelatin. Pour into 4 individual

ring molds that have been rinsed in cold water. Let stand until set. To serve, turn out of molds and garnish with watercress.

## PORK RAGOUT

2 onions, sliced
¼ cup fat or oil
2 pound shoulder of pork, boned and cubed
2 small green peppers, seeded and sliced
2 cloves garlic, crushed
⅝ cup red wine
⅝ cup stock or water
¼ teaspoon chili powder
1 teaspoon celery salt
1 bay leaf
Salt and pepper
¼ cup raw rice
1 package herb stuffing mix

*Tomato jelly rings to serve as a first course at a dinner party*

Cook the onions in hot fat for about 5 minutes. Remove from pan and brown the meat in remaining fat for 8–10 minutes. Drain off any excess fat. Return the onions to the pan with the peppers, garlic, wine, stock, chili powder, celery salt, bay leaf and seasoning. Cover tightly and simmer for 1½ hours or until meat is tender. Meanwhile, cook the rice in boiling salted water according to package directions. Make up the stuffing mix accord-ing to package directions. Shape into 12 small balls. Fry in a small amount of fat until golden brown, 3–4 minutes. Add to the meat with the rice just before serving.

## FRESH GARDEN SALAD

1 clove garlic
½ head iceberg lettuce
½ head romaine lettuce
2 tomatoes, cut into bite-sized pieces
4 green onions, sliced
½ bunch radishes, sliced
½ cucumber, sliced
½ head cauliflower, cut into flowerets
French dressing
3 hard-cooked eggs, peeled and sliced
¼ cup sliced stuffed olives

Rub salad bowl with cut garlic. Tear the lettuce into bite-sized pieces and place in a salad bowl. Add vegetables and toss together with French Dressing to taste. Garnish with egg slices and stuf-fed olives.

### Handy hint

To remove the skin from tomatoes, drop them one at a time into boiling water and leave for a few seconds. This will loosen the skin so that it comes off easily. But do not leave the tomatoes in the water too long or they will start to cook. Alternatively, hold each tomato on a fork in a gas flame for a moment, until the skin comes off easily.

## CHOCOLATE SOUFFLE

3 large eggs, separated
6 tablespoons sugar
2½ tablespoons water
2½ teaspoons unflavored gelatin
2½ tablespoons water
3 squares semi-sweet chocolate
1 tablespoon brandy
1¼ cups heavy cream

Prepare a 1-quart soufflé dish by tying a double piece of oiled aluminum foil around it, extend-ing about 3 in. above the top. Beat the egg yolks and sugar with the water in a deep bowl. Place over a pan of hot water and con-tinue beating until thick and creamy. Remove from the heat and continue beating until cool. Soften the gelatin in the water in a bowl. Place the bowl in a pan of hot water and heat until gelatin is dissolved. Let cool slightly. Pour into the egg mixture in a slow stream, stirring all the time. Melt the chocolate in a bowl over hot water. Stir until smooth. Stir the melted chocolate and brandy into the egg mixture. Cool until the mixture is close to setting. Lightly whip half the cream and fold into the chocolate mixture. Beat the egg whites until stiff but not dry. Quickly, lightly and evenly fold into the chocolate mixture. Pour the mixture into the soufflé dish. Chill until set. Beat the remaining cream. Just before serving, remove the paper collar from soufflé dish. Pipe the cream over top of soufflé.

## TUILES D'AMANDES

3 egg whites
¾ cup sugar
¾ cup all-purpose flour
¾ cup finely chopped almonds
6 tablespoons butter, melted

Beat the egg whites in a large bowl until stiff. Fold in the sugar, sifted flour and almonds. Mix well. Fold in the cooled melted butter. Place teaspoonfuls of the mixture on a greased cookie tray, keeping cookies well apart. Smooth out each one thinly with the back of a spoon, retaining the round shape. Bake in a fairly hot oven (375°F.) for 8–10 minutes or until lightly browned.
Use a spatula to lift each one from the cookie tray and place it over a rolling pin so that it sets in a curled shape. Allow a moment or two for the wafer to harden and then remove to a wire rack to cool. Store in an airtight tin.

# More Dinner Party Specials

More dinner party menus for small numbers, with wine suggestions and timetables. Make your dinners a pleasure for your friends and yourself.

*Fresh pineapple in liqueur Kirsch is a favorite choice*

**PASTA HORS D'OEUVRE**
**SALTIMBOCCA ALLA**
**ROMANA**
**PETIT POIS A LA**
**FRANCAISE, CROUTONS**
**PRALINE BOMBE**
Wine – Red or white Chianti

**Timetable** *for dinner at 8.00 p.m.*
**Day before:** *Make bombe.*
*Prepare mayonnaise for pasta.*
**5.00** *Collect ingredients and equipment. Prepare first course. Prepare veal rolls ready for frying. Fry croûtons; keep warm. Prepare vegetables.*
**7.45** *Cook main course and vegetables; keep warm. Unmold bombe on to chilled plate and return to freezing compartment.*
**8.00** *Serve first course.*

## PASTA HORS D'OEUVRE

¼ **cup macaroni shells**
1 **egg yolk**
⅝ **cup salad oil**
1 **tablespoon vinegar**
**Pinch sugar**
¼ **teaspoon dry mustard**
**Salt**
**Freshly ground black pepper**
1 **tablespoon milk**
1 **onion, chopped**
1 **teaspoon tomato paste**
¼ **pound garlic salami**
¼ **pound cooked tongue**
2 **crisp green apples, cored and finely diced**
**Chopped parsley**

Cook the macaroni shells in boiling water until tender. Drain and rinse under cold running water.
Beat the egg yolk with a rotary beater or a whisk. Add the oil, a little at a time, beating constantly. When thick stir in the vinegar, sugar, mustard and seasoning. Blend in the milk, onion and tomato paste.
Cut the garlic salami and tongue into strips; toss with macaroni shells and apple. Add mayonnaise mixture and toss together. Serve on individual plates garnished with chopped parsley.

## SALTIMBOCCA ALLA ROMANA

8 **thin slices veal**
**Lemon juice**
**Freshly ground black pepper**
1 **teaspoon dried marjoram**
8 **thin slices prosciutto ham**
**Butter**
2½ **tablespoons Marsala**
½ **in. squares day-old bread, fried in butter or oil**

*Saltimbocca alla romana is a traditional dish from Italy*

Place the veal between 2 pieces of waxed paper. Pound with the side of a cleaver so that each piece is about 4 in. by 5 in. and very thin. Season with lemon juice and pepper. Place a pinch of marjoram in center and cover with a slice of ham. Roll up and fasten with toothpicks.
Melt enough butter to cover the bottom of a skillet, large enough to take the rolls in a single layer. Gently fry the veal rolls until golden brown. Add the Marsala. Cover tightly and simmer gently until the veal is tender.
Place the rolls on a platter. Pour the juices from the pan over and surround with bread cubes.

## PETITS POIS A LA FRANCAISE

¼ **head lettuce, washed and finely shredded**
6 **scallions, halved and trimmed**
**A little parsley and fresh mint, tied together**
1½ **pounds peas, shelled**
⅝ **cup water**
2 **tablespoons butter**
**Salt and pepper**
2½ **teaspoons sugar**
**Butter**

Put all the ingredients, except the extra butter, in a pan. Cover closely and simmer for about 20–30 minutes or until cooked. Remove the parsley and mint. Drain the peas. Serve with extra butter.

## PRALINE BOMBE

½ **cup sugar**
⅝ **cup boiling water**
4 **egg yolks, beaten**
½ **cup crushed almond toffee**
1 **teaspoon vanilla flavoring**
**Pinch of salt**
1¼ **cups heavy cream, whipped**
2½ **cups vanilla ice cream**

Put the sugar in a heavy saucepan and heat very gently until coffee-colored. Add the boiling water and stir carefully to dissolve the caramel. Cool the mixture.
Put the egg yolks in the top of a double boiler. Add the cooled caramel mixture. Cook and stir over hot water until the mixture thickens. Cool.
Stir in the crushed toffee, vanilla and salt. Fold in the whipped cream. Turn into an ice cube tray. Freeze until half-frozen. Chill a bombe mold and line it to about 1 in. thickness with the vanilla

ice cream. Fill the center with the half-frozen praline mixture. Cover the top with vanilla ice cream. Press on lid of mold or cover with aluminum foil. Return to freezing compartment and freeze until very firm.
Turn out of mold on to serving platter just before serving.

**MENU** *serves 6*

**CONSOMME**
**TOURNEDOS BEARNAISE**
**POTATO STICKS**
**APFELSTRUDEL**
Wine – Beaujolais

**Timetable** *for dinner at 8.00 p.m.*
**Day before:** *Make apfelstrudel and parsley butter.*
**5.00** *Collect ingredients and equipment.*
**7.20** *Prepare béarnaise sauce and keep warm in a bain-marie. Fry bread croûtes lightly and keep them warm.*
**7.45** *Heat consommé and potato sticks. Reheat apfelstrudel at 350°F.*
*Fry the tournedos, heat the artichokes and keep them warm without boiling. Garnish just before serving.*
**8.00** *Serve first course.*

## CONSOMME

2 cans (10½ ounces each) beef
    consommé
Water
Salt
Lemon juice

Heat the consommé gently with
water added according to directions on the can. Stir in salt if
needed, and lemon juice to taste.
Serve piping hot.

## TOURNEDOS BEARNAISE

1½ teaspoons chopped parsley
1½ cups butter, softened
3 cans (7½ ounces each)
    artichoke bottoms
Six 3 in. bread squares
7½ tablespoons white wine
    vinegar
2 tablespoons chopped shallots
6 peppercorns
1 bay leaf
Sprig of fresh tarragon
Sprig of fresh chervil
3 egg yolks
Salt and pepper
½ teaspoon dried tarragon
½ teaspoon dried chervil
3¾ tablespoons salad oil
6 tournedos (fillet of beef), about
    ½ in. thick

Blend the parsley with 5 tablespoons of butter. Form into a
square and wrap in waxed paper.
Chill until firm. Drain the
artichokes and rinse them in cold
water. Simmer in a little water for
about 7 minutes. Drain and keep
warm.
Melt 6 tablespoons of the butter
in a skillet. Fry bread squares on
both sides until golden. Drain on
paper towels and keep warm.
Put the wine vinegar, shallots,
peppercorns, bay leaf, fresh tarragon and chervil in a saucepan.
Boil rapidly until reduced to
about 1½ tablespoons liquid.
Cream the egg yolks with about 1
tablespoon butter and a pinch of
salt in a bowl. Place the bowl over
a pan of hot water. Cook, stirring,
until mixture thickens. Strain the
vinegar mixture into the cooked
egg mixture and blend thoroughly. Add ½ cup butter, in small
amounts, stirring constantly with
a wooden spoon. Continue beating until the sauce is thick. When
all of the butter has been added to
the sauce, season with salt and
pepper and add the dried tarragon
and chervil. Keep warm, not too
hot as it may separate.
Melt remaining ¼ cup butter
with the salad oil in a heavy skillet. Season the steaks with pepper
and fry quickly in the hot fat

*Apfelstrudel is a universal favorite – always with cream*

about 3 minutes on each side.
Cook a shorter length of time if
you like them very rare, longer if
you like them well done. Place
the fried toast squares on a
warmed serving platter and place
1 steak on each piece of toast.
Arrange the artichoke bottoms
between the steaks and fill with
the bearnaise sauce. Just before
serving, top each steak with a pat
of the firm parsley butter.

## APFELSTRUDEL

2 cups all-purpose flour
½ teaspoon salt
1 egg, lightly beaten
2½ tablespoons salad oil
5 tablespoons lukewarm water
3 tablespoons seedless raisins
3 tablespoons currants
6 tablespoons sugar
½ teaspoon cinnamon
2½ pound cooking apples, pared
    and grated
3 tablespoons butter, melted
1 cup ground almonds
Confectioners' sugar

Put the flour and salt in a large
bowl, make a well in the center
and pour in the egg and oil. Add
the water gradually, stirring with
a fork to make a soft, sticky

dough. Work the dough in the
bowl until it leaves the sides.
Turn it out on to a lightly floured
board and knead for 15 minutes.
Form into a ball on a clean cloth.
Cover with a warmed bowl and let
stand in a warm place 1 hour.
Combine the raisins, currants,
sugar, cinnamon and apples.
Blend thoroughly. Set aside.
Warm the rolling pin. Spread a
clean old cotton cloth on a table
and sprinkle lightly with 1–2 tablespoons flour. Place the dough
on the cloth and roll out into a
rectangle about ⅛ in. thick, lifting and turning it to prevent it
sticking to the cloth. Gently
stretch the dough, working from
the center to the outside and
using the backs of the hands,
until it is paper-thin (traditionally
it should be thin enough to read
through). Let stand to dry out a
little for 15 minutes.
Cut the dough into strips 9 in. by
6 in. Take each piece in turn,
place it on a damp tea towel,
brush it with melted butter and
sprinkle with ground almonds.
Spread the apple mixture over the
dough, leaving a ½ in. border
uncovered all around the edge.
Fold the pastry edges over the

apple mixture towards the center.
Lift the corners of the cloth
nearest you up and over the pastry, causing the strudel to roll up,
but stop after each turn to pat it
into shape and to keep the roll
even. As each roll is completed
slide it on to a lightly buttered
cookie tray. Brush the individual
strudels with melted butter. Bake
in a fairly hot oven (375°F.) for
about 40 minutes or until golden
brown. Dust with confectioners'
sugar. Serve warm with cream.

---

**MENU** *serves 6*

**MUSHROOMS A LA
GRECQUE
DUCKLING WITH
PINEAPPLE
MANGE-TOUT
PARISIENNE POTATOES
ICED ZABAIONE**
Wine – Claret (Pauillac –
Cabernet Sauvigon)

**Timetable** *for dinner at 8.00 p.m.*
**Day before:** *Make iced zabaione.
Prepare giblet stock for duckling.*
**5.00** *Joint ducklings and start to
cook. Prepare mushrooms and
chill.*
**5.45** *Place casserole in oven. Cut
potato balls and trim mange-tout.*
**7.45** *Add brandy and parsley to
casserole and keep warm.
Mange-tout (sugar peas) only take
about 5 minutes to cook in boiling
salted water. Start cooking
potatoes.*
**8.00** *Serve first course.*

---

## MUSHROOMS A LA
## GRECQUE

1 onion, finely chopped
5 tablespoons olive oil
⅝ cup dry white wine
Bouquet garni
1 clove garlic
Salt and black pepper
1 pound button mushrooms
½ pound tomatoes, peeled and
    cut up
Chopped parsley

Sauté the onion in 2½ tablespoons oil until soft. Add the wine,
bouquet garni, garlic and seasoning. Wipe the mushrooms and
seed the tomatoes. Add to onion
mixture and cook gently, uncovered, for about 10 minutes.
Remove from heat and cool.
Remove the bouquet garni and
garlic. Add the remaining oil if
needed. Chill thoroughly. Serve
sprinkled with chopped parsley.

*Nasi goreng is a popular dish in Holland. It originated in Indonesia*

## DUCKLING WITH PINEAPPLE

**Two 3½ pound ducklings**
**2 medium onions**
**4 cloves**
**Flour**
**2½ tablespoons salad oil**
**3 tablespoons butter**
**1 teaspoon ground ginger**
**2½ tablespoons honey**
**1 can (16 ounces) pineapple pieces, drained**
**8 maraschino cherries**
**1 chicken bouillon cube**
**2½ tablespoons cornstarch**
**Juice of ½ lemon**
**5 tablespoons brandy**
**Chopped parsley**

Put the duck giblets in a pan with 1 onion, stuck with cloves and water to cover. Bring to a boil. Cover and simmer for about 45 minutes. Strain and allow to cool. When cold, skim off any fat. Cut each duckling into 4 portions and remove the skin, except from the wing joints.

Dredge the duckling pieces with flour. Heat the oil and butter in a large, shallow skillet. Add the duckling pieces, flesh side down. Fry for 10 minutes or until golden brown. Remove and place in a casserole.
Finely chop the remaining onion and add to the skillet. Sauté gently for a few minutes. Add the ginger, honey, pineapple and cherries. Measure 2½ cups of the strained duck stock and add the crumbled bouillon cube. Combine the cornstarch with a little pineapple juice. Add with the stock and lemon juice to the juices in the skillet. Bring to a boil, stirring. Pour over the duck in the casserole, cover and cook in a warm oven (325°F.) for about two hours or until the duck is tender.
Remove the excess fat from the surface of the casserole with a spoon or crumpled paper towels. Warm the brandy in a small pan, ignite with a kitchen match and pour into the casserole while it is still flaming. Stir and sprinkle with chopped parsley.

## ICED ZABAIONE (Zabaglione)

**6 egg yolks**
**¾ cup sugar**
**1 cup Marsala**

Beat the yolks to a cream and mix in the sugar and Marsala. Cook in the top of a double boiler, over hot water, stirring constantly until the custard coats the back of a spoon. Pour into individual soufflé dishes. Cool. Place in the freezer and freeze until firm. Serve in individual soufflé dishes with crisp cookies.

---

**MENU** *serves 4*

### SALADE NICOISE
### NASI GORENG
### LEMON SORBET
**To drink – Lager, chilled**

**Timetable** *for dinner at 8.00 p.m.*
**Day before:** *Make lemon sorbet. (Unless you have a freezer or a refrigerator with a separate low temperature compartment it is wise not to try to keep the lemon sorbet overnight. In this case, buy the sorbet mixture on the day.)*
**5.00** *Collect ingredients and equipment.*
*Prepare dressing and vegetables for salade niçoise.*
**7.00** *Combine ingredients for salade niçoise.*
**7.15** *Cook main course except for egg and tomato garnish and keep warm. Add egg and tomato at the last possible minute.*
**8.00** *Serve first course.*

---

## SALADE NICOISE

**1 clove garlic, cut up**
**1 head lettuce**
**1 cup cooked green beans, chilled**
**1 green pepper, cut into thin rounds**
**1 red pepper, cut into thin rounds**
**1 can (2 ounces) anchovy fillets, drained**
**1 large Spanish onion, finely sliced**
**6 tomatoes, peeled and cut up**
**½ cucumber, peeled and thinly sliced**
**1 can (7 ounces) tuna, drained and flaked**
**16 black olives**
**Chopped chives**
**Vinaigrette dressing, recipe below**
**4 hard-cooked eggs, cut up**

Rub the inside of a salad bowl with the cut clove of garlic. Break up the cleaned head of lettuce and place in the bowl. Add the green beans and remaining ingredients, except the dressing and eggs. Stir the dressing in very gently, just enough to make sure all ingredients are glistening. Refrigerate for 30 minutes. Just before serving, add the hard-cooked eggs.

## VINAIGRETTE DRESSING

**⅝ cup salad oil**
**½ teaspoon dry mustard**
**¼ teaspoon French mustard**
**¼ teaspoon salt**
**Little freshly ground black pepper**
**1 teaspoon sugar**
**2 teaspoons lemon juice**
**5 tablespoons wine or cider vinegar**
**1 clove garlic, crushed**
**½ small onion, finely chopped**
**1 teaspoon mixed chopped fresh herbs**

Place all the ingredients in a screw-top jar and shake well.

## NASI GORENG

**2 onions, chopped**
**1 clove garlic, crushed**
**¼ cup butter**
**1 cup long grain rice**
**⅛ teaspoon coriander powder**
**½ teaspoon caraway seeds**
**½ teaspoon chili powder**
**1 teaspoon curry powder**
**1¼ tablespoons soy sauce**
**1 pound cold roast pork, diced**
**½ pound freshly cooked peas**
**1 egg**
**2½ tablespoons water**
**Salt and pepper**
**Tomato wedges**

Fry the onion and garlic in the butter until soft but not browned. Cook the rice in plenty of boiling salted water until cooked but still firm, about 12 minutes. Drain and rinse in cold water. Stir the spices and soy sauce into the onion and cook for 1–2 minutes. Stir in the meat and heat thoroughly. Add the cooked rice, blending all the ingredients. When the meat and rice are thoroughly heated, stir in peas. Break the egg into a bowl, beat lightly, add the water, salt and pepper. Lightly grease the bottom of a small skillet and pour in the beaten egg. When set, turn out on a warm, greased cookie tray. Cut into strips.

*A salt taste of the south of France in salade niçoise*

Turn the rice and meat mixture into a heated serving platter. Decorate top with a lattice of egg strips. Garnish with tomato.

## LEMON SORBET

**2 medium lemons**
**4 very large lemons**
**1¼ cups water**
**¾ cup sugar**

Thinly pare the rind from the smaller lemons, making sure it is free from all traces of white part. Put in a pan with the water. Bring to a boil and simmer for 10 minutes. Cut the tops off the larger lemons and scoop out all the fruit with a spoon. Squeeze the juice from the fruit and from the pared lemons.

Strain the water to remove the rind. To the water add 12½ tablespoons lemon juice and the sugar. Heat gently until the sugar dissolves. Cool. Pour the mixture into ice cube trays and place in the freezer. Chill lemon cases. Freeze the lemon mixture until it has almost set. Turn the mixture into a well-chilled bowl. Beat well. Pile into the pre-chilled lemon cases. Return to the freezer for 2–3 hours or until the mixture is firm. Cover with lemon tops and serve at once.

*Lamb cutlets wrapped in pastry and served with salad*

---

**MENU** *serves 4*

**COQUILLES ST. JACQUES**
**LAMB CUTLETS EN CROUTE**
**AVOCADO, TOMATO AND ONION SALAD**
**REMOULADE SAUCE**
**PINEAPPLE IN LIQUEUR WITH COCONUT MACAROONS**
**Wine – Claret**

**Timetable** *for dinner at 8.00 p.m.*
**Day before:** *Make coconut macaroons and store in an airtight tin.*
**5.00** *Collect ingredients and equipment. Prepare dessert. Wrap cutlets in pastry and place on cookie tray. Make salad dressing and prepare pepper, tomatoes and onion. Make rémoulade sauce.*
**6.00** *Prepare scallops ready to broil. Keep cool. Cut bread and butter.*
**6.30** *Cut avocado and combine salad ingredients, arrange as individual side salads.*
**7.45** *Put cutlets en croûte in oven.*
**7.55** *Turn down oven temperature. Brown scallops under broiler.*
**8.00** *Serve first course.*

## COQUILLES ST. JACQUES

**½ pound scallops**
**Bouquet garni**
**⅝ cup dry white wine**
**⅝ cup water**
**½ cup butter**
**2½ tablespoons lemon juice**
**1 onion, chopped**
**¼ pound button mushrooms, chopped**
**6 tablespoons flour**
**1 egg yolk**
**⅓ cup heavy cream**
**Salt**
**Freshly ground black pepper**
**½ cup fresh white breadcrumbs**
**Watercress**
**Lemon wedges**

If scallops are large, cut in pieces. Place in a saucepan with bouquet garni, wine and water. Bring to a boil, cover and simmer for 10–15 minutes or until tender.

Melt 2 tablespoons of the butter in a small pan. Add 1 tablespoon lemon juice. Stir in the onion and mushrooms. Cover and cook gently, without browning, for 10 minutes. Strain off juices and reserve.

Drain the scallops and reserve stock. Melt 3 tablespoons of the butter in a pan. Stir in the flour and cook for 1–2 minutes without browning, stirring constantly. Remove from heat and stir in the stock from the scallops. Cook over moderate heat, stirring constantly, until mixture comes to a boil. Lower heat and simmer for 3 minutes.

Blend together the egg yolk and cream. Stir in a little of the hot sauce. Pour back into the pan and stir thoroughly. Reheat the sauce over low heat but *do not boil*. Stir in the scallops, mushrooms and onions. Season to taste. Keep warm. Melt remaining butter in a

small pan, and use a little to brush the inside of 4 scallop shells or individual ramekins. Stir the breadcrumbs into the rest of the melted butter. Remove from heat and stir in 2 teaspoons lemon juice. Divide the scallop mixture between the shells. Sprinkle with the crumbs. Brown quickly under a preheated broiler. Garnish with watercress and lemon wedges. Serve immediately.

## LAMB CUTLETS EN CROUTE

**1 package (10 ounces) frozen patty shells**
**2 tablespoons butter**
**1 clove garlic, crushed**
**Salt**
**Freshly ground black pepper**
**4 lamb cutlets, trimmed**
**2 medium tomatoes, peeled and sliced**
**1 egg, beaten**

Let patty shells defrost. Remove from package and press edges together to make a sheet. Roll out on a lightly floured board into a rectangle 15 in. by 4 in. Let stand while preparing cutlets.

Cream the butter and beat in the garlic. Season to taste. Spread the garlic butter over one side of each cutlet and top with slices of tomato. Cut the pastry lengthwise into 4 narrow strips and brush with beaten egg. Use one strip to wrap around each cutlet; over-wrap each turn fractionally and keep the egg glazed side uppermost. Place the pastry-wrapped cutlets on a cookie tray. Bake in a very hot oven (450°F.) for 10 minutes. Reduce temperature to 350°F. and cook for 20 minutes. Serve piping hot.

## AVOCADO, TOMATO AND ONION SALAD

*For dressing:*
**5 tablespoons salad oil**
**2½ tablespoons wine vinegar**
**½ teaspoon sugar**
**¼ teaspoon salt**
**¼ teaspoon dry mustard**
**¼ teaspoon Dijon mustard**
**Freshly ground black pepper**

**1 avocado**
**Juice of ½ lemon**
**½ medium green pepper, thinly sliced**
**2 tomatoes, peeled and sliced**
**1 small onion, thinly sliced**
**Chopped parsley**

To make the dressing, place all the ingredients in a screw-top jar and shake vigorously.

Cut the avocado in half lengthwise. Discard the pit. Peel and slice the fruit. Squeeze a little lemon juice over to prevent discoloration.

Combine the avocado with the pepper, tomatoes and onion. Moisten with dressing to taste and garnish with parsley.

## REMOULADE SAUCE

**⅝ cup mayonnaise**
**1¼ tablespoons finely chopped mixed pickles**
**1 tablespoon prepared mustard**

Combine all the ingredients and allow to stand for a while for the flavors to mellow.

## PINEAPPLE IN LIQUEUR

**1 medium pineapple**
**Kirsch**
**Sugar, optional**

Cut the pineapple into rings about ½ in. thick. Cut around the rings in a zig-zag pattern to remove all skin and eyes. Remove the core with an apple corer. Divide the rings between individual dishes or glasses and sprinkle each with a few drops of Kirsch.
Serve with sugar if desired.

## COCONUT MACAROONS

**2 egg whites**
**1 teaspoon vanilla extract**
**½ teaspoon salt**
**1 cup sugar**
**2 cups flaked coconut**

Beat the egg whites until stiff. Gradually beat in the vanilla, salt and sugar, 1 tablespoon at a time. Fold in the coconut. Drop by teaspoons on to unglazed brown paper on a cookie tray. Bake in a warm slow oven (325°F.) for about 20 minutes or until golden.

---

## MENU *serves 6*

### CUCUMBER PORTUGAISE
### TURBOT AU FOUR
### BROCCOLI SPEARS
### CREAMED POTATOES
### STRAWBERRIES ROMANOFF

**Wine – White Wine (Pouilly Fuissé – Chenin Blanc)**

**Timetable** *for dinner at 8.00 p.m.*
**Day before:** *Make feuilles royales. Prepare fish stock, strain and refrigerate.*
**5.00** *Collect ingredients and equipment.*
*Clean mussels. Bake fleurons, prepare orange garnish and prepare vegetables.*
**5.30** *Prepare cucumber portugaise.*
**6.00** *Start to prepare dessert (decorate just before serving).*
**7.15** *Start to cook main course. Leave fish and sauce to keep warm separately.*
**7.50** *Finish off main course and keep warm.*
**8.00** *Serve first course.*

---

## CUCUMBER PORTUGAISE

**2 large cucumbers**
**1 large onion, finely chopped**
**5 tablespoons salad oil**
**4 firm ripe tomatoes, peeled and seeded**
**2 teaspoons tomato paste**
**2½ tablespoons garlic vinegar**
**Pinch of dried thyme**
**Salt**
**Freshly ground black pepper**

Thinly pare the cucumbers, using a potato peeler. Cut into

**Handy hint**

When making a crushed cookie crust for a flan, place the cookies in a plastic bag, or between sheets of waxed paper wrapped in a tea towel, before crushing. This prevents both mess and wastage.

1 in. lengths. Cut each piece into quarters lengthwise. Remove the center seeds with the point of a knife. Plunge the cucumbers into boiling salted water for 5 minutes. Drain and rinse under cold running water.
Sauté the onion in the hot oil until tender. Add the diced tomatoes, tomato paste, vinegar and thyme. Blend the cucumber with the tomato. Season well and turn into a serving platter. Chill. Serve as a first course with crusty bread.

## TURBOT AU FOUR

**¼ pound cod or fish trimmings**
**1 large onion, chopped**
**1 bay leaf**
**6 peppercorns**
**1 quart mussels**
**½ cup butter**
**5 tablespoons dry white wine**
**6 turbot steaks or cutlets, about 2½ pound**
**½ cup all-purpose flour**
**½ pound cooked, shelled shrimp**
**2 egg yolks**
**Salt**
**Freshly ground black pepper**
**1 tablespoon lemon juice**
**½ cup grated Parmesan cheese**
**1 orange**

Put the cod or fish trimmings in a saucepan with ½ the chopped onion, the bay leaf and peppercorns. Cover with water and bring to a boil. Cover and simmer for about 1 hour. Add more water during cooking time if necessary. Meanwhile place the mussels in a large bowl under running water and scrape off any mud, barnacles, seaweed and 'beards' with a sharp knife. Discard any that are cracked, open or loose. Rinse until there is no trace of sand in the bowl.
Melt 2 tablespoons butter in a pan. Sauté the remaining chopped onion until soft. Add the wine and mussels. Cover and steam, shaking often, for about 5 minutes or until mussel shells are open. Strain, reserving the liquid. Remove the mussels from their shells and discard the shells. Add the mussels and onion to the liquid in which they were cooked. Lay the fish in 1 layer in a roasting pan. Strain 2 cups of the fish stock over them. Cover with a sheet of buttered aluminum foil. Bake in a cool oven (325°F.) for about 20 minutes. The fish when cooked should offer no resistance to a skewer inserted into the thickest part of the flesh. Remove the

fish from the stock and keep warm.
Strain the stock. Melt 6 tablespoons butter in a pan. Stir in the flour and cook for 1 minute. Remove from heat and stir in the strained stock. Cook over moderate heat, stirring constantly, until mixture thickens and comes to a boil. Stir in the shrimp and mussels in their liquid. Add a little of the hot liquid to the egg yolks, beat well and return mixture to the hot sauce. Heat through. Season to taste and add lemon juice. Place the fish on a heatproof platter. Cover with sauce and sprinkle with grated cheese. Broil in a hot broiler just until lightly browned on the top. Garnish with sections of orange and serve immediately.

## STRAWBERRIES ROMANOFF

**1 quart strawberries, hulled**
**5 tablespoons port wine**
**2 tablespoons sugar**
**1 cup heavy cream**
**Vanilla sugar**

*For feuilles royales:*
**1¼ cups confectioners' sugar**
**1 egg white**

Put aside 6 whole strawberries. Thickly slice the remainder and place in a bowl with the port and sugar. Turn lightly and let stand for at least 1 hour. Spoon the fruit into individual glasses.
Beat the cream with vanilla sugar, just until it holds its shape. Spoon over the strawberries. Before serving, decorate with whole strawberries and feuilles royales.
To make feuilles royales, gradually stir the confectioners' sugar into the egg white and beat well. Make a pastry bag out of waxed paper. Spoon the icing into the bag and snip off the tip of the bag to allow the icing to flow through. Pipe the icing into leaf shapes on a sheet of aluminum foil, starting with the outline and then filling in the leaf itself. Allow to dry for about 1 hour then pipe in the center vein.
Place the leaves on foil in the broiling compartment about 8 in. from the source of heat. Broil gently for about 10 minutes or until dried out and lightly browned. The leaves should now come away from the foil easily. Turn them over and dry for a little longer. Cool on a wire rack. Wrapped in foil, feuilles royales will store for up to 2 weeks.

*Strawberries Romanoff, topped with feuilles royales*

# DINNER PARTIES FOR SLIMMERS

You can't give a dinner party and expect to lose weight, but there is no need to add any. These menus are 'maintenance' meals – delicious and filling, but not too full of carbohydrates and calories

*grilled sole with grapes*

*A really refreshing start to a meal – frozen pineapple cocktail*

## MENU *serves 6*

**FROZEN PINEAPPLE
COCKTAIL
PORK CHOPS WITH
CREAMED CABBAGE
CARROT RINGS AND
SMALL BAKED POTATOES
APRICOT YOGURT
CUSTARD**
Wine – Valpolicella – Zinfandel

**Timetable** *for dinner at 8.00 p.m.*
**In the morning:** *Make the frozen
pineapple cocktail.*
**5.00** *Collect ingredients and
equipment. Make up the apricot
yogurt custard, cook and allow to
cool. Meanwhile prepare the
cabbage to the stage of placing half
in the casserole. Scrape and slice
carrots. Scrub even-sized potatoes.*

*Pork chops with creamed cabbage are simple to prepare but tasty*

**7.00** *Put potatoes in oven at
400 °F. Grill chops, finish pork
dish and place in oven (reduce
temperature to 350°F.). Spoon
pineapple cocktail into glasses,
decorate and keep in refrigerator.
Put carrots on to cook (when they
are ready, drain, toss in butter and
parsley and keep warm).*
**8.00** *Serve first course.*

### FROZEN PINEAPPLE
COCKTAIL

**1 can (16 ounces) crushed
pineapple
1¼ cups unsweetened orange
juice
1¼ cups unsweetened grapefruit
juice
⅝ cup low calorie ginger ale
2–3 drops liquid sweetener
Mint sprigs**

Mix together all the ingredients,
except the mint. Pour into an ice
cube tray and freeze.
When frozen, but not solid, spoon
into stemmed glasses and garnish
with mint sprigs.

### PORK CHOPS WITH
CREAMED CABBAGE

**1 cabbage, trimmed and
shredded, about 3 pound
Salt
Freshly ground black pepper
1⅞ cup low fat unflavored yogurt
6 pork chops, well trimmed
Salad oil
Sage
4 tablespoons dry white wine
⅜ cup grated American cheese
Paprika**

Plunge the shredded cabbage into
boiling salted water; bring to a
boil and boil for 3 minutes.
Drain. Add the yogurt, some pepper and toss the mixture together.
Place half the cabbage in a shallow casserole, large enough to
take the chops in a single layer.
Brush the chops with oil and broil
until golden brown on both sides.
Arrange in a single layer on the
cabbage and season lightly.
Add a sprinkling of sage and the
wine to the drippings in broiler
pan. Stir well to loosen any
residue. Spoon the liquid evenly
over the chops and cover with the
remainder of the cabbage.
Bake in a moderate oven (350°F.)
for 45 minutes. If there is too
much liquid, drain it off and
reduce it to the required amount
by fast boiling in a separate pan.
Return liquid to the casserole.
Just before serving, sprinkle the
top with cheese. Garnish with
paprika before serving.

### APRICOT YOGURT
CUSTARD

**1⅞ cup low fat unflavored yogurt
3 egg yolks, beaten
1 cup dried apricots, soaked
overnight**

Beat the yogurt and egg yolks
together. Cut the apricots in half
and arrange in 6 ovenproof custard cups. Pour over the yogurt
mixture. Place the cups in a baking pan and add hot water to come
halfway up the sides of the cups.
Cook in a warm oven (325°F.) for
15–20 minutes or until set. Chill
before serving.

## MENU *serves 6*

**WATERCRESS SOUP OR
CHILLED CANTALOUP
MELON
CROWN ROAST OF LAMB
PEAS, DICED CARROTS
APPLE FOOL**
Wine – Claret
(St. Estèphe Cabernet
Sauvignon)

**Timetable** *for dinner at 8.00 p.m.*
**In the morning:** *Prepare the
watercress. Cook to purée stage if
serving hot or finish completely if
serving cold. Make the apple fool
and keep it in the refrigerator.
Prepare the crown of lamb.*
**5.00** *Pare and dice carrots. Fill the
center of crown and put to roast.*
**7.45** *Put carrots and peas on to
cook. If serving soup hot, blend the
yogurt and yolks with the soup and
put over a gentle heat.*
**8.00** *Serve first course.*

### WATERCRESS SOUP

**3 large bunches watercress,
washed
3 tablespoons butter or
margarine
3 scallions, chopped
1 chicken bouillon cube
dissolved in 3¾ cups water
1 cup low fat unflavored yogurt
3 egg yolks
Salt and pepper**

Reserve a few sprigs of watercress
for garnish. Discard any coarse
stems and chop the rest. In a large
pan, melt the butter and cook the
onions until soft. Add the watercress and stock and bring to a
boil. Purée in a blender or push
through a sieve.
Return the soup to a clean saucepan. Beat together the yogurt and
egg yolks and gradually add to the
soup. Adjust seasoning. Reheat,
but *do not boil*. Serve hot or chilled garnished with watercress.

### CROWN ROAST OF LAMB

**¼ cup salad oil
½ cup chopped green pepper
1 cup chopped mushrooms
1 cup small white onions, cooked
2 cups cooked wild or brown rice
Salt and pepper
½ teaspoon dried marjoram
5–6 pounds crown roast of lamb**

Heat the oil. Cook the green pepper and mushrooms until barel
tender. Add the onions, rice, sal
pepper and marjoram. Fill lam
with this mixture. Place on a rac

a roasting pan. Bake in a pre-
eated warm oven (325°F.) for
½–3 hours, until cooked to taste.

## PPLE FOOL

oranges
¼ cups fresh apple sauce, see
  below
½ teaspoons lemon juice
 teaspoon ground ginger
iquid sweetener
cup buttermilk
envelope unflavored gelatin
¾ tablespoons water
egg whites

ut the oranges in halves, using a
harp pointed, serrated knife and
aking a zig-zag edge on each
alf. Carefully remove the orange
uit, making sure it is free of
hite part, membranes and seeds.
ut into small pieces. Clean out
e shells and chill.

ix together the apple sauce,
mon juice, ginger and
weetener to taste. Add the
range pieces and buttermilk.
often the gelatin in the water in
small bowl. Place over a pan of
ot water and heat until gelatin is
issolved. Stir the dissolved gela-
n into the buttermilk mixture.
eat the egg whites until stiff.
hen apple mixture is beginning
 set, fold in the egg whites. Pile
to the orange cases and top with
 twist of fresh orange. Chill
efore serving.

ote: To make 1¼ cups apple
auce, pare and slice 1 pound
oking apples. Cook in very lit-
e water until soft. Purée in an
lectric blender or put through a
od mill.

**7.00** *Take out the mint freeze (if it
is solid, let it stand in the body of
the refrigerator to soften).
Complete the cocktail and leave in
the refrigerator. Skin grapes and
remove seeds.
Put the potatoes on to cook in
boiling salted water.*
**7.45** *Put the peas on to cook.
Cream the potatoes and keep them
warm. Broil soles and keep warm;
garnish just before serving.
Drain peas, toss with butter and
keep warm.*
**8.00** *Serve first course.*

fruit pieces. Pile into the grapefruit shells. Top with the mint
freeze and serve immediately.

## GRILLED SOLE WITH GRAPES

**4–8 fillets of sole, depending on
  size**
**Butter or margarine, melted**
**Salt**
**Pepper**
**Lemon wedges**
**Green grapes**
**Parsley**

*Apple fool has an added zest when made with orange juice and served in the orange skins*

imetable *for dinner at 8.00 p.m.*
 the morning: *Make up the mint
eeze and put in the freezing
mpartment.*
.00 *Pare potatoes, leave in cold
ater.*
'ash grapes and parsley. Prepare
e oranges and grapefruit.
ut out the cheeses to allow the
avors to develop – leave covered.*

## GRAPEFRUIT AND ORANGE COCKTAIL

*For mint freeze:*
**1¼ tablespoons lemon juice**
**1 cup low calorie lemonade**
**2½ tablespoons finely chopped
  fresh mint**

**2 large grapefruit**
**2 large oranges**

Combine the lemon juice,
lemonade and mint and pour into
an ice tray. Freeze until it is soft
ice but not solid.
Meanwhile, halve the grapefruit,
using a zig-zag cutter to give a
decorative edge. Remove the fruit
from the halves.
Pare and section the oranges,
remove the membranes and cut
into pieces.
Combine the orange and grape-

Preheat broiling compartment
and pan. Brush the pan with butter and place the fillets on it.
Brush with melted butter. Place
the pan about 3 in. from source of
heat. Broil fish for 5–8 minutes,
depending on thickness of fish,
brushing twice during cooking
period with melted butter.
Sprinkle with salt and pepper.
Place on a heated serving platter
and garnish with lemon wedges,
green grapes and parsley.

**Timetable** *for dinner at 8.00 p.m.*
**In the morning:** *Make the orange
pots and allow to chill. Wash
lettuce and other salad
ingredients, shake well, put in a
plastic bag and crisp in the
refrigerator. Make up the salad
dressing.*
**5.00** *Prepare the avocado soup.*
**6.00** *Make up the casserole and put
in the oven at about 7.00.*
**7.45** *Toss the salad. Pour soup into
bowls; garnish.*
**8.00** *Serve first course.*

## CHILLED AVOCADO SOUP

**3 ripe avocados**
**Juice of 1 lemon**
**1 can (10½ ounces) consommé**
**¾ cup low fat unflavored yogurt**
**Salt and pepper**
**Chopped chives**

Halve the avocados, scoop out the
fruit and press through a nylon
sieve, using a wooden spoon. Add
the other ingredients, except the
chives, and season well.

Alternatively, place all the ingredients (except the chives) in an electric blender and blend until smooth. Serve chilled with a few chopped chives.

## ITALIAN VEAL CASSEROLE

**3¾ tablespoons salad oil**
**2 pound lean veal, trimmed and diced**
**Salt**
**Freshly ground black pepper**
**2 cloves garlic, chopped**
**1¼ cups dry white wine**
**½ pound tomatoes, peeled and chopped**
**1½ tablespoons tomato paste**
**2 sprigs rosemary**
**Strip of lemon rind**

Heat the oil in a skillet. Add the meat, salt and pepper and continue cooking until the meat is golden brown, about 8–10 minutes. Add the garlic. Stir in the wine, tomatoes, tomato paste, rosemary and lemon rind. Add just enough water to cover.

Pour into a casserole, cover with a tightly fitting lid. Cook in a moderate oven (350°F.) for about 1 hour or until meat is tender. Remove rosemary and lemon rind before serving.

## ORANGE POTS

**3¾ tablespoons orange juice**
**2 tablespoons lemon juice**
**½ package unflavored gelatin**
**1½ cups cottage cheese**
**7½ tablespoons buttermilk**
**Liquid sweetener, optional**
**1 sliced orange**

Put the orange juice and lemon juice in a small bowl. Soften gelatin in juices. Place bowl in a pan of hot water and heat gently until the gelatin is dissolved.

Put the orange gelatin into a blender container. Add the cottage cheese and buttermilk. Blend until smooth. Add a few drops of sweetener, if desired. Divide mixture between small dishes or dessert glasses. Chill. Decorate with quarters of sliced orange just before serving.

---

**MENU** *serves 4*

**APPLE-TUNA SALAD**
**MARINATED LAMB KEBABS**
**BOILED RICE AND BROILED TOMATOES**
**CRUNCHY SPICED PEARS**
Wine – Beaujolais – Gamay

224

*Chicken Louisette is a delicious way to serve chicken in its own gravy*

**Timetable** *for dinner at 8.00 p.m.*
**In the morning:** *Make up the marinade. Dice the lamb and leave to marinate during the day. Poach the pears. Make up the cheese dressing.*
**5.00** *Prepare ingredients for the kebabs. Make up the kebabs on skewers.*
**6.30** *Make up the apple-tuna salad (the apple should not discolor if sufficient lemon juice is used).*
**7.15** *Finish preparing the pears, but do not broil them.*
**7.30** *Put rice on to cook.*
**7.45** *Drain the rice; keep hot. Broil the kebabs and tomatoes and keep hot. (When the kebabs are cooked, leave the broiler on a low heat and turn it up again shortly before the end of the main course. Then broil the pears.)*
**8.00** *Serve first course.*

---

## APPLE-TUNA SALAD

**1 can (7 ounces) tuna fish**
**1 small green pepper, seeded and chopped**
**4 medium red-skinned apples**

*For dressing:*
**½ cup cottage cheese**
**Juice of ½ lemon**
**Salt and pepper**

Drain and flake the tuna and mix with the pepper. Wash the apples, discard the core and scoop out the inside of each, leaving a ¼ in. wall. Chop the scooped-out apple and add to the tuna mixture.

Combine the cottage cheese, lemon juice and seasoning and sieve or blend until smooth and creamy. Add 1–2 tablespoons to the tuna mixture and mix thoroughly. Pile into the apple shells. Chill. Serve the rest of the dressing with the apples.

## MARINATED LAMB KEBABS

**1 pound lean lamb, trimmed and cut in 1 in. cubes**
**3¾ tablespoons olive oil**
**1¼ tablespoons lemon juice**
**Salt and pepper**
**1 clove garlic, crushed**
**4 small firm tomatoes, cut up**
**8 slices bacon, rolled up**
**8 button mushrooms, washed**
**A few bay leaves, optional**
**2 small onions, cut up, optional**
**Melted butter**

Combine the lamb cubes, olive oil, lemon juice, seasoning and garlic. Let stand at least 2 hours, tossing occasionally.

Thread 8 skewers alternately with meat cubes, halved tomatoes, bacon rolls and whole mushrooms. If desired, a bay leaf or an onion quarter may be placed on each side of the meat pieces to give more flavor.

Brush with melted butter. Preheat the broiling compartment and pan. Broil for 10–15 minutes, turning about 3 times, or until the meat is cooked to desired degree of doneness.

Serve with plain boiled rice.

## CRUNCHY SPICED PEARS

**1 pound eating pears, pared and sliced**
**⅝ cup water**
**Finely grated rind of ½ lemon**
**Small piece of cinnamon stick**
**Artificial sweetener**
**¼ cup cornflakes**
**2 tablespoons butter**

Poach the pear slices in the water combined with the lemon rind and cinnamon until tender. Add sweetener to taste. Drain the pears and place in a shallow heat-proof dish. Sprinkle with corn flakes and dot with butter. Broil under a heated broiler until pears are piping hot and bubbling.

*The perfect slimmers' dessert – orange pots are non-fattening, yet tasty and filling*

Beat together the egg yolks and milk, add the liquid from the pan. Return to the heat, in a double boiler over hot water, and heat very gently, without boiling, until the sauce thickens. Pour the sauce over the chicken and garnish with ham and parsley.

## RASPBERRY DELIGHT

**2 boxes fresh raspberries**
**½ cup orange juice**
**Mint leaves**

Divide the cleaned and well-drained raspberries between 6 dessert glasses. Divide orange juice between glasses. Chill. Serve decorated with mint leaves.

## MENU *serves 8*

**SHRIMP ZUCCHINI**
**SWISS VEAL**
**NEW POTATOES AND**
**GREEN BEANS**
**STRAWBERRY SPONGE**
**Wine – White Bordeaux (Graves)**

**Timetable** *for dinner at 8.00 p.m.*
**In the morning:** *Make the strawberry sponge and leave in the refrigerator. Make up the cheese dressing.*
*Prepare the vegetables.*
**6.15** *Make the Swiss veal and put on to cook.*
**7.00** *Blanch the zucchini, drain and cool.*
**7.15** *Put the potatoes to cook. When ready, drain, toss in butter and keep hot. (Sprinkle the potatoes with chopped parsley before serving.) Fill the zucchini with shrimp and finish off.*
**7.45** *Put beans to cook. When ready, drain and toss in butter. Remove the Swiss veal from the heat. Thicken the sauce, reheat and pour over the meat. Keep hot. Decorate the strawberry sponge.*
**8.00** *Serve first course.*

## SHRIMP ZUCCHINI

**8 small even-sized zucchini**
**1 can (7 ounces) shrimp, drained**
**1¼ tablespoons lemon juice**
**Freshly ground black pepper**

*For cheese dressing:*
**½ cup cottage cheese**
**Juice of ½ lemon**
**Salt and pepper**

Remove a thin slice lengthwise from each zucchini. Scoop out the seeds and discard. Blanch for 3–4 minutes in boiling water. Remove zucchini and cool. Fill

## MENU *serves 6*

**CRAB DIP PLATTER**
**CHICKEN LOUISETTE**
**HERBED RICE AND**
**BROCCOLI**
**RASPBERRY DELIGHT**
**Wine – Gewürz Traminer**

**Timetable** *for dinner at 8.00 p.m.*
**In the morning:** *Put the chicken wings out to thaw. Squeeze sufficient orange juice.*
**4.00** *Pick over the raspberries. Wash in ice-cold water; drain on paper towels. Put into glasses (do not pour on orange juice until just before serving). Make the crab dip. Prepare the dunks and keep in plastic wrap. Prepare the broccoli (if fresh) and the vegetables for the chicken.*
**5.30** *Make up the chicken louisette, put in the oven at about 7.00. Arrange the crab dip platter.*
**7.15** *Put rice into fast boiling water with a teaspoon of mixed herbs.*
**7.30** *Cook the broccoli. Drain rice and keep hot.*
**7.45** *Drain broccoli, toss in butter and keep hot. Finish the chicken and keep hot.*
**8.00** *Serve first course.*

## CRAB DIP PLATTER

**1 can (6 ounces) crab meat**
**⅝ cup low fat unflavored yogurt**
**Salt and freshly ground black pepper**
**2 tomatoes, cut up**
**Celery sticks**
**Olives**
**Radishes**
**Cauliflower flowerets**
**Carrot sticks**

Combine the crab meat and yogurt. Season. Put in a small dish and chill.
Place the dish on a large platter

### Handy hint

Almonds are best bought with their skins on and blanched as you need them – this way they are juicier. If you have only blanched almonds in your store cupboard, soak them in hot water for 30 minutes to make them plump and juicy again

and garnish with tomato quarters, celery sticks, olives, radishes, cauliflower and carrot sticks.

## CHICKEN LOUISETTE

**6 chicken breasts with wings attached**
**Salt and pepper**
**2½ tablespoons salad oil**
**1 onion, sliced**
**2 cloves garlic, crushed**
**1¼ cups stock**
**1¼ cups dry white wine**
**Bouquet garni**
**1 small cucumber, pared and thinly sliced**
**4 egg yolks**
**2½ tablespoons milk**
**¼ pound lean cooked ham, chopped**
**Chopped parsley**

Season the chicken and fry in the hot oil until well browned on all sides. Pour off any excess drippings. Add the onion, garlic, stock, wine and bouquet garni. Bring to a boil. Reduce heat, cover and simmer for about 45 minutes or until tender. Discard the bouquet garni. Add the cucumber and simmer for 5 minutes. Arrange the chicken and vegetables on a hot serving platter. Keep warm.

*Chilled avocado soup is just right for a summer evening*

## MENU *serves 4*

**OYSTERS AU NATUREL**
**ORANGE-APPLE STEAK**
**GREEN BEANS**
**GINGER FRUIT SALAD**
**Wine – With the oysters,**
**White Bordeaux**
**(Entre-deux-Mers)**
**With the main course,**
**Red Burgundy**
**(Nuits St. Georges – Pinot Noir)**

**Timetable** *for dinner at 8.00 p.m.*
**In the morning:** *Make the ginger fruit salad. Leave in refrigerator.*
**5.30** *Top and tail the beans. Mix together the stuffing for the steak.*
**7.00** *Prepare brown bread and butter; cut up lemon wedges. Prepare bed of cracked ice for the oysters; keep frozen.*
**7.30** *Put the beans on to cook. Prepare the steaks. Open the oysters and arrange on the serving platter.*
*Drain the beans, toss in butter and keep warm.*
**7.50** *Broil steaks and keep warm (remember that steaks will continue cooking while keeping warm, so be careful not to broil for too long).*
**8.00** *Serve first course.*

## OYSTERS AU NATUREL

**24 oysters**

Scrub the oyster shells. Hold the deep half of the shell in the left hand (protected by a thick cloth) and work the point of an oyster knife into the hinge between the shells to cut the ligament. Trim off the beard and any threads attached to the shell. Place them on a bed of cracked ice, arranged so that the pointed end is towards the center of the dish.
Serve with thin slices of brown bread and butter and lemon wedges. Provide seafood cocktail sauce for those who like it.

## ORANGE-APPLE STEAK

**4 individual top round or**
 **boneless sirloin steaks, cut**
 **1 in. thick**
**5 tablespoons fresh**
 **breadcrumbs**
**2½ teaspoons coarsely chopped**
 **parsley**
**Grated rind and juice of 1 orange**
**1 cooking apple, not pared but**
 **grated**
**2 tablespoons butter, melted**
**1 egg yolk**
**Salt and pepper**
**Salad oil**

Trim all visible fat from steaks. Using a sharp knife, slit each one horizontally to within ½ in. of the edge and open it out. Mix the breadcrumbs, parsley, orange rind, apple, melted butter and egg yolk together. Season to taste. Spread this mixture on one half of the steak, fold the other half over. Brush steak with oil.
Preheat broiling compartment and pan. Place steaks on pan and broil for 3–7 minutes on each side, according to taste. Heat the orange juice and pour over the steaks.

with shrimp. Sprinkle with lemon juice and freshly ground black pepper.
Combine the cheese, lemon juice, salt and pepper. Beat until smooth and creamy. Spread on top of shrimp. Chill and serve.

## SWISS VEAL

**4 pound boneless veal, cut in**
 **cubes**
**Seasoned flour**
**2½ tablespoons salad oil**
**1 bunch carrots, diced**
**½ pound shallots, chopped**
**1¼ tablespoons lemon juice**
**1¼ cups stock**
**⅝ cup dry white wine**
**Bouquet garni**
**4 egg yolks, beaten**
**1¼ cups unflavored yogurt**
**Salt and pepper**
**Chopped parsley**

Dust the veal lightly with seasoned flour. Heat the oil in a heavy Dutch oven. Add the veal and fry until pale golden in colour. Add the carrots, shallots, lemon juice, stock, wine and bouquet garni. Simmer gently for about 1½ hours or until the meat is tender.

Blend the egg yolks with the yogurt. Add a little of the hot stock from the veal and stir well. Return to veal mixture in Dutch oven. Reheat gently, but *do not boil.* Adjust seasoning. Serve sprinkled with chopped parsley.

## STRAWBERRY SPONGE

**2 envelopes unflavored gelatin**
**1¼ cups water**
**2½ cups strawberry purée, made**
 **from 2 pints berries**
**2 egg whites**
**½ cup evaporated milk**
**Small whole strawberries**

Soften the gelatin in the water in a bowl. Place the bowl in a pan over hot water and heat until gelatin is dissolved. Add to the puréed strawberries, stirring continuously and evenly until the mixture begins to thicken. When it is just starting to set and is the consistency of unbeaten egg white, add the egg whites and evaporated milk and beat until foamy with a rotary beater or electric mixer.
Divide the mixture between 8 dessert glasses. Chill until set. Just before serving garnish with whole strawberries.

### Handy hint

When baking bread, to test if a loaf is cooked, tap it underneath with your knuckles. If it is cooked it will sound hollow.

## GINGER FRUIT SALAD

**2 apples, cored**
**2 apricots, pared and pitted**
**1 orange, pared and sectioned**
**¾ cup low-calorie ginger ale**
**2 bananas**
**2½ tablespoons lemon juice**
**Small bunch green grapes**

Dice the apples and apricots, add the orange sections and ginger ale and let stand. Slice the bananas and mix with the lemon juice and grapes. Mix all the fruits and juices together and serve in dessert dishes.

# MAXI-MENUS
# FOR DINNER

Whether your dinner party is a family
occasion or something more formal, choose
a menu that is simple to prepare and
that will give you time to welcome your guests.

## SMOKED TROUT WITH LEMON WEDGES
## LAMB EN CROUTE
## ZUCCHINI AND CARROTS
## CREME ST. VALENTINE
## RUM GLAZED PEARS

Wine – Loire (Pouilly-Fumé) – Savignon Blanc

**Timetable** *for dinner at 8.00 p.m.*
**Day before:** *Marinate, stuff and cook leg of lamb; cool and store in refrigerator.*
**In the morning:** *Roll out pastry and wrap lamb; return to refrigerator. Prepare carrots.*
**6.30** *Assemble ingredients and equipment. Start to cook pears; when cooked keep warm. Skin trout if wished (leave on the head and tail) and serve on individual plates. Make crème St. Valentine.*
**7.15** *Put lamb en croûte in oven and make gravy.*
**7.45** *Cook carrots; when ready, keep hot. Cook zucchini for about 10 minutes.*
**8.00** *Serve first course.*

A leg of lamb, stuffed and served 'en croûte' serves 10 easily

## LAMB EN CROUTE

**4½ pound leg of lamb, boned**
**⅝ cup red wine**
**1 pound pork sausage meat**
**¼ pound sliced bacon, chopped**
**2 tablespoons pistachio nuts, blanched and peeled**
**Salt**
**Freshly ground black pepper**
**2 tablespoons butter or margarine**
**½ pound onions, sliced**
**Sprig of fresh thyme or a little dried thyme**
**1 bay leaf**
**3 parsley stalks**
**1 clove garlic, crushed**
**1 can (10½ ounces) consommé**
**2 packages (10 ounces each) frozen patty shells**
**2 eggs, beaten**
**Flour**
**2 tablespoons cornstarch**

Marinate the lamb in the wine for 2–3 hours, turning occasionally. Combine the sausage meat, bacon and nuts. Season well. Remove the lamb from wine and dry well on paper towels. Stuff the bone cavity of the lamb with the sausage meat mixture. Sew up both ends with fine string.
Melt the butter in a large skillet. Brown the lamb quickly on all sides. Transfer to a large casserole. Reheat the fat, add the onions and sauté lightly. Add to the casserole with the herbs, wine and consommé. Cover and cook in a warm oven (325°F.) for 2 hours. Remove the meat and cool quickly. Reserve pan juices.
Remove patty shells and let thaw. Place close together on a board and press edges together. Roll out into an oblong 20 in. by 10 in. Brush the surface of the meat with beaten egg and dust lightly with flour. Place meat in the center of the pastry and make a parcel by folding the short pastry ends into the center. Trim off the excess and brush the pastry with beaten egg. Bring together the long edges and seal with beaten egg. Place the croûte, seam side down, on a cookie tray.
Roll out the pastry trimmings and cut some leaves to decorate. Place these on the croûte and brush again with the egg.
Bake in a very hot oven (450°F.) for 45 minutes. Cover with aluminum foil if the pastry is in danger of over-browning.
To make the gravy, remove the fat from the pan juices by pressing a sheet of paper towel on the surface. There should be about 2½–3 cups juices. Thicken with the cornstarch blended with a little of the cold liquid. Bring to a boil, simmer until thickened and adjust the seasoning.

## CREME ST. VALENTINE
*6 servings*

**2 packages (3 ounces each) cream cheese, softened**
**4 large eggs, separated**
**⅝ cup heavy cream**
**3 tablespoons coffee flavoring**
**6 tablespoons sugar**
**Milk chocolate**

Beat together the cream cheese, egg yolks and cream until thick. Stir in the coffee flavoring. Beat the egg whites until they stand in peaks, gradually add sugar and continue beating. Pour the coffee cream over the egg whites and fold through. Pour into 6 dessert dishes and chill thoroughly. Decorate with curls of milk chocolate, pared from a block with a potato peeler.

## RUM GLAZED PEARS
*6 servings*

**6 large firm eating pears**
**Juice and finely grated rind of 1 lemon**
**⅝ cup sugar**
**1¼ tablespoons rum**
**1¼ tablespoons arrowroot**
**2½ tablespoons cold water**

Pare the pears thinly, keeping the stems intact. Dip in lemon juice to prevent discoloration. Place the pears in a single layer in a saucepan. Pour over the lemon juice, the grated rind and sufficient water to cover the pears to a depth of 1 in. Cover and bring to a boil. Lower heat and simmer for 20 minutes or until the pears are tender.
Meanwhile, place the sugar in a heavy saucepan. Place over medium heat and cook without stirring until the sugar caramelizes. Cool slightly. Remove the pears from the pan. Gradually stir the poaching liquid and the rum into the caramel. Work with a wooden spoon to remove the caramel sediment from the base of the pan. Blend the arrowroot with the water and gradually add it to the

*Offer Crème St. Valentine and Rum Glazed Pears as alternative desserts*

sauce, stirring all the time. Bring to a boil.

Replace the pears in the sauce. Cover and simmer gently for 15–20 minutes. Serve warm with whipped cream.

---

## MENU *serves 12*

**AVOCADO, GRAPEFRUIT AND SHRIMP COCKTAIL**
**CHICKEN WITH GINGER**
**BOILED RICE**
**STRAWBERRY TIMBALE**
**NORWEGIAN CREAM**

**Wine – White Burgundy (Chablis – Chardonnay)**

**Timetable** *for dinner at 8.00 p.m.*
**A few days before:** *Make meringue cases; store in an airtight tin.*

**In the morning:** *Prepare and cook custard for Norwegian cream. Hull strawberries. If wished fry chicken joints and get ready to put in oven; keep in refrigerator.*
**6.00** *Prepare grapefruit and dressing for cocktail. Start to cook chicken with ginger. Decorate desserts.*
**7.00** *Prepare avocados and finish*

preparing cocktails.
**7.30** *Boil rice; when cooked, keep hot.*
**8.00** *Serve first course.*

---

## AVOCADO, GRAPEFRUIT AND SHRIMP COCKTAIL

**2 grapefruit**
**1 cup salad oil**
**¼ cup wine vinegar**
**Salt and pepper**
**Sugar**
**1¼ teaspoons French mustard**
**3 ripe avocados**
**1 large head lettuce, well cleaned and drained**
**2½ cups mayonnaise**
**¾ pound cooked shrimp**

Pare the grapefruit with a sharp knife, removing all the white part. Section the grapefruit over a bowl to catch all the juice.
Blend together the oil, vinegar, seasoning, a little sugar and the mustard. Set aside.
Cut the avocados in half lengthwise, discard the pits and pare away the skin. Cut most of the fruit into small dice, but reserve half an avocado to cut 24 thin slices for garnish. Toss the avocado in the grapefruit juice to

prevent discoloration. Drain the avocado. Shred the lettuce and toss with the avocado and the mixed dressing. Arrange in the bottom of 12 medium-sized glasses. Lightly fold the shrimp into the mayonnaise and spoon over the avocado. Garnish with slices of avocado and grapefruit.

---

## CHICKEN WITH GINGER

**7½ tablespoons salad oil**
**¾ cup butter or margarine**
**12 chicken breasts with wings**
**¾ cup seasoned flour**
**3 large onions, sliced**
**1¼ tablespoons powdered ginger**
**6 teaspoons French mustard**
**5⅝ cup chicken stock**
**7½ tablespoons medium dry sherry**
**Salt**
**Freshly ground black pepper**
**¾ pound button mushrooms, wiped and stalks removed**

Heat the oil and half the butter in a skillet. Toss the chicken pieces in seasoned flour to coat and fry in hot fat until evenly browned on all sides. Remove from pan and place in a large casserole.

Reheat the fat, add the onions and fry until soft but not browned. Stir in any excess seasoned flour, ginger and mustard. Cook, stirring, for a few minutes.
Remove from heat and stir in the stock and sherry. Cook over medium heat, stirring, until mixture comes to a boil. Adjust seasoning and pour over the chicken. In a clean skillet, melt the remaining butter. Quickly sauté the mushrooms. Add to the casserole. Cover tightly. Cook in a warm oven (325°F.) for 1½ hours or until chicken is tender.

---

## STRAWBERRY TIMBALE
*6 servings*

**4 egg whites**
**1 cup sugar**
**2 cups heavy cream**
**1 quart strawberries, hulled and sliced**

Draw an 8-in. circle on non-stick paper and place on a cookie tray. Beat the egg whites until they stand in stiff peaks. Add half the sugar, beating constantly until very stiff. Fold in the remaining sugar. Spread some of the meringue mixture within the circle to form a base. Place the rest of the meringue in a pastry bag with a large star nozzle. Pipe a circle of shell shapes to border the base. Pipe a circle of meringue just inside the shelled border to form an interior wall. Pipe a similar double wall of shells in a circle on top and complete the case by piping a final single border. This forms the timbale shape, with a deep hollow in the center. Dry just below the center of the oven at 300°F. for about 3 hours or until crisp. Let cool on a wire rack. Remove the paper.
Whip the cream until it holds its shape. Heap the cream and two-thirds of the strawberries in the meringue case. Decorate with the remaining berries.

---

## NORWEGIAN CREAM
*6 servings*

**¾ cup apricot preserves**
**3 large eggs**
**1 tablespoon sugar**
**Few drops vanilla flavoring**
**1⅞ cups milk**
**3 squares semi-sweet chocolate**
**1¼ cups heavy cream, whipped**

Cover the bottom of a 1½-quart soufflé dish with apricot preserves. In a bowl, mix together 2 whole eggs, 1 egg yolk, the sugar and vanilla flavoring. Heat the

229

milk but do not boil. Pour the hot milk over the egg mixture, stirring constantly. Strain over the preserves in the soufflé dish. Cover dish with aluminum foil and place in a baking pan with hot water to come halfway up the sides of the dish. Cook in a moderate oven (325°F.) for about 1 hour 45 minutes or until the custard is set. Remove dish from hot water and let stand until cold.

Pare the chocolate with a potato peeler so that it forms curls. Cover the surface of the custard with about half of these.

Beat the remaining egg white until stiff. Fold into about a third of the whipped cream. Spoon over the chocolate. Pipe the remaining cream around the edge of the dish and fill the center with the remaining chocolate curls.

*Fonds d'artichauts is simple, but looks luxurious*

## MENU serves 8

**FONDS D'ARTICHAUTS**
**CROWN ROAST OF PORK WITH ORANGE RICE**
**BUTTERED CAULIFLOWER**
**FRUIT MERINGUE**
Wine – Hock (Liebfraumilch)

**Timetable** *for dinner at 8.00 p.m.*
**In the morning:** *Prepare crown of pork and make stock; strain and cool. Prepare flavoring vegetables for orange rice. Make pastry base for dessert.*
**5.00** *Assemble ingredients and equipment. Marinate artichokes and boil eggs. Finish dessert. Prepare cauliflower and keep covered.*
**5.30** *Put pork to cook.*
**6.00** *Make up first course.*
**7.15** *Cook rice and keep warm.*
**7.45** *Dish up pork and keep hot. Make gravy. Cook cauliflower.*
**8.00** *Serve first course.*

## FONDS D'ARTICHAUTS

1 can (6½ ounces) artichoke bottoms, drained
Juice of 1 lemon
2½ tablespoons salad oil
Salt and pepper
8 small hard-cooked eggs
⅝ cup thick mayonnaise
Pinch of sugar
Paprika
Lemon slices
Parsley

Marinate 8 of the artichoke bottoms for 1 hour in 1¼ teaspoons

lemon juice, the oil, salt and pepper. Drain and arrange on serving platters. Shell the eggs and slice off the bottoms so they will stand. Place an egg upright on each artichoke bottom. Add the remaining lemon juice and sugar to the mayonnaise. Spoon it into a pastry bag fitted with a small star nozzle and pipe it around the base of the artichokes. Dust the eggs with paprika. Garnish with lemon slices and parsley.

## CROWN ROAST OF PORK WITH ORANGE RICE

2 loin of pork, 7 ribs on each
¼ cup shortening, melted
Salt and pepper
¼ cup butter or margarine
2 stalks celery, finely diced
1 large onion, finely chopped
¼ teaspoon curry powder
1½ cups long grain rice
Juice of 2 large oranges
1 cup seedless raisins
1 tablespoon finely grated orange rind
1¼ tablespoons sherry
1 orange, sliced

*For stock:*

1 onion, peeled and stuck with 5 cloves
1 carrot, peeled
1 stalk celery
8 peppercorns

Ask your butcher to skin the meat, remove the chine bones and trim the rib bones to an equal length. Keep the bone trimmings for the stock.

Score across both joints 1½ in. down from the bone tips. Remove

the fatty ends and carefully scrape the bone tips free of meat. Place the joints back to back, with the rib bones outermost. Sew the joint ends together, using a trussing needle and fine string. Tie the string.

Place the crown shaped pork in a roasting pan and tightly pack the cavity with aluminum foil to maintain the shape while cooking. Brush the outside of the meat with melted fat. Season. Cover the tips of the bones with foil to prevent charring. Roast in a hot oven (425°F.) for about 2¼ hours, basting frequently.

Meanwhile, place the bone pieces, meat trimmings, onion, carrot, celery and peppercorns in a pan. Cover with water and simmer for 2 hours, adding more water if necessary during cooking time. Strain stock and set aside. Melt the butter in a large saucepan. Add the diced celery and onion and sauté until tender. Stir

### Handy hint

To refresh a stale loaf, wrap it in aluminum foil and place it in the oven at 450°F. for 8–10 minutes. Cool in the foil.

in the curry powder and cook for 1 minute. Add the rice, 3 cups of the pork stock and the orange juice. Season well. Cover and simmer for 20 minutes or until the rice is tender. Add the raisins and orange rind. Reheat gently. Remove the foil from the pork crown and transfer meat to a serving platter. Pour off the fat from the roasting pan. Add about 1¼ cups stock to the sediment and season well. Stir the sediment into the stock and add the sherry. Cook for 1 minute. Strain into a gravy boat. Spoon the hot orange rice into the center of the crown and around the meat. Garnish with orange slices that have been warmed in the oven.

## FRUIT MERINGUE

1 package (10 ounces) frozen patty shells
1¼ tablespoons milk
1 large juicy lemon
1¼ cups sugar
2 pears, pared, cored and sliced
2 apples, pared, cored and sliced
2 peaches, pared, pitted and sliced
2 oranges, peeled and sectioned
¼ pound black grapes, halved and seeded
1 can (16 ounces) pineapple pieces, drained
1 can (8 ounces) red cherries, drained and pitted
3 egg whites
Glacé cherries, halved
Angelica
2 tablespoons toasted, flaked almonds
1 lemon, sliced

Thaw patty shells. Remove from package and place together on a board. Press together. Roll out into a 9 in. circle. Place on a cookie tray. Brush with milk and prick all over with a fork. Bake in a very hot oven (450°F.) for 15 minutes or until well risen and golden brown. Cool.

Thinly pare the rind from the lemon with a potato peeler. Put the rind in a small pan with the juice of the lemon and 1¼ cups water. Bring to a boil and continue boiling until the liquid is reduced by half. Strain. Return to the pan and add ½ cup sugar. Dissolve the sugar over low heat. Bring back to a boil and continue boiling until the syrup is reduced by half. Cool.

Place the pastry base on a cookie tray and top it with the fruit, arranged in layers to a height of 3–4 in. Flatten the top slightly.

Spoon the lemon syrup carefully over the fruit, allowing it to run through to the pastry base.
Beat the egg whites until stiff but not dry. Beat in remaining sugar, a little at a time, beating until mixture stands in stiff peaks. Frost entire cake and fruit with the meringue, smoothing over top and sides. Place in a very cool oven (200°F.) for 2–2½ hours until the meringue is firm but not colored. Cool, then transfer to a serving platter. Decorate the meringue with halved glacé cherries, strips of angelica and toasted almonds. Halve the lemon slices and arrange around the base of the meringue.

*Baked ham with an orange caramel glaze*

---

## MENU *serves 12*

### CHILLED CREAM OF SPINACH SOUP
### SPICED ORANGE HAM
### BROAD BEANS, CARROTS AND RICE
### COFFEE CREAM RING
### FRESH FRUIT SALAD
**Wine – Claret (Pauillac Cabernet – Sauvignon)**

**Timetable** *for dinner at 8.00 p.m.*
**Day before:** *Make soup; store in refrigerator. Prepare orange caramel glaze; store in refrigerator. Make choux ring and store in an airtight tin.*
*Soak ham.*

**In the morning:** *Make fruit salad. Prepare vegetables ready for cooking.*
**5.30** *Start ham cooking. Finish coffee cream ring.*
**7.15** *Glaze ham and heat remaining glaze. Cook rice and keep hot. When ham is cooked, keep hot. Make croûtons.*
**7.45** *Cook vegetables. Pour soup into individual cups and add cream.*
**8.00** *Serve first course.*

---

## CHILLED CREAM OF SPINACH SOUP

**2 pound spinach**
**½ cup butter or margarine**
**2 onions, chopped**
**7½ cups chicken stock**
**½ teaspoon salt**
**Freshly ground black pepper**
**1½ tablespoons lemon juice**
**2 bay leaves**
**¼ cup all-purpose flour**
**⅝ cup light cream**
**Croûtons of fried bread**
**Grated cheese**

Wash and drain the spinach and discard tough stalks. In a large pan, melt half the butter and sauté the onions until soft but not colored. Add the spinach and sauté for 5 minutes, stirring frequently. Add the stock, salt, pepper, lemon juice and bay leaves. Bring to a boil. Cover and simmer for about 20 minutes. Discard bay leaves. Purée in an electric blender.
In a clean pan melt the remaining butter. Stir in the flour and cook for 1 minute. Remove from heat and stir in the soup. Cook over moderate heat, stirring until mixture comes to a boil. Simmer for 5 minutes. Adjust seasoning. Turn into a bowl and chill.
Just before serving, pour into soup cups and add a little cream to each serving. Sprinkle grated cheese on the croûtons and melt under a hot broiler. Serve with chilled soup.

## SPICED ORANGE HAM

**6 pound smoked ham**
**¾ cup butter or margarine**
**¾ cup soft brown sugar**
**Grated rind and juice of 3 oranges**
**6¼ tablespoons cider vinegar**
**½ teaspoon ground ginger**
**Salt**
**Freshly ground black pepper**
**2 whole oranges**

Soak the ham in cold water 2–3 hours. Drain and place skin side down in a large pan. Cover with fresh water. Bring to a boil, skim off the scum. Reduce the heat and cook for 55 minutes. Make sure that the ham is always covered with water, topping it up with fresh boiling water if necessary. Drain the ham. Wrap in aluminum foil and place in a roasting pan. Bake in a moderate oven (350°F.) for 65 minutes.
Meanwhile, prepare the orange glaze. Melt the butter and brown sugar together over low heat. When the sugar is dissolved, raise heat and cook until golden. Remove from heat and add rind and juice of 3 oranges, vinegar and ginger. Continue to heat gently, uncovered, for 7–10 minutes. Season to taste.
Slice the whole oranges and poach in water to cover until the rinds are soft. Drain and add to the orange syrup. Heat gently for a further 5 minutes.
About 20 minutes before the end of the cooking time, remove the ham from the oven. Unwrap the foil and strip off the rind. Coat the fat with a little of the orange glaze. Return it to the oven and raise the temperature to 425°F. Cook for 20 minutes. Serve the ham hot with the rest of the glaze on the side.

## COFFEE CREAM RING
*Make 2 for the party*

*For the ring:*
**1 cup water**
**½ cup butter or margarine**
**¼ teaspoon salt**
**1 cup sifted all-purpose flour**
**4 large eggs**

*For decoration:*
**¼ cup butter**
**⅓ cup soft dark brown sugar**
**½ cup chopped mixed nuts**
**1¼ cups heavy cream**
**1 tablespoon coffee extract**

In a saucepan heat the water, butter and salt to a full rolling boil. Reduce heat and quickly stir in the flour, mixing vigorously with a wooden spoon until the mixture leaves the sides of the pan in a ball. Remove from heat and add eggs, one by one, beating until very smooth after each addition. Lightly grease a cookie tray and dredge with flour. Mark a 7 in. circle in the flour. Spoon the batter into a pastry bag with a large plain nozzle. Pipe it in a ring just outside the marked circle on the cookie tray. Bake in a very hot oven (450°F.) for 40 minutes. Lower heat to 325°F. and bake for 15 minutes. If the ring starts to over-brown, cover with foil.
Cool the ring and split in half, crosswise. In a small saucepan, melt the butter and sugar over low heat. When the sugar has dissolved, boil the syrup for 1–2 minutes and stir in the nuts. Drizzle the sauce over the top half of the ring.
Beat the cream until it holds its shape. Add the coffee extract. Spoon the cream inside the lower ring and top with the nut-encrusted ring.

## FRESH FRUIT SALAD

*For syrup:*
**½ cup sugar**
**⅝ cup water**
**2½ tablespoons lemon juice**
**1¼ tablespoons orange liqueur**

*For salad:*
**2 eating apples, pared and thinly sliced**
**2 pears, pared and diced**
**2 oranges, pared and sectioned**
**2 large bananas, sliced**

Dissolve the sugar in the water over low heat. Bring to a boil and boil for 2–3 minutes. Cool the syrup, then stir in the lemon juice and liqueur.
Combine all the fruits with the syrup. Chill well before serving.

*Potted shrimp are easily prepared a day in advance*

## MENU *serves 10*

**POTTED SHRIMP**
**ROAST SIRLOIN OF BEEF**
**ROAST POTATOES,**
**GLAZED CARROTS AND**
**GREEN BEANS**
**BERRIES IN BRANDY**
Wine – Burgundy (Morey
St-Denis, Chambertin Clos de
Bèze, Pinot Noir)

**Timetable** *for dinner at 8.00 p.m.*
**Day before:** *Prepare the potted
shrimp.*
**In the morning:** *Prepare
vegetables.*
**5.30** *Start cooking beef.*
**6.00** *Prepare berries with brandy.
Whip the cream.
Turn out the shrimp. Cut the bread
and butter, cover and keep in a
cool place.*
**7.00** *Put potatoes to roast, below
the meat.*
**7.45** *Cook carrots and green
beans. Dish up beef and make
gravy. Keep hot.*
**8.00** *Serve first course.*

## POTTED SHRIMP

1½ pound cooked, peeled tiny
  shrimp
1¼ cups butter, melted
Ground mace
Cayenne
Ground nutmeg
Clarified butter
Sliced cucumber and lemon

Heat the shrimp very slowly in
the warm butter, without allowing them to come to a boil. Add
seasonings to taste. Pour the
shrimp into small pots or glasses.
Let stand to become cold. Cover
the top of the shrimps with a thin
layer of clarified butter. Chill
before serving.

To serve, turn out the shrimp on
to individual plates, retaining the
shape of the pots. Garnish with
cucumber slices and lemon
twists. Serve with brown bread
and butter.

## ROAST SIRLOIN OF BEEF

Choose a sirloin of beef weighing
about 7½ pound. Place on a rack
in a roasting pan. Roast in a hot
oven (425°F.) for about 15
minutes per pound, plus 20
minutes extra.

## BERRIES IN BRANDY

2 quarts hulled small
  strawberries
7½ tablespoons honey
7½ tablespoons brandy
2½ cups heavy cream, lightly
  whipped

Pile the prepared fruit in a bowl.
Blend together the honey and
brandy and spoon over the berries. Turn the berries gently to
coat them well. Chill for about 2
hours, stirring once or twice.
Serve in dessert dishes with
whipped cream.

## MENU *serves 8*

**CHAMPIGNONS MARIE**
**ROAST STUFFED VEAL**
**BRAISED CELERY**
**HEARTS AND**
**CREAMED POTATOES**
**GRAPE DELIGHT**
Wine – Claret (Château
Haut-Brion)

**Timetable** *for dinner at 8.00 p.m.*
**In the morning:** *Stuff veal and
return to refrigerator. Prepare
potatoes, keep under water. Halve
and seed grapes; store in
refrigerator.*
**5.00** *Assemble ingredients and
equipment. Prepare all
ingredients for first course but do
not start to cook.*
**5.30** *Start to cook veal.*
**7.00** *Start to braise celery.
Make up grape delight.*
**7.30** *Cook mushrooms and make
toast. Dish up mushroom starter at
the last minute. Cook potatoes.
Keep vegetables hot.*
**7.45** *Dish up veal and make gravy.
Keep hot.*
**8.00** *Serve first course.*

## CHAMPIGNONS MARIE

1½ pound button mushrooms,
  wiped and stalks removed
7½ tablespoons salad oil
4 shallots, finely chopped
5 tablespoons fine, dry
  breadcrumbs
Salt and pepper
2½ tablespoons lemon juice
5 tablespoons chopped parsley

Quarter the mushroom caps and
half of the stalks. Heat the oil in a
heavy skillet and fry the mushrooms for 10 minutes, until
brown. Chop the remaining
stalks finely, mix with the chopped shallots and add to the mushrooms in the pan. Fry for 2–3
minutes. Drain any excess fat
from the pan and mix with the
breadcrumbs. Add to pan and stir
gently. Season and stir in the
lemon juice and chopped parsley.
Spoon into individual dishes.
Serve with hot buttered toast.

## ROAST STUFFED VEAL

3½ pound boned shoulder of
  veal
Salt
Freshly ground black pepper
½ pound sliced bacon
*For stuffing:*
1 onion, finely chopped
¼ pound mushrooms, wiped
  and chopped
2 cloves garlic, crushed
1¼ teaspoons grated lemon rind
3¾ tablespoons chopped parsley
2 cups fresh white breadcrumbs
¼ pound pork sausage meat,
  lightly cooked
Salt
Freshly ground black pepper
1 egg
2½ tablespoons melted butter

Cut through the veal and open it
out flat. Beat it lightly with a
heavy knife or the side of a cleaver
until it is of a fairly even thickness. Season lightly.
Mix together the onion, mushrooms, garlic, lemon rind, parsley, breadcrumbs, sausage meat,
salt and pepper. Add the egg and
butter to make the mixture stick
together. Pile into the center of
the veal and fold each flap over it.
Tie with string.
Stretch the bacon slices as long as
possible with the back of a knife,
cover the meat completely with
bacon and tie in place with string.
Wrap loosely in aluminum foil,
weigh, and then place the meat in
a roasting pan. Roast in a hot
oven (425°F.) for 35 minutes per
pound. Remove the foil for the
last 30 minutes, to allow the meat
to brown.

## GRAPE DELIGHT

½ pound black grapes, halved
  and seeded
½ pound white grapes, halved
  and seeded
1⅞ cup apricot flavored yogurt
3 egg whites

Turn the yogurt into a bowl. Beat
the egg whites until stiff and fold
into the yogurt.
Layer the yogurt and grapes into
dessert glasses. Decorate with a
few grapes on top.

*Grape delight – a light dessert after a rich meal*

# SAVORIES

*These are some of our favorite savories. Pick the lighter ones for after dinner – the classics are angels and devils on horseback, anchovy toasts, Scotch woodcock, Welsh rarebit and chicken livers on toast.*

*Prepare the more substantial recipes for snack meals such as lunch or supper.*

## DEVILS ON HORSEBACK
*4 servings*

**4 blanched almonds, optional**
**Olive oil, optional**
**Salt, optional**
**Cayenne, optional**
**4 large, plump prunes**
**2 slices bacon**
**4 rounds of bread, about 2 in. in diameter**
**2 tablespoons butter**
**Watercress**

If you are using the almonds, heat the oil in a small pan and fry them for 2–3 minutes, until they are golden. While they are still hot, toss in salt and a very little cayenne. Remove the pits from the prunes and put almonds in their place. Alternatively, simply remove the pits.

Flatten and stretch the bacon slices with the back of a knife. Cut each slice in half and roll around a prune. Secure with a toothpick. Broil in a broiling pan, turning the rolls until all the bacon is golden brown.

Meanwhile melt the butter in a skillet and fry the bread for 2–3 minutes until golden. Put a hot broiled prune and bacon roll on each piece, garnish with watercress and serve at once.

## ANGELS ON HORSEBACK
*4 servings*

**4 rounds of bread, about 2 in. in diameter**
**2 tablespoons butter**
**2 slices bacon**
**4 oysters**
**Cayenne**
**Lemon juice**
**Watercress**

Fry the bread rounds in hot butter until golden. Stretch the bacon slices with the back of a knife and cut in half. Put an oyster in the middle of each piece of bacon, sprinkle with cayenne and a squeeze of lemon juice. Roll the bacon around the oyster. Secure with a wooden toothpick.

Place an oyster roll on top of each bread round and place on a cookie tray. Bake in a fairly hot oven (400°F.) for about 5 minutes or until bacon is cooked. Serve at once, garnished with watercress.

## CHICKEN LIVERS ON TOAST
*4 servings*

**¼ pound chicken livers**
**Seasoned flour**
**Butter or margarine**
**4 rounds of bread, about 2 in. in diameter**
**2 tablespoons sherry or Madeira**
**4 mushrooms, sliced, optional**

Wash and dry the chicken livers. Cut them in small pieces, using kitchen scissors, and coat with seasoned flour. Melt a little butter in a small skillet and fry the bread 2–3 minutes until golden brown. Remove and keep warm. Add more butter, put in the prepared livers and stir them over the heat until browned. Add the sherry or Madeira, mix well and simmer very slowly for 10–15 minutes.

Serve the livers on bread rounds. If mushrooms are used, sauté them before the livers; when livers are cooked add the mushrooms and adjust seasoning.

## CHICKEN LIVER SAVORY
*4 servings*

¼ pound chicken livers
2 tablespoons butter or
   margarine
Salt
Cayenne
2 tablespoons sherry or Madeira
A few mushrooms, optional
8 fingers of fried bread
Parsley

Wash and dry the chicken livers. Melt 1 tablespoon butter in a small skillet and cook the livers until browned, about 10 minutes. Put livers through a sieve or purée in an electric blender. Blend in 1 tablespoon butter, salt, cayenne and sherry. If the mushrooms are used, cook them lightly in about 1 tablespoon butter for 3–5 minutes.
Spread the liver mixture on the fried bread and arrange the mushrooms on top, if used. Garnish with parsley and serve hot.

## WELSH RAREBIT
*4 servings*

½ pound Cheddar cheese, grated
2 tablespoons butter
1¼ teaspoons dry mustard
Salt and pepper
4 tablespoons ale
4 small slices toast

Place the cheese, butter, mustard, salt, pepper and ale in a very heavy pan. Heat very gently until a creamy mixture is obtained. Pour over the toast. Put under a hot broiler until golden and bubbling.

## CHEESE FRITES
*4 servings*

2 egg whites
2½ tablespoons grated Parmesan
   cheese
Salt
Cayenne
Fat for deep frying
Parsley

Beat the egg whites until stiff. Fold in the cheese and seasonings. Heat the fat to 350°F. on a fat thermometer or until a 1 in. cube of bread turns brown in 60 seconds. Drop in 1 tablespoon of the cheese mixture at a time and cook until golden brown, about 3 minutes. Drain well on paper towels. Garnish with parsley.

234

## SOFT ROE SAVORY
*4 servings*

12 herring roes
Butter for frying
4 fingers of bread
Salt and pepper
Squeeze of lemon juice
Parsley

Wash the roes, dry them well and fry gently in butter in a small pan for 8–10 minutes or until golden. Remove from pan. Wipe out the pan with paper towels, heat a little more butter and fry the bread fingers for 2–3 minutes or until golden. Place the cooked roes on the fried bread, season, add lemon juice and garnish with parsley.

## SCOTCH WOODCOCK
*4 servings*

1 large slice of bread
Butter
1 can (2 ounces) anchovies,
   drained
1 tablespoon butter
2 tablespoons milk
1 large egg
Salt and pepper
Pimiento

Toast the bread, remove the crusts, butter the toast and cut it into triangles. Reserve 2 anchovy fillets for garnish, sieve the rest and spread on the toast triangles. Melt the butter in a saucepan. Beat together the milk, egg and seasoning. Pour into the hot pan and stir slowly over low heat until the mixture begins to thicken. Remove from heat and stir until creamy. Spread the mixture on top of the anchovy toast, garnish with thin strips of anchovy fillet and pimiento.

## CHEESE SOUFFLES
*4 servings*

2 tablespoons butter
2 tablespoons flour
⅝ cup milk
¾ cup grated Cheddar cheese
3 eggs, separated
Salt and pepper

Grease 4 individual soufflé dishes. Melt butter in a pan. Stir in the flour and cook for about 1 minute. Remove from heat and stir in the milk. Cook over medium heat, stirring constantly, until the mixture comes to a boil and thickens. Cool slightly and stir in the cheese. Add the egg yolks, one at a time, beating well. Season. Beat the egg whites until stiff and fold into the cheese mixture. Divide between prepared

*Individual cheese soufflés make a tasty snack*

soufflé dishes. Bake in the center of a fairly hot oven (400°F.) for about 25 minutes or until well risen.

## SCALLOPS AND BACON
*4 servings*

8 scallops
Salt and pepper
Lemon juice
8 slices bacon
Tartare sauce

Sprinkle the scallops with salt, pepper and lemon juice. Flatten and stretch the bacon with the back of a knife. Wrap 1 slice bacon around each scallop and secure with a toothpick. Place in a pan under a hot broiler and broil several inches from source of heat until cooked, about 5 minutes on each side. Serve accompanied with tartare sauce.

## MEXICAN FIRE
*4 servings*

1 tablespoon butter
1½ tablespoons flour
⅝ cup milk
Salt and pepper
¼ teaspoon dry mustard
½ teaspoon chili powder
¼ pound Gruyère cheese, finely
   chopped
1 tablespoon chopped green
   pepper

Melt the butter, stir in the flour and cook for 2–3 minutes. Remove from heat and stir in the milk. Cook over moderate heat, stirring constantly, until the mixture comes to a boil and thickens. Add the seasonings. Remove from heat and add the cheese and green pepper. Stir until the cheese has melted. Serve hot with deep-fried shrimp.

*Deep fried shrimp with Mexican fire dip*

## CROQUE MONSIEUR

*4 servings*

¼ **cup butter**
8 **large slices white bread**
¼ **pound sliced ham**
¼ **pound Gruyère or Emmenthal**
   **cheese, sliced**
8 **gherkins**

Butter the bread slices on 1 side only. Sandwich in pairs with a slice of ham and enough cheese to cover. Toast each sandwich on both sides until evenly browned. Cut each in half crosswise and place a gherkin fan on top.

## HAM FINGERS

*4 servings*

2 **large slices of bread with crusts**
   **removed**
**Butter**
½ **cup finely chopped cooked**
   **ham**
2 **eggs, beaten**
2 **tablespoons milk**
**Salt and pepper**

Fry the bread in a little butter for 2–3 minutes or until golden. Cut into fingers. Add more butter to the pan and fry the ham gently for 2–3 minutes. Beat the eggs with the milk and seasoning, pour the mixture into the pan and stir slowly over gentle heat until it begins to thicken. Remove from heat and stir until creamy. Pile on the bread and serve hot.

## EGGS EN COCOTTE

*4 servings*

2 **slices bacon, chopped**
4 **eggs**
**Salt and pepper**
**Butter**

Divide the bacon between 4 ramekins or individual soufflé dishes. Bake towards the top of a moderate oven (350°F.) for about 10 minutes or until bacon is lightly cooked. Break an egg into each dish. Sprinkle with salt and pepper. Put a few dots of butter on each and bake for 7–10 minutes or until the eggs are lightly set. Serve hot.

## ANCHOVY TOASTS

*4 servings*

2 **slices bread**
1 **tablespoon butter**
**Squeeze of lemon juice**
5 **anchovy fillets, chopped**
**Pepper**
**Pinch of nutmeg**
**Pinch of ground mace**
**Parsley**

*Fluffy cheese boats are good after dinner or with evening drinks*

Toast the bread and cut into fingers. Melt the butter, add a squeeze of lemon juice, the anchovies, pepper, nutmeg and mace. Beat well and rub through a sieve. Spread this mixture on the fingers of hot toast and garnish with parsley. Similar savories can be made with sardines or herrings.

## CURRY PUFFS

*4 servings*

*For pastry:*

1 **cup all-purpose flour**
**Pinch of salt**
6 **tablespoons butter or**
   **shortening and butter, mixed**
**Squeeze of lemon juice**
4–5 **tablespoons cold water**
1 **egg, beaten**

*For filling:*

2½ **teaspoons curry powder**
1 **cup thick white sauce**
¼ **pound cooked, peeled shrimp**

Sift together the flour and salt. Cut a quarter of the butter into the flour with a pastry blender or two knives until it resembles breadcrumbs. Add the lemon juice and enough water to make a soft, elastic dough.
On a lightly floured board, roll the pastry into an oblong 3 times as long as it is wide. Put another portion of the fat over the top two-thirds of the pastry in dots, so that it looks like buttons on a card. Fold the bottom third up and top third down and turn it 90° around, so that the folds are now at the sides.
Seal the edges of the pastry by pressing firmly with a rolling pin. Re-roll as before and continue until all the fat is used up. Wrap loosely in wax paper or plastic wrap and chill for 30 minutes in the refrigerator.
Roll out the pastry thinly and cut into rounds with a 1½ in. cutter. Stir the curry powder into the white sauce. Roughly chop the shrimp and mix with enough sauce to hold them together. Put a little of this mixture into the centers of half the rounds of pastry. Moisten the edges with water and place another round of pastry on top of each to make a lid. Seal the edges by pressing with the fingers and pierce the tops gently once or twice with a fork.
Brush the puffs with beaten egg and place on a cookie tray. Bake towards the top of a very hot oven (450°F.) for 10–15 minutes or until golden brown. Serve hot.

## SHRIMP IN ANCHOVY SAUCE

*4 servings*

*For anchovy sauce:*

1½ **tablespoons butter**
3 **tablespoons all-purpose flour**
1¼ **cups milk or milk and fish**
   **stock mixed**
2½ **teaspoons anchovy paste**
**Salt**
**Freshly ground black pepper**
**Pinch of nutmeg**

½ **pound cooked, shelled shrimp**
**Chopped parsley**

Melt the butter in a small pan. Stir in the flour and cook over low heat 2–3 minutes. Remove from heat and stir in the milk. Cook over medium heat, stirring constantly, until mixture comes to a boil. Simmer for 1–2 minutes. Remove from heat, stir in the anchovy paste and season with salt, pepper and nutmeg.
Add the shrimp to the sauce and heat through. Divide the mixture between 4 individual dishes or scallop shells. Garnish with parsley and serve immediately.

## FLUFFY CHEESE BOATS

*4 servings*

*For pastry:*

1 **cup all-purpose flour**
**Pinch of salt**
2 **tablespoons shortening**
2 **tablespoons margarine**
4½ **teaspoons water,**
   **approximately**

*For filling:*

2 **tablespoons butter or**
   **margarine**
¼ **cup flour**
1¼ **cups milk**
¼ **pound Cheddar cheese, grated**
**Salt**
**Freshly ground black pepper**
2 **eggs, separated**

Sift together the flour and salt. Cut in the shortening and margarine with a pastry blender or two knives until the consistency of fine breadcrumbs. Add the water a little at a time, stirring with a fork until the mixture begins to stick together. With 1 hand, collect the dough together and knead lightly to give a smooth, firm dough. Wrap in waxed paper or plastic wrap and chill for 15 minutes.
Roll the pastry out on a lightly floured board and use to line small boat-shaped molds or small patty tins. Carefully fit a small piece of foil into each case, fill with dried beans and place on a cookie tray. Bake near the top of a hot oven (425°F.) for 15 minutes or until cooked but still pale in color. Remove foil and beans and let cool.
Melt the butter in a small saucepan. Stir in the flour and cook for 2–3 minutes. Remove from heat and stir in the milk. Cook over medium heat, stirring constantly, until mixture comes to a boil and thickens. Remove from heat and stir in three-quarters of the cheese, seasoning and the egg yolks. Pour the mixture into the baked shells. Beat the egg whites until stiff. Spoon a little on top of each boat and sprinkle with the remaining cheese. Reduce the oven temperature to 350°F. Return cases to the oven and bake for 10 minutes or until the filling is heated through and the meringue is golden. Serve at once.

# PETITS FOURS

*A few petits fours are the perfect finish for a big dinner party. Serve them with the coffee, either at the table or after you have moved to easy chairs. These are the little details that make your guests feel really special!*

*Toffee grapes, marzipan toffees and chocolate rum truffles*

## ALMOND FOURS
*makes 20–24*

**2 egg whites**
**1½ cups ground almonds**
**6 tablespoons sugar**
**A few drops almond extract**
**Glacé cherries, angelica and toasted almonds**

Line 2 cookie trays with non-stick paper.
Beat the egg whites until stiff. Fold in the ground nuts, sugar and almond extract. Place the mixture in a pastry bag fitted with a ½ in. star-shape nozzle. Pipe out into small whirls on the trays. Decorate each with a small piece of glacé cherry, angelica or toasted almond. Bake in a cool oven (300°F.) for 15–20 minutes until meringues begin to color.

## BRANDY WAFERS
*makes about a dozen*

**¼ cup molasses**
**¼ cup butter**
**¾ cup sifted cake flour**
**⅛ teaspoon salt**
**⅓ cup sugar**
**½ tablespoon ground ginger**
**1½ tablespoons brandy**

Heat the molasses to boiling, add the butter. Add the sifted dry ingredients gradually, stirring constantly. Stir in the brandy. Drop by half teaspoonfuls 3 in. apart on to greased cookie trays. Bake, 6 cookies at a time, in a cool oven (300°F.) for 8–10 minutes. Remove from oven and cool 1 minute. Remove with a spatula and roll them around the handle of a wooden spoon with the upper surface of each brandy wafer on the outside. When the biscuits have hardened enough to hold the shape, slip them gently off the spoon handles. If the wafers cool too much while still on the tray and become too brittle to roll, return the tray to the oven for a moment to soften them.

## COFFEE ECLAIRS
*makes about 24*

**1 cup water**
**½ cup butter or margarine**
**¼ teaspoon salt**
**1 cup sifted all-purpose flour**
**4 large eggs**

*For filling:*
**1¼ cups heavy cream, whipped**
**Coffee-flavored confectioners' sugar glaze**

In a saucepan heat the water, butter and salt to a full rolling boil. Reduce heat and quickly stir in the flour, mixing vigorously with a wooden spoon until the mixture leaves the sides of the pan in a ball. Remove from heat and beat in eggs, one by one, beating until very smooth after each addition. Put the mixture into a pastry bag fitted with a plain round 1 in. nozzle. Pipe the dough out on to greased cookie tray in fingers about 1½ in. long. Keep the lengths very even, cutting the paste off with a wet knife against the edge of the nozzle.
Bake toward the top of a fairly hot oven (400°F.) for about 35 minutes until well risen, crisp and golden brown. Remove from the tray, slit down the sides with a sharp pointed knife to allow the steam to escape. Let cool on a wire rack.
When the éclairs are cold, fill with whipped cream. Ice the tops with coffee-flavored icing.

## COCONUT KISSES
*makes about 1½ pound*

**2 cups sugar**
**½ cup powdered glucose**
**⅝ cup water**
**1½ cups shredded coconut**
**Glacé cherries**
**Crystalized violets**

Put the sugar, glucose and water into a pan and heat gently until the sugar has dissolved. Then boil to the soft ball stage, 240°F. on a candy thermometer. Remove from heat and stir in the coconut. Form into small rocky heaps on a sheet of waxed paper. Place a small piece of glacé cherry or crystalized violet on each. Let stand to cool and harden.

## TOFFEE GRAPES

**¼ pound black grapes**
**¼ pound white grapes**
**1 cup sugar**
**1¼ cups water**

Wipe the grapes clean and divide into pairs, keeping the stalks on. Dissolve the sugar in the water over low heat, then bring to a boil and boil steadily until the syrup turns a pale caramel color. Allow to cool a little, then dip the grapes in the caramel, holding them by the stalks. Leave on a greased plate to harden, then pile in a glass dish to serve.
*Note:* Prepare about 1 hour before serving. If wished, serve the grapes in individual paper cases.

## MARZIPAN TOFFEES

**Almond paste trimmings**
**Grated rind and juice of ½ lemon**
**1 cup sugar**
**1¼ cups water**
**Whole blanched almonds**

Sharpen the almond paste with lemon rind and juice and roll into little balls. Dissolve the sugar in the water over low heat. Bring to a boil and boil steadily until the syrup turns a pale caramel color. Remove from heat and allow to cool slightly. Hold each ball of marzipan on a skewer and dip into the caramel. Place on a greased plate or waxed paper. Decorate with a blanched almond and let stand to harden.

## CHOCOLATE RUM TRUFFLES
*makes 1 pound*

**4 squares semi-sweet chocolate**
**2¼ cups confectioners' sugar, sifted**
**½ cup unsalted butter**
**Rum**
**Chocolate shot**

Place the chocolate in a small bowl over a pan of hot water until melted. In a bowl, beat together the chocolate, sugar and butter until well blended. Add rum to taste. Form into small balls and roll in chocolate shot. Allow to harden before serving.

236

# CHILDREN'S PARTY MENUS

Make the party fun for yourself as well as the children. Plan it in advance and save your energies for the day.

## SAVORY CHOUX BUNS
## HOT DIGGETY DOGS
## CHEESE PICTURES
## ALASKA EXPRESS
## GINGERBREAD MEN

**Timetable** *for preparing the food.*
**Day before:** *Bake choux buns but do not fill; bake gingerbread men; store both in airtight containers.*
**In the morning:** *Make cheese pictures, arrange and cover with plastic wrap. Cook and stuff frankfurters, wrap in bacon and put ready for broiling; split and butter rolls.*
*Slice jelly roll for Alaska express and place on dish. Assemble the other ingredients. Refresh, cool and fill choux buns.*
**Just before tea:** *Broil and assemble hot diggety dogs.*
*As tea is served finish Alaska express.*

---

### SAVORY CHOUX BUNS

*For choux pastry:*
**3 tablespoons butter**
**⅝ cup water**
**⅝ cup all-purpose flour**
**2 eggs, lightly beaten**

*For filling:*
**1 package (3 ounces) cream cheese**
**¼ cup butter**
**Lemon juice**
**Salt**
**Freshly ground black pepper**
**Chopped parsley**

Melt the butter in the water in a saucepan and bring to a boil. Remove the pan from the heat and add the flour all at once. Beat until the paste is smooth and leaves the side of the pan, forming a ball. Cool slightly, then gradually beat in the eggs.
Put the batter in a pastry bag fitted with a ½ in. plain nozzle. Pipe the mixture into about 24 walnut-sized balls on greased cookie trays. Bake in a fairly hot oven (400°F.) for 15–20 minutes, until golden brown and cooked through.
Make a slit in the side of each bun to release the steam; if necessary, put them in the oven to dry out. Cool on wire racks.
Beat together the cream cheese, butter, lemon juice, seasoning and parsley until smooth. Pipe into the hollow of each bun, using a ½ in. plain nozzle. Pile the buns in a pyramid on a flat serving platter.

*Alaska express is a children's favorite*

### HOT DIGGETY DOGS

**24 frankfurters**
**½ cup cottage cheese**
**Chopped chives**
**12 slices bacon**
**24 hot dog rolls**
**Butter**

To cook the frankfurters, bring a large pan of water to a boil. Turn off the heat and immerse the frankfurters in the water for 5 minutes. Do not boil.
Slit the frankfurters lengthwise, almost to the ends. Mix the cottage cheese well with the chives. Fill the mixture into the split frankfurters.
Cut the bacon slices in half and stretch each one with the blade of a knife. Wrap each frankfurter spirally in a piece of bacon. Fasten the ends with toothpicks. Broil in a hot broiler until the bacon is crisp.
Split the rolls, leaving a hinge, and butter them. Toast lightly under the broiler if desired. Just before serving, remove the toothpicks and place a hot, bacon wrapped frankfurter in each roll. Serve with tomato relish, catsup and mustard.

### CHEESE PICTURES

**24 small slices bread**
**Butter**
**24 slices cold luncheon meat**
**12 slices processed American cheese**

Butter the bread and top each slice with a slice of luncheon meat. Trim the edges.
Using a fancy cookie cutter, cut the centers out of the cheese slices. Top half the slices of luncheon meat with the fancy shapes, using the outsides of the cheese squares as 'frames' for the remaining 12 slices.

### ALASKA EXPRESS

**1 large chocolate, cream-filled jelly roll, store bought**
**1 can (11 ounces) mandarin oranges**
**5 egg whites**
**1¼ cups sugar**
**1 package (1 quart) vanilla ice cream**
**Chocolate morsels**
**Dark cardboard**
**Cotton**

Cut the jelly roll into 10 slices. Arrange 6 of the slices on a flat, oblong, ovenproof dish to form a rectangle. Spoon over 2 tablespoons mandarin juice from the can. Beat the egg whites until stiff. Beat in the sugar gradually and continue beating until egg whites stand in stiff peaks. Spoon the meringue into a pastry bag fitted with a large star nozzle. Place the ice cream on the jelly roll slices and arrange all but 3 of the drained mandarins on top.
Quickly pipe the meringue over the ice cream to form an engine shape completely enclosing the ice cream and the cake.
Pipe meringue rosettes along the top and decorate with the reserved mandarins and chocolate morsels. Quickly bake the engine in a very hot oven (450°F.) for 4 minutes or just until lightly browned. The meringue will be slightly crisp on the outside and soft inside.
Position the extra 4 slices of jelly roll for wheels. Form a roll from the cardboard to resemble a smokestack with a piece of cotton for smoke. Place on top of the engine. Serve at once.
*Note:* The Alaska express, complete except for wheels and smoke, can be packed in a container and frozen. Remove from the freezer 1 hour before slicing and keep in a cool place.

*Sausage kebabs, with bacon rolls and cheese*

## GINGERBREAD MEN

**3 cups all-purpose flour**
**1¼ teaspoons baking soda**
**2½ teaspoons ground ginger**
**½ cup butter or margarine**
**1 cup brown sugar, firmly**
**packed**
**5 tablespoons corn syrup**
**1 egg, beaten**
**Currants**
**White icing**

Sift together the flour, soda and ginger. Rub the butter into the sifted ingredients with the fingertips, add the sugar and mix well. Warm the syrup slightly and stir into the rubbed mixture, with the egg, to give a smooth dough. Knead until smooth and roll out on a lightly floured board to ⅛ in. thickness. Draw a gingerbread man about 5½ in. high and 4½ in. broad on waxed paper. Cut out the shape and use as a pattern. Place it on the dough and cut around it with a sharp-pointed knife. Carefully lift the men on to a greased cookie tray, keeping them well apart.

On to each man, put 3 currants for buttons and 3 more for his eyes and mouth.

Bake in a fairly hot oven (375°F.) for 10–15 minutes, until evenly browned. Cool on a wire rack. To decorate, outline the neck, sleeve ends and feet with white icing.

## MENU *serves 12*

**HOT SAUSAGES**
**POPCORN**
**CHICKEN PUFFS**
**DECKER SANDWICHES**
**MONEY CAKE**
**STRAWBERRY AND**
**ORANGE CUPS**
**CHEESE AND CHERRY**
**HEDGEHOG**

**Timetable** *for preparing food.*
**Day before:** *Make and decorate the cake; store in an airtight container in a cool place.*
*Cook the chicken puffs and store in a cool place.*
*Make the strawberry and orange cups but do not add cream and decoration.*
**In the morning:** *Decorate the strawberry and orange cups.*
*Twist the sausages and put in pan ready for cooking.*
*Make the sandwiches and chill.*
**1 hour before:** *Make the hedgehog.*
**Just before tea:** *Refresh the chicken puffs in the oven at 350°F.*
*for about 15 minutes. Cook sausages.*
*Cut sandwiches into fingers.*

## CHICKEN PUFFS

**1 pound cooked chicken meat**
**¼ cup butter or margarine**
**2 onions, finely chopped**
**½ cup flour**
**1¼ cups milk**
**Lemon juice**
**Salt and pepper**
**1 package (10 ounces) frozen**
**patty shells**
**Beaten egg**

Discard the skin from the chicken and cut the meat into small pieces. In a saucepan, melt the fat. Add the onion and sauté until soft but not browned. Stir in the flour and cook for 2 minutes. Remove from heat and stir in the milk. Cook over medium heat, stirring constantly, until mixture comes to a boil. Lower heat and simmer for 3 minutes, stirring. Add the chicken, lemon juice and seasoning to taste. Turn into a bowl, cover closely with waxed paper and let cool.

Remove patty shells from package and thaw. Place close together on a lightly-floured board. Press together and roll out very thin. Cut out twenty-four 4 in. rounds. Brush the edge of each round with beaten egg. Put a teaspoon of the chicken mixture in the center of each, fold the pastry over, seal and brush with more egg to glaze.

Place on a cookie tray. Bake in a fairly hot oven (400°F.) for 20 minutes, until puffed and golden. Serve warm rather than hot.

## DECKER SANDWICHES

**1½ pound unsliced sandwich**
**loaf**
**Butter**

*For first layer:*
**6 eggs, hard-cooked and mashed**
**½ cup butter, softened**
**Salt and pepper**

*For second layer:*
**2 cans (4⅜ ounces each)**
**sardines, drained**
**1 can (4 ounces) pimiento,**
**drained and chopped**
**1¼ tablespoons lemon juice**
**Salt and pepper**

*For third layer:*
**1 can (8 ounces) liver pâté**
**2 sweet gherkins, finely chopped**
**Salt and pepper**

*For fourth layer:*
**1 package (8 ounces) cream**
**cheese, softened**
**½ bunch watercress, chopped**
**Salt and pepper**

Remove the crusts from the bread. Slice the loaf in half and cut each half into 12 slices, lengthwise. Butter and assemble the bread slices with different fillings, in 4 blocks of 6 slices. Wrap in foil and chill until required. Cut into fingers or small triangles.

## MONEY CAKE

*For cake:*

**½ cup butter**
**½ cup margarine**
**1 cup sugar**
**4 eggs**
**1½ cups self-rising flour**
**¼ cup cocoa**

*For butter cream:*
**1 cup butter**
**3½ cups confectioners' sugar,**
**sifted**
**5 tablespoons evaporated milk**
**Vanilla extract**
**¼ cup cocoa blended with a little**
**water**

*For decoration:*
**Foil-covered chocolate coins**

Grease three 8 or 9-in. cake pans. Line the bottoms with a round of waxed paper and grease again. Cream the butter, margarine and sugar together until light and fluffy. Add the eggs, one at a time, beating well after each addition. Sift together the flour and cocoa and fold half into the creamed mixture and blend well. Fold in the rest of the flour and cocoa. Blend well.

Divide the cake mixture between the pans. Bake in a fairly hot oven (375°F.) for 20–25 minutes. Turn out the cakes and cool on wire racks.

Meanwhile, make the butter cream. Cream the butter and gradually beat in half the confectioners' sugar, with the evaporated milk and a few drops of vanilla. Then beat in the rest of the sugar. Divide the butter cream into 2 portions. Flavor half with the blended cocoa, mixing well. When the cakes are cool, sandwich them together with the white butter cream. Coat the top and sides with chocolate butter cream and decorate with the foil-covered chocolate coins.

### STRAWBERRY AND ORANGE CUPS

**6 medium oranges**
**1 package (6 ounces) orange flavored gelatin**
**4 cups cake crumbs**
**12 fresh strawberries, hulled**
**⅞ cup heavy cream**
**12 small chocolate peppermint or orange sticks**

Halve the oranges and squeeze out the juice without damaging the skins. Scrape out as much as possible of the white part. Dissolve the gelatin in 1 cup boiling water. Put the orange juice in a 1 quart measure and add water to make up to 3 cups liquid. Stir this into dissolved gelatin.

Soak the cake crumbs in 2½ cups of the liquid gelatin and divide among the orange cups. Chill until set. Pour the remaining gelatin into a shallow pan to set. When the gelatin is set, chop it roughly and pile it on to the cake crumb base.

Pipe a whirl of cream in the center of each cup and place a strawberry in the center. Decorate with a chocolate peppermint or orange stick.

### FOR THE EXTRAS

You will need 1½ pound cocktail sausages. Broil them or bake in the oven and spear with tooth-

*Roundabout cake – allow a ribbon for each guest*

picks. Open bags of popcorn and serve in small dishes. For the cheese and cherry hedgehog, use about ¾ pound Cheddar cheese, cut into ½ in. cubes. Spear each cube on a toothpick with a pitted black cherry and spike the sticks into a hard white cabbage.

---

**MENU** *serves 8*

**SAUSAGE KEBABS**
**PINWHEEL SANDWICHES**
**POTATO CHIPS**
**KNICKERBOCKER GLORIES**
**ROUNDABOUT CAKE**
**OWL COOKIES**

**Timetable** *for preparing the food.*
**Several days before:** *Make roundabout cake but do not decorate; make owl cookies; store in airtight containers.*
**Day before:** *Divide the sausages, make bacon rolls and cut cheese cubes; store in separate plastic bags in refrigerator. Make jellies, leave in a cool place.*
**In the morning:** *Make sandwich rolls and refrigerate. Decorate cake.*

**Before tea:** *Slice the pinwheel sandwiches, cook sausages and bacon and finish kebab arrangement. Make knickerbocker glories just before serving.*

---

### SAUSAGE KEBABS

**1 pound link pork sausages**
**¾ pound sliced bacon**
**½–¾ pound Cheddar cheese**
**Potato chips**

Place the sausages in a baking pan. Bake in a fairly hot oven (400°F.) for about 30 minutes. Cut each sausage in half.

On a flat surface, stretch the bacon slices with the back of a knife. Cut each slice in half and form into rolls. Place in a pan and cook in the oven until the bacon begins to brown. Cut the cheese into cubes and spear with toothpicks. Spear the sausages and bacon rolls separately on toothpicks. Spike all the kebabs into a cabbage. Surround with potato chips.

The sausages and bacon are best eaten warm.

### PINWHEEL SANDWICHES

**1 large, square unsliced loaf**
**Butter**

*For sandwich fillings:*
**Mashed canned salmon mixed with chopped cucumber**
**Scrambled eggs mixed with chopped chives**
**Cream cheese mixed with diced tomatoes**

Trim the crust from the loaf and cut into lengthwise slices. Butter

**Handy hint**

Remove the syrup from glacé cherries before using them in a cake. Halve large cherries, place them in a sieve and rinse under cold running water. Dry them thoroughly on paper towels before using.

*Owl cookies can be made well in advance*

each slice right up to the edges and spread with fillings.
Roll each slice up like a jelly roll. Wrap the rolls in plastic wrap or foil and chill for several hours. Just before serving, slice the rolls across into pinwheels and arrange on serving platters.

## KNICKERBOCKER GLORIES

1 package (3 ounces) raspberry flavored gelatin
1 can (16 ounces) sliced peaches, drained and chopped
1 can (8 ounces) pineapple tidbits, drained
Vanilla ice cream
Whipped cream
8 glacé cherries

Make up the gelatin as directed on the package. Pour into a shallow pan and let set. When set, chop in small pieces. Put small portions of the chopped fruit in the bottom of tall dessert glasses and cover with a thin layer of chopped gelatin. Put a scoop of ice cream on top and add another layer of chopped gelatin. Repeat the layers if necessary, finishing with a layer of whipped cream and topped with a cherry.

## ROUNDABOUT CAKE

1 cup butter
1 cup sugar
4 eggs
2 cups self-rising flour
Juice of ½ lemon

*For butter icing:*
1 cup butter
2⅝ cups confectioners' sugar, sifted
Juice of ½ lemon

*For decoration:*
½ pound orange and lemon slices, candied
1 lemon candy stick
Colored ribbons

Grease two 8-in. cake pans. Line the bottoms with a circle of waxed paper and grease again.
Cream the butter and sugar together until light and fluffy. Add the eggs one at a time, beating well after each addition. Fold in half the flour and blend. Fold in remaining flour and blend well. Stir in the lemon juice. Divide the mixture between the two pans. Bake in a fairly hot oven (375°F.) for about 25 minutes. Cool on a wire rack.
To make the butter icing, cream the butter until fluffy then gradually add the confectioners' sugar

and lemon juice. Beat well.
Sandwich the layers together with a little icing then spread the remainder over the top and sides. Place the cake on a serving platter and draw a fork around the edges to make ridges.
Using scissors or a sharp knife, cut the orange and lemon slices into little boys and girls. Arrange them around the sides of the cake. Fix the ribbons on to the lemon candy stick with icing, then press the stick into the center of the cake. Arrange the ribbons so that each figure is holding one.

## OWL COOKIES

1¼ cups all-purpose flour
1¼ teaspoons baking powder
Pinch of salt
6 tablespoons butter
½ cup light brown sugar, firmly packed
½ large egg, beaten
Vanilla extract
1 square unsweetened chocolate
Pinch of baking soda
Whole almonds, blanched
Chocolate morsels

Sift together the flour, baking powder and salt. Cream the butter and sugar together until light and fluffy. Add the egg and a few

drops of vanilla. Melt the chocolate in a small bowl over a pan of warm water; cool it slightly but keep it liquid, add the soda and blend well.
Add the dry ingredients to the creamed mixture and stir until evenly blended. Remove two-thirds of the dough to a floured board. Stir the melted chocolate into the remaining third.
Lightly shape both mixtures into sausage shapes. Chill in the refrigerator for ½–1 hour, until the dough is a rolling consistency. Divide the light-colored dough into 2 portions and roll each into an oblong 5 in. by 4 in. Divide the chocolate dough into 2 portions and roll each into a 5 in. sausage length. Place each chocolate roll on a piece of light dough and roll up. Leave both rolls in the refrigerator for a further 1–2 hours to firm.
Cut into slices about ⅛–¼ in. thick. To form the owl's head, place 2 circles side by side and press lightly together. Pinch the top corners of each head to form ears. Cut the almonds diagonally across and place a piece in the center of each head for the beak; place chocolate morsels for eyes. Bake in a moderate oven (350°F.) for 8–10 minutes. Remove carefully to a wire rack to cool.

---

**MENU** *serves 6*

**Timetable** *for preparing the food.*
**Day before:** *Make cake but do not decorate; store in an airtight container. Make sausage beehives; store in an airtight container in a cool place.*
**In the morning:** *Decorate Jumbo the clown. Cut sandwiches and refrigerate, make dips. Prepare rabbit faces and ears.*
**Just before tea:** *Reheat sausage beehives if serving warm. Make rabbit mousses at the last possible moment.*

---

## SAUSAGE BEEHIVES

2 packages (10 ounces each) frozen patty shells
1 egg, beaten
1 pound pork sausage meat

Remove patty shells from package and allow to thaw. Place close together on a lightly floured board and press edges together. Roll each package into a strip 20 in. long by 2½ in. wide. With a 2 in. cutter, stamp out 2 rounds from each end of each strip, making 8 rounds altogether. Cut the remainder of each strip into 4 long strips, each ½ in. wide. Brush the pastry strips and round with beaten egg. Divide the sausage meat into 8 pieces and shape each piece into a pyramid. Place the pastry rounds on a cookie tray; top each with a sausage pyramid. Then, starting at the base of the pyramid, coil a pastry strip around the sausage meat with the egg side outermost. Slightly overlap each layer to make it look like a beehive. Brush the finished beehives with beaten egg. Bake in a fairly hot oven (400°F.) for about 30 minutes or until golden brown.

## DIP-IN SALAD

**2 large carrots**
**½ small cucumber**
**2 stalks celery**
**7½ tablespoons salad dressing**
**2½ tablespoons white raisins**
**¼ cup chopped peanuts**

Pare the carrots and cut them into chunky sticks, about 1½–2 in. long. Cut the cucumber into sticks about the same size, without removing the skin. Cut the celery into pieces about 2 in. long. Make small cuts down into the celery to within ½ in. of one end; leave the pieces in very cold water for about 1 hour until the ends start to curl.
Mix together the remaining ingredients in a small bowl. Stand the bowl on a plate and arrange the vegetables around.

## SANDWICH CHECKERBOARD

**Butter**
**9 thin slices white bread**
**9 thin slices whole wheat bread**
**1 egg, scrambled with butter, milk and seasoning**
**1 can (5 ounces) tuna, drained and flaked**
**1 teaspoon lemon juice**
**Bunch of watercress**

Lightly butter bread slices. Use the white bread to make egg sandwiches. Season the tuna with lemon juice and use to sandwich the whole wheat bread

*Jumbo the clown is fun to make as well as eat*

together. Cut off all the crusts and cut each sandwich into 4 squares. (The 9th slice in each case should be cut in half and sandwiched to give 2 squares.)
Cover a 10-in. square board with foil. Arrange alternating whole wheat and white breads to form a square. Garnish with small sprigs of watercress.

## CHIVE DIP

**1 package (3 ounces) cream cheese, softened**
**2 tablespoons chopped chives**
**1 tablespoon light cream**

Blend all the ingredients to a soft cream. Serve in a small dish surrounded with crackers.

## RABBIT MOUSSES

**¼ cup chocolate morsels**
**12 marshmallows**
**6 individually paper wrapped ice cream slices**
**12 short pretzel sticks**

Melt the chocolate morsels in a small bowl over hot water. Stir with a teaspoon and then spoon into a paper cone for piping.
Dip a pair of kitchen scissors in water and cut 6 of the marsh-

mallows almost completely in half. Snip off the very tip of the chocolate filled bag and pipe rabbit faces on to the 6 whole marshmallows. Leave to set.
Unwrap the vanilla ice cream slices and place side by side on a flat dish. Decorate each with a rabbit face, using the split marshmallows for ears. Use the pretzel sticks for legs. Serve at once.

## JUMBO THE CLOWN

*For cake:*
**1 cup butter**
**1 cup sugar**
**4 eggs, beaten**
**Grated rind and juice of 1 orange**
**2 cups self-rising flour**

*For frosting:*
**3 egg whites**
**2¼ cups sugar**
**Pinch of salt**
**7½ tablespoons water**
**Pinch of cream of tartar**
**Orange coloring**

*For decoration:*
**1 ice cream cone**
**1 ping-pong ball**
**Orange ribbon**
**Colored shot**

Grease two 8-in. cake pans. Line the bottoms with a circle of waxed paper and grease again.
Cream together the butter and sugar until light and fluffy. Gradually beat in the eggs, orange rind and juice. Sift the flour, fold it into the creamed mixture and mix well. Turn into prepared pans. Bake in a moderate oven (350°F.) for about 30 minutes or until golden brown. Turn out carefully, peel off paper and cool on a wire rack.
For the frosting, put the egg whites, sugar, salt, water and cream of tartar in the top part of a double boiler. Place over hot water and keep water just at boiling point. Beat with a rotary beater or electric hand beater until the mixture thickens enough to form peaks – approximately 7 minutes. Color with a few drops of orange coloring; take care not to over-color.
Sandwich the layers together with 2–3 tablespoons of the frosting. Spread all but 2–3 tablespoons of remaining frosting over cake and whirl into a pattern.
Cut the ice cream cone, removing the base for a collar. Fix this in the center of the cake. Paint a clown's face on the ping-pong ball and fix this to the collar; tie a bow around with the ribbon.
Cover the top of the ice cream cone with the frosting, peaking it up and sprinkle with the colored shot. Attach it carefully to the face with the remaining frosting to make a tall clown's hat. Sprinkle more shot on the cake around the base of the collar to make a ruff. Serve the cake on a flat platter or board.

*Sausage beehives and dip-in salad*

# Parties for Young Teenagers

*Now is the time for you to leave the youngsters to themselves.*
*If you have a suitable attic or spare room which you can hand over, they may even wish to decorate it to their own taste permanently.*
*Provide lots of food, preferably hot, plenty of soft drinks and a good punch or cup. They will enjoy organizing the music and decor themselves, but be around in case advice is needed.*

*Baked apples, stuffed with orange butter and topped with fruit*

## HAMBURGERS ON SAVORY RICE

1½ cups rice
Salt and pepper
½ cup white raisins
5 teaspoons chopped parsley
1 red pepper, seeded and diced
1 green pepper, seeded and diced
¼ pound boiled ham, chopped
Stock
16 frozen hamburger patties
Olive oil

Cook the rice according to package directions. Do not overcook. Place in a large, shallow casserole. Stir in the seasoning, raisins, parsley, peppers and chopped ham. Add just enough stock to cover top of rice. Brush the patties with oil and place on top of the rice. Cover with a piece of foil and cook in a moderate oven (350°F.) for 45 minutes. Remove foil during last 10 minutes of cooking time.

## WHITE CABBAGE SALAD

1½ pound cabbage, finely shredded
2 carrots, grated
1 eating apple, cored and cubed
1 small green pepper, seeded and very finely chopped
1¼ tablespoons chopped onion
2½ tablespoons sugar
1¼ tablespoons lemon juice
⅝ cup dairy sour cream
4 tablespoons mayonnaise
Salt and pepper
Celery seeds

Toss together the cabbage, carrot, apple, pepper and onion. Blend together the sugar, lemon juice, sour cream and mayonnaise. Season to taste.
Add the salad ingredients and lightly toss together; sprinkle with celery seeds.

## ORANGE BAKED APPLES

8 large cooking apples, cored
½ cup butter
½ cup sugar
2 large oranges
1¼ cups heavy cream, whipped

Make a cut through the skin around the center of each apple and place them in a large baking dish. Cream together the butter and sugar. Grate the rind from 1 of the oranges and squeeze out the juice; beat the rind into the butter with as much of the juice as it will take. Fill this orange butter into the apples.
Pare the rind finely from the remaining orange, shred it and blanch in boiling water for 5 minutes. Meanwhile remove all the white part from the orange and chop the orange roughly.
Bake in a moderate oven (350°F.) for about 30 minutes. Top each apple with a spoonful of chopped orange and a few shreds of rind. Serve hot with whipped cream.

## MULLED CIDER
*24 servings*

6 in. stick cinnamon
2½ teaspoons whole allspice
20 cups cider
1 cup sugar, approximately
1 orange, sliced
1 lemon, sliced
Whole cloves

Put the cinnamon stick and allspice in a small square of cheesecloth and tie tightly. Heat the cider, sugar and spices in a saucepan and bring almost to a boil. Remove the spices. Stud the center of each fruit slice with a clove, float the slices on top of the mull and simmer gently for a few minutes. Ladle into mugs.

## BROWN ONION SOUP

2½ tablespoons salad oil
¼ cup butter or margarine
2 pounds onions, finely sliced
2 cloves garlic, crushed
8 beef bouillon cubes
7½ cups boiling water
Salt and pepper

Heat the oil and butter in a large heavy soup pot or Dutch oven. Fry the onion over gentle heat for about 20 minutes until soft but not browned. Add the garlic, bouillon cubes and boiling water. Cover and simmer for 30 minutes. Adjust seasoning.

## POTATO MOUSSAKA

½ cup margarine, divided
2 large onions, finely chopped
2 cloves garlic, crushed
2 pounds cooked lamb, finely chopped
2 beef bouillon cubes, dissolved in 1¼ cups boiling water
2½ tablespoons tomato paste
1 teaspoon dried oregano
Salt and pepper
½ cup shortening
3 pounds potatoes, sliced
½ cup flour
1⅞ cup milk
Pinch of ground nutmeg
2 egg yolks
½ cup grated Cheddar cheese
2 tomatoes, sliced

Melt half the margarine in a large skillet, add the onions and fry for 5 minutes until golden. Add the garlic, lamb, stock, tomato paste, oregano, salt and pepper. Melt the shortening in a large skillet and fry the potato slices for about 10 minutes or until golden. Drain off the fat.
Melt the remaining margarine in a saucepan. Stir in the flour and cook over medium heat for 2 minutes. Remove from heat and stir in the milk. Cook over medium heat, stirring constantly, until mixture comes to a boil. Simmer for 2 minutes. Stir in the nutmeg and season to taste. Remove from heat and beat in the egg yolks, one at a time.
Cover the bottom of a large buttered casserole with a layer of potatoes and season. Spread half

the meat mixture over the potatoes, top with half the remaining potatoes and half the cream sauce. Repeat the layers. Sprinkle the cheese on top and bake in a fairly hot oven (375°F.) for 35 minutes. Garnish with tomato slices.

## POOR MAN'S FONDUE

*you may find it easier to make this quantity in 2 pans*

**1 clove garlic, cut in half**
**6 tablespoons butter**
**5 tablespoons all-purpose flour**
**2½ cups medium sweet cider**
**1½ pounds Cheddar cheese, grated**
**½ pound Gruyère cheese, grated**
**Salt and pepper**
**½ teaspoon grated nutmeg**
**French bread cut in small cubes**

Rub the cut garlic around the sides and bottom of a large flame-proof pan – this will impart just the faintest garlic flavor. Melt the butter in the pan. Stir in the flour and cook for 1–2 minutes. Remove from heat and stir in the cider. Cook over moderate heat, stirring constantly until mixture thickens and comes to a boil. Simmer for 2 minutes.
Stir the grated cheeses into the sauce and heat very gently until melted. Season lightly with salt, pepper and nutmeg.
Transfer the pan to a candle warmer or table heater for serving so that it remains hot. Serve with French bread.

## WHITE WINE CUP

**Fresh fruit in season**
**1¼ tablespoons sugar**
**5 tablespoons Kirsch or maraschino**
**1 bottle medium dry white wine**
**1 bottle champagne**

Slice the fruit (strawberries, peaches, apricots, etc.) and place in the bottom of a bowl. Sprinkle with sugar, pour on the Kirsch and let stand 30 minutes. Pour on the wine and chill for 30 minutes. Add champagne and serve at once.

*Potato moussaka is a good filler for young people*

## CREAM OF CELERY AND TOMATO SOUP

**¾ pound onions, sliced**
**¾ cup butter or margarine**
**3 pound celery, sliced**
**3 pounds tomatoes, peeled and sliced**
**10 cups chicken bouillon**
**1 teaspoon sweet basil**
**Salt**
**Freshly ground black pepper**
**1 cup flour**
**5 cups milk**
**Chopped parsley**

Fry the onions gently in ¼ cup of the butter in a large pan for 5 minutes. Add the celery and cook for another 5 minutes.
Add the tomatoes, chicken bouillon and basil. Season well and bring to a boil. Reduce heat, cover and simmer for about 45 minutes. Put the soup through a sieve or purée in an electric blender.
Melt the remaining butter in a saucepan. Stir in the flour and cook over low heat for 2–3 minutes. Remove from heat and stir in the milk. Cook over moderate heat, stirring constantly, just until hot. Gradually add the vegetable purée and bring to a boil. Adjust the seasoning and simmer for 15 minutes. Sprinkle in the chopped parsley and serve.

## STUFFED BAKED POTATOES

**12 large baking potatoes, approximately the same size**
**Salad oil**

*For curried egg filling:*
**4 eggs, hard-cooked**
**¼ pound onions, chopped**
**2 tablespoons butter or margarine**
**1 teaspoon curry powder**
**¼ pound cooking apples, pared and diced**
**Salt**
**Freshly ground black pepper**

*For bacon filling:*
**2 onions, chopped**
**2 tablespoons butter**
**6 slices bacon, chopped**
**½ teaspoon marjoram**
**1¼ tablespoons milk**
**Salt**
**Freshly ground black pepper**
**1 cup grated Cheddar cheese**

Wash and scrub the potatoes. Dry thoroughly. Prick with a fork and brush with oil, then place on cookie trays and bake in a moderate oven (350°F.) for about 1½ hours or until cooked through.
For the first filling, mash 2 of the eggs, fry the onion in the butter until soft but not browned, add the curry powder and apple and sauté for another 5 minutes, then stir in the mashed egg.
Cut lids from the tops of 6 of the

potatoes when they are cooked and scoop out the centers, leaving a wall of skin. Mix the soft potato with the curried mixture and season well. Replace the mixture in the potato shells and garnish with the remaining eggs, sliced. Serve with mango chutney.
For the second filling, sauté the onion in the hot butter until soft but not browned, remove the onion and set aside. Add the bacon to the pan and fry until crisp. Stir in the marjoram.
Scoop out the centers from the remaining 6 potatoes, cream the soft potato with the milk, add the onion and bacon and season well. Refill the potato cases. Top with grated cheese and keep warm in a very slow oven. Brown under a hot broiler just before serving.

## HOT DOGS

**32 frankfurters**
**1 pound sliced bacon**
**32 hot dog rolls**
**Butter**

Wrap each frankfurter in a half-slice of bacon. Broil until bacon is cooked. Split the rolls, toast if desired, and butter them. Insert hot dogs. Serve with sweet corn relish, catsup and mustard.

## WINTER FRUIT SALAD

**Juice of 6 large lemons**
**3 pound bananas, sliced**
**1½ pound black grapes, halved and seeded**
**1½ pound white grapes, halved and seeded**
**3 cans (16 ounces each) pineapple slices, drained**
**12 tangerines, pared and sectioned**
**3¾ cups water**
**2 cups brown sugar, firmly packed**
**4 tablespoons Kirsch**
**3 trays ice cubes**
**Vanilla ice cream**

Pour the juice of the lemons into a large bowl. Add the bananas, grapes, quartered pineapple slices and tangerines. Turn the fruit lightly in the juice. Make up the water to 5⅝ cups liquid with the juice from the pineapple.
In a saucepan, heat the liquid with the sugar until dissolved, then reduce to 3¾ cups by boiling rapidly. Cool. Pour over the fruit. Chill. Add the Kirsch. Just before serving, stir in the ice cubes. Serve with ice cream.

*Sweet and sour meat balls with buttered noodles*

## MENU *serves 8*

**WEST AFRICAN BEEF CURRY**
**BOILED RICE**
**SAMBALS**
**CHICKEN, RICE AND CORN SALAD**
**FRUIT SALAD**
**MERINGUE SHELLS**
**SHANDY**

### WEST AFRICAN BEEF CURRY

**4 pounds boneless chuck steak**
**½ cup all-purpose flour**
**¼ teaspoon paprika**
**¼ teaspoon cayenne**
**¼ teaspoon chili powder**
**Corn oil**
**1 pound onions, chopped**
**2½ tablespoons flaked coconut**
**6 tablespoons curry powder**
**1 clove garlic, crushed**
**Few drops Tabasco sauce**
**5 cups beef stock**

Trim steak and cut into serving-size pieces. Toss in the flour seasoned with paprika, cayenne and chili powder, using just enough flour to coat the steak thoroughly.

Heat 3 tablespoons oil in a large saucepan and fry the onions until browned. Add the coconut, curry powder, garlic, Tabasco and stock. Bring to a boil.

In a large skillet, heat enough oil just to cover the bottom. Fry the meat a little at a time, until well browned on all sides. Remove the meat and add to the curry sauce. Cover and simmer for about 2 hours or until meat is tender.

As sambals or accompaniments, serve sliced fruit, raw vegetables, flaked coconut and pappadums.

### CHICKEN, RICE AND CORN SALAD

**4 pound stewing chicken, cooked**
**7½ tablespoons French dressing**
**1¼ cups lemon mayonnaise**
**2½ tablespoons lemon juice**
**2½ tablespoons light cream**
**Salt and pepper**
**1½ cups cooked rice**
**2 cans (8 ounces each) kernel corn, drained**
**2 green peppers, seeded and finely diced**
**1 head lettuce**

Strip the chicken meat from the bones and cut into 1 in. pieces. Toss the meat in French dres-

sing. Put the mayonnaise, lemon juice, cream and seasoning in a bowl. Gently fold in the chicken, rice, corn and green peppers. Adjust seasoning.

Line a large salad bowl with lettuce leaves and fill the bottom with torn lettuce. Pile the chicken salad in the center. .

## MENU *serves 12*

**SWEET AND SOUR MEAT BALLS**
**NOODLES**
**DUTCH APPLE PIE**
**VERANDAH PUNCH**

### SWEET AND SOUR MEAT BALLS

**3 pound ground beef**
**2 cloves garlic, finely chopped**
**1 cup all-purpose flour**
**1 cup fresh white breadcrumbs**
**Salt and pepper**
**3 egg yolks**
**6 tablespoons shortening**

*For sauce:*

**1⅛ cups sugar**
**15 tablespoons cider vinegar**
**15 tablespoons soy sauce**
**5 tablespoons cornstarch**
**3¾ cups water**
**3 green peppers, seeded and sliced**
**1½ pound tomatoes, peeled and cut up**
**4 cans (8 ounces each) crushed pineapple, drained**

In a large bowl, mix together the beef, garlic, 6 tablespoons flour, breadcrumbs, salt and pepper. Add the egg yolks and blend thoroughly. Form the mixture into small balls (this amount of meat should make 50–60 balls). Toss the meat balls in the remaining flour.

Melt the shortening in a heavy skillet. Fry the meat balls in batches for 20 minutes; turn frequently during cooking time. Keep each batch hot.

Meanwhile prepare the sauce. Place the sugar, vinegar and soy sauce in a pan. Blend the cornstarch with a little of the measured water and add to the pan with the remaining water. Bring to a boil, stirring, simmer for 5 minutes. Blanch the pepper and add to the sauce with the tomatoes and pineapple. Simmer for 5–10 minutes.

When the meat balls are cooked divide them between 2–3 large pans. Pour over the sauce and simmer for 3 minutes. Serve in large dishes with cooked noodles.

### DUTCH APPLE PIE
*make 3 for the party*

**1½ pound cooking apples, pared and cut up**
**5–7½ tablespoons water**
**⅔ cup soft brown sugar, firmly packed**
**1¼ tablespoons cornstarch**
**½ teaspoon salt**
**1 teaspoon cinnamon**
**2½ tablespoons lemon juice**
**2 tablespoons butter**
**½ teaspoon vanilla extract**
**1½ cups all-purpose flour**
**1¼ teaspoons salt**
**2 tablespoons shortening**
**¼ cup butter**
**Milk**

Simmer the apples with the water until soft. Combine the sugar, cornstarch, salt and cinnamon and stir into the apples. Stir in the lemon juice and cook, stirring occasionally, until fairly thick. Remove from heat, stir in the butter and vanilla. Cool.

Sift the flour and salt into a bowl. Cut in the shortening and butter with a pastry blender or two knives until the mixture resembles fine breadcrumbs. Add enough ice cold water to make a stiff dough.

Roll out a little over half the dough and use to line a 6–7 in. pie plate, preferably metal. Put the apple mixture in the pastry case. Roll out the remaining pastry and use to cover the top of the pie. Press the edges together, seal and crimp and brush with milk. Bake in a hot oven (425°F.) for 10 minutes. Reduce oven temperature to 375°F. and cook for 20 minutes or until the pastry is golden brown.

Serve hot or cold with whipped cream or ice cream.

### VERANDAH PUNCH

**2 large juicy oranges**
**3 thin-skinned lemons**
**⅝ cup sugar syrup**
**1¼ cups freshly made tea**
**2 bottles (12 ounces each) ginger ale, well chilled**
**2 bottles (12 ounces each) soda water, well chilled**
**Ice cubes**
**Orange slices**

Squeeze out the fruit juices and mix with the sugar syrup and the tea. Cool. Strain into a bowl and chill.

Just before serving, mix in the ginger ale and soda water. Add ice cubes and orange slices.

*Verandah punch is ideal for a teenage party*

# Christmas

Turkey and Christmas pudding must form the center of most families' traditional meal, but there's more to it than that. Here are some recipes both old and new to try.

## ROAST TURKEY

To help you calculate what size turkey you need, use this chart:

| Turkey (oven-ready weight) | Servings |
|---|---|
| 6–8 pounds | 6–10 |
| 8–12 pounds | 10–20 |
| 14–16 pounds | 20–40 |

It's useful to know that a 10 pound turkey yields about 2¾ pounds white meat and about the same amount of dark meat. As a straight roast meal, with trimmings, this will serve 8, plus a further 4 servings as cold cuts and should leave you enough for a réchauffé dish as well.

ing wrap or bag.
Approximate cooking times for the quick oven method using foil wrap, at 450°F. are:
6–8 pounds 2½ hours
8–10 pounds 2½–2¾ hours
10–12 pounds 2 hours 50 minutes
12–14 pounds 3 hours
14–16 pounds 3–3¼ hours
16–18 pounds 3¼–3½ hours
If wished, open the foil for the last 30 minutes and cover the bird with bacon slices. Turn the bird about half-way through the cooking time so that it cooks evenly. To check if the turkey is cooked, pierce the deepest part of the

thigh with a skewer. If the juices are colorless, the bird is ready; if tinged pink, cook it a little longer. Calculate the cooking time to have the bird ready 30 minutes before serving. When ready, lower the oven temperature and keep the bird warm.
If you wish to use the slow oven method, don't wrap the bird in foil, but if it just about fills the oven it is wise to protect the legs and breast. Approximate cooking times at 325°F. are:
6–8 pounds 3–3½ hours
8–10 pounds 3½–3¾ hours
10–12 pounds 3¾–4 hours

browned. Finely dice the apple, add to the pan and cook a little longer. Stir in the breadcrumbs, lemon rind, 1 tablespoon lemon juice and sage. Toss lightly and season well with salt and pepper. Add just enough liquid to hold the mixture together but do not make it soggy.

## NUT STUFFING

½ cup walnuts
¼ cup cashews
¼ cup Brazil nuts
¼ cup butter or margarine
2 small onions, finely chopped
¼ pound mushrooms, finely chopped
Pinch of dried herbs
1¼ tablespoons chopped parsley
3 cups fresh white breadcrumbs
1 large egg, beaten
Giblet stock, if needed
Salt
Freshly ground black pepper

Finely chop the nuts. Melt the butter and sauté the onion until soft but not brown. Add mushrooms and sauté 5 minutes.
Toss together the nuts, herbs and breadcrumbs. Stir in the onion-mushroom mixture with the beaten egg. Toss well. If necessary, moisten with a little stock. Season to taste.

*A tasty risotto makes a change the day after Christmas*

If your turkey is frozen, make sure it arrives in good time. Remove it from the container, cover with muslin and leave it to thaw, preferably in the refrigerator, for 2–3 days. If refrigerator space is not available store in the coldest possible place.
To prepare the bird for the oven, first remove the giblets and use them to make a stock for the gravy. Wipe the turkey inside, then put in the stuffing. Most people use 2 kinds of stuffing in a turkey, 1 at the neck end and 1 at the vent. Allow about ½ pound stuffing to each 5 pound of turkey; do not stuff too tightly. Brush the skin with melted butter or dripping and season with salt, pepper and lemon juice. Either put it in a roasting pan and cover with foil or use plastic film roast-

12–14 pounds 4–4¼ hours
14–16 pounds 4¼–4½ hours
16–18 pounds 4½–4 hours 50 minutes

**Handy hint**

Stuffings are best made with fresh breadcrumbs. If only dry crumbs are available, soak in a little milk or stock for 1 hour and squeeze out the excess moisture before use.

## CELERY STUFFING

¼ pound onions, finely chopped
2–3 celery stalks, finely diced
¼ cup butter or margarine
¼ pound cooking apples, pared and cored
3 cups fresh white breadcrumbs
Juice and finely grated rind of 1 small lemon
2½ teaspoons dried sage
Salt
Freshly ground black pepper
3 tablespoons liquid from cooked giblets

Fry the onion and celery in hot butter until tender but not

## MUSHROOM AND BACON STUFFING

3 cups fresh white breadcrumbs
1¼ tablespoons chopped parsley
½ teaspoon dried thyme
1 clove garlic, crushed
¼ cup butter or margarine
¼ pound onions, chopped
¼ pound sliced bacon, chopped
¼ pound mushrooms, chopped
Salt
Freshly ground black pepper
1 egg yolk, optional
Giblet stock, optional

In a large mixing bowl toss together the breadcrumbs, parsley, thyme and garlic.
Melt the butter in a skillet and sauté the onions until soft but not browned. Stir in the bacon and cook for 3–4 minutes. Add the mushrooms and blend well. Combine this mixture with the breadcrumbs in the bowl.
Season well. Add the egg yolk and a little stock if needed to hold mixture together.

## CRANBERRY SAUCE

¾ cup sugar
⅝ cup water
½ pound fresh cranberries, washed
Sherry

Gently heat the sugar with the water in a pan until the sugar dissolves. Add the cranberries and cook uncovered over medium heat for about 10 minutes or until cranberries pop. Allow to cool. Add sherry to taste before serving.

## CRANBERRY AND BACON BALLS

*makes 16–20*

3 small onions, finely chopped
¼ pound bacon, chopped
2 tablespoons butter or margarine
¼ pound fresh cranberries, washed
¼ cup shredded suet
1 teaspoon dried thyme
Finely grated rind of 1 orange
3 cups fresh white breadcrumbs
1 teaspoon salt
Freshly ground black pepper
1 large egg, beaten
Orange juice
Fat for cooking

Sauté the onion and bacon in the hot butter until tender. Add the cranberries and cook until they 'pop'. Cool a little. Add the suet, thyme, orange rind and breadcrumbs. Toss the mixture together and add the salt and pepper. Stir in the egg and enough orange juice to moisten and make the mixture stick together. Form the mixture into balls.
Heat some shortening or dripping to give ¼ in. depth in a baking pan. Add the stuffing balls and bake in a fairly hot oven (400°F.) for about 20 minutes. Turn the balls over once during the cooking time.

## TURKEY RISOTTO

*4 servings*

3 small onions, finely chopped
2 tablespoons butter or margarine
¼ pound bacon, diced
½ pound cooked turkey, diced
¼ pound button mushrooms, sliced
1 small green pepper, seeded and sliced
1 cup raw rice
Celery salt
Freshly ground black pepper
5 tablespoons dry white wine
2½ cups turkey stock
Tomato wedges

Sauté the onion in the butter until tender, add the bacon and cook until bacon is almost cooked. Add the cooked, diced turkey, mushrooms, pepper, rice and seasonings. Stir well and pour in the wine and the stock. Bring this mixture to a boil, stirring gently, and turn into a casserole.
Cover tightly and bake in a warm oven (325°F.) for 35 minutes until the stock is absorbed and the rice is fluffy and tender.
Turn out into a heated serving platter and garnish with tomato wedges.

*Traditional Christmas pudding with a fluffy brandy flavored sauce*

## TURKEY CRANBERRY SALAD

*4 servings*

2½ tablespoons unflavored gelatin, divided
⅝ cup water
5 tablespoons lemon juice, divided
1 can (8 ounces) whole berry cranberry sauce
1¼ cups turkey stock
¼ teaspoon Tabasco sauce
6¼ tablespoons lemon mayonnaise
2½ teaspoons finely chopped onion
2–3 stalks celery, chopped
1 small green pepper, seeded and chopped
1 red-skinned eating apple, cored and diced
¾ pound cooked turkey, diced

Sprinkle 1 tablespoon of the gelatin over the water in a bowl to soften. Place the bowl over a pan of hot water and dissolve the gelatin. Add 2 tablespoons lemon juice and the cranberry sauce. Stir thoroughly. Pour into a 4-cup mold. Let stand until firm.
Place the turkey stock in a saucepan. Sprinkle remaining gelatin over the top to soften. Dissolve the gelatin over very low heat but do not boil. Add the Tabasco sauce and remaining lemon juice and pour into a bowl. Leave to cool. Gradually beat in the mayonnaise. When mixture is beginning to set, fold in the onion, celery, pepper, apple and turkey. Adjust seasoning. Spoon on to the cranberry layer and let stand until firm. To serve, unmold and garnish as desired.

## TURKEY BROTH

*4 servings*

3 carrots, coarsely grated
3 onions, finely chopped
2 tablespoons butter or margarine
3¾ cups strong turkey stock
1 bay leaf
¼ cup small pasta
½ cup chopped celery leaves

Sauté the carrot and onion in the hot butter until soft but not browned, about 10 minutes. Pour in the stock and add the bay leaf and pasta. Bring to a boil. Cover and simmer for 30 minutes. Discard the bay leaf, adjust seasoning and add the celery leaves. Serve with grated cheese and hunks of bread.

## ROAST HAM

*10 servings*

½ smoked ham, about 4–5 pounds
⅔ cup light brown sugar
Cloves
2½ tablespoons honey
2½ tablespoons orange juice
Glacé cherries, canned apricots and sliced oranges

Soak the ham for several hours in cold water. Drain. To calculate the cooking time, allow 20–25 minutes per pound. Place the ham in a pan, skin side down. Cover with water and half the sugar. Bring slowly to boil and remove the scum. Reduce the heat and simmer, covered, for half the cooking time. Top up with boiling water when necessary. Drain the ham. Carefully strip off the rind and score the fat into squares. Stud with cloves. Blend the remaining sugar, honey and orange juice and spread over the ham. Place in a roasting pan, and roast in a moderate oven (350°F.) for the remaining cooking time. Baste two or three times during cooking and, 20 minutes before the end of the cooking time, raise the temperature to 425°F.
Serve hot, garnished with drained apricot halves and glacé cherries impaled on toothpicks or with slices of orange.

## CHRISTMAS PUDDING

*6–8 servings*

1½ cups all-purpose flour
1¼ teaspoons cinnamon
½ teaspoon nutmeg
¼ pound apples, pared and cored
1½ cups fresh white breadcrumbs
¼ pound suet, shredded
½ cup seedless raisins, chopped
1 cup currants
1 cup white raisins
½ cup light brown sugar
Grated rind of 1 lemon
Grated rind of 1 orange
2 eggs, beaten
⅞ cup strong ale

Grease a 1½-quart pudding bowl or mold. Sift together the flour, cinnamon and nutmeg. Dice the apple and add to the flour along with the breadcrumbs, suet, dried fruits, sugar, lemon and orange rinds. Combine the eggs and ale and blend well. Gradually stir into the mixed flour and fruit and stir thoroughly. If possible, let stand overnight at this stage.

Turn the mixture into the prepared bowl, then cover with waxed paper and aluminum foil or a pudding cloth. Tie the foil or cloth firmly in place with cord. Either place in a pan half-filled with water and, after bringing to a boil, reduce heat and boil gently for about 6 hours, or place in a steamer and cook for 8 hours. A piece of lemon in the water will prevent discoloration of the pan. Top up with more boiling water at intervals.

To store, leave the waxed paper in position, but re-wrap with fresh foil. On the day of serving, reboil for about 3 hours.

## EASY CHRISTMAS PUDDING
*makes 2 puddings*

**1 cup all-purpose flour**
**1 teaspoon cinnamon**
**½ teaspoon nutmeg**
**2 cups fresh white breadcrumbs**
**⅓ cup light brown sugar**
**Grated rind of 1 lemon**
**½ cup glacé cherries, chopped**
**¼ cup chopped almonds**
**3 pounds prepared mincemeat**
**3 eggs, beaten**

Grease two 3-cup pudding molds or bowls.

Sift together the flour, cinnamon and nutmeg into a large bowl. Add the breadcrumbs, sugar, lemon rind, cherries and almonds. Mix together and stir in the mincemeat and eggs. Mix the ingredients together well with a wooden spoon.

Divide the mixture evenly between the 2 bowls. Cover tightly with waxed paper and aluminum foil or pudding cloths. Tie the foil or cloths in place with cord.

Place in a saucepan half-filled with water. Bring to a boil, reduce heat and simmer for about 4¾ hours. Top up with boiling water when necessary.

To store, leave waxed paper in position but cover with fresh foil. To reheat, boil gently for about 2 hours.

## FLUFFY SAUCE

**¼ cup butter**
**⅞ cup confectioners' sugar, sifted**
**2 eggs, separated**
**2½ tablespoons brandy**
**⅝ cup heavy cream**

*Snowman cake for the children*

Cream together the butter and confectioners' sugar. Beat in the egg yolks and then gradually beat in the brandy. Add the heavy cream. Place in the top part of a double boiler. Cook over hot water until the mixture is the consistency of thick custard. Beat the egg whites until stiff but not dry. Pour the custard mixture on to the egg whites, beating all the time. Return to the double boiler and keep warm over water. Stir well before serving.

## RUM BUTTER

**½ pound unsalted butter**
**⅔ cup light brown sugar, firmly packed**
**2–3 tablespoons rum**
**Confectioners' sugar**

Cream the butter in a bowl with a wooden spoon and beat in the sugar. When the mixture is soft, slowly beat in the rum to taste. Pile into the bowl in which it is to be served and chill.

Just before serving, dredge with confectioners' sugar.

## MINCEMEAT
*makes about 6 pounds*

**¾ pound currants**
**½ pound white raisins**
**¾ pound seedless raisins**
**¼ pound cut mixed candied peel**
**¾ pound firm, hard cooking apples, peeled and cored**
**1 pound light brown sugar**
**1 pound shredded suet**
**1 teaspoon nutmeg**
**½ teaspoon cinnamon**
**Grated rind and juice of 1 lemon**
**Grated rind and juice of 1 small orange**
**⅞ cup brandy**

Roughly chop the currants, raisins, peel and apples. Combine with the sugar, suet, spices, lemon and orange rind and juice and brandy. Mix all the ingre-

dients together thoroughly. Cover the mincemeat and let stand overnight.

Next day stir the mincemeat well and put into jars. Cover with a thin layer of paraffin. Store in a cool, dry, well ventilated place and allow to mature for at least 2 weeks before using.

A quarter of a cup of almonds may be added to each pound of mincemeat just before use.

## MINCE TARTS
*makes 20*

**Double recipe Shortcrust Pastry. page 75**
**¾ pound mincemeat**
**Confectioners' sugar**

Grease twenty 2½ in. patty pans. Roll out the pastry about ⅛ in. thick. Using a 3 in. round fluted cutter, cut out 20 rounds for the bottoms and then cut 20 smaller rounds with a 2¼ in. fluted cutter, rerolling pastry as necessary. Line the patty pans with the larger rounds, fitting in carefully with the fingers. Fill two-thirds full with mincemeat and place the smaller rounds on top. Make a slit in the top of each round and place on a cookie tray. Bake in a fairly hot oven (400°F.) for about 20 minutes or until light golden brown.

Serve warm or cold, lightly dusted with confectioners' sugar. If preferred, the tops may be brushed with a little milk before baking to glaze them.

## CHRISTMAS CAKE

**½ pound seedless raisins**
**½ pound white raisins**
**½ pound currants**
**¼ pound chopped mixed candied peel**
**1 cup ground almonds**
**1 cup glacé cherries, cut up**
**2 cups all-purpose flour**
**½ teaspoon cinnamon**
**½ teaspoon nutmeg**
**Pinch of salt**
**1 cup butter**
**1 cup light brown sugar, firmly packed**
**4 large eggs**
**2 tablespoons brandy**

Grease an 8-in. spring-form pan. Line the bottom with a circle of waxed paper and grease again.

Combine the raisins, white raisins, currants, peel, almonds and cherries. Set aside.

Sift the flour, cinnamon, nutmeg and salt together. Cream the butter and sugar together until light and fluffy. Beat in the eggs, one at a time, beating well after each addition. Fold in the dry ingredients and blend well. Stir in the fruit mixture and brandy. Turn the mixture into the prepared pan. Place the spring-form pan in a 9-in. cake pan. Place the cake pan on a cookie tray which has been covered with a sheet of brown paper.

Bake in the lower part of a cool oven (300°F.) for 3½ hours. Let stand in pan until cool. Remove ring and bottom pan, remove paper from bottom and let stand on wire rack until thoroughly cool. If desired, baste with a little more brandy before storing. Wrap in foil, put in an airtight tin and store in a cool, dry place. Decorate not more than 1 week before Christmas.

## SNOWMAN CAKE

**1 cup butter or margarine**
**1 cup sugar**
**4 large eggs**
**2 cups self-rising flour**
**¼ cup cocoa**
**2½ tablespoons hot water**

*For decoration:*
**2 egg whites**
**4 cups confectioners' sugar, sifted**
**1¼ tablespoons glycerin**
**1¼ teaspoons lemon juice**
**¼ pound store-bought marzipan**
**Few drops red coloring**
**Colored mint patties**
**Liquorice pipe**

Grease a 2-cup and a 1½-quart, ovenproof bowl or baking mold. Dust lightly with flour, shaking out any excess.

Cream the butter and sugar together until light and fluffy. Add the eggs, one at a time, beating well after each addition. Fold in the flour. Blend the cocoa with the hot water until smooth and stir into the mixture. Fill both bowls two-thirds full. Put them in the center of a moderate oven (350°F.). Bake the small one 40–45 minutes and the large one 1 hour and 15 minutes. Let stand on a wire rack about 5 minutes, then turn out and cool. Brush the loose crumbs off both cakes and place the larger one on a flat serving platter.

Beat the egg whites in a bowl. Beat in the sugar, a little at a time, with a wooden spoon. Add the glycerin and lemon juice. The icing should be soft, but firm enough to hold the shape of peaks. Spread the icing over the

*No need to pipe elaborate decorations on the Christmas cake – icing 'snow' is just as pretty*

*Home-made mincemeat, with almonds and a little brandy, makes the best mince tarts*

251

larger cake to cover completely and rough up into soft peaks. Place the small cake on top and cover with icing in the same way. Let stand until frosting is set. Meanwhile, add a few drops of coloring to the marzipan, roll out fairly thinly into a circle and shape into a brimmed hat. When the icing is nearly set, place the hat in position and put the colored mints in place to make the eyes, nose and buttons. Add the liquorice pipe. When the icing is firmly set, secure a colored ribbon around the snowman's neck to make a scarf.

## YULE LOG PUDDING

*6 servings*

**2 tablespoons chopped candied ginger**
**½ cup chopped glacé cherries**
**2 tablespoons brandy**
**¼ cup blanched almonds**
**1 package (3 ounces) vanilla pudding and pie filling mix**
**2 cups milk**
**⅝ cup heavy cream, whipped**
**1 egg white**

Combine the ginger, cherries and brandy and let stand 30–60 minutes. Chop the nuts roughly. Make up the mix with the milk according to package directions. Cool thoroughly. Turn the pudding into ice cube tray and freeze until it is half frozen. Fold in the fruit, nuts and cream. Beat the egg white until stiff, fold it into the custard mixture and freeze until almost set then beat well with a spoon.
Pour the mixture into a loaf pan that has been rinsed with cold water. Freeze until hard. To serve, turn out and cut into slices.

## MARZIPAN AND RAISIN TRUFFLES

**½ pound semi-sweet chocolate**
**¾ cup seedless raisins**
**1¼ tablespoons rum**
**½ pound ready-made marzipan**
**1 teaspoon coffee extract**
**Chocolate shot**
**Cocoa**

Melt half the chocolate in a bowl over hot water. When melted and smooth, add the raisins and rum. Blend thoroughly. When firm enough, shape into 24 small balls. Chill.
Knead the marzipan until pliable and work in the coffee extract. Roll out to about ¼ in. thick and stamp out 24 rounds, using a 2 in. plain cutter. Shape the marzipan around the chocolate and raisins

*Christmas preserves – rich or spicy – for cold meats*

to form balls.
Melt the remaining chocolate in a small, deep bowl over hot water. Dip each ball in the melted chocolate, drain a little, then coat half of them with the chocolate shot. Let the remainder dry on waxed paper, then roll in cocoa. Serve in small paper cases.

# CHRISTMAS PRESERVES

*After Christmas, some special preserves will add to the pleasure of meals. These make good presents, too, in attractive jars.*

## SPICED ORANGE RINGS

**8 thin-skinned oranges**
**3¾ cups water**
**3 cups sugar**
**1¼ cups white vinegar**
**½ tablespoon whole cloves**
**1½ sticks cinnamon**
**6 blades of mace**

Wipe the oranges, cut into ¼ in. thick slices and remove the seeds. Place the sliced oranges in a pan, cover with water, cover the pan and simmer for about 40 minutes or until the orange rind is soft. Make a syrup by dissolving the sugar in the vinegar, add the spices and boil for 3–4 minutes. Drain the oranges, place in a shallow pan and cover with the vinegar syrup. Simmer, covered, for 30–40 minutes, until the orange slices look clear. Remove from heat and let stand in the syrup for 24 hours.
Drain the orange rings and pack into sterilized jars. Cover the fruit

with the syrup. Do not seal at once, but keep adding the syrup for the next 3 to 4 days until the syrup is all used. Then seal with tight lids.
Allow to mature for at least 6 weeks before using.

## BRANDIED PEACHES

**1 pound fresh peaches**
**1 cup sugar**
**⅝ cup brandy or Cointreau, approximately**

Peel the peaches by plunging them into boiling water, then gently removing the skins. Halve the peaches and remove the pits. Make a light syrup by dissolving ½ cup sugar in 1¼ cups water. Poach the peaches gently for 4–5 minutes. Remove from the heat, lift out the peaches and arrange in small, sterilized jars.
Add the remaining sugar to the syrup and dissolve slowly. Bring to a boil and boil to 230°F. Remove from heat and cool. Add an equal quantity of brandy or Cointreau to the syrup. Pour over the peaches. Cover with a layer of melted paraffin.

## SPICED CRAB APPLES

**6 pound crab apples**
**3¾ cups water**
**2–3 strips lemon peel**
**2 cups sugar**
**1⅞ cup wine vinegar**
**1 stick cinnamon**
**1–2 whole cloves**
**3 peppercorns**

Wash and trim the crab apples. Simmer in the water with the lemon rind until just tender, remove from the heat.

Place the sugar and vinegar in a saucepan and add 3¾ cups of the liquid from the fruit. Tie the spices in a square of cheesecloth and add to the liquid. Heat gently to dissolve the sugar, then bring to a boil and boil for 1 minute. Remove the pan from the heat and add the crab apples. Simmer gently until the syrup has reduced to a coating consistency, 30–40 minutes. Remove the spices after 30 minutes. Place the fruit in small sterilized jars. Cover with syrup. Cover with a layer of melted paraffin.

## SPICED PEARS

**1¾ cups sugar**
**1½ tablespoons salt**
**5 cups water**
**6 pound small, hard pears, pared and cored**
**5 cups white vinegar**
**2 sticks cinnamon**
**1 tablespoon whole cloves**

Dissolve ¼ cup of the sugar and the salt in the water and bring to a boil. Cut the pears in quarters and add to the boiling water; remove the pan from the heat, cover and let stand until cool.
Boil together the vinegar, remaining sugar and spices. Remove the pears from the water and drain. Place them in the vinegar syrup and bring to a boil. Remove from heat and allow to cool. Bring back to a boil. Repeat this process 3 times.
Finally allow to cool and place the pears in small sterilized jars. Pour the syrup over them, retaining the surplus, but do not seal. Top up each day for the next 4 days with the reserved syrup, or until no more syrup can be absorbed. Cover with a layer of melted paraffin.

## BRANDIED PINEAPPLE

**1 can (1 pound 13 ounces) pineapple chunks**
**3 cloves**
**2 in. stick cinnamon**
**⅝ cup brandy or Kirsch**

Drain the juice from the pineapple and place in a saucepan. Add the cloves and cinnamon and simmer gently until of a syrupy consistency. Add the pineapple chunks and simmer for 10 minutes. Remove from the heat and add the brandy or Kirsch. Let stand to cool.
Pack the fruit in a wide-necked bottle. Pour in the syrup. Cover with a tight lid or top with a layer of melted paraffin.

# EASTER

**Warm hot cross buns on Good Friday,
Easter bread for Sunday breakfast,
simnel cake and Easter cookies for
tea. In between, all children love a
chocolate egg.**

## HOT CROSS BUNS
*makes 18*

¾ cup milk, scalded
½ cup shortening
⅓ cup sugar
1 teaspoon salt
¼ cup warm water (105–115°F.)
1 package of cake yeast, active
    dry or compressed
1 egg, beaten
¾ cup currants
½ teaspoon mace
4 cups all-purpose flour,
    approximately
Salad oil
1 egg white, slightly beaten

Combine the milk, shortening, sugar and salt. Cool to lukewarm. Measure the warm water into a large warm mixing bowl. Sprinkle or crumble in the yeast. Stir until dissolved. Add the milk mixture, egg, currants and mace. Stir in about 3½ cups flour to make a stiff dough. Add more flour if needed. Place the dough in an oiled bowl. Turn once to bring oiled side up. Cover and let rise in a warm place, free from draft, for about 2 hours or until doubled in bulk. Turn out on to a lightly floured surface and knead for 1 minute. Cut dough in half then cut each half into 9 pieces. Shape each one into a ball. Arrange in 2 oiled 8 in. square pans. With oiled scissors, snip a deep cross in top of each bun. Brush with egg white. Cover and let rise in a warm place, free from draft, until doubled in bulk. Bake in a hot oven (425°F.) for 25 minutes or until well browned. Cool on a wire rack.

## EASTER COOKIES
*makes 15-20*

6 tablespoons butter or
    margarine
5 tablespoons sugar
1 egg, separated
1½ cups self-rising flour
Pinch of salt
¼ cup currants
1 tablespoon chopped mixed
    candied peel
1–2 tablespoons milk or brandy
Sugar

Grease 2 cookie trays. Cream the butter and sugar together until light. Beat in the egg yolk. Sift the flour with the salt and fold into the creamed mixture with the currants and finely chopped mixed peel. Add enough milk or brandy to give a fairly soft dough. Cover and let stand in a cool place to become firm.
Knead lightly on a floured board

*Buy an Easter egg mold and make your own chocolate eggs*

and roll out to about ¼ in. thick. Cut into rounds, using a 2½ in. fluted cutter.
Place well apart on cookie trays. Bake in a fairly hot oven (400°F.) for about 20 minutes, or until lightly browned. After 10 minutes, brush the cookies with egg white and sprinkle with sugar, then continue baking.
Cool on a wire rack.

## SIMNEL CAKE

1 pound ready-made almond
    paste
2 cups all-purpose flour
Pinch of salt
½ teaspoon nutmeg
½ teaspoon cinnamon
½ pound currants
¼ pound white raisins
½ cup chopped mixed candied
    peel
¼ pound glacé cherries, cut up
¾ cup butter
¾ cup sugar
3 eggs
Milk, if required
1 egg white

Grease a 7 or 8 in. spring-form pan. Line the bottom with a circle of waxed paper and grease again. Roll out one-third of the almond paste into a round slightly smaller than the pan.
Sift together the flour, salt and spices. Mix together all the fruit. Cream the butter and sugar together until light and fluffy. Beat in the eggs, one at a time, beating well after each addition. Fold in the flour, adding a little milk if necessary to make a heavy batter. Fold in the fruit.
Put half of the cake mixture into the prepared pan and place the round of almond paste on top.

Cover with the rest of the mixture, spreading it evenly. Bake in a cool oven (300°F.) for 2½–3 hours, until the cake is a rich brown and firm to the touch. Cool on a wire rack. It is not possible to test this cake with a skewer as the almond paste remains soft and may give a false impression.
From the remaining almond paste, shape 11 small balls, then cut the rest into a round to fit the top of the cake. Remove the cooled cake from the pan, brush with egg white and place the almond paste on top. Smooth it down with a rolling pin. Pinch the edges into scallops with finger and thumb. Score the surface into a lattice with a knife, brush with egg white, arrange the almond paste balls around the top of the cake and brush these with egg white.
Put under a heated broiler until a light, golden brown.

## EASTER BREAD
*makes 2 loaves*

5¼–6¼ cups all-purpose flour
¾ cup sugar
½ teaspoon salt
1 teaspoon ground cardamom
1 tablespoon grated orange rind
1 teaspoon grated lemon rind
2 packages active dry yeast
¾ cup milk
½ cup water
½ cup butter or margarine
2 eggs
½ cup chopped almonds
½ cup white raisins

In a large bowl thoroughly mix 1½ cups flour, the sugar, salt, cardamom, orange and lemon rinds, and yeast. Combine the

milk, water and butter in a saucepan. Heat over low heat until the liquids are very warm (120–130°F.); the butter does not need to melt. Gradually add to the dry ingredients and beat for 2 minutes at medium speed with electric mixer, scraping bowl occasionally. Add the eggs and 1 cup flour. Beat at high speed for 2 minutes, scraping bowl occasionally. Stir in enough additional flour by hand to make a soft dough. Turn out on to a lightly floured board, knead until smooth and elastic, about 8–10 minutes. Place in a greased bowl, turning to grease top. Cover and let rise in a warm place, free from draft, until doubled in bulk, about 1 hour.
Punch dough down; turn out onto a lightly floured board. Knead in almonds and white raisins. Divide in half. Shape into 2 smooth balls. Place in 2 greased 8-in. round cake pans. Cover and let rise in a warm place, free from draft, until doubled in bulk, about 1 hour.
Bake in a fairly hot oven (375°F.) for 35–40 minutes or until done. Remove from pans and cool on wire racks. Frost with confectioners' sugar frosting if desired.

## CURRANT CAKE

¾ cup butter, softened
⅔ cup sugar
3 eggs
2 cups sifted all-purpose flour
1 teaspoon baking powder
½ teaspoon salt
1 cup currants
¾ cup chopped, pitted dates
¼ cup white raisins
½ cup chopped mixed candied
    peel
3 tablespoons split blanched
    almonds

Cream the butter and sugar together until light and fluffy. Add the eggs, one at a time, beating well after each addition. Reserve 2 tablespoons of the flour; sift remaining flour with baking powder and salt. Add the flour mixture to the butter mixture, blending thoroughly. Mix the reserved flour with the fruits until they are well coated. Stir the fruits into the butter mixture. Spoon into an oiled 8-in. square cake pan. Bake in a moderate oven (325°F.) for 30 minutes. Arrange the almonds on top. Reduce temperature to 325°F. and bake 30 minutes longer. Cool on a wire rack.

# ANNIVERSARY SUPPERS

*There are no traditional anniversary dishes, but a celebration of this importance merits something special.*

*Coffee brandy gâteau and sunshine fruit salad for an anniversary*

## MENU *serves 12*

**SALMON MOUSSE**
**BAKED HAM SLICES**
**BOILED RICE WITH ALMONDS**
**MIXED SALAD**
**GREEN BEAN VINAIGRETTE**
**COFFEE BRANDY GATEAUX**
**SUNSHINE FRUIT SALAD**

**Day before:** *Wash the salad ingredients and pack them in plastic wrap in the refrigerator to keep crisp. Make up the salad dressing, keep it in a screw-top jar. Cook the beans.*
*Make the gâteaux and leave them in the refrigerator.*
*Make the mousse, but do not leave it in the mold overnight if it is a metal one.*

**In the morning:** *Make up the fruit salad.*

**2 hours before:** *Turn out the mousse and garnish. Turn out the gâteaux and decorate.*

**1 hour before:** *Prepare the ham and put it on to cook. Boil the rice. Toss the salads.*

## SALMON MOUSSE

**2 envelopes unflavored gelatin**
**½ cup water**
**2 cans (16 ounces each) salmon**
**1 cup diced celery**
**½ cup finely chopped green pepper**
**½ cup chopped pimiento**
**¼ cup fresh lemon juice**
**3 cups mayonnaise**
**1 tablespoon grated onion**
**¼ teaspoon pepper**
**Cooked shrimp**
**Watercress**
**3 tablespoons chopped chives**

Soften the gelatin in cold water in a small bowl. Place the bowl in a

pan of hot water to dissolve. Cool. Mash the salmon, including the liquid. Add the celery, green pepper, pimiento, lemon juice, 1½ cups mayonnaise, onion and pepper. Mix well. Stir in the cool gelatin. Pack the mixture into a 2 quart mold or bowl. Chill overnight. Unmold on serving platter and garnish with cooked shrimp and watercress. Fold chives into remaining mayonnaise and serve on the side.

## BAKED HAM SLICES

**12 center cut fully cooked ham slices, ½ in. thick**
**3 teaspoons dry mustard**
**4 cups pared chopped tart apples**
**1 cup firmly packed brown sugar**
**2 cups claret**

Put the ham slices in a large shallow baking dish, or in two baking dishes, so that they are flat. Sprinkle with the dry mustard.

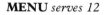

**Handy hint**

1 tablespoon oil added to the water when cooking pasta prevents the pasta sticking together and also improves the flavor.

Top with the chopped apples and sprinkle with brown sugar. Pour the claret over the ham. Cover and bake in a moderate oven (350°F.) for 40 minutes. Uncover and bake 30 minutes longer.
Serve hot with cooked rice, that has been tossed with almond halves, green beans vinaigrette and a mixed green salad.

## COFFEE BRANDY GATEAU
*make 2 for the party*

**¾ cup butter**
**¾ cup sugar**
**3 large eggs**
**2½ tablespoons coffee extract**
**1¼ tablespoons brandy**
**12 lady fingers**
**⅝ cup heavy cream, whipped**
**Chopped walnuts**

Line the bottom of a loose-bottomed 8-in. cake pan with waxed paper.
Cream the butter and sugar together until light and fluffy and the sugar has lost its grittiness. Beat in the eggs, one at a time. Beat in the coffee extract and brandy. Split the lady fingers in half lengthwise. Arrange 8 pieces in the base of the prepared pan. Pour in half the coffee mixture. Cover with 8 more lady finger halves, then pour in the remaining coffee mixture. Arrange the remaining lady fingers on top. Press down well. Cover with a small plate and put a weight on the plate. Leave in the refrigerator for about 3 hours or until set.
Shortly before serving, run a spatula around the edge of the pan. Turn the gâteau out on to a serving platter and remove the

waxed paper. Cover the top with cream and pipe the remaining cream around the top and base of the gâteau, using a large star nozzle. Cluster a few chopped walnuts in the center.

## SUNSHINE FRUIT SALAD
*make 2 for the party*

**½ cup sugar**
**1¼ cups water**
**Juice of ½ lemon**
**1 medium-sized melon**
**3 oranges**
**3 grapefruit**
**1 pint box strawberries**
**2½ tablespoons Grand Marnier**

Make the syrup by dissolving the sugar in the water over gentle heat and boiling for 5 minutes. Allow to cool then stir in the lemon juice.
Halve the melon, discard the seeds and scoop out the fruit. Chop it roughly. Remove the rind and white part from the oranges and grapefruit and cut into sections. Discard the hulls from the strawberries and cut in half.
Put all the fruit into the syrup, add the Grand Marnier and refrigerate for 2–3 hours.

## MENU *serves 12*

**ROCK LOBSTER TAILS WITH TARRAGON DRESSING**
**CRUMBED LAMB CHOPS**
**BEEF AND PORK SKEWERS**
**SOUR CREAM AND GARLIC DIP**
**CONFETTI SALAD**
**FRENCH BREAD AND BUTTER**
**TUTTI FRUTTI**
**CHERRY FLAN**

**Day before:** *Prepare rock lobster but do not slice.*
*Marinate meats.*
*Make sponge flan case; when cold store in a plastic bag.*

**In the morning:** *Prepare salad dressing.*
*Cook chops.*
*Prepare sour cream dip.*
*Finish the cherry flan and make the tutti frutti.*

**1½ hours before:** *Cook the meats and arrange on skewers.*

**1 hour before:** *Arrange rock lobster and garnishes.*

**Before serving:** *Spoon juices over meat.*
*Add dressing to salad.*

## ROCK LOBSTER TAILS WITH TARRAGON DRESSING

**12 frozen rock lobster tails, 2–3 ounces each**
**2 limes or lemons**
**2½ tablespoons tarragon vinegar**
**1¼ cups salad oil**
**Thinly pared rind of 1 lemon**
**2 eggs, hard-cooked**
**Sprigs of parsley**
**Salt**
**Freshly ground black pepper**
**Sugar to taste**

Drop frozen rock lobster tails into boiling salted water. When water reboils, cook for 2 minutes. Drain. Drench immediately with cold water. When cold, cut away underside membrane. Remove meat in one piece and reserve shells. Slice thickly and return meat to shells. Garnish with wedges of lime or lemon.
Put the remaining ingredients into an electric blender and blend until creamy. Or chop the parsley, roughly chop the eggs and beat with a whisk into the remaining ingredients until creamy.
Arrange on a serving platter with salads such as tomatoes stuffed with coleslaw, onions and sweet peppers, marinated mushrooms and sliced cucumbers. Serve with the dressing on the side.

## CRUMBED LAMB CHOPS

**4 cups fresh white breadcrumbs**
**¼ pound sliced bacon, cooked until crisp**
**1 onion, chopped**
**Sprig of parsley**
**Thinly pared rind of 1 lemon**
**Salt**
**Freshly ground black pepper**
**12 rib lamb chops, trimmed**
**2 eggs, beaten**
**7½ tablespoons salad oil**

Put the breadcrumbs in an electric blender with the bacon, onion, parsley, lemon rind and seasoning. Blend until well mixed. Turn the mixture on to a plate. Dip each chop into the beaten egg, then coat with the seasoned crumbs, pressing the crumbs in well. Chill well.
Divide the oil between 2 roasting pans. Add the chops, turning them in the oil so that both sides are covered. Cook in a fairly hot oven (400°F.) for 45 minutes or until meat is tender. Drain well and cool on paper towels.
To serve, put a paper frill on the end of each bone.

*A special salad for a celebration supper – rock lobster tails*

## BEEF AND PORK SKEWERS

**2½ pound top round steak, 1 in. thick**
**2½ pound lean pork**
**1¼ cups red wine**
**7½ tablespoons corn oil**
**2½ teaspoons dried rosemary**
**1¼ teaspoons dried sage**
**Freshly ground black pepper**

Cut the beef and pork into 1 in. cubes. Place each in separate bowls with ⅝ cup of the wine. Turn well, cover and chill several hours or overnight. Turn occasionally during this time.
Drain the meat, reserving the wine. Add half the oil and the rosemary to the beef and the remaining oil and sage to the pork. Turn lightly to distribute the oil and herbs. Season with freshly ground pepper.
Place in separate baking pans. Roast in a hot oven (400°F.) for 1 hour. Reduce temperature to 350°F. and cook for 30 minutes. Baste frequently with pan juices and add a little of the wine marinade. Turn the meat 2–3 times during cooking.
When tender, skewer the meats and keep hot. Reduce the juices by boiling rapidly. Adjust seasoning and spoon over meats. Serve with sour cream and garlic dip.

## SOUR CREAM AND GARLIC DIP

**1¼ cups dairy sour cream**
**2 cloves garlic, crushed**
**Salt**
**Freshly ground black pepper**

Mix the sour cream and the garlic. Season to taste.

## CONFETTI SALAD

**1½ large cucumbers**
**1½ pound firm tomatoes, peeled and cut up**
**1 bunch young carrots, scraped**
**Bunch of radishes, cleaned**
**Celery seed dressing**

Cut the unpeeled cucumber in ¼ in. slices and then cut each slice into sticks. Remove the seeds from the tomatoes and cut the fruit into strips. Slice the carrots in rings and cut into sticks as for the cucumber. Slice the radishes thinly.
Combine these ingredients in a large salad bowl. Add enough French dressing, made with lemon juice and flavored with celery seeds, to moisten.

## TUTTI FRUTTI
*6 servings*

**1 cup vanilla cookie crumbs**
**3 oranges**
**1 pint strawberries, hulled and sliced**
**⅓ cup light brown sugar**
**⅝ cup dairy sour cream**
**Toasted shredded coconut**

Divide half of the cookie crumbs between 6 individual dishes. Pare the oranges and divide into sections. Place on the cookie crumbs.
Layer the strawberries, sugar and sour cream on top of the oranges, using half of each. Repeat the layers with the remaining ingredients, finishing with a layer of sour cream. Chill for 1 hour. Garnish with toasted, shredded coconut.

## CHERRY FLAN
*6–8 servings*

*For flan case:*
**2 eggs**
**¼ cup sugar**
**½ cup all-purpose flour**

*For filling:*
**1 can (16 ounces) cherries**
**⅝ cup cherry juice (if necessary make up with water)**
**2½ teaspoons arrowroot**
**4 tablespoons red-currant jelly**
**1¼ cups heavy cream, lightly whipped**

Grease an 8-in. loose-bottomed cake pan. Place a round of waxed paper in the bottom and grease. Put the eggs and sugar in a large bowl. Stand it over hot water and beat with a whisk until the mixture is light and creamy and thick enough to show a trail when the whisk is lifted. Remove from the heat and whisk until cool.
Sift half the flour over the egg mixture and fold in lightly with a rubber scraper. Add the remaining flour in the same way. Pour the mixture into the pan, spread it evenly with a spatula. Bake above the center of a hot oven (425°F.) for about 15 minutes. Loosen the edges carefully and turn the flan case out on to a wire rack; leave to cool.
Drain the cherries thoroughly. Remove pits if there are any and place in the sponge flan case. Combine the cherry juice, arrowroot and red-currant jelly. Cook over moderate heat until the mixture comes to a boil and thickens. Simmer for 2 minutes. Allow to cool, but not become cold. Pour over top of cherries to glaze. Serve with whipped cream.

### Handy hint

To make pork crackling really crisp, score deeply and evenly, brush with oil and sprinkle with salt before cooking.

# CHRISTENINGS

## PATE FLEURONS

*makes about 50*

1 package (10 ounces) frozen
  patty shells, thawed
Beaten egg

*For filling:*
1 can (4¼ ounces) liverwurst
  spread
¼ cup butter

Place the frozen patty shells close
together on a lightly-floured
board. Press shells together. Roll
out the dough as thin as possible.
Using a 1½ in. fluted round cutter, cut out about 50 rounds.
Brush with beaten egg and fold
over in semi-circles. Place on a
cookie tray and refrigerate for 30
minutes. Brush with beaten egg.
Bake in a fairly hot oven (400°F.)
for about 15 minutes or until puffed and lightly browned.
With a sharp knife, cut almost
through the pastry to allow steam
to escape. Cool on wire racks.
Combine the liverwurst spread
and butter and beat well. Spoon
the mixture into a pastry bag
fitted with a tiny nozzle. Pipe
down the center of each fleuron.

## CHEESE OLIVES

*makes 30*

1 package (8 ounces) cream
  cheese
15 stuffed green olives
Chopped walnuts

Cream the cheese.
Using about 1 heaped teaspoon
cheese for each, roll the cheese
around the olives to enclose them
completely. Toss lightly in chopped walnuts. Chill for about 1
hour. Just before serving, cut in
half with a sharp knife.

## HARE TERRINE

1 hare, boned and filleted
1 medium carrot, grated
1 medium onion, grated
1½ pound pork sausage meat
4 egg yolks
1¼ cups raisins
5 tablespoons stock
Salt and pepper
Sliced bacon

Reserve the best pieces of hare
and grind the remainder. Mix the
ground hare with the carrot,
onion, sausage meat, egg yolks,
raisins, stock and seasonings.
Blend well. Line a terrine with
overlapping bacon strips and fill
with alternate layers of sausage
mixture and hare fillets. Wrap the
bacon over the top to cover. Bake
in a moderate oven (350°F.) for
about 2½ hours. Pour off most of
the fat. Let stand until cool.
Chill. Serve in thick slices.

## SALMON RICE SALAD

*make 2 for the party*

1½ cups long grain rice
1 can (16 ounces) salmon
1 pound tomatoes, peeled and
  chopped
10 tablespoons chopped chives
6¼ tablespoons heavy cream
15 tablespoons mayonnaise
2½ teaspoons celery seeds
Grated rind of 2 lemons
Salt and pepper
Lettuce
Sliced radishes

Cook the rice in boiling salted
water until tender. Allow to cool.
Drain the salmon, remove the
skin and bones and flake the fish.
Add the salmon, tomatoes and
chives to the rice. Whip the cream
and fold into the mayonnaise.
Add the celery seeds, with the
lemon rind and seasoning. Fold
in the rice mixture. Press into a
lightly oiled 2½ quart ring mold.
When firm, turn out onto a serving platter lined with lettuce
leaves. Garnish with radishes.

## COFFEE CREAM FLAN

*make 3 for the party*

½ pound graham crackers
6 tablespoons butter, melted
2 eggs, separated
⅜ cup sugar
2–2½ tablespoons instant coffee
  powder
5 tablespoons water
2½ tablespoons Tia Maria
2½ teaspoons unflavored gelatin
⅝ cup heavy cream
36 hazelnuts, toasted and peeled

*Coffee cream and nuts for a delicious flan*

Crush the graham crackers and
blend with the melted butter. Use
the mixture to line a 10-in.
French fluted loose-bottomed
flan case or a 9-in. deep cake pan.
Press crumbs well on to the base
and up the sides. Chill the flan
case.
Beat the egg yolks and sugar in a
deep bowl until thick and creamy.
Blend the instant coffee with 2
tablespoons water and the Tia
Maria. Gradually beat into egg
mixture.
Soften the gelatin in the remaining water. Dissolve over hot
water. When cool, stir into the
coffee mixture and refrigerate
just until mixture begins to set.
Beat the egg whites until stiff and
fold into coffee mixture. Turn
into flan case and chill well.
Before serving, beat the cream
just until thick. Pipe 12 whirls of
cream around the flan edge and
arrange three toasted hazelnuts
on top of each.

## BANANA AND MANDARIN CHARTREUSE

1 package (6 ounces) lemon
  flavored gelatin
1 package (3 ounces) orange
  flavored gelatin
Juice of 1 orange
Juice of 1 lemon
2 cans (11 ounces each)
  mandarin oranges
2–3 bananas
Lemon juice

Place the gelatin in a large bowl.
Pour over 2½ cups boiling water.
Stir until dissolved.
Pour the fruit juices into a 1-quart
measure. Add the syrup from the
mandarins and make up to 3 cups
with cold water. Strain into the
hot liquid. Spoon enough of the
gelatin into a 2-quart fancy mold
to cover the base. Allow to set
until firm.
Slice the bananas thinly, dip
them in lemon juice. Dip the fruit
in a little of the gelatin and

*The cake is the center of the Christening meal*

arrange banana and mandarins alternately in the bottom of the mold. Let stand until set.

Cover the fruit with another layer of gelatin and let stand until set. Then coat the sides of the mold with gelatin. To help it set quickly, rotate the mold at an angle over a shallow dish containing water with ice cubes added.

Arrange orange and banana alternately around the sides; allow to set. Layer the sides and middle alternately with fruit and then gelatin. Chill until firm, for at least 2 hours.

To serve, unmold and serve with heavy pouring cream.

*Tasty snacks to serve with pre-lunch drinks*

## TEA MENU *serves 20–25*

**OPEN SANDWICHES**
**ORANGE TEABREAD**
**ALMOND GINGERBREAD**
**COFFEE WALNUT**
**GATEAU**
**CUP CAKES**
**CHRISTENING CAKE**

## OPEN SANDWICHES

*Danish rye bread, sold in a packet, makes a firm-to-handle base. The butter on the bread provides a useful anchor for the topping, so be generous. Choose both fillings and garnishes with an eye for color.*

Here is a selection of toppings:

Slices of tomato with a good sized piece of crab, garnished with cottage cheese and black olives.

Slices of salami topped with stuffed olives and tomato slices.

Slices of hard-cooked egg and a sardine, with a few slivers of tomato and stuffed olive.

Luncheon meat topped with a spoonful of potato salad, raw onion rings and radish slices.

A slice of strong blue cheese, with rings of green pepper and a black olive on top.

A few shrimp, with a slice or two of hard-cooked egg.

A slice of luncheon meat, garnished with tomato, cucumber, cottage cheese and a black olive.

## ORANGE TEABREAD

*make 2 for the party*

**¼ cup butter or margarine**
**¾ cup sugar**
**1 egg, beaten**
**Grated rind of ½ orange**
**2½ tablespoons orange juice**
**2½ tablespoons milk**
**2 cups all-purpose flour**
**3 teaspoons baking powder**
**Pinch of salt**

Grease the bottom of an 8½ in. by 4½ in. loaf pan. Line the bottom with a piece of waxed paper and grease again.

Cream the butter and sugar together until light and fluffy. Gradually beat in the egg until smooth and creamy. Slowly add the orange rind and juice; don't worry if the mixture curdles. Lightly beat in the milk alternately with the sifted flour, baking powder and salt.

Turn the batter into the pan. Bake in the center of a fairly hot oven (375°F.) for 40–45 minutes. Let stand in pan a few minutes. Then turn out on to a wire rack to cool. Wrap in foil and keep 1–2 days before using. Slice thinly and spread with honey and cream cheese spread or butter.

## ALMOND GINGERBREAD

**¼ cup flaked almonds**
**3 cups all-purpose flour**
**1 tablespoon ginger**
**2 tablespoons chopped candied ginger**
**6 tablespoons shortening**
**½ cup light brown sugar, firmly packed**
**¾ cup corn syrup**
**½ cup water**
**1 egg, beaten**
**2 scant teaspoons baking soda**

Grease a 2-quart ring mold generously. Sprinkle the almonds in the bottom.

Sift together the flour and ginger. Stir in the candied ginger.

Gently heat together the shortening, sugar, syrup and half the water, making sure it does not boil. Stir the syrup into the flour, add the egg and beat well. Dissolve the baking soda in the remaining water and pour into the mixture. Stir thoroughly.

Pour the batter into the ring mold. Bake in a warm oven (325°F.) for 50 minutes or until well risen and spongy to the touch. Let stand in mold 5 minutes. Turn out on to a wire rack and cool with the nut side uppermost.

## COFFEE WALNUT GATEAU

*make 3 for the party*

*For sponge cakes:*

**6 large eggs**
**¾ cup sugar**
**1¼ cups all-purpose flour**
**3 tablespoons cornstarch**
**1 tablespoon glycerin**

*For crème au beurre:*

**3 egg yolks**
**½ cup sugar**
**⅝ cup milk**
**1¼ tablespoons instant coffee powder**
**¾–1 cup butter**
**4 tablespoons coffee liqueur**

*For topping and decoration:*

**¾ cup chopped walnuts**
**1¾ cups confectioners' sugar**
**1¼ teaspoons instant coffee powder**
**2½ tablespoons hot water**

Grease two 9-in. cake pans. Line the bottoms with a circle of waxed paper and grease again. Sprinkle with sugar.

Break the eggs into a deep bowl. Add the sugar and beat with an electric mixer or rotary beater until the mixture is thick and pale and leaves a trail when the beater is lifted out.

Sift the flour and cornstarch together twice. Sift half of this mixture on to the surface of the egg mixture. Fold in quickly with a rubber spatula. Spoon glycerin in a thin stream over the surface, sieve in the remaining flour and fold in until no pockets of flour are left. Pour the mixture quickly

into the cake pans. Bake in a fairly hot oven (375°F.) for about 30 minutes.

Meanwhile, beat together the egg yolks and sugar until light and creamy. Bring the milk and coffee to a boil. Pour the milk into the beaten eggs, stirring well. Return the mixture to the saucepan and cook over gentle heat, stirring constantly, until the mixture thickens. Remove from the heat and cool, stirring occasionally. Beat the butter until light and creamy. Pour the cold coffee sauce in a thin stream into the butter, beating all the time. Store in a cool (not cold) place until needed.

Sprinkle the sponges with coffee liqueur and sandwich together with one-third of the crème au beurre. Coat the sides with another third. Press the chopped walnuts on to the sides of the cake with a small spatula. Spoon the remaining crème au beurre into a pastry bag fitted with a medium size star nozzle. Pipe stars around the edge, touching each other.

Beat together the confectioners' sugar and coffee blended with the hot water. Add a little more water if necessary to give a thick, flowing consistency. Pour into the center of the cake, tilting the plate slightly so that the top is evenly coated. Before the icing sets, burst air bubbles with a fine skewer or pin.

## CUP CAKES

*makes 24*

**2½ cups sifted cake flour**
**1⅔ cups sugar**
**1 teaspoon salt**
**¾ cup soft shortening**
**¾ cup milk**
**4½ teaspoons baking powder**
**5 egg whites, unbeaten**
**¼ cup plus 2 tablespoons milk**
**1 teaspoon vanilla extract**

Line 24 3-in. cup cake pan cups with paper liners. Into a large bowl, sift the flour, sugar and salt. Drop in the shortening and pour in ¾ cup milk.

With electric mixer at low to medium speed, mix until all flour is dampened then beat 2 minutes, scraping bowl and beaters occasionally. Stir in the baking powder. Add the egg whites, remaining milk and vanilla. Beat 2 more minutes. Half fill cup cake pans. Bake in a fairly hot oven (375°F. for 20 minutes or until a cake tester inserted in center, comes out clean. Cool and frost as desired.

# PICNIC MENUS

Summer or winter, given good weather, a picnic is always fun. Our menus offer a variety of foods that are far removed from the usual sandwich.

**POTTED SMOKED SALMON**
**FRIED SALAMI CHICKEN**
**ITALIAN CAULIFLOWER SALAD**
**STUFFED FRENCH LOAF**
**JELLIED BEET AND APPLE SALAD**
**DANISH BAKED FRUIT SALAD**

## POTTED SMOKED SALMON

**2 packages (3 ounces each) cream cheese**
**Finely grated rind of 1 lemon**
**2 egg yolks**
**1¼ cups heavy cream**
**Salt**
**Freshly ground black pepper**
**Cayenne**
**1 clove garlic, crushed**
**⅓ pound smoked salmon**
**5 tablespoons finely chopped parsley**
**1 cup fresh white breadcrumbs**
**¼ cup butter**

Put the cheese, lemon rind, egg yolks and cream in a small bowl and blend very well. Place the bowl over a pan of hot water and cook until smooth and thick. Remove from heat. Season with salt, pepper, cayenne and garlic. Chop the smoked salmon finely and add to the cheese mixture with the chopped parsley and breadcrumbs. Blend well.
Spoon into 6–8 individual soufflé dishes or ramekins until about two-thirds full. Melt the butter and pour a little into the top of each dish. Chill until firm.

## FRIED SALAMI CHICKEN

**12–16 chicken drumsticks, skinned**
**12–16 thin slices salami**
**3–4 large eggs, beaten**
**⅔ large loaf of white bread, made into breadcrumbs**
**Oil for deep frying**
**1 can (16 ounces) grapefruit segments, drained**
**¼ cucumber, sliced**

Make an incision to the bone along one side of each drumstick and loosen the meat around the bone. Place a slice of salami around the bone, pull the chicken meat together and secure with toothpicks.
Dip the salami-filled chicken first

*Fried salami chicken is as good cold as hot*

into beaten egg and then into breadcrumbs. Pat the crumbs in well. Repeat the egg and breadcrumb process to coat well.
Deep fry in hot oil (360°F.) for 7–10 minutes or until golden brown and cooked through. Drain on paper towels. Cool. Pack the drumsticks in several plastic boxes with the drained grapefruit segments and slices of cucumber.

## ITALIAN CAULIFLOWER SALAD

**1 medium cauliflower**
**7 anchovy fillets, cut into small pieces**
**10 pitted ripe olives, sliced**
**1¼ tablespoons capers**
**1¼ tablespoons ground shallot or onion**
**Freshly ground black pepper**
**4 tablespoons olive oil**
**1¼ tablespoons wine vinegar**

Wash and trim the cauliflower and break into small flowerets. Cook in a small amount of boiling water for about 10 minutes or until tender but still crisp. Drain thoroughly. Cool and chill.
Place the chilled cauliflower, anchovy fillets, olives, capers and shallot in a bowl. Shake the pepper, oil and vinegar together in a screw-top jar. Toss the salad very gently in the dressing and serve in a salad bowl.

## STUFFED FRENCH LOAF

**1 long loaf French bread**
**5 stalks celery, chopped**
**Butter**
**1 package (3 ounces) cream cheese**
**Milk**
**Salt**
**Freshly ground black pepper**

Cut off the top of the loaf at a slight angle, so that you remove the top and part of the inside. Scoop out some of the inside to make room for the filling. Mix the celery, a little butter, cream cheese, milk and seasoning. Pile into the loaf. Replace the top. Wrap the stuffed loaf in foil until

**Handy hint**

To make Melba toast, toast bread from a thin sliced loaf on both sides, cut off the crusts and slice into 2 with a sharp knife (this is easier after toasting); open out and toast the insides.

required at the picnic. To serve, cut the loaf into 2–3 in. slices.

## JELLIED BEET AND APPLE SALAD

**1 package (3 ounces) lemon flavored gelatin**
**1 cup boiling water**
**⅝ cup vinegar**
**2½ tablespoons lemon juice**
**1 pound cooked beets**
**2 eating apples**
**¼ cup shelled walnuts**

Dissolve the gelatin in the boiling water. Combine the vinegar and lemon juice, make up to 1¼ cups with cold water. Stir into dissolved gelatin.
Pare and dice or slice the cooked beets. Pare, core and slice the apples. Place the walnuts in the bottom of a 1½-quart ring mold and add the beets and apple in layers. Pour on the liquid gelatin and let stand in a cool place to set. To serve, unmold on a flat plate and garnish as desired.

## DANISH BAKED FRUIT SALAD

**¾ cup dried prunes**
**¾ cup dried apricots**
**6 bananas, cut up**
**¼ cup seedless raisins**
**5 tablespoons honey**
**1⅞ cup fresh orange juice**
**Grated rind of 1 lemon**

Soak the prunes and apricots in warm water for several hours or overnight. Butter a large, flat ovenproof dish and arrange the fruit in it. Add the honey to the orange juice and mix well. Pour it over the fruit. Sprinkle the lemon rind over the top. Bake in a moderate oven (350°F.) for about 30 minutes. Serve cold with cream.

## CURRIED KIPPER SALAD

1 pound smoked kipper fillets or smoked mackerel
10 tablespoons mayonnaise
2½ teaspoons curry powder
2½ teaspoons vinegar
1 cup cooked rice
1 pound tomatoes, peeled and sliced
8 stalks celery, sliced
Salt and pepper
Watercress

Cook the kippers as directed on the package. Remove the skins and cut into thin slivers. Combine the mayonnaise, curry powder and vinegar. Stir in the fish, rice, tomatoes and celery. Blend well and adjust the seasoning with a little salt and pepper. Pile in plastic box. Garnish with watercress, if desired.

## PARTY CHICKEN MOLD

½ a cooked chicken
2 eggs, hard-cooked
1 envelope unflavored gelatin
2 cups chicken bouillon
Sherry
Cooked peas

Cut the chicken into small pieces, removing all the bone and skin. Slice the eggs neatly.
Soften the gelatin in the chicken bouillon. Put over low heat until gelatin is dissolved. Remove from heat and stir in a dash of sherry. Let stand until cool and starting to set.
Rinse a 5-cup ring mold in cold water. Coat the ring mold with the gelatin. Set some cooked peas in the bottom.
Dip each slice of egg in the gela-

tin and position them around the side of the mold. Chill in refrigerator until eggs are firmly set. Fill up the mold with the chicken and pour in the rest of the gelatin. Refrigerate until set. Unmold just before leaving for the picnic and carry in an insulated container.

## CABBAGE SALAD

1 small head cabbage
1 onion, chopped
4 tablespoons French dressing
1 teaspoon caraway seeds
½ teaspoon dried marjoram

Trim the cabbage, remove the outer leaves and shred the cabbage. Place it in a bowl and pour boiling water over it. Let stand 10 minutes. Drain and rinse under cold running water. Drain the cabbage well. Place in a plastic picnic box and add the chopped onion.
Combine the French dressing, caraway seeds and marjoram. Put into a screw-top jar and pour over the salad at the picnic.

## LEEK AND TOMATO SALAD

4 young tender leeks, washed carefully and thoroughly
4 small tomatoes, peeled
1 head lettuce
1 teaspoon chopped fresh basil
1 teaspoon chopped fresh chervil
4 tablespoons French dressing

Slice the white part of the leeks very finely. Cut the tomatoes into sections. Wash and drain the lettuce. Put the lettuce leaves, leeks and tomatoes into a plastic container and sprinkle on the basil and chervil. Put the dressing in a screw-top jar and pour it over the salad at the picnic.

## CHERRY AND ALMOND PIE
*make 2 for the picnic*

Double recipe Shortcrust Pastry, page 75
Raspberry preserves
½ cup ground almonds
¼ cup sugar
1 large egg, beaten
¾ pound pie cherries, pitted
Sugar

Roll out half the pastry and use to line a 7 or 8 in. foil pie plate. Spread preserves over the bottom. Blend together the almonds, sugar and egg and spread half this mixture over the preserves. Add the cherries and cover with the remaining almond mixture. Roll out the pastry into a lid to cover

the pie. Seal the edges and flute. Decorate with leaves cut from pastry trimmings.
Bake in a fairly hot oven (375°F.) for 30–40 minutes or until cherries are cooked and pastry is lightly browned. Cool and dredge with sugar.

*This is an elegant salad for a garden lunch*

## MIXED MEAT PATE

½ pound sliced bacon
¼ pound lambs' liver, chopped
¼ pound lean raw pork, chopped
¼ pound pork sausage meat
½ cup fresh white breadcrumbs
1¼ tablespoons milk
1 small onion, finely chopped
Beaten egg
2 tablespoons brandy
Salt and pepper
Pinch of ground nutmeg
½ pound cold roast chicken, sliced

Line a 7 or 8 in. round deep, straight sided casserole or baking pan with foil, leaving enough to cover the top later.
Stretch the bacon slices with the back of a knife and use to line the casserole or pan.
Mix together the liver, pork,

*A mixture of fresh and dried fruit for Danish baked fruit salad*

sausage meat, breadcrumbs, milk, onion, egg, brandy and seasoning. Fill the pan, starting with a layer of sliced chicken and alternating with layers of the meat mixture. Cover with foil. Place the casserole or pan in a baking pan half-filled with water. Cook in a warm oven (325°F.) for about 2½ hours.

Remove from the oven, cover with a plate and put a weight on top. Chill overnight.

To pack for the picnic, turn out of the casserole or pan, wrap the extra foil over the top and slip the pâté into a plastic bag.

## MEAT LOAF

½ pound stewing veal
½ pound stewing beef
½ pound lean bacon
¼ pound onions
2 carrots, grated
¼ pound tomatoes, peeled and chopped
1 tablespoon thyme
2 tablespoons chopped parsley
¼ cup fresh breadcrumbs
1 teaspoon salt
Freshly ground black pepper
1 egg, beaten

Put the veal, beef, bacon and onion through the food chopper two times. Combine with the remaining ingredients.

Place the mixture on a piece of aluminum foil and shape it into a loaf about 3 in. by 7 in. Wrap it neatly in the foil and place it in a baking dish or loaf pan. Cook in a moderate oven (350°F.) for 1¼ hours. Open the foil and cook 1¼ hours more.

Remove from oven and cool. When cold, wrap in clean aluminum foil and pack in a large plastic box for the picnic.

## EGG AND VEGETABLE FLAN

⅔ recipe (1 cup flour) Shortcrust Pastry, page 75
2 tablespoons butter
¼ cup all-purpose flour
1¼ cups milk
¾ cup grated Cheddar cheese
Salt and pepper
3 eggs, hard-cooked and sliced
1 package (10½ ounces) frozen mixed vegetables

Roll out the pastry and fit into a 7 in. flan ring or cake pan. Fit in a piece of aluminum foil and fill with dried beans. Bake in a fairly hot oven (400°F.) until lightly

*A pâté covered with bacon rashers always looks attractive*

browned. Cool. This can be done a day in advance.

Melt the butter. Stir in the flour and cook slowly for 2–3 minutes. Remove from heat and stir in the milk. Cook over moderate heat, stirring constantly, until thickened and the mixture comes to a boil. Stir in the cheese and season to taste.

Arrange the sliced eggs in the cooled flan case, retaining 2–3 slices for garnish. Cook the frozen vegetables according to package directions. Mix them with the cheese sauce. Cool. Spoon into the flan case. Refrigerate until cold. Garnish with the remaining slices of egg just before packing. Cover the flan with foil, but be careful not to stand anything on top of it. Slice it, as required, at the picnic.

## GOLDEN SLAW

1 small Savoy cabbage
¼–⅓ pound Gruyère cheese, cut in thin strips
½ pound red-skinned apples, cored and chopped
⅝ cup mayonnaise
1 tablespoon prepared mustard
1 teaspoon sugar
Salt and pepper

Wash the cabbage well. Curl back the outer leaves, cut around the base of the heart and scoop out the heart, to leave a 'bowl'. Finely shred the cabbage heart and put in a bowl with the cheese and apples. Combine the mayonnaise, mustard, sugar and seasoning. Toss with the cabbage mixture until the ingredients are well coated. Spoon into the scooped-out cabbage 'bowl' and pack in kitchen foil or plastic bag.

## FILLED BEETS

8 small cooked beets
Salt and pepper
2½ tablespoons lemon juice
8 stalks celery, chopped
2 oranges, pared and chopped
2½ teaspoons horseradish sauce
2½ teaspoons sugar
French dressing

Peel the beets. Trim the base of each one so that it will stand firmly. Hollow out the center to form a cup. Season with salt and pepper and sprinkle with lemon juice. Mix the celery and orange and fill the beet centers. Add the horseradish sauce and sugar to the French dressing, mix well and spoon over the beets. Wrap each beet separately.

## SMOKED SALMON SPREAD

1 package (8 ounces) cream cheese, softened
½ cup finely diced smoked salmon
1 teaspoon black pepper
2 tablespoons lemon juice

Combine the ingredients, blending thoroughly with a fork until of a spreading consistency. Serve with French bread and butter.

## PINEAPPLE SOUFFLES

1 can (16 ounces) crushed pineapple
2 envelopes unflavored gelatin
4 large eggs, separated
6 tablespoons sugar
2½ tablespoons whiskey
1¼ cups heavy cream
Frosted grapes, optional

Drain the crushed pineapple. Reserve 2 tablespoons juice and place it in a small bowl. Sprinkle gelatin into juice to soften. Set the bowl over a pan of hot water to dissolve the gelatin.

Beat the egg yolks, sugar and whiskey in a large bowl over a pan of hot water until they are thick and pale. Remove from the heat and stir in the crushed pineapple. Stir in the dissolved gelatin. Let

*Use frozen mixed vegetables for this tasty flan*

stand to cool, beating from time to time.

Beat the cream until soft peaks are formed. Fold into the pineapple mixture. Beat the egg whites until stiff but not dry. Pour the pineapple mixture over the whites and fold in lightly. Divide between chilled soufflé dishes and chill until set. Garnish with frosted grapes, if desired.

**PICNIC MENU** *serves 8*

**APPETIZER SOUP**
**RAISED BACON AND EGG PIE**
**PORK LOAF**
**ENDIVE SALAD**
**TOMATO COLESLAW**
**GREEN SALAD**
**BAPS**
**SUMMER PUDDING**

## APPETIZER SOUP

6¼ cups water
3 beef bouillon cubes
3 chicken bouillon cubes
2 cans (16 ounces each) tomatoes
2 onions, chopped
½ bunch carrots, thinly sliced
4 stalks celery, cut into ½ in. lengths
6 peppercorns
½ teaspoon dried sage
Salt
Freshly ground black pepper
Grated Parmesan cheese

Put the water in a saucepan. Add the bouillon cubes, tomatoes, onion, carrots, celery, peppercorns and sage. Mix well. Bring to a boil. Cover and simmer for 1 hour. Adjust seasoning.

Pour while still hot into a warmed, wide-necked vacuum jug. Take the cheese separately to sprinkle on each serving.

## RAISED BACON AND EGG PIE

*For hot water crust:*
1 pound (4 cups) all-purpose flour
2½ teaspoons salt
½ cup shortening
⅞ cup milk or water
Beaten egg for glaze
*For filling:*
2 pound sliced bacon, cooked but not too crisp
1 egg, lightly beaten
2½ tablespoons tomato paste
4 tablespoons chopped parsley
Freshly ground black pepper
3 eggs, hard-cooked
½ envelope unflavored gelatin
1 cup beef bouillon

Sift the flour and salt into a bowl and put in a warm place. Melt the shortening and add the liquid. Bring the mixture to a boil and pour into the flour. Mix to a paste quickly, using a wooden spoon, turn it out on to a floured board and knead until the dough is smooth and free from cracks.

Cut off one quarter of the dough and put aside. Roll out the rest and use to line a 7-in. straight sided casserole or soufflé dish, at least 3 in. deep. Take care to work quickly and keep the pastry warm while it is being molded or it will crack.

Put one pound of the cooked bacon through a meat grinder or chop very fine with a French knife. Mix with the beaten egg, tomato paste, parsley and pepper to make a smooth mixture. Chop the remaining bacon roughly and toss lightly with 2 of the hard-cooked eggs, cut up.

Line the pastry case with the smooth bacon mixture. Fill the center with the chopped bacon and eggs, placing the remaining hard-cooked egg in the center. Roll out the remaining piece of pastry for the top. Place over the top of the mixture, press the pieces together and flute the edges. Make a cut in the center to allow steam to escape and decorate the pie with leaves cut from the pastry trimmings. Brush with egg.

Bake in the center of a very hot oven (425°F.) for 30 minutes. Reduce the temperature to 350°F. and bake for 15 minutes. Let cool in the pan for a while until firm. Carefully remove from the casserole and allow to cool.

Soften the gelatin in the beef bouillon. Set over low heat and heat until the gelatin is dissolved. Cool and when gelatin is on the point of setting, pour it into the pie through the hole in the center of the top. Chill to set the gelatin completely. Pack in foil.

## PORK LOAF

1 pound lean pork, cubed
1 pound lean ham, cubed
1¼ tablespoons onion, finely chopped
⅝ cup thick white sauce
1 egg, beaten
Salt and pepper
Pinch of rosemary
Sliced bacon
Vinegar

Put the pork, ham and onion through a meat chopper two times. Blend very thoroughly with the white sauce, egg, seasoning and rosemary. Place the mixture on a sheet of aluminum foil. Form it into a loaf shape and cover with slices of bacon. Fold foil over and seal tightly.

Place in a large pan of boiling water with a little vinegar and salt and boil gently for 2½ hours. (A saucer placed on the bottom of the pan will prevent the foil coming into contact with the metal.)

*A plastic mold is ideal for a picnic jelly*

Remove the loaf from the pan and let stand to cool. Remove the foil. Pack in fresh foil for the picnic.

## ENDIVE SALAD

4 heads endive, cleaned
12 black olives, pitted
2½ tablespoons vinegar
2½ teaspoons honey
2 onions, finely chopped
5 tablespoons salad oil
2½ tablespoons lemon juice
Pinch each of sugar and salt

Cut the endive into thin slices. Mix in the olives. In a screwtop jar, shake together the vinegar, honey, onion, oil, lemon juice, sugar and salt. Pack the salad and dressing separately and toss together at the picnic.

## TOMATO COLESLAW

¾ pound white cabbage, cleaned
1 red pepper, seeded
4 tomatoes, peeled
½ cucumber
1 cup mayonnaise
5 tablespoons dairy sour cream
2½ teaspoons honey
2½ teaspoons catsup
Salt
Freshly ground black pepper
Juice of 1 lemon

Shred the cabbage finely. Slice the pepper, tomatoes and cucumber. Beat the mayonnaise with the remaining ingredients and toss the salad ingredients in this dressing. Pack in a plastic container for the picnic.

## SUMMER PUDDING
*make 2 for the picnic*

1 pound berries (raspberries, currants, blackberries)
Sugar
Thin slices of white bread, crusts removed

Stew the fruit gently with sugar and water, if necessary, keeping it as whole as possible and not too runny. Line a mixing bowl with bread slices and fill with alternate layers of fruit and bread, retaining some of the juice. When the last layer of fruit is in the bowl, pour the juice over and cover with a slice of bread. Cover the pudding with a plate and press down with a heavy weight. Chill in the refrigerator overnight.
Remove the weight and plate and cover the bowl with foil for carrying. Turn out before serving. Serve with cream, if desired.

---

**PICNIC MENU** *serves 12*

**ZUCCHINI AND
CARROT SOUP OR
CHILLED VEGETABLE
JUICE
PICNIC SANDWICH BOX
SALMON RICE
FENNEL AND
GRUYERE SALAD
COFFEE AND VANILLA
MILK JELLY**

## ZUCCHINI AND
## CARROT SOUP

½ cup butter or margarine
1 bunch carrots, sliced
1 pound zucchini, thinly sliced
½ teaspoon dried thyme
2 bay leaves
10 cups chicken stock
5 teaspoons tomato paste
½ cup instant potato flakes
Salt
Freshly ground black pepper
Chopped parsley

Melt the butter in a large saucepan. Add the carrots, zucchini, thyme and bay leaves. Cover and sauté, shaking the pan occasionally, for ten minutes.
Add the stock and tomato paste. Stir. Bring to a boil. Lower heat, cover and simmer for 30 minutes. Add the potato, stir and bring back to a boil. Adjust seasoning. Pour into a vacuum flask and garnish with chopped parsley at serving time.

## PICNIC SANDWICH BOX
*make 2 for the picnic*

1 small loaf French bread
6 tablespoons butter, melted
½ pound pork sausage meat
¼ pound cooked ham, finely chopped
½ pound cooked tongue, finely chopped
1 onion, chopped
2 eggs
⅝ cup milk
Salt
Freshly ground black pepper
2 eggs, hard-cooked and cut up

Cut horizontally across the loaf, two-thirds of the way up. Remove the lid, gently ease away the bread from around the crust edge of both pieces. From the soft bread make 2 cups of breadcrumbs. Brush the cavity of the loaf and lid with some of the melted butter. Combine the sausage meat, ham, tongue, breadcrumbs and onion. Beat together the raw eggs and milk and combine with the meat mixture. Place one-third of this down the center of the loaf. Arrange the halved hard-cooked eggs lengthwise on top and pack around with more of the meat mixture. Top with the lid.
Tie the loaf up like a parcel with string and brush all over with the remaining melted butter. Place on a cookie tray and bake in a hot oven (400°F.) for 15 minutes. Cover with foil and continue cooking for another 45 minutes. Unwrap, remove the string and cool on a wire rack. Pack in clean foil. Serve cut into thick slices.

## SALMON RICE
*make 2 for the picnic*

1 cup long grain rice
1 can (2 ounces) anchovy fillets, drained
Milk
3¾ tablespoons corn oil
1¼ tablespoons wine vinegar
1¼ tablespoons lemon juice
1¼ teaspoons French mustard
Salt
Freshly ground black pepper
2 onions, finely chopped
2½ tablespoons chopped parsley
1 can (1 pound) salmon
1 small ripe avocado
Extra lemon juice

Cook the rice in boiling salted water until tender. Cool quickly. Separate the anchovies, cover with milk and let stand 30 minutes to marinate.
Beat together the oil, vinegar, lemon juice and mustard. Season well with salt and pepper and fork this dressing through the cooled rice with the onion, parsley and drained, chopped anchovies. Discard the dark skin and bone from the salmon and flake the fish. Lightly fold it through the rice, but take care not to break down the salmon too finely. Pack in a rigid plastic container.
To serve, cut the avocado in half lengthwise and discard the pit. Pare and slice the avocado and toss in lemon juice to prevent discoloration. Use the avocado slices to garnish the salad.

## FENNEL AND GRUYERE
## SALAD

2 fennel roots
½ pound Gruyère cheese
Freshly ground black pepper
Lemon and oil dressing

Shed the fennel finely and cut the cheese into slivers. Mix the fennel and Gruyère, season well with freshly ground black pepper and pack in a plastic box.
Take the dressing separately and pour over the salad at the picnic.

## COFFEE AND VANILLA
## MILK JELLY
*make 2 for the picnic*

¼ cup sugar
⅝ cup strong coffee
1⅞ cup milk
1½ envelopes unflavored gelatin
5 tablespoons water
Vanilla pod

Add 2 tablespoons sugar to the coffee and ⅝ cup milk. Soften half the gelatin in 2 tablespoons water in a bowl. Place the bowl in a pan of hot water until gelatin is dissolved. Remove from heat and stir in coffee and milk mixture. Pour one-third of the gelatin into a plastic mold and refrigerate until set (keep the rest warm so that it does not set).
Put the vanilla pod in the remaining milk for a short time. Soften the remaining gelatin in the remaining water. Put over hot water until gelatin has dissolved. Stir into the milk mixture. Remove the vanilla pod. Pour half of this vanilla mixture over the set coffee gelatin and refrigerate until set. Repeat the layers, finishing with the coffee mixture. Transport in an ice-box if possible and unmold at the picnic.

# BARBECUE MENUS

Eating out of doors adds a zest to any appetite, and what better way to entertain friends on a summer evening than to have a barbecued meal in your own garden? Salads, sauces and vegetable accompaniments can all be prepared beforehand in your kitchen, and you'll find that most men enjoy being in charge of the barbecue – which leaves you free to enjoy yourself. Choose simple menus with desserts that can be cooked either in foil in the charcoal embers or in a pan under the broiler.

---

**MENU** *serves 8*

**TANDOORI CHICKEN**
**SYRIAN BREAD**
**MELON AND BANANA SALAD**
**SLICED TOMATOES AND GHERKINS**
**BOILED RICE**
**PEACHES WITH BUTTERSCOTCH SAUCE**

---

## TANDOORI CHICKEN

8 chicken legs and thighs
Salt and pepper
1 cup unflavored yogurt
1½ teaspoons chili powder
Pinch of ginger
Pinch of ground coriander
1 large clove garlic, crushed
Juice of 1½ lemons
4 tablespoons melted butter

Remove any protruding bones from the chicken legs, wipe and season with salt and pepper. Combine the yogurt, chili powder, ginger, coriander, garlic, lemon juice, 1¼ teaspoons black pepper and 2½ teaspoons salt. Mix well and add the chicken pieces. Let stand 3–4 hours, turning several times.
Remove the chicken from the marinade, shaking off as much of the liquid as possible, then pour a little melted butter over each chicken piece. Place chicken on a hot barbecue and brown quickly on all sides. Remove and place each piece in aluminum foil about 15 in. square. Make a double drug-store fold in the top and a double fold on each end of the foil to seal thoroughly.
Place each packet on the grill. Cook for 20 minutes, turning once during the cooking time. Gently heat marinade on top and serve separately with the chicken.

## SYRIAN BREAD

*Syrian bread can be purchased in most grocery stores. Just pop it in a hot oven to heat and you will find it delicious. Allow 1 per person. It also makes fantastic sandwiches, split open and the pockets filled with favorite filling and then heated and served piping hot.*

## MELON AND BANANA SALAD

2 ripe cantaloupes
8 bananas
Lemon juice

Cut the melons in half, scoop out the seeds and discard. Remove the skin and cut the fruit into cubes. Slice the bananas thinly. Turn in lemon juice to prevent browning, then mix the melon and bananas together.

## PEACHES WITH BUTTERSCOTCH SAUCE

¼ cup butter
2 cans (16 ounces each) peach halves, drained
Soft brown sugar

Melt the butter in a skillet over the barbecue and add the peach halves, cut side up. Fill each with brown sugar. Simmer until the sugar melts and runs into the butter to form a sauce.
Serve with heavy pouring cream or ice cream.

---

**MENU** *serves 12*

**FOIL-ROASTED CORN**
**HAMBURGERS**
**HOT DOGS**
**BAKED POTATOES**
**TOMATO SAUCE**
**CREAMY MUSTARD SAUCE**
**APPLE AND TOMATO SALAD**
**HOT WEATHER GREEN SALAD**
**FRUIT AND CHEESE**
**ORANGE WAFERS**

## FOIL-ROASTED CORN

12 ears of corn
½ cup butter
Freshly ground black pepper

Remove the husks and silks from the corn. Combine the butter with a generous amount of pepper. Spread some butter on each ear of corn. Place each one on a square of aluminum foil. Bring the sides together with a double fold in the center and make double folds or twists on each end to seal completely.

Cook at the sides of the barbecue grill for 25–30 minutes, turning occasionally.

## HAMBURGERS

3 pounds lean ground beef
3¾ teaspoons mixed herbs
Salt and pepper
Butter or oil
3 onions, sliced
12 hamburger buns

Combine the meat, herbs and seasonings and toss together lightly. Shape into 12 flat patties and brush with a little oil or melted butter. Broil over hot coals for 6–10 minutes, depending on the degree of doneness desired. Turn patties once during cooking. Meanwhile, fry the onion rings in a skillet in a little fat until soft and golden. Place the buns, split side down, on the barbecue and toast for 2–3 minutes.

To serve, top each hamburger with a few onion rings and put between 2 toasted bun halves. Serve with a selection of relishes.

## HOT DOGS

12 frankfurters
12 hot dog buns

Grill the frankfurters over low coals and put inside a split roll. Serve with mustard, tomato sauce, catsup or relish.

## TOMATO SAUCE

1 slice bacon
1 pound tomatoes, chopped
2 onions, sliced
¼ cup butter or margarine
Bouquet garni
2½ cups stock
Salt and pepper
2½ teaspoons sugar
2 tablespoons flour
Milk

Dice the bacon. Put in a pan with the tomatoes, onions and butter. Cook with a lid on for about 10 minutes, shaking frequently. Add the herbs, stock, seasoning

*Hamburgers and hot dogs are traditional barbecue fare*

and sugar. Simmer gently, uncovered, for 30 minutes. The mixture should now be pulpy and well reduced.

Put the mixture through a sieve. Return to the pan and bring to a boil. Blend the flour with a little cold milk to a smooth paste. Add to the pan and bring to a boil, stirring constantly. Cook for 2–3 minutes and adjust seasoning. Serve hot or cold with the hot dogs and hamburgers.

## CREAMY MUSTARD SAUCE

⅝ cup dairy sour cream
2½ tablespoons prepared mustard
1¼ tablespoons ground onion
½ teaspoon salt
⅛ teaspoon pepper

Mix all ingredients together in a pan and heat gently for a few minutes. Serve warm with the hot dogs and hamburgers.

## APPLE AND TOMATO SALAD

4 eating apples, pared and cored
1 pound tomatoes, peeled and sliced
French dressing
Watercress, optional

Dice the apples and put in a bowl with the tomato slices. Add enough French dressing to coat lightly. Toss. Garnish with watercress, if desired.

## HOT WEATHER GREEN SALAD

1 head lettuce
1 large bunch watercress
1 large cucumber, peeled
12–15 scallions
French dressing
1¼ tablespoons dry white wine

Wash the lettuce and watercress. Discard stems and coarse leaves. Slice the peeled cucumber and scallions very fine. Mix all the ingredients together in a salad bowl. Add the French dressing and wine and toss lightly.

## ORANGE WAFERS
*makes about 8 dozen*

½ cup butter or margarine
¾ cup sugar
1 egg
1 teaspoon grated orange rind
1 tablespoon orange juice
1½ cups all-purpose flour
½ teaspoon baking powder
¼ teaspoon salt

Cream the butter and sugar until fluffy. Beat in the egg. Stir in the orange rind and juice. Sift together the dry ingredients and stir into creamed mixture. Drop by level teaspoonfuls on to greased cookie tray. Press flat with the bottom of a glass dipped in sugar. Bake in a fairly hot oven (375°F.) for about 7 minutes or until lightly browned. Cool on wire racks.

**Handy hint**

To remove the fat from gravy, place a double thickness of absorbent kitchen towels on the gravy and press lightly. The paper will soak up a little of the gravy and all of the fat. Alternatively use a bulb-type gravy syphon.

*Stuffed apples, baked in the oven or in the embers*

## MENU *serves 8*

**LAMB CHOPS**
**SAUSAGES**
**BARBECUE SAUCE**
**RICE**
**LAYERED COLESLAW**
**ENDIVE AND**
**ORANGE SALAD**
**STUFFED BAKED APPLES**

### BARBECUE SAUCE

5 tablespoons Worcestershire
  sauce
5 tablespoons catsup
2½ teaspoons sugar
1¼ tablespoons vinegar
2 tablespoons butter or
  margarine, melted
Cayenne
Salt
⅝ cup water
1 small onion, thinly sliced

Blend all the ingredients
together, adding the onion last.

Be very sparing with the cayenne.
Pour the sauce over the meat to be
cooked and baste frequently
while it is cooking.

### LAYERED COLESLAW

1 small head white cabbage
½ cucumber
1 large green pepper
2 onions
Bunch of radishes

*For golden dressing:*
1¼ cups mayonnaise
½ teaspoon salt
⅛ teaspoon pepper
⅛ teaspoon paprika
2½ teaspoons sugar
2½ tablespoons vinegar
2½ tablespoons milk
2½ teaspoons prepared mustard
2 egg yolks

Shred the cabbage very fine.
Score the cucumber from end to
end with the prongs of a fork and
slice very thinly. Wash and seed
the pepper and cut into fine rings.

Cut the onion into wafer thin
rings. Prepare and wash the
radishes and slice very thinly.
Arrange about a quarter of the
cabbage in a salad bowl. Arrange
the cucumber in a layer on top,
cover with another quarter of the
cabbage, then a layer of green
pepper rings. Cover with more of
the cabbage, then add a layer of
onion rings. Heap the remaining
cabbage in the center. Arrange
radish slices around the outside
of the salad.
Combine the mayonnaise with
the remaining ingredients and
beat until well blended. Pour over
the salad.

### ENDIVE AND ORANGE SALAD

3 large endive
3 oranges
French dressing

Remove the roots and outer
leaves of the endive and wash.
Cut into chunks. Pare the
oranges and divide into sections.
Mix the two together in a bowl
and sprinkle with French dressing.

### STUFFED BAKED APPLES

8 medium cooking apples
7½ tablespoons water
Mixture of currants, white
  raisins, chopped dried
  apricots, mixed candied peel
  or glacé fruits
Sugar
Butter

Wipe the apples and make a shallow cut through the skin around
the middle of each. Core the
apples and stand them in an
ovenproof dish. Pour the water
around and fill each apple with
the fruit mixture. Sprinkle a little
sugar over the apples and top each
one with a lump of butter. Bake in
the center of a fairly hot oven
(400°F.) for 45 minutes to 1 hour
or until apples are soft.
Alternatively, wrap individual
apples in foil (omitting the water)
and bake in the embers of the hot
coals in the barbecue unit.

## MENU *serves 12*

**FISH CHOWDER**
**MIXED KEBABS**
**ROLLS AND BUTTER**
**GREEN SALAD**
**BANANES AU CARAMEL**

### FISH CHOWDER

6 slices lean bacon, chopped
3 onions, sliced
3 pound fresh haddock, cooked
  and flaked
2 cans (16 ounces each) tomatoes
6 potatoes, diced
3¾ cups fish stock or bottled
  clam juice
Salt
Freshly ground black pepper
3 bay leaves
6 cloves
1⅞ cups milk
Chopped parsley

Fry the bacon until the fat runs
add the onion and fry until soft
Add the fish, tomatoes and
potatoes with the stock and seasonings. Simmer gently for about
30 minutes or until potatoes are
tender. Add the milk. Remove the
bay leaves and cloves, then rehea
gently. Serve in mugs with a little
chopped parsley sprinkled on top.

### MIXED KEBABS

*For the marinade:*
2 parts olive oil
1 part wine vinegar
Clove garlic, crushed
Few peppercorns

Lean, tender steak, cubed
Sausages, halved
Button mushrooms, wiped
Cherry tomatoes
Bacon slices
Tiny onions, par-boiled
Bay leaves

Marinate the steak in the mixture
several hours. Thread a selection
of the ingredients on skewers;
allow 2 skewers per person.
Refrigerate until cooking time.
Brush with melted butter and
grill over hot coals, basting and
turning as they get brown.

### BANANES AU CARAMEL

12–15 bananas
1½ cups sugar
7½ tablespoons water

Choose bananas which are
slightly under-ripe. Using a
strong, deep skillet, dissolve the
sugar in the water over low heat.
Bring to a boil and bubble until
the syrup is lightly colored. Lay
the bananas in the sauce and
spoon the caramel over them
until they are coated.
Cook for about 10 minutes on top
of the barbecue. Serve the
bananas with the caramel poured
over them.

*Mix steak with sausages and bacon for tasty kebabs*

# EASY WEEKENDS

Weekend guests become part of your family for a short time – yet somehow they seem to merit more than family treatment!

*Liver and bacon provençale*

*Make a change from everyday bacon and eggs*

## BREAKFAST

*A good breakfast goes a long way towards keeping your guests happy for the rest of the day. It may be a meal they don't bother with at home, and the sheer luxury of having someone else prepare it is bound to make them appreciate your efforts. Most of the dishes in our menus can be prepared all at once, and then kept hot in the oven or on a hot tray.*

### MENU 1

**CEREAL or
ORANGE WAKE ME UP
PLAIN OMELET
PRUNE AND BACON ROLLS
BROILED TOMATOES
PECAN BUTTERMILK
MUFFINS
TOAST
MARMALADE**

*Home-made muesli is wholesome and different from packet cereals*

270

### ORANGE WAKE ME UP

*For each person:*
**Juice of 1 orange
1¼ tablespoons clear honey
1 egg**

Place all the ingredients in an electric blender and blend for 30 seconds. Or place in a bowl and beat with a rotary beater until thoroughly blended.

### PRUNE AND BACON ROLLS

**Prunes
Lean bacon slices
Prepared mustard**

Soak the prunes (allow 2 prunes for each slice of bacon) overnight in enough water to cover. Drain and remove the pits. Stretch the bacon slices with the back of a knife. Cut each slice in half and spread with mustard. Roll one

piece around each prune, place on small skewers under a hot broiler until the bacon is cooked.

### PECAN BUTTERMILK MUFFINS
*makes 2 dozen*

**2 cups sifted cake flour
1 teaspoon baking powder
½ teaspoon salt
2 tablespoons sugar
½ teaspoon baking soda
1 cup buttermilk
3 tablespoons melted butter
1 egg, beaten
½ cup chopped pecans**

Sift dry ingredients together into a mixing bowl. Combine buttermilk, butter and egg and add mixture all at once to the dry ingredients. Add pecans and mix only enough to moisten dry ingredients. Do not beat. Mixture will be slightly lumpy. Two-thirds fill well-buttered muffin pans. Bake in a fairly hot oven (400°F.) 20–25 minutes or until muffins are puffed and lightly browned.
*Note:* Reheat leftover muffins, loosely wrapped in aluminum foil, in a very hot (450°F.) oven for 5 minutes.

### MENU 2

**YOGURT
MIXED SALAD OF DRIED
FRUITS – PRUNES,
APRICOTS, APPLES,
PEARS
FINNAN HADDIE or
BACON
MUSHROOMS
ROLLS
HONEY**

### FINNAN HADDIE
*4 servings*

*These are smoked haddock named after the Scottish fishing village Findon, near Aberdeen.*

**2 finnan haddock (or smoked cod
fillets), about 1½ pound
2½ cups milk
¼ cup butter
½ cup all-purpose flour
Chopped parsley
Salt and pepper
2 hard-cooked eggs**

Place the fish skin side up under a hot broiler for a few minutes – this makes skinning very simple. Peel the skin off and cut the fish into 8 pieces. Poach in milk for 15 minutes or until tender. Drain off the milk into a 1–quart measure and make up to 2½ cups with

more milk if necessary.
Melt the butter in a pan, stir in the flour and cook for 1 minute. Remove from the heat and stir in the milk. Cook over moderate heat, stirring constantly, until thickened. Flake the fish, removing any bones, and add to the sauce with the parsley, salt and pepper. Heat thoroughly. Pour into individual serving platters and garnish with wedges of hard-cooked egg.

### MENU 3

**FRUIT JUICE or
HONEY MUESLI
BREAKFAST BROIL –
Kidneys, bacon, sausages,
tomatoes
POACHED EGGS
TOAST
BRAN MUFFINS**

### HONEY MUESLI
*4–6 servings*

**4 oranges
Grated rind of ½ lemon
4 eating apples
2½ tablespoons white raisins
1 banana, sliced
2½ tablespoons ground almonds
2½ tablespoons rolled oats
1¼ tablespoons honey
5 tablespoons light cream
1 red eating apple, cored
2½ tablespoons lemon juice
Black and white grapes, seeded**

Squeeze the juice from 2 of the oranges into a large bowl. Add the grated lemon rind. Grate 4 apples into the juice, discarding the cores. Add the raisins, banana, almonds, oats, honey and cream. Turn into a serving platter.
Divide the remaining 2 oranges into sections. Slice the red apple and dip it into the lemon juice to prevent discoloration. Decorate the muesli with alternate slices of orange, apple and a few grapes. Serve chilled.

### BRAN MUFFINS
*makes 20*

**1¾ cups all-purpose flour
1¼ teaspoons salt
7½ teaspoons baking powder
1 cup whole bran cereal
1¾ cups milk, plus 2 teaspoons
5 tablespoons soft butter or
margarine
5 tablespoons sugar
2 eggs, beaten**

Grease twenty 2½-in. muffin pans, or line with paper cup cake liners. Sift the flour, salt and baking powder together. Soak the bran in the milk for 5 minutes. Meanwhile, cream the butter and sugar together until light. Add the egg and stir until smooth. Add the bran mixture and stir. Add the flour and stir only until just mixed, no longer. Two-thirds fill the muffin pans. Bake in the center of a fairly hot oven (400°F.) for 25 minutes or until well browned. Turn out on a wire rack to cool. Serve hot with butter.

## WEEKEND LUNCHES

*Nobody expects a 3-course meal twice a day, but you probably feel you want to offer something a little more organized than your usual family lunch. These menus are quick and easy to prepare, even for a full house.*

## MENU *serves 4*

### LIVER AND BACON PROVENCALE
### BUTTERED NOODLES
### GREEN SALAD
### ICE CREAM CAKE

## LIVER AND BACON PROVENCALE

**1 pound lambs' liver**
**½ cup all-purpose flour**
**2½ tablespoons salad oil**
**½ pound lean sliced bacon, chopped**
**1 pound onions, chopped**
**1 can (16 ounces) tomatoes**
**1 teaspoon dried marjoram**
**1 bay leaf**
**1¼ tablespoons Worcestershire sauce**
**2 cups beef stock or bouillon**
**Salt and pepper**

Slice the liver into long, thick strips, coat with flour and fry in hot oil until golden brown. Place in a casserole.

Add the bacon and onions to the skillet and cook until golden. Stir in any flour left over from coating the liver. Add the tomatoes, marjoram, bay leaf and Worcestershire sauce. Stir in the stock, season well, and pour into the casserole. Cover with a tightly fitting lid and cook in a cool oven (300°F.) for about 1½ hours. Serve with a green salad and hot cooked noodles.

## ICE CREAM CAKE

**7 or 8 in. sponge layer cake**
**Preserves**
**Ice cream**
**⅔ cup heavy cream, whipped**

*Double crust blackcurrant pie to finish a Saturday lunch*

Split the sponge cake and spread one half with preserves. Cover with ice cream, piling it up in the center. Cut the other half of the cake into wedges and arrange around the cake so that they open at the center to show the ice cream. Fill the gaps between the wedges with whipped cream.

## MENU *serves 4*

### DEVILLED HAM SLICES WITH PINEAPPLE
### SPINACH
### CREAMED POTATOES
### DOUBLE CRUST BLACKCURRANT PIE

## DEVILLED HAM SLICES WITH PINEAPPLE

**Two ¾ pound ham slices**
**5 teaspoons dry mustard**
**¾ cup brown sugar**
**1 can (8 ounces) pineapple slices**
**8 maraschino cherries**

Trim excess fat from ham slices and snip at intervals to keep from curling. Combine the mustard, sugar and 10 tablespoons syrup from the can of pineapple. Lay the ham slices on the rack in a preheated broiling compartment.

Spread evenly with some of the sugar mixture. Cook, about 5 in. from source of heat for 15 minutes, basting every 5 minutes. Turn the ham slices, spread with remaining sugar mixture and cook until bubbly and piping hot. Place 2 pineapple slices and 4 cherries on each slice. Baste and cook for 3–4 minutes. Each slice will make 2 servings.

## DOUBLE CRUST BLACKCURRANT PIE

**2 cups sifted all-purpose flour**
**1 teaspoon salt**
**⅔ cup shortening**
**4 tablespoons cold water**
**1–1½ pounds blackcurrants**
**½ cup sugar**
**1¼ tablespoons flour**
**Milk**

Mix together the flour and salt. Cut in the shortening with a pastry blender or two knives, until mixture looks like cornmeal. Sprinkle the water over, a little at a time, and mix lightly with a fork until all dry ingredients are moistened. Press firmly into a ball. Divide the pastry in two – one piece should be larger than the other. Roll out the larger piece on a lightly floured board and fit into

an 8-in. pie pan.

Pick over and wash the currants. Mix with sugar and 1¼ tablespoons flour. Fill the lined pie pan with the fruit mixture. Roll out the remaining dough in a circle and place on top of fruit. Press the edges together to seal firmly. Scallop or flute the edges. Brush the top with a little milk. Bake in a hot oven (425°F.) for 10–15 minutes or until the pastry begins to brown. Reduce the temperature to 350°F. and continue cooking for 20–30 minutes or until the fruit is cooked. Serve warm or cold with cream or ice cream.

### Handy hint

Sour cream is not the same as fresh pasteurized cream that has gone 'off'. It is specially treated to give a fresh, sharp flavor. If a recipe calls for sour cream and you have none available, add a little lemon juice to fresh cream.

## MENU *serves 4*

**HERRING FILLETS
NORMANDY STYLE
BROILED TOMATOES
POTATO CHIPS
FRESH FRUIT
CHEESE BOARD**

### HERRING FILLETS NORMANDY STYLE

**4 herrings or 1 pound other oily
  fish
Seasoned flour
2½ tablespoons corn oil
¼ cup butter
2 eating apples
Juice of ½ lemon
Pepper
Chopped parsley**

Bone the fish and cut each in half
down the center. Dip the fillets in
seasoned flour and fry in hot oil
mixed with 2 tablespoons of the
butter until crisp and golden on
each side. Remove from pan and
keep warm. Wipe out the pan
with paper toweling.
Pare and core the apples and cut
each one into 8 pieces. Add
remaining butter to the pan and
sauté the apple until tender but
still in pieces. Add the lemon
juice and a dusting of freshly
ground pepper. Arrange the fillets
in a dish, spoon the apple mixture
over the top and sprinkle with
chopped parsley.

### TEAS

*Tea-time at the weekend may be
anything from toast and muffins
around the fire, to a quick
mouthful of something in the
kitchen. If you have guests, you
may find they do not want tea, but
something must be available for
the hungry types. Even those who
don't bother at home will probably
develop a healthy appetite when
they see some of your goodies.*

### TOASTED TEAS

*Ideal in winter, particularly if
dinner is to be late. Your guests
will be grateful for one of these
snacks if they have spent the
afternoon walking briskly in the
snow – if they have just dozed in
front of the fire, try some tempting
pastries instead! Toasted
sandwiches usually need a knife
and fork for eating.
Apart from the recipes given here
you can also serve traditional
crumpets and muffins toasted.*

*Herrings Normandy style – quick to prepare*

*A huge toasted sandwich will satisfy tea-time appetites*

### TRIDENT TOASTED SANDWICHES
*4–6 servings*

**2 large hard-cooked eggs
1 cup grated strong Cheddar
  cheese
1 can (7 ounces) tuna, drained
  and flaked
5 sweet pickled onions, chopped
5 tablespoons mayonnaise
Juice of ½ lemon
Few drops Tabasco sauce
Salt
Freshly ground black pepper
3 tablespoons butter
12 large slices white bread**

#### Handy hint

Aluminum pans will go
black when in contact with
boiling water for long
periods. To prevent this,
add a little vinegar to the
water (e.g. when boiling
eggs or steaming) or a
little lemon juice (e.g. when
boiling rice). If vinegar or
lemon juice would spoil the
flavor of the food being
cooked, boil up a fresh pan
full of water afterwards with
a little vinegar added.

Chop the eggs and combine with
the cheese, tuna, onions, mayonnaise, lemon juice, Tabasco, salt
and pepper. Melt the butter in a
small pan. Brush it on one side of
each slice of bread. Place 6 of the
slices, butter side down, on a
board. Spread each with part of
the filling. Top with another slice
of bread, butter side up. Broil in a
hot broiler until golden brown on
both sides. Cut in half and serve.

### SMOKED ROE SALAD
*4 servings*

**1 lemon
⅝ cup mayonnaise
Few drops Tabasco sauce
Salt
Freshly ground black pepper
4 slices white bread
Butter
Lettuce leaves
3 large eggs, hard-cooked
½–¾ pound smoked cod or
  salmon roe
Paprika**

Blend the juice from ½ the lemon
into the mayonnaise, add the
Tabasco and adjust seasoning.
Toast the bread until golden
brown on both sides. Butter liberally. Lay 3 or 4 lettuce leaves on

each slice of toast and spoon the
mayonnaise down the center.
Slice the eggs and position overlapping down one side of the
toast. Place the roe on the other
side. Take 4 slices from the
remaining ½ lemon, make a cut
in the center of each slice, twist
and place on top. Dust the egg
with paprika.

### PIZZA BAMBINI
*4 servings*

**¼ pound salami
6 anchovy fillets
1 cup grated cheese
4 hamburger rolls
Butter
½ pound firm tomatoes, peeled
  and thickly sliced
1 small green pepper, seeds
  removed and thinly sliced**

Roughly chop the salami and
anchovy fillets. Combine with the
cheese.
Cut the rolls in half and toast
lightly. Butter and spoon cheese
mixture on to each half. Spread
evenly. Top each with a thick
slice of tomato. Broil until cheese
bubbles and browns.
Garnish with thin rings of green
pepper.

### BEANS AND BACON SANDWICH
*4 servings*

**½ cup canned baked beans in
  tomato sauce
8 slices lean bacon
Horseradish sauce
Prepared mustard
8 slices white bread
Butter**

Heat the beans gently in a small
pan. Fry the bacon until crisp,
then crumble on to a plate. When
the beans are hot, add a little
horseradish and mustard to taste.
Stir in the crumbled bacon.
Toast the bread on both sides,
butter and spread on filling.

### SANDWICHES

*Sandwiches are the easiest to eat if
you don't want to sit down to a
table with a knife and fork. Ring
the changes with different types of
bread – white, brown, wholewheat,
granary, rye and so on – and slice it
very thinly and butter it well.
Fillings need to be well-flavored;
anything very delicate is muted to
the point of tastelessness when
encased in a double layer of bread.*

For some unusual sandwich fillings, try the following mixtures:
Shrimp, chopped celery, shredded pineapple and mayonnaise.
Cream cheese, chopped walnuts and seeded raisins or dates.
Chopped tongue, chopped hard-cooked egg, mayonnaise and a pinch of curry powder.
Flaked, canned crabmeat, chopped avocado and mayonnaise.
Ground chicken, ground ham and finely chopped pineapple.
Cream cheese, chopped celery and chopped green pepper.

## CAKES

*A large cake is always welcome at tea-time, either on its own or with sandwiches. These two are firm family favorites.*

### BRANDY, ORANGE AND RAISIN CAKE

*This is a moist cake and keeps well for 2–3 weeks.*

1½ pound white raisins
2 medium oranges
⅝ cup brandy
1 cup sugar
1 cup butter
4 large eggs
2 cups all-purpose flour
½ cup self-rising flour

The day before baking, place the raisins in a deep bowl. Grate the rind from the oranges, add to the raisins with the juice squeezed from the oranges (about 10 tablespoonfuls) and the brandy. Stir well. Leave for at least 12 hours for the raisins to plump up, stirring occasionally. Grease an 8-in. spring-form pan. Line the bottom with 2 layers of waxed paper and grease again. Tie a band of brown paper around the outside.
Cream the butter and sugar together until light and fluffy. Beat in the eggs one at a time, beating well after each addition. Lightly beat in the sifted flours. Fold in the fruit and its juices. Turn the mixture into the prepared pan. Bake in a warm slow oven (325° F.) for about 3 hours. If the top of the cake appears to be getting too brown, cover with a sheet of waxed paper. To test whether the cake is cooked, insert a hot skewer into the center of the cake. It should come out perfectly clean. If any cake mixture is sticking to it, the cake requires longer cooking. Turn out and

*Cream horns are a real weekend luxury – make the horns in advance*

cool on a wire rack. Store in an airtight tin.

### WALNUT BUTTER CAKE

6 tablespoons unsalted butter
½ cup all-purpose flour
2 tablespoons cornstarch
3 large eggs
½ cup sugar
1 cup finely chopped walnuts

Grease and lightly flour a 9-in. tube cake pan. Shake out any excess flour.
Heat the butter gently until melted, remove from heat and let stand until any sediment settles. Sift the flour and cornstarch together. Put the eggs and sugar in a large bowl. Stand the bowl over a saucepan of hot, not boiling, water and beat until light and creamy. The mixture should be stiff enough to retain the impression of the beater for a few seconds. Remove from heat and beat until mixture is cool.
Pour the tepid, but still flowing, butter around the edge of the mixture. Lightly fold in the butter until most of it is worked in. Sift half the flour over the surface and fold in lightly with a rubber scraper. Fold in remaining flour and nuts. Pour the mixture into the prepared pan. Bake in the center of a fairly hot oven (375° F.) for about 20 minutes.
Serve plain or frosted as desired.

### PASTRIES

*Introduce a touch of luxury into the weekend, without hard labor. The pastry cases can be made a day or two in advance and stored in an airtight tin. Fill them the day you intend serving them.*

### TARTLETTES AUX FRUITS
*makes 6*

*For pâté sucrée:*
1 cup all-purpose flour
Pinch of salt
¼ cup sugar
¼ cup butter, at room temperature
2 egg yolks

*For crème pâtissière:*
2 egg yolks
¼ cup sugar
3 tablespoons all-purpose flour
2 tablespoons cornstarch
1¼ cups milk
1 egg white
Vanilla extract
Confectioners' sugar

1 can (16 ounces) black cherries
⅝ cup cherry juice
1¼ teaspoons arrowroot
1 cup heavy cream

Sift the flour and salt together onto a pastry board. Make a well in the center and put in the sugar, butter and egg yolks. Using the fingertips of one hand, pinch and work the sugar, butter and egg yolks together until well blended. Gradually work in all the flour and knead lightly until smooth. Put the paste in a cool place for at least 1 hour to relax.
Roll out the pastry and use it to line 4½-in. shallow patty or tart pans. Line the pastry with aluminum foil and a few dried beans. Bake in a fairly hot oven (375° F.) for 12–15 minutes. Remove foil and bake 4–5 minutes longer or until browned and set. Let stand a few minutes, then cool on a wire rack.
Make up the crème pâtissière a

day in advance to save time. Cream the egg yolks and sugar together until really thick and pale in color. Beat in the flour and the cornstarch. Add a little cold milk to make a smooth paste. Heat the rest of the milk in a saucepan until almost boiling, pour slowly on to the egg mixture, beating well all the time. Return the mixture to the saucepan. Cook over very low heat, stirring constantly, until the mixture boils. Beat the egg white until stiff. Remove the custard mixture from the heat and fold in the egg white. Return the pan to the heat, add a few drops of vanilla and cook for 2–3 minutes. Remove and let cool. Sprinkle the top of the custard with confectioners' sugar to prevent a skin forming. Before serving, spread a layer of crème pâtissière over the bottom of each tart. Drain the cherries (reserving the juice) and remove pits, if necessary. Blend ⅝ cup of the juice with the arrowroot in a saucepan. Bring to boil and cook until the mixture thickens. Remove from heat and cool.
Whip the cream until stiff. Pipe around the edges of the pastry cases. Arrange the cherries in the center and spoon the thickened juice over the top.

### CREAM HORNS
*makes 8*

1 package (10 ounces) frozen patty shells, thawed
1 egg, beaten
Raspberry preserves
1 cup heavy cream
Confectioners' sugar

Place the patty shells close together on a board and press edges together. Roll out into a strip 26 in. by 4–4½ in. Brush with beaten egg. Cut into eight ½ in. ribbons with a very sharp knife. Wind each ribbon around a cream horn pan, glazed side uppermost. Start at the tip, overlapping ⅛ in. all the way and finish neatly on the underside. The pastry should not overlap the metal rim. Place on a damp cookie tray, with the seams underneath. Bake near the top of a hot oven (425° F.) for 8–10 minutes or until golden brown. Cool for a few minutes.
Carefully twist each pan, holding the pastry lightly in the other hand, to ease off the case. When cold, fill the tip of each horn with a little preserves. Whip the cream and fill the horns. Dust with confectioners' sugar.

*Dinner when you have weekend guests has to be fairly informal, since you are not free yourself to make elaborate preparations in the shops or kitchen.*

## MENU *serves 4*

**AVOCADO AND MELON COCKTAIL**
**ROLLED STUFFED BREAST OF LAMB**
**SAUTE POTATOES**
**BROCCOLI WITH BROWNED ALMONDS**
**ANANAS GLACE**

## AVOCADO AND MELON COCKTAIL

2 small honeydew or cantaloupe melons
4 avocados
Lemon juice
¼ watermelon
Fresh mint

Cut the melons in half and discard the seeds. Scoop out as much of the fruit as is practical with a small melon ball cutter and retain the melon halves. Cut the avocados in half lengthwise, remove the pits and scoop out the fruit with the same size melon ball cutter. Sprinkle the avocado balls with lemon juice to prevent discoloration. Make watermelon balls in the same fashion.
Pile the melon and avocado balls back into the melon halves. Top with a sprig of mint. Chill for 20–30 minutes before serving.
*Note:* The melon balls can be prepared 1–2 hours in advance, but the avocado should be left until just before serving.

## ROLLED STUFFED BREAST OF LAMB

3 pound breast of lamb, boned
Salt and pepper
¼ pound lean veal
5 slices lean bacon
1 onion, chopped
2 tablespoons butter or margarine
1½ cups fresh white breadcrumbs
1 large mushroom, chopped
1 teaspoon finely chopped parsley
Cayenne
Ground mace
1 egg, beaten
Milk, optional

Spread the lamb out flat on a board, sprinkle with salt and pep-

*Refreshing and simple to make – avocado and melon cocktail*

per and rub into the meat.
Put the veal and bacon through a meat chopper two times, then beat well in a bowl. Sauté the onion in a little of the butter until soft but not browned. Add to the meat. Add the breadcrumbs, mushroom, remaining butter and parsley. Season with salt, pepper, very little cayenne and mace. Lastly add the egg and mix well. If the mixture is too stiff add a little milk.
Spread the meat mixture over the lamb and roll the meat up loosely to allow the stuffing to expand during cooking. Tie the roll in several places with fine string to hold its shape. Weigh it and calculate the cooking time, allowing 27–30 minutes per pound plus 27 minutes. Place the meat on a rack in a shallow roasting pan. Roast in a moderate oven (350°F.) for the calculated time.
Remove the string and serve sliced fairly thickly, accompanied by a thickened gravy. Any stuffing left over can be cooked in a separate small dish and served with the meat.

## ANANAS GLACE

2 small or 1 large pineapple
5 tablespoons Kirsch
2 oranges
2 pears
2½ tablespoons lemon juice
12 glacé cherries
2 tablespoons thinly sliced candied citron
Vanilla ice cream

Cut the pineapple in half lengthwise and scoop out the fruit, taking care not to damage

the shells. Remove the core and cut the rest of the fruit into cubes. Put these into a bowl with the Kirsch. Chill the pineapple shells. Pare the oranges, remove all the white part and cut into sections, discarding the membrane. Add the oranges and any juice to the pineapple. Pare, core and slice the pears and dip them into the lemon juice before adding to the other fruit. Add the cherries and citron. Chill for at least 2 hours.
Pile the fruit and juice into the pineapple shells and top with scoops of ice cream.

## MENU *serves 6*

**FLORIDA COCKTAIL**
**CARBONNADE OF BEEF**
**GREEN BEANS**
**CREAMED POTATOES**
**PEAR AND ALMOND PIE**

## FLORIDA COCKTAIL

3 large grapefruit
6 oranges
Sugar
Sherry, optional

Cut the grapefruit in half across the center and divide into sections using a curved grapefruit knife. Divide the pieces between 6 small dessert glasses, pouring any juice over the top. Pare the oranges, removing all the white part, and divide into sections. Add to the grapefruit, with the juice. Sprinkle with sugar and add a dash of sherry, if desired. Serve chilled.

## CARBONNADE OF BEEF

3 pound lean beef stew, cut into ½ in. cubes
Salt and pepper
6 tablespoons fat or oil
¼ pound lean bacon, chopped
½ cup all-purpose flour
2 cups beer
2 cups stock or water
4–5 tablespoons vinegar
1½ pound onions, chopped
2 cloves garlic, chopped
Bouquet garni

Season the meat and fry a little at a time in the hot fat or oil until brown, about 5 minutes for each batch. Add the bacon and continue cooking for a few minutes. Remove the meat and bacon from the pan, stir in the flour and brown lightly. Gradually add the beer, stock and vinegar, stirring constantly until the mixture thickens. Fill an ovenproof casserole with layers of meat, bacon, onion and garlic. Pour the beer sauce over and add the bouquet garni. Cover and cook in a cool oven (300° F.) for about 4 hours. Add a little more stock during cooking if sauce seems too thick. Remove the bouquet garni before serving.

## PEAR AND ALMOND PIE

2 pound cooking pears
5 tablespoons brandy
¼ cup butter
1½ cups ground almonds
1 cup sugar
1 teaspoon cinnamon
1 package (10 ounces) frozen patty shells, thawed
1 egg, beaten
a little sugar
1¼ cups heavy cream, whipped

Pare and core the pears. Cut them lengthwise into eighths, and lay in a round, shallow 10-in. pie dish. Pour the brandy over them and dot with the butter cut into small pieces. Combine the almonds, sugar and cinnamon and spoon evenly over the fruit. Place the patty shells on a lightly floured board and press edges together. Roll out pastry into a large round and place on top of dish. Trim and crimp the edges. Decorate with leaves cut from the pastry trimmings. Brush the beaten egg over the top. Chill for 20 minutes. Bake in a very hot oven (425°F.) for 15 minutes, reduce temperature to 375°F. and bake for 25–30 minutes or until the pastry is well risen and golden brown. Sprinkle with a little sugar 5 minutes before the end of the cooking time. Serve hot or cold with whipped cream.

## HOT STUFFED TOMATOES

**6 even-sized tomatoes**
**¼ cup chopped cooked ham**
**2 teaspoons chopped onion**
**1½ tablespoons butter**
**1 teaspoon chopped parsley**
**4 tablespoons fresh white breadcrumbs**
**Salt and pepper**
**4 tablespoons grated cheese, optional**

Cut a small round from each tomato at the end opposite the stalk and scoop out the centers. Lightly fry the ham and onion in the butter for 3 minutes. Add the parsley, breadcrumbs, salt and pepper, cheese if used and the pulp removed from the tomatoes. Fill the tomato cases with this mixture, pile it neatly on top and put on the lids. Place in a baking dish and bake in a fairly hot oven (400° F.) for about 15 minutes, or until piping hot.

## WIENER BEEF BRAISE

**1½ pound round steak, cut into 12 very thin slices**
**12 cocktail frankfurters**
**6 tablespoons fat or pan drippings**
**2 onions, chopped**
**4 carrots, cubed**
**1 large rutabaga, peeled and cubed**
**3 stalks celery, sliced**
**2 cups beef bouillon**
**Salt and pepper**
**1½ pound potatoes, creamed**
**3¾ teaspoons cornstarch**

Beat the beef with a rolling pin until very thin. Roll each slice around a frankfurter and tie with fine string.
Melt half the fat and brown the beef rolls on all sides. Remove the rolls from the pan and add the remaining fat. Sauté the vegetables until the fat is absorbed. Place the beef rolls on top of the vegetables, add the stock and season with salt and pepper. Bring to a boil, cover, reduce heat and simmer for about 2 hours or until the meat is tender.
Lift the beef rolls out and arrange on a platter in a ring of creamed

*Cheese topped gammon with peas lyonnaise for an informal dinner*

potatoes. Keep hot. Strain the cooking liquid, thicken it with the cornstarch and check the seasoning. Pour over the beef rolls.

## BLACKCURRANT STREUSEL

**1½ cups all-purpose flour**
**½ cup butter**
**¾ cup sugar**
**1 pound blackcurrants**
**1¼ cups heavy cream, whipped**

*For topping:*
**¾ cup all-purpose flour**
**6 tablespoons butter**
**6 tablespoons sugar**

Sift the flour. Rub in the butter and then add ¼ cup sugar. Knead the mixture until it forms a dough then press out to fit a 9-in. square baking pan. Wash and pick over the blackcurrants. Mix with the remaining sugar and sprinkle over the dough. To make the topping, sift the flour and rub in the butter very lightly. Add the sugar and toss with a fork. Sprinkle over the blackcurrants.
Bake in a fairly hot oven (375° F.) for about 1 hour or until golden brown. Serve warm or cold, cut into squares and topped with cream.

## EGG MAYONNAISE

**4 hard-cooked eggs**
**Lettuce leaves**
**⅝ cup mayonnaise**
**Chopped parsley**

Cut the eggs lengthwise into halves or quarters. Put a few lettuce leaves on each plate. Serve the eggs on the lettuce, cut side down, coat with the mayonnaise and garnish with parsley.

## CHEESE TOPPED HAM

**4 thick boiled ham slices, about ⅓ pound each**
**2 green eating apples**
**Melted butter**
**4 slices Cheddar cheese**

Snip the edges of the ham slices to keep from curling. Line the broiler pan with foil and put in the ham slices. Broil under a hot broiler for 4–5 minutes, turning halfway through the cooking time. Core the apples but do not pare. Slice thinly into rounds. Lay the apple slices over the ham. Brush a little melted butter over the apple slices and continue broiling for 2–3 minutes. Lay the cheese slices over the apples and broil for 1 minute or until the cheese is hot and bubbling.

## LYONNAISE PEAS

**¼ cup butter**
**2 large onions, finely sliced**
**1 pound frozen peas**
**Salt**

Melt the butter in a small pan. Add the onion and cook over low heat for 3 minutes. Meanwhile cook the peas in boiling salted

water for 3 minutes, or just until tender. Drain the peas and mix with the onions. Heat thoroughly and serve.

## GALETTE JALOUSIE

**1 package (10 ounces) frozen patty shells, thawed**
**1 egg, beaten**
**½ pound preserves**
**1 egg white, beaten**
**Sugar**

Put the patty shells close together on a lightly floured board. Press the edges together. Roll out into a strip 18 in. by 4 in. Cut into 2 portions, one 2 in. shorter than the other. Roll out the smaller piece to the same size as the larger and place on a dampened cookie tray. Brush a border ½ in. wide at the end of each strip with beaten egg. Spread the preserves over the center of the pastry. Fold the thicker strip of pastry in half lengthwise. Using a sharp knife, cut across the fold at intervals to within ½ in. of the edge. Unfold the pastry and lift it carefully on to the portion on the cookie tray. Press edges together and seal. Bake in the center of a very hot oven (425° F.) for about 20 minutes. Remove from the oven. Brush with egg white, dredge with sugar and return to the oven for 5 minutes to frost the top.

### Handy hint

To cook a perfect omelet, you need the pan evenly heated. Place the pan on a very gentle heat to ensure that it is heated evenly right to the edges. When the pan is ready for the mixture it will feel comfortably hot to the back of your hand about 1 in. from the surface. Add the butter or oil when the pan is ready.

# FONDUE BOURGUIGNONNE

A meat fondue is a pleasant Swiss way of giving an informal dinner party for 6–8 people. It entails very little by way of preparation by the hostess, and what has to be done can all be done well in advance. In fact, the guests cook their own meat in a pot at the table, which adds to the interest of the evening.

You need a fondue set consisting of a flameproof pot over a spirit burner, and a set of long handled forks. If you have no fondue set you could improvize with an electric table cooker – but the atmosphere won't be quite the same. The traditional meat fondue pots are copper or iron; there are also some attractive stainless steel pots available.

Allow ⅓ pound good tender steak per person, cut into 1 in. cubes. Fill the pot two-thirds full with salad oil (corn oil is suitable) and heat on your ordinary cooker to 375°F., using a frying thermometer for accuracy. Transfer the pot to the spirit burner or a table cooker that will keep the oil at just the correct temperature (the oil should not smoke or spit as this indicates a dangerous heat, but it must be hot enough to seal the meat quickly, so that the fat is not absorbed). It helps to have a second pot of oil heated so that the first can be replaced when the temperature of the oil begins to drop.

Place a plate of raw steak and a long-handled fork in front of each person and equip them with a second fork with which to eat the meat (if they use the same forks as those on which the meat is cooked someone will get a nasty burn). Each person impales a piece of steak on the long-handled fork and puts it into the oil until it is cooked. It is then transferred to the cold fork and dipped into one of the sauces on the table.

## TARTAR SAUCE

⅝ cup mayonnaise or salad
  dressing
1¼ teaspoons chopped tarragon
  or chives
2½ teaspoons chopped capers
2½ teaspoons chopped gherkins
2½ teaspoons chopped parsley
1¼ tablespoons lemon juice or
  tarragon vinegar

Mix all the ingredients well, then
leave the sauce for at least 1 hour
before serving, to allow the
flavors to blend.

## HOLLANDAISE SAUCE

2½ tablespoons wine or tarragon
  vinegar
1¼ tablespoons water
2 egg yolks
½ cup butter
Salt and pepper

Put the vinegar and water in a
small pan and boil until reduced
to about 1 tablespoon; cool slightly. Put the egg yolks in a bowl and
stir in the vinegar. Put over a pan
of hot water and heat gently, stirring all the time, until the egg

mixture thickens (never let the
water go above simmering point).
Divide the butter into small
pieces and gradually beat into the
sauce. Season to taste. If the
sauce is too sharp add a little
more butter – it should be slightly
piquant, almost thick enough to
hold its shape and warm rather
than hot when served.

## TOMATO MAYONNAISE

Blend ⅝ cup mayonnaise with
tomato paste to taste.

## CURRY MAYONNAISE

Blend ⅝ cup mayonnaise with a
little curry powder to taste.

## HORSERADISH SAUCE

Mix whipped heavy cream with
horseradish relish to flavor.

## SIDE DISHES

Chopped banana
Sliced gherkins
Sliced olives
Green salad
Tomato wedges, cucumber
slices, whole radishes, carrot
sticks.

Information

# PARTY PLANNERS' CHECK LIST

## Countdown

### A MONTH BEFORE

What sort of party will it be? You've a good idea of the numbers by now and have probably decided more or less what to serve, but now you must finalize your ideas.

### THE WEEK BEFORE

All replies will be in by now, and you'll be able to confirm your drinks and glasses orders, as well as anything else you may be hiring. Make a hair appointment for the day of the party, and have a manicure as well.

### THE DAY BEFORE

Clean the house thoroughly. Put away superfluous or precious ornaments to prevent damage. Move furniture away from main traffic areas, but don't let your main room get too bare.

### ON THE DAY

Remember it's your party and you should enjoy it as well. Clear your dressing table and put out hair spray, tissues, pins and so on for your women guests. A needle and thread might also come in useful. When the family has finished in the bathroom have a tidy-up and put out fresh soap and several guest towels. A clean glass, with drinking water, aspirins and Alka Seltzer would probably be welcome. And don't forget your hairdresser's appointment!

## Food and drink

Order wine and/or spirits from the liquor store preferably on 'sale or return'. If you have a freezer, you can start cooking for your party now. Pastry cases, meringues, sauces and pâtés can all be made and packed away.

Non-freezer owners can make meringues and pâtés – both keep happily for up to 5 days. Buy the 'nibblers' – olives, peanuts, crisps, etc. and check you have everything you need in the cupboard. Order meat, fish and any special fruit. Make a complete list of other foods you need, including coffee, tea and soft drinks.

Take food out of the freezer. Prepare pastry and pie fillings. Make up fruit salad (except for bananas) and leave to mature. Order extra milk and cream. Make sure the liquor is delivered. Make up the salad dressings; prepare salad stuffs and vegetables as much as possible; cut garnishes. Make up a lot of extra ice cubes – keep them in plastic bags.

Do as much of the cooking as possible as early as possible. If you're having cold roast meat, this will give your husband a chance to carve it during the afternoon. If anything has a tendency to dry out – wrap it in self-clinging plastic film. Put out the nibblers at the last moment. If you're making a cold wine cup do it in the early afternoon to give it time to mellow. Rice or pasta can be cooked early and reheated by plunging into hot water for 5 minutes if necessary.

## Extras

Investigate the possibility of hiring glasses or buying cheap ones. Will you need extra chairs – china – speakers for your stereo? There's sure to be a firm locally which hires these out.

Order the flowers. Buy in a stock of cigarettes (make sure you have plenty of ashtrays to go around). Buy a quantity of paper napkins and whatever covering you plan to use for the table. Check the linen is all clean and re-iron during the week if necessary. Check your serving dishes and hire or borrow any extras necessary. Buy some candles.

Check that you have tissues, cotton, safety pins and so on for your women guests. Arrange the flowers. Make up the spare bed – there's always someone who's left at the end. Check that you have enough cutlery – borrow some from a friend if it's too late to hire any. Clean any silver. Collect the meat, fish and green groceries. Don't forget extra bread.

Set out the china, glass and cutlery (don't forget to leave room for last minute serving dishes). Try to arrange your buffet so that you achieve a flow of traffic around the room. Put out *plenty* of ashtrays; put out some of the cigarettes, but keep a couple of packs in reserve for late-night desperation. Make sure your stereo and speakers are all functioning properly. Make a note of local all-night taxi services and put it near the phone. Leave yourself time to have half an hour's relaxation – even if it's in the bath.

# CATERING QUANTITIES

## APPROXIMATE QUANTITIES FOR BUFFET PARTIES

| | 1 portion | 24–26 portions | Notes |
|---|---|---|---|
| **Soups:** cream, clear or iced | 1 cup | 1 gallon | Serve garnished in mugs or cups |
| **Fish cocktail:** shrimp, tuna or crab | 2–3 tablespoons | 1½ pound fish<br>2–3 lettuces<br>1½ pints sauce | In stemmed glasses, garnished with a shrimp |
| **Meat** with bone | ⅓ pound | 7–8 pounds | Cold roasts or barbecue chops |
| boneless | ¼ pound | 5–6½ pounds | Casseroles, meat balls, sausages, barbecue steaks |
| **Poultry:** turkey | ¼ pound (boneless) | 16 pound (dressed) | |
| chicken | 1 piece (⅓–½ pound) | Six 2½–3 pound (dressed) | Serve hot or cold |
| **Delicatessen:**<br>ham or tongue | ¼ pound | 5–6½ pounds | Halve the amounts if making stuffed cornets |
| pâté for wine-and-pâté party | ¼ pound | 5–6½ pounds | Half the amount if pâté is starter course |
| **Salad vegetables**<br>lettuce<br>cucumber<br>tomatoes<br>white cabbage<br>boiled potatoes | sixth<br>1 in.<br>1–2<br>2 tablespoons<br>1 tablespoon | 3–4<br>2 cucumbers<br>3 pounds<br>1½ pounds<br>3 pounds | Dress at last minute<br><br><br>for winter salads<br>for potato salads |
| **Rice or pasta** | ¼ cup (uncooked) | 2 pounds | Can be cooked a day ahead, reheated in 5 min. in boiling water |
| **Cheese** (for wine-and-cheese party) | ¼ pound | 4½–5 pounds of at least 4 types | You'll need more if you serve a cheese dip too |
| **Cheese** (for biscuits) | ⅛ pound | 1½–2 pounds cheese<br>1 pound butter<br>2 pounds biscuits | Allow the larger amounts for an assorted cheese board |

## SAVORIES AND SWEETS

| | Ingredients | Portions | Notes |
|---|---|---|---|
| **Sausage rolls** | 1½ pounds shortcrust or flaky pastry<br>2 pounds sausage meat | 25–30 medium or 50 small rolls | Pastry based on 1½ pounds flour, ¾–1 pound fat |
| **Bouchées** | 1 pound puff pastry<br>3¼ cups thick white sauce<br>10 ounces prepared filling | 50 bouchées | Pastry based on 1 pound flour, ¾ pound butter. Fillings: chopped ham, chicken, egg, mushrooms, shrimp |
| **Cheese straws** | ½ pound cheese pastry | 100 cheese straws | 2 cups flour, ½ cup fat, 1 cup cheese |
| **Meringues** | 6 egg whites<br>1½ cups sugar<br>1¾ cups whipped cream | 50 (small) meringue halves | 2 halves per head with cream<br>1 half with fruit and cream, or ice cream |
| **Gelatin** | 2½ quarts | 25 | |
| **Trifle** | 10 cups custard<br>25 sponge fingers<br>1 large can fruit | 25 | Decorate with cream, glacé cherries, chopped nuts, angelica |
| **Fruit salad** | 6½ pounds fruit<br>7½–10 cups sugar syrup<br>3¾ cups cream | 25 | Can be prepared a day ahead and left submerged in syrup but bananas should be added just before serving |

# CATERING QUANTITIES

## QUANTITIES FOR PARTY DRINKS
Rough guide only, as drinking habits vary.

### BUFFET PARTIES
Allow for each, 1–2 shorts and
3–6 longer drinks plus coffee.
Reckon a half-bottle of wine
per person.

### DINNER PARTIES
One bottle of table wine is
sufficient for 4 people.

### DROP-IN-FOR-DRINKS
Reckon on 3–5 short drinks
each and 4–6 small savories
besides the usual olives
and nuts.

### DRINKS BY THE BOTTLE
Sherry and port and straight
vermouths give roughly 12–16
glasses. In single nips for
cocktails, vermouths and spirits
give just over 30 a bottle.
Reckon 16–20 drinks of spirit
from a bottle when serving them
with soda, tonic or other
minerals. Liqueurs served in
proper glasses — 30 portions.
A split bottle of soda or tonic
gives 2–3 drinks. A 1 pint can of
tomato juice gives 3–4 drinks.
Dilute a bottle of fruit cordial with
$8\frac{1}{2}$ pints water for 20–25 drinks.

## APPROXIMATE COFFEE AND TEA QUANTITIES

| | 1 Serving | 24–26 Servings | | Notes |
|---|---|---|---|---|
| **Coffee** | | | | |
| ground, hot | 1 cup | $1\frac{1}{4}$ cups coffee<br>15 cups water | $7\frac{1}{2}$ cups milk<br>1 pound sugar | If made in advance, strain it after infusion. Reheat without boiling. Serve sugar separately. |
| ground, iced | 1 cup | $1\frac{1}{2}$ cups coffee<br>15 cups water | $7\frac{1}{2}$ cups milk<br>Sugar to taste | Make coffee (half sweetened, half not), strain and chill. Mix with chilled milk. Serve in glasses. |
| instant, hot | 1 cup | 4–6 tablespoons coffee<br>15 cups water | 5 cups milk<br>1 pound sugar | Make coffee in jugs as required.<br>Serve sugar separately. |
| instant, iced | 1 cup | 6 tablespoons coffee<br>5 cups water | 15 cups milk<br>sugar to taste | Make black coffee (half sweetened, half not) and chill. Mix with chilled creamy milk. Serve in glasses. |
| **Tea** | | | | |
| Indian, hot | 1 cup | $\frac{1}{4}$ cup tea<br>10 pints water | $3\frac{1}{2}$ cups milk<br>1 pound sugar | It is better to make tea in several pots rather than one outsize one. |
| Indian, iced | 1 cup | 6 tablespoons tea<br>$8\frac{1}{2}$ pints water | 5 cups milk<br>sugar to taste | Strain tea immediately it has infused. Sweeten half of it. Chill. Serve in glasses with chilled creamy milk. |
| China | 1 cup | 4 tablespoons tea<br>11 pints water | 2–3 lemons<br>1 pound sugar | Infuse China tea for 2 or 3 minutes only. Put a thin lemon slice in each cup before pouring. Serve sugar separately. |

# STORAGE

Foods such as meat, fish, dairy produce, fruits and vegetables are all perishable and if they are kept too long the action of bacteria, mold and enzymes (called micro-organisms) will make changes in them so that milk will sour, fats go rancid, meat, fish and eggs decompose and fruits and vegetables discolor and go moldy. The lower the temperature, the less micro-organism activity there will be, so that the best way to store perishable foods is in a refrigerator at a steady temperature of 35°F.–45°F. The next best thing is a cool larder where the temperature does not exceed 50°F.

Bacon, cheese, eggs and fats should really be bought at least once a week – or twice a week in hot weather if a refrigerator is not available. Meat, fish, poultry, soft fruits, green and salad vegetables should, ideally, be purchased as you need them – preferably not too much at a time.

### In the store cupboard (in covered containers)

**Flour**

| | |
|---|---|
| All-purpose, self-rising | Up to 6 months |
| Wheatmeal | 2–3 months |
| Wholewheat | Up to 1 month |
| Cake mixes (unopened) | Up to 6 months |

**Raising agents**

| | |
|---|---|
| Baking powder, baking soda, cream of tartar | 2–3 months |
| Dried yeast | Up to 6 months |

**Cereals**

| | |
|---|---|
| Cornstarch, custard powder | Up to 12 months |
| Dried vegetables – pearl barley, lentils, peas, etc. | Up to 12 months |
| Oatmeal | Up to 1 month |
| Rice, sago, tapioca | Up to 12 months |

**Nuts**

| | |
|---|---|
| Whole almonds, walnuts | Up to 1 month |
| Ground almonds, coconut | Up to 1 month |

**Preserves and bottled goods**

| | |
|---|---|
| Gravy browning | Up to 12 months |
| Sauces | Up to 6 months |
| Salad oil | Up to 18 months |
| Pickles and chutneys | Up to 12 months |
| Lemon curd, bought | 2–3 months |
| home-made | Up to 1 month |
| Preserves and mincemeat | Up to 12 months |
| Mayonnaise, salad dressing (bought) | Up to 12 months |
| Vinegar | At least 2 years |

**Cans**

| | |
|---|---|
| Fish, meat, fruit and juices | Up to 12 months |
| Ham | Up to 6 months |

**Sugars**

| | |
|---|---|
| Granulated, superfine, caster, cubes | Up to 12 months |
| Confectioners', brown | Up to 1 month |

**Syrups**

| | |
|---|---|
| Corn syrup, molasses | Up to 12 months |
| Honey | Up to 6 months |

**Dried fruit**

| | |
|---|---|
| Currants, white raisins, seedless raisins | 2–3 months |
| Prunes, figs, apricots | 2–3 months |
| Candied peel, glacé cherries | 2–3 months |

**Miscellaneous**

| | |
|---|---|
| Dried milk, whole | Up to 1 month |
| skimmed | 2–3 months |
| Gelatin | Up to 12 months |
| Breakfast cereals | Up to 1 month |
| Tea | Up to 1 year |
| Coffee (beans) | Up to 1 month |
| (ground) | 1 week |
| Soups (including condensed) | Up to 12 months |
| Vegetables (including tomato juice and purée) | Up to 12 months |
| Evaporated milk | 6–8 months |
| Condensed milk | 4–6 months |
| Cocoa, drinking chocolate | Up to 12 months |
| Packet soups | Up to 12 months |

**Herbs, spices and seasonings**

| | |
|---|---|
| Allspice, bay leaves, cloves, celery seeds, cinnamon, dried herbs, ginger, mace, mixed spice, curry powder | Up to 6 months |
| Curry paste, mustard, pepper | Up to 12 months |
| Salt | Up to 6 months (or longer if perfectly dry) |

**Colorings and flavorings**

| | |
|---|---|
| Flavoring extract | Up to 12 months |
| Chocolate squares or morsels | Up to 1 month |
| Colorings | Up to 12 months |
| Silver balls, vermicelli and other decorations | Up to 1 month |

Note: Many of these items will keep for longer than the recommended times if the packaging is not disturbed. In particular, most canned goods will keep for years if the tin is not exposed to damp that will cause it to rust. However, it is advisable to turn out your storecupboard 3 or 4 times a year, so as to ensure a regular turnover of stock.

| In the refrigerator | How to store | Time |
|---|---|---|
| **Milk produce** | | |
| Fresh milk | In the bottle or carton. If in a jug, keep covered | 3–4 days |
| Milk puddings, custards, etc. | In a covered dish | 2 days |
| Yogurt | Leave in the original container | 7 days |
| **Fats** | | |
| Butter, margarine, shortening, etc. | Leave in original wrapping and store in the special door compartment | 2–4 weeks |
| **Cheese** | | |
| Hard and blue cheeses | Wrapped in the original pack, in plastic wrap, or foil | 1–2 weeks |
| Cream cheese | Keep in a covered container, or wrap in plastic or foil | 5–7 days |
| **Poultry** | | |
| Whole, fresh birds | Draw, wash, dry and wrap in plastic or foil. Remove wrappings from ready-to-cook poultry | 2–3 days |
| Cooked birds | Cool and refrigerate straight away. Remove any stuffing and wrap or cover with plastic wrap or foil | 2–3 days |
| Frozen birds | Leave in the original wrapping and put while still frozen into the frozen food compartment | Depends on star rating (refer to manufacturer's instructions) 2–3 days in main cabinet |
| Cooked and made-up poultry dishes | Cool quickly and refrigerate in covered dish or container | 1 day |
| **Meat** | | |
| Roasts | Rinse off any blood and wipe dry. Cover lightly with plastic wrap or foil (do not seal tightly) and refrigerate straight away | 3–5 days |
| Steaks, chops, stewing veal | | 2–4 days |
| Smoked hams, sliced bacon | | 1 week |
| Variety meats, chopped meat | | 1–2 days |
| **Cooked meats** | | |
| Roasts | Wrap in foil or plastic or leave, covered, in the dish they were cooked in. Alternatively, store in any covered container | 3–5 days |
| Casseroles, made-up dishes | | 2–3 days |
| **Fish** | | |
| Raw | Cover loosely in plastic wrap or foil | 1–2 days |
| Cooked | Cover loosely in plastic wrap or foil, or place in covered container | 2 days |
| **Eggs** | | |
| Fresh in shells | Small end down | About 2 weeks |
| Yolks | Covered with water if whole | 2–3 days |
| Whites | In a covered container | 3–4 days |
| Hard-boiled in shell | Leave uncovered | Up to 1 week |
| **Fruit and vegetables** | | |
| Soft fruits | Clean and store in a covered container | 1–3 days |
| Hard fruits | Lightly wrapped, or in the crisper | 3–7 days |
| Bananas | *Never refrigerate* | |
| Salad vegetables | Wash and dry; store in crisper, plastic container or wrap lightly in plastic | 4–6 days |
| Greens | Prepare ready for use. Wrap lightly or place in the crisper | 3–7 days |

# OPERATION RESCUE

*If something goes wrong when you're cooking – be it for a family supper or a formal dinner – the essential rule is* don't panic. *Take a good look at the dish in question – taste it – and think what can be done to save it. If the flavor is wrong, it can often be saved (see our specific examples). If there's time, use it as the base for another dish altogether (if necessary, give your guests another drink to keep them happy).*

*If the result looks a disaster, but the flavor is fine, change its appearance – cover it up with sauce, for instance, or turn a collapsed cake into a delicious trifle. Whatever you do, don't serve something that* looks *a failure – it will make you feel bad and embarrass your guests. If you've under-calculated badly on quantities, serve an extra variety of vegetable – or try to serve another course (be inventive – see what you have in the store cupboard by way of canned soups, or hors d'oeuvre). Be sure you always have some cans of attractive vegetables available –* French beans, asparagus or artichoke hearts.

## SWEETS

### To eke out a scanty sweet course
Top each serving with a portion of bought ice cream.

### If a chocolate cake turns out rather too moist
Call it a pudding and serve it hot with a fluffy sauce.

### If homemade biscuits crumble badly
Use them to make a biscuit crumb flan case.

### If the top of a fruit cake gets burnt
Cut it off and use a well-flavored almond paste to disguise it.

### If apples or pears stew unevenly
Some fluffy and some still hard? Put them in the blender and purée to make a fool.

### If a gel won't set
Put in a warm place to melt completely, then add more dissolved gelatin and place in the coldest part of the refrigerator. If you haven't time to wait any longer, turn it into a trifle, with sherry-soaked sponge on the bottom, fruit and cream.

### If meringues break as you lift them from the cookie tray
Meringue shells can be served on top of fruit and cream if the pieces are large enough. A meringue gâteau can usually be stuck together and suitably disguised with plenty of whipped cream and fruit or grated chocolate.

### If your custard sauce curdles
Whip in 1–2 teaspoons cornstarch for 2½ cups; continue cooking.

### If a pastry flan case breaks
Put 5 tablespoons preserves in a small pan, boil and brush well into the broken edges. Press together and brush over the join again with more preserves. Allow

to cool before filling.

**If your sponge cake turns out a thin, flat, biscuity layer**
Cut into fancy shapes with a cookie cutter and sandwich together with jam and cream.

**If your cake rises unevenly**
Level the top, turn it over and ice the bottom.

**If a cake breaks up as you take it out of the pan**
It can often be disguised as a hot pudding by adding custard sauce or fruit.

**If a cake sinks in the middle**
Cut out the center and decorate with fruit, cream or butter cream. If it is a heavy fruit cake, cut out the center and turn into a ring cake, decorating with almond paste and royal icing if you wish.

## SAUCES

**If a sweet sauce is too sickly**
Add some lemon juice to give it zest. This is also a good ploy with puddings which are too bland.

**If a sauce turns lumpy**
Beat with a rotary whisk, purée in a blender or sieve finely.

**If a savory sauce lacks flavor but will not stand more seasoning**
Add lemon juice (especially good with sauces for fish).

**If French dressing tastes too oily**
Add more salt and a splash of vinegar or lemon juice.

**If mayonnaise curdles**
Start again with a fresh egg yolk in a clean bowl and slowly beat in the curdled mixture – the whole should then blend well.

## MEATS, POULTRY AND FISH

**If a chicken is over-cooked (flesh falls apart, skin breaks)**
Cut into pieces and mix with the vegetables instead of serving separately. Dish up on a bed of buttered noodles or rice.

**If fish breaks up**
Mix it with rice to make a kedgeree, or serve in piped potato nests, or allow it to cool, flake it and make up a fish salad.

**If a curry sauce is too hot**
Add yogurt, sour cream, milk, lemon juice or potato, or a combination of these.

**If a casserole is too spicy**
Add a few tablespoons of cream or milk.

**If a casserole has too much liquid**
Work together butter and flour in the proportion 2 tablespoons butter to 2 tablespoons flour with a fork and stir into the hot liquid in small pieces until the sauce is the desired consistency. Continue to cook a little longer.

## SOUPS

**If a soup is too salty but not too thick**
Add a small quantity of instant mashed potato.

## VEGETABLES AND FRUIT

**If your potatoes – or other vegetables – boil dry**
Cut off the burnt part and remove whatever is salvageable to another pan. If necessary, add more boiling water, or toss in butter and season well.

**If creamed potatoes are lumpy**
Purée in a blender with plenty of butter, salt and pepper.

**If rice is overcooked and soggy**
Rinse in a colander with cold running water to stop it cooking any further. Cool any other vegetables similarly, drain and mix together as a rice salad, using French dressing to moisten.

**If soft fruits are damaged**
Cut off the damaged parts and purée the remainder for use as a fruit sauce with ice cream.

**If preserves won't set**
Small quantities of runny preserves can be used as fruit sauce for hot puddings or ice cream.

# COOK'S TOOLS

It's difficult to be a successful cook without the right equipment. By that, we don't mean that you should go to your nearest big store and spend the month's housekeeping money in the kitchen gadget department! It simply means that if you *are* going to buy a piece of kitchen equipment, make sure it's something that is really useful – and that it's well made. It's far better to spend a little more and buy something that's going to last, rather than buy a cheaper version that will break the first time it has something tough to cope with. And if you're buying bakeware – cake pans and so on – do consider the easy clean type; they are well worth the extra money in time- and temper-saving. To give you an idea, a variety of pieces considered essential basic equipment have been assembled and photographed all together.

**Bottom row, left to right**

cutting board
set of French knives
serrated knife
timer
kitchen scissors
whisk
pancake turner
measuring spoons
bottle opener
vegetable peeler
corer
small spatula
large spatula
rubber scraper
wooden spoons
plastic spoons
roasting pan with rack
meat thermometer

**Top and middle, left to right**

mixing bowls
Mouli grater
glass measuring cups, 1 quart, 2 cups, 1 cup
pastry blender
strainer
electric hand mixer
muffin pans
pastry brush
4-sided grater
garlic press
peppermill
cake cooling rack
cake pan
metal measuring cup set
rolling pin
jelly roll pan
pie pan
pastry bag with nozzles
lemon juicer
egg slicer
3 saucepans
1 skillet
tongs
loaf pan

# CALORIES AND CARBOHYDRATES

| | Grams of carbohydrate per oz. | Calories per oz. |
|---|---|---|
| **FRUIT** | | |
| Apples | 3·5 | 13 |
| Apricots, raw | 1·9 | 8 |
| dried | 12·3 | 52 |
| Bananas | 5·5 | 22 |
| Blackberries | 1·8 | 8 |
| Blackcurrants | 1·9 | 8 |
| Cherries | 3·4 | 13 |
| Damsons | 2·7 | 11 |
| Gooseberries, ripe | 2·6 | 10 |
| Grapes, black | 4·4 | 17 |
| white | 4·6 | 18 |
| Grapefruit | 1·5 | 6 |
| Lemons | 0·9 | 4 |
| Melons | 1·5 | 7 |
| Olives in brine | trace | 30 |
| Oranges | 2·4 | 10 |
| Peaches | 2·6 | 11 |
| Pears | 3·1 | 12 |
| Plums | 2·7 | 11 |
| Prunes | 11·4 | 46 |
| Raspberries | 1·6 | 7 |
| Rhubarb | 0·2 | 1 |
| Seedless raisins | 18·3 | 70 |
| Strawberries | 1·8 | 7 |
| Tangerines | 18·4 | 71 |
| White raisins | 2·3 | 10 |

| | Grams of carbohydrate per oz. | Calories per oz. |
|---|---|---|
| **VEGETABLES** | | |
| Artichokes, globe | 0·8 | 4 |
| Asparagus | 0·3 | 5 |
| Avocados | 0·7 | 25 |
| Beans, broad | 2·0 | 12 |
| butter | 4·9 | 26 |
| French | 0·3 | 2 |
| haricot | 4·7 | 25 |
| runner | 0·3 | 2 |
| Beets | 2·8 | 13 |
| Broccoli | 0·1 | 4 |
| Brussels sprouts | 0·5 | 5 |
| Cabbage, raw | 1·1 | 7 |
| cooked | 0·2 | 2 |
| Carrots, raw | 1·5 | 6 |
| cooked | 1·2 | 5 |
| Cauliflower | 0·3 | 3 |

| | Grams of carbohydrate per oz. | Calories per oz. |
|---|---|---|
| Celery, raw | 0·4 | 3 |
| cooked | 0·2 | 1 |
| Endive | 0·4 | 3 |
| Cucumber | 0·5 | 3 |
| Leeks, cooked | 1·3 | 7 |
| Lentils | 5·2 | 27 |
| Lettuce | 0·5 | 3 |
| Mushrooms, raw | 0·0 | 2 |
| fried | 0·0 | 62 |
| Onions | 0·8 | 4 |
| Parsley | trace | 6 |
| Parsnips | 3·8 | 16 |
| Peas, boiled | 2·2 | 14 |
| dried, cooked | 5·4 | 28 |
| Potatoes, old | 5·6 | 23 |
| new | 5·2 | 21 |
| chips | 10·6 | 68 |
| crisps | 14·0 | 159 |
| Pumpkin | 1·0 | 4 |
| Radishes | 0·8 | 4 |
| Seakale | 0·2 | 2 |
| Spinach | 0·4 | 7 |
| Spring greens | 0·3 | 3 |
| Swedes | 1·1 | 5 |
| Tomatoes, raw | 0·8 | 4 |
| Turnips | 0·7 | 3 |
| Watercress | 0·2 | 4 |
| Zucchini | 0·4 | 2 |

| | Grams of carbohydrate per oz. | Calories per oz. |
|---|---|---|
| **NUTS** | | |
| Almonds | 1·2 | 170 |
| Brazils | 1·2 | 183 |
| Chestnuts | 10·4 | 49 |
| Coconut, shredded | 1·8 | 178 |
| Peanuts | 2·4 | 171 |
| Walnuts | 1·4 | 156 |

| | Grams of carbohydrate per oz. | Calories per oz. |
|---|---|---|
| **MEAT AND POULTRY** | | |
| Bacon, back | 0·0 | 169 |
| streaky | 0·0 | 149 |

| | Grams of carbohydrate per oz. | Calories per oz. |
|---|---|---|
| Beef, topside, roast | 0·0 | 91 |
| sirloin, roast | 0·0 | 109 |
| silverside | 0·0 | 86 |
| corned | 0·0 | 66 |
| Chicken, roast | 0·0 | 54 |
| Duck, roast | 0·0 | 89 |
| Ham, boiled | 0·0 | 123 |
| Heart | 0·0 | 68 |
| Kidney | 0·0 | 45 |
| Lamb, chop, broiled | 0·0 | 80 |
| leg, roast | 0·0 | 100 |
| Liver, calf, fried | 0·7 | 74 |
| ox, fried | 1·1 | 81 |
| Luncheon meat, canned | 1·4 | 95 |
| Pork, leg, roast | 0·0 | 90 |
| chops, broiled | 0·0 | 92 |
| Rabbit, stewed | 0·0 | 51 |
| Sausages, fried | 4·5 | 81 |
| Tongue, sheeps', stewed | 0·0 | 84 |
| Tripe | 0·0 | 29 |
| Turkey, roast | 0·0 | 56 |
| Veal, roast | 0·0 | 66 |

| | Grams of carbohydrate per oz. | Calories per oz. |
|---|---|---|
| **FISH** | | |
| Cod, steamed | 0·0 | 23 |
| Crab | 0·0 | 36 |
| Haddock | 0·0 | 28 |
| Hake | 0·0 | 30 |
| Halibut | 0·0 | 37 |
| Herring | 0·0 | 54 |
| Kippers | 0·0 | 57 |
| Lemon Sole | 0·0 | 26 |
| Lobster | 0·0 | 34 |
| Mackerel | 0·0 | 53 |
| Oysters | trace | 143 |
| Plaice | 0·0 | 26 |
| Prawns | 0·0 | 30 |
| Salmon, canned | 0·0 | 39 |
| fresh | 0·0 | 57 |
| Sardines, canned | 0·0 | 84 |
| Shrimp | 0·0 | 32 |
| Sole | 0·0 | 24 |

| | Grams of carbohydrate per oz. | Calories per oz. |
|---|---|---|

# SUGARS, PRESERVES

| | Grams of carbohydrate per oz. | Calories per oz. |
|---|---|---|
| Chocolate, sweet | 15·5 | 167 |
| Semi-sweet | 14·9 | 155 |
| Chutney, tomato | 11·0 | 43 |
| Glacé cherries | 15·8 | 137 |
| Honey | 21·7 | 87 |
| Ice cream | 5·6 | 56 |
| Jelly, packet | 17·7 | 73 |
| Lemon curd | 12·0 | 86 |
| Marmalade | 19·8 | 74 |
| Molasses | 19·1 | 73 |
| Sugar | 29·6 | 112 |
| Syrup, corn | 22·4 | 84 |
| Preserves | 19·7 | 74 |

# MILK PRODUCTS, etc.

| | Grams of carbohydrate per oz. | Calories per oz. |
|---|---|---|
| Butter | trace | 226 |
| Cheese, Cheddar | trace | 120 |
| Edam | trace | 88 |
| blue | trace | 103 |
| Gruyère | trace | 132 |
| Cream, heavy | 0·6 | 131 |
| light | 0·9 | 62 |
| Milk, whole | 1·4 | 19 |
| skimmed | 1·4 | 10 |
| Yogurt, low-fat | 1·4 | 15 |
| Eggs | trace | 46 |
| Margarine | 0·0 | 226 |
| Oil | 0·0 | 264 |
| Shortening | 0·0 | 262 |

# CEREAL PRODUCTS

| | Grams of carbohydrate per oz. | Calories per oz. |
|---|---|---|
| All-Bran | 16·5 | 88 |
| Arrowroot | 26·7 | 101 |
| Bread, Hovis | 13·5 | 67 |
| malt | 14·0 | 71 |
| Procea | 14·3 | 72 |
| Cornflakes | 25·2 | 104 |
| Cornstarch | 26·2 | 100 |
| Energen rolls | 13·0 | 111 |
| Flour, 100% | 20·8 | 95 |
| 85% | 22·5 | 98 |
| 80% | 22·9 | 99 |
| 75% | 23·2 | 99 |
| Macaroni, boiled | 7·2 | 32 |
| Pearl barley, cooked | 7·8 | 34 |
| Oatmeal porridge | 2·3 | 13 |
| Puffed wheat | 21·4 | 102 |
| Rice, polished | 8·4 | 35 |
| Ryvita | 21·9 | 98 |
| Sago | 26·7 | 101 |
| Semolina | 22·0 | 100 |
| Shredded Wheat | 22·4 | 103 |
| Spaghetti | 23·9 | 104 |
| Tapioca | 27·0 | 102 |
| Weetabix | 21·8 | 100 |
| Salt | 0·0 | 0 |
| Pepper | 19·3 | 88 |

# BEVERAGES

| | Grams of carbohydrate per oz. | Calories per oz. |
|---|---|---|
| Bovril | 0·0 | 23 |
| Cocoa | 9·9 | 128 |
| Coffee with chicory essence | 16·1 | 64 |
| Coffee, infusion | 0·1 | 1 |
| Drinking chocolate | 19·2 | 105 |
| Lemonade | 1·6 | 6 |
| Marmite | 0·0 | 2 |
| Tea, infusion | 0·0 | 1 |

# ALCOHOL BY THE GLASS: BEERS

| | Calories |
|---|---|
| Brown ale, bottled (½ pint) | 80 |
| Draught ale, bitter ,, | 90 |
| Draught ale, mild ,, | 70 |
| Pale ale, bottled ,, | 90 |
| Stout, bottled ,, | 110 |
| Stout, extra ,, | 110 |
| Strong ale ,, | 210 |

# CIDERS

| | Calories |
|---|---|
| Dry (1¼ cups) | 100 |
| Sweet ,, | 120 |
| Vintage ,, | 280 |

# TABLE WINES

| | Calories |
|---|---|
| Beaujolais (glass, 4 fl. oz.) | 76 |
| Champagne ,, | 84 |
| Chianti ,, | 72 |
| Graves ,, | 84 |
| Médoc ,, | 72 |
| Sauternes ,, | 104 |

# FORTIFIED WINES

| | Calories |
|---|---|
| Port, ruby (glass, 2 fl. oz.) | 86 |
| Port, tawny ,, | 90 |
| Sherry, dry ,, | 66 |
| Sherry, sweet ,, | 76 |

# SPIRITS, 70° PROOF

| | Calories |
|---|---|
| Whisky, Gin, Vodka, Rum (1 fl. oz.) | 63 |

# LIQUEURS

| | Calories |
|---|---|
| Bénédictine (glass, 2–3 oz.) | 69 |
| Crème de Menthe ,, | 67 |
| Anisette ,, | 74 |
| Apricot brandy ,, | 64 |
| Curaçao ,, | 54 |

# COGNAC

| | Calories |
|---|---|
| Brandy (pony, 1oz.) | 73 |

# Herbs and Spices

| | Meat | Fish | Poultry, game | Soups | Vegetables |
|---|---|---|---|---|---|
| **Basil**<br>*Use sparingly* | Lamb, pork, veal, beef casseroles | Shrimp, white fish | | Many soups, especially tomato | Tomatoes, broad beans |
| **Bay** | Kebabs, marinades for beef, casseroles | Baked or casseroled fish | Marinades | As a background seasoning, remove before serving | |
| **Chervil**<br>*Use generously* | Chervil butter for veal cutlets | Crab | Fricassees, rub into chicken before roasting/broiling | Herb soup | Chervil butter for peas, tomatoes, egg plants |
| **Chives**<br>*According to taste* | Hamburgers, meat loaves, garnish for casseroles | Fish cakes, fish stuffings | With dishes containing tomatoes | Garnish for vegetable soups, especially vichyssoise | Garnish to potatoes, other vegetables |
| **Dill**<br>*Use carefully* | Lamb and rich pork dishes, beef and chicken ragoût | All fish dishes, especially salmon, crab, mackerel | Creamed chicken, add a spray to roasting pan | Fish, pea, tomato and bean soups | With delicate vegetables |
| **Garlic**<br>*Use judiciously* | Continental cookery, pasta, sauces, casseroles | Use sparingly in most fish dishes | Together with other robust flavors | Most soups | Ratatouille |
| **Marjoram**<br>*Use judiciously* | Veal, lamb, pork, sausages, liver | Salt fish, shellfish | Stuffings, rub unstuffed chicken, duck before roasting | Onion, potato, lentil, pea soups | Tomatoes, peas, carrots, spinach, mushrooms |
| **Oregano**<br>*Use judiciously* | Veal, lamb, pork, sausages, liver | Many fish dishes | Stuffings | Onion, potato, lentil, pea soups | Tomatoes, peas, carrots, zucchini spinach, mushrooms |
| **Parsley**<br>*Use freely* | Stuffings, casseroles | Fish cakes, stuffings | Stuffings | Garnish for any soup | Parsley butter, new potatoes, celery |
| **Rosemary**<br>*Use sparingly* | Roast lamb, tripe, kidneys, marinades | Marinades for salmon, eel, mackerel | Sprinkle lightly inside before roasting, stuffings | Minestrone | Sauté potatoes, beans (cassoulet), spinach, tomatoes |
| **Sage**<br>*Use carefully* | Stuffing for pork | | Stuffing for duck, goose, turkey | Robust chicken, turtle, mushroom soups; fish chowder | |
| **Tarragon**<br>*Use carefully* | Marinades, steak, casseroles | Many fish dishes | Classic Tarragon chicken, chicken liver pâté, hare | | |
| **Thyme**<br>*Use very carefully* | Stuffings, gravies, sausages | All types of fish | Stuffing for chicken, rabbit; jugged hare | Thick soups | Tomatoes, sauté vegetables |
| **Allspice**<br>*ground*<br>Spicy-sweet, mild | Pot roasts, meat balls, baked ham, beef stews | Boiled fish, oyster stews | | Broths | Add a little to tomatoes, cream potatoes, carrots |
| **Cayenne**<br>*ground*<br>Hot, pungent | Use sparingly in meat dishes and gravies, mince | Shellfish | Chicken dishes | All soups | Baked beans, vegetable curries, egg plants |
| **Celery seeds**<br>*whole*<br>Slightly bitter | Casseroles | Most fish dishes | | Meat soups | |
| **Chilies**<br>*whole*<br>Spicy, hot | Mexican dishes | | Excellent in a chicken pie filling | | Use sparingly (crushed) in tomato dishes |
| **Cinnamon**<br>*stick or ground*<br>Sweet, spicy | Ham glaze, pork | | | | |
| **Cloves**<br>*whole or ground*<br>Strong and spicy | Ham, tongue | | Poultry and game casseroles, marinades | Beef, tomato, bean, pea, beets' soups | Pumpkin, spinach |
| **Curry**<br>*powder*<br>Strong and spicy | Casseroles, left-over meat dishes, meat loaves | Shellfish, devilled fish | Chicken | Mulligatawny, apple, tomato soups | Vegetable curries |
| **Ginger**<br>*root or ground*<br>Hot, rich, aromatic | Curries | Many fish dishes | Duck, rub into the meat of chicken and brush with butter | | |
| **Mace**<br>*blade or ground*<br>Sweet, softly spicy | Meat stuffings, mince dishes, veal, lamb chops, pâté | Potted shrimp, fish dishes with sauces | Chicken à la King | Cream of chicken soup | Mashed potato, creamed spinach |
| **Mustard**<br>*seed or ground*<br>Hot, pungent | Beef, ham, frankfurters, cold meats | | | Cream of celery, lentil, mushroom, chicken soups | |
| **Nutmeg**<br>*whole or ground*<br>Sweet, spicy | Veal, meat loaves | Fish cakes, croquettes | Chicken | | Spinach, carrots, beans |
| **Paprika**<br>*ground*<br>Colorful, mild | Lamb, pork, veal, mince dishes, goulash | Shellfish | Chicken | Cream soups, chowders | Beans, potatoes, cauliflower |
| **Pepper**<br>*whole or ground*<br>Strong | Most meat dishes | Most fish dishes | Most poultry and game dishes | | Most vegetable dishes |
| **Saffron** *powder*<br>Mildly spicy, golden color | Oriental cooking | Spanish cod dishes | Chicken, rabbit | Bouillabaisse, chicken, turkey | Rice |
| **Turmeric**<br>*powdered*<br>Aromatic, slightly bitter | Curries | Fish kedgeree, fish stew | | | Rice dishes |

| Salads and salad dressings | Cheese | Eggs | Sauces | Preserves | Baked goods | Other uses |
|---|---|---|---|---|---|---|
| Green, tomato, rice salads | | Fines herbes or tomato omelet | For pasta, rice | | | |
| | | | Infuse in milk for béchamel sauce | | | Rice pudding |
| Most salads, French dressing | Excellent with cream cheese | Fines herbes omelets and soufflés | Most lightly seasoned sauces, béarnaise, green | | | |
| All salads and dressings | Cottage and cream cheeses | Scrambled eggs, soufflés, fondue | In savory white and herb sauces, mayonnaise | | | |
| Most salads, sour cream dressing, avocado | Cream cheese and other dishes | Egg mayonnaise | Dill sauce with pike, eel | Pickled cucumber | | In egg sandwiches, dill tea |
| French dressing | Pizza | Pickled eggs | Use sparingly in many sauces especially for pasta | | | |
| Green, chicken salads | Cottage and cream cheeses | Egg based quiches, omelets | Cheese sauces | | | Pizza, tomato juice cocktail |
| Green and chicken Salads | Cottage and cream cheeses | Egg based quiches, omelets | Cheese sauces | | | Pizza |
| Most salads | Most cheese dishes | Fines herbes, omelets and other dishes | Sauces for ham, chicken, fish | | | |
| | Cottage and cream cheeses | | Apple jelly, jams | | | Herb tea, fruit salads, wine/cider cups, vegetable cocktail |
| | Many cheese dishes | | | | | |
| Asparagus, chicken salads; sour cream dressing | | Tarragon pickled eggs | Béarnaise, hollandaise, mousseline, tarragon | | | Tomato and fish cocktails, sandwich spread, aspic glaze |
| Many salads | Most cheese dishes, cheese herb bread | Many egg dishes | | | | Lemon thyme in fruit salads, liqueurs |
| Fruit salads | Cottage cheese | Egg dishes with sauce | Tomato and barbecue sauces | Pickles, chutneys, relishes, mincemeat | Fruit cakes, rice puddings, apple pies, poached fruit | Ingredient in mixed spice |
| Cocktail sauce for shrimp | | | Use sparingly in sauces for fish | | | Ingredient in curry powder |
| Salads and dressings, coleslaw | Cream cheese as a sandwich spread | | | Pickles, chutneys | Bread | |
| | | | Tomato sauce for pasta, also meat sauces | Pickles | Cakes, pies | |
| | | Egg nog | | Pickles, mincemeat | Fruit cake, milk pudding, pumpkin pie, Christmas fare | Mulled wine (stick), cinnamon toast (ground) |
| | | | Bread, apple, cranberry sauces | Chutneys, mincemeat, bottled sauces | Fruit cake, apple and pear pies | Mulled wine |
| Mayonnaise | | Curried eggs | For shellfish, chicken, eggs, meat | Chutneys, pickles | | |
| | | | | Fruit chutneys | Cakes, biscuits | With melon (ground), stewed fruit (root) |
| | Welsh rarebit or other cheese dishes | | For fish and vegetables | Chutneys, pickles | Fruit cakes, pies, cherry pie, chocolate | Tomato juice |
| French dressing, mayonnaise | Strengthens the flavor of cooked cheese | Stuffed eggs | For meat, fish, barbecues | Pickles | | Sandwiches |
| | | Scrambled eggs | Cheese sauce | | Cakes, pies, puddings, doughnuts | Milk, egg nog, puddings |
| Dressings, coleslaw | Cream cheese | Devilled eggs | Cream sauces | | | |
| Most dressings and salads | Many cheese dishes | Many egg dishes | Most sauces | Most preserves | | |
| Rice salads, seafood, chicken | Cream cheese | | Veal and fish sauces | | Buns, cakes | Risotto, paella |
| | | Devilled eggs, creamed eggs | Adds color and flavor to white sauces | Pickles, relishes | For coloring cakes | Ingredient of curry powder |

# HANDY CHARTS
## EVERYDAY MEASURES

## EQUIVALENT MEASURES

| | |
|---|---|
| $\frac{1}{3}$ of $\frac{1}{2}$ teaspoon | Pinch |
| $\frac{1}{2}$ of $\frac{1}{4}$ teaspoon | $\frac{1}{8}$ teaspoon |
| 3 teaspoons | 1 tablespoon |
| 4 tablespoons | $\frac{1}{4}$ cup |
| 5 tablespoons plus 1 teaspoon | $\frac{1}{3}$ cup |
| 8 tablespoons | $\frac{1}{2}$ cup |
| 12 tablespoons | $\frac{3}{4}$ cup |
| 16 tablespoons | 1 cup |
| 1 cup | 8 fluid ounces |
| 2 cups | 1 pint |
| 2 pints | 1 quart |
| 4 quarts | 1 gallon |
| 1 pound | 16 ounces (dry measure) |

## HANDY EQUIVALENTS

| Food | Weight | Equivalent |
|---|---|---|
| Apples | 1 pound | $3\frac{1}{2}$ cups, pared and sliced |
| Berries | 1 quart | $3\frac{1}{2}$ cups |
| Bread | 1 slice | $\frac{1}{4}$–$\frac{1}{3}$ cup dry breadcrumbs |
| Bread | 1 slice | $\frac{3}{4}$–1 cup soft breadcrumbs |
| Cheese, Cheddar, | $\frac{1}{2}$ pound | 2 cups grated |
| Cream | 3 ounce package | 6 tablespoons |
| Crackers, graham | 15 | 1 cup fine crumbs |
| Egg whites | 8–11 | 1 cup |
| Egg yolks | 12–16 | 1 cup |
| Gelatin | $\frac{1}{4}$ ounce package | 1 tablespoon |
| Lemon | 1 medium | 3 tablespoons juice |
| Orange | 1 medium | $\frac{1}{3}$ cup juice |
| Rice | 1 cup raw | 3 cups cooked |
| Spaghetti | 1 pound uncooked | 7 cups cooked |
| Sugar, brown | 1 pound | $2\frac{1}{4}$–$2\frac{1}{3}$ cups, firmly packed |
| Sugar, confectioners' | 1 pound | about 4 cups, sifted |
| Sugar, granulated | 1 pound | $2\frac{1}{2}$ cups |

## A WORD ABOUT CANS

Be a label reader when it comes time to shop. Can labels give a variety of information such as grade of produce, what is in the can if it is a mixture, and most important when following recipes, the size of the can and how much it contains. Here is a chart to help you just in case all information is not available on the can.

| Industry Term | Approximate New Weight or Fluid Measure | Approx. Cups |
|---|---|---|
| 6 ounces | 6 ounces | $\frac{3}{4}$ cup |
| 8 ounces | 8 ounces | 1 cup |
| Picnic | $10\frac{1}{2}$–12 ounces | $1\frac{1}{4}$ cups |
| 12 ounces | 12 ounces | $1\frac{1}{2}$ cups |
| No. 300 | 14–16 ounces | $1\frac{3}{4}$ cups |
| No. 303 | 16–17 ounces | 2 cups |
| No. 2 | 1 pound 4 ounces or 20 ounces | $2\frac{1}{2}$ cups |
| No. $2\frac{1}{2}$ | 1 pound 13 ounces or 29 ounces | $3\frac{1}{2}$ cups |
| No. 3 | 3 pounds 3 ounces or 46 fluid ounces | $5\frac{3}{4}$ cups |

# GLOSSARY OF COOKING TERMS

**Aspic jelly** Savory gelatine used for setting and garnishing savory dishes.

**Au gratin** Food coated with sauce, sprinkled with breadcrumbs (and sometimes grated cheese) and browned under the broiler. Usually served in the dish in which it has been cooked.

*Making a sauce in a bain marie*

**Bain marie** A flat, open vessel, half-filled with water, which is kept at a temperature just below boiling point; used to keep sauces, etc., hot without further cooking. Also a baking pan half-filled with water in which custards and other egg dishes stand while cooking to prevent overheating.

**Baking** Cooking in the oven by dry heat. The method used for most cakes, cookies and pastries, and for many other dishes.

**Baking blind** Baking pastry shapes without a filling. Line the flan case or pie dish with pastry and trim. Line with waxed paper and fill with dry beans, rice or stale crusts of bread. Or press aluminum foil into the pastry case and omit beans, etc. When pastry has set, remove the paper or foil and return to the oven to dry out.

**Barding** Covering the breast of poultry or game birds with pieces of fat bacon to prevent it drying out during roasting.

**Basting** Moistening meat, poultry or game during roasting by spooning over it the juices and melted fat from the pan, to prevent the food from drying out.

**Beating** Agitating an ingredient or mixture by vigorously turning it over with an upward motion so as to introduce air, using a spoon, fork, whisk or electric mixer.

**Béchamel** A rich white sauce, one of the four basic sauces.

**Binding** Adding a liquid, egg or melted fat to a dry mixture to hold it together.

**Blanching** Treating food with boiling water in order to whiten it, preserve its natural color, loosen the skin or remove a flavor which is too strong. Two methods are:

1. To plunge the food into boiling water; used to peel tomatoes or to prepare vegetables for freezing.

2. To bring it to the boil in the water; used to whiten veal and sweetbreads or to reduce the saltiness of kippers or pickled meat.

**Blending** Mixing flour, cornstarch and similar ground cereals to a smooth cream with a cold liquid (milk, water or stock) before a boiling liquid is added, as in the preparation of soups, stews, or gravies.

**Boiling** Cooking in liquid at a temperature of 212°F. The chief foods that are boiled are vegetables, rice, pasta and suet puddings; syrups that need to be reduced are also boiled. Meat, fish and poultry should be simmered – fast boiling makes them shrink, lose flavor, and toughen.

**Bouquet garni** A small bunch of herbs tied together in cheesecloth and used to give flavor to stews, etc. Usually consists of a sprig of parsley and thyme, a bay leaf, 2 cloves and a few peppercorns.

**Braising** A method of cooking either meat or vegetables which is a combination of roasting and stewing. A casserole or pan with a tightly fitting lid is used to prevent evaporation. The meat is placed on a bed of vegetables (a mirepoix), with just sufficient liquid to cover the vegetables and to keep the food moist.

**Brining** Immersing food (mainly meat or fish which is to be pickled and vegetables which are to be preserved) in salted water.

**Broiling** Cooking food by direct heat under a broiler or over a hot fire. Good quality, tender meat (steak, chops), whole fish (herring, trout) and fish cutlets are the foods most generally cooked in this way. Some cooked dishes are put under the broiler to give them a brown top surface or to heat them through before serving.

**Browning 1.** Giving a dish (usually already cooked) an appetizing golden brown color by placing it under the broiler or in a hot oven for a short time.

**2.** Preparing food for stewing or casseroling, by frying to seal and color the meat.

**Caramel** A substance obtained by heating sugar syrup very slowly in a thick pan until it is a rich brown color. Used for flavoring cakes and puddings and for lining pudding molds.

**Casserole** A baking dish with a tightly fitting lid, used for cooking meat and vegetables in the oven. The food is usually served straight from the dish. May be 'ovenproof' (for oven use only) or 'flameproof' (suitable for use on top of the stove and in the oven).

**Chaudfroid** A jellied sauce with a béchamel base, used for masking cold fish, poultry and game.

**Chining** Severing the rib bones from the backbone by sawing through the ribs close to the spine (on roasts such as loin or neck of lamb, mutton, veal or pork).

*Use a special saw for chining*

**Chopping** Dividing food into very small pieces. The ingredient is placed on a chopping board and a very sharp knife is used with a quick up-and-down action.

**Clarifying** Clearing or purifying fat from water, meat juices or salt.

**1.** Butter or margarine – heat the fat gently until it melts, then continue to heat slowly without browning until all bubbling ceases (this shows the water has been driven off). Remove from the heat and allow to stand for a few minutes until the sediment has settled. Pour the fat off gently. It is not usually necessary to strain through cheesecloth.

**2.** Dripping – melt the fat and strain into a large bowl to remove any big particles. Then pour over it 2–3 times as much boiling water, stir well and leave to cool; the clean fat will rise to the top. When it has solidified, lift it off, dab the underside dry and scrape off any sediment.

**Coating 1.** Covering food which is to be fried with flour, egg and breadcrumbs, batter, etc.

**2.** Covering food which is cooked or ready to serve with a thin layer of mayonnaise, sauce, etc.

**Coddling** A method of softboiling eggs: they are put into a pan of boiling water, withdrawn from the heat and allowed to stand for 8–10 minutes.

**Compôte** Fruit stewed in sugar syrup and served hot or cold.

**Consistency** The term used to describe the texture of a dough, batter, etc.

**Creaming** The beating together of fat and sugar to resemble whipped cream in color and texture, i.e., until pale and fluffy. This method of mixing is used for cakes and puddings containing a high proportion of fat.

**Crimping 1.** To remove the skin in strips from cucumber and similar foods, to give the finished slices a ridged appearance.

**2.** To decorate the double edge of

*Use thumbs and forefingers to crimp the edge of a pastry case*

a pie or tart or the edge of a shortbread by pinching it at regular intervals, giving a fluted effect.

**Croquettes** A mixture of meat, fish, poultry or potatoes, bound together and formed into various shapes, then coated with egg and breadcrumbs and fried in deep fat.

**Croûte** A large round or finger of toasted or fried bread, about ¼ in. thick, on which game and some entrées and savories are served.

**Croûtons** Small pieces of bread which are fried or toasted and served as an accompaniment or garnish to soup.

**Curd 1.** The solid part of soured milk or junket.

**2.** A creamy preserve made from fruit – usually lemons or oranges – sugar, eggs and butter.

**Dariole** A small, narrow mold with sloping sides, used for setting creams and gels and for baking or steaming puddings, especially castle puddings. Also used to prepare English madeleines.

**Devilled** Food which has been broiled or fried with sharp, hot seasonings.

**Dough** A thick mixture of uncooked flour and liquid, often combined with other ingredients. As well as the usual yeast dough, it can also mean mixtures such as pastry, scones and biscuits.

**Dredging** The action of sprinkling food lightly and evenly with flour, sugar, etc. Fish and meat are often dredged with flour before frying, while pancakes, etc., may be dredged with fine sugar to improve their appearance. A pierced container of metal or plastic (known as a dredger) is generally used.

**Dripping** The fat obtained from roasted meat during cooking or from small pieces of new fat that have been rendered down.

**Dropping consistency** The term used to describe the texture of a cake or pudding mixture before cooking. To test, fill a spoon with the mixture and hold it on its side without jerking the spoon – the mixture should fall in 5 seconds.

**Egg-and-crumbing** A method of coating fish, cutlets, rissoles, etc., before they are fried or baked. Have a beaten egg on a plate and some breadcrumbs on a piece of paper towel; dip the food in the egg and lift out, letting it drain for a second or two. Transfer it to the crumbs and tip the paper until the food is well covered. Press in the crumbs, then shake the food to remove any surplus.

**Entrée** A hot or cold dressed savory dish consisting of meat, poultry, game, fish, eggs or vegetables, served complete with sauce and garnish.

**Escalope** A slice of meat (usually veal) cut from the top of the leg. Escalopes are generally egg-and-crumbed and fried.

**Espagnole** A rich brown sauce, one of the four basic sauces.

**Farce, forcemeat** Stuffing used for meat, fish or vegetables. A farce is based on meat, bacon, etc., while the basic forcemeat is made from breadcrumbs, suet, onion and herbs.

**Fillet** A term used for the undercut of a loin of beef, veal, pork or game, for boned breasts of poultry and for boned sides of fish.

**Fines herbes** A combination of finely chopped herbs. In practice, the mixture is usually parsley, chervil, tarragon and chives, and it is most commonly used in omelets. When fresh herbs are used one can add enough to make the omelet look green, but when dried ones are used, ½ teaspoon of the mixture is plenty for a 4-egg omelet. For other dishes, the blend is sometimes varied.

**Flaking** Breaking up cooked fish into flakes with a fork.

**Folding in** (Sometimes called cutting-and-folding). Combining a whisked or creamed mixture with other ingredients so that it retains its lightness. It is used for certain cake mixtures and for meringues and soufflés. A typical example is folding dry flour into a whisked sponge cake mixture. Important points to remember are that the mixture must be folded very lightly and that it must not be agitated more than absolutely necessary, because with every movement some of the air bubbles are broken down. Do not use an electric mixer.

**Fricassee** A white stew of chicken, veal or rabbit.

**Frosting 1.** A method of decorating the rim of a glass in which a cold drink is to be served. Coat the edge with whipped egg white, dip into sugar and allow to dry. **2.** An icing.

*Iced and creamy desserts look good in a frosted glass*

**Frying** The process of cooking food in hot fat or oil. There are two main methods:

**1. Shallow frying** A small quantity of fat is used in a shallow pan. Used for steak, chops, sausages, fish steaks and white fish, which need only sufficient fat to prevent their sticking to the pan. Made-up dishes such as fish cakes can also be shallow-fried, but need enough fat to half-cover them. In most cases food requires coating.

**2. Deep frying** The food is cooked in sufficient fat to cover it completely. Used for batter-coated fish, whitebait, potato chips, doughnuts and dishes such as croquettes and fritters.

A deep pan and a wire basket are needed, with fat to come about ¾ up the pan; clarified beef fat, shortening and salad oil are suitable. The fat must be pure and free from moisture, to avoid spurting or boiling over, and it must be heated to the right temperature or the food will be either grease-sodden or burnt. If the fat is strained into a bowl, jug or wide-necked jar and covered, it may be stored in a cool place for further use. A frying thermometer should always be used with oil for deep fat frying.

**Galantine** White meat, such as poultry or veal, which has been cooked, rolled and pressed. Sometimes glazed or finished with toasted breadcrumbs.

**Garnish** An edible decoration, such as parsley, watercress, hard-cooked egg or lemon added to a savory dish to improve the appearance and flavor.

**Glaze** Beaten egg, egg white, milk, etc., used to give a glossy surface to certain sweets and to savories such as galantines. The meat glaze used for savories is home-made meat stock reduced by rapid boiling. Stock made from a cube cannot be treated this way.

**Grating** Shaving foods such as cheese and vegetables into small shreds. Foods to be grated must be firm and cheese should be allowed to harden.

**Grinding 1.** The process of reducing hard foodstuffs, such as nuts and coffee beans, to small particles by means of a food mill, grinder or electric blender. **2.** Chopping or cutting into very small pieces with a knife or, more commonly, in a food chopper.

**Hors d'oeuvre** Small dishes served cold, usually before the soup, as an appetizer. Hors d'oeuvre are generally piquant.

**Infusing** Extracting flavor from spices, herbs, etc., by pouring on boiling liquid and then covering and standing in a warm place.

**Jardinière** A garnish of diced, mixed spring vegetables, plus peas, cauliflower sprigs, etc.

**Julienne** A garnish of fine strips of mixed vegetables.

**Kneading** Working a dough firmly, using the knuckles for bread-making, the fingertips in pastry-making. In both cases the outside of the dough is drawn into the center.

**Knocking up** Preparing a pastry edge ready for crimping. Hold a spatula parallel with the pastry and knock against the knife, to open up the pastry in ridges.

**Larding** Inserting small strips of fat bacon into the meat of game birds, poultry and meat before cooking, to prevent its drying out when roasting. A special larding needle is used for the process.

**Liaison** A thickening agent, such as flour, cornstarch or arrowroot, which is used for thickening or binding sauces and soups.

**Lukewarm** Moderately warm; approximately 100°F. (38°C.).

**Macedoine** A mixture of fruits or vegetables cut into evenly sized dice, generally used as a decoration or garnish. Alternatively, the fruits may be set in gelatin.

**Marinade** A seasoned mixture of oil and vinegar, lemon juice or wine, in which food is left for a given time. This helps to soften the fibres of meat and fish and adds flavor to the food.

**Masking 1.** Covering or coating a cooked meat or similar dish with savory gelatin, glaze or sauce. **2.** Coating the inside of a mold with gelatin.

*Ice helps to set the thin layer of gelatin quickly*

**Meringue** Egg white beaten until stiff, mixed with sugar and dried in a cool oven till crisp.

**Mixed herbs** These most commonly consist of a blend of dried parsley, tarragon, chives, thyme and chervil, but other variations may occur in certain recipes.

**Mirepoix** A mixture of carrot, celery and onion, often including some ham or bacon, cut into large pieces, lightly fried in fat and used as a 'bed' for braising meat.

**Noisettes** Neatly trimmed round or oval shapes of lamb, mutton or beef, not less than ½ in. thick.

**Panada** A thick binding sauce (using 2 tablespoons fat and 4 tablespoons flour to 10 tablespoons liquid) made by the roux method and used for binding croquettes and similar mixtures.

**Parboiling** Part-boiling; the food is boiled for part of the normal cooking time, then finished by some other method.

**Paring** Peeling or trimming, especially vegetables or the rind of citrus fruits.

*A vegetable peeler makes paring a lemon easy*

**Petits fours** Very small fancy cakes, often iced, and almond cookies, served at the end of a formal meal.

**Piping** Forcing cream, icing or butter out of a pastry bag through a nozzle, to decorate cakes, etc. Also used for potatoes and meringues. The bag may be made of cotton fabric, nylon or plastic.

**Poaching** Cooking in an open pan at simmering point with sufficient seasoned liquid to cover. Used in egg, fish and some meat dishes.

**Pot-roasting** Cooking meat in a saucepan with fat and a very small amount of liquid; particularly good for small and less tender cuts.

**Pulses** Dried beans, peas, split peas and lentils.

**Purée** Fruit, vegetable, meat or fish which has been pounded, sieved or pulverized in an electric blender (usually after cooking), to give a smooth pulp. A soup made by sieving vegetables with the liquid in which they were cooked is also called a purée.

**Raspings** Fine crumbs made from stale bread; used for coating fried foods and for au gratin dishes. The bread is first dried in a cool oven and then crushed.

**Réchauffé** Reheated left-over foods.

**Reducing** Boiling a liquid in an uncovered pan in order to evaporate it and give a more concentrated result, especially when making soups, sauces, or syrups.

**Refreshing 1.** After cooking vegetables, pouring cold water over them to preserve the color; they are then reheated before serving. **2.** Crisping up already-cooked pastry in the oven. **3.** For home-freezing, plunging partly-cooked or blanched vegetables and meat into ice-cold water immediately after removing from the heat.

**Rendering** Extracting fat from meat trimmings by cutting them up small and heating in a cool oven (300°F.) until the fat has melted out, or boiling them in an uncovered pan with very little water until the water is driven off and the fat is melted; the fat is then strained into a basin.

**Rennet** An extract from calves' stomachs. It contains rennin and is used for curdling and coagulating milk for junket and for cheese-making.

**Rissoles** Small portions of minced meat enclosed in rounds of pastry and folded to form a semi-circle, then egg-and-crumbed and fried in deep fat. Now loosely applied to a round cake of a meat or fish mixture, egg-and-crumbed and fried.

**Roasting** In its true sense, roasting means cooking by direct heat in front of an open fire. Thus rôtisserie cooking is true roasting, but the modern method of cooking in a closed oven is really baking. Only good-quality poultry, and the best cuts of meat, should be cooked in this way.

**Roux** A mixture of equal amounts of fat and all-purpose flour cooked together to form the basis for a sauce and for thickening sauces and stews.

**Rubbing in** Incorporating fat into flour; used when making shortcrust pastry, plain cakes and cookies, when a short texture is required. Put the fat in small pieces in the flour, then rub it into the flour with the fingertips.

**Rusks** Fingers or slices of bread dried in a slow oven.

**Salmi** A ragoût or stew, usually of game.

**Sauté** To cook in an open pan over a strong heat in fat or oil, shaking the pan to make whatever is in it 'sauter' or jump, to keep it from sticking. The pan used should be heavy, wide and shallow. This may be used as a complete cooking method or as the initial cooking before finishing in a sauce.

**Scalding** Pouring boiling water over food to clean it, to loosen hairs (as from a joint of pork) or to remove the skin (as on tomatoes or peaches). The food must not be left in the boiling water or it will begin to cook.

**Scalloped dishes** Food (often previously cooked) baked in a scallop shell or similar small container; it is usually combined with a creamy sauce, topped with breadcrumbs and surrounded with a border of piped potato.

**Scalloping** A means of decorating the double edge of the pastry covering of a pie. Make close short cuts with a knife around the edge of the pie, giving a flaked effect (see **knocking up**) then, with the back of the knife, pull the edge up vertically at regular intervals to form scallops. Traditionally these should be close together for a sweet pie and wider apart for a savory one.

**Scoring** To make shallow, parallel cuts in the surface of food in order to improve its flavor or appearance or to help it cook more quickly (e.g. fish).

**Searing** Browning meat quickly in a little fat before broiling or roasting.

**Seasoned flour** Used for dusting meat and fish before frying or stewing. Mix about 2 tablespoons flour with about 1 teaspoon salt and a good sprinkling of pepper. Either pat it on to the food or dip the pieces in the flour and shake them gently before cooking.

**Shredding** Slicing a food such as cheese or raw vegetables into very fine pieces. A sharp knife or coarse grater is generally used.

**Sieving** Rubbing or pressing food (e.g. cooked vegetables) through a sieve; a wooden spoon is used to force it through.

**Sifting** Shaking a dry ingredient through a sieve or flour sifter to remove lumps and aerate it.

**Simmering** Keeping a liquid just below boiling point (approximately 205°F. or 96°C.). First bring the liquid to the boil, then adjust the heat so that the surface of the liquid is kept just moving or 'shivering'; continuous bubbling indicates the temperature is too high.

**Skimming** To take fat off the surface of stock, gravy or stews, or scum from other foods (e.g. preserves) while they are cooking. A piece of paper towel or a metal spoon may be used.

**Steaming** An economical method of cooking food in the steam from rapidly boiling water. There are several ways of steaming, according to the equipment available.

**Steeping** The process of pouring hot or cold water over food and leaving it to stand, either to soften it or to extract its flavor and color.

**Stewing** A long, slow method of cooking in a liquid which is kept at simmering point; particularly suitable for coarse-fibered foods. The liquid is served with the food, so that flavor is not wasted.

**Stock** The liquid produced when meat, bones, poultry, fish or vegetables are simmered in water with herbs and flavorings for several hours, to extract their flavor. Stock forms the basis of soups, sauces and stews and many savory dishes.

**Sweating** Cooking a food (usually a vegetable) very gently in a covered pan with melted fat until it exudes juices. The food should not color.

**Syrup** A concentrated solution of sugar in water, prepared by boiling and used in making water ices, drinks and fruit desserts. Corn syrup is a by-product of sugar refining. Maple syrup is extracted from the North American sugar maple.

**Tammy** To strain soups, sauces, etc., through a fine woollen cloth.

**Tepid** Approximately at blood heat. Tepid water is obtained by adding 2 parts cold water to 1 part boiling water.

**Thickening** Giving body to soups, sauces or gravies by the addition of flour, cornstarch or arrowroot.

**Trussing** Tying or skewering a bird into a compact shape before cooking.

**Vol-au-vent** A round or oval case made of puff pastry and filled with diced meat, poultry, game or fish in a well-flavored sauce.

**Whipping** To beat air rapidly into a mixture:
**1.** By hand, using an egg beater or whisk or two forks.
**2.** By rotary beater.
**3.** By electric beater.

*Beat eggs and sugar over gentle heat for best results*

**Zest** The colored part of orange or lemon peel containing the oil that gives the characteristic flavor. To obtain zest, remove the rind very thinly, with no white part, by grating, or use a zester. If it is required for a sweet dish, you can rub it off with a lump of sugar.

# A B C

 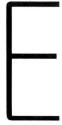

94–5; with ginger, 221; hot pie, 77; Kiev, 96–7; liver pâté, 3, 168; liver savory, 234; livers on toast, 233; Louisette, *224*, 225; marsala, 211; Maryland, 32; mille feuilles, 181; pâté stuffed, 184, *184*; party mold, 261; in a pot, 39, *39*; pie, jellied, 198, *198*; puffs, 239; ramekins, 202; roasting, 44; roast Italienne, 213; roast with pecan stuffing, 193, *193*; salad, 52, 200; Swedish, 52; Tandoori, 266; tetrazzini, 154; see also Poulet

**Chocolate,** Bavarois au, 108–9; butter cream, 84; éclairs, 78, *78*; German ice cream, 67; nut sundae, 159, *159*; rum mousse, 184; rum truffles, 236, *236*; sauce, 59, 60; soufflé, 214; sponge, 173; superb mousse, 176; uncooked cake, 81

**Choux savory buns,** 238

**Clam dip,** 180

**Coconut,** kisses, 236; maca-roons, 219

**Cod,** fluffy balls, 33; Provençale, 164; roe pâté, 175, *175*

**Coffee,** 133; Borgia, 206; cream ring, 231; éclairs, 236

**Compote,** red-currant, 193

**Consommé,** 8, 217; indienne, 189; lemon, 198; princesse, 9; sherried, 157

**Cookies,** cream cheese, 196; Easter, 254; lace, 171; one-two-three, 170; owl, 241, *241*

**Coquilles St. Jacques,** 153, 219

**Corn,** on the cob, 49, 134; foil roasted, 267; fritters, 32

**Cornish pasties,** 76

**Crab,** and asparagus soup, 161; dip, platter, 225; toasts, 204

**Crab apples,** spiced, 252

**Cranberry,** and bacon balls, 249; salad of turkey and, 249

**Cream(s),** coffee, 173; ginger meringue, 198; jellied chicken, 175, *175*; Norwegian, 229; puffs, 73; tunafish, 183

**Crème,** andalouse, 157; caramel, 106–7; marron, 162; St. Valentine, 228, *229*

**Crêpes,** pear and almond, 63, *63*; Suzette, 110–11

**Croissants,** 91

**Croque monsieur,** 235

**Croûtons,** 15

**Cuba libré,** 128

**Cucumber,** chartreuse, 189; chilled soup, 212, *212*; Portu-gaise, 220; sauté, 30; salad, 198; sweet and sour, 194

**Cumberland sauce,** 27

**Curry,** beef, 154; chicken cornets, 158; kipper salad, 261; mayon-naise, 277; puffs, 235; sauce, 154; scramble, 204; vegetable, 51; West African beef, 246

**Custard,** apricot caramel, 169

**Cutlets,** lamb, en croûte, 219

**Daiquiri,** 129

**Date,** cakes of ginger and, 171; scone bars, 155

**Desserts,** blackberry and pine-apple brioche, 65, *65*; iced Charlotte russe, 66; mandarin liqueur gâteau, 64, *64*; melon and pineapple salad, 64; nutty caramel pies, 65; pistachio apple flan, 64; pudding glace, 66; strawberry galette, 66, *66*; strawberry palmiers, 64; tranche aux fruits, 65

**Devils on horseback,** 233

**Dip(s),** cheddar, 180; chive, 242; clam, 180; in salad, 242, 243; sour cream and garlic, 256

**Doughnuts,** 33

**Dressings,** blue cheese, 22; foamy mayonnaise, 54; French, 54, 183; green mayonnaise, 54; mayonnaise, 54; Thousand Islands mayonnaise, 54; vinai-grette, 218

**Drinks,** mixing, 128–9

**Duck,** 44; liver and pork terrine, 14; roast, 45; terrine of, 14; wild roast, 45

**Duckling,** with pineapple, 218; with turnips, 40

**Eclairs,** chocolate, 78, *78*; coffee, 236

**Egg(s),** à la Florentine, 166; brains with, 166; cheesy, 166; crumbling, 31; en cocotte, 235; fritura, 166; gulls', 134; hot stuffed, 165; mayonnaise, 275; nog, 206; -nog ice cream, 68; oeufs à la maison, 202; pie of raised bacon and, 263; quails, 134; salad with yogurt dressing, 53; scrambled archiduchesse, 165; scrambled nests, 165; shirred with chicken livers, 166; stuffed, au gratin, 203; and vegetable flan, 262

**Eggplant,** 49

**Endive,** braised, 39, *40*; dressed spears, 211; and orange salad, 268

**Equipment for the kitchen,** 286–7

**Escalopes,** veal, with marsala and cheese, 162; veal, au poivre rose, 192–3

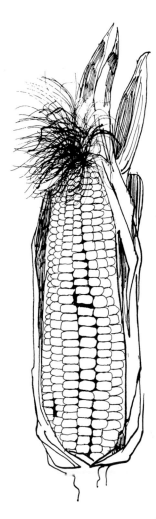

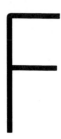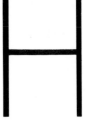

# F G H

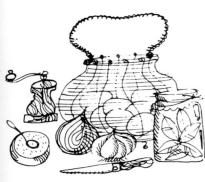

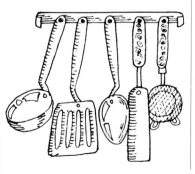

# M N O

  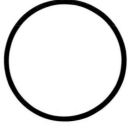

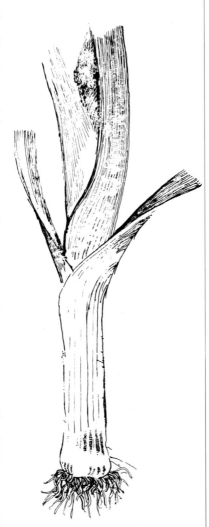

# P

# Q

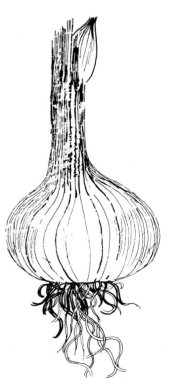

# R

# S

# T   V

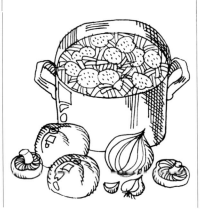

**The publishers would like to
acknowledge the help of the following
in providing photographs for this book:**
American Dairy Association (p. 67);
Peter Bilyard (pp. 133, 286);
Fleischmann's Yeast (pp. 89, 91);
General Electric (pp. 172, 173);
National Presto Industries (pp. 167,
169); Sunbeam Corporation (p. 174).

**The publishers wish to thank the
following companies in England for
the loan of accessories for
photography:**
Bosch; Bourne and Hollingsworth;
Casa Pupo; Civil Service Stores;
Collets Chinese Art Gallery; Cona;
Craftsmen Potters' Association;
Cucina; Dartington; David Mellor;
Denby; Design and Crafts, Farnham;
Divertimenti; Domecq; Elizabeth
David; Garrards; Grants of St James;
Gratnel; Habitat; Heal's; Henry's;
Hoover; John Lewis; Kenco;
Kenwood; Langley London; Loon
Fung Supermarket; Macdonald
Imports and Exports, Exeter; Melita;
Midwinter; Optima; Philips; Presents,
Farnham; Prestige; Robert Carrier
Cookshop; Robert Jackson; Robinson
and Cleaver; Rosenthal; Russell
Hobbs; Selfridges; Shaplans; Staines
Kitchen Supplies; Tiarco; Viners;
Wedgwood; Wilson and Gill.